DEFINING AND MEASURING DIVERSITY IN ARCHAEOLOGY

DEFINING AND MEASURING DIVERSITY IN ARCHAEOLOGY

Another Step Toward
an Evolutionary Synthesis of Culture

Edited by
Metin I. Eren and Briggs Buchanan

berghahn
NEW YORK · OXFORD
www.berghahnbooks.com

First published in 2022 by
Berghahn Books
www.berghahnbooks.com

Library of Congress Cataloging-in-Publication Data
Names: Eren, Metin I., 1982- editor. | Buchanan, Briggs (Briggs Wheeler), editor.
Title: Defining and measuring diversity in archaeology : another step toward an
    evolutionary synthesis of culture / edited by Metin I. Eren and Briggs Buchanan.
Description: New York : Berghahn, 2022. | Includes bibliographical references and index.
Identifiers: LCCN 2022004639 (print) | LCCN 2022004640 (ebook) |
    ISBN 9781800734296 (hardback) | ISBN 9781800734302 (ebook)
Subjects: LCSH: Archaeology—Statistical methods. | Material culture. | Cultural
    pluralism. | Biodiversity.
Classification: LCC CC80.6 .D44 2022 (print) | LCC CC80.6 (ebook) |
    DDC 930.1072/7—dc23/eng/20220302
LC record available at https://lccn.loc.gov/2022004639
LC ebook record available at https://lccn.loc.gov/2022004640

British Library Cataloguing in Publication Data
A catalogue record for this book is available from the British Library

ISBN 978-1-80073-429-6 hardback
ISBN 978-1-80073-430-2 ebook

DOI: https://doi.org/10.3167/9781800734296

Contents

List of Illustrations   vii

Foreword   xx
   Michael J. O'Brien and David Hurst Thomas

Introduction. On the Challenges of Measuring Diversity
in Archaeology   1
   Briggs Buchanan and Metin I. Eren

Chapter 1. Dispersion and Diversity: Parfleche Variation on
the Great Plains vs. the Columbia Plateau   26
   Stephen J. Lycett

Chapter 2. The Diversity of North America's "Old Copper"
Projectile Points   43
   Michelle R. Bebber and Anne Chao

Chapter 3. Diversity in Hunter-Gatherer Architecture   64
   Brian Andrews, Danielle Macdonald, and Brooke Morgan

Chapter 4. The Potential of Coverage-Based Rarefaction in
Zooarchaeology   81
   J. Tyler Faith and Andrew Du

Chapter 5. Diversity and Lithic Microwear: Quantification,
Classification, and Standardization   97
   W. James Stemp and Danielle A. Macdonald

Chapter 6. Intensification Mechanisms Driving Dietary Change
among the Great Plains Big Game Hunters of North America   125
   Erik Otárola-Castillo, Melissa G. Torquato, and Matthew E. Hill

   Appendix 6.1. Summary Information for Archaeological
   Sites Used in This Study   159

Chapter 7. Challenges and Prospects of Richness and Diversity
Measures in Paleoethnobotany   178
Alan Farahani and R. J. Sinensky

    Appendix 7.1. Abundance of Reproductive Plant Parts
    Recovered from the Las Capas Site, Southeastern Arizona,
    1220–730 BCE   205

Chapter 8. Quantifying Evenness of Paleoindian Projectile Point
Forms within Geographic Regions of Eastern North America   213
Matthew T. Boulanger, Ryan P. Breslawski, and Ian A. Jorgeson

Chapter 9. Thinking about Diversity in Material Culture at
Multiple Scales   247
Steven L. Kuhn

Chapter 10. Measuring and Comparing Class Diversity in
Archaeological Assemblages: A Brief Guide to the History and
State-of-the-Art in Diversity Statistics   263
Robert K. Colwell and Anne Chao

Epilogue. Diversity Metrics are Convenient, but Their
Archaeological Meanings Are Still Obscure   295
R. Lee Lyman

Index   322

Illustrations

Figures

F.1. Graph showing annual fluctuations (1915–1970) in percentage of articles in four major anthropological journals—*American Anthropologist*, *American Journal of Physical Anthropology*, *American Antiquity*, and *Language*—that employed statistical inference (after Thomas 1976).   xxvii

0.1. Google NGram of the term "archaeological diversity" shows that it peaked in 1989.   2

0.2. An illustration of two hypothetical assemblages' data with respect to a single character. The distribution of data can potentially influence the number of character states present in an assemblage, which in turn can potentially influence relative richness.   12

1.1. Examples of the contrasts in parfleche form and decorative features across tribes. Redrawn and modified after Lycett 2017 and Morrow 1975.   29

1.2. Map showing the geographic extent of the tribes in Plateau (hatching) and Plains (stippling) regions considered in the analyses.   31

1.3. The extent of latitudinal distributions (variance) of the various ethnolinguistic tribes is statistically higher for Plains than for Plateau tribes. Boxes delimit the 25–75 percent quartiles, and the median is indicated by the horizontal line inside each box. Termination of the lines (whiskers) extending from the boxes indicate minimal and maximal values in each case.   32

1.4. Average geographic distance between the center points of territories for Plains tribes is statistically higher than is the case for Plateau tribes.   33

1.5. Boxplots showing the average among-tribe parfleche distance value for each tribe of the Plateau versus the Plains (median value for each region indicated). Contrary to predictions based on geographic dispersion, parfleche distances (i.e., cultural diversity) is not significantly different between the Plateau and Plains tribes.   35

1.6. PCo plot showing patterns of parfleche attribute affinities between the ethnolinguistic tribes considered here. Polygons indicate the maximum extent of distributions for the Plains tribes (triangles) versus the Plateau tribes (circles). PCo 1 and 2 cumulatively account for 35.2 percent of the variability among parfleches; all remaining PCo each account for ≤11 percent of variation.   39

2.1. Map of Archaic Period copper tools. Approximate archaeological area of the North American "Old Copper" Culture.   44

2.2. Core and peripheral zones. The core region was determined by the density of artifacts located in southern and eastern Wisconsin. The counties shown here with red circles have the greatest number of Archaic copper artifacts on record. The peripheral region was simply all other areas surrounding the core where Archaic copper artifacts have been found. These peripheral counties are demarcated with white circles.   47

2.3. Archaic Period copper projectile points. Projectile points are the most common type of "heavy" copper artifact from the Archaic Period. They come in a variety of shapes and sizes, as shown here.   48

2.4. Paradigmatic class construction. Classes were created using five formal characters: (1) spear point haft form; (2) spear point tip morphology; (3) presence of blade ridge; (4) presence of hole; and (5) overall length.   50

2.5. Four most common classes in the core and periphery. The core and periphery share the same two most common classes, 11222 and 11122. However, the periphery has a different class of equal prominence, 31221, followed by 32221, which are both much smaller in size compared to the other point classes.   51

2.6. Graphs of class richness, Shannon, and Simpson diversity. Although core has higher observed class richness (34 vs. 32), it is mainly due to larger sample size and higher sample completeness. When we standardize sample size at a finite value (left columns in the Figure) or sample completeness at a value < 1 (right columns in the Figure), the periphery turns out to be consistently more diverse in class richness (q=0, upper row of the Figure), common class richness (q=1, middle row), and dominant class richness (q=2, lower row). However, all confidence intervals overlap, therefore there is insufficient evidence to demonstrate a statistically significant difference.   55

3.1. General location of sites used in the sample.   69

3.2. Average and variability in floor area for non-organic and organic constructed architecture.   71

3.3. Relationship between average structure floor area per site and the total number of inside features per site.   72

3.4. Variability in floor area of individual structures divided as circular or non-circular in shape.   73

3.5. Average floor area per site through time for the entire sample used in this study.   74

3.6. Average floor area per site over the Pleistocene to Holocene transition.   75

4.1. (A) The species abundance distributions for hypothetical assemblages A and B. Taxa ranked from most to least abundant. (B) Specimen-based rarefaction curves for assemblages A and B (95 percent confidence limits omitted for sake of clarity). (C) The ratio of rarefied richness for assemblage B relative to assemblage A (B:A) as a function of assemblage sample size (NISP = number of identified specimens).   83

4.2. The concept of coverage. (A) Population A, which includes 2,500 specimens distributed across ten taxa. The species abundances for Population A are: A = 900, B = 690, C = 250, D = 230, E = 120, F = 100, G = 80, H = 50, I = 50, J = 50. (B) Sample A, which is drawn from Population A and includes 25 specimens distributed across seven taxa. The species abundances for Sample A are: A = 10, B = 6, C = 3, D = 2, E = 2, F = 1, G = 1. Those seven taxa account for 95 percent of the specimens in Population A, so the coverage for Sample A is 0.95.   84

4.3. (A) The species abundance distributions for hypothetical assemblage A and assemblage B (identical to those in Figure 4.1). Taxa ranked from most to least abundant. (B) Coverage-based rarefaction curves for assemblages A and B (95 percent confidence limits omitted for sake of clarity). (C) The ratio

of rarefied richness for assemblage B relative to A (B:A)
as a function of coverage.   85

4.4. (A) Estimated coverage for the Boomplaas Cave faunas
according to NISP versus MNI counts. (B) Assemblage
sample size for NISP counts versus MNI counts. (C) The
number of singletons according to NISP counts versus
MNI counts. Solid lines in A–C indicate unity. Data from
Table 4.2.   87

4.5. (A) The relationship between the number of singletons and
estimated coverage for a hypothetical case where sample size
is held constant at 100 and the number of singletons ranges
from 1 to 20 (no doubletons). (B) The relationship between
sample size and estimated coverage for a hypothetical case
where sample size ranges from 10 to 100 and the number
of singletons is held constant at 2 (no doubletons).   88

4.6. The relationship between rarefied richness for the NISP
counts (rarefied to coverage = 0.79) versus the MNI
counts (rarefied to coverage = 0.52) across assemblages at
Boomplaas Cave. Errors indicate 95 percent confidence
limits. Solid line indicates unity.   89

4.7. The relationship between assemblage sample size and
estimated coverage for the Boomplaas Cave Pleistocene
aggregate (NISP counts and MNI counts).   90

4.8. The relationship between rarefied richness at a coverage
of 0.79 versus 0.5 across assemblages at Boomplaas Cave
(NISP data). Errors indicate 95 percent confidence limits.   90

4.9. The difference between true coverage and estimated coverage
(using the coverage estimator) as a function of subsample
size for the Boomplaas Cave Pleistocene aggregate. Black
line indicates the mean difference over 500 iterations. Grey
shading indicates 95 percent confidence intervals.   91

5.1. Richness (S) graphs for microwear (IUZs) on obsidian
artifacts from Alamilla's, Elvi's, Nuñez's, and Sands Hotel/
Parham's properties.   100

5.2. Richness (S) graphs for microwear (IUZs) on obsidian
artifacts from Actun Uayazba Kab, Belize, based on analyses
by Stemp and Awe (2014) and Stemp, Peuramaki-Brown,
and Awe (2019).   104

5.3. Mean relative areas (Srel) calculated for two unused
surfaces on a flint flake (left).   112

5.4. F-test results based on mean relative areas (Srel) indicating
     no discrimination of the two surface microtopographies
     at any scale above the 95 percent confidence level as
     represented by the solid horizontal line.   112

5.5. Mean relative areas (Srel), with standard deviations for two
     experimental obsidian blade segments (OBS1-u, OBS3-u)
     used to slice raw beef for thirty strokes, versus scale.   113

5.6. F-test results based on mean relative areas (Srel) indicating
     no discrimination of the two surface microtopographies at
     scales below the 95 percent confidence level as represented
     by the solid horizontal line. Discrimination at coarser
     scales (above the solid horizontal line) represents the
     natural microtopographies of each of the blade segments,
     whereas lack of discrimination at finer scales (below the
     solid horizontal line) represents the similarly used/worn
     microtopographies of each blade segment.   114

6.1. Graphic depiction of variation in prey richness in an
     idealized forager's diet on a one-dimensional gradient
     from a specialized diet focused on large game to one with
     high prey diversification.   138

6.2. Graphic depiction of variation in prey richness and
     evenness. This "diversification space" illustrates an
     idealized forager's diet on a two-dimensional gradient
     from a hyper-specialized diet composed of low species
     representation and dominated by the large game, to a
     diet that is hyper-diversified representing many species
     at a similar abundance.   139

6.3. Map of the Great Plains and adjacent Rocky Mountains,
     including site locations for the archaeological components
     used in this study.   143

6.4. Estimates of mean Diversity Index (DMg) values of
     species (with standard error [SE]). This plot illustrates
     estimates across habitats (alluvial valleys, plains and rolling
     hills, and foothills and mountains) for the Paleoindian,
     Archaic, Woodland and Late Prehistoric periods. Means
     and SEs were calculated using a generalized linear model
     (GLM) and a gamma distribution. Estimates without SEs
     had small sample size (see text).   147

6.5. Estimates of mean Simpson's Index (1-D′) values with
     SE. This plot illustrates estimates across time and habitats

(alluvial valleys, plains and rolling hills, and foothills and mountains) for the Paleoindian, Archaic, Woodland and Late Prehistoric periods. Means and SEs were calculated using a GLM using a beta distribution. Estimates without SEs had small sample size (see text).   148

6.6. Estimates of mean Large Mammal Abundance Index (AI_lg) values with standard errors. This plot illustrates estimates across time and habitats (alluvial valleys, plains and rolling hills, and foothills and mountains) for the Paleoindian, Archaic, Woodland, and Late Prehistoric periods. Means and SEs were calculated using a GLM using a beta distribution. Estimates without SEs had small sample size (see text).   150

6.7. Bivariate plot exhibiting the variability in Margalef's Diversity Index (DMg) and Simpson's Index (1-D′) values of site components in the three different habitats (alluvial valleys, plains and rolling hills, and foothills and mountains). Each panel separately illustrates the Paleoindian, Archaic, Woodland, and Late Prehistoric periods. Habitat means value with 95 percent confidence intervals are depicted for each habitat.   152

6.8. Stacked bar graph illustrating the variability in mean large-bodied Abundance Index (AIlg), medium-bodied Abundance Index (AIme), and small-bodied Abundance Index (AIsm) for three different habitats (alluvial valleys, plains and rolling hills, and foothills and mountains) during the Paleoindian, Archaic, Woodland and Late Prehistoric periods.   153

7.1. Hypothetical relationship between the number of identified specimens (usually counts of plant seeds, or similar disseminules) to the total number of taxa represented among them.   185

7.2. A comparison of the sampling outcomes of two archaeological sites from Jordan (Dhiban, DHB) and Arizona (Las Capas, LCA). (A) illustrates the total volume associated with increasing numbers of samples collected, (B) illustrates the average number of plant remains recovered from each site by total volume, while (C) does the same but by total number of samples. The ribbons in all cases are one standard deviation.   188

7.3. Sample-based rarefaction curves, comparing the number of identified specimens (NISP), or the total number of samples

(N), or the total sample volume (in liters) to total richness (S): (A) An annotated sample-based rarefaction curve illustrating the component parts of a typical visualization for paleoethnobotanical data; (B & C) Sample-based rarefaction curves comparing richness to NISP and N for the data presented in Table 7.4. Here the hypothetical data are calculated on abundance data, hence the unit of resampling is the physical sample, not the number of individuals (NISP), although the average number of identified specimens (individuals) per sample is calculated as well in a sample-based rarefaction.   191

7.4. Taxonomic density (A) and diversity (B) computed from the three temporal phases at Las Capas, as reported in Sinensky and Farahani 2018. In both cases, analyses were conducted using a sample-based rarefaction. The color and fill of each curve represent a different temporal phase, as shown in the legend.   196

7.5. An inventory of Hill numbers calculated from *sample*-based rarefaction on *incidence* data using the *iNEXT* package. When q=0, the curves yield species richness; when q=1, the curves represent Shannon diversity; and when q=2, the curves represent Simpson diversity.   198

7.6. An inventory of Hill numbers calculated from *individual*-based rarefaction on *abundance* data using the *iNEXT* package. When q=0, the curves yield species richness; when q=1, the curves represent Shannon diversity; and when q=2, the curves represent Simpson diversity.   199

8.1. Measurements and nominal attributes recorded from each fluted-point specimen.   218

8.2. Graphical summary of the paradigmatic classification used in this study, as well as the distributions of observed measurements for each dimension in the sample (n = 1480).   219

8.3. Locations and quantities of fluted-point specimens included in the present study. Note: Fluted points from localities in Canada were excluded because of limitations of the GIS files used in this study.   221

8.4. Extent of glaciation at ca. 20,000 cal BP (ca. 18,000 ^{14}C YBP) from Dalton et al. (2020) and Dyke et al. (2003), showing United States counties from which projectile point specimens are included. Note: Darker shading indicates greater numbers of specimens.   227

8.5. 13,000 cal BP biomes calculated for eastern North America by Williams et al. (2004). Glacial boundaries, proglacial lakes, and the Champlain Sea inlet at 11,000 ^{14}C YBP are shown from Dalton et al. (2020) and Dyke et al. (2003). As in Figure 8.4, counties with fluted-point specimens are shown and shaded by the number of specimens.   228

8.6. Physiographic provinces (Fenneman 1946) in the eastern United States. As in Figure 8.4, counties with fluted-point specimens are shown and shaded by the number of specimens.   229

8.7. Results of modeling point-form evenness in glaciated and unglaciated landscapes showing the posterior probabilities for evenness values. (A) Distributions of modeled evenness values over 30 permutations of the model. (B) Samples drawn from the pooled posterior probability distribution of all models showing the estimated median evenness value, and the uncertainty in those estimations (X axis is jittered to enhance visibility). (C) Proportions of each point class within glaciated and unglaciated portions of the East across all permutations of the model. Note that the order of point classes in C is the same as in Table 8.2.   231

8.8. Results of modeling point-form evenness within reconstructed biomes of 13,000 cal BP (Williams et al. 2004). (A) Distributions of modeled evenness values over 30 permutations of the model. (B) Samples drawn from the pooled posterior probability distribution of all models showing the estimated median evenness value, and the uncertainty in those estimations (X axis is jittered to enhance visibility). (C) Proportions of each point class within each biome. Note that certain point classes are much more prevalent in some regions than in others.   234

8.9. Results of modeling point-form evenness within physiographic provinces (Fenneman 1946). (A) Distributions of modeled evenness values over 30 permutations of the model. (B) Samples drawn from the pooled posterior probability distribution of all models showing the estimated median evenness value, and the uncertainty in those estimations (X axis is jittered to enhance visibility). Note the extreme uncertainty in evenness estimates within several of the provinces.   236

8.10. Proportions of each point class within physiographic provinces across all permutations of the model. Note that certain point classes are much more prevalent in some provinces than in others. 239

10.1. Why incidence frequencies closely reflect abundance, for random samples. (A) A frequency distribution of colors. (B) An urn of colored balls, sorted by color, matching the relative abundance of balls of different colors in frequency distribution A. Red balls are the commonest, light blue balls the rarest. (C) The urn is shaken to randomize the position of the balls in B. (D) Balls are drawn at random from the mixed urn in C, creating 10 random samples, each with 8 to 12 balls. (E) The incidence frequencies (the number of samples in which each color occurs at least once—the numbers next to the color bar) closely match the abundance frequencies in A. Red balls are the most frequent, light blue balls the least frequent. 270

10.2. The perils of using abundance-based R/E when samples are spatially or temporally heterogeneous. The filled circles are a smaller and a larger reference sample, each from a different but (not known to the researcher) identical assemblage. The diversity (any Hill number) of the two assemblages is to be compared. The solid curved line is the sample-based rarefaction curve for the larger sample. Because the assemblages are actually identical, however, the sample-based rarefaction curve for the smaller sample coincides, up to its reference sample size, with the curve for the larger sample. The curved dashed lines are the abundance-based rarefaction curves for the two samples. The open circle marks the expected diversity of the larger sample, when rarefied by abundance-based rarefaction to the reference sample size of the smaller assemblage. The inference that the large sample is more diverse is erroneous, when spatial or temporal structuring is taken into account. 271

10.3. Results for incidence analysis for the Alta Toquima intramural and extramural datasets. (A) Estimated sample-completeness profile for diversity orders $0 \leq q \leq 2$. (B) Sample-based rarefaction (solid curve segments) and extrapolation (dashed curve segments); extrapolation is extended to double the size of the reference sample. (C) Observed (dotted lines) and asymptotic (solid lines, with confidence intervals) diversity profiles, for diversity orders $0 \leq q \leq 2$. (D) Coverage-based rarefaction (solid curve segments) and extrapolation (dashed curve segments); solid dots and triangles mark observed data points. (E) Evenness profiles for diversity orders $0 < q \leq 2$, computed for the coverage value of C_{max}, in this case 97.5 percent. Shaded areas in (a)-(d) show 95 percent confidence bands obtained with a bootstrap method with 100 replications. The numerical values for the three special cases of $q = 0, 1,$ and 2 appear in Table 10.3 (left half).   282

10.4. Results for abundance analysis for the Alta Toquima intramural and extramural datasets. See the Figure 10.3 caption for explanation. All numerical values for the three special cases of $q = 0, 1,$ and 2 are shown in Table 10.3 (right half).   287

10.5. Comparison of incidence-based (blue) vs. abundance-based (red) rarefaction curves for the Alta Toquima intramural and extramural datasets. "Ratio" means rarefied fraction. See the text for interpretation.   288

11.1. Paleontological model of how gaps in the stratigraphic record create gaps in the fossil record that can be conveniently used as boundaries between species. Each shaded bar labeled with a capital letter represents a stratum; each "gap" represents missing populations and strata. Each unimodal curve represents a population and its included formal variation; solid portions of each curve represent the parts of the population that are present; dashed portions of the curve represent the parts of the population that are absent from the fossil record. After Newell 1956.   306

11.2. Illustration of alpha (α), beta (β), and gamma (γ) diversity. Each large circle represents an aggregate such as an artifact assemblage, and each symbol (open squares, diamonds, etc.) within a circle represents a different category (e.g., artifact type). The dashed box encloses all assemblages, and might represent a stratum or a site. For simplicity, diversity is calculated as richness. Alpha diversity is calculated for each assemblage (= 2, 3, or 4); gamma diversity is calculated for all assemblages combined (= 4); the magnitude of beta diversity, calculated as shared types, varies from one pair of assemblages to the next (= 1, 2, or 3) and is signified by the breadth of the gray line connecting two assemblages (greater breadth

signifies more shared types). Modified after Jurasinski et al.
2009.   307

11.3. Models of variability in the abruptness of biological
      community boundaries along an environmental gradient.
      Each curve represents the frequency distribution of a species
      along the environmental gradient: (A) boundaries between
      communities are abrupt and self-evident; (B) boundaries
      between communities are diffuse and not apparent; (C)
      boundaries between communities are diffuse but evident;
      and (D) boundaries between communities are diffuse and
      not apparent. Note that each frequency curve could represent
      frequencies of a kind of artifact across geographic space (e.g.,
      think site boundaries along the x-axis) or over time (e.g.,
      think assemblage boundaries without stratigraphic breaks
      along the x-axis). After Whittaker 1975.   308

Tables

0.1. Studies that have used paradigmatic classification to classify
     archaeological or other types of data.   7

1.1. Ethnolinguistic tribes incorporated in this study.   30

2.1. Data summary for the periphery and core. Note: In the
     periphery, frequency counts (f_k values) are complete; in the
     core, there are four additional frequency counts (f_{17}=1, f_{21}=1,
     f_{24}=1, and f_{26}= 1).   53

2.2. Observed diversities and estimated asymptotic diversities in
     the periphery.   53

2.3. Observed diversities and estimated asymptotic diversities in
     the core.   54

3.1. Sites used in the analysis. Note that each site may contain
     multiple structures.   67

4.1. Taxonomic abundances (NISP/MNI) across stratigraphic
     units for Boomplaas Cave (from Klein 1983).   86

4.2. Summary of the Boomplaas Cave data for NISP and MNI
     tallies: variables involved in generating the coverage estimator
     (n = sample size; f_1 = singletons; f_2 = doubletons) and estimates
     of richness (S) at different levels of coverage (C).   88

5.1. Microwear (IUZs) on obsidian artifacts from Late
     Postclassic/Early Colonial (AD 1400–1700) San Pedro,
     Ambergris Caye, Belize.   99

5.2. Diversity measures for microwear (IUZs) on obsidian artifacts from Late Postclassic/Early Colonial (AD 1400–1700) San Pedro, Ambergris Caye, Belize. 100

5.3. Microwear (IUZs) on obsidian artifacts from Actun Uayazba Kab, Belize, based on analyses by Stemp and Awe (2014) and Stemp, Peuramaki-Brown, and Awe (2019). 103

5.4. Diversity measures for microwear (IUZs) on obsidian artifacts from Actun Uayazba Kab, Belize, based on analyses by Stemp and Awe (2014) and Stemp, Peuramaki-Brown, and Awe (2019). 104

5.5. Summary table of results of collated data from the published lithic microwear blind-tests (from Evans 2014: Table 1). 107

5.6. Some ISO 25178-2 surface roughness/texture parameters. 109

5.7. Surface roughness/texture data for the experimental antler and dry hide scraping flint flakes. 110

5.8. Welch's t-test of surface roughness/texture data for the experimental antler and dry hide scraping flint flakes (p = 0.05). 110

6.1. Site frequency by time period and habitat setting. 146

6.2. Mean Margalef D_{mg} values (and SE) by time period and habitat setting, calculated using a GLM with gamma function. 147

6.3. Mean Simpson's Index 1-D' values (and standard errors) by time period and habitat setting, calculated using beta regression. 149

6.4. Mean large-bodied Abundance Index (AI) values (and standard errors) by time period and habitat setting, calculated using beta regression. 150

7.1. Two hypothetical assemblages (a_1, a_2) illustrating the counts of individuals across nine distinct taxa ($T_1 ... T_9$). 180

7.2. Common measures of richness and diversity. 181

7.3. Hypothetical inventory of identified plant remains from one assemblage, with taxonomic categories and richness (S) at the top. 183

7.4. Two hypothetical assemblages, with accompanying sampling information. 187

7.5. Summary statistics for the assemblages described in Figure 7.2. 188

7.6. Summary data for the Las Capas paleoethnobotanical assemblage discussed in this chapter, including the date range associated with sampled deposits, the number of analyzed samples (N), the total volume of those samples (in liters), the number of identified plant remains NISPN, the base richness (S), and an Inverse Simpson's index value (1/D).   195

8.1. Number of fluted points from each state in the East by the scale of reported provenience.   217

8.2. Paradigmatic classes defined by our classification, the total number of specimens assigned to each class, and the most-commonly represented point type names (as assigned by reporting authors) within each class. Serial order corresponds to that used in Figures 8.7, 8.8, and 8.10.   220

8.3. Median evenness (E_H) values modeled for different biogeographic regions, as well as the 95 percent highest probability density interval (HPDI) of the modeled distributions. The final two columns provide the probability of each region having the minimum and the maximum evenness within each set of model comparisons.   232

8.4. Comparison of modeled evenness (E_H) distributions for projectile-point classes in (A) unglaciated and (B) glaciated regions, and the probabilities of each distribution being greater than the other.   233

8.5. Comparison of modeled evenness (E_H) distributions for projectile-point classes in reconstructed biomes at 13,000 cal BP, and the probabilities of each distribution being greater than the other.   235

8.6. Comparison of modeled evenness (E_H) distributions for projectile-point classes in modern physiographic provinces, and the probabilities of each distribution being greater than the other.   238

10.1. Terminology for diversity statistics, with archaeological examples.   265

10.2. Data summary for incidence and abundance data.   281

10.3. The numerical values for the three special cases of $q = 0, 1,$ and 2 for incidence-based data (left half) and abundance data (right half) for Alta Toquima intramural and extramural datasets. Blue font marks the higher value between the intramural and extramural datasets/assemblages.   284

11.1. Definitions of assemblage and site. Listed in chronological order of publication.   302

Foreword

Michael J. O'Brien and David Hurst Thomas

———— ∞∞∞ ————

The ideas discussed at the "Defining and Measuring Diversity in Archaeology" symposium held at the 2019 annual meeting of the Society for American Archaeology (SAA) in Albuquerque, New Mexico, planted the seeds that led to the organization of this volume. The timing purposely coincided with the thirtieth anniversary of the publication of *Quantifying Diversity in Archaeology* (Leonard and Jones 1989), a volume that itself grew out of a 1984 SAA symposium in Portland, Oregon, organized by Bob Leonard and Tom Jones. Both of us attended that symposium, which was divided into fifteen presentations—including one by Thomas—and two wrap-up discussions, one by George Cowgill and the other by Bob Dunnell.

Leonard and Jones noted in their preface to the book that the idea for the 1984 symposium had emerged from their graduate work at the University of Washington. Both had trained under Don Grayson, and as they told it, it was his research on faunal diversity that not only prepared them to be suspicious of straightforward comparisons of faunal assemblages but also offered directions they could take for making valid comparisons of diversity generally. A number of archaeologists of the 1980s, including both of us, could have made similar remarks about Grayson's influence on their own work. Over his long career, Grayson trained several generations of graduate students, including twenty-two doctoral students whom he directly supervised, with Jones and Leonard being numbers two and three (behind Lee Lyman).

Grayson did not introduce diversity measures into archaeology single-handedly—there had been earlier efforts in the 1970s and early 1980s (e.g., Cannon 1983; Jefferies 1982; Kintigh 1984; Rice 1981; Schiffer 1973; Yellen 1977)—but no one played a bigger role in emphasizing the utility of diversity measures in archaeology. In addition to his book *Quantitative Zooarchaeology* (Grayson 1984) and his chapters in *Quantifying Diversity in Archaeology*—one single authored (Grayson 1989) and one co-authored (Jones et al. 1989)—Grayson published several pivotal papers on diversity (Grayson 1981; Jones et al. 1983). In addition to Jones and Leonard, several other students and colleagues at Washington got the message and began applying diversity measures to a wide range of archaeological phenomena, concentrating in particular on the role of sample size in influencing those measures (e.g., Kirch et al. 1987; Meltzer, Leonard and Stratton 1992; Rhode 1988).

At the time, there was no synthetic treatment of diversity in archaeology, so Leonard and Jones decided to fill the gap, first with the 1984 symposium and, five years later, with *Quantifying Diversity in Archaeology*. The promotional blurb on the back cover of the book presented both its purpose and its goals:

> One of the enduring aims of archaeological research has been to explain why human material culture is so diverse, both across the world and through history. Recognising that diversity exists is not, however, to explain it nor to measure it effectively. The aim of the contributors to *Quantifying Diversity in Archaeology* is therefore to examine what we mean by diversity, to review the methods of measurement and formulae we can apply, and to assess the pitfalls that exist. Richness and evenness, the two main components of diversity measures developed in the biological sciences, are considered, as are the value of diversity measures in the study of style, ecology, cultural geography and faunal, lithic and spatial analysis. Subsequent papers consider critically why the archaeological remains of particular cultures vary so markedly between sites, localities and regions.

Given the reception the 1984 symposium received—large crowds throughout the morning and early afternoon—interest in diversity measures appeared to be high, even though the subject itself was relatively new to the discipline. The 2019 SAA symposium, organized by Metin I. Eren and Briggs Buchanan, was also packed throughout the afternoon—luckily the conference organizers had set aside a large room—signifying a still considerable interest in diversity some thirty-five years later. The papers in the session were excellent, and we were pleased when the organizers asked us to write a foreword to the volume that was being put together. Forewords oftentimes read like publicity blurbs—"You really need to read this book!"—or at worst like shameless self-promotion—"I'm an important person in the field (in my mind, at least), which is undoubtedly why I was asked to add a few comments to the front of the book."

Neither of us feels that way. Rather, we perceive ourselves as two archaeologists trained in the early 1970s, a time when statistics was just becoming an integral part of undergraduate and, especially, doctoral programs.

Here, we provide some historical context for why diversity measures, a specialized subset of statistics, entered the archaeological picture during that decade. We think it is easier for the reader to appreciate the papers in the present volume with an appreciation of what came before—and how and why things unfolded as they did. Although forewords normally do not cite references, we break with tradition and include relevant citations to help readers better explore points of interest.

Archaeologists have long experienced a tenuous relationship with statistics. Low-level statistics such as chi-squared and t-tests do not raise too many issues, because both are fairly straightforward and not too scary. But far fewer archaeologists are familiar with diversity measures, first formalized by the American mathematician Claude Shannon (1948) and the British codebreaker Edward Simpson (1949), among others.[1] Chi-squared and t-tests are directly applicable to archaeological data, but not so much with diversity measures, which carry steep epistemological and methodological requirements. As a prelude to the following chapters, we look at how authors of earlier efforts handled such requirements. As you read this volume, you might want to keep those requirements in mind.

Good Reviews . . . and a Few Admonitions

The Leonard and Jones volume received several positive reviews. Colin Pardoe (1992: 72), for example, noted that "the volume is logically set out and shows commonalty of purpose and extremely good editing. The openers introduce diversity from its ecological . . . and evolutionary . . . bases. These set the stage for the following chapters, and apart from historical overviews, concentrate on the many measures of diversity in which the authors bring out the range of diversity studies and theoretical underpinnings." Similarly, Fred Limp (1991: 523) stated that "*Quantifying Diversity in Archaeology* is an important volume. It should sensitize all archaeologists to the critical problem that small and differing sample sizes present, and suggest some avenues for future research. It is not the last word on the subject but does represent a pioneering effort in an area that will undoubtedly see much more study in the future."

In emphasizing "the critical problem that small and differing sample sizes present," Limp underscored a central issue in measuring diversity, namely that sample size affects the measurement in important ways. Consider the two first-order measures of diversity: *richness*—the number of different categories (classes, taxa, and the like) in an assemblage; and *evenness*—the degree of homogeneity among the objects or individuals per unit. Sample size can impact both measures, but it becomes an even greater issue when working with second-order measures, in which richness and evenness are measured simultaneously.

Grayson's chapter in *Quantifying Diversity in Archaeology* emphasized that "the scope of sample-size effects on the relative abundances of classes in archaeological assemblages has yet to be generally recognized" (Grayson 1989: 79). We would add a caveat to his point: even when archaeologists do recognize a problem, it does not mean they can come up with a simple solution. Several authors in the earlier volume, including Kintigh (1989), Grayson (1989), and Thomas (1989), offered different probabilistic methods for correcting for sample size (see Sanders 1968 for a pioneering, but flawed, effort in ecology, and Simberloff 1972 for an early, valid approach), but most authors sidestepped the issue. And, curiously, almost unmentioned— Rindos (1989) was an exception—was the worrisome fact that Shannon's index, perhaps the most-used diversity measure in archaeology at the time, was meant to be applied only to *infinite* populations (see Cowgill 2015).

Albert Ammerman's (1991: 95) review of the Leonard and Jones volume extended Grayson's point. Ammerman wondered if perhaps archaeologists had borrowed the ecological concept of diversity without having a "larger body of knowledge and theory about populations and their interactions with one another. Might not the archaeologist want to consider alternative, less reductive approaches to the measurement of diversity: ones that are, in a word, more diversified?" Ammerman's polite question highlighted a long-standing problem in archaeology, and one not limited to diversity measures: the often uncritical borrowing of theory, concepts, and methods from other disciplines—what Don Hardesty (1980: 161) referred to as "crossing disciplinary boundaries on search-and-seizure missions." Much of the archaeological borrowing over the years was from ecology (Keene 1983): adaptive response, behavioral ecology, competitive exclusion, niche, optimal foraging, patch, and resource partitioning, to name but a few of the concepts lifted wholesale and applied to archaeological data.

Ammerman's point had been made a bit more forcefully in Dunnell's chapter in *Quantifying Diversity in Archaeology*, "Diversity in Archaeology: A Group of Measures in Search of Application?" Dunnell concluded with a prophetic warning: "The explanation of diversity . . . is going to take us into largely unexplored methodological ground if archaeology is to be more than a dog wagged by a borrowed technical tail or an exercise in the writing of uncontested fiction" (Dunnell 1989: 149). Dunnell noted that archaeological uses of the diversity concept displayed "all of the classic symptoms of concept borrowing, symptoms largely initiated by the efforts to treat it quantitatively" (ibid.: 142).

Dunnell also pointed out the less-than-clear distinction between samples and the populations from which they were drawn (see Colwell and

Chao, this volume). There was confusion, or perhaps a bit of sleight-of-hand, over the units used to measure diversity—the implications of which, in Dunnell's mind, were far more fundamental and wide-reaching than the simple choice of which diversity measure to use. Cowgill (1989) raised the same point in his discussion. We cannot overstate that any measure of diversity must be linked to the categories used to classify an assemblage, whether it be an assemblage of fish bones or stone tools. Standard taxonomic categories in ecology include species, genera, and the like, but archaeological categories tend to be spread across the board. For us, the bottom line is simple: Analytical categories need to be clearly defined, meaning they must be replicable by other investigators.

Ammerman's (1991: 95) review raised another issue mirrored in the Cowgill and Dunnell discussions: "Is it really appropriate to treat part of an object (for example, a design motif in the [chapters] by Conkey and Schiffer) as equivalent to an individual or to a species? Would we be willing to let the ecologist measure diversity by counting the spots on a leopard's back? Probably not." Leaving that sticky issue for others, we suggest here simply that archaeologists have failed to reach widespread agreement over how to represent the relationship between parts and wholes when measuring diversity.

As Dunnell correctly predicted, "the unexplored methodological ground" facing diversity studies in archaeology began with problems in basic measurement. Following the publication of *Quantifying Diversity in Archaeology*, archaeology experienced some limited success in refining archaeodiversity measures, notably Kaufman's (1998) jackknife technique and the improvements made by Grayson and Cole (1998) in regression analysis (see also Cannon 2001; Cochrane 2003; Kintigh 2006; Lepofsky and Lertzman 2005; Magguran 1988; Meltzer et al. 1992), but nearly a quarter-century would pass without any significant breakthrough in the field of biodiversity generally. A wide range of diversity indices were applied without addressing the attendant problems of sampling and species abundance. Although attempts were made to combine species richness and a proportional representation of taxa into a single metric, these units of measure were counterintuitive and/or difficult to interpret. Only within the last decade have sample-size-based and coverage-based methods been developed that provide workable ways of estimating species richness and developing statistical inferences based on those estimates (Chao et al. 2014; Colwell et al. 2012). Archaeologists are now beginning to take full advantage of recent progress in analyses of biodiversity (e.g., Buchanan et al. 2017; Eren et al. 2012; Eren et al. 2016), as the papers in this volume clearly attest.

Statistical Roots

Some will disagree with us, but we link the emergence of diversity measures in archaeology directly to the New Archaeology of the 1960s and 1970s—often referred to as "processual archaeology." Statistics in general emerged at the time as a central issue in archaeology, and diversity measures eventually tagged along as part of the extended statistical package. Those of us who became archaeologists in that era remember the intense and long-standing debates over whether archaeology was properly considered to be history or science. If the former, then statistics were unnecessary, but if archaeology is to be science, then statistics becomes a primary requirement. The debate, of course, overlooked the fact that history is not, as some archaeologists dismissed it, simply storytelling or chronicling. Rather, history is quite capable of providing explanations in its own right. Here is how biologist Robert O'Hara (1988: 144) made the distinction:

> A *chronicle* is a description of a series of events, arranged in chronological order but not accompanied by any causal statements, explanations, or interpretations. A chronicle says simply that A happened, and then B happened, and then C happened. A *history*, in contrast to a chronicle, contains statements about causal connections, explanations, or interpretations. It does not say simply that *A* happened before *B* and that *B* happened before *C*, but rather that *B* happened because of *A*, and *C* happened because of *B*.

So when causal statements are proposed, statistics can come in mighty handy—provided we keep in mind the key distinction between correlation and cause, which several authors in *Quantifying Diversity in Archaeology* appear to have overlooked. They were by no means alone.

As processual archaeology gained a foothold, it changed the way archaeology courses were designed, especially at the graduate level. Based on a survey of anthropology graduate programs in the United States regarding the kind of statistical requirements set for their doctoral and master's students, one of us found that over half the programs in the early 1970s either required or strongly suggested a competency in statistics (Thomas 1976). Although we lack data for earlier periods, we know that the percentage was much less—and we'd guess that the percentage has declined since the 1970s.

Given that anthropology students were being exposed to statistics at a fairly high rate, it seems fair to ask whether this translated into useful results. Depending on whom you asked at the time, the answer would have ranged from "absolutely yes," to a lukewarm "maybe," to an emphatic "no!"

Maybe a better question would be, did the results of statistical analysis have broad and, more importantly, lasting effects on archaeology? Or put another way, how disruptive were statistically centered studies in changing the course of archaeology? Let us take a quick look.

As another part of his study of statistical training in anthropology, Thomas (1976) analyzed the literature to see how the use of statistical inference had changed over the years. Using articles in four major journals—*American Anthropologist, American Journal of Physical Anthropology, American Antiquity*, and *Language*—as a sample, he calculated the percentage by year of those that employed statistical inference. The percentages by subdiscipline are shown in Figure F.1. O'Brien, Lyman and Schiffer (2005) suggest that the marked increase around 1950 in the percentage of ethnological articles containing statistical inference (as reflected in *American Anthropologist*) was a result of the availability and early popularity of cross-cultural studies employing the Human Relations Area Files (Murdock 1940). But look at the percentage of archaeological articles in *American Antiquity* (the flagship American archaeology journal) using statistical inference in 1970—a whopping 2 percent. This was near the apex of the processual "revolution" in American archaeology, and one must wonder what could account for this intuitively upside-down proportion, especially in light of the build-up of statistical training in anthropology generally at the time.

Addressing this counterintuitive result invites a bit deeper reflection on the general history of statistics in archaeology. We might trace the beginnings to Leslie Spier's early twentieth-century use of normal frequency distributions and a form of simple least-squares regression to determine if the frequencies of types of Southwestern pottery in collections he had seriated fluctuated monotonically (Lyman, O'Brien and Dunnell 1997). A later, and perhaps better-known, statistical technique is the "Brainerd–Robinson coefficient." Archaeologist George Brainerd had long advocated the use of what he termed "statistical manipulations" to clarify archaeological systematics, and he enlisted statistician William Robinson to help solve the problem of ordering artifact collections based on the relative frequencies of types (Brainerd 1951). Robinson calculated an "agreement coefficient" to measure the similarity of two collections—based on richness and evenness—and then arranged several such coefficients in a matrix with the largest values on the diagonal and the coefficients decreasing toward the opposite corners (Robinson 1951).

Don Lehmer (1951) claimed that the Brainerd–Robinson coefficient failed to consider varying sample sizes, and he advocated using the mean standard error of each type's abundance in two samples. Robinson and Brainerd (1952: 60) responded that "Lehmer has confused two very different statistical problems, *viz.*, the problem of estimating a population

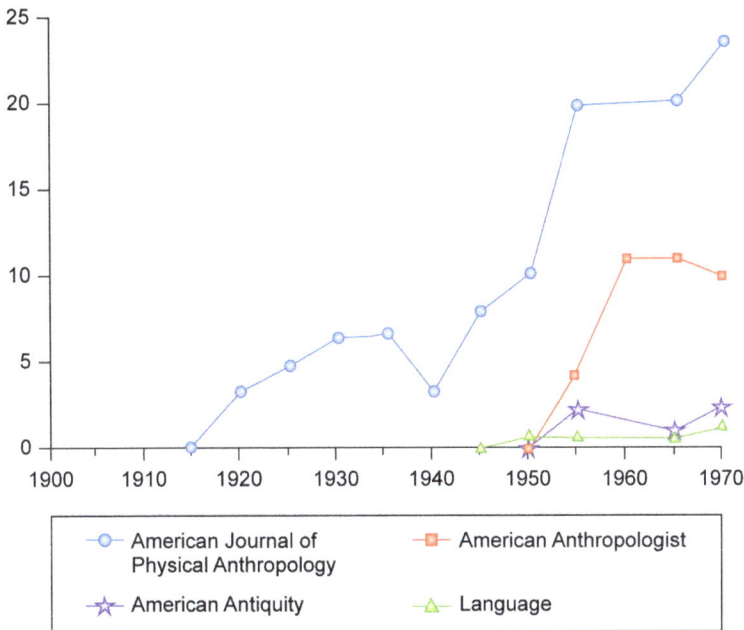

Figure F.1. Graph showing annual fluctuations (1915–1970) in percentage of articles in four major anthropological journals—*American Anthropologist, American Journal of Physical Anthropology, American Antiquity*, and *Language*—that employed statistical inference (after Thomas 1976). © The authors.

parameter and the problem of testing the statistical significance of an observed result," concluding their response with an acerbic comment: "We regret that we have had to expound in an archaeological journal upon matters which ought to be relegated to a course in elementary statistics" (ibid.: 61). But let us give Lehmer credit for at least trying to stimulate archaeological debate over the use and misuse of statistics, especially as they relate to sample size and what small samples might be missing in terms of, say, certain pottery types.

Despite the stir over individual methods in the 1950s, the vast majority of archaeologists had no real—or imagined—understanding of basic statistics. This had begun to change, albeit slowly, by the late 1950s, especially with the rise of radiocarbon dating, which required that archaeologists understand, if even in a rudimentary way, what a mean and standard deviation were (Thomas 1978). A specially convened symposium on quantitative methods in archaeology held in 1959 made several more far-reaching recommendations, including that (1) archaeologists should become familiar with the basic principles of sampling theory, and (2) agreement should be reached on standard descriptive statistical methods (Heizer and Cook 1960). Many archaeologists seem to have taken these recommendations to heart as they searched for patterning in their data sets. By the mid-to-late 1970s, archaeologists were routinely incorporating at least rudimentary statistical methods in their work, whether it be calculating a z-score or a Pearson's r, or performing a chi-squared or t-test.

The small percentage of archaeological articles incorporating statistics reported by Thomas (1976) began to rise as processualists demanded not only quantification but also deduction and hypothesis testing. That demand carried both good and bad news. *Good intentions are one thing, but skillful execution is another.* Whereas statistical inference rather than seat-of-the-pants inference *can* yield significant insights into archaeological data, many of the resulting products were flawed. We see the blind (if not strident) allegiance to hypothesis testing and the devotion to formulating general principles (often referred to as "covering statements") as a low point in American archaeology—Leroy Johnson (1972) referred to it as "avant-garde" archaeology—resulting in dozens (if not more) of what Kent Flannery (1973) called "Mickey Mouse laws."

O'Brien and colleagues (2005) considered 1976 to be something of a watershed year in statistical archaeology for two entirely different reasons. First, Lew Binford invited Albert Spaulding to present the 1976–77 Harvey Lecture at the University of New Mexico, which Spaulding titled "On Growth and Form in Archaeology: Multivariate Analysis," which subsequently appeared in the *Journal of Anthropological Research* (Spaulding 1977). Binford's invitation to present this prestigious lecture signified both the growing importance of statistics in archaeology (and Spaulding's role in that growth) and the tendency among the majority of archaeologists to stick to culture history, thereby ignoring the New Archaeology and its call for statistical applications. Second, Thomas's *Figuring Anthropology: First Principles of Probability and Statistics* appeared in 1976. Because Thomas feels more than a little awkward discussing his own work, O'Brien will step in and note that *Figuring Anthropology*—the first statistics textbook with purely anthropological examples—was hugely popular, seeing widespread adoption in graduate courses across the discipline. For many years it was the only such book on the market.

Why did Thomas feel compelled to write a textbook on statistics? He did not come right out and say it in the book, but a few years later he underscored his irritation at the growing number of inappropriate statistical applications in an article solicited for a special issue of *American Antiquity*, "Contributions to Archaeological Method and Theory," edited by Mike Schiffer. In "The Awful Truth about Statistics in Archaeology," Thomas

(1978) addressed what he perceived as statistical excesses, many of them emanating from multivariate analysis. He suggested that the rationale for using multivariate statistics came from a false logic that just because culture is a complex and multivariate phenomenon, the methods and techniques we use to study phenomena must also be complex and multivariate. This nonsensical view led more than a few archaeologists to simply throw some data in a hopper, search the manual to find the "on" switch, and flip it. Statistical operations always produce a result, but whether it means anything is quite another matter.

Thomas also emphasized some problems with sampling and statistics in archaeology—a topic addressed by many of the contributors to both the 1989 volume and the current volume. There was a feeling in the late 1970s that if you did not "sample," you were not a good processualist. Overlooked was the fact that archaeology has always been about sampling. The true concern should be about the *nature* of the sampling. Traditional archaeologists tended to think "more is better," meaning that larger samples better approximate the target population (whatever that is). For their part, processualists tended to work toward empirically deriving a universal sample size that in some sense was representative or adequate (e.g., Mueller 1975). But this approach was also flawed because it ignored variation in population parameters (more heterogeneous populations require greater sample sizes).

Archaeologists eventually recognized, though certainly not in all quarters, that accurate estimates of different population parameters often require samples of *different* sizes. Even in a single population, a sample that is adequate for estimating one parameter may not be adequate for estimating others. Cowgill (1989) and Dunnell (1989) pointed out in their critiques in *Quantifying Diversity in Archaeology* that several authors failed to recognize the distinction. You might want to keep an eye on this issue as you read through the chapters included here.

Into the Future

It is fair to ask whether the discipline has improved over the three decades since *Quantifying Diversity in Archaeology* appeared. Are archaeologists today embracing diversity measures as a meaningful part of routine archaeological analysis? Our guess is "no," in part because day-to-day archaeology does not ordinarily require that diversity be measured at all. Citation analysis demonstrates that the number of publications in archaeological diversity trailed off dramatically after the publication of *Quantifying Diversity in Archaeology* (Buchanan and Eren, this volume). This surprising finding recalls the point made by Dunnell (1989: 149) that if archaeologists end up overemphasizing diversity studies, many will object to the "dog wagged by a borrowed technical tail."

Exactly this unintended consequence surfaced when Steve Plog and Michelle Hegmon (1993, 1997) questioned the research priorities of controlling sample-size effects first, and only later turned to substantive questions of prehistoric behavior. Sample size sometimes reflects excavation strategies or natural formation processes, they argued, but ancient behavior feeds in as well—people can live longer in some places than in others, and two sites can be involved in different activity mixes. Plog and Hegmon directly echoed Dunnell's earlier concerns, disparaging what they saw in diversity studies as a "substitute [of] statistical theory for anthropological theory, a substitution that we find unacceptable" (Plog and Hegmon 1997: 718; see also Leonard 1997). We agree.

We conclude by applauding the editors of the present volume for assembling chapters that cover such a wide range of archaeological applications of diversity measures. Some chapters take diversity measures as a given and apply them to impressive datasets, from projectile points to lithic microwear, and from architecture to plants. Other chapters are more methodologically driven and are innovative and groundbreaking, picking up on themes covered in papers in *Quantifying Diversity in Archaeology* but moving us well ahead of where we were three decades ago. Perhaps as important, there is a clear tendency to involve statisticians in archaeological analysis, particularly those with expertise not only in measuring biodiversity but also in developing new methods with which to measure it. This bodes well for the discipline.

Acknowledgments

We thank Robert Colwell for his many helpful suggestions for improving the manuscript, Lee Lyman for suggesting additional references, and an anonymous referee for their positive comments.

Michael J. O'Brien is a Professor at Texas A&M University–San Antonio.

David Hurst Thomas is a Curator at the American Museum of Natural History, New York.

Note

1. The term "index of diversity" seems to have emanated from the work of statistician Sir Ronald Fisher and colleagues in biology even earlier (Fisher, Corbet and Williams 1943).

References

Ammerman, A. J. 1991. "Review of *Quantifying Diversity in Archaeology*, by R. D. Leonard, G. T. Jones." *American Journal of Archaeology* 95: 341–42.

Brainerd, G. W. 1951. "The Use of Mathematical Formulations in Archaeological Analysis." In *Essays on Archaeological Methods*, ed. J. B. Griffin, 117–27. Anthropological Papers No. 8. Ann Arbor: Museum of Anthropology, University of Michigan.

Buchanan, B., A. Chao, C.-H. Chiu, R. K. Colwell, M. J. O'Brien, A. Werner, and M. I. Eren. 2017. "Environment-Induced Changes in Selective Constraints on Social Learning during the Peopling of the Americas." *Scientific Reports* 7: 44431.

Cannon, A. 1983. "The Quantification of Artifactual Assemblages: Some Implications for Behavioral Inferences." *American Antiquity* 48: 785–92.

Cannon, M. D. 2001. "Archaeofaunal Relative Abundance, Sample Size, and Statistical Methods." *Journal of Archaeological Science* 28: 185–95.

Chao, A., N. J. Gotelli, T. C. Hsieh, E. L. Sander, K. H. Ma, R. K. Colwell, and A. M. Ellison. 2014. "Rarefaction and Extrapolation with Hill Numbers: A Framework for Sampling and Estimation in Species Diversity Studies." *Ecological Monographs* 84: 45–67.

Cochrane, G. W. G. 2003. "Artefact Attribute Richness and Sample Size Adequacy." *Journal of Archaeological Science* 30: 837–48.

Colwell, R. K., A. Chao, N. J. Gotelli, S.-Y. Lin, C. X. Mao, R. L. Chazdon, and J. T. Longino. 2012. "Models and Estimators Linking Individual-based and Sample-based Rarefaction, Extrapolation and Comparison of Assemblages." *Journal of Plant Ecology* 5: 3–21.

Cowgill, G. L. 1989. "The Concept of Diversity in Archaeological Theory." In *Quantifying Diversity in Archaeology*, ed. R. D. Leonard and G. T. Jones, 131–41. Cambridge: Cambridge University Press.

———. 2015. "Some Things I Hope You Will Find Useful Even If Statistics Isn't Your Thing." *Annual Review of Anthropology* 44: 1–14.

Dunnell, R. C. 1989. "Diversity in Archaeology: A Group of Measures in Search of Application?" In *Quantifying Diversity in Archaeology*, ed. R. D. Leonard and G. T. Jones, 142–49. Cambridge: Cambridge University Press.

Eren, M. I., A. Chao, C.-H. Chiu, R. K. Colwell, B. Buchanan, M. T. Boulanger, J. Darwent, and M. J. O'Brien. 2016. "Statistical Analysis of Paradigmatic Class Richness Supports Greater Paleoindian Projectile-Point Diversity in the Southeast." *American Antiquity* 81: 174–92.

Eren, M. I., A. Chao, W. H. Hwang, and R. K. Colwell. 2012. "Estimating the Richness of a Population When the Maximum Number of Classes Is Fixed: A Nonparametric Solution to an Archaeological Problem." *PLoS ONE* 7(5): e34179.

Fisher, R. A., A. S. Corbet, and C. B. Williams. 1943. "The Relation between the Number of Species and the Number of Individuals in a Random Sample of an Animal Population." *Journal of Animal Ecology* 12: 42–58.

Flannery, K. V. 1973. "Archaeology with a Capital S." In *Research and Theory in Current Archaeology*, ed. C. L. Redman, 47–53. New York: Wiley.

Grayson, D. K. 1981. "The Effects of Sample Size on Some Derived Measures in Vertebrate Faunal Analysis." *Journal of Archaeological Science* 8: 77–88.

———. 1984. *Quantitative Zooarchaeology: Topics in the Analysis of Archaeological Faunas.* Orlando, FL: Academic Press.

———. 1989. "Sample Size and Relative Abundance in Archaeological Analysis: Illustrations from Spiral Fractures and Seriation." In *Quantifying Diversity in Archaeology*, ed. R. D. Leonard and G. T. Jones, 79–84. Cambridge: Cambridge University Press.

Grayson, D. K., and S. C. Cole. 1998. "Stone Tool Assemblage Richness during the Middle and Early Upper Palaeolithic in France." *Journal of Archaeological Science* 25: 927–38.

Hardesty, D. L. 1980. "The Use of General Ecological Principles in Archaeology." *Advances in Archaeological Method and Theory* 3: 157–87.

Heizer, R. F., and S. F. Cook, eds. 1960. *The Application of Quantitative Methods in Archaeology.* Publication in Anthropology No. 28. New York: Viking Fund, Wenner-Gren Foundation for Anthropological Research.

Jefferies, R. W. 1982. "Debitage as an Indicator of Intraregional Activity Diversity in Northwest Georgia." *Midcontinental Journal of Archaeology* 7: 99–132.

Johnson, L. 1972. "Problems in 'Avante-Garde' Archaeology." *American Anthropologist* 74: 366–77.

Jones, G. T., C. Beck, and D. K. Grayson. 1989. "Measures of Diversity and Expedient Lithic Technologies." In *Quantifying Diversity in Archaeology*, ed. R. D. Leonard and G. T. Jones, 69–78. Cambridge: Cambridge University Press.

Jones, G. T., D. K. Grayson, and C. Beck. 1983. "Artifact Class Richness and Sample Size in Archaeological Surface Assemblages." In *Lulu Linear Punctated: Essays in Honor of George Irving Quimby*, ed. R. C. Dunnell and D. K. Grayson, 55–73. Anthropological Papers No. 72. Ann Arbor: Museum of Anthropology, University of Michigan.

Kaufman, D. 1998. "Measuring Archaeological Diversity: An Application of the Jackknife Technique." *American Antiquity* 63: 73–85.

Keene, A. S. 1983. "Biology, Behavior and Borrowing: A Critical Examination of Optimal Foraging Theory in Archaeology." In *Archaeological Hammers and Theories*, ed. J. A. Moore and A. S. Keene, 137–55. New York: Academic Press.

Kintigh, K. W. 1984. "Measuring Archaeological Diversity by Comparison with Simulated Assemblages." *American Antiquity* 49: 44–54.

———. 1989. "Sample Size, Significance, and Measures of Diversity." In *Quantifying Diversity in Archaeology*, eds. R. D. Leonard and G. T. Jones, 25–36. Cambridge: Cambridge University Press.

———. 2006. "The Promise and Challenge of Archaeological Data Integration." *American Antiquity* 71: 567–78.

Kirch, P. V., M. S. Allen, V. L. Butler, and T. L. Hunt. 1987. "Is There an Early Far Western Lapita Province? Sample Size Effects and New Evidence from Eloaua Island." *Archaeology in Oceania* 22: 123–27.

Lehmer, D. J. 1951. "Robinson's Coefficient of Agreement—A Critique." *American Antiquity* 17: 151.

Leonard, R. D. 1997. "The Sample Size–Richness Relation: A Comment on Plog and Hegmon." *American Antiquity* 62: 713–16.

Leonard, R. D., and G. T. Jones, eds. 1989. *Quantifying Diversity in Archaeology.* Cambridge: Cambridge University Press.

Lepofsky, D., and K. Lertzman. 2005. "More on Sampling for Richness and Diversity in Archaeobiological Assemblages." *Journal of Ethnobiology* 25: 175–88.

Limp, W. F. 1991. "Review of *Quantifying Diversity in Archaeology*, ed. R. D. Leonard and G. T. Jones." *Journal of Field Archaeology* 18: 520–23.

Lyman, R. L., M. J. O'Brien, and R. C. Dunnell. 1997. *The Rise and Fall of Culture History*. New York: Plenum.

Magguran, A. E. 1988. *Ecological Diversity and Its Measurement*. Princeton, NJ: Princeton University Press.

Meltzer, D. J., R. D. Leonard, and S. K. Stratton. 1992. "The Relationship between Sample Size and Diversity in Archaeological Assemblages." *Journal of Archaeological Science* 19: 375–87.

Mueller, J. W., ed. 1975. *Sampling in Archaeology*. Tucson: University of Arizona Press.

Murdock, G. P. 1940. "The Cross-Cultural Survey." *American Sociological Review* 5: 361–70.

O'Brien, M. J., R. L. Lyman, and M. B. Schiffer. 2005. *Archaeology as a Process: Processualism and Its Progeny*. Salt Lake City: University of Utah Press.

O'Hara, R. J. 1988. "Homage to Clio, or, Toward an Historical Philosophy for Evolutionary Biology." *Systematic Zoology* 37: 142–55.

Pardoe, C. 1992. "Review of *Quantifying Diversity in Archaeology*, ed. R. D. Leonard and G. T. Jones." *Australian Archaeology* 35: 72–73.

Plog, S., and M. Hegmon. 1993. "The Sample Size–Richness Relation: The Relevance of Research Questions, Sampling Strategies, and Behavioral Variation." *American Antiquity* 58: 489–96.

———. 1997. "An Anthropological Perspective on the Sample Size–Richness Relation: A Response to Leonard." *American Antiquity* 62: 717–18.

Rhode, D. 1988. "Measurement of Archaeological Diversity and the Sample-Size Effect." *American Antiquity* 53: 708–16.

Rice, P. M. 1981. "Evolution of Specialized Pottery Production: A Trial Model." *Current Anthropology* 22: 219–40.

Rindos, D. 1989. "Diversity, Variation and Selection." In *Quantifying Diversity in Archaeology*, ed. R. D. Leonard and G. T. Jones, 13–23. Cambridge: Cambridge University Press.

Robinson, W. S. 1951. "A Method for Chronologically Ordering Archaeological Deposits." *American Antiquity* 16: 293–301.

Robinson, W. S., and G. W. Brainerd. 1952. "Robinson's Coefficient of Agreement—A Rejoinder." *American Antiquity* 18: 60–61.

Sanders, H. L. 1968. "Marine Benthic Diversity: A Comparative Study." *American Naturalist* 102: 243–82.

Schiffer, M. B. 1973. "The Relationship between Access Volume and Content Diversity of Storage Facilities." *American Antiquity* 38: 114–16.

Shannon, C. E. 1948. "A Mathematical Theory of Communication." *Bell System Technical Journal* 27: 379–423.

Simberloff, D. 1972. "Properties of the Rarefaction Diversity Measurement." *American Naturalist* 106: 414–18.

Simpson, E. H. 1949. "Measurement of Diversity." *Nature* 163: 688.

Spaulding, A. C. 1977. "On Growth and Form in Archaeology: Multivariate Analysis." *Journal of Anthropological Research* 33: 1–15.

Thomas, D. H. 1976. *Figuring Anthropology: First Principles of Probability and Statistics*. New York: Holt, Rinehart, and Winston.

———. 1978. "The Awful Truth about Statistics in Archaeology." *American Antiquity* 43: 231–44.

———. 1989. "Diversity in Hunter-Gatherer Cultural Geography." In *Quantifying Diversity in Archaeology*, ed. R. D. Leonard and G. T. Jones, 85–91. Cambridge: Cambridge University Press.
Yellen, J. R. 1977. *Archaeological Approaches to the Present: Models for Reconstructing the Past.* New York: Academic Press.

Introduction

On the Challenges of Measuring Diversity in Archaeology

Briggs Buchanan and Metin I. Eren

───⊗⊗⊗───

Calculating the diversity of biological or cultural classes is a fundamental way of describing, analyzing, and understanding the world around us. Diversity can be understood simply in terms of richness, the number of classes in an assemblage, and evenness, the relative proportion of those classes, or some combination of those measures. And as archaeology inevitably continues to mature as an evolutionary science, the regular integration of diversity measures and concepts into archaeological practice—along with hypothesis testing; quantitative methods, morphometrics, and inferential statistics; experimentation; cultural transmission theory; and population thinking (Lycett 2011; Lycett and Chauhan 2010 [cf. Shott 2020]; Lycett and von Cramon-Taubadel 2015; Lycett, von Cramon-Taubadel, and Foley 2006; Lycett et al. 2016; Mesoudi 2011)—will become increasingly important.

The idea for this volume stemmed from a symposium we organized at the 2019 annual meeting of the Society for American Archaeology (SAA) in Albuquerque, New Mexico. That year marked the 30th anniversary of the landmark volume on archaeological diversity, *Quantifying Diversity in Archaeology* (Leonard and Jones 1989) (see O'Brien and Thomas Foreword, this volume). The Leonard and Jones volume included several theoretical and methodological contributions, as well as case studies using diversity measures to analyze an array of different artifact types and datasets from the archaeological record. Despite the success of that book, and several other important studies involving diversity that preceded and succeeded it (e.g., Cruz-Uribe 1988; Kaufman 1998; Meltzer, Leonard, and Stratton 1992; Nagaoka 2001; Rhode 1988; Shott 1989, 1997, 2010), 1989 seems to mark a high point in the archaeological use of diversity concepts and measures (Figure 0.1). Our intent in organizing the symposium, and subsequently this volume, was to try to reverse the declining trend by illustrating both the range of datasets to which diversity measures can be applied, and the new methods now available to examine archaeological diversity.

As so often happens in science, we each began to work with concepts of diversity independently of each other. Buchanan started his work on archaeological diversity in his dissertation comparing the proportions of stone tools in Clovis-aged tool assemblages recovered in different regions of the United States (Buchanan 2005). To account for varying sample sizes of tool assemblages, he made use of rarefaction techniques, although very small and homogenous Clovis toolkits in the Western United States made comparisons across regions difficult. Later, working with Collard and colleagues, Buchanan applied measures of diversity to toolkits recorded among more recent hunter-gatherer (Collard et al. 2011a, 2011b, 2013a) and food-producing (Collard et al. 2011b, 2012, 2013b) populations across the world. In these studies, Buchanan and colleagues counted the number of tools and tool parts recorded by ethnographers to investigate hypotheses concerning the drivers of technological diversity.

Eren also began his work with diversity concepts in his dissertation, which focused entirely on Clovis unifacial tool diversity in the North

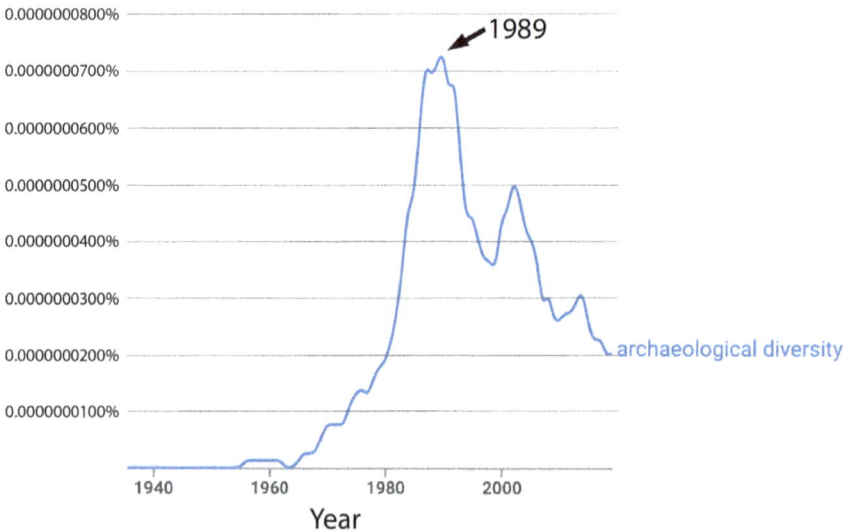

Figure 0.1. Google NGram of the term "archaeological diversity" shows that it peaked in 1989. © The authors.

American Lower Great Lakes region (Eren 2011; see also Eren 2012, Eren et al. 2012). It was during his attempts to apply the Chao1 Richness Estimator (Chao 1984) to his paradigmatic artifact classes that he found an anomaly using paradigmatic classification (for description see below). Paradigmatic classification produces a fixed number of classes, which is different than the typical situation in ecology or biogeography, where established upper limits for the number of species that can be found in a particular region are rarely, if ever, known. When the Chao1 estimator was used to estimate paradigmatic class richness, an impossible estimate emerged: the upper 95 percent confidence interval of unifacial tool class richness sometimes exceeded the maximum number of possible classes. Eren contacted Robert Colwell and Anne Chao, shared his results, and all agreed that a new method was needed to address richness estimation when both upper and lower bounds are known. This collaboration resulted in a new method, doubly-bounded confidence intervals (both lower and upper bounds fixed), for class richness (Eren et al. 2012).

We (Buchanan and Eren) began to formally collaborate a few years later, and, having taken a short break from archaeological diversity, returned to the subject, along with Colwell, Chao, and others, in order to explore Clovis stone point diversity across North America (Buchanan et al. 2017; Eren et al. 2016). It was after these latter studies had been published that we felt, given the 30th anniversary of the 1989 Leonard and Jones volume was upon us, that archaeological diversity should once again be brought to the fore.

Challenges in the Study of Archaeological Diversity

This volume features studies of archaeological diversity ranging from the data-driven to the theoretical, from the Paleolithic to the Historic periods. Most importantly, however, is the application of diversity concepts and measures to a broad range of *kinds* of archaeology data. Chapters in this volume focus on the diversity of parfleche (Lycett), metal artifacts (Bebber and Chao), architecture (Andrews, Macdonald, and Morgan), faunal remains (Faith and Du; Otárola-Castillo, Torquato, and Hill), ethnobotanical remains (Farahani and Sinensky), and flaked stone on macroscopic (Boulanger, Breslawski, and Jorgeson) and microscopic (Stemp and Macdonald) scales. A Forward by Mike O'Brien and David Hurst Thomas, and discussion chapters by Steve Kuhn, by Robert Colwell and Anne Chao, and by Lee Lyman reflect on important issues remaining in the methodological and theoretical treatment of diversity.

Rather than summarize the findings of the chapters above, as is typical for an introductory chapter, we instead outline three challenges that we have already encountered in our study of archaeological diversity, but that are also addressed in various ways, either fully or partly, within the chapters of this volume.

Challenge #1: Creation of Units

The analysis of diversity requires classes of phenomena. In some subfields of archaeology, such as zooarchaeology, the data translate easily into explicit, discrete classes. In other subfields, such as flaked stone artifact analysis, data are less readily translatable into explicit, discrete classes. In these latter subfields the use of paradigmatic classification is a very robust solution (Dunnell 1971). Paradigmatic classification is a procedure specifically intended to document and monitor artifact variation in a manner that is explicit, and unbiased by the experience of the analyst. Specimen classes arise from the unique combinations of character states, scoring each specimen with one character state for each character, to classify it. This procedure makes paradigmatic classes explicit, equivalent, and comparable. Thus, we are not saying the paradigmatic classification is always necessary for analyses of archaeological diversity, but in many cases it will substantially facilitate and strengthen such analyses. It is important to note that "classes" are theoretical/ideational/conceptual units, just like inches and grams. In other words, paradigmatic classes are not empirical; instead, they are measurement units, where "measurement" means "description."

In his landmark, although arguably still underappreciated, work *Systematics in Prehistory*, Dunnell explored "the lowest order of theory in any discipline, that of the definition and conception of data, the creation of meaningful units for the purposes of a particular field of inquiry" (Dunnell 1971: 6). His reasons for discussing archaeological systematics and introducing paradigmatic classification are varied and complex, but they broadly involve the maturity of archaeology (prehistory) as a scientific discipline. Paradigmatic classification is a dimensional classification procedure in which the units (i.e., classes) are defined by intersection, with each dimension (henceforth "character") being a set of mutually exclusive alternate features (henceforth "character states"). All character states belonging to a single character share the ability to combine with character states of each other character. Dunnell specified: "In paradigmatic classification, all of the class definitions are drawn from the same set of dimensions [characters] of features [character states]. Individual classes are distinguished from one another by the unique product obtained in the combination, permutation, or intersection of features [character states] from the set of dimensions [characters]" (ibid.: 71).

Dunnell (1971: 73–76) noted that paradigmatic classes possess three important properties given their creation via intersection of character states. First, all of the characters and character states are equivalent; none is or can be weighted more or less than any other. Second, paradigmatic classes are unambiguous, given that character states within a single character are mutually exclusive, and the intersection of character states from different characters prevent internal contradiction. Third, paradigmatic classes are comparable; that is, one class is comparable with all other classes in the same classification. In other words, "the structure of paradigmatic classification always specifies that all classes within it differ from one another in the same manner" (ibid.: 74). O'Brien and Lyman (2002: 47) note a fourth property of the procedure, namely that any paradigmatic classification is infinitely expandable, meaning that attribute states can be added as needed. Similarly, deletion of a dimension or of an attribute found to be analytically useless or ambiguous does not require another examination of specimens (Beck and Jones 1989).

Of course, as Dunnell clearly spelled out, the field of a particular classification must be established *prior* to the creation of the classification. This field, what Dunnell (1971: 74) termed the "root of the paradigm", is a statement of what the classes are classes of, and it is usually expressed as a trait or set of traits common to all the classes within the paradigm. That said, Dunnell emphasized that the root or common trait(s) is not a product of the paradigmatic classification, but is instead a symbolic record of one of the decisions made prior to the construction of the classification.

The fact that paradigmatic classification is not more frequently used in formal artifact analyses in archaeology is not altogether surprising, although it is disappointing. This is probably mostly attributable to the difficulty in giving up traditional extensionally defined classifications (see O'Brien and Lyman 2000), and the associated type names that are in common use within archaeology. There have been several implicit or explicit criticisms of paradigmatic classification and its use in archaeological or cultural evolutionary studies (e.g., Araujo 2015; Read 2015; Shott 2011; Thulman 2006; Whallon 1972). Such assertions can arise from the identification of true shortcomings of paradigmatic classification in particular instances, but can also arise from a misunderstanding of Dunnell's (1971) jargon-laden prose, from confusion as to how paradigmatic classification works, from a misunderstanding of pattern versus noise, from a lack of experience with hypothesis-driven archaeology, or simply from unfounded skepticism that paradigmatic classes—given their inherent properties—are useful. One can easily contrast criticisms of paradigmatic classification with the substantive ones about typology. Indeed, Thomas (1989) pointed out in his contribution to *Quantifying Diversity in Archaeology* (Leonard and Jones 1989) that typology and its extensionally defined taxonomic units can be subjective, often defined by overlapping and inconsistent criteria (see also Bisson 2000; Dunnell 1971; Eren et al. 2012; Fish 1978; O'Brien, Darwent, and Lyman 2001; O'Brien et al. 2014; Whittaker, Caulkins, and Kamp 1998). Yet, none of the above should be taken to mean that paradigmatic classes are perfect or that types are useless (e.g., see Lyman 2021). Instead, our point is that both classes and types (and, for that matter, "modes," Clark 1969; Shea 2013) are tools that should be judiciously used or designed when the question asked or analysis performed requires, or at least benefits from, the employment of one or more of these tools to arrive at a robust conclusion.

Paradigmatic classification can be applied to *any* kind of archaeological data, as illustrated by Table 0.1, and has been used outside of archaeology as well (Adriano and Ricarte 2012; Deetz 1965; Shaw 1969; Strong 1935). Distinct paradigmatic classifications can also be applied to the same artifactual datasets, depending on the question being asked. For example, Eren (2011, 2012; Eren et al. 2012) applied two distinct paradigmatic classifications to the same set of Clovis unifacial tools. The first classification was designed to categorize overall unifacial tool morphology, while the second classification was designed to categorize unifacial tool edge morphology. Although each of these classifications and subsequent diversity analyses explored specific questions, the subsequent side-by-side comparison of the diversity results from each classification is also productive. For example, Eren (2011) found an inverse relationship between sample size and tool class evenness, but a positive relationship between sample size and edge class evenness. This means that as sample size increases, every additional discarded *tool* specimen is increasingly likely to be a class that is already abundantly represented in the sample. It also means that every additional discarded *edge* specimen is increasingly likely to be a rare class minimally represented in the sample or a class not yet represented. He reasoned that this difference lies in the distinction between the *potential of a tool* and the *function of an edge*. The potential of a tool involves whether or not its edges can be modified. This is largely determined by the tool's shape. Relatively thick, spherical tools are more difficult to modify and resharpen than other shapes. If a person is going to discard a tool, it is more likely to be thick and spherical than any other shape. Thus the "bins" of spherical, thick tools will continually be filled as sample size increases. However, this pattern does not appear to be the case for edge classes. As sample size increases, rarer edge classes are more likely to be discarded because their function is presumably more limited than that of more common edge classes. When it comes time to decide which tools to discard and which tools to keep, the tools with edges that are not functionally limited are more likely to be kept.

Table 0.1. Studies that have used paradigmatic classification to classify archaeological or other types of data.

Year	Authors	Material Classified	Time Period	Geographic Location
1969	Shaw	Conodonts	Devonian	n/a
1971	Dunnell	Pottery (Hypothetical)	n/a	n/a
1973	Dancey	Use Wear	Prehistoric	Washington, USA
1974	Dunnell and Lewarch	Use Wear	Prehistoric	Washington, USA
1975	Dancey	Use Wear	Prehistoric	Washington, USA
1975	Dunnell and Fuller	Use Wear	Prehistoric	Washington, USA
1976	Dunnell et al.	Flaked Stone Tools (Core Tools)	Prehistoric	Washington, USA
1976	Dunnell et al.	Flaked Stone Tools	Prehistoric	Washington, USA
1976	Dunnell et al.	Use Wear	Prehistoric	Washington, USA
1977	Aikens and Minor	Use Wear	Prehistoric	Oregon, USA
1977	Dunnell and Campbell	Use Wear	Prehistoric	Washington, USA
1977	Croes	Woven textiles (Basketry, hats, mats)	1050 BC – AD 1300	Pacific Northwest
1978	Thompson	Use Wear	Prehistoric	Pacific Northwest
1979	Duncan	Use Wear	Prehistoric	Washington, USA
1979	Dunnell and Beck	Use Wear	Prehistoric	Washington, USA
1980	Hanford Arundale	Flaked Stone Tools	2000 BC – AD 1600	Baffin Island, Canada
1980	O'Brien et al.	Architecture (Houses)	AD 1800 – 1900	Missouri, USA
1981	Campbell	Bone Technology	Prehistoric	Washington, USA
1981	Campbell	Clay Concretions	Prehistoric	Washington, USA
1981	Campbell	Subsurface Features	Prehistoric	Washington, USA
1981	Campbell	Flaked Stone Tools	Prehistoric	Washington, USA
1981	Campbell	Use Wear	Prehistoric	Washington, USA
1981	Meltzer	Flaked Stone Tools (Endscrapers)	Various	Various
1982	Johnson et al.	Groundstone Tools	3000 BC – AD 1000	Kansas, USA
1982	Mason et al.	USDA Soil Series	n/a	Missouri, USA
1982	Lewarch	Use Wear	n/a	Missouri, USA
1982	Zeier	Cultural-Historic Integration Systems	Misc.	North American Plains
1983	Futato	Projectile Points	Prehistoric	Southeastern USA
1983	Lyman et al.	Use Wear	Prehistoric	Oregon, USA

(continued)

Table 0.1. *Continued*

Year	Authors	Material Classified	Time Period	Geographic Location
1984	Chatters	Use Wear	Prehistoric	Washington, USA
1984	Goodwin et al.	Ceramics	AD 19th/20th centuries	Louisiana, USA
1984	Meltzer	Flaked Stone Tools (Projectile Points)	Paleoindian	Eastern North America
1984	Jones	Flaked Stone Tools	Prehistoric	Oregon, USA
1984	Beck	Flaked Stone Tools	Prehistoric	Oregon, USA
1984	Campbell et al.	Flaked Stone Tools	Prehistoric	Washington, USA
1984	Beck	Use Wear	Prehistoric	Oregon, USA
1984	Campbell et al.	Use Wear	Prehistoric	Washington, USA
1984	Jones	Use Wear	Prehistoric	Oregon, USA
1984	O'Brien and Lewarch	Architecture (Houses)	AD 1800 – 1900	Missouri, USA
1985	O'Brien and Warren	Flaked Stone Tools (Projectile Points)	7500 – 5000 BC (Early-Middle Archaic)	Missouri, USA
1985	Currey et al.	Flaked Stone Tools (Projectile Points)	Prehistoric	Missouri, USA
1986	Winterhalder	Behavioral Responses	n/a	n/a
1987	Chatters	Use Wear	Prehistoric	Columbia Plateau, USA
1987	Lyman	Faunal Processing (butchery) marks	n/a	n/a
1987	Leonard and Jones	Societies	n/a	Various
1987	Miss	Use Wear	Prehistoric	Washington, USA
1988	Clark	Flaked Stone Tools	AD 1575 – 1790	Oregon, USA
1988	Clark	Lithic Raw Materials	AD 1575 – 1790	Oregon, USA
1991	Dockall	Flaked Stone Tools	AD 200 – 1150	New Mexico, USA
1993	Thorpe and Brown	Lithic Raw Materials (Volcanic)	n/a	Pacific Northwest
1994	Rafferty	Flaked Stone Tools (Projectile Points)	Archaic and Woodland Periods	Mississippi, USA
1995	Gunn and Graves	Ceramics	Prehistoric	Philippines
1995	Lewarch and Bangs	Use Wear	Prehistoric	Washington, USA
1996	Allen	Fishhooks (heads only)	AD 1250 – 1650	Cook Islands
1996	Allen	Fishhooks	AD 1250 – 1650	Cook Islands
1996	Jones	Flaked Stone Tools (Projectile Points)	Paleoindian	Montana, USA
1996	Loughran-Delahunt	Spindle whorls	AD 750 – 1800	Pacific Northwest

Year	Authors	Material Classified	Time Period	Geographic Location
1997	McCutheon	Lithic Raw Materials (Volcanic)	n/a	Pacific Northwest
1998	Blackham	Ceramics	Various	Southern Levant
1998	Cogswell and O'Brien	Ceramics	Early Mississippian Period	Missouri, USA
1998	Lohse	Use wear and Flaked Stone Tools	n/a	n/a
1998	Seong	Flakes Stone Tools (Microblades)	Paleolithic	Korea / Northeast Asia
1998	Weitzel	Hair	n/a	n/a
1999	Lohse and Sammons	Flaked Stone Tools	n/a	n/a
1999	Pierce	Ceramics (Coil Dimensions)	AD 650 – 1450	Southwestern USA
2000	Carr and Bradbury	Flaked Stone Tools (Bifaces)	n/a	n/a
2000	Weisler	Shell Rings	AD 1st – 11th centuries	Marshall Islands
2001	Cagle	Sediment deposits	2500 – 2290 BC (Old Kingdom)	Egypt
2001	Cochrane	Architecture	ca. AD 1250	Society Islands
2001	Pfeffer	Fishhooks	AD 1400 – 1750	Hawai'i, USA
2001	Lipo	Ceramics (Pottery Decorations)	AD 1400 – 1600	Central Mississippi River Valley, USA
2001	Sterling	Ceramics (Pottery Rims)	3500 – 2100 BC	Egypt
2001	Wilhelmsen	Flaked Stone Tools (Projectile Points)	Pleistocene & Holocene	Central Mississippi River Valley, USA
2003	Gjesfjeld	Architecture	Historic	Great Plains, USA
2003	VanPool	Flaked Stone Tools (Projectile Points)	8050 BC – AD 1900	Arizona, USA
2003	McElroy	Groundstone Tools (poi pounders)	Prehistoric	Hawai'i, USA
2003	McElroy	Groundstone Tools (poi pounders)	Prehistoric	Hawai'i, USA
2004	Emery	Ceramics	A.D. 1700 – 1970	Louisiana, USA
2004	Cochrane	Ceramics	Prehistoric	Fiji
2005	Commendador	Archaeological Structures	Prehistoric	Rapa Nui, Chile
2005	Darwent	Flaked Stone Tools (Projectile Points)	8950 – 6000 BC (Late Paleoindian-Early Archaic)	Missouri, USA

(continued)

Table 0.1. *Continued*

Year	Authors	Material Classified	Time Period	Geographic Location
2006	Burris	Flaked Stone Tools (Projectile Points)	Early Holocene	Mississippi, USA
2006	Harmon et al.	Ceramics (Pottery Decorations)	100 BC – AD 1450	Mexico
2006	Darwent and O'Brien	Flaked Stone Tools (Projectile Points)	8950 – 6000 BC (Late Paleoindian-Early Archaic)	Missouri, USA
2007	Beck and Jones	Flaked Stone Tools (Projectile Points)	Paleoindian	Great Basin, USA
2008	Egerer	Ceramics	Mayan	Belize–Guatemala Border
2008	VanPool et al.	Horned Serpent Motifs (pottery, murals, rock art)	AD 1000 – 1500	Southwestern USA
2009	Allen	Architecture (Foundations)	AD 17th Century and later	Marquesas Islands
2009	Edmonds	Flaked Stone Tools (Projectile Points)	Pleistocene & Holocene	Mississippi, USA
2009	Miksic et al.	Ceramics	AD 11th Century	Cambodia
2009	Ramenofsky et al.	Ceramics (glaze-paint types)	AD 1200 – 1700	New Mexico, USA
2009	Rorabaugh	Bone/Antler Barbed Tools	ca. 650 BC	Pacific Northwest
2009	Riede	Table Cutlery (forks)	AD 1500 – 1600	Northern Europe
2009	Riede	Table Cutlery (knives)	AD 1500 – 1600	Northern Europe
2009	Tehrani and Collard	Woven textiles	Modern/ Ethnographic	Iran
2009	Zedeño	Hunting Objects	n/a	North America
2010	Brown	Adzes and Fishhooks	Prehistoric	New Zealand
2010	García Rivero	Decorated slate plaques/ gorgets	3800 – 1800 BC (Neolithic)	Southwestern Iberian Peninsula
2010	Nolan	Subsurface Features	Late Prehistoric Period	Ohio, USA
2011	Bradbury et al.	Flaked Stone Tools (Projectile Points)	AD 1000 – 1500	Kentucky, USA
2011	Eren	Flaked Stone Tools (Unifacial tools)	Paleoindian	North American Lower Great Lakes
2011	Nolan and Cook	Time Periods	Late Prehistoric Period	Middle Ohio River Valley, USA
2012	Adriano and Ricarte	Digital Annotation Systems	n/a	n/a

Year	Authors	Material Classified	Time Period	Geographic Location
2012	Bradbury et al.	Flaked Stone Tools (Projectile Points)	AD 1000 – 1500	Kentucky, USA
2012	Eren	Flaked Stone Tool (Unifacial tool edges)	Paleoindian	North American Lower Great Lakes
2012	Eren et al.	Flaked Stone Tools (Unifacial tools)	Paleoindian	North American Lower Great Lakes
2013	Darwent et al.	Architecture (Houses)	AD 1150 – 1850	Alaska, USA
2014	Crema et al.	Flaked Stone Tools (Projectile Points)	Neolithic	Western Europe
2014	Gjesfjeld	Ceramics (Pottery Decorations)	6000 BC – AD 1850	Kuril Archipelago, Northeast Asia
2014	García Rivero and O'Brien	Decorated slate plaques/ gorgets	3800 – 1800 BC (Neolithic)	Southwestern Iberian Peninsula
2014	Letham	Archaeological Sites	Prehistoric and Historic	British Columbia, Canada
2014	O'Brien et al.	Flaked Stone Tools (Projectile Points)	Paleoindian	Eastern North America
2014	Okumura and Araujo	Flaked Stone Tools (Projectile Points)	11600 – 7540 cal. BP	Brazil
2015	Cardillo and Alberti	Flaked Stone Tools (Projectile Points)	Middle-Late and Final-Late Holocene	Argentina
2015	Lipo et al.	Flaked Stone Tools (Stemmed obsidian tools [mata'a])	Prehistoric	Rapa Nui, Chile
2015	Nolan et al.	Flaked Stone Tools (Bifaces)	1520 – 1370 BP	Ohio, USA
2015	O'Brien et al.	Flaked Stone Tools (Projectile Points)	Paleoindian	Eastern North America
2015	Sheldon	Subsurface Features, Lithic Technology	3500 – 2400 BP	Washington, USA
2015	VanPool et al.	Flaked Stone Tools (Projectile Points)	Paleoindian	Southwestern USA
2016	O'Brien et al.	Flaked Stone Tools (Projectile Points)	Paleoindian (Clovis)	Ohio, Indiana, Kentucky, USA
2016	O'Brien et al.	Flaked Stone Tools (Projectile Points)	Paleoindian	Eastern North America
2016	Eren et al.	Flaked Stone Tools (Projectile Points)	Paleoindian	Eastern North America
2017	Buchanan et al.	Flaked Stone Tools (Projectile Points)	Paleoindian (Clovis)	North America

Challenge #2: Scale of Analysis

As described above, the use of paradigmatic classification requires the use of mutually exclusive characters and character states in each dimension. This is one area in which a researcher can potentially exercise subjectivity—specifically in terms of character state breadth and character presence—thereby influencing an archaeological assemblage's relative observed richness of paradigmatic classes.

There is reason to suspect that character state breadth can potentially, in individual cases, influence the relative difference of observed class richness. For a simple example, consider hypothetical assemblages A and B, each classified via a paradigmatic classification consisting of three characters, each character in turn initially possessing two "character states." In this initial iteration, assemblage A is richer than assemblage B. However, what if the data necessary for the first character are more evenly distributed in assemblage B, but more clustered overall in assemblage A (Figure 0.2)? In this circumstance, as character state breadth becomes narrower in character 1, say expanding from two character states to four, observed richness

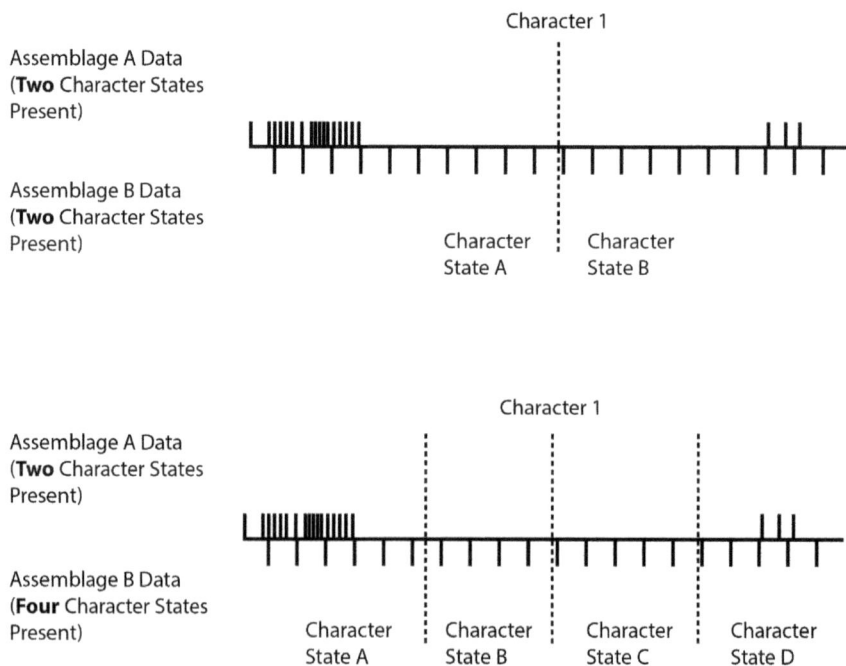

Figure 0.2. An illustration of two hypothetical assemblages' data with respect to a single character. The distribution of data can potentially influence the number of character states present in an assemblage, which in turn can potentially influence relative richness. © The authors.

in assemblage B increases at a faster rate than in assemblage A. All other things being equal, this faster rate of increasing richness could potentially erode substantially or even erase the relative difference of observed richness between the two assemblages.

A similar situation could potentially arise with respect to character presence. Again, consider hypothetical assemblages A and B, each classified via a paradigmatic classification consisting of five characters, but this time each character in turn initially possesses ten character states. In this initial iteration, assemblage A is again richer than assemblage B. However, it is soon discovered that the first character is found to be ambiguous, biased, or problematic, and must be discarded. If this first character was a principal driver of richness because of the way its character states combined with other characters' states, then when removed we may again see the relative difference of observed richness between the two assemblages be affected.

Due to these concerns, we incorporated a sensitivity analysis of characters and character states into our study of Clovis point diversity. This study, carried out by the authors and several colleagues (Buchanan et al. 2017), investigated differences in the diversity of Clovis point forms made in the western and eastern halves (split at the Mississippi River) of North America. This study used paradigmatic classification of seven characters that were defined to capture the shape and technological attributes of Clovis points (ibid.: Fig. 5). Because the samples from the west and east were different in sample size and completeness, we compared our three measures of class diversity—richness (the number of classes), Shannon diversity (the effective number of common classes), and Simpson diversity (the effective number of dominant classes)—using sample-size-based rarefaction and extrapolation, and coverage-based rarefaction and extrapolation. The results indicated that Clovis points in the east are more diverse relative to Clovis points in the west.

To assess the impact that our choice of characters and character states had on the outcome of this analysis, we iteratively removed from the analysis each of the seven characters that we had originally defined to measure the Clovis points. After each iteration we compared the three measures of class diversity between the west and east, and found that the removal of any of the seven characters from the analysis did not change its outcome. Next, we modified the breadth of the four characters in our paradigmatic classification that measured continuous variables by reducing the number of character states from three to two. The results of these analyses also showed them to be qualitatively similar to our initial results with the full range of characters and character states.

Lastly, in the study by Buchanan et al. (2017) we also modified the scale of our analysis by investigating the impact of excluding the largest assemblages in our dataset from each region and rerunning the analyses, and comparing the results to the original findings in order to evaluate the influence of these large assemblages on the results. As with the sensitivity analyses described above, the removal of large and potentially influential assemblages from both the east and west regions did not change the results of the study. Taken together, the results of our sensitivity analyses which altered the number of characters, character states, and assemblages in our study demonstrated that our results were robust to these perturbations.

Challenge #3: The Meaning of Diversity

After measuring diversity, and comparing measures of diversity between archaeological assemblages, it was not always immediately clear how to explain patterns or differences. Of course, the better defined the research questions and the implications of each set of predictions are at the outset of a study—that is, a well-developed and deductively derived set of hypotheses—the more compelling the explanations will be. In practice, however, archaeological hypotheses associated with diversity analyses are not always derived in a rigorous deductive manner, and many studies might start as exploratory endeavors or re-evaluations of older hypotheses that were not well justified at the outset. The latter issue is something that we have contended with in our study of Paleoindian point technology in the Eastern United States (Eren et al. 2016). In brief, our study re-examined the long-standing hypothesis put forth by Ronald Mason in the 1960s (Mason 1962) that the Southeastern United States possesses greater Paleoindian point diversity than other regions. We used paradigmatic classification and rarefaction techniques to compare the point-class richness of 1,056 Paleoindian points in different regions of the east. In our first set of analyses, we compared the Southeast region to the Northeast and found that the Southeast did indeed have more point-class richness than the Northeast. Next, we split Eastern North America into three regions—the Lower Southeast, the Upper Southeast, and the Northeast—and made similar comparisons among the three regions as we did with the two regions. We found that the Upper Southeast had greater point class richness than the other two regions. Thus, our first set of results supported Mason's initial claim, and our second set of results provided more specific details on the regional differences in the Eastern United States.

Our support for Mason's (1962) original claim does not however immediately imply that his explanation for this pattern should also be accepted. Mason assumed that greater diversity of Paleoindian point types was a consequence of greater time depth in the region. This explanation was based on a once-held belief that greater time depth was necessarily linked to greater diversity. However, Eren et al. (2016) pointed out other explanations for the greater point-class richness in the Southeast (and more specifically the Upper Southeast), including demographic processes that led to the isolation of specific populations. Founder effects and cultural drift can be associated with population isolation that might lead to reduced cultural richness and diversity. Eren et al. did not propose a specific explanation for the pattern of point-class richness in the Eastern United States, but rather emphasized that the goal of their study had been to use more rigorous quantitative methods to document diversity. Attributing meaning to the observed pattern of diversity requires the evaluation of multiple competing hypotheses for why there are differences in diversity.

Faced with a similar situation, the study by Buchanan et al. (2017), as described above, evaluated several competing hypotheses to narrow down an appropriate explanation for the patterns they found. To reiterate, the study by Buchanan et al. compared Clovis point-class richness between the broad eastern and western regions of North America. Using interpolation and extrapolation rarefaction techniques, they concluded that the eastern region had a richer and more uneven set of Clovis points compared to the west. Although this study was exploratory in its evaluation of the point-class richness and diversity pattern across the continent, Buchanan et al. attempted to assess the likelihood of several competing hypotheses. The first hypothesis was related to Mason's original proposal that diversity is a function of age. Buchanan et al. evaluated the current radiocarbon and genetic evidence that clearly indicates a west-to-east dispersal of Paleoindians rather than an east-to-west dispersal, thus rejecting this hypothesis. Next, they evaluated the population fissioning and isolation hypothesis, which, as described above, suggests that population budding and subsequent isolation during dispersal from west-to-east would result in more isolated populations in the east. These populations would then be subject to founder effects and drift. Buchanan et al. constructed a network of Clovis point-classes to evaluate this hypothesis and to determine if eastern Clovis assemblages appeared less connected than western assemblages. The results indicated that the east was well connected internally and connected with assemblages in the west, thus rejecting the isolation hypothesis. Lastly, Buchanan et al. assessed differential learning within the different environments of the east and west. They argued that the environment of the east was more heterogenous than the environment of the west, and consequently that learning in the east was more trial-and-error or experimental relative to the west. This difference in learning translated to more point class diversity in the east. To be sure, the hypothesis favored by Buchanan et al. (2017) requires further testing, but their evaluation of multiple hypotheses in this case was able to reject two hypotheses.

The Future

In conclusion, as archaeologists we commonly compare artifacts and assemblages, and the future is bright for such comparisons to occur via assessments of diversity. Indeed, the diverse approaches to archaeology—culture-history, processual archaeology, aspects of post-processual archaeology (e.g., agency)—are in many ways melding, as the social sciences in general undergo a culture evolutionary revolution (e.g., Boyd and Richerson 1988; Lycett 2015; Lyman and O'Brien 1998, 2001, 2006; Mesoudi 2007a, 2007b, 2011, 2017, 2020; Mesoudi, Whiten, and Laland 2004, 2006; O'Brien and Lyman 2000, 2002, 2003; O'Brien et al. 2001, 2003; Prentiss 2021; Richerson and Boyd 2008). Understanding archaeological diversity is but one small step in this more general, positive trend in understanding human culture.

Acknowledgments

We would like to thank all of the volume's contributors for their hard work, ingenuity, and patience. These sorts of volumes are truly a team effort, and we are extremely grateful to our colleagues who fulfilled their commitments. We would also like to thank Caryn Berg for her help, interest, patience, and guidance during the production of this book. We are appreciative of the contributions from Matt Boulanger and Lee Lyman in the assembly of Table 0.1, and from P. J. C.-E., who helped to put everything in proper perspective for M. I. E.

Briggs Buchanan is an Associate Professor at the University of Tulsa, Oklahoma, USA.

Metin I. Eren is an Associate Professor at Kent State University, Ohio, and a Research Associate at the Cleveland Museum of Natural History, Ohio, USA.

References

Adriano, C. M., and I. L. M. Ricarte. 2012. "Essential Requirements for Digital Annotation Systems." *Revista de Sistemas de Informação da FSMA* 9: 24–44.
Aikens, C. M., and R. Minor. 1977. *The Archaeology of Coffeepot Flat, South Central Oregon.* Portland: University of Oregon Anthropological Papers No. 11.

Allen, M. S. 1996. "Style and Function in East Polynesian Fish-Hooks." *Antiquity* 70(267): 97–116.

———. 2009. "Morphological Variability and Temporal Patterning in Marquesan Domestic Architecture: Anaho Valley in Regional Context." *Asian Perspectives* 48(2): 342–82.

Araujo, A. G. 2015. "On Vastness and Variability: Cultural Transmission, Historicity, and the Paleoindian Record in Eastern South America." *Anais da Academia Brasileira de Ciências* 87(2): 1239–58.

Beck, C. 1984. "Steens Mountain Surface Archaeology: The Sites." PhD dissertation. University of Washington, Seattle.

Beck, C., and G. T. Jones. 1989. "Bias and Archaeological Classification." *American Antiquity* 54: 244–62.

———. 2007. "Early Paleoarchaic Point Morphology and Chronology." In *Paleoindian or Paleoarchaic? Great Basin Human Ecology at the Pleistocene–Holocene Transition*, ed. K. E. Graf and D. N. Schmitt, 23–41. Salt Lake City: University of Utah Press.

Bisson, M. S. 2000. "Nineteenth-Century Tools for Twenty-First-Century Archaeology? Why the Middle Paleolithic Typology of François Bordes Must Be Replaced." *Journal of Archaeological Method and Theory* 7(1): 1–48.

Blackham, M. 1998. "The Unitary Association Method of Relative Dating and its Application to Archaeological Data." *Journal of Archaeological Method and Theory* 5(2): 165–207.

Bordes, F. 1961. *Typologie du Paléolithique Ancien et Moyen*. Bordeaux: Publications de l'Institut de Préhistoire de l'Université de Bordeaux, Mémoire 1.

Boyd, R., and P. J. Richerson. 1988. *Culture and the Evolutionary Process*. Chicago: University of Chicago Press.

Bradbury, A. P., D. R. Cooper, and R. L. Herndon. 2011. "Kentucky's Small Triangular Subtypes: Old Theories and New Data." *Journal of Kentucky Archaeology* 1(1): 2–24.

———. 2012. "Points on Points: A Reply to Pollack et al." *Journal of Kentucky Archaeology* 1(2): 65–88.

Brown, A. 2011. "Material Culture Traditions of Prehistoric Murihiku." Master's thesis. University of Otago, Dunedin, NZ.

Buchanan, B. 2005. "Cultural Transmission and Stone Tools: A Study of Early Paleoindian Technology in North America." PhD dissertation. University of New Mexico, Albuquerque, USA.

Buchanan, B., A. Chao, C. H. Chiu, R. K. Colwell, M. J. O'Brien, A. Werner, and M. I. Eren. 2017. "Environment-Induced Changes in Selective Constraints on Social Learning during the Peopling of the Americas." *Scientific Reports* 7: 44431.

Burris, A. 2006. "Defining an Alternative Typology for Early Holocene Projectile Points from the Hester Site (22MO569), Northeast Mississippi: A Systematic Approach." Master's thesis. Mississippi State University, Starkville, USA.

Cagle, A. J. 2001. "The Spatial Structure of Kom el-Hisn: An Old Kingdom Town in the Western Nile Delta, Egypt." PhD dissertation. University of Washington, Seattle.

Campbell, S. K. 1981. "The Duwamish No. 1 Site: A Lower Puget Sound Shell Midden." Office of Public Archaeology Research Report 1. Seattle: University of Washington Office of Public Archaeology.

Campbell, S. K., R. C. Dunnell, D. K. Grayson, M. E. Jaehnig, and J. V. Jermann. 1984. *Research Design for the Chief Joseph Dam Cultural Resources Project*. Seattle: University of Washington Office of Public Archaeology.

Cardillo, M., and J. Alberti. 2014. "The Evolution of Projectile Points and Technical Systems: A Case from the North Patagonian Coast (Argentina)." *Journal of Archaeological Science: Reports* 2: 612–23.

Carr, P. J., and A. P. Bradbury. 2000. "Contemporary Lithic Analysis and Southeastern Archaeology." *Southeastern Archaeology* 19(2): 120–34.

Chao, A. 1984. "Nonparametric Estimation of the Number of Classes in a Population." *Scandinavian Journal of Statistics* 11(4): 265–70.

Chatters, J. C. 1984. "Dimensions of Site Structure: The Archaeological Record from Two Sites in Okanogan County Washington." Central Washington University, Ellensburg: Report to the Seattle District, US Army Corps of Engineers. Central Washington Archaeological Survey.

———. 1987. "Hunter-Gatherer Adaptations and Assemblage Structure." *Journal of Anthropological Archaeology* 6: 336–75.

Clark, G. 1969. *World Prehistory: A New Synthesis.* Cambridge: Cambridge University Press.

Clark, L. A. 1988. "Archaeological Investigations at the Seal Rock Site, 35LNC14: A Late Prehistoric Shell Midden Located on the Central Oregon Coast." Master's thesis. Oregon State University, Corvallis, USA.

Cochrane, E. E. 2001. "Style, Function, and Systematic Empiricism: The Conflation of Process and Pattern." In *Style and Function: Conceptual Issues in Evolutionary Archaeology,* ed. T. D. Hurt and G. F. M. Rakita, 183–202. Westport, CT: Bergin & Garvey.

———. 2004. "Explaining Cultural Diversity in Ancient Fiji: The Transmission of Ceramic Variability." PhD dissertation. University of Hawaii, Manoa, USA.

Cogswell, J. W., and M. J. O'Brien. 1998. "Analysis of Early Mississippian Period Pottery from Kersey, Pemiscot County, Missouri." *Southeastern Archaeology* 17(1): 39–52.

Collard, M., B. Buchanan, J. Morin, and A. Costopoulos. 2011a. "What Drives the Evolution of Hunter-Gatherer Subsistence Technology? A Reanalysis of the Risk Hypothesis with Data from the Pacific Northwest." *Philosophical Transactions of the Royal Society B* 366:1129–1138.

Collard, M., B. Buchanan, M. J. O'Brien, and J. Scholnick. 2013a. "Risk, Mobility, or Population Size? Drivers of Technological Richness among Contact-Period Western North American Hunter-Gatherers." *Philosophical Transactions of the Royal Society B* 368: 20120412.

Collard, M., B. Buchanan, A. Ruttle, and M. J. O'Brien. 2011b. "Niche Construction and the Toolkits of Hunter-Gatherers and Food Producers." *Biological Theory* 6: 251–59.

Collard, M., A. Ruttle, B. Buchanan, and M. J. O'Brien. 2012. "Risk of Resource Failure and Toolkit Variation in Small-Scale Farmers and Herders." *PLoS ONE* 7: e40975.

———. 2013b. "Population Size and Cultural Evolution in Nonindustrial Food-Producing Societies." *PLoS ONE* 8: e72628.

Commendador, A. S. 2005. "Measuring Variability in Prehistoric Stone Construction on Rapa Nui, Chile." PhD dissertation. University of Hawaii, Manoa, USA.

Crema, E. R., K. Edinborough, T. Kerig, and S. J. Shennan. 2014. "An Approximate Bayesian Computation Approach for Inferring Patterns of Cultural Evolutionary Change." *Journal of Archaeological Science* 50: 160–70.

Croes, D. R. 1977. "Basketry from the Ozette Village Archaeological Site: A Technological, Functional, and Comparative Study." PhD dissertation. Washington State University, Pullman, USA.

Cruz-Uribe, K. 1988. "The Use and Meaning of Species Diversity and Richness in Archaeological Faunas." *Journal of Archaeological Science* 15(2): 179–96.

Currey, M., M. J. O'Brien, and M. K. Trimble. 1985. "The Classification of Pointed, Hafted Bifaces." In *Archaeology of the Central Salt River Valley: An Overview of the Prehistoric Occupation,* ed. M. J. O'Brien, 77–189. Missouri Archaeologist 46.

Dancey, W. S. 1973. "Prehistoric Land Use and Settlement Patterns in the Priest Rapids Area, Washington." PhD dissertation. University of Washington, Seattle.

———. 1975. "The Wood Box Spring Site (45-KT-209): A Preliminary Report." Reports in Highway Archaeology no. 1. Office of Public Archaeology, University of Washington, Seattle.

Darwent, J. 2005. "Late Paleoindian Period and Early Archaic Period Projectile-Point Phylogeny in the Salt River Valley, Northeastern Missouri." PhD dissertation. University of Missouri, Columbia, USA.

Darwent, J., O. K. Mason, J. F. Hoffecker, and C. M. Darwent. 2013. "1,000 Years of House Change at Cape Espenberg, Alaska: A Case Study in Horizontal Stratigraphy." *American Antiquity* 78(3): 433–55.

Darwent, J., and M. J. O'Brien. 2006. "Using Cladistics to Construct Lineages of Projectile Points from Northeastern Missouri." In *Mapping Our Ancestors: Phylogenetic Approaches in Anthropology and Prehistory*, ed. C. P. Lipo, M. J. O'Brien, M. Collard, and S. J. Shennan, 185–208. New Brunswick, NJ: Transaction.

Deetz, J. 1965. *The Dynamics of Stylistic Change in Arikara Ceramics*. Champaign: University of Illinois Press.

Dockall, J. 1991. "Chipped Stone Technology at the Nan Ruin, Grant County, New Mexico." Master's thesis. Texas A&M University, College Station, USA.

Duncan, M. A. 1979. *Archaeological Assessment of the Proposed Horsethief Lake Interpretive Facility*. Reconnaissance Report no. 25. Office of Public Archaeology, University of Washington, Seattle.

Dunnell, R. C. 1971. *Systematics in Prehistory*. New York: Free Press.

Dunnell, R. C., and C. Beck. 1979. "The Caples Site, 45-SA-5, Skamania County, Washington." Reports in Archaeology no. 6. Department of Anthropology, University of Washington, Seattle.

Dunnell, R. C., and S. K. Campbell. 1977. "Aboriginal Occupation of Hamilton Island, Washington." Reports in Archaeology no. 4. Department of Anthropology, University of Washington, Seattle.

Dunnell, R. C., S. K. Campbell, M. A. Duncan, D. E. Lewarch, and J. Rafferty. 1976. *Archaeological Test Investigations at the Caples Site, 45-SA-5, Skamaia County, Washington*. San Francisco: National Park Service.

Dunnell, R. C., and J. W. Fuller. 1975. *An Archaeological Survey of Everett Harbor and the Lower Snohomish Estuary-Delta*. San Francisco, CA: National Park Service.

Dunnell, R. C., and D. Lewarch. 1974. *Archaeological Remains in Home Valley Park, Skamania County, Washington*. Portland, OR: US Army Corps of Engineers.

Dunnell, R. C., D. E. Lewarch, and S. K. Campbell. 1976. *Test Excavations at the Hamilton Island Site, 45-A-12*. San Francisco: National Park Service.

Edmonds, J. L. 2009. "Mobility and Population Change in Northeast Mississippi: An Object-based Seriation of Projectile Points as a Relative Paleodemographic Indicator." Master's thesis. Mississippi State University, Starkville, USA.

Egerer, C. T. 2008. "The Ancient Maya Ceramics of El Pilar–Characteristics and Comparison." Master's thesis. University of Bonn, Germany.

Emery, J. A. 2004. "What Do Tin-Enameled Ceramics Tell Us? Explorations of Socioeconomic Status through the Archaeological Record in Eighteenth-Century Louisiana: 1700–1790." PhD dissertation. Louisiana State University, Baton Rouge, USA.

Eren, M. I. 2011. "Behavioral Adaptations of Human Colonizers in the North American Lower Great Lakes Region." PhD dissertation. Southern Methodist University, Dallas, Texas.

———. 2012. "Were Unifacial Tools Regularly Hafted by Clovis Foragers in the North American Lower Great Lakes Region? An Empirical Test of Edge Class Richness and Attribute Frequency among Distal, Proximal, and Lateral Tool-sections." *Journal of Ohio Archaeology* 2: 1–15.

Eren, M. I., A. Chao, C. H. Chiu, R. K. Colwell, B. Buchanan, M. T. Boulanger, J. Darwent, and M. J. O'Brien. 2016. "Statistical Analysis of Paradigmatic Class Richness Supports Greater Paleoindian Projectile-Point Diversity in the Southeast." *American Antiquity* 81: 174–92.

Eren, M. I., A. Chao, W. H. Hwang, and R. K. Colwell. 2012. "Estimating the Richness of a Population When the Maximum Number of Classes is Fixed: A Nonparametric Solution to an Archaeological Problem." *PLoS ONE* 7(5): e34179.

Fish, P. 1978. "Consistency in Archaeological Measurement and Classification: A Pilot Study." *American Antiquity* 43: 86–89.

Futato, E. M. 1983. "Projectile Point Morphology: Steps Toward a Formal Account." *Southeastern Archaeological Conference Bulletin* 21: 38–55.

García Rivero, D. 2010. "Evolución Cultural y Filogenias en Arqueología: El Caso de los Denominados Ídolos Placa Prehistóricos del Suroeste de la Península Ibérica." PhD dissertation. Universidad de Sevillas, Seville.

García Rivero, D., and M. J. O'Brien. 2014. "Phylogenetic Analysis Shows that Neolithic Slate Plaques from the Southwestern Iberian Peninsula Are Not Genealogical Recording Systems." *PLoS ONE* 9(2): e88296.

Gjesfjeld, E. W. 2003. "New Approaches to Understanding Cultural Continuity in the Great Plains." Master's thesis. University College London.

———. 2014. "Of Pots and People: Investigating Hunter-Gatherer Pottery Production and Social Networks in the Kuril Islands." PhD dissertation. University of Washington, Seattle.

Goodwin, R. C., J. K. Yakubik, and P. A. Gendel. 1984. *Archeological Data Recovery at Algiers Point*. New Orleans: Goodwin and Associates.

Gunn, M. M., and M. W. Graves. 1995. "Constructing Seriations from the Guthe Collection, the Central Philippines: Implications for Southeast Asian Ceramic Chronologies." *Asian Perspectives* 34: 257–82.

Hanford Arundale, W. 1980. "Functional Analysis of Three Unusual Assemblages from the Cape Dorset Area, Baffin Island." *Arctic* 33(3): 464–86.

Harmon, M. J., T. L. VanPool, R. L. Leonard, C. S. VanPool, and L. A. Salter. 2006. "Reconstructing the Flow of Information across Time and Space: A Phylogenetic Analysis of Ceramic Traditions from Prehispanic Western and Northern Mexico and the American Southwest." In *Mapping Our Ancestors: Phylogenetic Approaches in Anthropology and Prehistory*, ed. C. P. Lipo, M. J. O'Brien, M. Collard, and S. J. Shennan, 209–29. New Brunswick, NJ: Transaction.

Johnson, A. E., P. E. Brockington Jr., M. Adair, E. Anderson, and J. A. Artz. 1982. "Archaeological Investigation at El Dorado Lake, Butler County, Kansas. Phase III." Museum of Anthropology, Lawrence, Kansas.

Jones, G. T. 1984. "Prehistoric Land Use in the Steens Mountain Area, Southeastern Oregon." PhD dissertation. University of Washington, Seattle.

Jones, J. S. 1996. "The Anzick Site: Analysis of a Clovis Burial Assemblage." Master's thesis. Oregon State University, Corvallis, USA.

Kaufman, D. 1998. "Measuring Archaeological Diversity: An Application of the Jackknife Technique." *American Antiquity* 63: 73–85.

Leonard, R. D., and G. T. Jones. 1987. "Elements of an Inclusive Evolutionary Model for Archaeology." *Journal of Anthropological Archaeology* 6: 199–219.

———, eds. 1989. *Quantifying Diversity in Archaeology*. Cambridge: Cambridge University Press.

Letham, B. 2014. "Settlement and Shell-Bearing Site Diversity in the Sechelt Inlet System, British Columbia." *Canadian Journal of Archaeology* 38(1): 280–328.

Lewarch, D. E. 1982. "Analysis of Lithic Artifacts." In *The Cannon Reservoir Human Ecology Project: An Archaeological Study of Cultural Adaptations in the Southern Prairie Peninsula*, ed. M. J. O'Brien, R. E. Warren, and D. E. Lewarch, 145–70. New York: Academic Press.

Lewarch, D. E., and E. W. Bangs. 1995. "Lithic Artifacts." In *The Archaeology of West Point, Seattle, Washington: 4000 Years of Hunter-Fisher-Gatherer Land Use in Southern Puget Sound*, ed. Lynn L. Larson and Dennis E. Lewarch, pp. 7.1–7.181. Seattle, WA: Larson Anthropological/Archaeological Services, report to CH2M Hill, Bellevue, Washington, and King County Department of Metropolitan Services.

Lipo, C. P. 2001. "Community Structures among Late Mississippian Populations of the Central Mississippi River Valley." In *Posing Questions for a Scientific Archaeology*, ed. T. L. Hunt, C. P. Lipo, and S. L. Sterling, 175–216. Westport, CT: Berlin & Garvey.

Lipo, C. P., T. L. Hunt, and B. Hundtoft. 2015. "An Analysis of Stylistic Variability of Stemmed Obsidian Tools (Mata'a) on Rapa Nui (Easter Island)." In *Lithic Technological Systems and Evolutionary Theory*, ed. N. Goodale and W. Andrefsky, 225–38. Cambridge: Cambridge University Press.

Lohse, E. S. 1998. "Manual for Archaeological Analysis: Field and Laboratory Analysis Procedures." *Archaeological Survey Miscellaneous Paper* 98-1.

Lohse, E. S., and D. Sammons. 1999. "A Computerized Data Base for Lithic Use-Wear Analysis." In *Archaeology in the Age of the Internet*, ed. L. Dingwall, S. Exon, V. Gaffney, S. Laflin, and M. van Leusen, 280-5 to 280-14. Computer Applications and Quantitative Methods in Archaeology. Proceedings of the 25th Anniversary Conference, University of Birmingham, April 1997. Oxford: Archaeopress.

Loughran-Delahunt, I. 1996. "A Functional Analysis of Northwest Coast Spindle Whorls." Master's thesis. Western Washington University, Bellingham, USA.

Lycett, S. J. 2011. "'Most Beautiful and Most Wonderful': Those Endless Stone Tool Forms." *Journal of Evolutionary Psychology* 9(2): 143–71.

———. 2015. "Cultural Evolutionary Approaches to Artifact Variation over Time and Space: Basis, Progress, and Prospects." *Journal of Archaeological Science* 56: 21–31.

Lycett, S. J., and P. R. Chauhan. 2010. "Analytical Approaches to Palaeolithic Technologies: An Introduction." In *New Perspectives on Old Stones*, ed. S. J. Lycett and P. R. Chauhan, 1–22. New York: Springer.

Lycett, S. J., and N. von Cramon-Taubadel. 2015. "Toward a 'Quantitative Genetic' Approach to Lithic Variation." *Journal of Archaeological Method and Theory* 22(2): 646–75.

Lycett, S. J., N. von Cramon-Taubadel, and R. A. Foley. 2006. "A Crossbeam Co-ordinate Caliper for the Morphometric Analysis of Lithic Nuclei: A Description, Test, and Empirical Examples of Application." *Journal of Archaeological Science* 33(6): 847–61.

Lycett, S. J., K. Schillinger, M. I. Eren, N. von Cramon-Taubadel, and A. Mesoudi. 2016. "Factors Affecting Acheulean Handaxe Variation: Experimental Insights, Microevolutionary Processes, and Macroevolutionary Outcomes." *Quaternary International* 411: 386–401.

Lyman, R. L. 1987. "Archaeofaunas and Butchery Studies: A Taphonomic Perspective." In *Advances in Archaeological Method and Theory*, ed. M. B. Schiffer, 249–338. San Diego: Academic Press.

———. 2021. "On the Importance of Systematics to Archaeological Research: The Co-variation of Typological Diversity and Morphological Disparity." *Journal of Paleolithic Archaeology* 4: 3.

Lyman, R. L., M. A. Gallagher, C. G. Lebow, and M. K. Weber. 1983. *Reconnaissance in the Redmond Training Area, Central Oregon*. Salem: Oregon Military Department.

Lyman, R. L., and M. J. O'Brien. 1998. "The Goals of Evolutionary Archaeology: History and Explanation." *Current Anthropology* 39: 615–52.

———. 2001. "The Direct Historical Approach, Analogical Reasoning, and Theory in Americanist Archaeology." *Journal of Archaeological Method and Theory* 8: 303–42.

———. 2006. "Evolutionary Archaeology Is Unlikely to go Extinct: Response to Gabora." *World Archaeology* 38: 697–703.

Mason, R. J. 1962. "The Paleo-Indian Tradition in Eastern North America." *Current Anthropology* 3: 227–78.

Mason, R. E., R. E. Warren, and M. J. O'Brien. 1982. "Historic Settlement Patterns." In *The Cannon Reservoir Human Ecology Project: An Archaeological Study of Cultural Adaptations in the Southern Prairie Peninsula*, eds. M. J. O'Brien, R. E. Warren, and D. E. Lewarch, 369–88. New York: Academic Press.

McCutheon, P. T. 1997. "Archaeological Investigations of Stone Tool Heat Treatment in Southeast Missouri: An Experimental Approach." PhD dissertation. University of Washington, Seattle.

McElroy, W. K. 2003a. "Rethinking the Traditional Classification of Hawaiian Poi Pounders." *Rapa Nui Journal* 17(2): 85–93.

———. 2003b. "Variability in Poi Pounders from Kaua'i Island, Hawai'i." PhD dissertation. University of Hawaii, Manoa, USA.

Meltzer, D. J. 1981. "A Study of Style and Function in a Class of Tools." *Journal of Field Archaeology* 8(3): 313–26.

———. 1984. "Late Pleistocene Human Adaptations in Eastern North America." PhD dissertation. University of Washington, Seattle.

Meltzer, D. J., R. D. Leonard, and S. K. Stratton. 1992. "The Relationship between Sample Size and Diversity in Archaeological Assemblages." *Journal of Archaeological Science* 19(4): 375–87.

Mesoudi, A. 2007a. "Biological and Cultural Evolution: Similar but Different." *Biological Theory* 2(2): 119–23.

———. 2007b. "A Darwinian Theory of Cultural Evolution Can Promote an Evolutionary Synthesis for the Social Sciences." *Biological Theory* 2(3): 263–75.

———. 2011. *Cultural Evolution*. Chicago: University of Chicago Press.

———. 2017. "Pursuing Darwin's Curious Parallel: Prospects for a Science of Cultural Evolution." *Proceedings of the National Academy of Sciences* 114(30): 7853–60.

———. 2020. "The Study of Culture and Evolution across Disciplines." In *Cambridge Handbook of Evolutionary Perspectives on Human Behavior*, ed. L. Workman, W. Reader, and J. Barkow, 61–74. Cambridge: Cambridge University Press.

Mesoudi, A., A. Whiten, and K. N. Laland. 2004. "Is Human Cultural Evolution Darwinian? Evidence Reviewed from the Perspective of The Origin of Species." *Evolution* 58(1): 1–11.

———. 2006. "Towards a Unified Science of Cultural Evolution." *Behavioral and Brain Sciences* 29(4): 329–47.

Miksic, J., C. Rachna, H. Piphal, and C. Visoth. 2009. "Archaeological Report on the Thnal Mrech Kiln Site, TMK 02, Anlong Thom, Phnom Kulen, Cambodia." *Asia Research Institute Working Paper* 16: 1–43.

Miss, C. J. 1987. "Lithic Artifact Analysis." In *The Duwamish No. 1 Site, 1986 Data Recovery*, by URS Corporation and BOAS, Incorporated, pp. 6.1–6.65. Report to the Municipality of Metropolitan Seattle (METRO). Seattle, WA.

Nagaoka, L. 2001. "Using Diversity Indices to Measure Changes in Prey Choice at the Shag River Mouth site, Southern New Zealand." *International Journal of Osteoarchaeology* 11(1–2): 101–11.

Nolan, K. C. 2010. "Multi-staged Analysis of the Reinhardt Village Community: A Fourteenth-Century Central Ohio Community in Context." PhD dissertation. The Ohio State University, Columbus, USA.

Nolan, K. C., and R. A. Cook. 2010. "An Evolutionary Model of Social Change in the Middle Ohio Valley: Was Social Complexity Impossible during the Late Woodland but Mandatory during the Late Prehistoric?" *Journal of Anthropological Archaeology* 29(1): 62–79.

———. 2011. "A Critique of Late Prehistoric Systematics in the Middle Ohio River Valley." *North American Archaeologist* 32(4): 293–325.

Nolan, K. C., P. Sciulli, S. Blatt, and C. K. Thompson. 2015. "A Late Woodland Red Ocher Burial Cache from Madison County, Ohio." *North American Archaeologist* 36(3): 197–236.

O'Brien, M. J., M. T. Boulanger, B. Buchanan, R. A. Bentley, R. L. Lyman, C. P. Lipo, M. E. Madsen, and M. I. Eren. 2016. "Design Space and Cultural Transmission: Case Studies from Paleoindian Eastern North America." *Journal of Archaeological Method and Theory* 23: 692–740.

O'Brien, M. J., M. T. Boulanger, B. Buchanan, M. Collard, R. L. Lyman, and J. Darwent. 2014. "Innovation and Cultural Transmission in the American Paleolithic: Phylogenetic Analysis of Eastern Paleoindian Projectile-Point Classes." *Journal of Anthropological Archaeology* 34: 100–119.

O'Brien, M. J., M. T. Boulanger, R. L. Lyman, and B. Buchanan. 2015. "Phylogenetic Systematics". In *Mathematics in Archaeology*, ed. J. Barcelo and I. Bogdanovic, 232–46. Boca Raton, FL: CRC Press.

O'Brien, M. J., B. Buchanan, and M. I. Eren. 2016. "Clovis Colonization of Eastern North America: A Phylogenetic Approach." *STAR: Science & Technology of Archaeological Research* 2(1): 67–89.

O'Brien, M. J., J. Darwent, and R. L. Lyman. 2001. "Cladistics is Useful for Reconstructing Archaeological Phylogenies: Palaeoindian Points from the Southeastern United States." *Journal of Archaeological Science* 28(10): 1115–36.

O'Brien, M. J., and D. E. Lewarch. 1984. "The Built Environment." In *Grassland, Forest, and Historical Settlement: An Analysis of Dynamics in Northeast Missouri*, ed. M. J. O'Brien, 231–65. Lincoln: University of Nebraska Press.

O'Brien, M. J., D. E. Lewarch, J. E. Saunders, and C. B. Fraser. 1980. "An Analysis of Historic Structures in the Cannon Reservoir Area, Northeast Missouri." Technical Report 80-17. Department of Anthropology, University of Nebraska, Lincoln, USA.

O'Brien, M.J., and R. L. Lyman. 2000. *Applying Evolutionary Archaeology: A Systematic Approach*. New York: Springer.

———. 2002. "The Epistemological Nature of Archaeological Units." *Anthropological Theory* 2(1): 37–56.

———, eds. 2003. *Style, Function, Transmission: Evolutionary Archaeological Perspectives*. Salt Lake City: University of Utah Press.

O'Brien, M. J., R. L. Lyman, and R. D. Leonard. 2003. "What Is Evolution? A Response to Bamforth." *American Antiquity* 68: 573–80.

O'Brien, M. J., and R. E. Warren. 1985. "Archaeology of the Central Salt River Valley: An Overview of the Prehistoric Occupation; Stratigraphy and Chronology at Pigeon Roost Creek." *The Missouri Archaeologist* 46: 203–25.

Okumura, M., and A. G. Araujo. 2014. "Long-Term Cultural Stability in Hunter-Gatherers: A Case Study Using Traditional and Geometric Morphometric Analysis of Lithic Stemmed Bifacial Points from Southern Brazil." *Journal of Archaeological Science* 45: 59–71.

Pfeffer, M. T. 2001. "The Engineering and Evolution of Hawaiian Fishhooks." In *Posing Questions for a Scientific Archaeology*, ed. T. L. Hunt, C. P. Lipo, and S. L. Sterling, 73–96. Westport, CT: Berlin & Garvey.

Pierce, C. 1999. "Explaining Corrugated Pottery in the American Southwest: An Evolutionary Approach." PhD dissertation. University of Washington, Seattle.

Prentiss, A. M. 2021. "Theoretical Plurality, the Extended Evolutionary Synthesis, and Archaeology." *Proceedings of the National Academy of Sciences* 118(2): e2006564118.

Rafferty, J. 1994. "Gradual or Step-Wise Change: The Development of Sedentary Settlement Patterns in Northeast Mississippi." *American Antiquity* 59: 405–25.

Ramenofsky, A. F., F. D. Neiman, and C. D. Pierce. 2009. "Measuring Time, Population, and Residential Mobility from the Surface at San Marcos Pueblo, North Central New Mexico." *American Antiquity* 74: 505–30.

Read, D. 2015. "Statistical Reasoning and Archaeological Theorizing: The Double-Bind Problem." *Mathematics in Archaeology*, ed. J. Barcelo and I. Bogdanovic, 100–122. Boca Raton, FL: CRC Press.

Rhode, D. 1988. "Measurement of Archaeological Diversity and the Sample-Size Effect." *American Antiquity* 53: 708–16.

Richerson, P. J., and R. Boyd. 2008. *Not by Genes Alone: How Culture Transformed Human Evolution*. Chicago: University of Chicago Press.

Riede, F. 2009. "Tangled Trees: Modeling Material Culture Evolution as Host–Associate Cospeciation." In *Pattern and Process in Cultural Evolution*, ed. S. Shennan, 85–98. Berkeley: University of California Press.

Rorabaugh, A. N. 2009. "Barbed Bone and Antler Technologies: Cultural Transmission and Variation in the Gulf of Georgia, Northwest North America." Master's thesis. Western Washington University, Bellingham, USA.

Seong, C. 1998. "Microblade Technology in Korea and Adjacent Northeast Asia." *Asian Perspectives* 37: 245–78.

Shaw, A. B. 1969. "Adam and Eve, Paleontology, and the Non-Objective Arts." *Journal of Paleontology* 43: 1085–98.

Shea, J. J. 2013. "Lithic Modes A–I: A New Framework for Describing Global-Scale Variation in Stone Tool Technology Illustrated with Evidence from the East Mediterranean Levant." *Journal of Archaeological Method and Theory* 20(1): 151–86.

Sheldon, D. J. 2015. "Determination of Site Functionality and Subsistence Patterns at the Bray Archaeological Site (45PI1276) in Edgewood, Washington." Master's thesis. Central Washington University, Ellensburg, USA.

Shott, M. J. 1989. "Diversity, Organization, and Behavior in the Material Record: Ethnographic and Archaeological Examples." *Current Anthropology* 30(3): 283–315.

———. 1997. "Activity and Formation as Sources of Variation in Great Lakes Paleoindian Assemblages." *Midcontinental Journal of Archaeology* 22: 197–236.

———. 2010. "Size Dependence in Assemblage Measures: Essentialism, Materialism, and 'SHE' Analysis in Archaeology." *American Antiquity* 75: 886–906.

———. 2011. "History Written in Stone: Evolutionary Analysis of Stone Tools in Archeology." *Evolution: Education and Outreach* 4(3): 435–45.

———. 2020. "Toward a Theory of the Point." In *Culture History and Convergent Evolution*, ed. H. Groucutt, 245–59. Cham, Switzerland: Springer.

Sterling, S. L. 2001. "Social Complexity in Ancient Egypt: Functional Differentiation as Reflected in the Distribution of Standardized Ceramics." In *Posing Questions for a Scientific Archaeology*, ed. T. L. Hunt, C. P. Lipo, and S. L. Sterling, 145–75. Westport, CT: Bergin & Garvey.

Strong, W. D. 1935. "An Introduction to Nebraska Archeology." *Smithsonian Miscellaneous Collections* 93(10).

Tehrani, J., and M. Collard. 2009. "The Evolution of Material Culture Diversity among Iranian Tribal Populations." In *Pattern and Process in Cultural Evolution*, ed. S. Shennan, 99–112. Berkeley: University of California Press.

Thomas, D. H. 1989. "Diversity in Hunter-Gatherer Cultural Geography." In *Quantifying Diversity in Archaeology*, ed. R. D. Leonard and G. T. Jones, 85–91. Cambridge: Cambridge University Press.

Thompson, G. 1978. *Prehistoric Settlement Changes in the Southern Northwest Coast: A Functional Approach*. Reports in Archaeology 5. Department of Anthropology, University of Washington, Seattle.

Thorpe, R. S., and G. C. Brown. 1993. *The Field Description of Igneous Rocks*. Chichester, UK: John Wiley & Sons.

Thulman, D. K. 2006. "A Reconstruction of Paleoindian Social Organization in North Central Flordia." PhD dissertation. Florida State University, Tallahassee.

VanPool, C. S., T. L. VanPool, and M. Harmon. 2008. "Plumed and Horned Serpents of the American Southwest." In *Touching the Past: Ritual, Religion, and Trade of Casas Grandes*, ed. G. Nielsen-Grimm and P. Stavast, 47–58. Brigham Young University, Provo, Utah: Museum of Peoples and Cultures.

VanPool, T. L. 2003. "Explaining Changes in Projectile Point Morphology: A Case Study from Ventana Cave, Arizona." PhD dissertation. University of New Mexico, Albuquerque.

VanPool, T. L., M. J. O'Brien, and R. L. Lyman. 2015. "Innovation and Natural Selection in Paleoindian Projectile Points from the American Southwest." In *Lithic Technological Systems and Evolutionary Theory*, ed. N. Goodale and W. Andrefsky, 61–82. Cambridge: Cambridge University Press.

Weisler, M. I. 2000. "Burial Artifacts from the Marshall Islands: Description, Dating and Evidence for Extra-Archipelago Contacts." *Micronesia Agana* 33(1/2): 111–36.

Weitzel, M. A. 1998. "A New Method for the Analysis of Human Hair: A Morphological Case Study of Five Sample Populations." Master's thesis. Oregon State University, Corvallis, USA.

Whallon Jr., R. 1972. "A New Approach to Pottery Typology." *American Antiquity* 37: 13–33.

Whittaker, J., D. Caulkins, and K. Kamp. 1998. "Evaluating Consistency in Typology and Classification." *Journal of Archaeological Method and Theory* 5: 129–64.

Wilhelmsen, K. H. 2001. "Building the Framework for an Evolutionary Explanation of Projectile Point Variation: An Example from the Central Mississippi River Valley." In *Posing Questions for a Scientific Archaeology*, ed. T. L. Hunt, C. P. Lipo, and S. L. Sterling, 97–144. Westport, CT: Bergin & Garvey.

Winterhalder, B. 1986. "Diet Choice, Risk, and Food Sharing in a Stochastic Environment." *Journal of Anthropological Archaeology* 5(4): 369–92.

Zedeno, M. N. 2009. "Animating by Association: Index Objects and Relational Taxonomies." *Cambridge Archaeological Journal* 19(3): 407–17.

Zeier, C. D. 1982. "The Willey and Phillips System Revisited: A Proposed Expansion of the Paradigm." *Plains Anthropologist* 27: 29–36.

Chapter 1

Dispersion and Diversity

Parfleche Variation on the Great Plains
vs. the Columbia Plateau

Stephen J. Lycett

Artifactual diversity is one of the ways in which differences in the socially
learned behaviors and conventions of different communities and subcom-
munities of peoples (what might also be called different "social networks"
or "communities of practice" [Lave and Wenger 1991]) manifest themselves. Accordingly, the issue of artifactual diversity and its causes has long
found itself at the heart of many archaeological questions. Indeed, in many
respects, understanding the link between artifactual diversity and its direct
anthropogenic causes (behavioral, social, functional, and so forth) could be
considered *the* prime directive of all archaeological research (Reid, Schiffer,
and Rathe 1975).

Artifactual diversity might also be considered to relate directly to another two key factors in archaeological work: variation in time and space
(Clarke 1968; Lyman, O'Brien, and Dunnell 1997). At whatever scale, artifactual "diversity" is a comparison or measure of variation within a specific unit of time and/or space. Even precisely defined "classes" of artifacts
have a dispersion in time and space, whether large or small. A reasonable
working assumption, if not null hypothesis, is that when either the dimension of space and/or time is increased, then artifactual diversity will
increase. The greater the time span examined, the greater the artifactual
diversity one might expect. Equally, the greater the spatial unit examined,
the more artifactual diversity one might expect to see (cf. Wright 1943).

Indeed, in principle, a linear relationship between spatial and artifactual variation might be accelerated if the increase in geographical area correlates with greater ecological diversity (cf. Báldi 2008).

A relationship between archaeological diversity and time is something that is at the core of many (often unspoken) concepts. It was key to the development of issues such as seriation, for example, by which changes in artifactual form directly measure change along the axis of time (Lyman and O'Brien 2006). This is because artifactual form and its variation in time and space can also be linked directly with the issue of cultural transmission, whereupon variations in socially learned concepts concerning the manufacture, use, and form of artifacts are replicated with varying degrees of error, or are deliberately modified as they are socially transmitted between individuals over time and space (Clarke 1968; Lycett and Shennan 2018; O'Brien and Lyman 2000). In fact, archaeologists some time ago noted the interrelationships between time, space, and artifactual form as a compounding—but interesting—factor when trying to organize (i.e., seriate) artifactual change along the temporal dimension (Deetz and Dethlefsen 1965; Phillips, Ford, and Griffin 1951). This is not to say that factors work to sometimes inflict stability in artifactual traditions (Lycett et al. 2016; Martin 2000; Okumura and Araujo 2014), nor that other complications arise, but in many different contexts a relationship between increased time span and increased diversity of artifactual form (however measured) can be demonstrated (e.g., Bouma and Keyser 2004; Deetz and Dethlefsen 1967; O'Brien and Lyman 1999).

In this chapter, I wish to focus more on the relationship between the areal dispersion of artifacts and their diversity. Archaeologists frequently examine archaeological variability on a relatively limited geographic scale, yet may also examine archaeological units at virtually continental-wide scales. The ceramic "Beaker" phenomenon of early Bronze Age Europe (Vander Linden 2007), the Paleoindian "Clovis" points of North America (Buchanan et al. 2016), or—most geographically monstrous of all—the Pleistocene bifaces of the Old World "Acheulean" (Lycett et al. 2016) are prime examples. In these cases, singular classes of artifacts are used to define a "pattern" or unit worthy of further consideration. Much ink has been spilled in using these units as strawmen to be easily knocked down with evident shortcomings as effective or singular ethnic or linguistic units. The fact remains that, as archaeological patterns, these units attest that people made pots, bifaces, and projectile points of a particular form over large spans of space. As such, they form a legitimate—but different—starting point for interesting questions (Clarke 1968; Lycett 2017).

Parfleches: Equestrian Suitcases of the Post-Contact Plains and Plateau Regions of North America

Here, I wish to examine the relationship between increased geographic space and increased artifactual diversity by using a singular artifactual class spread over a large geographic region. As has been noted elsewhere, ethnographically derived data can form the basis for particularly useful insights for archaeologists into these kinds of questions, since broader contextual, historical, linguistic, and other key factors are often known with greater security than is typically the case in archaeological situations (Clarke 1968; Hodder 1982; Lycett 2017).

An issue arising with ethnographically derived data, however, is that they are often (understandably) obtained from relatively discrete geographical areas. In the case of detailed artifactual data, for example, a single craftsperson, community, or, at best, region, comprise the most frequently encountered forms of detailed data. Parfleches made by Indigenous communities during the Historic period in western North America may potentially provide something of the richness of context that ethnographic data deliver, but can also be studied on a geographic scale that is more applicable to many equivalent archaeological cases (Lycett 2015, 2017). Parfleches (Figure 1.1) are painted and folded rawhide bags (sometimes referred to as "envelopes") that came to be used by many Indigenous peoples in western North America following the introduction of the horse in the post-Contact Period (Morrow 1975; Torrence 1994). The majority of parfleches average between 56–74 cm in length and 30–41 cm in width (Torrence 1994: 63). They were used as storage and transportation devices, often as saddle bags strapped to the side of horses and mules (Ewers 1955: 113). Although containers of a similar form were perhaps used prior to the late 1700s, their better-known form and size was likely a direct development of the "horse culture" period, with many tribes potentially adopting these for the first time as part of the broader cultural changes that occurred during this period (Torrence 1994). Indeed, recent work has shown that trade networks were a major means by which stylistic variants were transmitted across groups (Lycett 2017).

Parfleches were used most extensively in the Great Plains and Columbia Plateau regions, and were made and decorated by the skilled craftswomen of numerous ethnolinguistic tribes inhabiting those regions (Morrow 1975). Although simply decorated with paints—predominantly red, blue, green, and yellow—and with geometric designs that included triangles, rhomboids, and rectangles made of curved and/or straight lines, diversity and tribal distinctiveness in design and decorative features could be created. In fact, one scholar of parfleche design noted, "it is remarkable that such

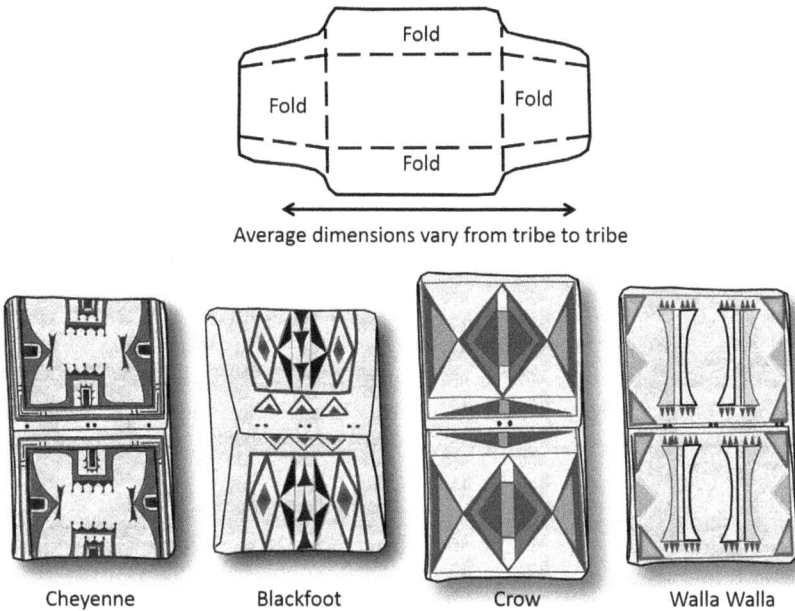

Figure 1.1. Examples of the contrasts in parfleche form and decorative features across tribes. Redrawn and modified after Lycett 2017 and Morrow 1975. © The author.

diverse effects were achieved by artists using essentially the same limited palette" (Torrence 1994: 78). It should be emphasized, however, that it was not merely the painted decorations that created the visual distinctions in these items (Morrow 1975). The form of the folding flaps, the number of lace holes, as well as the overall shape and dimensions of parfleches combined to create the distinctive forms that varied across different ethnolinguistic groups. Parfleche attributes also varied from tribe to tribe in terms of whether the decorative designs were outlined, whether small black or brown decorative units were used, whether bands were used to join design areas, and whether the sides of parfleches were decorated in addition to the flaps. In this study, twenty-three of these different attributes were used to consider diversity in parfleche designs across the Plateau and Great Plains regions (see Morrow 1975, and Lycett 2015, 2017, for further details).

The Great Plains and Columbia Plateau Regions

Both the Great Plains and the Columbia Plateau regions have long been considered two of the classic "culture areas" of post-Contact western North America (Holmes 1914; Kroeber 1939). In other words, on the basis of combined topographical, ecological, subsistence, and cultural features, these regions were considered distinctive. The Great Plains, is a semiarid region, which, during the post-Contact Period, was home to many of the classic "horse culture" peoples (Hämäläinen 2003; Mitchell 2015). Buffalo (*Bison bison*) hunting is a feature of these peoples that has most famously entered the popular imagination, but only tribes in the far west of the Great Plains adopted this as their primary economic base; many tribes in the eastern reaches of the Great Plains were also agriculturalists (Holder 1970). Tipis were the favored form of dwelling among the fully equestrian tribes due to their portability, while villages with structures of timber and earth were also used by the farming peoples (DeMallie 2001). On the Columbia Plateau, fishing of both anadromous and resident species in the region's lakes and rivers was a major subsistence base, which was supplemented with a variety of wild game and the gathering of root vegetables (Walker 1998). Facilitated by the region's trade fairs (especially at The Dalles), contact with peoples of the Plains region was extensive for many tribes situated along the Columbia River and its tributaries, as was contact among many tribes of the Plateau itself (Lycett 2017, 2019; Walker 1998).

In the present study, parfleche data from twenty-six ethnolinguistic tribes were analyzed: fifteen from the Great Plains and eleven from the Columbia Plateau (Table 1.1). The high linguistic diversity among the peoples of both

Table 1.1. Ethnolinguistic tribes incorporated in this study.

Plains (language family)	Plateau (language family)
Arapaho (Algonquian)	Cayuse (Cayuse)
Gros Ventre (Algonquian)	Klikitat (Sahaptian)
Blackfoot (Algonquian)	Umatilla (Sahaptian)
Cheyenne (Algonquian)	Walla Walla (Sahaptian)
Assiniboine (Siouan)	Nez Perce (Sahaptian)
Crow (Siouan)	Yakima (Sahaptian)
Lakota (Siouan)	Wishram (Chinookan)
Hidatsa (Siouan)	Wasco (Chinookan)
Mandan (Siouan)	Kootenai (Isolate)
Osage (Siouan)	Flathead (Salishan)
Pawnee (Caddoan)	Kalispel (Salishan)
Wichita (Caddoan	
Sarcee (Athapaskan)	
Kiowa (Kiowa-Tanoan)	
Comanche (Uto-Aztecan)	

regions is a feature that has long been noted, with as many as six different language families represented in the Plains tribes considered here, and five in the Plateau tribes, with multiple languages and distinct dialects spoken in both cases (Campbell 1997). One startling feature of contrast between the two regions, however, is their geographic extent. Figure 1.2 maps the total extent of tribal territories during the nineteenth century (taken from Walker 1998 and DeMallie 2001) for the Plateau tribes versus the Plains tribes. The tribes of the Great Plains covered areas that would now be designated as the US states of Arkansas, Missouri, Oklahoma, Texas, Kansas, Colorado, Wyoming, Montana, Nebraska, North Dakota, and South Dakota, as well as southern portions of the Canadian Provinces of Alberta and Saskatchewan. Tribes of the Columbia Plateau were situated in what is now northern Idaho, eastern Washington, northeastern Oregon, western portions of Montana, and a southeast portion of Canada's British Columbia (Figure 1.2).

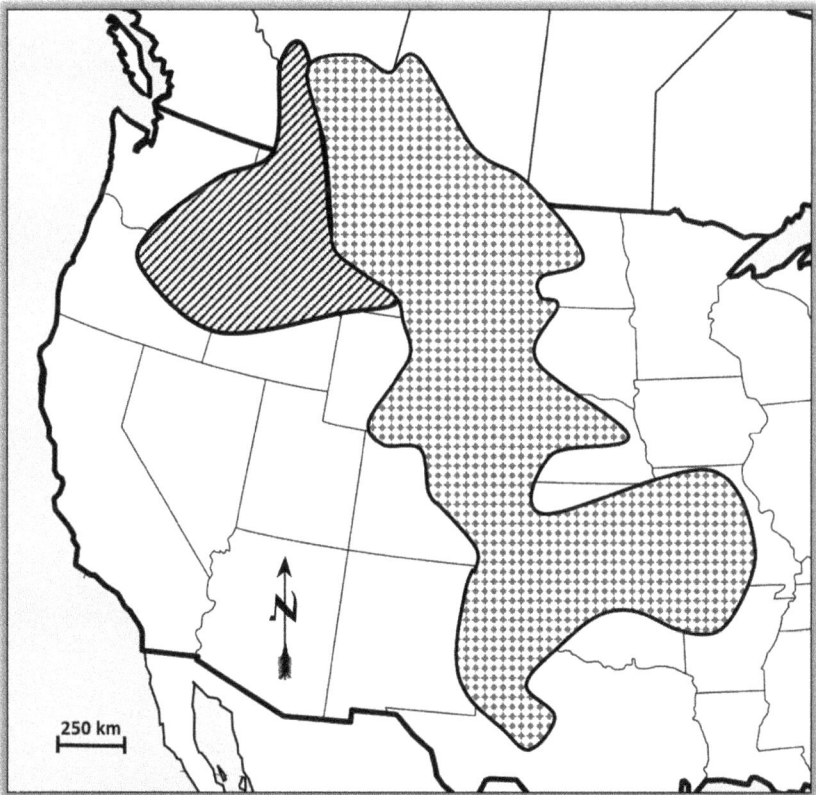

Figure 1.2. Map showing the geographic extent of the tribes in Plateau (hatching) and Plains (stippling) regions considered in the analyses. © The author.

While the contrast in geographic scale of the Plateau and Great Plains tribal territories might be evident from the foregoing, it is useful given the purposes of this chapter to draw out these contrasts more formally, especially in terms of the dispersion and distribution of the various ethnolinguistic units across both regions. The center points of tribal territories can form the basis for a series of geographic comparisons of the two study regions. While tribal territorial boundaries were inevitably somewhat malleable during the Historic period, the center points of each tribe's main occupation area during these years provide a locality point that can be used in comparative analysis. As implied by the map shown in Figure 1.2, there is marked variation in both the latitudinal and longitudinal distribution of the Plains and the Plateau tribes. However, more formally, the variance in latitudinal distribution (as measured by the center points of their territories) for the Plateau tribes is 2.3, while the equivalent variance for the Plains tribes is 42.8, a difference which is, unsurprisingly, statistically significant ($F[11, 15] = 18.58, p < 0.001$). Figure 1.3 visually illustrates this

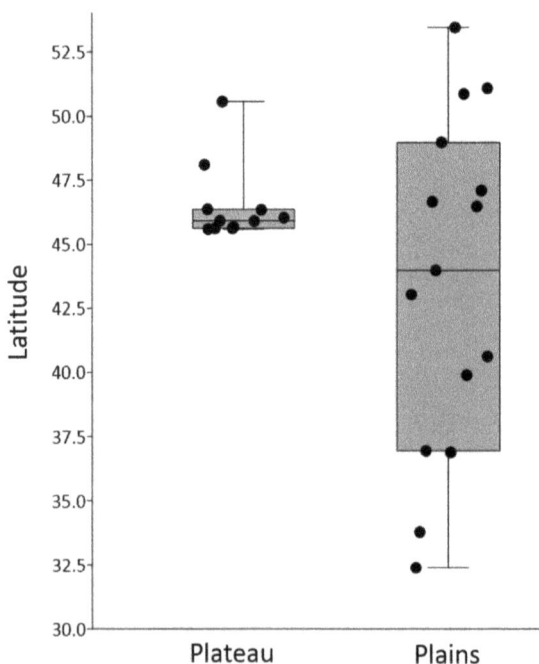

Figure 1.3. The extent of latitudinal distributions (variance) of the various ethnolinguistic tribes is statistically higher for Plains than for Plateau tribes. Boxes delimit the 25–75 percent quartiles, and the median is indicated by the horizontal line inside each box. Termination of the lines (whiskers) extending from the boxes indicate minimal and maximal values in each case. © The author.

difference in latitudinal distributions. A similar pattern is found for the longitudinal distributions of the tribes in both regions: the longitudinal variance for the Plateau tribes is 9.5, whereas for the Plains tribes it is 35.7. Again, this difference in longitudinal variance is statistically significant (F [11, 15] = 3.78, p = 0.04). In basic terms, both longitudinal and latitudinal distributions are far more variable for Plains tribes than they are for Plateau tribes.

Comparing geographic distances between the center points for each tribe's territory reinforces the geographic contrasts in these two regions. The geographic distance from the center of each tribe's territory to all other tribes was computed, as were average and median among-tribe values for the Plains region versus the Plateau region respectively. Figure 1.4 shows boxplots for the average geographic distances from other tribes of the same region, clearly showing that the median of these values is higher for the Plains region than for the Plateau. Again, unsurprisingly, this difference between median values for each region is statistically significant

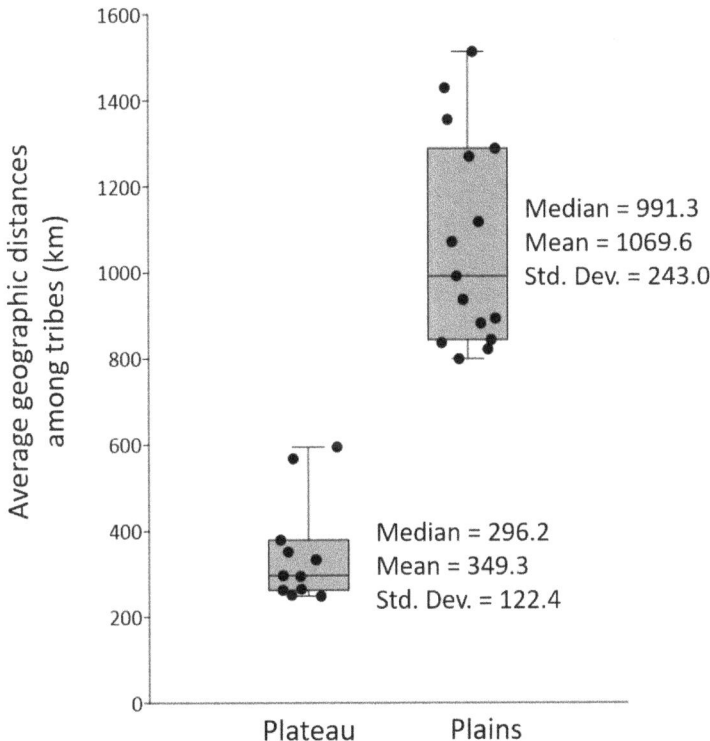

Figure 1.4. Average geographic distance between the center points of territories for Plains tribes is statistically higher than is the case for Plateau tribes. © The author.

(Mann-Whitney $z = -4.256$, $p < 0.001$). The same effect can be shown in statistical comparison of the mean average distances among tribes in each region ($t_{\text{Unequal variance}} = 9.8971$, $p < 0.001$). The tribes of the Plains sprawl out over a far larger area than is the case for the Plateau tribes. Accordingly, the ratio of average among-group distances compared to the number of tribes on the Plains is 71.3, while the equivalent ratio for the Plateau is only 31.75. In sum, all of these comparisons more formally demonstrate what is readily visible on the map shown in Figure 1.2: the total areal extent of tribes in the Great Plains is much higher than it is for the Plateau region. However, by stating the differences between the two regions in formal terms, we can now compare the extent of parfleche attribute diversity in specific geographic terms.

Comparing Parfleche Diversity in the Plateau versus the Plains

The analyses undertaken so far have unequivocally demonstrated that the Historic-period Plains tribes were distributed over a broader geographic sprawl compared to the more discretely distributed Plateau tribes, both longitudinally and latitudinally. Moreover, on average, there are significantly greater geographic distances between the center points of tribal territories on the Plains versus the Plateau. Using the logic described earlier, the larger area covered and the greater average geographic distances between Plains tribes might be expected to lead to higher parfleche diversity (i.e., material culture diversity) among Plains groups compared to those on the Columbia Plateau.

As noted earlier, twenty-three attributes describing differences in the form and decorative attributes of parfleches can be used to compute among-tribe diversity measures for the Plains and Plateau regions. Three of the parfleche characters used for this purpose were treated as nominal (i.e., categorical) variables, while the additional twenty features may be described simply on a "present versus absent" (i.e., binary) basis (Morrow 1975; Lycett 2015, 2017). Different categories of variable require different measures of intergroup artifactual "distance" (Shennan 1997). The nominal variables were examined using the Hamming distance measure, while for the binary characters the Jaccard measure was used, which is particularly appropriate for presence/absence data. This latter distance measure places greater emphasis on shared presences rather than absences in computing distances between groups, the latter of which are more prone to sampling errors or observational errors that create spurious absences (Shennan 1997).

Effectively, the higher the "distance" value between two tribes, the greater the number of attribute differences that exist between them. Such distances were calculated on a pairwise basis for all the tribes of the Plains and the Plateau. From these values, an average among-tribe distance measure can be computed for each of the tribes of the Plateau versus those of the Plains region. In other words, this procedure provides an among-tribe diversity measure of parfleche attributes for each region. If spatial dispersion is a preeminent factor in driving among-tribe diversity of parfleche attributes, then the Plains region should have a higher diversity measure than the Plateau.

Figure 1.5 illustrates boxplots that describe the average among-tribe parfleche distance values for each tribe of the Plateau versus those of the Plains. Contrary to predictions, the median value of these measures for the Plains region (0.603) is not higher than for the Plateau (0.658). However, the difference between these values for each region is not statistically different (Mann-Whitney $z = -1.557$, $p = 0.12$). Likewise, the mean of these

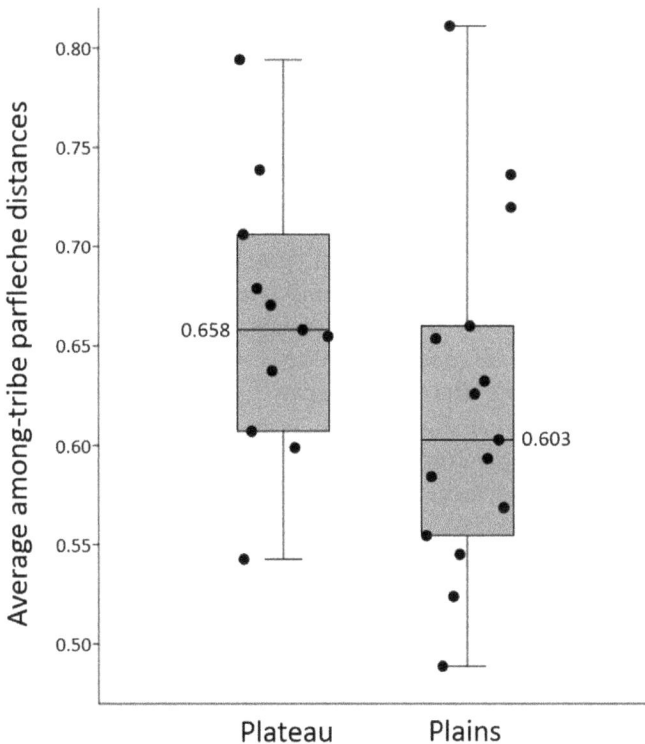

Figure 1.5. Boxplots showing the average among-tribe parfleche distance value for each tribe of the Plateau versus the Plains (median value for each region indicated). Contrary to predictions based on geographic dispersion, parfleche distances (i.e., cultural diversity) is not significantly different between the Plateau and Plains tribes. © The author.

data is actually higher for the Plateau tribes (0.66) than for the Plains tribes (0.62), but again these values are statistically equivalent ($t_{\text{Unequal variance}}$ = 1.39, p = 0.18). It is also worth directly comparing Figure 1.5 to figures 1.3 and 1.4, which on the one hand graphically illustrate the marked geographic differences between the two regions, yet on the other illustrate the general comparability of inter-tribe distances of parfleche attributes for these two regions. In other words, on average, parfleche attributes are about as different from each other among the tribes of the Columbia Plateau as they are among the tribes of the Great Plains. Moreover, this equivalence of artifactual diversity exists despite the geographic differences between these two regions.

Discussion and Conclusions

At a most basic level, the analyses undertaken here show that greater dispersion of peoples (specifically, ethnolinguistically defined peoples) across one geographic region does not automatically result in greater artifactual diversity compared to a smaller region. It is perhaps important to emphasize, however, that the analysis does not entirely dismiss a relationship between increased parfleche diversity at increased geographic scales. The sum of the diversity in the two regions is inevitably greater than the diversity seen within a single region. Equally, the analysis certainly does not rule out use of the idea that a larger area will contain greater artifactual diversity than a smaller one as a worthwhile null hypothesis, especially because, as here, it can be rejected—which is actually a strength rather than weakness of all effective null models. A key point, however, is that the units of space examined here—the Plains versus the Plateau regions—were not arbitrarily defined on spatial grounds alone. They have long been seen as representing differing cultural, social, economic, and ecological conditions. It appears likely, therefore, that these are the kinds of variables that are more pertinent drivers of parfleche diversity than spatial issues alone.

Given the results obtained, a basic question to ask is what is going on to create this apparent equivalency: is parfleche diversity unexpectedly low on the Plains, or is parfleche diversity relatively high on the Plateau? In over a century of research, many commentaries on parfleche design and decorative features have noted the marked contrasts among those produced by the various tribes of the Great Plains (e.g., Douglas 1936; Kroeber 1908; Lycett 2017; Morrow 1975; Spier 1925; Torrence 1994). Indeed, among the nomadic tribes of the High Plains at least, there is evidence that parfleche designs were deliberately being used either consciously or unconsciously as highly visible signals of ethnolinguistic affiliation (Lycett 2015).

In other words, there is absolutely no reason to propose that parfleche designs were "uniform" on the Plains, nor that they show low disparity in design and decorative attributes; all evidence points to the contrary. Given the results of the analysis, therefore, what is even more intriguing is that at least as much diversity was seen over the relatively more discrete space of the Plateau region.

An additional factor, adding further intrigue, is the social contrast between the two regions. During the Historic period, the Great Plains are known to have seen marked levels of inter-tribal conflict, which was not only violent, but frequently fatal in form (Clark and Bamforth 2018; McGinnis 1990; Smith 1938). This conflict was driven by demands for territory, horses, and firearms, with competition for all of these stoked by the Euro-American fur trade. Recall that parfleches were used as "saddle bags," strapped to the sides of horses while groups were moving across the Plains. This is exactly the kind of circumstance in which we might expect highly visible items of material culture such as parfleches to act as markers of group identity (Lycett 2015; Wobst 1977). As Wobst (1977: 332) observed, such devices effectively "allow one to decide whether contact and interaction with an unknown person would be advantageous or not, before one gets uncomfortably close to the individual." In other words, cultural selection relating to social conditions (Lycett 2015) seems to explain something of the diversity in parfleche designs of the Great Plains, which scholars have noted for decades.

In direct contrast to this, however, the Plateau region has long been seen as a region marked by strong levels of intergroup transmission and mutual cooperation. This is observed to have created high levels of cultural homogeneity across the region, with Walker (1998: 3) noting that the Plateau was characterized by "relatively uniform mythology, art styles, and religious beliefs and practices." Recent work has shown that clothing styles and fishing practices (but not funerary practices) were readily transmitted across groups possessing different languages, with geographically proximate peoples sharing more in common with each other than those farther away (Lycett 2019). This cultural exchange was facilitated by extensive resource sharing and cross-utilization of sites, intermarriage, and trade (Anastasio 1972; Walker, 1967, 1998). Anastasio (1972: 152–54) noted that Plateau peoples would form "task groups" composed of people from different ethnolinguistic groups, specifically to engage in joint cooperative activities such as fishing, hunting, root gathering, and trade. The region's trade fairs were a major means of facilitating contact between peoples from both within and outside of the Plateau region (Stern 1998). Such inter-group alliances were cemented by marriage (Anastasio 1972) and would, in theory, have made ideal conditions for parfleche attributes to have been shared among the craftswomen of various groups, who ultimately were responsible for their manufacture and who learned this skill from each other (Morrow 1975).

Given the foregoing, the level of parfleche diversity in the Plateau might appear all the more puzzling. However, as is now widely recognized in archaeology, the interactions of peoples might also structure differentiation of material attributes as much as lead to "homogeneity" in others, particularly where social tensions arise (Hodder 1982). Given their primary function as storage and transportation containers, parfleches inevitably played an important role in Indigenous trade networks (Lycett 2017; Morrow 1975: 17–18). Trade in the Plateau was a complex affair, involving what can be seen as forms of generalized reciprocity, balanced reciprocity, and negative reciprocity, at various scales of interaction (Stern 1998). Trade, even in the form of gift exchange, inevitably has the potential to take on competitive elements, while certainly either facilitating social relationships or raising tensions (Sahlins 1972). Lycett (2017) has noted that stylistic patterns in parfleches often tend to define trade zones (spheres of interaction), with boundaries between the zones being marked by "trade tones," with tribes at these edges often trying to exploit the benefits of two spheres of interaction, and the resources that flowed through them. Hence, in a social environment involving high degrees of cultural exchange, the specific role of parfleches in trade systems (which again are particularly visible items) might have invoked differentiation in a situation that otherwise tended toward commonality (or conformity) of material patterns.

An additional factor arising from trade and political alliance patterns is that some groups in each culture area may have parfleches more similar to those of the other area than they do their own. This may induce additional between-group variability within both areas than might be expected solely through their assignment to "culture area." Again, Lycett's (2017) analysis of parfleche attributes over a broader area than considered here, confirmed earlier suggestions that Plains tribes such as the Crow often had parfleches that more closely resembled Plateau groups than they did other Plains tribes. The same phenomenon can also be shown using the tribes considered in this chapter through the multivariate statistical technique of Principal Coordinates (PCo) analysis. Exactly the same measures of distances used in the earlier analysis can be used for this purpose.

Figure 1.6 shows the resultant PCo plot, which ultimately describes patterns of parfleche attribute affinities across the various groups. The polygons indicate the maximum extent of distributions for Plains peoples versus the Plateau peoples. As can be seen, while there is some separation between regions, specific groups are causing high levels of overlap between the two "culture areas." Most notably, the Crow are again shown to share

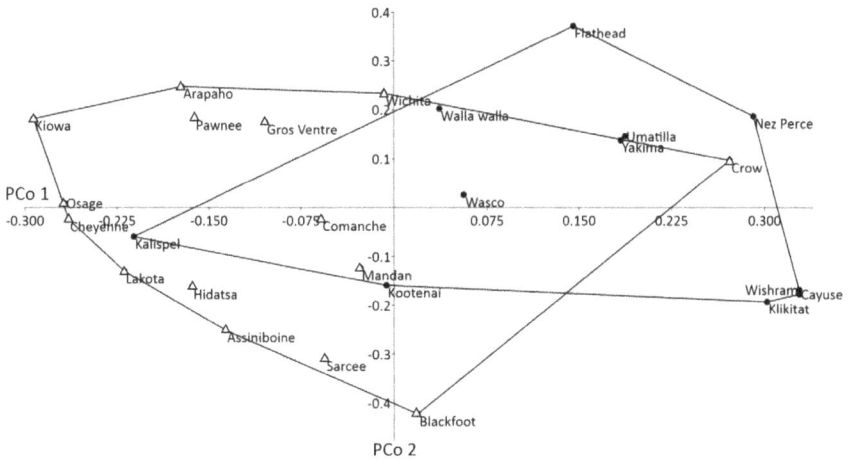

Figure 1.6. PCo plot showing patterns of parfleche attribute affinities between the ethnolinguistic tribes considered here. Polygons indicate the maximum extent of distributions for the Plains tribes (triangles) versus the Plateau tribes (circles). PCo 1 and 2 cumulatively account for 35.2 percent of the variability among parfleches; all remaining PCo each account for ≤11 percent of variation. © The author.

strong parfleche affinities with the Plateau region. Moreover, the parfleches of Kootenai and Kalispel peoples show strong affinities with Plains groups.

It is important to underline what are perhaps the main take-home implications of the analyses undertaken here. Along with time, space is a powerful concept in archaeology, and has been so since the earliest days of the modern discipline (Lyman et al. 1997). In a field where hard data are always in shorter supply than is desired, the fact that space can be measured and directly inputted within empirical analyses adds to its importance. In such circumstances, however, there is an ever-present danger that causal agency can be inadvertently or unconsciously attributed to a spatial dimension. Changes in artifactual diversity, whether an increase, decrease, or imposed "stability," are ultimately a cultural evolutionary question, not a geographic one in the strictest sense. At risk of making an axiomatic point, geographic "space" per se is a relatively meaningless concept unless it is related to broader concepts and features, specifically the cultural gradients that traverse the exact spatial dimensions under consideration. This is not to say spatial analysis is unimportant—far from it. It merely underlines that increased numbers of kilometers alone are not what are important in driving artifactual diversity: it is the ecological and cultural vectors that correlate with those kilometers that are actually underlying any spatial patterning or change in artifactual diversity observed. Put another way, it is small-scale (cultural) *microevolutionary* variables that matter in underpinning artifactual diversity, even when examined or observed at a broader macroscale. These include the errors in manufacture that will occur across space (itself a small-scale temporal dimension) and the rate of innovations or deliberate modifications that will occur in response to local cultural conditions, whether social, economic, or technological in motivation. It also includes the culturally specific factors that are either facilitating cultural exchange among individuals and groups across space (i.e., the rate of culture flow), and those that impede such exchange (such as cultural biases) in specific cases. In other words—analogous to the situation when considering within- and between-population genetic diversity—the major cultural (evolutionary) forces underling artifact diversity are innovation rate, error rate, migration rate of concepts, the strength of drift, and the strength of selection biases. Space itself is not an anthropogenic variable, but many anthropogenic variables will often correlate with a spatial dimension. In terms of their effects on artifactual diversity, it is always these that must be given primacy, not space.

Acknowledgments

I am grateful to Briggs Buchanan and Metin Eren for their invitation to contribute this chapter. I also thank Lee Lyman and two anonymous reviewers for their helpful comments.

Stephen J. Lycett earned his MSc from University College London and his PhD from the University of Cambridge, UK. He is currently a member of faculty in the Department of Anthropology, University at Buffalo (SUNY), New York, USA. His major research interests include the study of social learning and the application of cultural evolutionary theory to material culture.

References

Anastasio, A. 1972. "The Southern Plateau: An Ecological Analysis of Intergroup Relations." *Northwest Anthropological Research Notes* 6: 109–229.
Báldi, A. 2008. "Habitat Heterogeneity Overrides the Species–Area Relationship." *Journal of Biogeography* 35(4): 675–81.
Bouma, J., and J. D. Keyser. 2004. "Dating the Deadmond Bison Robe: A Seriation of Blackfeet Biographic Art." *Plains Anthropologist* 49: 9–24.

Buchanan, B., M. J. Hamilton, J. D. Kilby, and J. A. Gingerich. 2016. "Lithic Networks Reveal Early Regionalization in Late Pleistocene North America." *Journal of Archaeological Science* 65: 114–21.

Campbell, L. 1997. *American Indian Languages.* New York: Oxford University Press.

Clark, A., and D. Bamforth, eds. 2018. *Archaeological Perspectives on Warfare on the Great Plains.* Louisville: University Press of Colorado.

Clarke, D. L. 1968. *Analytical Archaeology.* London: Methuen.

Deetz, J., and E. Dethlefsen. 1965. "The Doppler Effect and Archaeology: A Consideration of the Spatial Aspects of Seriation." *Southwestern Journal of Anthropology* 21(3): 196–206.

———. 1967. "Death's Head, Cherub, Urn and Willow." *Natural History* 76(3): 29–37.

DeMallie, R. J. 2001. "Introduction." In *Handbook of North American Indians: Plains, vol. 13,* ed. R. J. DeMallie, 1–13. Washington, DC: Smithsonian Institution.

Douglas, F. H. 1936. *Parfleches and Other Rawhide Articles: Leaflet 77–78.* Denver, CO: Denver Art Museum.

Ewers, J. C. 1955. *The Horse in Blackfoot Indian Culture.* Washington, DC: Smithsonian Institution, Bureau of American Ethnology.

Hämäläinen, P. 2003. "The Rise and Fall of Plains Indian Horse Cultures." *Journal of American History* 90: 833–62.

Hodder, I. 1982. *Symbols in Action: Ethnoarchaeological Studies of Material Culture.* Cambridge: Cambridge University Press.

Holder, P. 1970. *The Hoe and the Horse on the Plains.* Lincoln: University of Nebraska Press.

Holmes, W. H. 1914. "Areas of American Culture Characterization Tentatively Outlined as an Aid in the Study of the Antiquities." *American Anthropologist* 16: 413–46.

Kroeber, A. L. 1908. "Ethnology of the Gros Ventre." *Anthropological Papers of the American Museum of Natural History* 1:145-281.

———. 1939. *Cultural and Natural Areas of Native North America.* Berkeley: University of California Press.

Lave, J., and E. Wenger. 1991. *Situated Learning: Legitimate Peripheral Participation.* Cambridge: Cambridge University Press.

Lycett, S. J. 2015. "Differing Patterns of Material Culture Intergroup Variation on the High Plains: A Quantitative Analysis of Parfleche Characteristics vs. Moccasin Decoration." *American Antiquity* 80: 714–31.

———. 2017. "Cultural Patterns Within and Outside of the Post-Contact Great Plains as Revealed by Parfleche Characteristics: Implications for Areal Arrangements in Artifactual Data." *Journal of Anthropological Archaeology* 48: 87–101.

———. 2019. "Cultural Transmission in the Post-Contact Plateau Region and Beyond: Insights from Funerary Practices, Fishing Practices, Clothing, and Languages." *Journal of Anthropological Archaeology* 54: 207–17.

Lycett, S. J., K. Schillinger, M. I. Eren, N. von Cramon-Taubadel, and A. Mesoudi. 2016. "Factors Affecting Acheulean Handaxe Variation: Experimental Insights, Microevolutionary Processes, and Macroevolutionary Outcomes." *Quaternary International* 411: 386–401.

Lycett, S. J., and S. J. Shennan. 2018. "David Clarke's *Analytical Archaeology* at 50." *World Archaeology* 50: 210–20.

Lyman, R. L., and M. J. O'Brien. 2006. *Measuring Time with Artifacts: A History of Methods in American Archaeology.* Lincoln: University of Nebraska Press.

Lyman, R. L., M. J. O'Brien, and R. C. Dunnell. 1997. *Americanist Culture History: Fundamentals of Time, Space, and Form.* New York: Plenum.

Martin, G. 2000. "Stasis in Complex Artefacts." In *Technological Innovation as an Evolutionary Process*, ed. J. Ziman, 90–100. Cambridge: Cambridge University Press.

McGinnis, A. R. 1990. *Counting Coup and Cutting Horses: Intertribal Warfare on the Northern Plains, 1738–1889*. Evergreen, CO: Cordillera Press.

Mitchell, P. 2015. *Horse Nations: The Worldwide Impact of the Horse on Indigenous Societies Post-1492*. Oxford: Oxford University Press.

Morrow, M. 1975. *Indian Rawhide: An American Folk Art*. Norman: University of Oklahoma Press.

O'Brien, M. J., and R. L. Lyman. 1999. *Seriation, Stratigraphy, and Index Fossils: The Backbone of Archaeological Dating*. New York: Kluwer Academic/Plenum.

———. 2000. *Applying Evolutionary Archaeology: A Systematic Approach*. New York: Kluwer Academic/Plenum.

Okumura, M., and A. G. Araujo. 2014. "Long-Term Cultural Stability in Hunter-Gatherers: A Case Study Using Traditional and Geometric Morphometric Analysis of Lithic Stemmed Bifacial Points from Southern Brazil." *Journal of Archaeological Science* 45: 59–71.

Phillips, P., J. A. Ford, and J. B. Griffin. 1951. *Archaeological Survey in the Lower Mississippi Alluvial Valley*. Cambridge: Peabody Museum of American Ethnology and Archaeology.

Reid, J. J., M. B. Schiffer, and W. L. Rathe. 1975. "Behavioral Archaeology: Four Strategies." *American Anthropologist* 77: 864–69.

Sahlins, M. 1972. *Stone Age Economics*. Chicago: Aldine-Atherton.

Shennan, S. J. 1997. *Quantifying Archaeology*. Edinburgh: Edinburgh University Press.

Smith, M. W. 1938. "The War Complex of the Plains Indians." *Proceedings of the American Philosophical Society* 78(3): 425–64.

Spier, L. 1925. *An Analysis of Plains Indian Parfleche Decoration*. Publications in Anthropology Vol. 1, No. 3. Seattle: University of Washington Press.

Stern, T. 1998. "Columbia River Trade Network." In *Plateau: Handbook of North American Indians, Vol. 12.*, ed. D. E. Walker, 641–52. Washington, DC: Smithsonian Institution.

Torrence, G. 1994. *The American Indian Parfleche: A Tradition of Abstract Painting*. Seattle: University of Washington Press.

Vander Linden, M. 2007. "What Linked the Bell Beakers in the Third Millennium BC Europe?" *Antiquity* 81: 343–52.

Walker, D. E. 1967. *Mutual Cross-Utilization of Economic Resources in the Plateau: An Example from Aboriginal Nez Perce Fishing Practices*. Pullman: Washington State University, Laboratory of Anthropology, Report of Investigation, No. 4.

———. 1998. "Introduction." In *Plateau: Handbook of North American Indians*, ed. D. E. Walker, 1–7. Washington, DC: Smithsonian Institution.

Wobst, H. M. 1977. "Stylistic Behavior and Information Exchange." In *For the Director: Research Essays in Honor of James B. Griffin*, ed. C. Cleland, 317–342. Ann Arbor: University of Michigan.

Wright, S. 1943. "Isolation by Distance." *Genetics* 28(2): 114–38.

Chapter 2

The Diversity of North America's "Old Copper" Projectile Points

Michelle R. Bebber and Anne Chao

❦

The copper technology that developed during the Archaic Period (10,000–3,000 BP) in North America has long been of interest to archaeologists and laypeople alike (Martin 1999). Despite early debate as to the origins of these ancient copper toolmakers, it is now well established that during the Archaic Period, indigenous peoples, over an extensive area, made a wide variety of copper tools including functional items such as knives, spear points, axes, awls, and fishing gear (Fogel 1963; Gibbon 1998; Griffin 1961; Martin 1999; Ritzenthaler 1957; Steinbring 1966; Wittry 1951; Wittry and Ritzenthaler 1956). These native copper tools represent the earliest examples in the world of metal being used as tool media, with models predicting copper use began between 9000-8000 BP (Bebber and Key 2022).

Early research on North American Archaic copper implements focused on broad topics of cultural origins and delineation, primarily using excavation data from cemeteries (Ritzenthaler 1946, 1957; Wittry 1951; Wittry and Ritzenthaler 1956) and analysis of artifacts collected from the surface or other non-mortuary archaeological contexts (Griffin 1961; Johnson 1964; McHugh 1973; Phillips 1925; Wittry 1951). Later studies focused on the role of copper in Archaic society (Binford 1962), the nature of tool use (Fregni 2009; Leader 1988; Penman 1977), tool production techniques (LaRonge 2001; Peterson 2003a, 2003b), and copper sourcing (Ehrhardt 2009; Hancock et al. 1991; Levine 2007; Mauk and Hancock 1998; Rapp et al. 1980, 1990, 2000). More recent research has focused on the nature of trade relationships (Hill 2006, 2012), population dynamics and changing social structure (Pleger 1998, 2000, 2002; Pleger and Stoltman 2009), and copper tool comparative functional efficiency (Bebber and Eren 2018; Bebber et al. 2019a, Bebber et al. 2019b).

North America's Archaic copper-using groups—commonly referred to as the Old Copper Culture (Steinbring 1966; Quimby and Spaulding 1957; Ritzenthaler 1957), the Old Copper Complex (Gibbon 1998; Martin and Pleger 1999; Wittry and Ritzenthaler 1956), or the Old Copper Industry (McKern 1942; Miles 1951)—were centered around the Western Great Lakes, with most copper implements found in southern and eastern Wisconsin (Miles 1951; Wittry 1951). However, despite the predominance of copper artifacts found in Wisconsin, many copper implements have been found as far west as Alberta (Gibbon 1998; Ritzenthaler 1960; Steinbring 1966, 1975) and as far east as the Ottawa Valley (Chapdelaine 2003; Clermont and Chapdelaine 1998) and into eastern maritime environments (Fitzhugh 1978; Hood 1993) (Figure 2.1). It is the dispersal of these copper implements, and the nature of their provenience, that is the focus of this study.

Although many copper artifacts are held in museums and by collectors, few Archaic copper culture habitation sites have been systematically excavated (although see Griffin and Quimby 1961; Hill 2006; Martin 1993; Moffatt and Speth 1999; and Olson 2018). Due to this relative dearth of

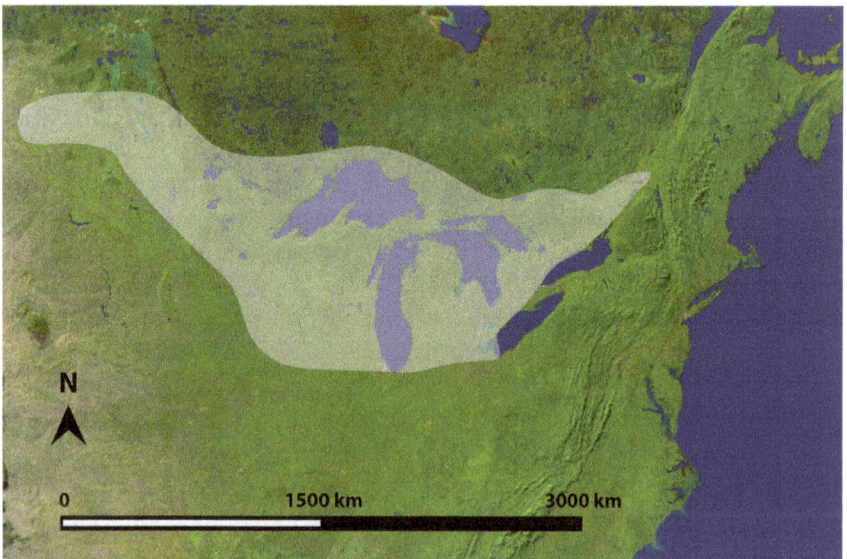

Figure 2.1. Map of Archaic Period copper tools. Approximate archaeological area of the North American "Old Copper" Culture. © The authors.

in situ cultural material, most data regarding Archaic copper culture life-ways comes from a handful of professional excavations of mortuary sites, namely Reigh (Baerreis, Daifuku, and James 1954; Ostberg 1956; Ritzen-thaler et al. 1956), Osceola (Ritzenthaler 1946), and Oconto (Ritzenthaler and Wittry 1952; Ritzenthaler 1970) in Wisconsin, and the Riverside site (Hruska 1967) in Michigan. In a summary article discussing their work at Oconto and Osceola, Wittry and Ritzenthaler (1956: 252) state that the "scattered occurrence of Old Copper implements in some of the cultures of the Great Lakes area is, *in many instances, the result of trade.*" Here we seek to better understand the nature of this trade by determining the man-ner in which copper was moving around the landscape. Along these lines, we use artifact attributes to assess whether or not there is in fact an "Old Copper" cultural core.

This study has two main objectives, both achievable via diversity analysis using class richness estimators. The first is to test whether or not there is an identifiable *culture core*. Here, culture is defined as "socially transmitted knowledge" (Mesoudi 2011, modified from Boyd and Richerson 2005), therefore, if there is in fact a unified "Old Copper" culture, we should be able to detect a pattern of tool form continuity between the core and the peripheral zones. The second is to assess the *nature of the movement of cop-per*. Although evidence shows that, at least in some areas (Hill 2006, 2012), high-quality cherts were likely traded as finished curated tools into copper-using areas in exchange for copper material; the precise form of the cop-per traded out to other areas is not known. Was it being traded as raw unworked copper nuggets, or was it being traded as finished copper tools? Native copper is commonly found as small nuggets as a result of glacial activity. This "float copper" is dispersed across a vast landscape far to the south of the massive copper deposits of the Keweenaw Peninsula. In addi-tion to float copper, there is substantial evidence for ancient mining around Lake Superior (Holmes 1901; Martin 1999; Pompeani et al. 2013, 2015; Whittlesey 1863). These ancient mining activities would have produced small copper pieces, as large nodules of copper would have been nearly impossible to extract and transport.

The question addressed here is whether or not copper was traded in this raw nugget form and then transformed into tools by people living in the peripheral zones. Or, alternatively, was it first worked into a finished object in the copper culture core and then traded out in this finished form. Gib-bon (1998) provides an overview of Old Copper in Minnesota, and brings up a question similar to that posed here: were copper tools obtained as gifts via trade or were they primarily manufactured locally? He suggests that if copper tools were in fact alliance-cementing gifts from the core cultural region, then they would be transported in their final form, from other areas. In contrast, he suggests that if the items were primarily utilitarian, they would be manufactured locally in various regions (ibid.: 42). Here, this idea is built upon using a class richness analysis to assess diversity between core and peripheral zones.

Methods and Materials

Prior research has successfully used class richness analysis to resolve lingering questions about regional Paleoindian tool diversity (Buchanan et al. 2017; Eren 2012; Eren et al. 2012, 2016). Here, we use class richness in a similar manner to assess differences between the core and peripheral regions. We hypothesize that, if copper tools were being manufactured in a highly controlled manner in the "Old Copper" heartland, and then traded out to the peripheral regions as finished tools, we can predict that that there will be no difference in class richness and no difference in kind between tools found in the core and those found in the periphery. In contrast, if there was less "control," and copper raw material was moving around more freely as unmodified raw material (i.e., the native copper nuggets) we can predict that there will be a significant difference in class richness, and that the greatest richness will be in the peripheral regions where there was less cultural affiliation to the core ideals.

Core and Periphery Delineation

For this analysis, the core region was determined by the quantity of artifacts located in southern and eastern Wisconsin. Based on data from the Milwaukee Public Museum, the southeastern counties (Figure 2.2) have the greatest number of Archaic copper artifacts on record; and this area has traditionally been thought of as the Old Copper heartland (Gibbons 1998; Wittry 1951). The peripheral region was delineated as "all other areas surrounding the core" where Archaic copper artifacts have been found. This area includes other counties in Wisconsin with lower frequencies of copper artifacts, counties in the northern and southern peninsulas of Michigan, parts of Minnesota, and northeast into Canada. Two very important sites of the Middle Archaic Period are those found at Allumette Island and Morrison Island in the Ottawa River, Ontario (Chapdelaine 2003; Clermont and Chapdelaine 1998). These two sites are especially notable for the large quantities of Lake Superior native copper objects found there. These artifacts represent the copper implements furthest from the core region used in this analysis.

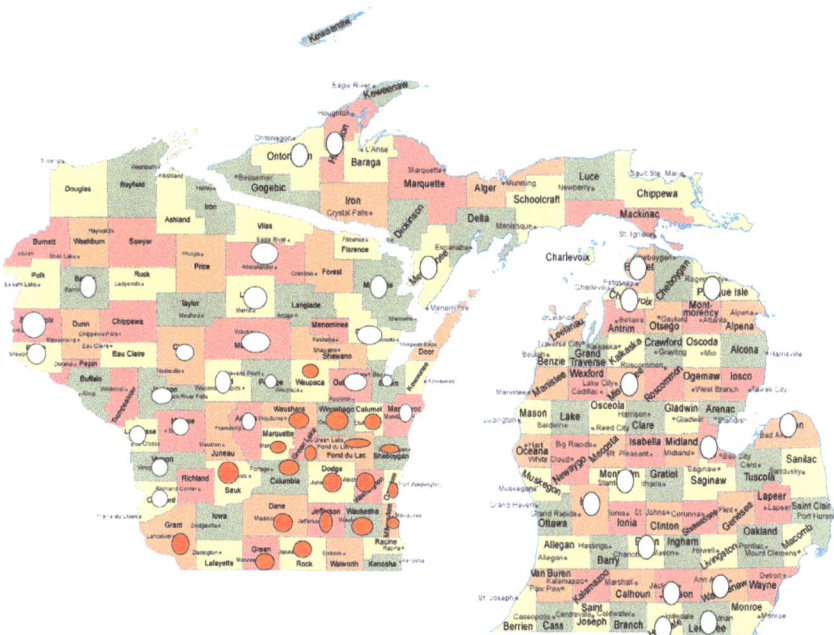

Figure 2.2. Core and peripheral zones. The core region was determined by the density of artifacts located in southern and eastern Wisconsin. The counties shown here with red circles have the greatest number of Archaic copper artifacts on record. The peripheral region was simply all other areas surrounding the core where Archaic copper artifacts have been found. These peripheral counties are demarcated with white circles. © The authors.

Data Collection

To begin the analysis, data collection was conducted at four museum collections: the Milwaukee Public Museum, the Chicago Field Museum, the Canadian Museum of History, and the University of Michigan Museum of Anthropological Archaeology. Although data has been collected for well over a thousand artifacts, this analysis is focused specifically on copper projectile point diversity. Copper projectile points represent the greatest quantity of copper tools held in museum collections, and were thus ideal as the focus of our diversity analysis.

Copper Spear Points

Copper projectile points were made in a variety of forms (Figure 2.3) and are the most common type of Archaic copper tools found in North America (Gibbon 1998; Martin 1999). For this study, data were collected from 378 archaeological copper point specimens. Archaic copper spear points

Figure 2.3. Archaic Period copper projectile points. Projectile points are the most common type of "heavy" copper artifact from the Archaic Period. They come in a variety of shapes and sizes, as shown here. © The authors.

range widely in overall size. These data show a mean mass of 38.4 g with a standard deviation of 27.4 g, ranging from 1 g (minimum) to 148 g (maximum). Like Archaic copper knives, Old Copper spear points have a variety of blade shapes and haft types, with socketed tangs and rat-tailed tangs being the most common haft form. Some specimens have rounded tangs, stemmed tangs, serrated tangs, and, on occasion, hooked tangs. The socketed-tang points represent the type with the greatest mass, as the tang portion itself is quite large which increases the overall point mass compared to rat-tailed or flat-tang varieties.

Copper Point Classification

The most widely used classification for Archaic copper tools was created in 1951 by Warren Wittry. He analyzed 2,600 copper specimens from three museums—the Milwaukee Public Museum, the Neville Museum in Green Bay, and the Museum of the State Historical Society of Wisconsin in Madison. He created the typology using taxonomic units, specifically variations in shape, to construct the classification system. He separated copper implements into groups that had the same features, or a given combination of features. His resulting groups formed the "types," however he notes that these types lack the adequate data needed to function as true archaeological types (Wittry 1951: 4). In order to be of use to archaeologists, types need to have spatial, temporal, and cultural delineations, which are generally lacking for Archaic copper tools.

In Wittry's typology, projectile points are represented by Roman numeral I, knives by II, crescents by III, and so on. Under these major classes, the specific types have a letter. For example, a socketed tang point is delineated as type I-A or I-B depending on the shape of the socket. The problem with such classification is that not only are such distinctions subjective, but the resulting types are often not discrete. Wittry (1951) acknowledges that in instances where types are closely related, and differ in only one or two features, they have been lumped together as sub-types that are designated with an additional Arabic numeral after the letter; for example, I-A2. For analytical purposes, he states that these sub-types should be treated as true types until "their status is more fully realized" (ibid.: 4). One of the main problems of such typologies is that these types are defined by features, and these features can occur in various combinations on more than one type, thus making the characteristics that define one type or another rather arbitrary. Likewise, such methods of tool classification can generate overlap; and they can be ambiguous, especially for rare tool variants, as to which type assignment is correct. This problem of overlap, subjectivity, and bias has been discussed frequently in stone tool literature (Anderson 2013; Anderson et al. 2010; Dunnell 2002; O'Brien et al. 2014; Whittaker, Caulkins, and Kamp 1998), and we emphasize here that it is equally important for Archaic copper implements to also be categorized in a manner that allows for discrete unit assignment, thereby eliminating ambiguity and furthering the potential for scientific analyses.

Paradigmatic Classification

Here, in contrast to prior taxonomic classification, paradigmatic classification was used to generate tool classes prior to assessing diversity indices. Paradigmatic classification is a dimensional classification procedure in which each class is defined via the intersection of characters to create discrete classes constituted by mutually exclusive alternate features (Dunnell 2002). In practice, all character states belonging to a specific character can combine with any character state of other predefined characters. Paradigmatic classification eliminates analyst bias by first establishing discrete characters and then analyzing each specimen to record the character state, which are all mutually exclusive. These character states are then combined to generate a unique specimen class. Paradigmatic classes are explicit and unambiguous in terms of structure and membership criteria (Eren et al. 2016; O'Brien and Lyman 2000).

Class Construction

To assess Archaic copper spear point diversity, we created fully replicable and explicit classes using five formal characters. In toto, 307 specimens

Class Construction

Character I: Spear
point haft form
1) socket
2) rat tail
3) stem
4) conical
5) notched or ornate
6) no tang

Character II: Spear
point tip morphology
1) pointed
2) tapered

Character III: Spear
point blade ridge
1) presence
2) absence

Character IV: Hole
present on point
1) presence of hole
2) absence of hole

Character V: Overall
spear point length
1) < 112.0 mm
2) > 112.0 mm

Figure 2.4. Paradigmatic class construction. Classes were created using five formal characters: (1) spear point haft form; (2) spear point tip morphology; (3) presence of blade ridge; (4) presence of hole; and (5) overall length. © The authors.

were analyzed using the paradigmatic classification procedure: 189 specimens from the core region and 118 specimens from the periphery region.

To assess copper spear point diversity, we created classes using five formal characters. The first character was spear point haft form (Figure 2.4). For this character there were six character states: socket, rat tail, stem, conical, notched or other ornate, and no tang. The second character was spear point tip morphology, and this had two states: pointed, or tapered. The third character was spear point blade ridge, with two character states: the presence or absence of a blade ridge. The fourth character also had two character states: the presence or absence of a hole on the point. The fifth and final character was overall spear point length, for which two character states were used: overall length less than 112.0 mm and overall length greater than 112.0 mm (this was used, as 112.0 mm represented the mean point length of the sample).

Paradigmatic Results: Core

The paradigmatic classification produced 96 possible classes. For the core region, 34 classes were identified in our sample. The most common class is 11222, which represents a socketed tang point with a pointed tip, no blade ridge, no hole, and an overall length over 112.0 mm (Figure 2.5a). The second most common class for the core region is 11122, which represents a socketed tang point with a pointed tip, a distinct blade ridge, no hole, and

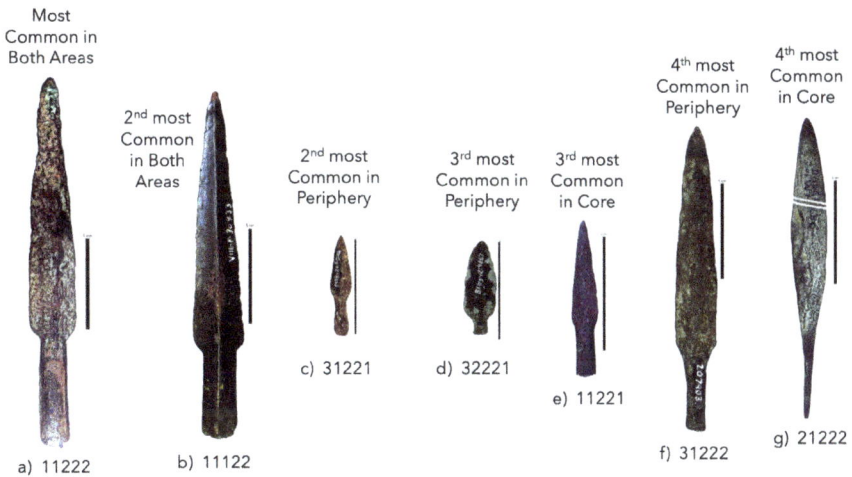

Figure 2.5. Four most common classes in the core and periphery. The core and periphery share the same two most common classes, 11222 and 11122. However, the periphery has a different class of equal prominence, 31221, followed by 32221, which are both much smaller in size compared to the other point classes. © The authors.

an overall length greater than 112.0 mm. This second most common class is essentially identical to the first most common except for the presence of a distinct ridge along the blade, which suggests it was made in some form of mold (Figure 2.5b). The third most common type for the core is 11221 which represents a socketed tang point with a pointed tip, no blade ridge, no hole, and an overall length less than 112.0 mm (Figure 2.5e). As you can see the socketed tang points are the dominant type, however the fourth most common class is 21222, which represents a rat tail point with a pointed tip, no blade ridge, no hole, and an overall length greater than 112.0 mm (Figure 2.5g). In total these four classes represent 88 of the 189 specimens analyzed.

There were 10 classes represented by only one specimen (the singletons) and there were 6 classes represented by only two specimens (the doubletons). The characters causing the most variation in these classes are those of haft type in combination with overall point length.

Paradigmatic Results: Periphery

For the periphery region, 32 classes were identified in our sample. The most common class for the peripheral region was once again 11222, which represents a socketed tang point with a pointed tip, no blade ridge, no hole, and an overall length over 112.0 mm. The second most common class for the peripheral region is 11122. However, in contrast to the core, tied for second place is class 31221, which represents a flat tang point with a pointed tip, no blade ridge, no hole, and an overall point length less than 112.0 mm (Figure 2.5c). Likewise, the third most common peripheral class is 32221 which represents a flat tang point with a tapered tip, no blade ridge, no hole, and an overall point length less than 112.0 mm (Figure 2.5d), and the fifth most common type is the same as 31221 but with a greater overall length and is thus coded as 31222 (Figure 2.5f). The top three categories represent 49 of the 118 specimens analyzed for the periphery zone, while flat tangs represent 36 of them.

In the periphery data, we identified 12 singletons and 6 doubletons. The character causing the most variation for the peripheral regions is related to haft type. Fifty percent of the singletons are socketed tang variants, which demonstrates how this one very common haft character can recombine with other character states to generate a wide range of discrete point classes. The remaining 6 singletons are either conical points, or ornate/side-notched bases. Half of the doubletons are also variations of notched bases.

Class Richness and Undersampling Bias

After the classes were identified, class richness was assessed to compare the two regions. Class richness refers to the number of classes or categories represented by the objects in a sample, but more important to the analysis here, is that it can also reveal the number of classes that are not present in the given sample, but that should exist in the total tool assemblage for a given area. Archaeological assemblages are characterized by uneven abundances of different classes. When doing an assemblage assessment, the most common classes are readily identified, but it may take a while before rare classes appear, or they may not appear at all. Such undersampling bias can substantially skew our interpretation of artifact diversity if there are actually many rare classes not being detected in the sample (Eren et al. 2016).

This is a problem for analyzing all past material remains; however, undersampling bias is even more problematic here because copper tools of North America have long been collected by hobbyists, and thus only a small sample of the total past assemblage is currently accessible for data collection. Given that there are believed to be thousands of undocumented copper artifacts in the hands of collectors, it is impossible to fully categorize every possible type, and so we can safely assume that there are many unidentified tools classes out there.

Class Richness: Chao1 Estimator

In such an instance of severely undersampled data, class richness can be inferred using a richness estimator. Here we use the Chao1 estimator (Chao

1984) to infer a lower bound for the number of classes and its associated confidence interval. The Chao1 estimator has been used successfully in archaeological stone tool research (Eren et al. 2016), and it is widely used in biological sciences to determine how many species there should be in a given area (Chao 2005). It is a nonparametric estimator that uses the number of singletons and doubletons, which are represented by the classes that were counted exactly once or exactly twice during the assessment. These counts are then used to estimate the number of undetected classes in an assemblage. This estimated count is then added to the actual observed class abundances to estimate true richness values. When there are no singletons in a sufficiently large sample, the observed class richness values are considered to be accurate, whereas the presence of numerous singletons suggests that there are likely to be many classes that have gone undetected in the sample.

Results

The data summary for the core region and peripheral regions, with statistical inference for estimated asymptotes of diversities, is presented in tables 2.1–2.3. The rarefaction and extrapolation curves for the diversity analyses are shown in Figure 2.6 using the online freeware application iNEXT (Hsieh, Ma, and Chao 2016).

Table 2.1. Data summary for the periphery and core. Note: In the periphery, frequency counts (f_k values) are complete; in the core, there are four additional frequency counts (f_{17} =1, f_{21} =1, f_{24} =1 and f_{26} = 1).

(f_k denotes the number of classes represented by exactly k individuals in the sample)

Area	Sample size n	Observed class richness	Sample completeness	CV	f_1	f_2	f_3	f_4	f_6	f_7	f_8	f_9	f_{11}	f_{13}	f_{14}
Periphery	118	32	89.92%	1.02	12	6	5	2	1	0	2	1	0	2	1
Core	189	34	94.74%	1.21	10	6	5	3	2	1	0	1	1	1	0

Table 2.2. Observed diversities and estimated asymptotic diversities in the periphery.

	Observed diversity	Estimated asymptote	Estimated s.e.	95% lower confidence nterval	95% upper confidence interval
Class richness	32	43.90	9.09	35.15	76.96
Shannon diversity (common class richness)	21.01	25.83	2.64	21.07	30.99
Simpson diversity (dominant class richness)	15.61	17.84	2.13	15.61	22.02

Table 2.3. Observed diversities and estimated asymptotic diversities in the core.

	Observed diversity	Estimated asymptote	Estimated s.e.	95% lower confidence interval	95% upper confidence interval
Class richness	34	42.29	6.87	36.01	68.21
Shannon diversity (common class richness)	19.52	22.05	1.65	19.52	25.29
Simpson diversity (dominant class richness)	13.73	14.73	1.47	13.73	17.61

Diversity Results: Class Richness, Shannon Diversity, and Simpson Diversity

In ecology, a consensus has now emerged that diversity can be completely characterized by a family of measures, called Hill numbers, indexed by a diversity order $q \geq 0$; see Colwell and Chao (this volume) for a review. Class richness, or "diversity of order $q = 0$", is the most intuitive diversity measure. As stated above, class richness is determined by the number of classes or categories represented by the items in a given assemblage, including not only the number of classes represented in samples but also the number of classes present in the assemblage that are not detected in the samples. Shannon diversity (diversity of order $q = 1$) or "common class" richness, unlike class richness, counts classes in proportion to their relative abundance. Common classes contribute relatively more to the total diversity than do rare classes. Thus, Shannon diversity (diversity of order $q = 2$) is interpreted as the (equivalent) number of common classes (Chao, Wang, and Jost 2013; Chao et al. 2014). Shannon diversity, unlike Chao1 (Chao 1984), is dependent upon all the observed frequencies of a given sample (Eren et al. 2016). Simpson diversity, or "dominant class richness," disproportionately discounts rare classes and emphasizes common classes, and is thus interpreted as the (equivalent) number of very common, or dominant, classes (Chao et al. 2014; Gotelli and Chao 2013).

Here we found that, although the core region has higher observed class richness (34 vs. 32), this is mainly due to it having a larger sample size and higher sample completeness. When we standardize sample size at a finite value (graphs on left, Figure 2.6) or sample completeness at a value < 1 (graphs on right, Figure 2.6), the periphery zone turns out to be consistently more diverse in class richness ($q = 0$, upper row graphs, Figure 2.6), common class richness (Shannon diversity, $q = 1$, middle row graphs, Figure 2.6), and dominant class richness (Simpson diversity, $q = 2$, lower row graphs, Figure 2.6). However, all confidence intervals overlap, thus we

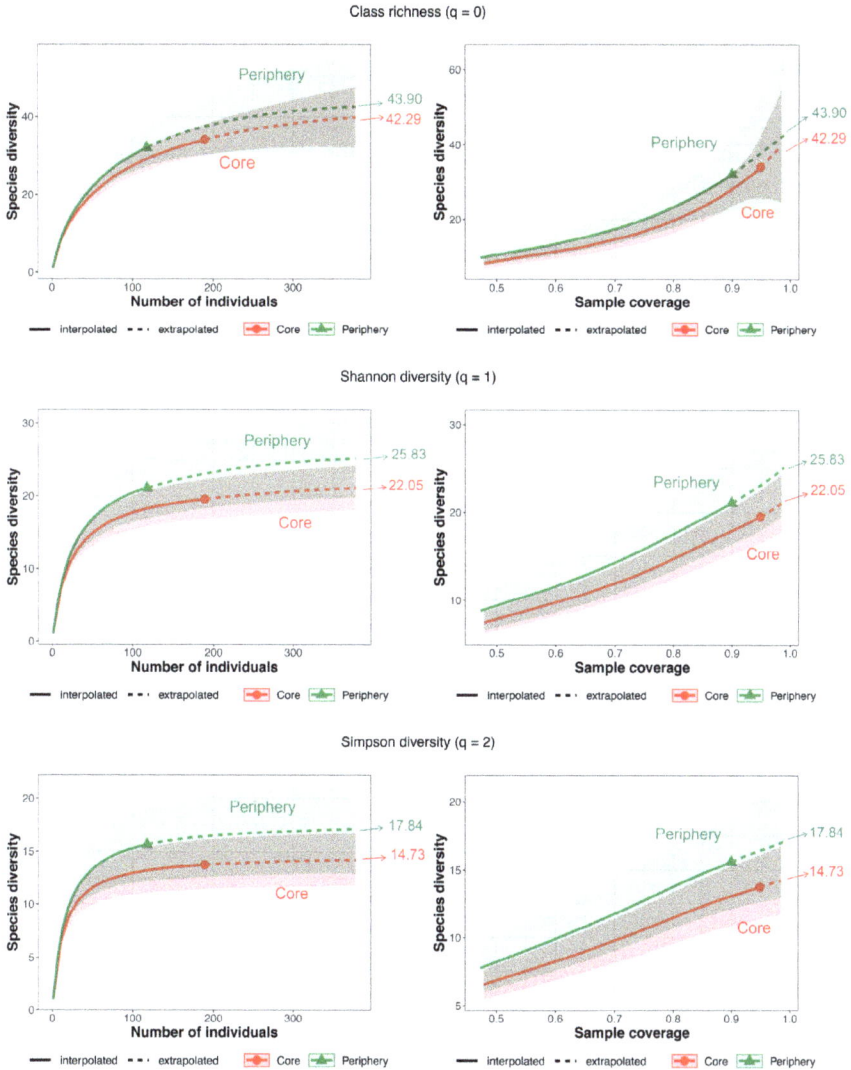

Figure 2.6. Graphs of class richness, Shannon, and Simpson diversity. Although core has higher observed class richness (34 vs. 32), it is mainly due to larger sample size and higher sample completeness. When we standardize sample size at a finite value (left columns in the Figure) or sample completeness at a value < 1 (right columns in the Figure), the periphery turns out to be consistently more diverse in class richness (q=0, upper row of the Figure), common class richness (q=1, middle row), and dominant class richness (q=2, lower row). However, all confidence intervals overlap, therefore, there is insufficient evidence to demonstrate a statistically significant difference. © The authors.

find insufficient evidence to demonstrate significant statistical difference by rigorous two-sample tests.

For asymptotic richness (i.e., richness for the entire assemblage; see tables 2.2–2.3, column 3), similar conclusions hold for the Chao1 estimates, common class richness, and dominant class richness. The periphery is consistently more diverse, but there is no evidence for significant difference, as all confidence intervals overlap.

We used the coefficient of variation (CV) based on the observed class abundances to quantify the degree of heterogeneity among abundances. The CV values (column 5, Table 2.1) imply that the classes in the core region are more heterogeneous than those in the peripheral zones. That is, the periphery is more diverse as shown by the analyses of class richness, Simpson diversity, and Shannon diversity (Figure 2.6), with classes exhibiting more evenness in their abundances (from CV values). Again, no evidence exists for significant difference.

Diversity Results: Kind

The results of the diversity analysis show that there is substantial overlap between the core and the peripheral regions. When looking at kind, there are almost equal numbers of classes that occur in one area and not in the other. There are 8 classes that occur only in the periphery and 10 classes that occur only in the core. For all of these unique classes, it is not surprising that they constitute the singletons and doubletons for each area (i.e., the rarest types). For the core region, the four most common types make up 47 percent (88/189) of the total sample. For the periphery, the four most common types constitute only 42 percent of the total sample (49/118). This suggests that although there is overlap in class richness, there seems to be greater diversity of classes in the peripheral area.

Discussion

Our main question asked was whether or not Archaic copper-using cultures represented one singular cultural identity—the "Old Copper Culture"—or were there in fact many different regional groups, all of whom happened to adopt and use copper as a raw material, without a unifying cultural affiliation. In essence, we wanted to determine whether or not there was evidence in tool form that would suggest that copper production was being controlled by the cultural core. In other words, was raw material procured from the copper source and then manufactured according to a set of identifiable cultural principles? Or, alternatively, was there less control of raw material, with copper being accessed and then used in peripheral regions by various groups not fully affiliated with "core values."

The results are somewhat equivocal, and show that there is slightly more diversity in the peripheral zones; thus, these results can be interpreted in a few ways. We saw that there is substantial overlap in the most common tool forms between the two areas, which suggests that the most prevalent tool types were finding their way into the peripheral region, either via trade or perhaps through being produced by specialists who lived outside the core but were familiar with the production techniques being used in the heartland. However, given the greater diversity in the periphery, this suggests that a substantial amount of unprocessed copper material was available to groups outside the core, and that these peripheral groups were manufacturing objects in their own way by generating novel haft forms and also by recombining stylistic attributes from the core to establish their own local conventions, such as those found far east of the Wisconsin heartland.

If we assume that there was in fact a unifying cultural identity throughout the broader copper-using area during the Archaic Period, then the greater copper tool diversity further from the core could be explained in a few ways. Perhaps peripheral artisans, who were in fact allied with the core values, were acquiring raw copper, and then trying to mimic the tool forms that they had acquired from the core on prior occasions. If there was a lack of social learning opportunities in the periphery, this would result in a reduced skill set that may have been required to produce the more "typical" or stylistic homogenous copper forms. This breakdown in knowledge transfer could explain the wider diversity occurring in the peripheral zones; even though they may have desired to align with the core styles, they may have lacked the artisanal know-how. In addition to a possible breakdown in social transmission of production knowledge, there may also be a technological constraint prohibiting the exact reproduction of core styles. Many of the most common core tool forms have blade ridges, suggesting the use of molds during manufacture, and it could be that such "accessory tools" were not as available in the peripheral areas.

Alternatively, if there was not a widespread, overarching "copper culture" identity, these diversity results suggest that raw material was being accessed by people in the non-core areas, either via trade or by direct procurement. Instead of one broad cultural identity with specific formal "rules," in this scenario there would have been fewer production constraints on formal qualities in peripheral zones, thus allowing for experimentation and expression, given that they were not closely affiliated with the styles of the people living in the "core," and nor would they have been invested in maintaining normative ideas. Another possibility is that in peripheral zones, copper implements that had arrived there via trade from the core were being reworked locally, either through necessity or because of regional stylistic preferences. Copper is a highly malleable raw material, and so it is possible that many of the novel haft variations, seen far to the east, were a result of reworking via heating, reshaping, and cutting away larger tangs that were either misshapen, damaged by use, or simply seen as no longer useful by peripheral craftspeople.

Our second question asked was: Were Archaic copper culture tools made in the core region and then traded to other regions as finished objects, or was the copper material moving around more freely, in its raw form, to other regions where it was then shaped via local convention? Well, the answer to this question is also rather ambiguous. The results suggest that both of these scenarios were taking place. There is overlap between the most common classes in the core and the peripheral zones. The most common class for the peripheral region is the same as in the core: a socketed tang point with a pointed tip, no blade ridge, and no hole present. Likewise, the second most common class for the peripheral region is a socketed tang point with a pointed tip and with no hole present, but it does have a distinct blade ridge. However, there is a tie for the second most common class in the periphery. Given that this second most common variant is very similar to the first two classes in all but haft type, we suggest that, as stated above, there may be some local modification to the socketed tang points. Perhaps, due to a desire for more raw copper, peripheral craftspeople were intentionally removing the large socketed tangs in order to repurpose the copper for the manufacture of other small implements such as awls, needles, beads, and smaller conical points. However, although the data show that there is overlap in the most common tool classes, there is more diversity in the periphery in general, which supports the idea put forth by others that peripheral craftspeople were in fact accessing raw material via trade, and then manufacturing items locally (Chapdelaine 2003; Levine 2007).

Overall, these results show that there is more diversity in the peripheral regions, and the precise reason for this requires more investigation. Future analyses will collect data from zones further from the core, specifically in areas to the west and north. Likewise, other tool forms, such as knives and fishing equipment, will be classified in order to better estimate richness for a variety of copper implements. Our analysis provides insight into lesser-known aspects of the Archaic copper tool production while elucidating the ways in which Archaic groups at the periphery of the copper culture heartland may have deviated from the core area. The precise cause of such deviation is not yet understood, however it is likely a combination of factors such as breakdowns in knowledge transmission, limitations due to technical specialization and accessory equipment, and the development of localized variants due to cultural experimentation or low core affiliation.

Continuing diversity-oriented research into Archaic copper technologies can clarify not only social and cultural patterns, but it may also offer insight into ecological and environmental constraints on copper point form during the Archaic Period.

Acknowledgments

M.R.B. is supported by the Kent State University College of Arts and Sciences. We would like to thank Briggs Buchanan and Metin I. Eren for inviting us to contribute to this volume.

Michelle R. Bebber is an Assistant Professor at Kent State University, Ohio, USA.

Anne Chao is a Professor at the Institute of Statistics, National Tsing Hua University, Hsin-Chu, Taiwan.

References

Anderson, D. G. 2013. "Paleoindian Archaeology in Eastern North America: Current Approaches and Future Directions." In *In The Eastern Fluted Point Tradition*, ed. J. Gingerich, 371–403. Salt Lake City: University of Utah Press.

Anderson, D. G., D. S. Miller, S. J. Yerka, J. C. Gillam, E. N. Johanson, D. T. Anderson, A. C. Goodyear, and A. M. Smallwood. 2010. "PIDBA (Paleoindian Database of the Americas) 2010: Current Status and Findings." *Archaeology of Eastern North America* 38: 63–89.

Baerreis, D. A., H. Daifuku, and E. L. James. 1954. "The Burial Complex of the Reigh Site, Winnebago County, Wisconsin." *The Wisconsin Archeologist* 35(1): 1–36.

Bebber, M. R., and M. I. Eren. 2018. "Toward a Functional Understanding of the North American Old Copper Culture 'Technomic Devolution.'" *Journal of Archaeological Science* 98: 34–44.

Bebber, M. R., A. J. Key, M. Fisch, R. S. Meindl, and M. I. Eren. 2019a. "The Exceptional Abandonment of Metal Tools by North American Hunter-Gatherers, 3000 BP." *Scientific Reports* 9(1) :1–4.

Bebber, M. R., J. D. Norris, K. Flood, M. Fisch, R. S. Mcindl, and M. I. Eren. 2019b. "Controlled Experiments Support the Role of Function in the Evolution of the North American Copper Tool Repertoire." *Journal of Archaeological Science:Reports* 26: 101917.

Bebber, M. R. and A. J. Key. 2022. 'Optimal Linear Estimation (OLE) Modeling Supports Early Holocene (9000–8000 RCYBP) Copper Tool Production in North America.' *American Antiquity* 87(2): 1–17.

Binford, L. R. 1962. "Archaeology as Anthropology." *American Antiquity* 28(2): 217–25.

Boyd, R., and P. J. Richerson. 2005. *The Origin and Evolution of Cultures*. Oxford: Oxford University Press.

Buchanan, B., A. Chao, C. H. Chiu, R. K. Colwell, M. J. O'Brien, A. Werner, and M. I. Eren. 2017. "Environment-Induced Changes in Selective Constraints on Social Learning during the Peopling of the Americas." *Scientific Reports* 7: 44431.

Chao, A. 1984. "Nonparametric Estimation of the Number of Classes in a Population." *Scandinavian Journal of Statistics* 11: 265–70.

———. 2005. "Species Estimation and Applications." In *Encyclopedia of Statistical Sciences*, 2nd edn, vol. 12, ed. N. Balakrishnan, C. B. Read, and B. Vidakovic, 7907–16. New York: Wiley.

Chao, A., N. J. Gotelli, T. C. Hsieh, E. L. Sander, K. H. Ma, R. K. Colwell, and A. M. Ellison. 2014. "Rarefaction and Extrapolation with Hill Numbers: A Framework for Sampling and Estimation in Species Diversity Studies." *Ecological Monographs* 84(1): 45–67.

Chao, A., Y. T. Wang, and L. Jost. 2013. "Entropy and the Species Accumulation Curve: A Novel Entropy Estimator via Discovery Rates of New Species." *Methods in Ecology and Evolution* 4(11): 1091–1100.

Chapdelaine, C. 2003. "Les Objets en Cuivre Natif." In *L'ile aux Allumettes: L'Archaique Superieur dans l'Outaouais*, ed. N. Clermont, C. Chapdelaine, and J. Cinq-Mars, 219–52. *Paleo-Quebec* No. 30.

Clermont, N., and C. Chapdelaine. 1998. "Ile Morrison: Lieu Sacre et Atelier de l'Archaique dans l'Outaouais." *Paleo-Quebec* No. 28.

Dunnell, R. C. 2002. *Systematics in Prehistory*. Caldwell, NJ: Blackburn Press.

Ehrhardt, K. L. 2009. "Copper Working Technologies, Contexts of Use, and Social Complexity in the Eastern Woodlands of Native North America." *Journal of World Prehistory* 22(3): 213–35.

Eren, M. I. 2012. "Were Unifacial Tools Regularly Hafted by Clovis Foragers in the North American Lower Great Lakes Region? An Empirical Test of Edge Class Richness and Attribute Frequency among Distal, Proximal, and Lateral Tool-Section." *Journal of Ohio Archaeology* 2: 1–15.

Eren, M. I., A. Chao, C. H. Chiu, R. K. Colwell, B. Buchanan, M. T. Boulanger, J. Darwent, and M. J. O'Brien. 2016. "Statistical Analysis of Paradigmatic Class Richness Supports Greater Paleoindian Projectile-Point Diversity in the Southeast." *American Antiquity* 81(1): 174–92.

Eren, M. I., A. Chao, W. H. Hwang, and R. K. Colwell. 2012. "Estimating the Richness of a Population When the Maximum Number of Classes is Fixed: A Nonparametric Solution to an Archaeological Problem." *PLoS ONE* 7(5): e34179.

Fitzhugh, W. 1978. "Maritime Archaic Cultures of the Central and Northern Labrador Coast." *Arctic Anthropology* 15(2): 61–95.

Fogel, I. L. 1963. "The Dispersal of Copper Artifacts in the Late Archaic Period of Prehistoric North America." *The Wisconsin Archeologist* 44(3): 129–80.

Fregni, G. 2009. "A Study of the Manufacture of Copper Spearheads in the Old Copper Complex." *The Minnesota Archaeologist* 67: 121–30.

Gibbon, G. 1998. "Old Copper in Minnesota: A Review." *Plains Anthropologist* 43(163): 27–50.

Gotelli, N. J., and A. Chao. 2013. "Measuring and Estimating Species Richness, Species Diversity, and Biotic Similarity from Sampling Data." In *Encyclopedia of Biodiversity*, 2nd edn, vol. 5, ed. S. A. Levin, 195–211. Waltham, MA: Academic Press.

Griffin, J. B. 1961. *Lake Superior Copper and the Indians: Miscellaneous Studies of Great Lakes Prehistory*. Ann Arbor: Museum of Anthropology, University of Michigan, Anthropological Papers, No. 17.

Griffin, J. B., and G. I. Quimby. 1961. "The McCollum Site, Nipigon District, Ontario." In *Lake Superior Copper and the Indians: Miscellaneous Studies of Great Lakes Prehistory*, ed.

J. B. Griffin, 91–102. Ann Arbor: Museum of Anthropology, University of Michigan, Anthropological Papers, No. 17.

Hancock, R. G., L. A. Pavlish, R. M. Farquhar, R. Salloum, W. A. Fox, and G. C. Wilson. 1991. "Distinguishing European Trade Copper and North-Eastern North American Native Copper." *Archaeometry* 33(1): 69–86.

Hill, M. A. 2006. "The Duck Lake Site and Implications for Late Archaic Copper Procurement and Production in the Southern Lake Superior Basin." *Midcontinental Journal of Archaeology* 31(2): 213–47.

———. 2012. "Tracing Social Interaction: Perspectives on Archaic Copper Exchange from the Upper Great Lakes." *American Antiquity* 77(2): 279–92.

Hood, B. 1993. "The Maritime Archaic Indians of Labrador: Investigating Prehistoric Social Organization." *Newfoundland Studies* 9(2): 163–84.

Holmes, W. H. 1901. "Aboriginal Copper Mines of Isle Royale, Lake Superior." *American Anthropologist* 3(4): 684–96.

Hruska, R. 1967. "The Riverside Site: A Late Archaic Manifestation in Michigan." *The Wisconsin Archeologist* 48(3): 145–260.

Hsieh, T. C., K. H. Ma, and A. Chao. 2016. "iNEXT: An R Package for Rarefaction and Extrapolation of Species Diversity (Hill Numbers)." *Methods in Ecology and Evolution* 7: 1451–56.

Johnson, E. 1964. "Copper Artifacts and Glacial Lake Aggasiz Beaches." *Minnesota Archaeologist* 26: 5–22.

LaRonge, M. 2001. "An Experimental Analysis of Great Lakes Archaic Copper Smithing." *North American Archaeologist* 22(4): 371–85.

Leader, J. M. 1988. "Technological Continuities and Specialization in Prehistoric Metalwork in the Eastern United States." PhD dissertation. Gainesville: University of Florida.

Levine, M. A. 2007. "Determining the Provenance of Native Copper Artifacts from Northeastern North America: Evidence from Instrumental Neutron Activation Analysis." *Journal of Archaeological Science* 34(4): 572–87.

Martin, S. R. 1993. "20KE20: Excavations at a Prehistoric Copper Workshop." *Michigan Archaeologist* 39(3–4): 127–93.

———. 1999. *Wonderful Power: The Story of Ancient Copper Working in the Lake Superior Basin.* Detroit, MI: Wayne State University Press.

Martin, S. R., and T. C. Pleger. 1999. "The Complex Formerly Known as a Culture: The Taxonomic Puzzle of Old Copper." In *Taming the Taxonomy: Toward a New Understanding of Great Lakes Archaeology*, ed. R. F. Williamson and C. M. Watts, 61–70. Toronto: Eastend Books.

Mauk, J. L., and R. G. Hancock. 1998. "Trace Element Geochemistry of Native Copper from the White Pine Mine, Michigan (USA): Implications for Sourcing Artefacts." *Archaeometry* 40(1): 97–107.

McHugh, W. P. 1973. "'New Archaeology' and the Old Copper Culture." *The Wisconsin Archaeologist* 54(2): 70–83.

McKern, W. C. 1942. "The First Settlers of Wisconsin." *The Wisconsin Magazine of History* 26(2): 153–69.

Mesoudi, A. 2011. *Cultural Evolution.* Chicago: University of Chicago Press.

Miles, S. W. 1951. "A Revaluation of the Old Copper Industry." *American Antiquity* 16(3): 240–47.

Moffat, C. R., and J. M. Speth. 1999. "Rainbow Dam: Two Stratified Late Archaic and Woodland Habitations in the Wisconsin River Headwaters." *The Wisconsin Archeologist* 80(2): 111–59.

O'Brien, M. J., M. T. Boulanger, B. Buchanan, M. L. Collard, R. L. Lyman, and J. Darwent. 2014. "Innovation and Cultural Transmission in the American Paleolithic: Phylogenetic Analysis of Eastern Paleoindian Projectile-Point Classes." *Journal of Anthropological Archaeology* 34: 100–119.

O'Brien, M. J., and R. L. Lyman. 2000. *Applying Evolutionary Archaeology: A Systematic Approach.* New York: Springer Science & Business Media.

Olson, S. J. 2018. "MCC Nipissing East 2 (20.IR.253) and MCC Nipissing East 3 (20. IR.254): A Cross Site Comparison of Archaic Sites on Isle Royale National Park." *Culminating Projects in Cultural Resource Management* 23.

Ostberg, N. J. 1956. "Additional Material from the Reigh Site." *The Wisconsin Archeologist* 42(4): 143–55.

Penman, J. 1977. "The Old Copper Culture: An Analysis of Old Copper Artifacts." *The Wisconsin Archeologist* 58(4): 3–23.

Peterson, D. H. 2003a. "Red Metal Poundings and the 'Neubauer Process': Copper Culture Metallurgical Technology." *Central States Archaeological Journal* 50(2): 102–6.

———. 2003b. "Native Copper Characteristics Demonstrated in the Neubauer Process." *Central States Archaeological Journal* 50(3): 168–72.

Phillips, G. B. 1925. "The Primitive Copper Industry of America." *American Anthropologist* 27(2): 284–89.

Pleger, T. C. 1998. "Social Complexity, Trade, and Subsistence during the Archaic/Woodland Transition in the Western Great Lakes (4000–400 BC): A Diachronic Study of Copper Using Cultures at the Oconto and Riverside Cemeteries." PhD dissertation. University of Wisconsin–Madison.

———. 2000. "Old Copper and Red Ocher Social Complexity." *Midcontinental Journal of Archaeology* 25: 169–90.

———. 2002. "A Brief Introduction to the Old Copper Complex of the Western Great Lakes: 4000–1000 BC." *Proceedings of the Twenty-Seventh Annual Meeting of the Forest History Association of Wisconsin* 5: 10–18.

Pleger, T. C., and J. B. Stoltman. 2009. "The Archaic Tradition in Wisconsin." In *Archaic Societies: Diversity and Complexity across the Midcontinent*, ed. T. Emerson, D. McElrath, and A. Fortier, 697–724. Albany, NY: SUNY Press.

Pompeani, D. P., M. B. Abbott, D. J. Bain, S. DePasqual, and M. S. Finkenbinder. 2015. "Copper Mining on Isle Royale 6500–5400 Years Ago Identified Using Sediment Geochemistry from McCargoe Cove, Lake Superior." *The Holocene* 25(2): 253–62.

Pompeani, D. P., M. B. Abbott, B. A. Steinman, and D. J. Bain. 2013. "Lake Sediments Record Prehistoric Lead Pollution Related to Early Copper Production in North America." *Environmental Science and Technology* 47(11): 5545–52.

Quimby, G. I., and A. C. Spaulding. 1957. "The Old Copper Culture and the Keweenaw Waterway." *Fieldiana Anthropology* 36(8): 189–201.

Rapp, G., J. Allert, V. Vitali, Z. Jing, and E. Henrickson. 2000. *Determining Geologic Sources of Artifact Copper: Source Characterization Using Trace Element Patterns.* Lanham, MD: University Press of America.

Rapp, G., E. Henrickson, and J. Allert. 1990. *Native Copper Sources of Artifact Copper in Pre-Columbian North America*, Vol. 4. Boulder, CO: Geological Society of America.

Rapp, G., E. Henrickson, M. Miller, and S. Aschenbrenner. 1980. "Trace-Element Fingerprinting as a Guide to the Geographic Sources of Native Copper." *JOM* 32(1): 35–45.

Ritzenthaler, R. E. 1946. "The Osceola Site: An 'Old Copper' Site Near Potosi, Wisconsin." *The Wisconsin Archeologist* 27(3): 53–70.

———, ed. 1957. *The Old Copper Culture of Wisconsin.* Milwaukee: Wisconsin Archaeological Society.

————. 1960. "An Old Copper Crescent from Alberta." *The Wisconsin Archeologist* 41(2): 34.

————. 1970. "Another Radiocarbon Date for the Oconto Site." *The Wisconsin Archeologist* 51(2): 77.

Ritzenthaler, R. E., N. Ostberg, K. Whaley, M. Greenwald, P. Foust, E. Schug, W. Wittry, H. Meyer, and E. Lundsted. 1956. "Reigh Site Report–Number 3." *The Wisconsin Archaeologist* 38(4): 278–310.

Ritzenthaler, R. E., and W. L. Wittry. 1952. *The Oconto Site: An Old Copper Manifestation.* Milwaukee: Wisconsin Archaeological Society.

Steinbring, J. 1966. "Old Copper Culture Artifacts in Manitoba." *American Antiquity* 31(4): 567–74.

————. 1975. "Taxonomic and Associational Considerations of Copper Technology during the Archaic." PhD dissertation. University of Minnesota, Minneapolis.

Whittaker, J. C., D. Caulkins, and K. A. Kamp. 1998. "Evaluating Consistency in Typology and Classification." *Journal of Archaeological Method and Theory* 5(2): 129–64.

Whittlesey, C. 1863. *Ancient Mining on the Shores of Lake Superior* (Vol. 155). Washington, DC: Smithsonian Institution.

Wittry, W. L. 1951. "A Preliminary Study of the Old Copper Complex." *The Wisconsin Archeologist* 32(1): 1–18.

Wittry, W. L., and R. E. Ritzenthaler. 1956. "The Old Copper Complex: An Archaic Manifestation in Wisconsin." *American Antiquity* 21(3): 244–54.

Chapter 3

Diversity in Hunter-Gatherer Architecture

Brian Andrews, Danielle A. Macdonald, and Brooke Morgan

———❦———

Architecture is a human universal. As far as is known, human groups have always constructed shelters—lean-tos, tents, wikiups, huts, houses—modern *Homo sapiens* have built things to live in, in all periods and in all geographic locations. Long after the abandonment of stone tools, which archaeologists spend a considerable amount of time and effort documenting, architecture remains as one of the central components of human material culture. Considering that much of our species' history was spent as hunter-gatherers, and that mobility is a key defining characteristic of 'non-complex' hunter-gatherer lifestyles, it is no surprise that so much research focuses on the impact of mobility rather than on other aspects of hunter-gatherer systems. With a few notable exceptions (Andrews and Macdonald *in press* and references therein; Andrews, Meltzer, and Stiger 2021; Bettinger 1991; Cuenca-Solana, Gutiérrez-Zugasti, and Marchand 2018; Dawson 2001; Maher and Conkey 2019; Milner, Conneller, and Taylor 2018; Schoenauer 2000; Steadman 2015; Thomas 2015; Vasil'ev, Soffer, and Kozlowski 2003; Whitelaw 1994; Zubrow, Audouze, and Enloe 2010), what is missing from studies of hunter-gatherer lifestyles, especially outside of discussions on complex hunter-gatherers, is an emphasis on the nature and role of permanent or semi-permanent architecture. The more archaeologically visible architecture of sedentary and semi-sedentary hunter-gatherer groups known from the Holocene (e.g., Cameron 1999; Coupland, Clark, and Palmer 2009; Diehl 1997; Hodder 1990), or terminal Pleistocene in the Levant (e.g., Bar-Yosef 1991, 1998), has received modest analytic attention, as these groups are seen as an important link to later, sedentary, complex societies that arise along with the change in adaptations from hunter-gatherer to agricultural strategies. As well, there are abundant studies examining diversity in domestic architecture among these complex agricultural societies (e.g., Banning 1996; Banning and Chazan 2006 and reference therein; Blanton 1994; Robin 2003 and references therein; Wilk and Ashmore 1988). That there have been far fewer detailed studies of variability in architecture among mobile hunter-gatherers from the Pleistocene and early Holocene is without doubt at least partly a result of the relative scarcity of well-documented architecture in the archaeological record of this period. But there are also other reasons for this lack of research beyond the actual scarcity of these types of architectural features.

The emphasis on mobility in hunter-gatherer studies has in some ways reduced the attention paid to architecture. This is particularly true in North America, where it is only in the past decade or so that archaeologists studying late Pleistocene Paleoindian adaptations have begun to recognize the importance of structures (Andrews 2010; Andrews et al. 2021; Morgan 2015; Morgan and Andrews 2016; Robinson et al. 2009; Smith and McNees 2016; Surovell and Waguespack 2007; Stiger 2006). The well-documented dependence on migratory or otherwise highly mobile large game that characterizes many late Pleistocene groups worldwide requires, at least theoretically, high levels of residential mobility. Emphasis on frequent movement of the entire camp should therefore result in little effort invested in any sort of substantial habitation features, and thus the theoretical de-emphasis on architecture by archaeologists.

But high residential mobility does not mean people do not need to build shelter. Cross-cultural studies of hunter-gatherer mobility and architecture, both archaeologically and ethnographically, have suggested that certain features of structures are influenced primarily by the degree of actual and anticipated mobility of the group building the structures (Kent 1991; McGuire and Schiffer 1983). Binford (1990), for example, in comparisons of nomadic, seminomadic, semisedentary, and fully sedentary groups, found that circular or semicircular dwelling structures were more common among the relatively highly mobile groups, and that these groups tend to utilize the same materials for both wall and roof construction—usually transportable materials such as hides or locally available plant resources like reeds, saplings, bark, and other plant thatching material. More substantial construction materials, as well as rectangular floor plans, are found among the more sedentary populations, as the increased labor that goes into it only makes sense if the residents plan to stay put for a relatively long time.

The archaeological scarcity, then, of architecture from relatively mobile hunter-gatherers is likely more a factor of the methodological difficulty of spotting these features in the archaeological record. The mostly organic composition of any superstructure means that direct evidence is usually only found in cases of exceptional preservation (e.g., Dillehay 1997; Maher et al. 2012; Nadel and Werker 1999; Ramsey et al. 2018); thus, it is through attention to the spatial patterning evident in artifact distributions that we are most likely to identify mobile hunter-gatherer structures. We strongly suspect that these types of architectural features are chronically under-reported for residentially mobile hunter-gatherers.

Hunter-Gatherer Structure Variability

Our analysis supports the suspicion that mobile hunter-gatherer architecture is underreported, as there is a relatively small number of sites that have the requisite documented information on architecture necessary to conduct a robust comparative analysis of architectural diversity among mobile hunter-gatherers. The goal in this study, then, is not to provide an exhaustive exploration of diversity in these features. Rather, this is a first step toward better understanding diversity, and as such focuses necessarily on defining and establishing classificatory variables and types evident in the limited available dataset. We assembled data on 121 architectural features from 37 late Pleistocene/early Holocene sites throughout the world (Table 3.1). These sites are from ten countries in North America, Western Europe, Eastern Europe, and the Middle East (Figure 3.1). Obviously, key areas occupied by humans during the late Pleistocene (Africa, South America, Asia, and Australia) are missing from the sample. This is a result of several factors, including reporting language variability and barriers, and, more notably, an overall lack of publications that report the type of data necessary to establish the quantitative variables and categories we propose below. Temporally, our sample of sites ranges from between about 9,000 to about 25,000 years ago (Table 3.1). The sample for the current study uses only sites from cultures or periods that are interpreted to be fully mobile, non-sedentary hunter-gatherer groups.

Classificatory Variables

Understanding diversity requires establishing a quantitative and objective means of classifying the data in question. There are several ways to do this. Geometric morphometric (GM) analysis is often used to objectively

Table 3.1. Sites used in the analysis. Note that each site may contain multiple structures.

Site Name	Approximate Date (rcybp)	Cultural Affiliation	References
Agate Basin Area 2 (Folsom)	10,400	Paleoindian	Frison and Stanford 1982; see Carlson et al. 2016
Andernach-Martinsberg 3	12,000	Final Paleolithic (Federmesser)	Gelhausen et al. 2004; Stevens et al. 2009
Azariq XIII	22,500	Early Epipalaeolithic	Goring-Morris and Belfer-Cohen 2003; Goring-Morris and Belfer-Cohen 2008
Barger Gulch Locality B	10,500	Paleoindian	Surovell and Wasguespack 2007; Waguespack and Surovell 2014
Berlin-Tegel concentration IX	12,000	Final Paleolithic (Federmesser)	Gelhausen et al. 2004
Bull Brook	10,410	Paleoindian	Robinson et al. 2009; Robinson and Ort 2013
Ein Gev I	15,700	Early Epipalaeolithic	Bar-Yosef 1970
Gagarino	21,800	Gravettian	Mongait 1959; Svezhentsev and Popov 1993
Gönnersdorf KI	12,800	Magdalenian	Joris et al. 2011
Gönnersdorf KII	13,100	Magdalenian	Joris et al. 2011
Gönnersdorf KIII	13,050	Magdalenian	Joris et al. 2011
Gönnersdorf KIV	13,000	Magdalenian	Joris et al. 2011; Moseler 2011
Grub-Kranawetberg	24,830	Gravettian	Nigst and Antl-Weiser 2011
Hell Gap Structure A, Locality I (Frederick level)	8,690	Paleoindian	Irwin-Williams et al. 1973; Larson et al. 2009
Hell Gap Structures A/B, Locality II (Midland level)	10,200	Paleoindian	Irwin-Williams et al. 1973
Hell Gap Structures C/D, Locality II (Agate Basin level)	10,260	Paleoindian	Irwin-Williams et al. 1973; Larson et al. 2009
Jiita II	22,500	Early Epipalaeolithic	Melki 2004
Jilat 6	16,162	Early Epipalaeolithic	Garrard and Byrd 2013; Garrard and Byrd 1992; Garrard et al. 1988
Kharaneh IV	19,000	Early Epipalaeolithic	Maher et al. 2012; Maher et al. 2021; Ramsey et al. 2018
Kostenki I-1	22,800	Gravettian	Grigor'ev 1967; Svezhentsev and Popov 1993

(continued)

Table 3.1. *Continued*

Site Name	Approximate Date (rcybp)	Cultural Affiliation	References
Kostenki IV (Alexandrovka) - lower horizon	24,790	Gravettian	Grigor'ev 1967; Reynolds et al. 2015
Kostenki IV (Alexandrovka) - upper horizon	24,710	Gravettian	Grigor'ev 1967; Reynolds et al. 2015
La Vigne Brun	22,000	Gravettian	Nigst and Antl-Weiser 2011
Mal'ta concentration 9	21,340	Mal'ta-Buret'	Vasil'ev 2003; Vasil'ev et al. 2002
Mal'ta concentrations 10-15	24,340	Mal'ta-Buret'	Vasil'ev 2003; Vasil'ev et al. 2002
Mal'ta concentrations 5-8	21,340	Mal'ta-Buret'	Vasil'ev 2003; Vasil'ev et al. 2002
Mezhirich	14,400	Late Upper Paleolithic	Soffer et al. 1997; Soffer 2003; Svezhentsev and Popov 1993
Mountaineer	10,440	Paleoindian	Andrews et al. 2008; Andrews 2010; Stiger 2006; Morgan 2014
Niederbieber Area IV	12,000	Final Paleolithic (Federmesser)	Gelhausen et al. 2004; Gelhausen 2011
Oelknitz	12,700	Magdalenian	Gaudzinski-Windheuser 2011
Ohalo II	19,500	Early Epipalaeolithic	Nadel and Werker 1999; Nadel 2003
Orp East	12,200	Magdalenian	Wenzel 2011; Stapert 1989; Vermeersch et al. 1984
Plasenn-al-Lomm	22,000	Gravettian	Nigst and Antl-Weiser 2011
Pushkari I	21,000	Gravettian/ Epigravettian	Mongait 1959; Demay et al. 2016
Sannyi Mys	12,000	Late Upper Paleolithic	Vasil'ev 2003
Ushki-1 Layer 7	11,185	Late Upper Paleolithic	Goebel et al. 2010
Ushki-5 Layer 6	10,350	Late Upper Paleolithic	Goebel et al. 2003

classify shape, especially in the analysis of stone tools (e.g., Adams, Rohlf, and Slice 2004; Buchanan and Collard 2010; Cardillo 2010; Lycett, von Cramon-Taubadel, and Gowlett 2010). However, the sample of well-documented hunter-gatherer architecture is, at this point, likely too small for a robust GM analysis. Furthermore, many of the documented hunter-gatherer architectural features are only mentioned in published texts, and

Figure 3.1. General location of sites used in the sample. © The authors.

do not include the detailed maps or photographs necessary for GM analysis. Although GM analysis for the classification and documentation of diversity in hunter-gatherer architecture is a promising way forward, this study uses the available data to define four objective categories around key architectural features that are normally reported in the literature.

These four categories include two directly quantifiable variables: floor size, measured as square meters of inside space, and number of inside features, measured as the number of reported features (hearths, storage pits, sleeping areas, or other identified special use areas) found in the interior space. Although both are directly quantifiable, there is still potential ambiguity. For floor size, it is sometimes difficult to determine the exact diameter or outline of a structure due to taphonomic factors, especially in cases of organic structures that have completely decayed. This means the structure can only be approximated through a spatial analysis of artifact distributions (e.g., Janes 1989; Robinson et al. 2009; Stapert 1989, 1990; Surovell and Waguespack 2007). Where possible, floor size is recorded here as directly reported by the analyst and/or authors of the given report. Where a floor size is not reported but scaled plan maps are available, floor size is determined from the map. Similar issues arise when calculating the number of interior features, as taphonomic factors, field methodologies, and reporting standards may have significant impact on the number of features found and/or reported. As with floor size, we record the number of interior features as reported by the analysts/authors, or, when not available, we calculate from features shown on maps.

The remaining two variables are construction material type and floor-plan shape. Construction material types are, of course, highly variable, depending on ecological settings, the available materials, and cultural/behavioral factors. In many cases, construction may involve a variety of different materials. For the sake of simplicity and quantifiability, here we define dichotomous categories for construction material: organic and non-organic. Organic materials are rarely preserved, so in many cases the use of organic materials in construction is identified primarily by the presence of compacted sediment, pit fill, artifact distributions, or some combination of these types of evidence. If any non-organic material is used in construction, the architecture is classified as "non-organic." While the most common type of non-organic material used in construction was stone, we also include bone or ivory in this category as it is generally more substantial (and certainly more likely to be preserved) than wood, grass, hides, or other types of thatching. Of course, non-organic construction materials are presumed to have been frequently combined with organic materials. For this classification system, though, the use of any non-organic materials requires classification as "non-organic."

Floorplan shape is more difficult to define, especially when no maps are published for a given site or structure. A variety of terms are used to describe the overall shape of architecture, so we have simplified this variable into two categories: circular and non-circular. Circular structures include those described as round, elliptical, oval, semi-circular, kidney bean-shaped, etc. Non-circular structures are any that are described as square, rectangular, trapezoidal, polygonal, or s imilar, in reports, or that have reported dimensions where the length is more than twice the width. This masks a good deal of variability in shape, but it is necessary to facilitate comparison between structure floorplans.

Relationships between Classificatory Variables

Out of this sample, nearly one-third (28.7 percent) of structures are thought to be made completely from organic material. They are identified primarily by the presence of compacted sediment, pit fill, artifact distributions, or some combination of this type of evidence. About 40 percent of the structures in our sample have no published data indicating the presumed type of construction material used. Although we cannot say for certain, it is likely that the structures in the "unknown" category were also made of organic materials, as the presence of stone-lined floors, rock ring or animal bone foundations, or other substantial inorganic materials are generally noted by archaeologists when encountered.

The average size of structures varies depending on construction material types, with the average floor area of non-organic structures about 46 square meters, and the average size for organic structures about 17 square meters. However, variability is very high (Figure 3.2), especially for non-organic examples, where the standard deviation of size approaches 60 square meters. The high degree of variability for non-organic structures makes it difficult to demonstrate a size difference statistically, but these data do suggest that the increase in labor investment represented by the utilization of rock, bone, and other substantial and semi-permanent materials also results in larger dwelling structures (or perhaps, the opposite: more effort to maintain larger-sized structures for longer periods of time is realized through more substantive construction techniques and materials). Another potential confounding variable impacting both organic and non-organic materials is the actual source location of the material; while we tend to think of higher labor investment in stone material, for example, that may be mitigated if the source of the stone is local. In many cases, stone used in construction may be immediately available at the construction site, which would act to reduce labor costs.

There is also evidence that labor investment in non-organic construction and larger structures are proportional to the intended intensity and length of use of inside space. Simple counts of the number of inside features (including hearths, storage pits, sleeping areas, and other special use areas) show that non-organic structures have a greater number of inside features (5.4 for non-organic, 3.8 for organic—albeit not a statistically significant difference) and that there is a strong positive correlation between

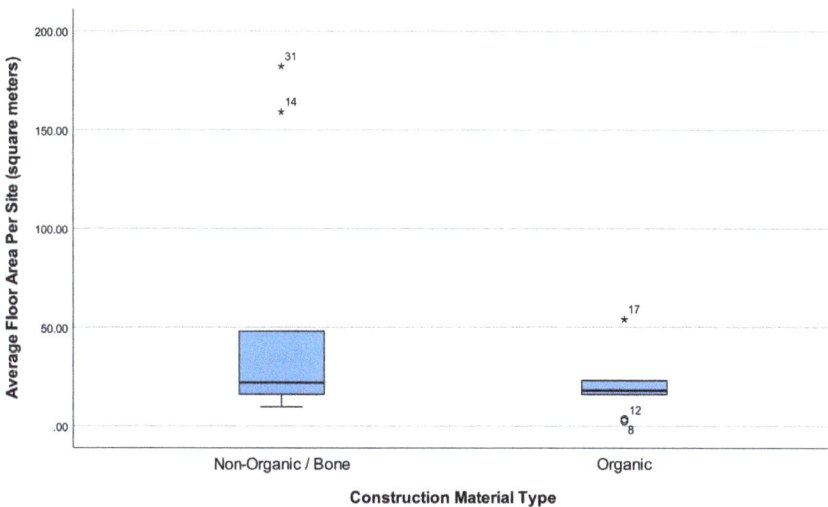

Figure 3.2. Average and variability in floor area for non-organic and organic constructed architecture. © The authors.

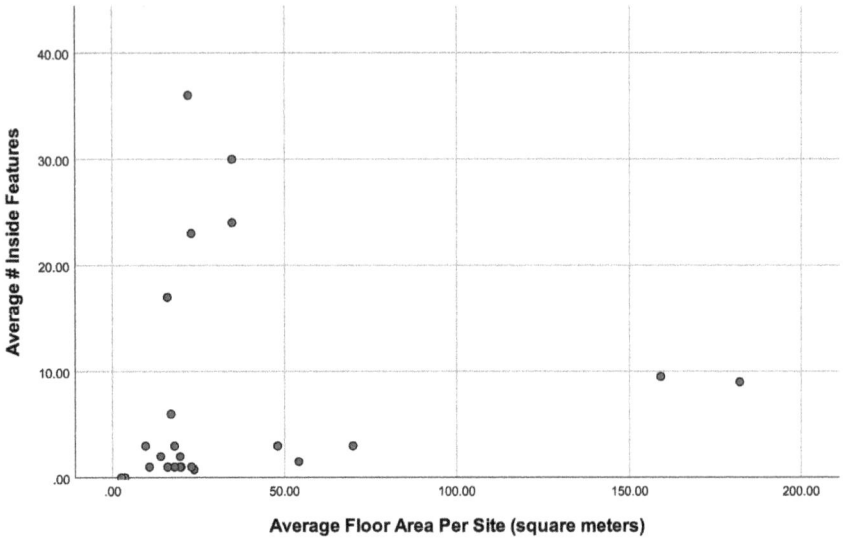

Figure 3.3. Relationship between average structure floor area per site and the total number of inside features per site. © The authors.

floor area and the number of interior features (Figure 3.3) (Spearman's rho =.472, p=.017).

Dwelling shape—circular versus non-circular—appears to be the result of activity differentiation present at a given site (Smith 2003), likely related to duration of occupation. Rectangular shapes are generally easier to "divide" into separate work areas, whereas circular shapes tend to have overlapping activity areas within them. As noted above, determining exact shape is problematic unless preservation is exceptional, hence the simplified dichotomous definition offered here. Defined in this way, there is a clear dominance of "circular" shaped structures (n=52) during this period. Non-circular structures (n=6) tend to be almost exclusively made of non-organic/bone materials, indicating more intensive labor in their construction and/or longer anticipated usage.

In terms of floor area, non-circular houses are significantly larger than circular houses (Figure 3.4) (p < 0.001). Kostenki is an extreme outlier, with one very large 35 by 16 meter rectangular mammoth bone structure known as the Kostenki "long house," which may actually be several smaller connected structures (Grigor'ev 1967). Even with this outlier removed, non-circular houses (mean floor area 68 m²) are much larger and much more variable in size than are circular shaped houses (mean floor area 19 m²), though in both cases there is a good deal of variability in floor area. There are undoubtedly practical explanations for this variability related to the

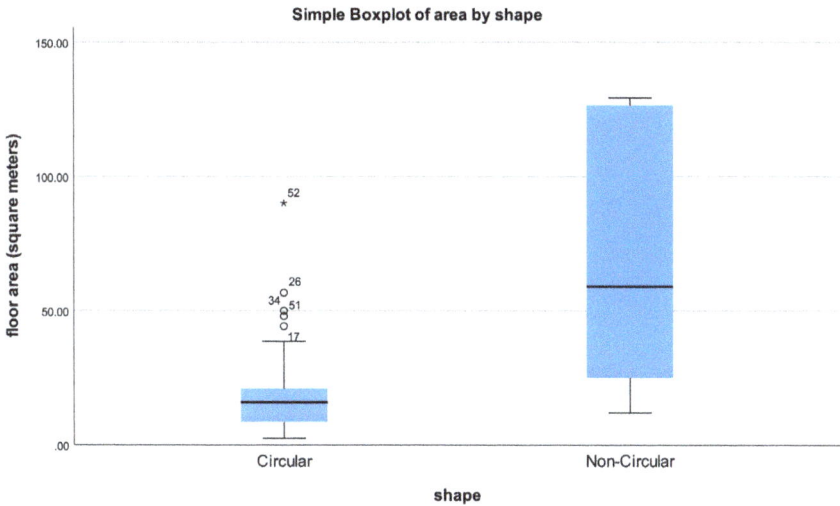

Figure 3.4. Variability in floor area of individual structures divided as circular or non-circular in shape. © The authors.

availability of construction materials. Large circular structures that rely on center pole supports would require significantly taller center poles in order to make the area near the perimeter functionally useful to the inhabitants. In environments with limited timber resources, animal bone may have been the only option for construction—even if this meant investing more time and labor. Further, there are functional explanations for this variability related to the types of activities planned for and carried out in different structures, which is also probably a function of the anticipated size of the group that would inhabit or utilize the structure, and the anticipated length of their stay. There is some evidence to support this, with structures interpreted as containing multiple separate occupations tending to be slightly larger than those thought to contain only a single occupation. However, this distinction between single and multiple occupations is difficult to make in the absence of stratigraphic separation of living floors, and only a small number of structures in our sample have definitive evidence with respect to the number of occupations. While seasonality information for the sample of sites is limited, it is notable that these larger structures are often interpreted as winter residences. Reduced mobility in winter and fewer outdoor activities may translate into a need for more inside space.

There is a significant relationship between structure size and date over the entire temporal span of our sample (R=.433, p=.017) (Figure 3.5). Older structures tend to be larger, though this pattern appears to be primarily driven by the fact that the largest structures are the oldest outliers

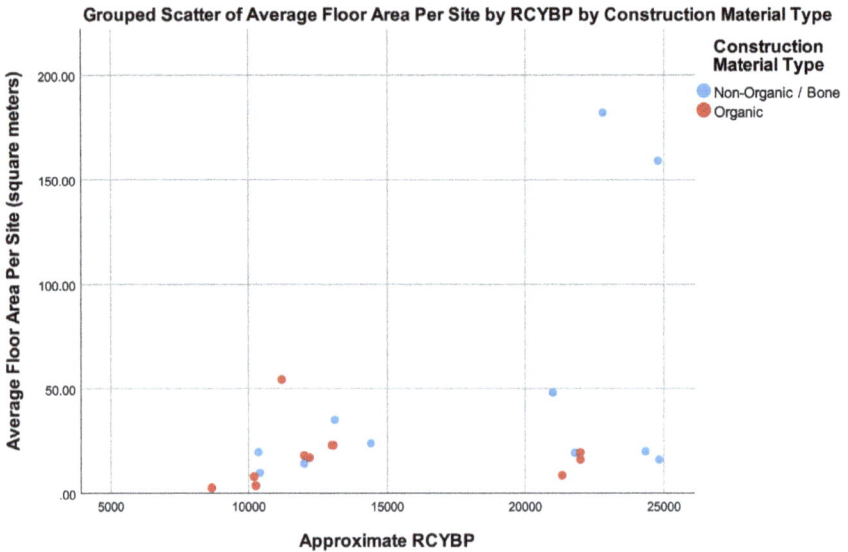

Figure 3.5. Average floor area per site through time for the entire sample used in this study. © The authors.

(both, notably, from Kostenki during the Gravettian). However, this trend in diminishing structure size continues during the terminal Pleistocene to Holocene transition (Figure 3.6), where we see a significant decrease in size over time (R=.502, p=.029). We hesitate to make any definitive statements about the possible causes behind these trends in decreasing structure size, but generally hypothesize that it may be related to changes in environmental and ecological conditions, especially during the terminal Pleistocene as more modern-like Holocene conditions take the place of Ice Age conditions. The resultant changes in resource distributions and characteristics may have had an impact on mobility and group structure in ways that exclude the use of larger structures. However, over this period from 14,500–8,000 RCYBP, there is still high variability in structure size and shape, and in construction techniques.

Conclusion

Much like stone tools, there are variable yet finite ways in which struc-tures can be made, variable yet finite morphologies they can take, and variable yet finite functions they can serve. The variability present in the construction, morphology, and function of structures is likewise related to

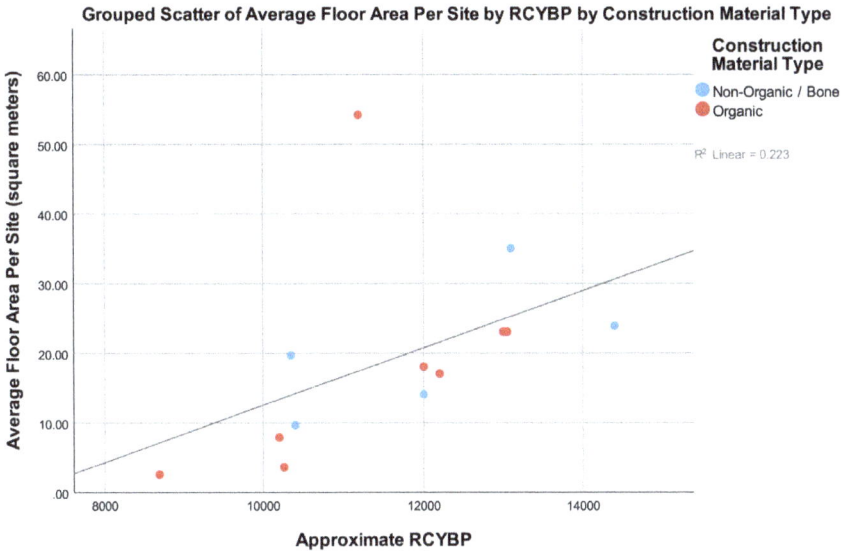

Figure 3.6. Average floor area per site over the Pleistocene to Holocene transition. © The authors.

a wide variety of factors, including functional/adaptive concerns, regional variability in environments, temporal variability, adaptive strategies, and ethnic and cultural identities. One way to make sense of variability is by narrowing the scope of empirical inquiry in such a way that many key variables are held constant (Bettinger 1993). Focusing on a limited suite of variables (floor size and shape among a sample of structures from similarly organized hunter-gatherer societies) and how they may relate to functional issues of mobility is, we believe, a productive path toward ultimately understanding variability in hunter-gatherer architecture.

Acknowledgments

We are grateful to Metin Eren and Briggs Buchanan for inviting us to participate in this book. We wish to thank our respective collaborators and field crews at Mountaineer and Kharaneh IV who helped excavate the hunter-gatherer structures at these sites. It inspired this comparative research, which would not have been possible without their hard work, insights, and good humor. Macdonald would also like to thank the Jordanian Department of Antiquities director general and representatives who worked at Kharaneh IV. Macdonald's research was funded by the National Endowment for the Humanities (grant number RZ-255635-17); and Andrews and Morgan would like to thank the Quest Archaeological Research Fund.

Brian Andrews is an Associate Professor at Rogers State University, Claremore, Oklahoma, USA.

Danielle A. Macdonald is an Associate Professor at the University of Tulsa, Oklahoma, USA.

Brooke Morgan is a Curator at the Illinois State Museum, Springfield, USA.

References

Adams, D. C., F. J. Rohlf, and D. E. Slice. 2004. "Geometric Morphometrics: Ten Years of Progress Following the 'Revolution.'" *Italian Journal of Zoology* 71: 5–16.

Andrews, B. N. 2010. "Folsom Adaptive Systems in the Upper Gunnison Basin, Colorado: An Analysis of the Mountaineer Site." PhD dissertation. Southern Methodist University, Dallas, Texas.

Andrews, B. N., and D. Macdonald, eds. In press. *More Than Shelter from the Storm: Hunter-Gatherers and the Built Environment*. Gainesville: University Press of Florida.

Andrews, B. N., D. J. Meltzer, and M. S. Stiger. 2021. *The Mountaineer Site: A Folsom Winter Camp in the Rockies*. Boulder: University of Colorado Press.

Banning, E. B. 1996. "Houses, Compounds and Mansions in the Prehistoric Near East." In *People Who Lived in Big Houses: Archaeological Perspectives on Large Domestic Structures*, eds. G. Coupland and E.B. Banning, 165-185. Madison: Prehistory Press.

Banning, E. B., and M. Chazan. 2006. "Structuring Interactions, Structuring Ideas: Domestication of Space in the Prehistoric Near East." In *Domesticating Space: Construction, Community and Cosmology in the Late Prehistoric Near East*, ed. E. B. Banning and M. Chazan, 5–14. Berlin: ex Oriente.

Bar-Yosef, O. 1970. "Epipalaeolithic Cultures of Palestine." PhD dissertation. Hebrew University of Jerusalem.

———. 1991. "The Archaeology of the Natufian Layer at Hayonim Cave." In *The Natufian Culture in the Levant*, ed. O. Bar-Yosef and F. Valla, 81–92. Ann Arbor, MI: International Monographs in Prehistory.

———. 1998. "The Natufian Culture in the Levant, Threshold to the Origins of Agriculture." *Evolutionary Anthropology* 6(5): 159–77.

Bettinger, R. L. 1991. "Aboriginal Occupation at High Altitude: Alpine Villages in the White Mountains of California." *American Anthropologist* 93: 656–79.

———. 1993. "Doing Great Basin Archaeology Recently: Coping with Variability." *Journal of Archaeological Research* 1: 43–66.

Binford, L. R. 1990. "Mobility, Housing, and Environment: A Comparative Study." *Current Anthropological Research* 46: 119–52.

Blanton, R. E. 1994. *Houses and Households: A Comparative Study*. New York: Plenum Press.
Buchanan, B., and M. Collard. 2010. "An Assessment of the Impact of Resharpening on Paleoindian Projectile Point Blade Shape using Geometric Morphometric Techniques." In *New Perspectives on Old Stones: Analytical Approaches to Paleolithic Technologies*, ed. S. Lycett and P. Chauhan, 255–74. New York: Springer.
Cameron, C. M. 1999. "Room Size, Organization of Construction, and Archaeological Interpretation in the Puebloan Southwest." *Journal of Anthropological Archaeology* 18: 201–39.
Cardillo, M. 2010. "Some Applications of Geometric Morphometrics to Archaeology." In *Morphometrics to Nonmorphometricians*, ed. A. M. T. Elewa, 325–41. Heidelberg: Springer.
Carlson, K. C., B. J. Culleton, D. J. Kennett, and L. C. Bement. 2016. "Tightening Chronology of Paleoindian Bison Kill Sites on the Northern and Southern Plains." *PaleoAmerica* 2: 90–98.
Coupland, G., T. Clark, and A. Palmer. 2009. "Hierarchy, Communalism, and the Spatial Order of Northwest Coast Plank Houses: A Comparative Study." *American Antiquity* 74: 77–106.
Cuenca-Solana, D., I. Gutiérrez-Zugasti, and G. Marchand, eds. 2018. "Mesolithic Dwelling Structures: From Methodological Approaches to Archaeological Interpretation." *Journal of Archaeological Science: Reports* 18: 902–4.
Dawson, P.C. 2001. "Interpreting Variability in Thule Inuit Architecture: A Case Study from the Canadian High Arctic." *American Antiquity* 66: 453–70.
Demay, L., S. Péan, V. I. Belyaeva, P. M. Vasil'ev, and M. Patou-Mathis. 2016. "Zooarchaeological Study of an Upper Paleolithic Site with Mammoth Remains, Pushkari I—Excavation VII (Chernigov Oblast, Ukraine)." *Quaternary International* 406 Part B: 183–201.
Diehl, M. W. 1997. "Changes in Architecture and Land Use Strategies in the American Southwest: Upper Mogollon Pithouse Dwellers, A.C. 200–1000." *Journal of Field Archaeology* 24: 179–94.
Dillehay, T. D. 1997. *Monte Verde: A Late Pleistocene Settlement in Chile, Vol 2.: The Archaeological Context and Interpretation*. Washington, DC: Smithsonian Institution Press.
Frison, G. C., and D. Stanford. 1982. *The Agate Basin Site: A Record of the Paleoindian Occupation of the Northwestern High Plains*. New York: Academic Press.
Garrard, A., and B. Byrd. 1992. "New Dimensions to the Epipalaeolithic of the Wadi El-Jilat in Central Jordan." *Paléorient* 18(1): 47–62.
———. 2013. *Beyond the Fertile Crescent: Late Palaeolithic and Neolithic Communities of the Jordanian Steppe*. Oxford: Council for British Research in the Levant.
Garrard, A., S. Colledge, C. Hunt, and R. Montague. 1988. "Environment and Subsistence during the Late Pleistocene and Early Holocene in the Azraq Basin." *Paléorient* 14: 40–49.
Gaudzinski-Windheuser, S. 2011. "An Introduction to Living Structures and History of Occupation at the Late Upper Palaeolithic Site of Oelknitz (Thuringia, Germany)." In *Site-Internal Spatial Organization of Hunter-Gatherer Societies: Case Studies from the European Palaeolithic and Mesolithic*, ed. S. Gaudzinski-Windheuser, O. Joris, M. Sensburg, M. Street, and E. Turner, 127–39. Druck: Strauss GmbH, Morlenbach.
Gelhausen, F. 2011. "Subsistence Strategies and Settlement Systems at the Federmessergruppen Site of Niederbieber (Central Rhineland, Germany)." In *Site-Internal Spatial Organization of Hunter-Gatherer Societies: Case Studies from the European Palaeolithic and Mesolithic*, ed. S. Gaudzinski-Windheuser, O. Joris, M. Sensburg, M. Street, and E. Turner, 159–73. Druck: Strauss GmbH, Morlenbach.

Gelhausen, F., J. Kegler, and S. Wenzel. 2004. "Latent Dwelling Structures in the Final Palaeolithic: Niederbieber IV, Andernach-Martinsberg 3, Berlin-Tegel IX." *Notae Praehistoricae* 24: 69–79.

Goebel, T., S. B. Slobodin, and M. R. Waters. 2010. "New Dates from Ushki-1, Kamchatka, Confirm 13,000 cal BP Age for Earliest Paleolithic Occupation." *Journal of Archaeological Science* 37: 2540–649.

Goebel, T., M. R. Waters, and M. Dikova. 2003. "The Archaeology of Ushki Lake, Kamchatka, and the Pleistocene Peopling of the Americas." *Science* 301: 501–5.

Goring-Morris, N., and A. Belfer-Cohen. 2003. "Structures and Dwellings in the Upper and Epi-Paleolithic (ca 42–10k BP) Levant: Profane and Symbolic Uses." In *Perceived Landscapes and Built Environments*, ed. S. Vasil'ev, O. Soffer, and J. Kozlowski, 65–81. Oxford: BAR International Series 1122.

———. 2008. "A Roof Over One's Head: Developments in Near Eastern Residential Architecture across the Epipalaeolithic-Neolithic Transition." In *The Neolithic Demographic Transition and Its Consequences*, ed. J.-P. Bocquet-Appel and O. Bar Yosef, 239–86. New York: Spring.

Grigor'ev, G. P. 1967. "A New Reconstruction of the Above-Ground Dwelling of Kostenki I." *Current Anthropology* 8: 344–49.

Hodder, I. 1990. *The Domestication of Europe*. Oxford: Basil Blackwell.

Irwin-Williams, C., H. Irwin, G. Agogino, and C. V. Haynes. 1973. "Hell Gap: Paleo-Indian Occupation on the High Plains." *Plains Anthropologist* 18: 40–53.

Janes, R. R. 1989. "An Ethnoarchaeological Model for the Identification of Prehistoric Tepee Remains in the Boreal Forest." *Arctic* 42: 128–38.

Joris, O., M. Street, and E. Turner. 2011. "Spatial Analysis at the Magdalenian Site of Gönnersdorf (Central Rhineland, Germany)." In *Site-Internal Spatial Organization of Hunter-Gatherer Societies: Case Studies from the European Palaeolithic and Mesolithic*, ed. S. Gaudzinski-Windheuser, O. Joris, M. Sensburg, M. Street, and E. Turner., 53–80. Druck: Strauss GmbH, Morlenbach.

Kent, S. 1991. "The Relationship between Mobility Strategies and Site Structure." In *The Interpretation of Archaeological Spatial Patterning*, ed. E. Krolland and T. Price, 33–59. New York: Plenum Press.

Larson, M. L., M. Kornfeld, and G. Frison. 2009. *Hell Gap: A Stratified Paleoindian Campsite at the Edge of the Rockies*. Salt Lake City: University of Utah Press.

Lycett, S. J., N. von Cramon-Taubadel, and J. Gowlett. 2010. "A Comparative 3D Geometric Morphometric Analysis of Victoria West Cores: Implications for the Origins of Levallois Technology." *Journal of Archaeological Science* 37: 1110–17.

Maher, L. A., and M. Conkey. 2019. "Homes for Hunters? Exploring the Concept of Home at Hunter-Gatherer Sites in Upper Palaeolithic Europe and Epipalaeolithic Southwest Asia." *Current Anthropology* 60(1): 91–137.

Maher, L. A., D. Macdonald, E. Pomeroy, and J. Stock. "Life, Death, and the Destruction of Architecture: Hunter-Gatherer Mortuary Behaviors in Prehistoric Jordan." *Journal of Anthropological Archaeology* 61: 101–262.

Maher, L. A., T. Richter, D. Macdonald, M. D. Jones, L. Martin, and J. Stock. 2012. "Twenty-Thousand-Year-Old Huts at a Hunter-Gatherer Settlement in Eastern Jordan." *PLoS ONE* 7(2): e31447.

McGuire, R. H., and M. B. Schiffer. 1983. "A Theory of Architectural Design." *Journal of Anthropological Archaeology* 2: 277–303.

Melki, E. 2004. "Jiita II; La Cabane Kebarienne." In *From the River to the Sea: The Palaeolithic and the Neolithic on the Euphrates and in the Northern Levant Studies in Honour of*

Lorraine Copeland, ed. O. Aurenche, M. Le Miere, and P. Sanlaville, 271–80. Oxford: BAR International Series.

Milner, N., C. Conneller, and B. Taylor, eds. 2018. *Star Carr Volume 1: A Persistent Place in a Changing World*. York: White Rose University Press.

Mongait, A. 1959. *Archaeology in the U.S.S.R.* Moscow: Foreign Languages Publishing House.

Morgan, B. M. 2015. "Folsom Settlement Organization in the Southern Rocky Mountains: An Analysis of Dwelling Space at the Mountaineer Site." PhD dissertation. Southern Methodist University, Dallas, Texas.

Morgan, B. M., and B. N. Andrews. 2016. "Folsom Stone Tool Distribution at the Mountaineer Site: Indoor and Outdoor Spaces as Activity Areas." *PaleoAmerica* 2: 179–87.

Moseler, F. 2011. "Spatial Analysis of Concentration K-IV of the Magdalenian Site of Gönnersdorf." In *Site-Internal Spatial Organization of Hunter-Gatherer Societies: Case Studies from the European Palaeolithic and Mesolithic*, ed. S. Gaudzinski-Windheuser, O. Joris, M. Sensburg, M. Street, and E. Turner, 103–26. Druck: Strauss GmbH, Morlenbach.

Nadel, D. 2003. "The Ohalo II Brush Huts and the Dwelling Structures of the Natufian and PPNA Sites in the Jordan Valley." *Archaeology, Ethnology & Anthropology of Eurasia* 1(13): 34–48.

Nadel, D., and E. Werker. 1999. "The Oldest Ever Brush Hut Plant Remains from Ohalo II, Jordan Valley, Israel (19,000 BP)." *Antiquity* 73: 755–64.

Nigst, P., and W. Antl-Weiser. 2011. "Intrasite Spatial Organization of Grub/Kranawet-Berg: Methodology and Interpretations." In *Site-Internal Spatial Organization of Hunter-Gatherer Societies: Case Studies from the European Palaeolithic and Mesolithic*, ed. S. Gaudzinski-Windheuser, O. Joris, M. Sensburg, M. Street, and E. Turner, 11–29. Druck: Strauss GmbH, Morlenbach.

Ramsey, M. N., L. A. Maher, D. A. Macdonald, D. Nadel, and A. Rosen. 2018. "Sheltered by Reeds and Settled on Sedges: Construction and Use of a Twenty-Thousand-Year-Old Hut According to Phytolith Analysis from Kharaneh IV, Jordan." *Journal of Anthropological Archaeology* 50: 85–97.

Reynolds, N., S. N. Lisitsyn, M. V. Sablin, N. Barton, and T. F. G. Higham. 2015. "Chronology of the European Russian Gravettian: New Radiocarbon Dating Results and Interpretation." *Quartär* 62: 121–32.

Robin, C. 2003. "New Directions in Classic Maya Household Archaeology." *Journal of Archaeological Research* 11: 307–56.

Robinson, B. S., and J. C. Ort. 2013. "Spatial Organization at Bull Brook." In *In The Eastern Fluted Point Tradition*, ed. J. Gingerich, 104–20. Salt Lake City: University of Utah Press.

Robinson, B. S., J. C. Ort, W. A. Eldridge, A. L. Burke, and B. G. Petellier. 2009. "Paleoindian Aggregation and Social Context at Bull Brook." *American Antiquity* 74: 423–47.

Schoenauer, N. 2000. *6,000 Years of Housing*. New York: W.W. Norton and Co.

Smith, C. S. 2003. "Hunter-Gatherer Mobility, Storage, and Houses in a Marginal Environment: An Example from the Mid-Holocene of Wyoming." *Journal of Anthropological Archaeology* 22: 162–89.

Smith, C. S., and L. M. McNees. 2016. "Folsom Structures in the Wyoming Basin of Southwest Wyoming: The Evidence from Site 48SW97." *Plains Anthropologist* 61: 76–95.

Soffer, O. 2003. "Mammoth Bone Accumulations: Death Sites? Kill Sites? Dwellings?" In *Perceived Landscapes and Built Environments*, eds. S. A. Vasil'ev, O. Soffer, and J. Kozlowski, 39–46. Oxford: BAR International Series 1122.

Soffer, O., J. M. Adovasio, N. L. Kornietz, A. A. Velichko, Y. N. Gribchenko, B. R. Lenz, and V. Y. Suntsov. 1997. "Cultural Stratigraphy at Mezhirich, an Upper Paleolithic Site in Ukraine with Multiple Occupations." *Antiquity* 71: 48–62.

Stapert, D. 1989. "The Ring and Sector Method: Intrasite Spatial Analysis of Stone Age Sites, with Special Reference to Pincevent." *Palaeohistoria* 31: 1–57.

———. 1990. "Middle Paleolithic Dwellings: Fact or Fiction? Some Applications of the Ring and Sector Method." *Palaeohistoria* 32: 1–19.

Steadman, S. R. 2015. *Archaeology of Domestic Architecture and the Human Use of Space.* Walnut Creek, CA: Left Coast Press.

Stevens, R. E., T. C. O'Connell, R. E. M. Hedges, and M. Street. 2009. "Radiocarbon and Stable Isotope Investigations at the Central Rhineland Sites of Gönnersdorf and Andernach-Martinsberg, Germany." *Journal of Human Evolution* 57: 131–48.

Stiger, M. A. 2006. "A Folsom Structure in the Colorado Mountains." *American Antiquity* 71: 321–52.

Surovell, T. A., and N. M. Waguespack. 2007. "Folsom Hearth-Centered Use of Space at Barger Gulch, Locality B." In *Emerging Frontiers in Colorado Paleoindian Archaeology*, ed. R. Brunswig and B. Pitblado, 219–59. Boulder: University of Colorado Press.

Svezhentsev, Y. S., and S. G. Popov. 1993. "Late Paleolithic Chronology of the East European Plain." *Radiocarbon* 35: 495–501.

Thomas, D. H. 2015. "Engineering Alta Toquima: Social Investments and Dividends at 11,000 Feet." In *Engineering Mountain Landscapes: An Archaeology of Social Investment*, ed. L. L. Scheiber and M. N. Zedeño, 49–74. Salt Lake City: University of Utah Press.

Vasil'ev, S. A. 2003. "The Upper Paleolithic Domestic Structures in Siberia: A Critical Review of Relevant Evidence." In *Perceived Landscapes and Built Environments*, ed. S. A. Vasil'ev, O. Soffer, and J. Kozlowski, 155–60. Oxford: BAR International Series 1122.

Vasil'ev, S.A., Y. V. Kuzmin, L. A. Orlova, V. N. Dementiev. 2002. "Radiocarbon-Based Chronology of the Paleolithic in Siberia, and Its Relevance to the Peopling of the New World." *Radiocarbon* 44: 503–30.

Vasil'ev, S.A., O. Soffer, and J. Kozlowski, eds. 2003. *Perceived Landscapes and Built Environments*. Oxford: BAR International Series 1122.

Vermeersch, P. M., R. Lauwers, H. van de Heyning, and P. Vynckier. 1984. "A Magdalenian Open Air Site at Orp, Belgium." In *Structures d'habitat du Paléolithique Supérieur en Europe: Colloque de Reisenburg/Günzburg, 8–14 mai 1983*, ed. H. Berke, J. Hahn, and C.-J. Kind, 195–208. Tübingen: Archaeologica Venatoria.

Waguespack, N. M., and T. A. Surovell. 2014. "A Simple Method for Identifying Households Using Lithic Assemblages: A Case Study from a Folsom Campsite in Middle Park, Colorado." In *Lithics in the West*, ed. D. MacDonald, W. Andrefsky Jr., and P.-L. Yu, 35–49. Salt Lake City: University of Utah Press.

Wenzel, S. 2011. "The Magdalenian Dwelling of Orp East (Belgium) and Its Spatial Organization." In *Site-Internal Spatial Organization of Hunter-Gatherer Societies: Case Studies From the European Palaeolithic and Mesolithic*, ed. S. Gaudzinski-Windheuser, O. Joris, M. Sensburg, M. Street, and E. Turner, 141–58. Druck: Strauss GmbH, Morlenbach.

Whitelaw, T. M. 1994. "Order Without Architecture: Functional, Social and Symbolic Dimensions in Hunter-Gatherer Settlement Organization." In *Architecture and Order: Approaches to Social Space*, ed. M. Parker Pearson and C. Richards, 217–43. New York: Routledge.

Wilk, R. R., and W. Ashmore, eds. 1988. *Household and Community in the Mesoamerican Past*. Albuquerque: University of New Mexico Press.

Zubrow, E., F. Audouze, and J. G. Enloe, eds. 2010. *The Magdalenian Household: Unraveling Domesticity*. New York: SUNY Press.

Chapter 4

The Potential of
Coverage-Based Rarefaction
in Zooarchaeology

J. Tyler Faith and Andrew Du

❈

In zooarchaeology and related disciplines that deal with biological data (e.g., paleobiology, ecology), taxonomic diversity is a concept that seems straightforward at first blush, but becomes increasingly complex the more it is scrutinized. This complexity stems from the numerous ways that diversity can be defined and measured (e.g., Hill 1973; Hurlbert 1971; Magurran 1988, 2004; Pielou 1966), and from the issues associated with its analysis (e.g., Faith and Lyman 2019; Gotelli and Colwell 2001; Magurran 1988, 2004). Perhaps the most straightforward and widely used diversity metric is taxonomic richness, which is simply the number of taxa (NTAXA) present in a sample. This variable is of interest to zooarchaeologists because it can be used to measure changes in human diet breadth (e.g., Grayson 1991; Grayson and Delpech 1998; Nagaoka 2002) or to inform on paleoecological change (e.g., Faith 2013; Faith and Lyman 2019; Grayson 1998).

Although tallying the richness of a faunal sample is simple enough, it is well known that if we wish to do anything meaningful with it, then we must contend with the effects of sampling (Faith and Lyman 2019; Grayson 1984; Lyman 2008). This is because the number of taxa recovered increases as a function of assemblage sample size, which means that a direct comparison of richness between assemblages is likely to tell us more about variation in sampling effort rather than provide useful information about the past. There are several analytical approaches that could be implemented to deal with these issues (Faith and Lyman 2019), and our concern here is with coverage-based rarefaction (Alroy 2010a; Chao and Jost 2012; Chao et al. 2020), a technique that has become increasingly popular in ecology and paleobiology, but has yet to gain traction among zooarchaeologists. In this chapter, we discuss what it is and how it differs from traditional rarefaction analysis, and highlight some of the analytical pitfalls that zooarchaeologists should be aware of when implementing the technique.

Specimen-Based versus Coverage-Based Rarefaction

Most zooarchaeologists are familiar with conventional specimen-based rarefaction analysis, which has a long history in paleobiology and ecology (Hurlbert 1971; Sanders 1968; Tipper 1979). It estimates the number of taxa that would be present in a faunal assemblage had fewer specimens been collected—and for this reason we refer to it here as specimen-based rarefaction. Note that ecologists use the term individual-based rarefaction for the same type of analysis because their taxonomic abundances are typically measured in terms of individuals (e.g., Colwell et al. 2012), whereas zooarchaeologists tally abundances according to the number of identified specimens (NISP) or some other measure derived from it (e.g., MNI, the minimum number of individuals). Specimen-based rarefaction facilitates comparison of richness between assemblages by standardizing them to the same sample size(s). Larger assemblages are typically rarefied down to a sample size equivalent to that of the smallest assemblage under consideration, or rarefaction curves are plotted to illustrate how richness varies as a function of sample size. An example of the latter is shown in Figure 4.1, which provides rarefaction curves for two hypothetical faunas, designated assemblage A and assemblage B (Figure 4.1A). Assemblage A has 258 specimens distributed across 10 species, and assemblage B has 516 specimens distributed across 20 species. The rarefaction curves, generated here using the Paleontological Statistics Package (Hammer, Harper, and Ryan 2001), show that for any given number of specimens, assemblage B includes more species than assemblage A, and at a sample size of 258 specimens (the observed sample size of assemblage A) it predicts 19.6 species in B compared to the 10 observed in A (Figure 4.1B). It is clear that assemblage B is richer than A.

Although specimen-based rarefaction is widely implemented, there is an important limitation to the technique. As discussed by Alroy (2010a) and Chao and Jost (2012), the ratio in rarefied richness calculated for two assemblages will vary depending on rarefied sample size, which means it provides no insight into the degree of difference between the two assem-

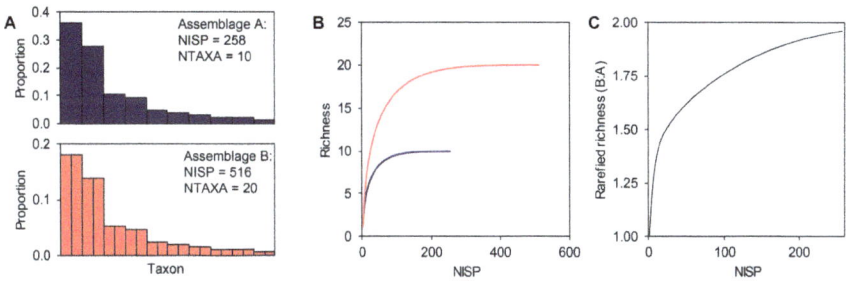

Figure 4.1. (A) The species abundance distributions for hypothetical assemblages A and B. Taxa ranked from most to least abundant. (B) Specimen-based rarefaction curves for assemblages A and B (95 percent confidence limits omitted for sake of clarity). (C) The ratio of rarefied richness for assemblage B relative to A (B:A) as a function of assemblage sample size (NISP = number of identified specimens). © The authors.

blages under comparison. This is illustrated in Figure 4.1C, which plots the ratio of rarefied richness of assemblage B relative to assemblage A (B:A) as a function of rarefied sample size. If we rarefy these assemblages down to a sample size of 25 specimens, for example, then the ratio of B to A is 1.5, but if we rarefy to a sample size of 100 specimens then the ratio increases to 1.8. The increase in B:A as a function of sample size means that specimen-based rarefaction allows us to say that assemblage B is richer than A, but not by how much.

Coverage-based rarefaction, also known as shareholder quorum subsampling in paleobiology (Alroy 2010b), provides a solution to this problem (Chao and Jost 2012). Rather than rarefying faunal assemblages down to an equivalent sample size, it involves rarefying assemblages down to a common coverage, which is a measure of sample completeness (Chao and Jost 2012; Chao et al. 2020; Close et al. 2018; Du and Alemseged 2018). Coverage ranges from 0 to 1 and represents the proportion of the total number of specimens in a statistical population (i.e., the community we are sampling from) that belong to the species represented in the sample. Subtracting coverage from 1 provides the coverage deficit, which represents the probability that the next sampled specimen will belong to a new species.

To illustrate the concept of coverage, consider a statistical population of 2,500 specimens distributed across ten species (Population A), and a zooarchaeological sample of that population (Sample A) that includes 25 specimens distributed across the seven most abundant species (Figure 4.2). Those seven species together account for 95 percent of the specimens in Population A, so the coverage for Sample A is 0.95. The coverage deficit for Sample A is 0.05, meaning there is a 5 percent chance that an increase

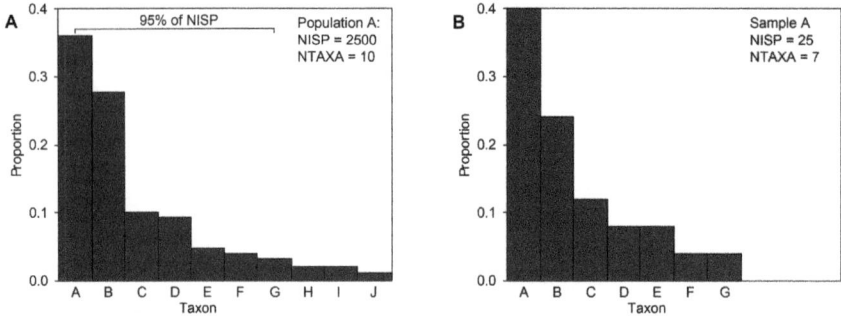

Figure 4.2. The concept of coverage. (A) Population A, which includes 2,500 specimens distributed across ten taxa. The species abundances for Population A are: A = 900, B = 690, C = 250, D = 230, E = 120, F = 100, G = 80, H = 50, I = 50, J = 50. (B) Sample A, which is drawn from Population A and includes 25 specimens distributed across seven taxa. The species abundances for Sample A are: A = 10, B = 6, C = 3, D = 2, E = 2, F = 1, G = 1. Those seven taxa account for 95 percent of the specimens in Population A, so the coverage for Sample A is 0.95. © The authors.

in sample size from 25 to 26 specimens will lead to the recovery of an additional species. Because the statistical population we are sampling from (e.g., Population A in Figure 4.2) is always unknown in zooarchaeological datasets, we cannot directly calculate coverage as we did here. Instead, coverage is estimated using a coverage estimator (Table 1 in Chao et al. 2020):

$$\widehat{C_n} = 1 - \frac{f_1}{n}\left[\frac{(n-1)f_1}{(n-1)f_1+2f_2}\right] \text{ if } f_2 > 0$$

$$\widehat{C_n} = 1 - \frac{f_1}{n}\left[\frac{(n-1)(f_1-1)}{(n-1)(f_1-1)+2}\right] \text{ if } f_2 = 0$$

where n is sample size, f_1 is the number of singletons (taxa represented by one specimen), and f_2 is the number of doubletons (taxa represented by two specimens). Estimated coverage for Sample A is 0.93, which is reasonably close to the true value of 0.95.

Figure 4.3 provides coverage-based rarefaction curves for the two assemblages examined earlier in Figure 4.1, using the analytical solutions provided by Chao and Jost (2012) in the R package *iNEXT* (Hsieh, Ma, and Chao 2016). These curves indicate the number of taxa recovered as coverage increases from 0.5 to 1. Importantly, the rarefied richness of assemblage B relative to assemblage A (B:A) is reasonably steady at ~2 (compare Figure 4.3C with Figure 4.1C). The ratio is a bit higher than 2 when coverage is less than 0.8, but this corresponds to very poorly sampled assemblages, so

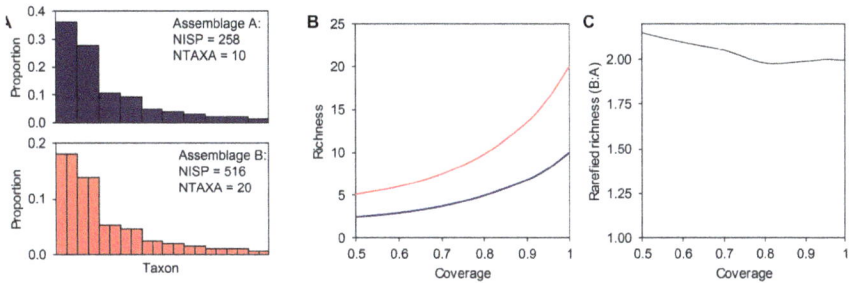

Figure 4.3. (A) The species abundance distributions for hypothetical assemblage A and assemblage B (identical to those in Figure 4.1). Taxa ranked from most to least abundant. (B) Coverage-based rarefaction curves for assemblages A and B (95 percent confidence limits omitted for sake of clarity). (C) The ratio of rarefied richness for assemblage B relative to A (B:A) as a function of coverage. © The authors.

some noise is not surprising (estimated NISP at coverage of 0.8 for assemblage A is only 11). This issue aside, Figure 4.3C indicates that the statistical population sampled by assemblage B is twice as rich as the one represented by assemblage A. Thus, coverage-based rarefaction not only tells us that assemblage B is richer than A (as in specimen-based rarefaction), but it also provides an indication of magnitude (unlike specimen-based rarefaction).

Coverage-Based Rarefaction with Zooarchaeological Data

Here we explore the quantitative behavior of coverage-based rarefaction using zooarchaeological data, with the goal of providing some straightforward recommendations for its implementation. We believe this is important considering that zooarchaeologists have not traditionally considered faunal data in terms of coverage, which opens the door to possible missteps when implementing coverage-based rarefaction. To illustrate the behavior of coverage-based rarefaction, we use Klein's (1983) abundance data (NISP and MNI) for the Late Pleistocene and Holocene ungulates from Boomplaas Cave in South Africa (Table 4.1). The Boomplaas ungulates sample much of the last ~65,000 years, and have a complex taphonomic history involving accumulation by humans, carnivores, and raptors (Faith 2013).

Zooarchaeological Counting Units

The variables involved in generating the coverage estimator—sample size (n), the number of singletons (f_1), and the number of doubletons (f_2)—pose a potential problem because zooarchaeological abundance data (e.g., NISP,

Table 4.1. Taxonomic abundances (NISP/MNI) across stratigraphic units for Boomplaas Cave (from Klein 1983).

Taxon	DGL	BLD	BLA	BRL	CL	GWA	LP	LPC	YOL	BP	OLP	BOL	OCH	LOH
Equus (small)	0	1/1	0	28/7	107/14	9/3	6/2	6/3	13/2	6/3	2/1	1/1	2/1	0
Equus capensis	0	0	0	0	9/5	1/1	0	0	0	0	0	0	0	0
Raphicerus spp.	8/5	8/3	6/2	69/14	7/4	0	1/1	0	1/1	6/3	8/3	15/4	39/8	3/2
Oreotragus oreotragus	2/1	9/3	3/1	71/12	0	0	1/1	2/1	6/2	5/3	9/3	3/1	62/10	1/1
Pelea capreolus	0	0	2/1	23/10	7/3	3/2	1/1	3/2	11/2	7/3	13/3	13/5	36/9	10/3
Redunca spp.	0	0	5/2	0	6/3	5/3	0	0	0	0	8/2	7/3	0	2/1
Antidorcas	0	0	0	0	2/1	1/1	1/1	1/1	0	0	1/1	1/1	2/2	1/1
Hippotragus spp.	1/1	0	1/1	9/4	12/5	2/1	3/2	0	1/1	0	0	0	2/2	0
Connochaetes/Alcelaphus	0	6/1	0	80/15	218/23	26/3	23/3	38/10	14/2	68/11	14/4	9/4	14/7	1/1
Damaliscus pygargus	0	0	0	5/3	1/1	1/1	1/1	1/1	0	6/2	2/1	2/1	4/3	1/1
Megalotragus priscus	0	0	0	0	0	0	0	1/1	0	0	0	0	0	0
Tragelaphus strepsiceros	0	0	0	2/1	1/1	0	0	0	0	0	0	0	0	0
Taurotragus oryx	0	0	0	15/6	36/10	4/1	0	2/1	0	2/2	0	0	6/4	0
Syncerus caffer	0	0	0	2/2	8/5	2/1	1/1	0	0	0	1/1	1/1	0	0
Syncerus antiquus	0	0	0	0	2/1	0	3/2	0	0	0	0	0	0	0

MNI) are not equivalent to counts of individuals. All three variables vary depending on which counting unit is used (Table 4.2), such that estimated coverage for the MNI counts is less than or equal to estimated coverage for the NISP counts (Figure 4.4A). This is because assemblage sample size tallied by MNI is always less than or equal to that provided by NISP (Figure 4.4B), and the number of singletons according to the MNI counts is always greater than or equal to that provided by NISP (Figure 4.4C). For example, a single specimen of a species (NISP = 1) must be associated with an MNI of 1, whereas two specimens of a species (NISP = 2) could be associated with an MNI of 1 or 2, three specimens of a species (NISP = 3) could be associated with an MNI of 1, 2, or 3, and so on. Doubletons are unimportant in the case of Boomplaas Cave—there are eighteen doubletons according to both the NISP and MNI data (Table 4.2).

The greater ratio of singletons to assemblage sample size when taxonomic abundances are quantified by MNI drives the coverage estimate down (see equation above). This is shown in Figure 4.5A, which illustrates how the coverage estimate changes as a function of the number of singletons for a case where sample size is constant at 100, the number of singletons ranges from 1 to 20, and the number of doubletons is held constant at 0. Figure 4.5B shows how the coverage estimate changes as a function of sample size for a hypothetical case where sample size ranges from 10 to 100, the number of singletons is held constant at 2, and the number of doubletons is held constant at 0. Because abundances quantified using MNI provide more singletons and smaller sample sizes, the outcome is a lower estimate of coverage compared to NISP tallies (Table 4.2).

Although our estimate of coverage clearly depends on which zooarchaeological counting unit is used, the good news is that the outcome of coverage-based rarefaction is consistent for both counting units. According to both counting units, the assemblage from member LOH is the most

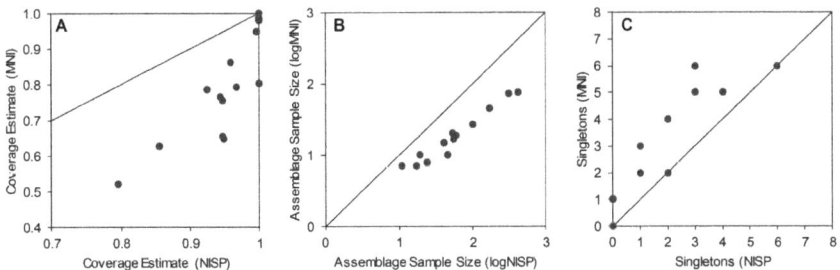

Figure 4.4. (A) Estimated coverage for the Boomplaas Cave faunas according to NISP versus MNI counts. (B) Assemblage sample size for NISP counts versus MNI counts. (C) The number of singletons according to NISP counts versus MNI counts. Solid lines in A–C indicate unity. Data from Table 4.2. © The authors.

Table 4.2. Summary of the Boomplaas Cave data for NISP and MNI tallies: variables involved in generating the coverage estimator (n = sample size; f_1 = singletons; f_2 = doubletons) and estimates of richness (S) at different levels of coverage (C).

				NISP						MNI	
Stratum	n	f_1	f_2	C	S (C= 0.79)	S (C= 0.5)	n	f_1	f_2	C	S (C= 0.52)
DGL	11	1	1	0.924	1.76	1.00	7	2	0	0.786	1.86
BLD	24	1	0	1.000	2.83	1.71	8	2	0	0.806	2.39
BLA	17	1	1	0.948	3.85	2.41	7	3	2	0.649	4.57
BRL	304	0	2	1.000	4.72	2.47	74	1	1	0.987	3.87
CL	416	2	2	0.995	3.01	1.65	76	4	0	0.948	3.78
GWA	54	3	2	0.946	5.74	2.31	17	6	1	0.654	6.72
LP	41	6	0	0.855	5.87	1.67	15	6	3	0.627	8.22
LPC	54	3	2	0.946	3.02	1.00	20	5	1	0.755	2.33
YOL	46	2	0	0.958	3.46	2.36	10	2	4	0.862	4.67
BP	100	0	1	1.000	3.16	1.00	27	0	2	1.000	3.03
OLP	58	2	2	0.967	5.32	3.15	19	4	1	0.795	5.28
BOL	52	3	1	0.943	5.02	3.04	21	5	0	0.768	4.48
OCH	167	0	3	1.000	3.74	2.34	46	1	2	0.980	3.82
LOH	19	4	1	0.795	6.79	1.71	10	5	1	0.521	6.50

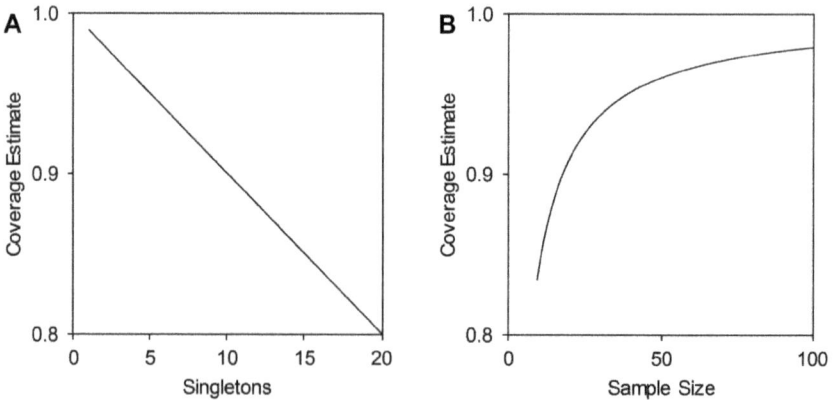

Figure 4.5. (A) The relationship between the number of singletons and estimated coverage for a hypothetical case where sample size is held constant at 100 and the number of singletons ranges from 1 to 20 (no doubletons). (B) The relationship between sample size and estimated coverage for a hypothetical case where sample size ranges from 10 to 100 and the number of singletons is held constant at 2 (no doubletons). © The authors.

poorly sampled at Boomplaas Cave, with a coverage of 0.79 according to the NISP counts and a coverage of 0.52 according to the MNI counts (Table 4.2). If we rarefy the Boomplaas Cave assemblages down to 0.79 for the NISP data and 0.52 for the MNI data, we observe similar trends in richness through the sequence and a strong correlation between the rarefied richness values provided by the two counting units (Figure 4.6) (r = 0.897, p < 0.001). The implication is that rarefied richness across the sequence is effectively identical, regardless of which counting unit is used. Note that the approximately 1:1 relationship shown in Figure 4.6 will not be observed if NISP counts and MNI counts are rarefied to the same level of coverage, because estimated richness for the MNI data will be higher than that for the NISP data.

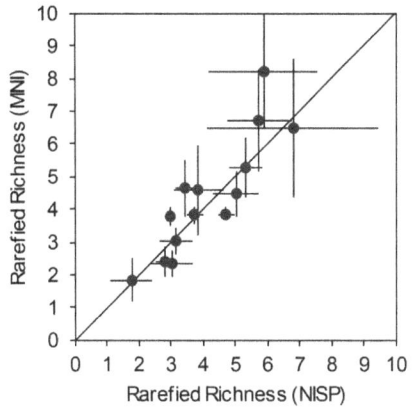

Figure 4.6. The relationship between rarefied richness for the NISP counts (rarefied to coverage = 0.79) versus the MNI counts (rarefied to coverage = 0.52) across assemblages at Boomplaas Cave. Errors indicate 95 percent confidence limits. Solid line indicates unity. © The authors.

Limitations of Small Samples

Because zooarchaeologists do not typically gauge sample adequacy in terms of coverage, it is worth exploring the implications of very incomplete samples. For example, though most analysts would be reluctant to use specimen-based rarefaction to rarefy assemblages down to a sample size of, say, 5 or fewer specimens, the appropriate cutoff for coverage may seem less intuitive. The R package *iNEXT* (Hsieh et al. 2016) will return the number of specimens (or individuals) associated with a given level of coverage, providing a simple solution to this problem. For illustrative purposes, Figure 4.7 plots the relationship between assemblage sample size and estimated coverage for the Boomplaas Cave Pleistocene aggregate (assemblages CL to LOH combined), including both NISP and MNI data. Although this relationship will differ for other assemblages depending on their richness and abundance distribution (and the counting units used), the Boomplaas Cave example is nonetheless informative. Rarefying the Boomplaas NISP data down to a coverage of 0.5, for example, is clearly ill-advised—it corresponds to a sample size of ~3.1 specimens. And just as one should not expect speci-men-based rarefaction to provide ecologically or behaviorally useful estimates of richness at a sample size of 3 specimens, one should not expect coverage-based rar-efaction to provide useful results at a coverage of 0.5. The situation is marginally better with respect to the MNI data, for which a cov-erage of 0.5 is expected at an as-semblage MNI of 6, though even this may be pushing the limits for some analysts.

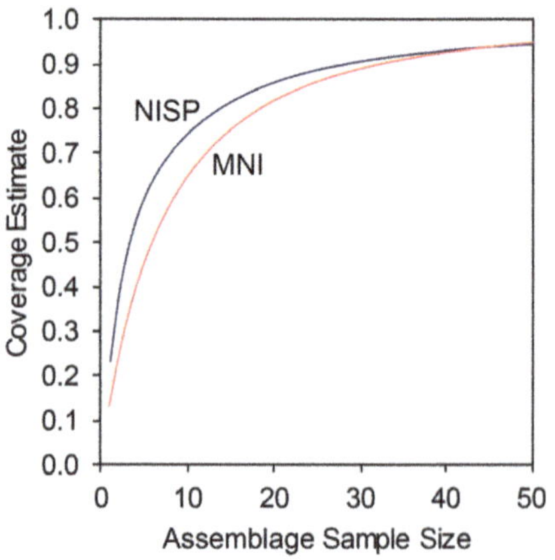

Figure 4.7. The relationship between assem-blage sample size and estimated coverage for the Boomplaas Cave Pleistocene aggregate (NISP counts and MNI counts). © The authors.

Not surprisingly, the analytical outcome of coverage-based rar-efaction can change in important ways if we rarefy down to very low coverage. For example, if we rarefy the NISP data down to a coverage of 0.5, which corresponds to a very poorly sampled assemblage (Figure 4.7), the estimates of richness are only weakly correlated with those obtained at a coverage of 0.79 ($r = 0.489$, $p = 0.076$) (Figure 4.8). This is not because the estimates of richness are noisy at a coverage of 0.5—the bootstrapped confidence limits are in fact low because a coverage of 0.5 always corre-

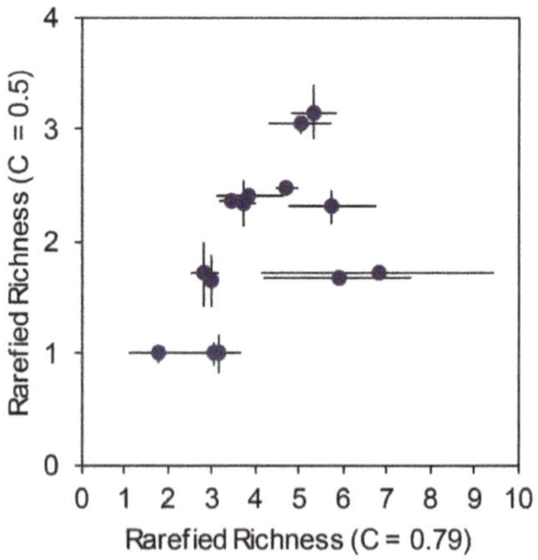

Figure 4.8. The relationship between rarefied richness at a coverage of 0.79 versus 0.5 across assemblages at Boomplaas Cave (NISP data). Errors indicate 95 percent confidence limits. © The authors.

sponds to very few species (Figure 4.8). The weak correlation occurs because when we rarefy to such a low level of coverage, we are look-ing at a very small portion of the assemblage, specifically the hand-ful of dominant taxa. At a cover-age of 0.5, assemblages dominated by a single taxon (e.g., stratum DGL and LPC) return an esti-mated richness of only 1, whereas those with several dominant taxa (e.g., stratum OLP and BOL) re-turn an estimated richness closer to 3 (see tables 4.1 and 4.2). Thus, the information provided about richness is very coarse, describ-ing the number of dominant taxa.

Most would agree that this is unlikely to provide useful zooarchaeological insights compared to a rarefaction analysis conducted at a higher level of coverage that encompasses a greater number of species.

An additional limitation of small samples concerns the coverage estimator, which is not always efficient when assemblage sample size is low (i.e., it requires a large sample size to provide a precise estimate). To illustrate this, we present a subsampling exercise in which we treat the Boomplaas Cave Pleistocene aggregate as the statistical population (NISP data). We randomly subsampled the population (without replacement) at sample sizes ranging from 5 to 250 specimens, with 500 iterations for each sample size. For each iteration, we calculate the difference between the 'true' level of coverage and the estimated level of coverage (using the coverage estimator). Note that, in this case, we are able to calculate the 'true' level of coverage represented by any subsample because the statistical population (i.e., the Boomplaas Cave Pleistocene aggregate) is known. Figure 4.9 illustrates the mean and 95 percent confidence intervals of subsampled values (true coverage – estimated coverage) as a function of sample size. Although the coverage estimator is unbiased, even at low sample sizes, it is very inefficient (i.e., the 95 percent confidence interval is broad), meaning that we cannot reliably estimate the level of coverage in a poorly sampled assemblage.

What are the implications of having a coverage estimator that is inefficient at low sample sizes? One problem is that we may choose the wrong

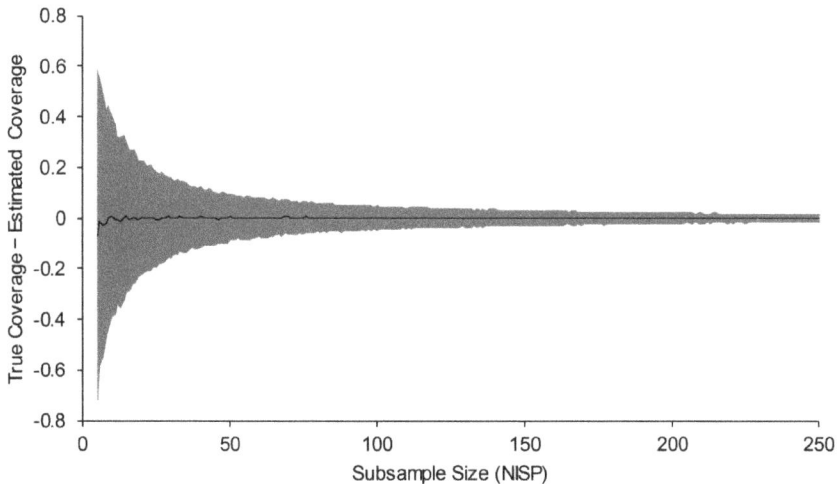

Figure 4.9. The difference between true coverage and estimated coverage (using the coverage estimator) as a function of subsample size for the Boomplaas Cave Pleistocene aggregate. Black line indicates the mean difference over 500 iterations. Grey shading indicates 95 percent confidence intervals. © The authors.

rarefaction target (i.e., the level of coverage that assemblages are rarefied down to). To illustrate potential consequences of this, we turn again to Boomplaas Cave, where the coverage estimate indicates that stratum LOH is the most incomplete (Table 4.2), so one would typically rarefy all other assemblages down to the level of coverage observed in LOH (as in Figure 4.6). However, given its small sample size (NISP = 19), it is not unreasonable to suppose—purely for illustrative purposes—that the true level of coverage of LOH is considerably higher than our estimate of 0.79 (it could also be much lower). If so, then rarefying all other assemblages down to 0.79 will depress their richness relative to LOH, the implication being that LOH would appear to be anomalously rich compared to other assemblages.

If the point of the rarefaction analysis is an examination of trends in richness across a long sequence of assemblages such as Boomplaas Cave, then a single anomalous value may not be hugely problematic. There is more potential for trouble, however, if one were instead comparing richness across only a handful of assemblages (e.g., Lyman 2014), where picking the wrong rarefaction target could lead to incorrect interpretations. The worst case would be a comparison of rarefied richness between two assemblages, in which one has been needlessly rarefied because the other is associated with an erroneously low estimate of coverage. The sensible solution is to exercise caution when small samples are involved. In addition, plotting coverage-based rarefaction curves (as in Figure 4.3B) along with their 95 percent confidence intervals can of course provide an indication of whether differences in richness between assemblages are statistically meaningful, even at low levels of coverage.

Discussion and Recommendations

Coverage-based rarefaction represents an improvement over traditional specimen-based rarefaction because it can allow zooarchaeologists to evaluate the magnitude of the difference in richness between two assemblages, something that is not possible from conventional specimen-based rarefaction (Chao and Jost 2012; Chao et al. 2020) or any other approach for circumventing the effects of sampling effort on richness (Faith and Lyman 2019). In addition, Chao and Jost (2012) show that coverage-based rarefaction is more effective than specimen-based rarefaction at correctly ranking the richness of various samples when their sizes are small. So, if one is trying to detect meaningful signals from poorly sampled faunas, then coverage-based rarefaction is the better option. These analytical advantages have led to rapid uptake of coverage-based rarefaction in paleo-biology (Alroy 2010b; Close et al. 2018; Du and Alemseged 2018; Faith, Du, and Rowan 2019). It has seen little use in the archaeological literature, though it is appropriate for any case where the focus is understanding the diversity of specimens across classes, be they species, raw materials, or ceramic types (i.e., categorical data). The only examples we are aware of have used coverage-based rarefaction to understand spatial patterns in projectile point diversity (Buchanan et al. 2017; Eren et al. 2016), and we are aware of none in the zooarchaeological literature. We suspect this simply reflects a lack of awareness of what is a relatively new analytical technique, and we hope this chapter will at the very least prompt our readers to consider it as an option.

Why might it be important to quantify the degree of difference in richness between assemblages? The obvious answer is that it can provide meaningful behavioral or ecological information that is otherwise inaccessible, allowing zooarchaeologists to ask questions about magnitude of difference and how it may vary through time or space. For example, previous analysis of the Boomplaas Cave faunas noted the decline in richness from the last glacial maximum through the Holocene (from stratum LP to BLD) (Faith 2013; see Table 4.2), but the magnitude of that decline was unclear. Coverage-based rarefaction of the NISP counts indicates that we should recover 3.0 species (95 percent CI: 2.6–3.4) from the BLD assemblage when it is rarefied to a level of coverage equivalent to LP (C = 0.855; Table 4.2). Given the observed number of taxa in the LP assemblage (NTAXA = 10; Table 4.1), the implication is that richness has declined by ~70 percent, in large part due to extinctions and extirpations (Faith 2013; Klein 1983). The ability to quantify the magnitude of this decline, and potentially compare it to other contemporary zooarchaeological records from southern Africa, sets the stage for comparative analyses that could provide deeper insight into the paleoenvironmental and perhaps anthropogenic factors underpinning diversity change in the region.

In addition to opening the door to new research questions by providing greater information content, knowing something about the magnitude of difference in richness between assemblages can also help us gauge the practical significance of our results. In their critique of statistics in zooarchaeology, Wolverton, Dombrosky, and Lyman (2014) argue that zooarchaeologists have paid undo attention to p-values while largely ignoring the arguably more important issue of effect size (see also Wasserstein and Lazar 2016). Although we routinely use p-values to determine whether a null hypothesis should be rejected, only measures of effect size can indicate whether the pattern we have detected is significant in any practical sense (i.e., one that is meaningful in the real world). Following this argument, we note that the ability to measure the magnitude of difference in richness between assemblages can provide faunal analysts with an indication of whether observed differences are relatively minor or substantial (e.g., a change in richness involving only a small handful of taxa versus a large number of taxa).

For zooarchaeologists interested in applying coverage-based rarefaction, our analyses highlight a few issues worth considering. The first is to ensure that only a single counting unit (NISP or MNI) is used, because the estimate of coverage for a given assemblage will vary depending on the unit (Table 4.2). The second is to be cognizant of the sample sizes associated with a given coverage level, and to avoid rarefying assemblages down to extremely low coverage. Such results will largely be an indication of the number of dominant taxa in an assemblage. We cannot make concrete recommendations about what level of coverage is too low because the answer will vary from assemblage to assemblage, depending on richness and the shape of the abundance distribution. Thus, some may find it useful to plot the relationship between assemblage sample size and coverage (as in Figure 4.7) to evaluate what a sensible cutoff might look like, with assemblages falling below a certain cutoff excluded from analysis. Plotting the coverage-based rarefaction curves and the diversity ratios between assemblages (e.g., Figure 4.3B and 4.3C) can also provide an indication of sample adequacy. And third, analysts should be aware of the fact that the coverage estimator can be extremely variable at small sample sizes (Figure 4.9). As discussed above, the potential implications of this can range from relatively minor to substantial, so caution is warranted when dealing with very incomplete samples. Provided that sufficient caution is exercised, however, we believe that coverage-based rarefaction should be a useful addition to the zooarchaeological toolkit.

Acknowledgments

We are grateful to Metin Eren and Briggs Buchanan for the invitation to contribute this chapter. Lee Lyman and two anonymous reviewers provided helpful feedback on a previous draft.

J. Tyler Faith is a Curator at the Natural History Museum of Utah, and an Associate Professor at the University of Utah, Salt Lake City, USA.

Andrew Du is an Assistant Professor at Colorado State University, Fort Collins, USA.

References

Alroy, J. 2010a. "Fair Sampling of Taxonomic Richness and Unbiased Estimation of Origination and Extinction Rates." In *Quantitative Methods in Paleobiology*, ed. J. Alroy and G. Hunt, 55–80. Paleontology Society Papers 16.

———. 2010b. "Geographical, Environmental and Intrinsic Biotic Controls on Phanerozoic Marine Diversification." *Palaeontology* 53: 1211–35.

Buchanan, B., A. Chao, C.-H. Chiu, R. K. Colwell, M. J. O'Brien, A. Werner, and M. I. Eren. 2017. "Environment-Induced Changes in Selective Constraints on Social Learning during the Peopling of the Americas." *Scientific Reports* 7: 44431.

Chao, A., and L. Jost. 2012. "Coverage-Based Rarefaction and Extrapolation: Standardizing Samples by Completeness Rather Than Size." *Ecology* 93: 2533–47.

Chao, A., Y. Kubota, D. Zelený, C.-H. Chiu, C.-F. Li, B. Kusumoto, M. Yasuhara, S. Thorn, C.-L. Wei, M. J. Costello, and R. K. Colwell. 2020. "Quantifying Sample Completeness and Comparing Diversities among Assemblages." *Ecological Research* 35: 292–314.

Close, R. A., S. W. Evers, J. Alroy, and R. J. Butler. 2018. "How Should We Estimate Diversity in the Fossil Record? Testing Richness Estimators Using Sampling-Standardized Discovery Curves." *Methods in Ecology and Evolution* 9: 1386–400.

Colwell, R. K., A. Chao, N. J. Gotelli, S.-Y. Lin, C. X. Mao, R. L. Chazdon, and J. T. Longino. 2012. "Models and Estimators Linking Individual-Based and Sample-Based Rarefaction, Extrapolation and Comparison of Assemblages." *Journal of Plant Ecology* 5: 3–21.

Du, A., and Z. Alemseged. 2018. "Diversity Analysis of Plio-Pleistocene Large Mammal Communities in the Omo-Turkana Basin, Eastern Africa." *Journal of Human Evolution* 124: 25–39.

Eren, M. I., A. Chao, C.-H. Chiu, R. K. Colwell, B. Buchanan, M. T. Boulanger, J. Darwent, and M. J. O'Brien. 2016. "Statistical Analysis of Paradigmatic Class Richness Supports Greater Paleoindian Projectile-Point Diversity in the Southeast." *American Antiquity* 81: 174–92.

Faith, J. T. 2013. "Taphonomic and Paleoecological Change in the Large Mammal Sequence from Boomplaas Cave, Western Cape, South Africa." *Journal of Human Evolution* 65: 715–30.

Faith, J. T., A. Du, and J. Rowan. 2019. "Addressing the Effects of Sampling on Ecometric-Based Paleoenvironmental Reconstructions." *Palaeogeography, Palaeoclimatology, Palaeoecology* 528: 175–85.

Faith, J. T., and R. L. Lyman. 2019. *Paleozoology and Paleoenvironments: Fundamentals, Assumptions, Techniques.* Cambridge: Cambridge University Press.

Gotelli, N. J., and R. K. Colwell. 2001. "Quantifying Biodiversity: Procedures and Pitfalls in the Measurements and Comparison of Species Richness." *Ecology Letters* 4: 379–91.

Grayson, D. K. 1984. *Quantitative Zooarchaeology.* Orlando: Academic Press.

———. 1991. "Alpine Faunas from the White Mountains, California: Adaptive Change in the Prehistoric Great Basin?" *Journal of Archaeological Science* 18: 483–506.

———. 1998. "Moisture History and Small Mammal Community Richness during the Latest Pleistocene and Holocene, Northern Bonneville Basin, Utah." *Quaternary Research* 49: 330–34.

Grayson, D. K., and F. Delpech. 1998. "Changing Diet Breadth in the Early Upper Paleolithic of Southwestern France." *Journal of Archaeological Science* 25: 1119–29.

Hammer, Ø., D. A. T. Harper, and P. D. Ryan. 2001. "Paleontological Statistics Software Package for Education and Data Analysis." *Palaeontologia Electronica* 4: 9.

Hill, M. O. 1973. "Diversity and Evenness: A Unifying Notation and its Consequences." *Ecology* 54: 427–32.

Hsieh, T. C., K. H. Ma, and A. Chao. 2016. "iNEXT: An R Package for Rarefaction and Extrapolation of Species Diversity (Hill numbers)." *Methods in Ecology and Evolution* 7: 1451–56.

Hurlbert, S. H. 1971. "The Nonconcept of Species Diversity: A Critique and Alternative Parameters." *Ecology* 52: 577–86.

Klein, R. G. 1983. "Palaeoenvironmental Implications of Quaternary Large Mammals in the Fynbos Region." In *Fynbos Palaeoecology: A Preliminary Synthesis*, ed. H. J. Deacon, Q. B. Hendey, and J. J. N. Lambrechts, 116–38. Mills Litho, Cape Town: South African National Scientific Programmes Report No. 75.

Lyman, R. L. 2008. *Quantitative Paleozoology*. Cambridge: Cambridge University Press.

———. 2014. "Terminal Pleistocene Change in Mammal Communities in Southeastern Washington State, USA." *Quaternary Research* 81: 295–304.

Magurran, A. E. 1988. *Ecological Diversity and Its Measurement*. Princeton, NJ: Princeton University Press.

———. 2004. *Measuring Biological Diversity*. Malden, MA: Blackwell Publishing.

Nagaoka, L. 2002. "The Effects of Resource Depression on Foraging Efficiency, Diet Breadth, and Patch Use in Southern New Zealand." *Journal of Anthropological Archaeology* 21: 419–42.

Pielou, E. C. 1966. "The Measurement of Diversity in Different Types of Biological Collections." *Journal of Theoretical Biology* 13: 131–44.

Sanders, H. L. 1968. "Marine Benthic Diversity: A Comparative Study." *American Naturalist* 102: 243–82.

Tipper, J. C. 1979. "Rarefaction and Rarefiction: The Use and Abuse of a Method in Paleoecology." *Paleobiology* 5: 423–34.

Wasserstein, R. L., and N. A. Lazar. 2016. "The ASA's Statement On p-Values: Context, Process, and Purpose." *The American Statistician* 70: 129–33.

Wolverton, S., J. Dombrosky, and R. L. Lyman. 2014. "Practical Significance: Ordinal Scale Data and Effect Size in Zooarchaeology." *International Journal of Osteoarchaeology* 26: 255–65.

Chapter 5

Diversity and Lithic Microwear

Quantification, Classification, and Standardization

W. James Stemp and Danielle A. Macdonald

———— ✦ ————

Although commonly employed for assessing diversity in ecological/biological populations (e.g., Hill 1973; May 1975; McCann 2000; Odum 1953; Peet 1974), measures of diversity have been variably applied to different types of material culture recovered archaeologically. The most noteworthy introduction of the potential value of diversity to archaeological questions was the edited volume *Quantifying Diversity in Archaeology* (Leonard and Jones 1989). In this volume, Leonard and Jones define diversity as "a measure of variation. Specifically, diversity refers to the nature or degree of apportionment of a quantity to a set of well-defined categories. This diversity is a referent for the structural properties of a population or sample made up of distinct categories" (ibid.: 2). Based on this understanding of diversity, a number of studies have looked at various aspects of measured variation in lithic assemblages (e.g., Buchanan et al. 2017; Eren 2012; Eren et al. 2012, 2016; Grayson and Cole 1998; Hiscock 2001; Jones, Beck, and Grayson 1989; Leonard, Smiley, and Cameron 1989; Lyman and O'Brien 2000; McCartney and Glass 1990; Simek 1989; Simek and Price 1990); however, to our knowledge, none have focused specifically on diversity of use traces on stone tools as observed with microwear (use-wear) methods. Moreover, to date, no one has incorporated methods to quantify microwear in diversity measures. In this chapter, we provide examples of diversity measures of microwear on obsidian assemblages from different sites, present issues of concern related to diversity and lithic microwear analysis, and explore the possibilities of the quantification of microwear in relation to diversity. Key to the use of diversity for lithic microwear analysis is the ability to establish "a set of well-defined categories." The existence of well-defined categories is connected to critical concerns about diversity and lithic microwear analysis in terms of the identification and classification of wear, the subjective nature of microwear analysis, and the need for improved standardization of methods to document microwear on stone tools.

Typology, Classification, Sample Size, and Microwear

Diversity can be determined in many ways using a variety of non-parametric measures (e.g., Gini 1912; Junge 1994; MacArthur 1965; Pielou 1977; Shannon and Weaver [1949] 1962; Simpson 1949; Solow and Polasky 1994; Weitzman 1992), as well as methods based on regression (Jones, Grayson, and Beck 1983), simulation (Kintigh 1984), and jackknifing (Kaufman 1998), or variations thereof. Whichever measure is utilized, there will be different properties emphasized (e.g., variety, evenness, disparity) and different advantages and disadvantages. Variables affecting the use of measures of diversity may include sample size and how the groups or classes are structured/determined in the first place. For archaeologists, obviously the sample sizes they have for analysis will be dependent on what they find and, for lithics, how the tools are typed, whether it be "technologically"—e.g., a biface—or "functionally—e.g., a projectile point (see Eren et al. 2012: 2; Eren et al. 2016: 177). The same is true for traditional visual lithic microwear, in that it is 'typed' and the identification of types will be, on some level, subjective (Whittaker, Caulkins, and Kamp 1998), as will the total number of 'types' that are considered to exist (O'Brien et al. 2014). The experience of the analyst will also play a crucial role in visual microwear identification and classification (Evans 2014).

The Application of Diversity to Microwear: The San Pedro Obsidian Example

Assuming microwear on stone tools is reliably observed and can be classified into different groups then diversity can be used to make inferences about assemblages. As an example, the example of microwear on obsidian artifacts recovered from the Late Postclassic/Early Spanish Colonial period (AD 1400–1700) Maya coastal site of San Pedro on Ambergris Caye, Belize, can be compared in terms of diversity, richness, evenness, and rarefaction. In this case, one analyst used the same method to divide the microwear, based on independent use zones (IUZs), into categories at four different loca-

Table 5.1. Microwear (IUZs) on obsidian artifacts from Late Postclassic/Early Colonial (AD 1400–1700) San Pedro, Ambergris Caye, Belize.

IUZs	Alamilla's	Elvi's	Nuñez's	Sands/Parham's
Antler/bone	0	2	8	22
Ceramic	0	1	4	18
Dry hide	0	2	6	0
Fish scales	0	0	0	6
Meat/fish/fresh hide	3	8	11	54
Meat/fish & bone	2	5	3	23
Plant	0	0	1	12
Plant (fiber)	0	2	0	8
Shell	0	5	2	21
Stone	0	1	0	2
Wood	2	4	19	63
Soft	3	4	3	35
Hard	0	6	7	16
Indeterminate	2	6	3	81

tions throughout the site where excavations were undertaken—Alamilla's property, Elvi's property, Nuñez's property, and the Sands Hotel/Parham's property (Stemp 2016a) (Table 5.1). The obsidian artifacts from each property were recovered from stratigraphic soil levels, identified by lot numbers, that contained Late Postclassic Maya ceramics and/or Early Spanish Colonial material culture. To demonstrate the calculation of alpha diversity[1] for microwear on the San Pedro obsidian, there are a number of options (Table 5.2). A simple calculation of richness (S) would rank the properties in terms of greatest richness as follows: Sands Hotel/Parham's, Elvi's, Nuñez's, and Alamilla's. Richness could also be presented using rarefaction curves (Figure 5.1). If we relied upon Simpson's index (D) of dominance, in which a higher value denotes less diversity, and the Shannon function (H′) of common richness, in which a higher value indicates greater diversity, then, based on microwear, the stone tool sub-assemblage from Elvi's property is the most diverse, followed by the sub-assemblages from the Sands Hotel/Parham's property, Nuñez's property, and Alamilla's property. Shannon's equitability (E_H), in which a value of 1 indicates complete evenness, also reveals that the sub-assemblage on Alamilla's property has the most equitable distribution of microwear types, followed by Elvi's, Nuñez's, and the Sands Hotel/Parham's.

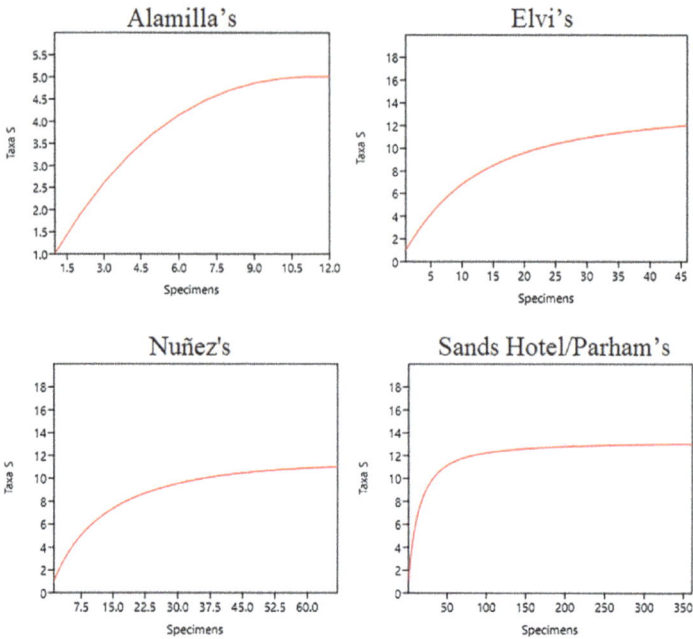

Figure 5.1. Richness (S) graphs for microwear (IUZs) on obsidian artifacts from Alamilla's, Elvi's, Nuñez's, and Sands Hotel/Parham's properties. © The authors.

These data could then potentially be used for interpretive purposes about sub-assemblage composition, tool function, and the organization of generalized versus specialized activities (Meltzer, Leonard, and Stratton 1992: 376). A specialist workshop focused on intensive production of specific objects would be expected to have lithic microwear that demonstrated low richness and low diversity. For example, comparing lithic sub-assemblages based on number of tools with specific microwear patterns at San Pedro may allow for the identification of a wide range of generalized subsistence and domestic activities versus a narrow specialization related to craft-

Table 5.2. Diversity measures for microwear (IUZs) on obsidian artifacts from Late Postclassic/Early Colonial (AD 1400–1700) San Pedro, Ambergris Caye, Belize.

	N (IUZs)	Richness (S)	ln S	Simpson Index (D)	Simpson Reciprocal Index (1/D)	Shannon Index (H')	Shannon Equitability Index (E$_H$)
Alamilla's	12	5	0.4167	0.1364	7.3333	1.5890	0.9873
Elvi's	46	12	2.4849	0.0899	11.1290	2.3182	0.9329
Nuñez's	67	11	2.3979	0.1384	7.2255	2.1129	0.8812
Sands Hotel/ Parham's	361	13	2.5649	0.1277	7.8327	2.2439	0.8748

production. The microwear in the former would be expected to have high diversity and high richness, or a low Simpson's index and a high Shannon function, whereas the latter would have a high Simpson's index and a low Shannon function. At San Pedro, the Alamilla's property sub-assemblage has lower richness and lower diversity, suggesting a narrow range of specialized activities. Elvi's sub-assemblage has higher richness and higher diversity, which could be used to argue for a wider range of more generalized activities. However, these interpretations may be affected or biased by a number of factors. Thus, issues related to the determination of diversity based on microwear need to be addressed in greater detail.

Diversity and Microwear Analysis: Issues of Concern

Standardization of Methodology

A significant issue associated with microwear analysis is the use of different microscopic methods (e.g., dark- vs. light-field illumination, cleaning protocols) and equipment (low-power, high-power, SEM), which means the process of data acquisition, identification, and classification may be highly variable. This raises the question of whether you can compare microwear between two assemblages or sub-assemblages if the method of data acquisition, identification, and classification is not standardized. Despite this concern about methods, many microwear analysts do compare microwear on tools that have been analyzed by different analysts using different methods. For example, Aoyama (1995) and Stemp (2016a) use two different systems to classify microwear on stone tools from ancient Maya sites into contact material categories, but Stemp and Awe (2014) and Stemp et al. (2018) have compared the results of their microwear analysis and those of Aoyama (2001, 2009) to comment on behaviors of ancient Maya populations. Whether this is appropriate or not is a question that requires further discussion.

The Exclusivity of Microwear Types

With standard typological classification, the method of classification is supposed to be the same and individual types/categories are typically expected to be mutually exclusive based on some combination of characteristics that will not be found in another type/category. This may not always be the case for microwear analysis if wear characteristics, such as those of different polishes, cannot be associated with specific contact materials, or if analysts rely on different combinations of microwear criteria to establish wear categories. There has been much debate about the exclusivity of polishes (and polish characteristics) to certain contact materials, and this issue is not necessarily resolved. This disagreement is also partly fueled by the lack of universal agreement among microwear analysts about the mechanisms responsible for wear formation (Brink 1978; Christenson 1998; Christenson et al. 1993; Christenson, Walter, and Menu 1992; Del Bene 1979; Diamond 1979; Fullagar 1991; Kamminga 1979; Lawn and Marshall 1979; Mansur 1982, 1997; Masson, Coqueugniot, and Roy 1981; Meeks et al. 1982; Ollé and Vergès 2008, 2014; Pedergnana and Ollé 2017; Schmidt et al. 2020; Šmit et al. 1998, 1999; Unger-Hamilton 1984; Yamada 1993). Essentially, this is the discussion about wear on stone tools being abrasive, additive, or some combination of abrasive and additive processes. Even within this simplified explanation, other factors are known to affect wear formation, wear characteristics, and rate of wear formation, including the structure and composition of the raw materials of the stone tools themselves (Bradley and Clayton 1987; Hurcombe 1997; Lerner 2007, 2014; Lerner et al. 2007; Lerner, Dytchkowskyj, and Nielsen 2010; Ollé et al. 2016; Pedergnana and Ollé 2017; Schmidt et al. 2020) and the contact materials, as noted above. The solution to exclusivity of wear (polishes) may be the use of paradigmatic classes of characters in quantification of wear (see below).

The Introduction of New Microwear Types

As noted by ecologists and biologists studying diversity, the discovery or introduction of new species within a region/ecological zone will affect diversity, and this has generally resulted in the absence of an upper bound set for richness. To some degree, this is true for microwear analysts in that microwear analysts can only identify microwear that they are already familiar with (i.e., known species); but new or previously unrecognized wear patterns (species) could potentially be observed. Such microwear categories may be established using a variety of approaches; however, 'paradigmatic classification', based on dimensional organization of sets of mutually exclusive variants of classificatory features might be difficult to implement because it is based on a fixed set of possible categories or classes (Dunnell 1971; Eren et al. 2012: 2; Eren et al. 2016: 178; Lyman and O'Brien 2000: 40); nevertheless, the use of paradigmatic classes might be possible with ranges of data for specific parameters using surface metrology (see below).

Non-Specific Microwear Types

Moreover, unlike ecologists or biologists, microwear analysts have classificatory options as default categories often referred to as "soft," "hard," "unknown," "undetermined," and "indeterminate," which are commonly used. These non-specific, non-exclusive categories have the potential to be problematic when attempting to calculate diversity, because they are not "a set of well-defined categories." Moreover, the identification of a previously unknown or unrecognized pattern of microwear, as noted above, means that an assemblage analyzed before the discovery of this new wear pattern will not contain it (because it did not previously exist to be observed), but analyses subsequent to the discovery of this wear pattern can potentially include it. An example of this is the analysis of the obsidian blades from Actun Uayazba Kab, a Maya cave site in Belize. In the original analysis (Stemp and Awe 2014), no contact material category called "bloodletting" existed because the analyst did not have a set of experimental microwear criteria for identification of this activity. Following experimentation (Stemp 2016b, 2016c; Stemp et al. 2015), microwear characteristics associated with bloodletting were defined. A reanalysis of some of the obsidian blades from the cave that were previously categorized as "indeterminate" revealed that some of them had been used for "bloodletting" (Table 5.3). When diversity and richness curves were calculated for the microwear on the blades before experimentation and after reanalysis, the results were different (Table 5.4; Figure 5.2).

Table 5.3. Microwear (IUZs) on obsidian artifacts from Actun Uayazba Kab, Belize, based on analyses by Stemp and Awe (2014) and Stemp, Peuramaki-Brown, and Awe (2019).

	Possible Blood-letting (pierce & twist)	Blood-letting (cut)	Possible blood-letting (cut)	Cut Skin/ Meat/ Hide	Scrape Hide	Cut Plant	Cut/Saw Wood
Stemp and Awe 2014	0	0	0	83	5	19	17
Stemp, Peuramaki-Brown, and Awe 2019	1	23	16	83	5	19	17

	Scrape/ Whittle Wood	Cut/Saw Bone	Cut Meat/ Skin/Hide & Bone	Scrape Bone/ Shell	Cut Indeter-minate	Scrape Indeter-minate	Indeter-minate
Stemp and Awe 2014	10	7	9	9	22	20	50
Stemp, Peuramaki-Brown, and Awe 2019	10	7	9	9	14	20	18

Table 5.4. Diversity measures for microwear (IUZs) on obsidian artifacts from Actun Uayazba Kab, Belize, based on analyses by Stemp and Awe (2014) and Stemp, Peuramaki-Brown, and Awe (2019).

	N (IUZs)	Richness (S)	ln S	Simpson Index (D)	Simpson Reciprocal Index (1/D)	Shannon Index (H')	Shannon Equitability Index (E_H)
Stemp and Awe 2014	251	11	2.3979	0.1754	5.7004	2.0249	0.8445
Stemp, Peuramaki-Brown, and Awe 2019	251	14	2.6391	0.1487	6.7256	2.2566	0.8551

Actun Uayazba Kab

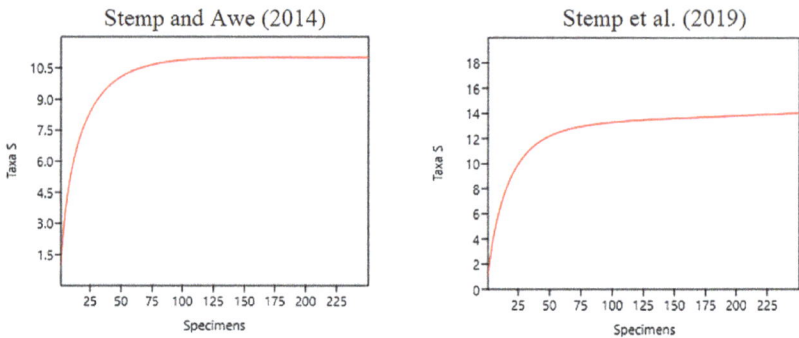

Figure 5.2. Richness (S) graphs for microwear (IUZs) on obsidian artifacts from Actun Uayazba Kab, Belize, based on analyses by Stemp and Awe (2014) and Stemp, Peuramaki-Brown, and Awe (2019). © The authors.

Microwear, Sample Size, and Transformation Processes

Much like any system of classification necessary for the calculation of diversity from a population, sample size is an important criterion. For lithic microwear, sample size is affected by many factors, including, first, the number of tools that were actually used in the total assemblage, and second, the number of tools with microwear that can be observed, correctly identified, and classified in the sample analyzed. The ability to observe, identify, and classify use-related wear can depend on equipment and methodology, as noted above, but will also be affected by past cultural modification of the tools and post-depositional processes (see Lévi-Sala 1986, 1993, 1996). For example, stone tool resharpening or reuse will potentially eliminate previous microwear evidence and replace it with other microwear. There is also evidence that post-depositional forces will differentially alter microwear on some stone tools. Clemente-Conte (1997: 533) notes that bone and wood polishes tend to survive exposure to burning better than polishes associated with soft contact materials, such as meat or fat. Additionally, there is a bias toward hard contact materials because they will modify surfaces at a faster rate than soft contact materials, and to a greater degree. These transformational processes can eliminate, obfuscate, or alter the microwear on stone tools such that the number of tools with specific types of wear may increase or decrease. Increases are potentially problematic, but more significant for measures of diversity is the possibility of very small sample sizes (Cochrane 2003; Hiscock 2001; Kaufman 1998: 83; Kintigh 1984; Meltzer et al. 1992: 385; Rhode 1988).

Microwear and Subjectivity

As noted by Eren et al. (2012: 2; also see Beck and Jones 1989; Bisson 2000; Whittaker et al. 1998), lithic typological classification, akin to classes or species in ecological or biological studies, has suffered from criticisms, "including its subjective, non-quantitative nature . . . and the unavoidable inter-observer variability that it yields." Similar criticisms have been leveled at traditional visual microwear analysis that depends on the experience of the analyst and relies on what the analyst 'sees' through the microscope (Grace, Graham, and Newcomer 1985; Stemp, Watson, and Evans 2016). However, as van Gijn (2014) notes, these issues may be addressed, at least in part, through more rigorous experimental design, incorporating more ethnographic and ethnohistoric comparative information, and increasing the sizes of the tool assemblages sampled. Related to this (and noted above) is the concern of microwear analysts for the standardization of results based on the specific method and technology used by the analyst, and how wear features are described or characterized. Another issue related to subjectivity is the aforementioned question of the exclusivity of polishes, or the stages of development at which polishes become exclusive ("a set of well-defined categories"). Concerns such as these led to attempts to objectively document microwear on stone tools using some form of technologically assisted assessment. These have varied significantly, including expert systems (Grace 1989, 1993; Lohse 1996; Lohse and Sammons 1999; Van den Dries 1994, 1998), grayscale imaging (Barceló, Pijoan, and Vicente 2001; Bietti 1996; González-Urquijo and Ibáñez-Estévez 2003; Lerner 2007, 2014; Pijoan et al. 2002; Vila and Gallart 1993), and documentation of surface roughness/texture using various measurement systems and surface data parameters (see below). Ideally, surface roughness/texture reduces elements of subjectivity by recording and expressing surface microstructures with numbers that are determined by machines and mathematical calculations. However, mathematical documentation of microwear is not without its problems or its critics (van Gijn 2014).

Diversity and Quantification of Lithic Microwear

In a number of ways, quantification of lithic microwear is still subject to some of the same concerns as traditional visual microscopic analysis of stone tools for use-related wear. Whether polishes are exclusive to particular contact materials (Evans and Donahue 2008; Pedergnana et al. 2020; Stemp et al. 2009), the development of wear (Evans et al. 2014; Ibáñez and Mazzucco 2021; Stemp and Stemp 2003), the effects of post-deposition (Werner 2018), and a number of other issues are currently being pursued using mathematical characterization of stone tool surfaces on the microscale using a variety of microscope systems and parameters. Different microscopes measure these surfaces using different techniques (e.g., Anderson et al. 2006; Astruc et al. 2011; Evans and Donahue 2008; Evans et al. 2014; Faulks et al. 2011; Kimball, Kimball, and Allen 1995; Kimball et al. 2017; Macdonald 2014; Macdonald, Bartkowiak, and Stemp 2020; Stemp and Chung 2011; Stemp, Lerner, and Kristant 2013, 2018; Stemp, Macdonald, and Gleason 2019), but a particular microscope will always measure the stone tool surface in the same way, assuming the settings for the microscope and its calibration, and data filtering, are consistent. Variation in the micro- or nanosurface data produced when measuring two or more different surfaces will not be the product of the process of acquisition itself (although two microscopes from the same manufacturer cannot be perfectly identical); this should be consistent from tool to tool, as long as the tools are made from the same raw material (see Lerner 2007, 2014; Lerner et al. 2007). The way in which the measurement data are processed using particular parameters should also be consistent because these are set/determined by professional industry-based standards ISO25178-2 (2012) and ASME B46.1 (2009). As long as the stone tool surfaces are measured following the same measurement protocols using the same calculation parameters then any source of variation should be the surface microstructures of the tools themselves. In this case, a huge potential source of variation in data acquisition and interpretation—the human factor—is avoided. Because analysts do not or cannot always 'see' the same microwear in the same way, it may be difficult to compare data and thus classify it in reliably exclusive ways. This may be demonstrated by previous blind-tests (Table 5.5) undertaken over the last five decades by microwear analysts (Evans 2014). Despite disagreements over how 'fair' these previous tests

Table 5.5. Summary table of results of collated data from the published lithic microwear blind-tests (from Evans 2014: Table 1).

Test	Year	Analysts/ Test	Unique Tools	Unique Edges	Total Tests	% Accuracy Material	% Accuracy Direction	% Accuracy Total
Newcomer and Keeley	1979	1	15	16	16	43.8%	75.0%	37.5%
Odell and Odell-Vereecken[2]	1980	1	31	31	31	35.5%	71.0%	32.3%
Vaughan*	1981	1	32	32	32			71.0%
Gendel and Pirnay	1982	1	23	23	23	65.2%	91.3%	65.2%
Knutsson and Hope	1984	1	4	4	4	75.0%	50.0%	50.0%
Newcomer et al. T1*	1986	4	10	10	40	37.5%		
Newcomer et al. T3*	1986	5	10	10	50	26.0 (6.0)[+]%	46.0%	14.0%
Unrath et al.	1986	4	20	28	112	42.9%	55.4%	36.6%
Bamforth et al.	1990	1	20	29	29	58.6%	82.8%	58.6%
Shea T8*, [1, 2]	1991	1	15	17	17	88.2 (64.7)[3]%	76.5%	70.6 (58.8)[3]%
Shea T2*, [1, 2]	1991	1	18	26	26	69.2%	88.5%	61.5%
Shea T7*, [1, 2]	1991	1	9	10	10	70.0%	80.0%	70.0%
Yamei	1992	1	9	9	9	55.6%	88.9%	55.6%
Shea and Klenck*, [1, 2]	1993	1	60	71	71	49.3%	49.3%	38.0%
van den Dries	1998	8	15	15	120	40.8%	76.7%	34.2%
Rots et al. T2b[2]	2006	1	10	10	10	80.0%	90.0%	80.0%
Rots et al. T2a[2]	2006	1	10	10	10	60.0%	100.0%	60.0%
Rots et al. T1	2006	1	8	8	8	75.0%	87.5%	75.0%
Rots et al. T3	2006	1	6	6	6	100.0%	83.3%	83.3%
Rots et al. T2c	2006	1	10	10	10	90.0%	100.0%	90.0%
Stevens et al. T1	2010	1	10	10	10	70.0%		
Stevens et al. T1x	2010	1	10	10	10	60.0%		
Stevens et al. T2	2010	1	10	10	10	60.0%		
Stevens et al. T2x	2010	1	10	10	10	60.0%		
Total		40	343	383	642	49.5%	68.7%	42.7%

*Only summary data available, [1] only category-based identifications, [2] low power, [+] with/without partially correct answers, [3] variable results based on category interpretation.

were, one thing they all suffer from is inter-observer error. In surface metrology, there may be calibration (or traceability) issues between different microscopes from the same manufacturers, as well as necessary calibration of parameters (Giusca, Leach, and Helary 2012; Giusca et al. 2012; Leach and Giusca 2011; see Evans et al. 2014; Stemp et al. 2016); however, once identified, these can be addressed.

Therefore, the process of acquiring the surface data and processing these data can be standardized, thus creating the possibility for establishing robust groups, categories, or classes of data under experimental conditions. However, what still needs to be established is: (1) whether a system of categorization for discriminating microwear (surface roughness/texture) resulting from different contact materials is possible; and (2) whether certain mathematical or quantitative measures of surface wear (surface roughness/texture) are exclusive to particular contact materials and could be used as "signatures" to establish "a set of well-defined categories." Thus far, experimental use of stone tools has generated microwear that can be reliably discriminated based on surface roughness/texture using a number of different measurement techniques to acquire the surface data and the application of parameters to ISO25178-2 (2012) or ASME B46.1 (2009) standards (e.g., Evans 2014; Evans and Donahue 2008; Evans and Macdonald 2011; Evans et al. 2014; Faulks et al. 2011; Kimball et al. 1995, 2017; Macdonald 2014; Macdonald, Harman, and Evans 2018; Macdonald, Xie, and Gallo 2019; Stemp 2014; Stemp and Chung 2011; Stemp, Morozov, and Key 2015; Stemp and Stemp 2001, 2003; Stemp et al. 2009, 2010, 2013, 2018). This means that, based on wear, a tool used on wood can be mathematically discriminated from one used on hide, for example. What has not been demonstrated, as of yet, is whether there is mathematical exclusivity of microwear based on surface roughness/texture data, meaning that a particular wear pattern documented mathematically will always be the product of contact with a specific material to the exclusion of all others.

Right now, current experimental research demonstrates that surface roughness/texture data generated by measuring surfaces cannot be used to identify a particular contact material to the exclusion of all others. Essentially, the data do not permit the establishment of "a set of well-defined categories" that are "paradigmatic" if one expects that the data for a single parameter will always be unique to one contact material. Given the complexity of surface micro- or nanostructures this will probably never occur. However, the solution to this problem likely lies in the application of multiple parameters calculated from large sets of surface data (many measurements of many experimentally used tools), such that certain combinations of parameter data are statistically much more likely to be associated with particular contact materials than others. This is similar to research results presented by Stevens, Harro, and Hicklin (2010); however, they did not use ISO25178-2 (2012) or ASME B46.1 (2009) parameters.

The application of multiple parameters calculated from large sets of surface data using ISO standards (Table 5.6) can be demonstrated by the following example. Using a Sensofar S neox imaging confocal microscope with the 50x objective [NA 0.80], five area scans were taken on each of three English chalk flint flakes used to scrape soaked antler and three flint flakes used to scrape dry hide for two thousand strokes. Prior to measurement each tool was cleaned in a 10 percent HCl solution in an ultrasonic bath, a 10 percent NaOH solution in an ultrasonic bath, and sonicated for 10 minutes in clean water, following Macdonald and Evans (2014). Confocal images were taken with blue light and a sampling area of 100 x 100 μm^2. Resulting scans were processed in SensoMap (by Digital Surf) using protocols outlined in Macdonald et al. (2019). Following surface measurement, seven different ISO25178-2 (2012) parameters were calculated for the five area scans for each flake (Table 5.7). By comparing the surface roughness/texture data statistically using Welch's t-test, the worn surfaces of the antler and hide scraping flakes can be statistically discriminated using the Sa parameter, but the worn surfaces were not significantly different from one another based on the other six parameters used in the example (Table 5.8). In this case, the Sa parameter calculated from the surface roughness/texture data could be used as a 'paradigmatic class' to discriminate antler scraping wear from dry hide scraping wear. With enough experimentation on more tools used to work different contact materials, more parameters could be found that would successfully discriminate worn stone tool surfaces, and these would be used to establish the 'paradigmatic signatures' for specific types of wear. This will mean that some paradigmatic classes (or parameters, such as Sp, Sq, and Sv, in this experimental example) did not produce surface roughness/texture data that could be considered exclusive to one contact material, and these parameters could not be

Table 5.6. Some ISO 25178-2 surface roughness/texture parameters.

Parameter	Description
Sa	Arithmetical mean height
Sp	Maximum peak height
Sq	Root mean square of height
Sv	Maximum pit depth
Sz	Maximum height of scale-limited surface
Sku	Kurtosis – sharpness of roughness profile
Ssk	Skewness – degree of bias of roughness shape (asperity)

Table 5.7. Surface roughness/texture data for the experimental antler and dry hide scraping flint flakes.

ISO 25178-2 Parameters	Antler Scraping Flake Scans (n = 15)	Dry Hide Scraping Flake Scans (n = 15)
Sa (μm) – range	0.103907208 – 0.521932544	0.160555977 – 0.563810313
Sa (μm) – mean	0.279108653	0.361172856
Sa (μm) – SD	0.103375622	0.113210815
Sp (μm) – range	0.8462 – 7.1004	0.8686 – 4.1236
Sp (μm) – mean	2.33456	2.247753333
Sp (μm) – SD	1.659869392	0.997511492
Sq (μm) – range	0.153545231 – 0.925179106	0.215248786 – 0.964127233
Sq (μm) – mean	0.402523348	0.519542893
Sq (μm) – SD	0.178785909	0.19174029
Sv (μm) – range	0.8634 – 8.6825	0.9236 – 11.2667
Sv (μm) – mean	2.571773333	3.41534
Sv (μm) – SD	1.855082484	2.755736822
Sz (μm) – range	1.7096 – 15.7829	2.0316 – 13.1922
Sz (μm) – mean	4.906333333	5.663093333
Sz (μm) – SD	3.368590743	3.077492631
Sku – range	4.106681785 – 14.73532418	4.243842305 – 54.56031532
Sku – mean	8.42892776	9.919370065
Sku – SD	5.245714849	12.67566693
Ssk – range	-2.535438464 – 0.44374744	-4.67979305 – 0.636990693
Ssk – mean	-0.542968984	-0.890314086
Ssk – SD	0.86094206	1.381133596

Table 5.8. Welch's t-test of surface roughness/texture data for the experimental antler and dry hide scraping flint flakes (p = 0.05).

ISO 25178-2 Parameters	t	p
Sa	-2.073174	0.0474725
Sp	0.173609	0.863692
Sq	-1.728761	0.0948655
Sv	-0.983492	0.334789
Sz	-0.642363	0.525863
Sku	-0.420787	0.678632
Ssk	0.826583	0.416967

used for wear classification purposes. The key will be in determining the parameters that most significantly discriminate wear resulting from contact with different materials. For some, the overlap in ranges and means, including standard deviations, will be so great that those parameters will not be good discriminators of surface wear. However, other parameters may demonstrate minimal (or no) overlap in data ranges for surface wear resulting from contact with different materials, such as Sa in this example. This endeavor still requires a tremendous amount of experimentation to generate the necessary comparative wear data to establish 'paradigmatic signatures' that consist of specific combinations of parameters as discriminators of surface roughness/texture data.

Another approach involves the use of scale-sensitive fractal analysis parameters, in which the surface data acquired from the stone tools permit the calculation of surface roughness/texture of the same region at multiple scales, using parameters such as relative area (Srel) or area-scale fractal complexity (Asfc) (Brown et al. 2018; Key et al. 2015; Stemp and Chung 2011; Stemp, Morozov, and Key 2015; Stemp et al. 2013, 2015, 2016, 2018); see ISO25178-2 (2012) or ASME B46.1 (2009). In this case, it would not be the use of combined ISO parameters as described above, but the use of multiple scales using a single parameter to determine at which scales the wear on stone tools used on the same contact materials could not be discriminated.

Data at those particular scales would become the 'signature' for that specific wear type. Eventually, every time those specific data for those multiple scales were generated, they would reliably indicate contact with a specific contact material. For example, using an Olympus LEXT OLS4000 laser scanning confocal microscope with the 20x objective [0.60 NA], three area scans were taken in two unused portions of a flint flake to mathematically document surface roughness/texture. Area scan sizes using the 20x objective were 643 x 643 μm^2. The two unused regions on the flint flake cannot be discriminated based on measures of mean relative area (Srel) (Figure 5.3) using Sfrax (by Digital Surf), and there is statistical confirmation of this using the F-test at the 95 percent confidence level because data at all scales is plotted below the horizontal confidence level line (Figure 5.4). As another example, six area scans on each of two obsidian blade segments (OBS1-u, OBS3-u) both used in experimental bloodletting (see Stemp et al. 2015) to slice raw beef for thirty strokes were also measured using the LEXT OLS4000 with the 20x objective [0.60 NA]. Area scan sizes using the 20x objective were 643 x 643 μm^2. Cleaning of the obsidian blades before surface measurement consisted of washing in warm water and a grit-free detergent, and then rinsing. Blades were subsequently soaked in

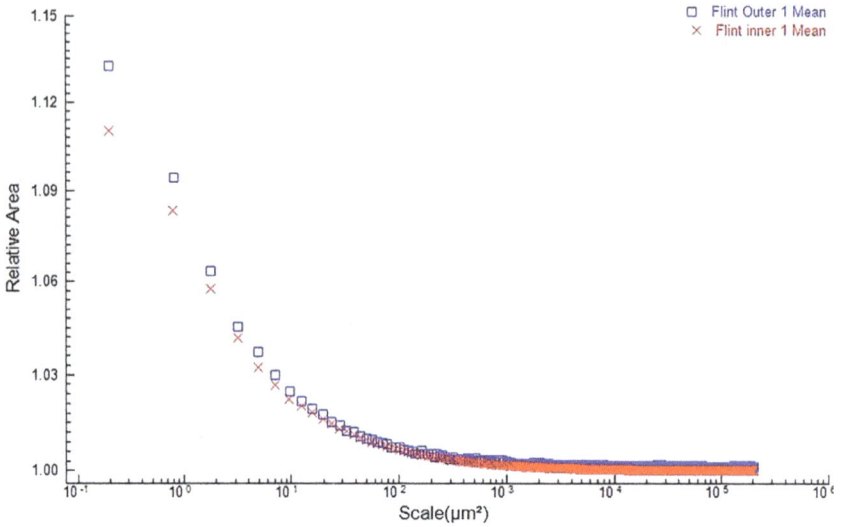

Figure 5.3. Mean relative areas (Srel) calculated for two unused surfaces on a flint flake (left). © The authors.

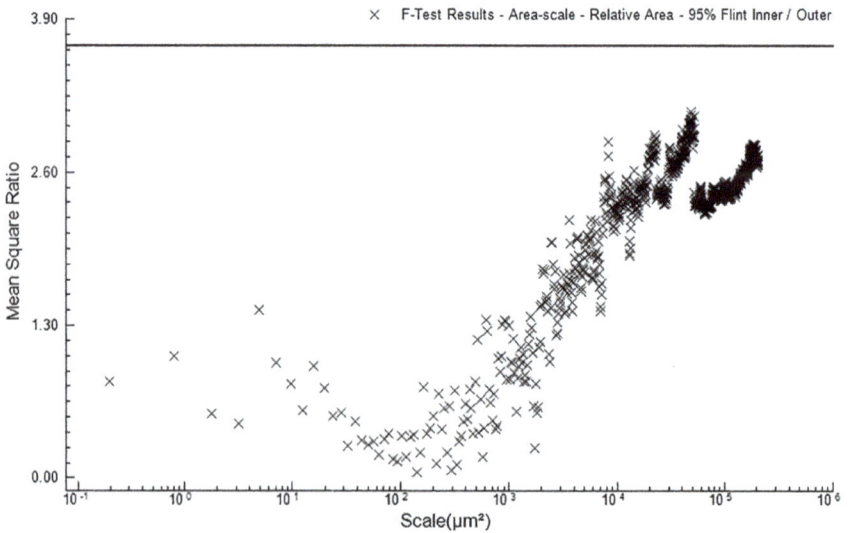

Figure 5.4. F-test results based on mean relative areas (Srel) indicating no discrimination of the two surface microtopographies at any scale above the 95 percent confidence level as represented by the solid horizontal line. © The authors.

a 15 percent solution of NaOH for 15 minutes, and then rinsed again in warm water. For the calculated surface roughness/texture for the two blades, there is significant overlap in their standard deviations of mean relative area (Srel) over some, but not all, scale ranges (Figure 5.5), and the F-test of mean relative area (Srel) demonstrates the specific scales at which the two blade segments' surface roughness/texture cannot be discriminated (i.e., below the 95 percent confidence level as indicated by the solid horizontal line) (Figure 5.6). In both the flint flake and the obsidian blade segment examples, the surface roughness/texture data at particular scales below the 95 percent confidence level for the F-test of mean relative areas (Srel) would become the 'paradigmatic signatures' for those specific wear types on those specific raw materials/stone types. Eventually, every time those specific data for those multiple scales were generated on tools made from those raw materials/stone types, they would reliably indicate contact with a specific material for a certain use-duration. As mentioned above, this will require a tremendous amount of experimentation.

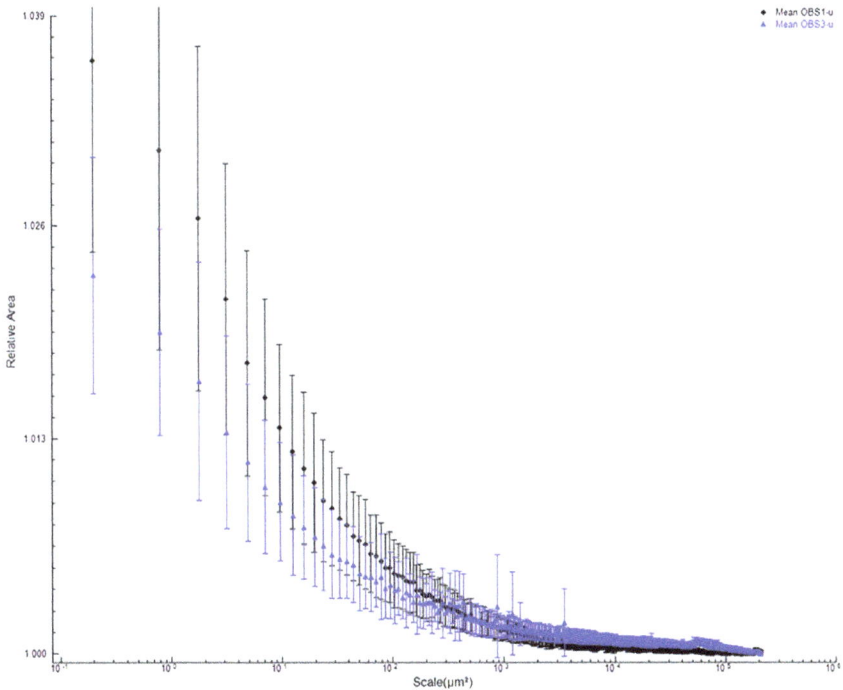

Figure 5.5. Mean relative areas (Srel), with standard deviations for two experimental obsidian blade segments (OBS1-u, OBS3-u) used to slice raw beef for thirty strokes, versus scale. © The authors.

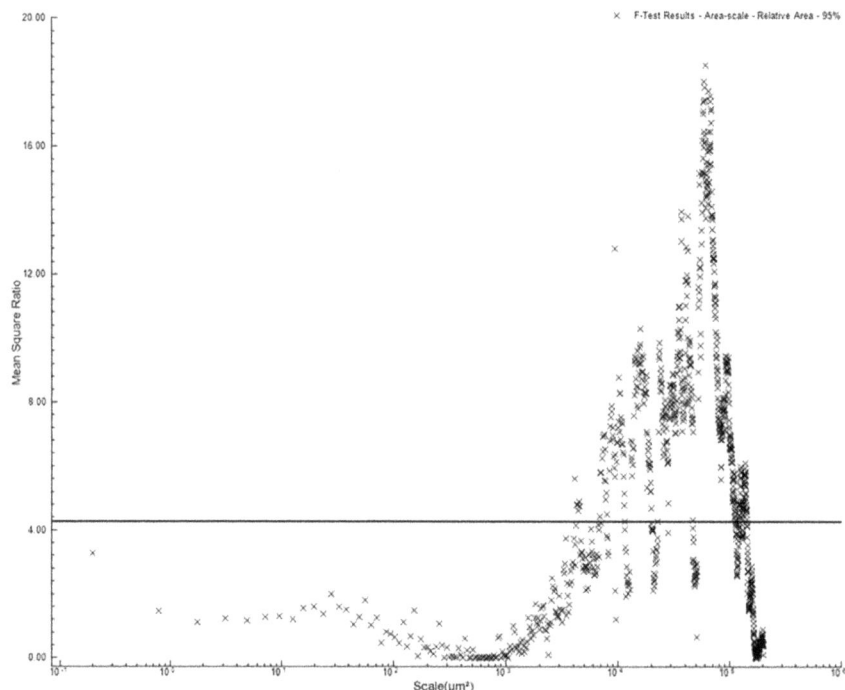

Figure 5.6. F-test results based on mean relative areas (Srel) indicating no discrimination of the two surface microtopographies at scales below the 95 percent confidence level as represented by the solid horizontal line. Discrimination at coarser scales (above the solid horizontal line) represents the natural microtopographies of each of the blade segments, whereas lack of discrimination at finer scales (below the solid horizontal line) represents the similarly used/worn microtopographies of each blade segment. © The authors.

Discussion and Conclusion

The application of measures of diversity to microwear on stone tools from archaeological sites has tremendous potential interpretive value. Thus far, however, there has been almost no use of diversity as a means to interpret similarities or differences in tool use in assemblages from different locations or over time. Reasons for this include the degree of standardization of methodologies and equipment that microwear analysts rely upon, discussions concerning the exclusivity of microwear types (including the mechanisms responsible for wear formation), the introduction of new microwear types, the difficulty of dealing with non-specific microwear, sample sizes, the preservation of traces of use-related wear on stone tools, and concerns over the subjectivity of microwear analysis (including inter-observer error).

Current visual microwear analysis techniques employed by various analysts tend to be individualized in many ways, even though they rely on the same basic principles devised by earlier researchers like Semenov (1964), Tringham et al. (1974), Keeley (1980), Anderson-Gerfaud (1981), Vaughan (1985), Knutsson (1988), van Gijn (1990), and Hurcombe (1992), among others. Although analysis based on visual observation and photomicrographs does have methodological or procedural expectations, often the verbal component of description of damage types or wear features, and the variable emphasis on which features are the most important, can make comparisons between analysts' results difficult to implement consistently. An example of this is the recent literature on fracture types and fracture characteristics associated with projectile use in the deep past, and how projectile point damage can be recognized (e.g., Rots and Plisson 2014; Wilkins, Schoville, and Brown 2014; Wilkins et al. 2012). Some of these disagreements are based on the lack of consensus concerning what counts as functional evidence for projectile use on stone tools. A system like the one proposed by Coppe and Rots (2017) would be practical in terms of implementation and application to diversity due to its terminology and its divisions of characteristics in what are essentially 'paradigmatic' classes.

The development of mathematical measurement techniques and parameters to establish 'exclusive' mathematical microwear data (classes) that can be assigned to particular contact materials requires a substantial amount of continued experimentation to identify the data of specific parameters like Sa, Sv, Sku, or specific scales using Srel or Asfc. What will also need to be demonstrated is the reproducibility and repeatability of the results to confirm their connections to specific contact materials before any reliable application to lithic artifacts is possible. Unfortunately, some microwear analysts have already opened Pandora's box and have attempted to quantify microwear on archaeological artifacts using quantitative methods (see Stemp, Evans, and Lerner 2012; Stemp, Watson, and Evans 2016). Their results cannot be considered reliable due to a number of factors, including the equipment/technology used, the design of the experiments upon which the analyses are based, failure to account for the influence of post-deposition on wear formation, issues associated with use-duration and wear development, and/or the inability to determine that the data generated using their parameters are specific to particular contact materials (e.g., Goodale et al. 2010; Ibáñez et al. 2016; Vardi et al. 2010). The more these types of applications to artifacts are published, the increasingly more difficult it will become to develop a robust quantitative methodology for microwear analysis that could be incorporated into lithic diversity studies. Measures of diversity should be combined with microwear analyses of stone tools, particularly for large assemblages, as a means to better determine similarities and differences between them, which can lead to more reliable interpretations about stone tool use in the past.

Acknowledgments

The authors would like to thank the volume editors, Metin Eren and Briggs Buchanan, for bringing together a fascinating collection of chapters on applications of diversity to the archaeological record. Thank you as well to Miriam Belmaker at the University of Tulsa for use of the Sensofar S Neox. Research was funded by a Keene State College Faculty Development Grant #KSC2013 and National Science Foundation Grant #1727357 (DM), USA.

W. James Stemp is a Professor at Keene State College, New Hampshire, USA.

Danielle A. Macdonald is an Associate Professor at the University of Tulsa, Oklahoma, USA.

Note

1. Alpha diversity (α-diversity) can be defined as the observed richness (number of taxa) or evenness/dominance (the relative abundances of those taxa) of an average sample within a particular area.

References

Anderson, P. C., J.-M. Georges, R. Vargiolu, and H. Zahouani. 2006. "Insights from a Tribological Analysis of the Tribulum." *Journal of Archaeological Science* 33: 1559–68.
Anderson-Gerfaud, P. C. 1981. *Contribution Méthologique: l'Analyse des Microtraces d'Utilisation sur les Outils Préhistoriques*. Bordeaux: Thèse de Troisième Cycle no.1607, Institut du Quatenaire, Université de Bordeaux 1.
Aoyama, K. 1995. "Microwear Analysis in the Southeast Maya Lowlands: Two Case Studies at Copan, Honduras." *Latin American Antiquity* 6: 129–44.
———. 2001. "Ritos de Plebeyos Mayas en la Cueva Gordon no. 3 de Copán (Honduras) Durante el Periodo Clásico: Análisis de las Microhuellas de Uso Sobre la Lítica Menor de Obsidiana." *Mayab* 14: 5–16.
———. 2009. *Elite Craft Producers, Artists, and Warriors at Aguateca: Lithic Analysis. Monographs of the Aguateca Archaeological Project First Phase, Volume 2*. Salt Lake City: University of Utah Press.

ASME B46.1. 2009. *Surface Texture (Surface Roughness, Waviness, and Lay): An American National Standard.* New York: The American Society of Mechanical Engineers.

Astruc, L., R. Vargiolu, M. Ben Tkaya, N. Balkan-Atli, M. Özbaşaran, and H. Zahouani. 2011. "Multi-scale Tribological Analysis of the Technique of Manufacture of an Obsidian Bracelet from Aşikli Höyük (Aceramic Neolithic, Central Anatolia)." *Journal of Archaeological Science* 38: 3415–24.

Barceló, J. A., J. Pijoan, and O. Vicente. 2001. "Image Quantification as Archaeological Description." In *Computing Archaeology for Understanding the Past*, ed. Z. Stančič and T. Veljanovski, 69–78. Oxford: BAR International Series 931.

Beck, C., and G. T. Jones. 1989. "Bias and Archaeological Classification." *American Antiquity* 54: 244–62.

Bietti, A. 1996. "Image Processing in Microwear Studies in Flint Artefacts." *Archeologia e Calcolatori* 7: 387–96.

Bisson, M. 2000. "Nineteenth-Century Tools for Twenty-First-Century Archaeology? Why the Middle Paleolithic Typology of François Bordes Must be Replaced." *Journal of Archaeological Method and Theory* 7: 1–48.

Bradley, R., and C. Clayton. 1987. "The Influence of Flint Microstructure on the Formation of Microwear Polishes." In *The Human Uses of Flint and Chert: Papers from the Fourth International Flint Symposium*, ed. G. de G. Sieveking and M. Newcomer, 81–89. Cambridge: Cambridge University Press.

Brink, J. W. 1978. "The Role of Abrasives in the Formation of Lithic Use-Wear." *Journal of Archaeological Science* 5: 363–71.

Brown, C. A., H. N. Hansen, X. J. Jiang, F. Blateyron, J. Berglund, N. Senin, T. Bartkowiak, B. Dixon, G. Le Goïc, Y. Quinsat, W. J. Stemp, M. K. Thompson, P. S. Ungar, and E. H. Zahouani. 2018. "Multiscale Analyses and Characterizations of Surface Topographies." *CIRP Annals of Manufacturing Technology* 76(2): 839–62.

Buchanan, B., A. Chao, C.-H. Chiu, R. K. Colwell, M. J. O'Brien, A. Werner, and M. I. Eren. 2017. "Environment-Induced Changes in Selective Constraints on Social Learning during the Peopling of the Americas." *Scientific Reports* 7: 44431.

Christensen, M. 1998. "Processus de Formation et Caractérisation Physico-Chimique des Polis d'Utilisation des Outils en Silex: Applications à la Technologie Préhistorique de l'Ivoire." *Bulletin de la Société Préhistoire Française* 95: 336–75.

Christensen, M., G. Grime, M. Menu, and P. Walter. 1993. "Usewear Studies of Flint Tools with MicroPIXE and MicroRBS." *Nuclear Instruments and Methods in Physics Research Section B: Beam Interactions with Materials and Atoms* 77(1–4): 530–36.

Christensen, M., P. Walter, and M. Menu. 1992. "Usewear Characterisation of Prehistoric Flints with IBA." *Nuclear Instruments and Methods in Physics Research Section B: Beam Interactions with Materials and Atoms* 64(1–4): 488–93.

Clemente-Conte, I. 1997. "Thermal Alterations of Flint Implements and the Conservation of Microwear Polish: Preliminary Experimental Observations." In *Siliceous Rocks and Culture. VI International Flint Symposium, Madrid, September 1991*, ed. A. Ramos-Millán and M. A. Bustillo, 525–35. Monográfica Arte y Arqueología 42. Granada: Universidad de Granada.

Cochrane, W. 2003. "Artefact Attribute Richness and Sample Size Adequacy." *Journal of Archaeological Science* 30: 837–48.

Coppe, J., and V. Rots. 2017. "Focus on the Target: The Importance of a Transparent Fracture Terminology for Understanding Projectile Points and Projecting Modes." *Journal of Archaeological Science: Reports* 12: 109–23.

Del Bene, T. A. 1979. "Once Upon a Striation: Current Models of Striation and Polish Formation." In *Lithic Use-Wear Analysis*, ed. B. Hayden, 167–77. New York: Academic Press.

Diamond, G. 1979. "The Nature of So-called Polished Surfaces on Stone Artifacts." In *Lithic Use-Wear Analysis*, ed. B. Hayden, 159–66. New York: Academic Press.

Dunnell, R. C. 1971. *Systematics in Prehistory*. New York: The Free Press.

Eren, M. I. 2012. "Were Unifacial Tools Regularly Hafted by Clovis Foragers in the North American Lower Great Lakes Region? An Empirical Test of Edge Class Richness and Attribute Frequency among Distal, Proximal, and Lateral Tool-Sections." *Journal of Ohio Archaeology* 2: 1–15.

Eren, M. I., A. Chao, C. H. Chiu, R. K. Colwell, B. Buchanan, M. T. Boulanger, J. Darwent, and M. J. O'Brien. 2016. "Statistical Analysis of Paradigmatic Class Richness Supports Greater Paleoindian Projectile-Point Diversity in the Southeast." *American Antiquity* 81: 174–92.

Eren, M. I., A. Chao, W. H. Hwang, and R. K. Colwell. 2012. "Estimating the Richness of a Population When the Maximum Number of Classes is Fixed: A Nonparametric Solution to an Archaeological Problem." *PLoS ONE* 7(5): e34179.

Evans, A. A. 2014. "On the Importance of Blind Testing in Archaeological Science: The Example from Lithic Functional Studies." *Journal of Archaeological Science* 48: 5–14.

Evans, A. A., and R. E. Donahue. 2008. "Laser Scanning Confocal Microscopy: A Potential Technique for the Study of Lithic Microwear." *Journal of Archaeological Science* 35: 2223–30.

Evans, A. A., H. J. Lerner, D. A. Macdonald, W. J. Stemp, and P. C. Anderson. 2014. "Standardisation, Calibration and Innovation: A Special Issue on Lithic Microwear Method." *Journal of Archaeological Science* 48: 1–4.

Evans, A. A., and D. Macdonald. 2011. "Using Metrology in Early Prehistoric Stone Tool Research: Further Work and a Brief Instrument Comparison." *Scanning* 33: 294–303.

Evans, A. A., D. A. Macdonald, C. L. Giusca, and R. K. Leach. 2014. "New Method Development in Prehistoric Stone Tool Research: Evaluating Use Duration and Data Analysis Protocols." *Micron* 65: 69–75.

Faulks, N. R., L. R. Kimball, N. Hidjrati, and T. S. Coffey. 2011. "Atomic Force Microscopy of Microwear Traces on Mousterian Tools from Myshtylagty Lagat (Weasel Cave), Russia." *Scanning* 33: 304–15.

Fullagar, R. L. K. 1991. "The Role of Silica in Polish Formation." *Journal of Archaeological Science* 18: 1–24.

Gini, C. W. 1912. "Variabilita e mutabilita." *Studi Economico-Giuridici della R. Universita di Cagliari* 3: 3–159.

Giusca, C. L., R. K. Leach, and F. Helary. 2012. "Calibration of the Scales of Areal Surface Topography Measuring Instruments: Part 2. Amplification, Linearity and Squareness." *Measurement Science Technology* 23: e065005.

Giusca, C. L., R. K. Leach, F. Helary, T. Gutauskas, and L. Nimishakavi. 2012. "Calibration of the Scales of Areal Surface Topography-Measuring Instruments: Part 1. Measurement Noise and Residual Flatness." *Measurement Science Technology* 23: e035008.

González-Urquijo, J. E., and J. J. Ibáñez-Estévez. 2003. "The Quantification of Use-Wear Polish Using Image Analysis: First Results." *Journal of Archaeological Science* 30: 481–89.

Goodale, N., H. Otis, W. Andrefsky, I. Kuijt, B. Finlayson, and K. Bart. 2010. "Sickle Blade Life-History and the Transition to Agriculture: An Early Neolithic Case Study from Southwest Asia." *Journal of Archaeological Science* 37: 1192–1201.

Grace, R. 1989. *Interpreting the Function of Stone Tools: The Quantification and Computerization of Microwear Analysis*. Oxford: BAR International Series 474.

———. 1993. "The Use of Expert Systems in Lithic Analysis." In *Traces et Fonction: Les Gestes Retrouvés, Éditions ERAUL 50, vol. 2*, ed. P. C. Anderson, S. Beyries, M. Otte, and

H. Plisson, 389–400. Liège: Centre de Recherches Archéologiques du CNRS, Études et Recherches Archéologiques de l'Université de Liège.

Grace, R., I. D. G. Graham, and M. H. Newcomer. 1985. "The Quantification of Microwear Polishes." *World Archaeology* 17: 112–20.

Grayson, D. K., and S. C. Cole. 1998. "Stone Tool Assemblage Richness during the Middle and Early Upper Palaeolithic in France." *Journal of Archaeological Science* 25: 927–38.

Hill, M. O. 1973. "Diversity and Evenness: A Unifying Notation and its Consequences." *Ecology* 54: 427–32.

Hiscock, P. 2001. "Sizing Up Prehistory: Sample Size and Composition of Artefact Assemblages." *Australian Aboriginal Studies* 1: 48–62.

Hurcombe, L. 1992. *Use Wear Analysis and Obsidian: Theory, Experiments and Results.* Sheffield Archaeological Monographs 4. Sheffield: J. R. Collis Publications, University of Sheffield.

———. 1997. "The Contribution of Obsidian Use-Wear Analysis to Understanding the Formation and Alteration of Wear." In *Siliceous Rocks and Culture*, ed. A. Ramos-Millan and M. A. Bustillo, 487–97. Grenada: Editorial Universidad de Grenada.

Ibáñez, J. J., P. C. Anderson, J. E. González-Urquijo, and J. F. Gibaja. 2016. "Cereal Cultivation and Domestication as Shown by Microtexture Analysis of Sickle Gloss through Confocal Microscopy." *Journal of Archaeological Science* 73: 62–81.

Ibáñez, J. J., and N. Mazzucco. 2021. "Quantitative Use-Wear Analysis of Stone Tools: Measuring How the Intensity of Use Affects the Identification of the Worked Material." *PloS one* 16: e0257266.

ISO 25178-2. 2012. *Geometrical Product Specifications (GPS)—Surface texture: Areal—Part 2: Terms, Definitions and Surface Texture Parameters.* Geneva: International Organization for Standardization.

Jones, G. T., C. Beck, and D. K. Grayson. 1989. "Measures of Diversity and Expedient Lithic Technologies." In *Quantifying Diversity in Archaeology*, ed. R. D. Leonard and G. T. Jones, 69–78. Cambridge: Cambridge University Press.

Jones, G. T., D. K. Grayson, and C. Beck. 1983. "Artifact Class Richness and Sample Size in Archaeological Surface Assemblages." In *Lulu Linear Punctuated: Essays in Honour of George Irving Quimby*, ed. R. C. Dunnell and D. K. Grayson, 55–73. Ann Arbor: Anthropological Papers 72, Museum of Anthropology, University of Michigan.

Junge, K. 1994. "Diversity of Ideas about Diversity Measurement." *Scandinavian Journal of Psychology* 35(1): 16–26.

Kamminga, J. 1979. "The Nature of Use-Polish and Abrasive Smoothing on Stone Tools." In *Lithic Use-Wear Analysis*, ed. B. Hayden, 143–57. New York: Academic Press.

Kaufman, D. 1998. "Measuring Archaeological Diversity: An Application of the Jackknife Technique." *American Antiquity* 63: 73–85.

Keeley, L. H. 1980. *Experimental Determination of Stone Tool Uses: A Microwear Analysis.* Chicago: University of Chicago Press.

Key, A. J. M., W. J. Stemp, M. Morozov, T. Proffitt, and I. de la Torre. 2015. "Is Loading a Significantly Influential Factor in the Development of Lithic Microwear? An Experimental Test Using LSCM on Basalt from Olduvai Gorge." *Journal of Archaeological Method and Theory* 22(4): 1193–214.

Kimball, L. R., T. S. Coffey, N. R. Faulks, S. E. Dellinger, N. M. Karas, and N. Hidjrati. 2017. "A Multi-instrument Study of Microwear Polishes on Mousterian Tools from Weasel Cave (*Myshtulagty Lagat*), Russia." *Lithic Technology* 42: 61–76.

Kimball, L. R., J. F. Kimball, and P. E. Allen. 1995. "Microwear Polishes as Viewed through the Atomic Force Microscope." *Lithic Technology* 20: 6–28.

Kintigh, K. 1984. "Measuring Archaeological Diversity by Comparison with Simulated Assemblages." *American Antiquity* 49: 44–54.

Knutsson, K. 1988. *Making and Using Stone Tools: The Analysis of the Lithic Assemblages from Middle Neolithic Sites with Flint from Västerbotten, Northern Sweden*. Uppsala: Societas Archaeologica Upsaliensis, AUN 11.

Lawn, B. R., and D. B. Marshall. 1979. "Mechanics of Micro-Contact Fracture in Brittle Solids." In *Lithic Use-Wear Analysis*, ed. B. Hayden, 63–82. New York: Academic Press.

Leach, R., and C. Giusca. 2011. "Calibration of Optical Surface Topography Measuring Instruments." In *Optical Measurement of Surface Topography*, ed. R. Leach, 49–70. Berlin: Springer.

Leonard, R. D., and G. T. Jones, eds. 1989. *Quantifying Diversity in Archaeology*. Cambridge: Cambridge University Press.

Leonard, R. D., F. E. Smiley, and C. M. Cameron. 1989. "Changing Strategies of Anasazi Lithic Procurement on Black Mesa, Arizona." In *Quantifying Diversity in Archaeology*, ed. R. D. Leonard and G. T. Jones, 100–8. Cambridge: Cambridge University Press.

Lerner, H. J. 2007. "Digital Image Analysis and Use-Wear Accrual as a Function of Raw Material: An Example from Northwestern New Mexico." *Lithic Technology* 32: 51–67.

———. 2014. "Intra-Raw Material Variability and Use-Wear Formation: An Experimental Examination of a Fossiliferous Chert (SJF) and a Silicified Wood (YSW) from NW New Mexico using the Clemex Vision Processing Frame." *Journal of Archaeological Science* 48: 34–45.

Lerner, H. J., X. Du, A. Costopoulos, and M. Ostoja-Starzewski. 2007. "Lithic Raw Material Physical Properties and Use-Wear Accrual." *Journal of Archaeological Science* 34: 711–22.

Lerner, H. J., D. Dytchkowskyj, and C. Nielsen. 2010. "Raw Material Variability, Use-Wear Accrual Rates and Addressing the Ambiguity of Some Use-Wear Traces: An Example from Northwestern New Mexico." *Rivista di Scienze Preistoriche* 60: 309–29.

Lévi-Sala, I. 1986. "Use Wear and Post-Depositional Surface Modification: A Word of Caution." *Journal of Archaeological Science* 13: 229–44.

———. 1993. "Use-Wear Traces: Processes of Development and Post-Depositional Alterations." In *Traces et fonction: Les Gestes Retrouvés, Éditions ERAUL 50, vol. 2*, ed. P. C. Anderson, S. Beyries, M. Otte, and H. Plisson, 401–16. Liège: Centre de Recherches Archéologiques du CNRS, Études et Recherches Archéologiques de l'Université de Liège.

———. 1996. *A Study of Microscopic Polish on Flint Implements*. Oxford: BAR International Series 629.

Lohse, E. S. 1996. "A Computerized Descriptive System for Functional Analysis of Stone Tools." *Tebiwa* 26(1): 3–66.

Lohse, E. S., and D. Sammons. 1999. "A Computerised Data Base for Lithic Use-Wear Analysis." In *Archaeology in the Age of the Internet CAA97. Computer Applications and Quantitative Methods in Archaeology*, ed. L. Dingwall, S. Exon, V. Gaffney, S. Laflin, and M. Van Leusen, 280-5 to 280-14. Oxford: BAR International Series 750 [CD-ROM].

Lyman, R. L., and M. J. O'Brien. 2000. "Measuring and Explaining Change in Artifact Variation with Clade-Diversity Diagrams." *Journal of Anthropological Archaeology* 19(1): 39–74.

MacArthur, R. H. 1965. "Patterns of Species Diversity." *Biological Reviews* 40(4): 510–33.

Macdonald, D. A. 2014. "The Application of Focus Variation Microscopy for Lithic Use-Wear Quantification." *Journal of Archaeological Science* 48: 26–33.

Macdonald, D. A., T. Bartkowiak, and W. J. Stemp. 2020. "Multiscalar 3D Curvature Analysis of Tool Edges as an Indicator of Cereal Harvesting Intensity." *Journal of Archaeological Science: Reports* 33: 102523.

Macdonald, D. A., and A. A. Evans. 2014. "Evaluating Surface Cleaning Techniques of Stone Tools Using Laser Scanning Confocal Microscopy." *Microscopy Today* 22: 22–26.

Macdonald, D. A., R. Harman, and A. A. Evans. 2018. "Replicating Surface Texture: Preliminary Testing of Molding Compound Accuracy for Surface Measurements." *Journal of Archaeological Science: Reports* 18: 839–46.

Macdonald, D. A., L. Xie, and T. Gallo. 2019. "Here's the Dirt: First Applications of Confocal Microscopy for Quantifying Microwear on Experimental Ground Stone Earth Working Tools." *Journal of Archaeological Science: Reports* 26: 101861.

Mansur, M. E. 1982. "Microwear Analysis of Natural and Use Striations: New Clues to the Mechanism of Striation Formation." In *Tailler! Pour quoi Faire: Préhistoire et Technologie Lithique II*, ed. D. Cahen, 213–33. Tervuren: Studia Praehistorica Belgica 2, Musée Royal de l'Afrique Central.

———. 1997. "Functional Analysis of Polished Stone-Tools: Some Considerations about the Nature of Polishing." In *Siliceous Rocks and Culture*, ed. A. Ramos-Millan and M. A. Bustillo, 465–86. Granada: Edicion Universidad de Granada.

Masson, A., E. Coqueugniot, and S. Roy. 1981. "Silice et Traces d'Usage: Le Lustre des Faucilles." *Nouvelles Archéologiques du Musée d'Histoire Naturel de Lyon* 19: 43–51.

May, R. 1975. "Patterns of Species Abundance and Diversity." In *Ecology and the Evolution of Communities*, ed. M. Cody and J. Diamond, 81–120. Cambridge: Belknap Press/Harvard University Press.

McCann, K. 2000. "The Diversity–Stability Debate." *Nature* 405: 228–33.

McCartney, P. H., and M. F. Glass. 1990. "Simulation Models and the Interpretation of Archaeological Diversity." *American Antiquity* 55(3): 521–36.

Meeks, N., G. Sieveking, M. Tite, and J. Cook. 1982. "Gloss and Use-Wear Traces on Flint Sickles and Similar Phenomena." *Journal of Archaeological Science* 9: 317–40.

Meltzer, D. J., R. D. Leonard, and S. K. Stratton. 1992. "The Relationship between Sample Size and Diversity in Archaeological Assemblages." *Journal of Archaeological Science* 19(4): 375–87.

O'Brien, M. J., M. T. Boulanger, B. Buchanan, M. Collard, R. L. Lyman, and J. Darwent. 2014. "Innovation and Cultural Transmission in the American Paleolithic: Phylogenetic Analysis of Eastern Paleoindian Projectile-Point Classes." *Journal of Anthropological Archaeology* 34: 100–119.

Odum, E. P. 1953. *Fundamentals of Ecology*. Philadelphia: W. B. Saunders, Co.

Ollé, A., A. Pedergnana, J. L. Fernández-Marchena, S. Martin, A. Borel, and V. Aranda. 2016. "Microwear Features on Vein Quartz, Rock Crystal and Quartzite: A Study Combining Optical Light and Scanning Electron Microscopy." *Quaternary International* 424: 154–70.

Ollé, A., and J. M. Vergès. 2008. "SEM Functional Analysis and the Mechanism of Microwear Formation." In *'Prehistoric Technology' 40 Years Later: Functional Studies and the Russian Legacy. Proceedings of the International Congress Verona (Italy), 20–23 April 2005*, ed. L. Longo and N. Skakun, 39–49. Oxford: BAR International Series 1783.

———. 2014. "The Use of Sequential Experiments and SEM in Documenting Stone Tool Microwear." *Journal of Archaeological Science* 48: 60–72.

Pedergnana, A., and A. Ollé. 2017. "Monitoring and Interpreting the Use-Wear Formation Processes on Quartzite Flakes through Sequential Experiments." *Quaternary International* 427B: 35–65.

Pedergnana, A., I. Calandra, A. A. Evans, K. Bob, A. Hildebrandt, and A. Ollé. 2020. "Polish Is Quantitatively Different on Quartzite Flakes Used on Different Worked Materials." *PloS one* 15: e0243295.

Peet, R. K. 1974. "The Measurement of Species Diversity." *Annual Review of Ecology Systematics* 5: 285–307.

Pielou, E. C. 1977. *Mathematical Ecology*. New York: Wiley.

Pijoan, J., J. A. Barceló, I. Clemente, and A. Vila. 2002. "Variabilidad Estadistica en Imagines Digitalizadas de Rastros de Uso: Resultados Preliminaries." In *Análisis Funcional. Su Aplicación al Estudio de Sociedades Prehistóricas*, ed. I. Clemente, R. Risch, and J. Gibaja, 55–64. Oxford: BAR International Series 1073.

Rhode, D. 1988. "Measurements of Archaeological Diversity and the Sample-Size Effect." *American Antiquity* 53: 708–16.

Rots, V., and H. Plisson. 2014. "Projectiles and the Abuse of the Use-Wear Method in a Search for Impact." *Journal of Archaeological Science* 48: 154–65.

Schmidt, P., A. Rodriguez, K. Yanamandra, R. K. Behera, and R. Iovita. 2020. "The Mineralogy and Structure of Use-Wear Polish on Chert." *Scientific Reports* 10: 1–9.

Semenov, S. A. 1964. *Prehistoric Technology*. New York: Barnes and Noble.

Shannon, C. E., and W. Weaver. (1949) 1962. *The Mathematical Theory of Communication*. Urbana: University of Illinois Press.

Simek, J. F. 1989. "Structure and Diversity in Intrasite Spatial Analysis." In *Quantifying Diversity in Archaeology*, ed. R. D. Leonard and G. T. Jones, 59–68. Cambridge: Cambridge University Press.

Simek, J., and H. Price. 1990. "Chronological Change in Perigord Lithic Assemblage Diversity." In *The Emergence of Modern Humans: An Archaeological Perspective*, ed. P. Mellars, 243–61. Edinburgh: University of Edinburgh Press.

Simpson, E. H. 1949. "Measurement of Diversity." *Nature* 163(4148): 688.

Šmit, Z., G. Grime, S. Petru, and I. Rajta. 1999. "Microdistribution and Composition of Use-wear Polish on Prehistoric Stone Tools." *Nuclear Instruments and Methods in Physics Research Section B: Beam Interactions with Materials and Atoms B* 150: 565–70.

Šmit, Z., S. Petru, G. Grime, T. Vidmar, M. Budnar, B. Zorko, and M. Ravnikar. 1998. "Use-wear-Induced Deposition on Prehistoric Flint Tools." *Nuclear Instruments and Methods in Physics Research Section B: Beam Interactions with Materials and Atoms B* 140: 209–16.

Solow, A., and S. Polasky. 1994. "Measuring Biological Diversity." *Environmental Ecology Statistics* 1: 95–107.

Stemp W. J. 2014. "A Review of Quantification of Lithic Use-Wear Using Laser Profilometry: A Method Based on Metrology and Fractal Analysis." *Journal of Archaeological Science* 48: 15–25.

———. 2016a. "Coastal Maya Obsidian Tool Use and Socio-Economy in the Late Postclassic–Early Spanish Colonial Period at San Pedro, Ambergris Caye, Belize." *Journal of Field Archaeology* 41(2): 162–76.

———. 2016b. "Explorations in Ancient Maya Blood-Letting: Experimentation and Microscopic Use-wear Analysis of Obsidian Blades." *Journal of Archaeological Science: Reports* 7: 368–78.

———. 2016c. "Twist and Shout: Experiments in Ancient Maya Blood-Letting by Piercing with Obsidian Blades and Splinters." *Journal of Archaeological Science: Reports* 9: 134–42.

Stemp, W. J., M. D. Andruskiewicz, M. A. Gleason, and Y. H. Rashid. 2015. "Experiments in Ancient Maya Blood-Letting: Quantification of Surface Wear on Obsidian Blades." *Archaeological and Anthropological Sciences* 7(4): 423–39.

Stemp, W. J., and J. J. Awe. 2014. "Ritual Use of Obsidian from Maya Caves in Belize: A Functional and Symbolic Analysis." In *Obsidian Reflections: Symbolic Dimensions of Obsidian in Mesoamerica*, ed. M. N. Levine and D. M. Carballo, 223–54. Boulder: University of Colorado Press.

Stemp, W. J., G. E. Braswell, C. G. B. Helmke, and J. J. Awe. 2018. "An Ancient Maya Ritual Cache at Pook's Hill, Belize: Technological and Functional Analyses of the Obsidian Blades." *Journal of Archaeological Science: Reports* 18: 889–901.

Stemp, W. J., B. E. Childs, and S. Vionnet. 2010. "Laser Profilometry and Length-Scale Analysis of Stone Tools: Second Series Experiment Results." *Scanning* 32: 233–43.

Stemp, W. J., B. E. Childs, S. Vionnet, and C. A. Brown. 2009. "Quantification and Discrimination of Lithic Use-Wear: Surface Profile Measurements and Length-Scale Fractal Analysis." *Archaeometry* 51: 366–82.

Stemp, W. J., and S. Chung. 2011. "Discrimination of Surface Wear on Obsidian Tools Using LSCM and RelA: Pilot Study Results." *Scanning* 33: 279–93.

Stemp, W. J., A. A. Evans, and H. J. Lerner. 2012. "Reaping the Rewards: The Potential of Well Designed Methodology, a Comment on Vardi et al. (*Journal of Archaeological Science* 37(2010): 1716–24) and Goodale et al. (*Journal of Archaeological Science* 37(2010): 1192–1201)." *Journal of Archaeological Science* 39: 1901–4.

Stemp, W. J., H. J. Lerner, and E. H. Kristant. 2013. "Quantifying Microwear on Experimental Mistassini Quartzite Scrapers: Preliminary Results of Exploratory Research using LSCM and Scale-Sensitive Fractal Analysis." *Scanning* 35: 28–39.

———. 2018. "Testing Area-Scale Fractal Complexity (Asfc) and Laser Scanning Confocal Microscopy (LSCM) to Document and Discriminate Microwear on Experimental Quartzite Scrapers." *Archaeometry* 60(4): 660–77.

Stemp, W. J., D. A. Macdonald, and M. A. Gleason. 2019. "Testing Imaging Confocal Microscopy, Laser Scanning Confocal Microscopy, and Focus Variation Microscopy for Microscale Measurement of Edge Cross-Sections and Calculation of Edge Curvature on Stone Tools: Preliminary Results." *Journal of Archaeological Science: Reports* 24: 513–25.

Stemp, W. J., M. Morozov, and A. J. M. Key. 2015. "Quantifying Lithic Microwear with Load Variation on Experimental Basalt Flakes Using LSCM and Area-Scale Fractal Complexity (Asfc)." *Surface Topography: Metrology and Properties* 3:3.

Stemp, W. J., M. Peuramaki-Brown, and J. J. Awe. 2019. "Ritual Economy and Ancient Maya Bloodletting: Obsidian Blades from Actun Uayazba Kab (Handprint Cave), Belize." *Journal of Anthropological Archaeology* 53: 304–24.

Stemp, W. J., and M. Stemp. 2001. "UBM Laser Profilometry and Lithic Use-Wear Analysis: A Variable Length Scale Investigation of Surface Topography." *Journal of Archaeological Science* 28: 81–88.

———. 2003. "Documenting Stages of Polish Development on Experimental Stone Tools: Surface Characterization by Fractal Geometry Using UBM Laser Profilometry." *Journal of Archaeological Science* 30: 287–96.

Stemp, W. J., A. S. Watson, and A. A. Evans. 2016. "Surface Analysis of Stone and Bone Tools." *Surface Topography: Metrology and Properties* 4(1): 013001.

Stevens, N. E., D. R. Harro, and A. Hicklin. 2010. "Practical Quantitative Lithic Use-Wear Analysis Using Multiple Classifiers." *Journal of Archaeological Science* 37: 2671–78.

Tringham, R., G. Cooper, G. Odell, B. Voytek, and A. Whitman. 1974. "Experimentation in the Formation of Edge Damage: A New Approach to Lithic Analysis." *Journal of Field Archaeology* 1: 171–96.

Unger-Hamilton, R. 1984. "The Formation of Use-Wear Polish on Flint: Beyond the 'Deposit vs. Abrasion' Controversy." *Journal of Archaeological Science* 11: 91–98.

Van den Dries, M. H. 1994. "WAVES: An Expert System for the Analysis of Use-Wear on Flint Artefacts." In *Methods in the Mountains*, ed. I. Johnson, 173–81. Sydney University Archaeological Methods Series 2.

———. 1998. *Archaeology and the Application of Artificial Intelligence: Case Studies on Use-wear Analysis of Prehistoric Flint Tools.* Archaeological Studies, Leiden University 1, Faculty of Archaeology.

van Gijn, A. L. 1990. *The Wear and Tear of Flint: Principles of Functional Analysis Applied to Dutch Neolithic Assemblages.* Leiden: Analecta Praehistorica Leidensia 22.

———. 2014. "Science and Interpretation in Microwear Studies." *Journal of Archaeological Science* 48: 166–69.

Vardi, J., A. Golan, D. Levy, and I. Gilead. 2010. "Tracing Sickle Blade Levels of Wear and Discard Patterns: A New Sickle Gloss Quantification Method." *Journal of Archaeological Science* 37: 1716–24.

Vaughan, P. C. 1985. *Use-Wear Analysis of Flaked Stone Tools.* Tucson: University of Arizona Press.

Vila, A., and F. Gallart. 1993. "Caracterización de los Micropulidos de Uso: Ejemplo de Aplicación del Análisis de Imagines Digitalizadas." In *Traces et Fonction: Les Gestes Retrouvés, Éditions ERAUL 50, vol. 2,* ed. P. C. Anderson, S. Beyries, M. Otte, and H. Plisson, 459–66. Liège: Centre de Recherches Archéologiques du CNRS, Études et Recherches Archéologiques de l'Université de Liège.

Weitzman, M. 1992. "On Diversity." *The Quarterly Journal of Economics* 107: 363–405.

Werner, J. J. 2018. "An Experimental Investigation of the Effects of Post-Depositional Damage on Current Quantitative Use-Wear Methods." *Journal of Archaeological Science: Reports* 17: 597–604.

Whittaker, J., D. Caulkins, and K. Kamp. 1998. "Evaluating Consistency in Typology and Classification." *Journal of Archaeological Method and Theory* 5: 129–64.

Wilkins, J., B. J. Schoville, and K. S. Brown. 2014. "An Experimental Investigation of the Functional Hypothesis and Evolutionary Advantage of Stone-Tipped Spears." *PLoS ONE* 9: e104514.

Wilkins, J., B. J. Schoville, K. S. Brown, and M. Chazan. 2012. "Evidence for Early Hafted Hunting Technology." *Science* 338: 942–46.

Yamada, S. 1993. "The Formation Process of 'Use-Wear Polishes.'" In *Traces et Fonction: Les Gestes Retrouvés, Éditions ERAUL 50, vol. 2,* ed. P. C. Anderson, S. Beyries, M. Otte, and H. Plisson, 433–45. Liège: Centre de Recherches Archéologiques du CNRS, Études et Recherches Archéologiques de l'Université de Liège.

Chapter 6

Intensification Mechanisms Driving Dietary Change among the Great Plains Big Game Hunters of North America

Erik Otárola-Castillo, Melissa G. Torquato, and Matthew E. Hill

⸺⸺⸻◯✖✖◯⸻⸺⸺

Studies of dietary diversity are prominent in the zooarchaeological literature, and have been pivotal to understanding prehistoric economies. Investigations of diachronic changes in economic strategies have focused on a broad selection of topics, including human–environment interactions, human ecological adaptations, the origins of farming, human-caused extinctions and animal translocation, and the development of social complexity (e.g., Boivin et al. 2016; Broughton 1999, 2002; DeAngelis and Lyman 2018; Munro et al. 2018; Nagaoka 2002; Stiner and Munro 2002; Weitzel 2019). Such studies often attempt to understand the factors contributing to changes in dietary diversity, focusing on the idea of resource intensification, or Boserup's Theory, which is commonly defined as the ability of human populations to obtain more food in a given unit of time, labor, or space (Binford 2001: 357; Boserup 1965; Broughton 1994b).

Boserup posited that when humans intensify food production, they incur a decline in productive efficiency, as increasing the food yield involves a disproportionate increase in costs relative to gains. Anthropologists have vigorously debated Boserup's Theory and the definition of intensification (Betts and Friesen 2004; Earle 1980; Matson 1983; Morrison 1994). Some have argued that intensification can occur even without a decline in efficiency (e.g., Brookfield 1972; Leach 1999; Morgan 2015; Morrison 1994). Others have focused on understanding what they call the "component strategies" of resource intensification, or what we term the "mechanisms" of intensification. We define a mechanism as an integrated process through which humans may achieve resource intensification. Some of the most studied intensification mechanisms are specialization, diversification, and investment (Betts and Friesen 2004; Morrison 1994). In zooarchaeology, specialization refers to economic strategies through which hunters focus on procuring a narrow range of species, typically with an associated decline in the procurement of other species (Lyman 1989, 1991). Diversification, meanwhile, is an intensification strategy through which hunters rely on a broader range of food species, or change the organization of the types of species procured.

Archaeologists have observed material culture representing both diversified and specialized economies across the North American Great Plains and its adjacent regions. Economic systems in this region have a record of at least thirteen thousand years of variation, likely due, at least in part, to diachronic (temporal) and synchronic (regional) variability in environmental conditions, and human and prey population pressures. Despite this variation, an apparent big-game hunting specialization seems to have persisted in this region alongside more diversified strategies, including a broad spectrum of small-to-medium-sized prey (Kelly and Todd 1988). This hunting-focused specialization lasted much longer than it did in many other regions of North America, where domesticates were adopted earlier (Fagan 2018; Neusius and Gross 2013). Early Great Plains archaeologists have proposed a simplified progression of subsistence intensification through time. This hypothesis starts with specialized big-game hunters in the Paleoindian period (13,500–9,000 BP) to the Late Prehistoric period (1,000–300 BP), which was then characterized by a diversified economy that included gathered, hunted, and domesticated resources (e.g., Lehmer 1971: 30–33; Liberty and Wood 1980: 37–41; Wedel 1940, 1953: 509).

Although recent research has presented much more nuanced inferences regarding the subsistence economies of peoples on the Great Plains, the hypothesized trend toward resource intensification has remained. For example, researchers have begun to question the traditional view of Paleoindians as big-prey hunting specialists (Blackmar and Hofman 2006; DeAngelis and Lyman 2018; Hill 2007a, 2008; Kornfeld and Larson 2008; Kornfeld et al. 2007). Studies of later periods on the plains have acknowledged a broader range of regional variability in subsistence practices, including an increasing diversity of hunted and gathered foods. Researchers have also documented the appearance and intensification of domesticated resources during the Woodland and Late Prehistoric periods (e.g., Adair and Drass 2011; Bozell, Falk, and Johnson 2011). Investigating the economic variability observed across this vast region has great potential to shed light on the broad range of behaviors and technologies driving the intensification mechanisms used by human populations to produce food.

Consequently, to evaluate the hypothesis that small-scale, prehistoric societies of the Great Plains increasingly and unidirectionally intensified their resource base over time, this study investigates the broad patterns of change in the economic strategies used by Great Plains indigenous communities. We examine the hunting and gathering economies of the Paleoindian period through to the farming societies of the Late Prehistoric period to compare how populations approached the intensification of a similar suite of faunal resources. It is important to note, however, that during the early Paleoindian period, some Great Plains foragers would have had access to species of megafauna that would be unavailable to their later counterparts. By the same token, bison seem to have filled the big game niche for the foragers and farmers living on the plains throughout the Holocene. We focus on the long-term use of intensification mechanisms within major habitat settings of the Great Plains and the Rocky Mountains, including alluvial valleys, foothills and mountains, and plains and rolling hills (Hill 2008; Knell and Hill 2012).

To test the hypothesis and track subsistence shifts through time, we use faunal evidence of more than two hundred zooarchaeological assemblages from across the North American Great Plains and adjacent regions, dating from the last 13,500 years. We assess the variability of dietary diversity via species richness and evenness, including the relative ratios of different sized prey, across the geographical extent of the Great Plains through time. In doing so, this study yields a better understanding of the long-term trends in the intensification of the human use of animals in this region.

Before describing the methods and results of this study, we provide a summary of prior zooarchaeological approaches to the study of animal resource intensification. In part, we discuss how our preceding work on Paleoindian subsistence has laid the foundation for a comparative study of later periods. The large temporal scale of our study provides a more comprehensive understanding of the economic strategies of prehistoric Great Plains foragers and farmers within the changing paleoenvironmental conditions in which these groups lived.

Zooarchaeological Approaches to Intensification

Boserup (1965) coined the term "resource intensification" in response to contemporary economists' application of the Malthusian paradigm (Malthus 1798) for understanding the population dynamics of small-scale farming societies. Boserup argued that, from a Malthusian perspective, small-scale farmers had little control over their population growth, which was instead controlled by the food supply available to these "primitive" farmers. In effect, the Malthusians viewed historical changes in human population sizes as the product of technological developments that generated increases in food productivity. For Boserup, however, the notion of food production as the ultimate limiting factor of population growth did not capture the reality of either ancient or contemporary small-scale populations. Instead, this idea likely reflected contemporaneous West European agricultural practices, which were characterized by extensive expansion to create new cultivation fields. By contrast, Boserup argued that human population growth was the driving force for increasing food productivity via *intensive* rather than *extensive* food production.

Over the past fifty years, archaeologists have elaborated many definitions of resource intensification, often depending on whether the focus of the research was on agricultural or hunter-gatherer societies (Moss 2012; Thurston and Fisher 2007). Zooarchaeologists have argued that the increase in foraging productivity via intensification arises through the mechanisms of specialization, diversification, and investment (Butler and Campbell 2004; Moss 2012). Diversification and specialization subsistence strategies are complex. Although some have hypothesized that for past societies these strategies would be mutually exclusive, or two ends of a continuum (e.g., Cleland 1976; Dunnell 1967), Betts and Friesen (2004: 359) argue that this is incorrect. In fact, when considered over a long period of time, specialization and diversification may emerge as complementary strategies. Investment in new technologies or behaviors is often directly tied to strategies of specialization and diversification (Binford 1980, 2001: 189). Yet, as Earle (1980) notes, increased investments and specialization may contribute to resource intensification up to a point, but only diversification will allow for further intensification. Below, we use these mechanisms to structure a summary of how recent zooarchaeologists have identified and used the concept of faunal resource intensification (Betts and Friesen 2004; Morrison 1994).

Especially in non-agricultural societies, archaeologists have often viewed specialization as a path to increased efficiency. In their discussion of the adaptations of the peopling of the Americas, Kelly and Todd (1988) hypothesized that a high-technology, highly specialized big-prey hunting strategy might have enabled early foragers to move through the new landscape, regardless of the environmental setting or seasonality. Recent research has inferred that early hunters in North America were indeed big-game hunting specialists (e.g., Surovell and Waguespack 2008, 2009); however, the hunting specialization hypothesis might be too simplistic to capture the variability of these foragers' hunting behaviors (e.g., Cannon and Meltzer 2008; DeAngelis and Lyman 2018; Haynes and Hutson 2014; Hill 2007a, 2008). In addition, in studies of Paleoindian foraging and prey use in the Great Plains and Rocky Mountains researchers (Hill 2007a, 2007b, 2008; Hill and Knell 2013; Knell and Hill 2012; and Otárola-Castillo 2016) have found statistically meaningful differences in prey use across habitats, potentially by the same hunting groups. For example, in the High Plains grasslands, there was low temporal and spatial predictability of important game and other biotic and non-biotic resources. This habitat likely provided a selective advantage for Paleoindian hunters to approach prey choice with a more specialist stance. At the same time, the same hunter may have found it better to practice a more generalist diet in an alluvial valley habitat, where resources were more predictable. These findings highlight the flexibility with which these early foraging groups behaved.

Researchers studying North America during later periods have also observed specialization among hunter-gatherers. In the northern plains, for example, researchers have proposed that Middle Holocene (~8,500–5,500 years ago) foragers were specialized bison hunters, perhaps in response to the paucity of alternative plant or animal resources in the region (Forbis 1982; Frison 1998a; Robertson 2011). Research from the Pacific Northwest has suggested a causal link between the economic surplus arising from fishing specialization and the region's increasing social complexity over the last 3,500 years (e.g., Butler and Campbell 2004; Coupland, Stewart, and Patton 2010; Fladmark 1975; Matson and Coupland 1995; Moss 2012).

Studies on the origins of herding and farming have frequently used Boserup's Theory to explain that domestication was rooted in a decline in foraging efficiency (Weitzel 2019). However, there has been disagreement about whether declines in foraging efficiencies were due to population increases (i.e., demographic packing; Broughton 1994b; Munro 2004; Munro et al. 2018; Stiner et al. 1999; 2000) or environmental change (Gremillion and Piperno 2009). Most researchers who have examined the rise of farming in connection with foraging declines have inferred that the mechanism of resource intensification was diversification (Munro 2009; Zeder 2012), as members of hunting and gathering economies adopted new strategies or technologies to exploit previously unrealized parts of their dietary niche. However, in this case, the increased cost of the behavioral or technological investment would have decreased the overall dietary efficiency (e.g., Bettinger, Winterhalder, and McElreath 2006; Munro 2009; Ugan, Bright, and Rogers 2003).

Flannery (1968) famously coined the term Broad Spectrum Revolution (BSR) to describe the dietary diversification strategy adopted by foraging societies, which led to the emergence of Neolithic farmer societies as part of a long-term trend of resource intensification caused by increasing population pressures (see review in Zeder 2012). To investigate the hypotheses of the BSR, researchers have increasingly employed Optimal Foraging

Theory (OFT) as a quantitative hypothesis testing framework (Broughton, Cannon, and Bartelink 2010; Byers and Broughton 2004; Gremillion
2004; Gremillion, Barton, and Piperno 2014; Winterhalder 1986; however, see a critique of OFT for studying the origins of domestication in
B. D. Smith 2011, 2015; Zeder 2012, 2015, 2016). Classic OFT heuristics
like the diet breadth model (DBM), also known as the prey model or prey
choice model, predict when and how foragers will diversify their diet base.
These models assume that foragers rank all prey according to their rate of
energy acquisition over the time spent foraging (E/T) and that they tend
to maximize this ratio. The DBM suggests that when high-ranked prey
become scarcer, foragers should diversify their diet by including low E/T-
ranked prey.

In this context, OFT and the DBM have been successful at generating testable hypotheses regarding foraging and farming populations (Bettinger and Grote 2016; Bird and O'Connell 2006). However, Stiner and
colleagues (Stiner 2001; Stiner and Munro 2002; Stiner et al. 2000; Stiner
et al. 1999; Zeder 2012) have challenged Flannery's original conceptual-
ization of the BSR in the Mediterranean Basin based on their application
of foraging theory. Rather than following traditional Linnaean taxonomic
categories, Stiner and colleagues used alternative classifications as the basis
for measuring the change in dietary diversity. They argued that there were
clear archaeological signals for the BSR when focusing on the practical
differences between prey—for example, the prey handling costs (e.g., pursuit, capture, and processing) associated with pursuing small versus large
prey. Results of Stiner and colleagues' work showed that Mediterranean
societies during the Late Pleistocene shifted away from slow-moving
prey, such as tortoises and shellfish, and increasingly began including fast-
moving prey, such as birds, hares, and rabbits, in their diet. The researchers
attributed these changes in prey use to demographically driven resource
pressures.

In North America, there have been numerous applications of OFT principles in order to understand the subsistence strategies of hunter-gatherer
and farming populations (Bettinger and Grote 2016; Bird and O'Connell
2006). For example, Barlow (2002) argued that increases in maize agriculture in the Great Basin were likely due to long-term decreases in wild
prey and plant resources. Broughton (1997, 1999) showed that occupants
of the Emeryville Shell mound in San Francisco Bay broadened their diet
breadth by including low-ranked prey such as marine mammals, mollusks,
small fish, and acorns. Broughton proposed that this type of resource intensification was a response to declines in high-ranked prey such as elk,
deer, and large fish. Likewise, the McElmo Dome area of Mesa Verde, in
southwestern Colorado, provides an example of macro-nutrient intensifi-

cation. In this study, Ellyson, Nagaoka, and Wolverton (2019) used predictions from OFT to contextualize their analysis of faunal remains left by farmer-gatherer-hunters who occupied the area during AD 900–1280. The subsistence system at Mesa Verde depended on both hunting and husbandry practices. However, when the availability of hunted prey declined, the people at Mesa Verde intensified turkey husbandry practices, likely in order to maintain appropriate levels of protein intake. In the Eastern United States, Weitzel (2019) demonstrated that the overall foraging efficiency of hunted prey gradually declined in the middle Tennessee River; occupants responded by gradually intensifying their resources through dietary diversification. Finally, in the Mimbres Valley of New Mexico, Cannon (2001) investigated whether people there adopted farming as a form of resource intensification. As in Flannery's BSR, dietary diversification might have played a precursory role in plant domestication in North America. Cannon documented that prey resource depression took place in the period immediately before the appearance of domestication in the region. Based on these results, Cannon argued that cultivation was indeed a form of resource intensification.

Recent studies have shown that, even in situations with long-term intensification trends, such tendencies may not be unidirectional or uniform across habitats. Weitzel (2019), for example, pointed out that, although foraging efficiency progressively declined in wetland patches, the same did not occur in terrestrial patches, where there was a general increase in foraging efficiency before initial domestication. Similarly, in a large faunal analysis from the Late Archaic through the Hohokam post-Classic period of the Sonoran Desert, Dean and colleagues identified a pattern of intensification via diversification of hunting strategies, which seems to have taken place in the time leading up to the adoption of farming (Beaver and Dean 2019; Dean 2007, 2017). However, for the Hohokam groups in this study, the adoption of agriculture created constraints on hunting intensification through gendered labor demands associated with canal irrigation and associated anthropogenic modifications to the landscape.

Investment is the last aspect of intensification. Humans and other animals differ in the degree to which they rely on technology to interact with their environment. Humans use a wide array of tools and features as part of their subsistence technology (Oswalt 1976). Hunters use weapons, tools, and structures to help them trap and kill their prey, process their carcasses, store animal products and then transform them into food and other useful products (e.g., clothes, shelter), and increase resource production when under population pressure (Flannery 1972: 417). As discussed above, there is an assumption that better technology increases the number of resources acquired. However, that technology comes with a cost of time (labor) to acquire the raw material, produce the technology, and maintain or repair that technology (e.g., Bleed 1986; Bright, Ugan, and Hunsaker 2002; Kuhn 1994; Metcalfe and Barlow 1992). As Ugan, Bright, and Rogers (2003) note, the costs of technology are just as substantial as the benefits derived from its use. We keep in mind two factors when comparing the time cost of technology. The first is the actual time invested in the creation and use of technology. The second is the time that hunters would otherwise spend foraging if the technology were not involved. As with all technology, its use is not always functional for maximizing returns. Decoration, construction, and use of technology also have symbolic or social values that are not viewed the same as caloric returns.

Since Flannery formulated and popularized the idea of the BSR as a type of resource intensification, researchers have focused on discovering other *formal* intensification mechanisms that have driven many large-scale human economic transitions, often using zooarchaeological data. This study documents the intensification mechanisms employed over time on the Great Plains. In the following section, we provide a brief background on the cultural history and environmental constraints of this region.

Great Plains Cultures and Paleoenvironment

This study expands on our earlier work examining the processes and resulting patterns of animal use across the Great Plains and adjacent regions during the Paleoindian period in the context of the longer-term cultural history of the area (see Fig 6.3 for map of region). In particular, we assess whether the apparent habitat differences in prey choice observed during the Paleoindian period are present later by tracking changes in the long-term foraging practices of peoples on the Great Plains. The archaeological record of this region covers a 13,500-year period of significant climatic and environmental changes. We discuss the degree to which shifts in human demography, mobility, and technology affected subsistence practices geared toward the intensification of resource production.

Before European settlement, a complex series of grassland plant and animal communities inhabited the North American Great Plains. The story of these biological communities began during the grassland expansion that occurred approximately 5–7 million years ago. Increased climatic aridity catalyzed this shift during the Miocene–Pliocene transition. The resulting decline in woodlands promoted an increased abundance of C_4 grasses, and facilitated the coevolution of mammals adapted to grazing and open habitats (Anderson 2006; Axelrod 1985; Mack and Thompson 1982). These factors shaped the composition of the Great Plains grasslands' biological communities and their organismal characteristics. Particularly crucial to the evolution of human occupation in this region, the plains hosted the coevolution of a mutually beneficial relationship between large mammal grazers and primary producers (grasses). At least as far back as the Pleistocene–Holocene transition, the structure of this and other community interactions varied according to the Great Plains' west to east precipitation cline and its north to south temperature gradient (Küchler 1965; Tieszen et al. 1997).

Tallgrass or mixed-grass prairies occurred across most of the eastern plains. Greater precipitation trends along the eastern borders of the plains supported tallgrass prairie grasses intermixed with oak, walnut, and hickory woodlands. Mixed-grass prairies and some gallery forest along major riverways covered the central plains (Iowa, Missouri, Kansas). The western portion of the plains became true shortgrass prairies, stretching to the front range of the Rocky Mountains (Coupland 1992; Küchler 1965; Tieszen et al. 1997; Weaver 1968). A high degree of spatial and temporal variability in climatic conditions over time influenced the distribution of vegetation and fauna, and instigated dramatic shifts in human land use and subsistence activities.

The gradients of temperature and precipitation on the Great Plains mean that the northwestern portions are generally cooler and drier. In comparison, the southern and eastern portions are generally warmer and wetter (Tieszen et al. 1997). This environmental variation underlies a gradient of grass adaptation, most notably reflected in the morphological cline ranging from tall to short grass species. Such evolutionary adaptations shaped an inverse relationship between grass height and the total edible portion of the grass (Frank, Kuns, and Guido 2002; Frank and McNaughton 1993; Frank, McNaughton, and Tracy 1998; McNaughton 1984). As a result, the western short grasses of the High Plains likely supported higher concentrations of large grazers than the mixed-grass or tallgrass prairies (Frank and McNaughton 1993; Otárola-Castillo 2016). Except in times of extreme drought, hunters would have likely found the High Plains region to be the most productive big-prey hunting area. After horticulture emerged in this region, the wetter and warmer conditions, including the higher levels of nitrogen in the soil, made the tallgrass prairie and eastern mixed-grass settings more attractive for dryland farming (Lauenroth, Burke, and Gutmann 1999).

Native cultures have existed on the Great Plains for at least 13,300 years, although claims that occupations of the plains and adjacent areas took place as much as 15,000 years ago are currently being debated (Miller 2018; Waters 2019). The first archaeological period (Paleoindian) on the Great Plains dates from approximately 13,300–8,000 BP. Paleoclimatic research of the Great Plains suggests that the Paleoindian period was generally cooler than later in the Holocene, with higher effective moisture and a high frequency of fluctuations in temperature regimes (e.g., Dansgaard et al. 1969; Williams, Brooks, and Seastedt 1998). Following the retreat of the Laurentide glacier by roughly 8,000 BP, the eastern portion of the northern plains saw a gradual transition from largely parkland vegetation to a mixed-grass savanna. Temperate grassland vegetation covered the northwestern plains, including more scattered forests and parklands (Betancourt et al. 2001; Dean and Schwalb 2000; Yansa 1998, 2006). In the southern plains, although some eastern regions have shown evidence of forests (especially before about 9,000 BP), grasslands or savanna conditions dominated most of the region, except with some scattered trees in well-watered valleys (Balinsky 1998; Betancourt et al. 2001; Bousman 1998; Fredlund, Bousman, and Boyd 1998; Holliday 1995; Johnson 1987; Theler 2003).

Groups living during this period maintained high degrees of residential mobility, but exhibited significant technological and economic differences from one another compared to later periods. There is a paucity of direct archaeological evidence for the use of plants or the presence of plant processing equipment (Adair and Drass 2011; Blackmar and Hofman 2006). Some Clovis-age plains sites have yielded evidence of human-produced artifacts in direct association with remains from extinct species, including mammoth, mastodon, bison, camels, and horses, suggesting that human predation may have been one factor contributing to the loss of those animals in North America (Broughton and Weitzel 2018; Meltzer 2015; Surovell and Waguespack 2009; Widga et al. 2017).

A research question that has generated much attention is whether Great Plains Paleoindians specialized in hunting big game. While there is little consensus on this topic, it is empirically challenging to rigidly categorize Paleoindian groups as solely specialized or generalized foragers, as evidence across sites shows substantial use of large, medium, and small prey. It is likely most appropriate to characterize these foragers as having practiced a seasonally and geographically flexible economy (Cannon and Meltzer 2008; DeAngelis and Lyman 2018; Hill 2007a, 2008; Kornfeld 2007; Kornfeld and Larson 2008; Surovell and Waguespack 2008). However, with the extinction of the Pleistocene megafauna, bison became the primary large-body prey, and archaeologists have discovered numerous single- and repeat-event bison kill localities across the plains (Bozell et al. 2011). Bison hunting was a year-round activity, with most kills being relatively small in size, and probably organized and executed by a single extended family (Hill 2013). Nonetheless, some Paleoindian groups, like the Cody complex, were skilled at conducting enormous, likely communal bison kills (>100 animals), at least on occasion (Bamforth 2011; Hill 2013; c.f. Hofman 1994).

The early to middle Holocene drying appears to have been a significant climatic event. The warmer, drier conditions led to the increasing dominance of drought-tolerant grasslands covering much of the plains. Primarily during severe drought, bare areas may have formed on the upland surface vegetation. Especially in central and southern regions of the Great Plains, the loss of surface vegetation resulted in massive eolian sedimentation and alluvial downcutting during this period (Bettis and Mandel 2002; Forman, Oglesby, and Webb 2001; Halfen and Johnson 2013). Drought conditions also resulted in significant declines in the availability of surface water. In the northeast, this often resulted in the appearance of more brackish wetlands, while in the south and far west, many springs and streams disappeared (Holliday 1995; Johnson 1987).

Starting around 6,000 BP (and established by about 4,000 BP), conditions across the Great Plains became cooler and wetter—conditions that have continued to modern times (Barnosky 1989; Clark et al. 2002). The expression and timing of this climatic amelioration varied across the region. In the dry western plains, increased precipitation reactivated spring-fed streams and marshes around 4,500 BP. In the northern plains, increased precipitation meant that short-grass prairie vegetation cover was sufficient to cease or at least dramatically slow soil erosion during the late Holocene. Despite the cooler and wetter conditions of this period, the late Holocene exhibited cyclical wet–dry periods. The drought periods could be quite severe and multidecadal, some even lasting a century (Clark et al. 2002; Halfen and Johnson 2013; Shuman and Marsicek 2016). These extended drought periods were so intense that they reactivated dune fields and increased eolian activity. In the warmer and drier central and southern plains, these droughts contributed to severe erosion in the small alluvial valleys, which would then aggregate in the more extensive alluvial valleys (Bettis and Mandel 2002; Robertson 2011).

Researchers have argued that generalized hunting-gathering economies characterized the Archaic period (8,000–2,000 BP), with increasing regional differences in terms of technology, subsistence, and mobility. In many parts of the Great Plains, the Archaic economies and lifeways differed greatly from those of Paleoindian groups (Blackmar and Hofman 2006; Frison 1998a, 1998b). Unlike in the Paleoindian period, however, periodic droughts during the Archaic may have resulted in the depleted use or even abandonment of the driest portions of the plains (Meltzer 1999). Bison procurement of mostly cow-calf herds continued throughout this period across much of the plains (Frison 1998a, 2001; Johnson 1987; Widga 2004, 2006). Mass communal kills were often conducted with the addition of jumps, arroyo traps, or surrounds, mostly in the northwestern and southern plains (Byerly et al. 2005; Frison 1970, 1998a, 2001; Lobdell 1973; Mulloy 1954). At least 5,000 years ago, these large-game hunters began to extract bone grease from carcasses (Walker 1992). Bison were, of course, not the only prey used by Archaic groups; evidence has indicated the importance of deer, pronghorn, elk, fish, rabbits, rodents, reptiles, and mussels in the diet, although these might have functioned as lower-ranked resources (Ahler and Toom 1995; Dyck and Morlan 2001; Haury 2005; Schmits 1978; Widga 2004).

On the eastern portions of the plains, Archaic groups demonstrated a higher degree of sedentism, and more complex and diversified adaptations than other plains Archaic groups (Adair and Drass 2011: 309; Kay 1998). Archaic groups introduced new technologies to the Great Plains, including bone and clay beads (Schmits 1978; Thies 1990), clay effigies (Witty and Reynolds 1982), fiber-tempered ceramics (Reid 1983), chipped-stone harvesting tools (Witty and Reynolds 1982), grinding stones, and earth ovens. Evidence for the use of plants became increasingly more common than in earlier periods, especially in the eastern plains during the Archaic (Adair 2006; Adair and Drass 2011; Kay 1998).

The Woodland period (2,500–1,000 BP) was a time of major regional social and economic innovation. Indigenous people across much of the plains began to make and use ceramic vessels regularly, enabling improved efficiency in cooking and grease extraction. Other economic shifts occurred as people gradually switched from the atlatl to the bow-and-arrow, and added the cultivation of domesticated plants to their repertoire of wild plant foods (Adair and Drass 2011; Johnson and Johnson 1998). Population size and residential sedentism significantly increased during the Woodland, especially in the eastern plains. People became more socially integrated during this period. This greater group cohesion is indicated by the communal use of burial mounds, and extensive sharing of technologies, symbols, and rituals (Adair 2012; Adair and Drass 2011).

In the drier western and the northern plains, some groups remained aceramic societies that continued to extensively use bison and pronghorn (Bozell et al. 2011; Frison 1998a, 2001; Johnson 1987; Kehoe 1973). In the far northwest, several Woodland sites, such as Head-Smashed-In, Gull Lake, and Wardell, reflect intensive and repeat mass harvesting of bison. At sites like these, very large, stratified bison bonebeds have been found at the base of cliff faces or associated with corral structures (Frison 2004; Kehoe 1973; Kornfeld, Frison, and Larson 2010). In the east, groups adopted a horticultural economy, became less mobile, and hunted fewer bison. However, they consumed a substantially broader diet of medium- and small-bodied animals. In these areas, Woodland people consistently exploited a wide range of taxa in their diets, including low-ranked fish, birds, turtles, and various small mammals, alongside larger prey such as deer and bison (Wismer 2018). Common elements at many Woodland sites were stone-filled pits and hearths associated with roasting and cooking meat, and grease extraction.

In the last 1,000 years of prehistory, a diverse array of Late Prehistoric groups appeared across the plains, characterized by considerably larger population sizes. Late Prehistoric people were more dependent on agriculture than their earlier Woodland counterparts. However, they used similar native seed crops, and introduced new cultigens (maize, bean, squash). Late Prehistoric sites reflect a high level of sedentism, usually marked by the construction of large houses used year-round, and a greater intensity of farming. Initially, farming communities were small, ranging from individual farmsteads to hamlets. Later, many people organized into large permanent villages. Ceramic technology became prominent, serving multiple functions (e.g., cooking, storage) and beginning to reflect regionally distinct technological traditions. These societies were economically largely self-sufficient, but often participated in extensive exchange networks involving groups within and outside the plains.

Despite the importance of agriculture, with few exceptions, hunting was still an essential part of Late Prehistoric economies. Massive bison kills took place, especially in the northwestern plains. Although communal hunts were probably not utilized everywhere, nonetheless, bison continued to be a central part of the subsistence across most of the plains (Bozell et al. 2011). Later groups developed a dual economic system composed of hunting and farming, organizing logistical parties for the long-distance hunting of bison scheduled around the planting and harvesting seasons. However, most hunting probably focused on more locally available resources, including deer and elk, and a diversity of smaller prey such as rabbits, turtles, dogs, furbearers, rodents, and a variety of fish. In this context, the central plains tradition in Kansas and Nebraska seems unique, as these groups relied on a generalized broad-spectrum economy; there is minimal evidence for the use of bison, except at localities in the High Plains.

In the next section, we introduce our framework for characterizing Great Plains' people's dietary strategies. We use this framework to develop predictions on the level of specialization and diversification expected across habitats (alluvial valleys, plains and rolling hills, and foothills and mountains) and time periods (Paleoindian, Archaic, Woodland, and Late Prehistoric).

Diversification and Specialization on the Great Plains

In general, behavioral signatures of diversification and specialization indicate a variable investment in "hardware" and "software." Hardware may consist of novel food procurement technologies—for example, storage or prey-capture facilities, development and use of nets, or new hunting equipment. Software refers to culturally normalized strategies for increasing food production, such as mass prey-capture events, increased labor inputs, divisions of labor by age and sex, degree of carcass processing, resource-life extension through storage, and the logistical organization of labor to resolve scheduling conflicts (Reitz and Wing 1999).

Dietary diversification and specialization strategies are likely the result of a continuum of subsistence behaviors. We assume that if small-scale societies practice such strategies, their archaeological record will reflect secular trends in their subsistence behaviors. Researchers have characterized these trends using sophisticated methods to account for the number of species (species richness) and the abundance of each species, included in the diet (species evenness). Patterns of species richness and evenness measures are not always straightforward, particularly when estimating them using archaeological faunal assemblages (e.g., Jones 2004). For example, Figure 6.1 illustrates a simple one-dimensional gradient of low to high

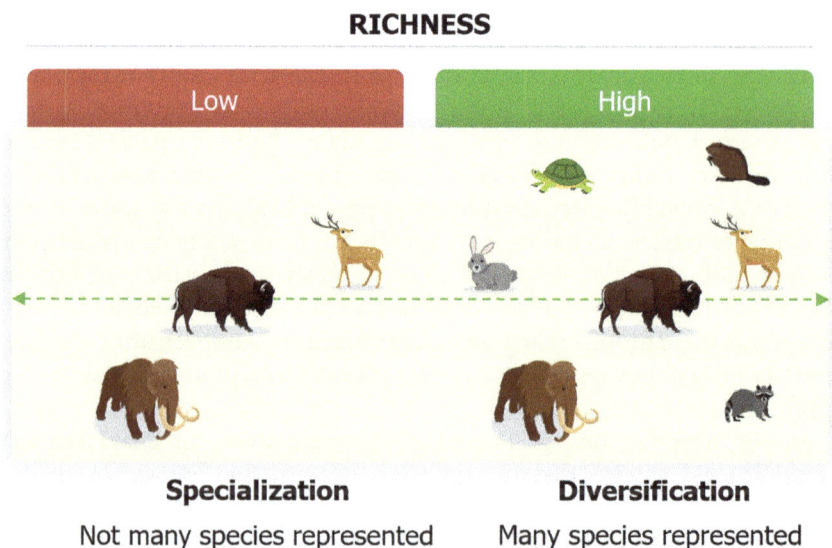

Figure 6.1. Graphic depiction of variation in prey richness in an idealized forager's diet on a one-dimensional gradient from a specialized diet focused on large game to one with high prey diversification. © The authors.

species richness. This figure visualizes the trend of an idealized forager diet focused on large-animal specialization (low diversity) versus one in which there is an increase in dietary diversification (high diversity). However, by not accounting for evenness, Figure 6.1 might mask a pattern of specialization, and characterize it as diversification. In Figure 6.2, the specialization–diversification continuum remains, but we add each species' abundance, characterized by evenness, as an additional axis to this space, creating four possible dietary configurations.

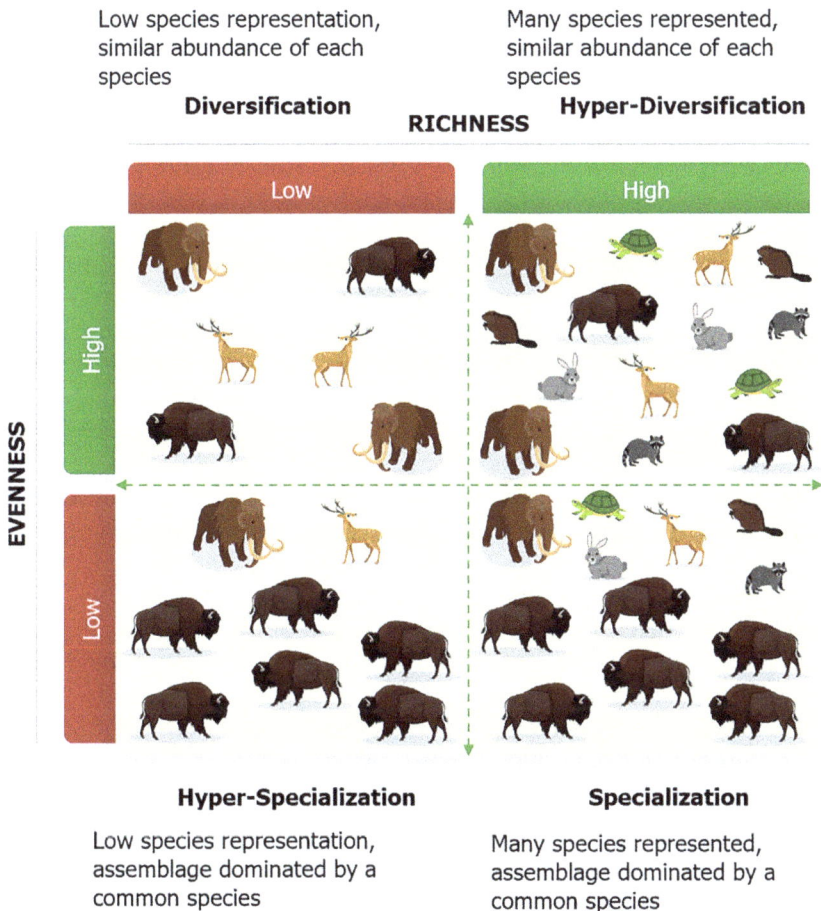

Figure 6.2. Graphic depiction of variation in prey richness and evenness. This "diversification space" illustrates an idealized forager's diet on a two-dimensional gradient from a hyper-specialized diet composed of low species representation and dominated by the large game, to a diet that is hyper-diversified representing many species at a similar abundance. © The authors.

Specialization. Here, we call specialization an assemblage exhibiting a pattern of high richness and low evenness. Although hunters target several species, there is a clear predominance of a single species or size-class.

Hyper-Specialization. We refer to hyper-specialization as the pattern characterized by low richness and low evenness. In this case, the low species representation is not only dominated by a single species but can also be a single species.

Diversification. We define diversification here to be assemblages that exhibit high evenness but low species richness. Evenness values show greater uniformity of hunting effort. This pattern no longer shows dominance by a single species or taxon, and even in low species representation, there is a tendency for equal species abundance.

Hyper-Diversification. This refers to a pattern of high evenness and high richness. This pattern of "jack of all trades, master of none" shows no apparent preference for any single species or taxon. High evenness values signify an equal abundance of all species represented, perhaps signifying hunting mastery of all species in the diet.

The literature shows that there has been limited systematic or quantitative work on changes in long-term animal use across the Great Plains (e.g., Bozell et al. 2011; Johnson 1986, 1987; Semken and Falk 1987). Despite this limitation, we expect there to be a trend of increasing dietary diversity among Great Plains hunters, as outlined above. The prehistoric people who lived on the North American Great Plains experienced a remarkable range of climatic, environmental, and cultural variability over a 13,000-year period. There is good reason to expect that their archaeological remains can track fundamental changes in human–animal interactions through time. We anticipate that Paleoindian and Archaic foragers had more specialized economies. The traditional perspective is that Paleoindians made extensive use of mammoth and bison. However, they also included a wide variety of lower-ranked resources in their diet, depending on the season and habitat.

The increasing temperatures and drought conditions during the Holocene Climatic Optimum likely negatively affected the natural abundance of large ungulates such as bison. We expect that this significant climatic change would have made it difficult to sustain heavy predation on bison across the region. In places where bison or other large game were less affected, Archaic groups likely maintained a fairly specialized diet; however, in places most affected by drought, we anticipate that hunters would have either abandoned these regions and/or increased their dietary diversification by increasingly procuring more readily available small animals.

The last few millennia likely witnessed a rebound of bison populations as more mesic conditions became established across the region. This recovery potentially caused a resurgence of bison hunting during the Woodland and Late Prehistoric periods. However, the economies of Woodland groups would have had to respond to increased population pressure and sedentism far beyond anything prior groups had experienced. This demographic packing probably amplified predation pressure on crucial prey. Hunters likely responded by further increasing the diversity of species in their diets, and by more evenly hunting all prey available. We therefore expect that the Woodland economies were the most diverse compared to the other periods, with small mammals, birds, and aquatic resources becoming more common in people's diets. However, the expected increase in bison on the landscape would have still made it quite attractive to hunt large prey, if small family groups could find ways to manage the competing labor demands of gathering wild plants, managing their horticultural pursuits, and making hunting forays increasingly farther away from human settlements.

The Late Prehistoric period witnessed a further increase in population sizes and the formation of aggregated settlements. In places across the Great Plains, Late Prehistoric groups were likely intensive agriculturists living in large, permanent villages. Under these demographic and land use conditions, we anticipate that hunting took on a dual nature, as hunters specialized in large and small prey alike. Large-prey hunting likely became more critical, especially seasonally; however, due to technological developments (e.g., bow and arrow) and social reorganization (e.g., a division of labor by age and sex), these groups likely also relied heavily on a broad spectrum of lower-ranked resources. Simultaneously, as settlements became more tethered to particular plots of land where farming was possible, the emphasis would have been on local resources. At the same time, it is also possible that the increasing social complexity and intergroup cooperation and competition among Late Prehistoric populations may have prompted some society members to undertake the increasingly inefficient and risky task of acquiring bison, despite the high risk of mortality and failure, and the low caloric returns involved in such strategies (Smith 2004; Wiessner 2002).

Materials and Methods

The current study examines faunal use at one of the largest geographic and spatial scales possible: trends across generations of multiple local groups. As noted previously (Cannon and Meltzer 2008; Moss 2012), the best approach to studying subsistence change is by determining how contemporary sites within a settlement function with resource variability. We accept that this large scale limits our ability to consider the effects of localized or, in some cases, even regional climatic and environmental changes on subsistence practices. We do not question the value of studies focusing on resource use within locally specific ecological, social, and historical frameworks; however, our study tries to consider large-scale trends in order to understand the full range of subsistence strategies. Organizing our analysis of faunal use around habitat setting differences is an attempt to factor in the natural effect that variation in resource availability might have had on the prey choice decisions of contemporary foragers.

Our project collected data on taxa abundance from 204 archaeological components from 116 archaeological sites across the Great Plains and the adjacent Rocky Mountains. Sites used in this study range in age from approximately 13,500 to 300 BP, with geographic distribution across all the major zones of the Great Plains and adjacent Rocky Mountains and its foothills (Figure 6.3). These data were derived primarily from published reports (see discussion of methods in Hill 2007b; Hill 2008; Otárola-Castillo 2016). We used only assemblages from residential camp localities because assemblages from special-use kill localities would likely have biased the sample toward a focus on large fauna. We expect kills to lack the dietary variation anticipated at residential camps. We followed the site function definitions established by Sellet (1999) and Wheat (1978), and followed Hill's (2008) criteria system for assigning sites to different habitats (alluvial valleys, plains and rolling hills, and foothills and mountains). We determined temporal associations (Paleoindian, Archaic, Woodland, and Late Prehistoric) for each assemblage using available dates and the presence of diagnostic artifacts. We chose habitat designations to reflect the key environmental zones exploited by past foragers and farmers, which differ in terms of resource productivity (e.g., patch caloric returns) and predictability (Knell 2007; Kornfeld 1997). As discussed previously (Hill and Knell 2013; Knell and Hill 2012), foragers and farmers would have found habitats to be quite different in terms of resource availability, abundance, and seasonal and spatial predictability. Mountains and foothills and alluvial valleys were likely calorie-rich areas with highly predictable and abundant biotic resources, and good sources of valuable abiotic resources (i.e., water, wood, and tool stone). By contrast, plains and rolling hills would have had a low abundance of biotic resources, as they were temporally and spatially unpredictable, and critical abiotic resources were spaced far apart.

In total, the sites used in this study contained 459,122 faunal specimens, including unidentified fragments. This dataset contained 332,099 specimens that could be quantified as Number of Identified Specimens (NISP), of which more than 176,364 (53 percent) were identified to genus or finer taxonomic distinction. Following the general criteria outlined by Grayson and Meltzer (2002) and Cannon and Meltzer (2004: 1959–60), we included only faunal remains that showed unequivocal evidence of human

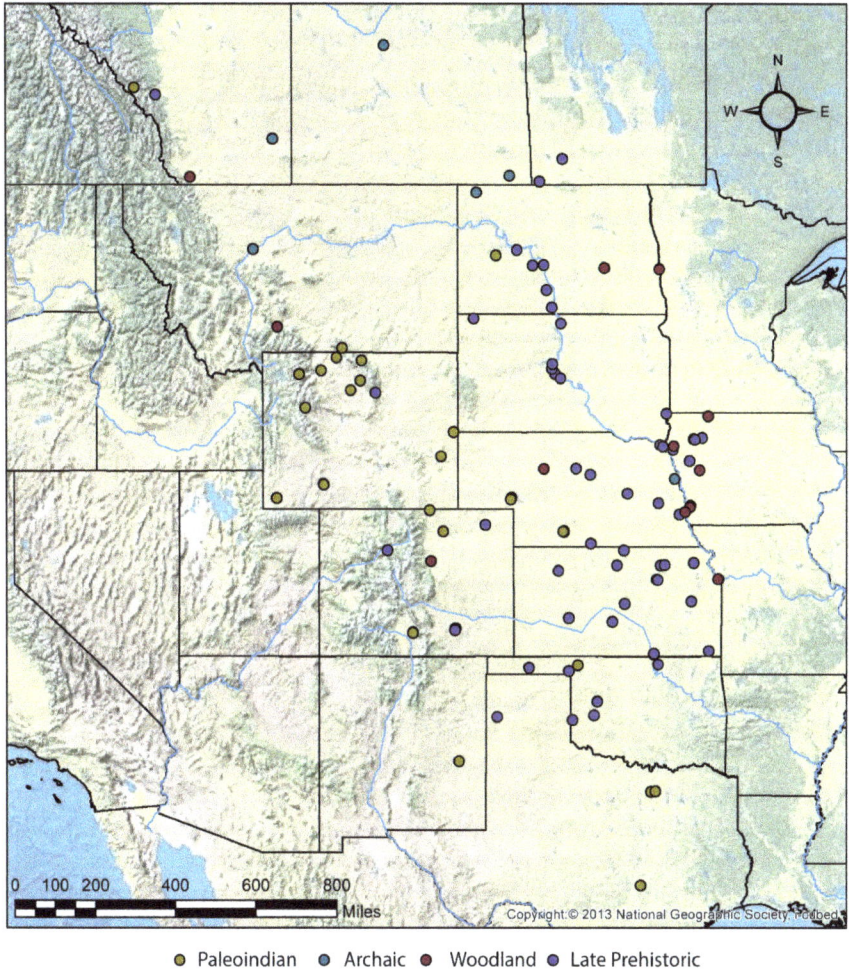

Figure 6.3. Map of the Great Plains and adjacent Rocky Mountains, including site locations for the archaeological components used in this study. © The authors.

butchery and consumption or were reported to be associated with cultural features or deposits.

We utilized three diversity measures to investigate multiple aspects of diet breadth in this study. The Margalef Diversity Index (D_{Mg}) (Clifford et al. 1975) is a simple richness measure that attempts to compensate for sample size differences by dividing the number of species present (S) by the total NISP in the assemblage (N), using the following equation (Magurran 2004: 77):

(1) $D_{mg} = \frac{S-1}{lnln\,(N)}$

An increase in D_{mg} indicates that a greater number of species are being consumed, which indicates a lack of specialization in the diet.

To explore the degree of hunting focus on any single species or group of species, we used the Simpson's Index (D′) (Levins 1968; Simpson 1949). This index is calculated using the formula:

$$(2) \quad D' = \sum \left(\frac{ni(ni-1)}{N(N-1)} \right)$$

where is the abundance of taxon i, and N is the total number of individuals (specimens) in the assemblage (Magurran 2004: 115). Because D′ decreases as evenness increases, we express the Simpson's Index as:

$$(3) \quad 1 - D'$$

Faith and Du (2018: 1428) note that, of various evenness measures used by zooarchaeologists, the Simpson's Index (1-D′) is superior because it is relatively insensitive to changes in richness and it has greater power to detect minor changes in evenness.

The final measure used was the Abundance Index (AI) (e.g., Bayham 1979; Broughton 1994a; Szuter and Bayham 1989). The AI value is calculated by combining NISP counts for all taxa within established body size classes (e.g., Brain 1981; Klein 1976; Thomas 1969) adapted by Hill (2007b: 219; 2008) to accommodate Great Plains prey: size class 1 (live body mass <22 kg; e.g., lagomorphs, birds, turtles), size class 2 (22–113 kg; e.g., bighorn sheep, pronghorn), size class 3 (113–340 kg; e.g., deer, elk), and size class 4 (>340 kg; e.g., bison, mammoth). We then determined the contribution of a specific body size class to the entire faunal assemblage. In this case, we used the following equation for large fauna:

$$(4) \quad AI_{lg} = \frac{\sum Size\ Class\ 4\ NISP}{\sum_{i=1}^{k} Size\ Class\ k_i\ NISP}$$

where k_i is the kth established body size class (1–4). The resulting index generates an AI_{lg} value ranging between 0 and 1. High values indicate greater representation of large-bodied fauna in the assemblage. For this study, large-bodied animals generally represented specimens identified as mammoth or bison, or indeterminate specimens that were the size of these animals.

The results from these three diversity measures can provide a perspective on where the foragers and farmers of the Great Plains and the Rocky Mountains fall along the diversification–specialization continuum of faunal use, as elaborated in Figure 6.2. The possible end values for the species richness and evenness of each assemblage, in this case, were measured by the Margalef Diversity Index and Simpson's Index, respectively.

We used the AI values to interpret the results further. For example, high values of in an assemblage with low evenness would indicate that bison or a comparable large-bodied species was the dominant prey species, whereas low in situations with low evenness would indicate that non-bison species were the dominant prey.

The data used in this study could not satisfy key assumptions. For example, sample values of D_{Mg}, 1-D' and AI_{lg} were not distributed, and thus exhibited Gaussian ("normal") errors. To account for this problem, we conducted statistical comparisons using generalized linear (GLM) in the R computing environment (R Core Team 2020). GLM allows users to apply a more appropriate distribution to model the sample's distribution error within a familiar ANOVA-like environment. Values of D_{Mg} were truncated at 0 and theoretically continued to infinity. The gamma function is a distribution that models such an outcome, and so was used to model this variable using the GLM() function in R's base statistics package. The AI_{lg} and 1-D' values are essentially proportions, distributed in a bimodal fashion with large proportions of 0s and 1s. As such, we analyzed these data using beta regression, using the R package *betareg* (Cribari-Neto and Zeileis 2010).

After modeling was complete, we estimated the means and standard errors in order to make comparisons within and between habitat and time group factors using the marginal means (least-squares means). Marginal means are recommended for ANOVA-like comparisons because they are more robust to sample size differences. We computed the marginal means using the *emmeans* package (Lenth 2020).

Results

We find clear differences in the representation of periods and habitat settings in the dataset, and not all groups are equally represented ($\chi2$ =42.09, df =6, p <0.00001, Cramer V =0.321; Table 6.1; Appendix 6.1). Based on standardized residuals from the χ^2 analysis, alluvial valley settings are underrepresented and foothill and mountain localities overrepresented in the Paleoindian period, whereas in the Archaic period there is a slight underrepresentation of plains/grassland localities. Both the Woodland and Late Prehistoric periods show an overrepresentation of alluvial valley sites and an underrepresentation of foothills/mountains and plains and rolling hills habitats. The Late Prehistoric period also has an overrepresentation of sites in the plains and rolling hills. Given that this study explicitly considers the interaction between period and habitat, minor differences in habitat

Table 6.1. Site frequency by time period and habitat setting.

Setting	Paleoindian	Archaic	Woodland	Late Prehistoric
Alluvial Valleys	11	25	22	48
Foothills/Mountains	29	20	2	14
Plains/Rolling Hills	11	2	4	16

X=42.09, df=6, p<.0001, Cramer V = .321

frequency over time should not significantly bias our results, especially as the sample size is adequate, at least for the Paleoindian, Archaic, and Late Prehistoric periods. At the same time, the very small size of the Woodland sample is problematic. Although the marginal means technique we outlined in the methods section can help with the sample size problem somewhat, we limited ourselves to making inferences about relatively larger samples (>10). Because of these sampling issues, we omit the standard error bars from some plots to show that the results come from small samples.

Our Margalef and Simpson's Index values are negatively related, with a statistically significant correlation of −76. While the relationship is not linear, it is visually evident that if it were linearized, the correlation would be more substantial.

Margalef Diversity Index

The plains and rolling hills habitat during the Paleoindian period has the lowest Margalef Diversity Index value (D_{Mg} = 0.237 ± 0.056) observed for any time or habitat (Figure 6.4; Table 6.2). Margalef values for Paleoindian sites in alluvial valleys (D_{Mg} = 1.237 ± 0.276) and foothills and mountains (D_{Mg} = 0.700 ± 0.081) are significantly higher than for the plains and rolling hills (p = 0.0004 and p < 0.0001, respectively), but do not differ from each other.

During the Archaic period, Margalef values for plains and rolling hills (D_{Mg} = 1.112± 0.556) more than quadruple compared to the Paleoindian values. However, it must be noted that there are only two Archaic plains sites, so these results could be a function of the small sample size. There are slight declines in the Margalef values for alluvial valleys (D_{Mg} = 0.821± 0.116) and a slight increase for foothills and mountains (D_{Mg} = 0.826 ± 0.130). These values do not indicate a significant change in species richness from the Paleoindian period, or significant differences between habitats.

In the Woodland period, species richness values rise to their highest levels in plains and rolling hills (D_{Mg} = 1.510 ± 0.534), alluvial valleys (D_{Mg} = 1.406 ± 0.212), and foothills and mountains (D_{Mg} = 2.406 ± 1.202).

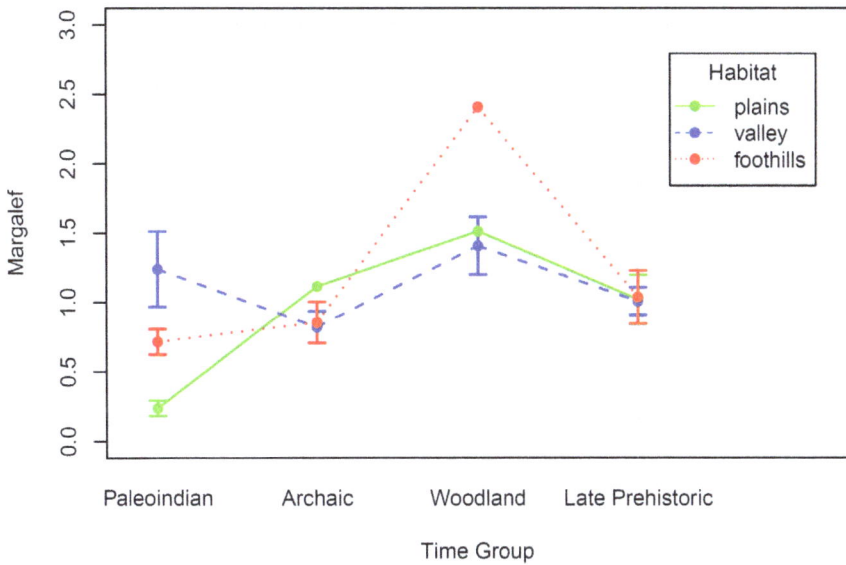

Figure 6.4. Estimates of mean Diversity Index (DMg) values of species (with standard error [SE]). This plot illustrates estimates across habitats (alluvial valleys, plains and rolling hills, and foothills and mountains) for the Paleoindian, Archaic, Woodland and Late Prehistoric periods. Means and SEs were calculated using a generalized linear model (GLM) and a gamma distribution. Estimates without SEs had small sample size (see text). © The authors.

However, this change represents a significant increase from the Archaic period only in alluvial valley settings. None of the differences between Woodland habitats are statistically significant, likely due to the very small sample sizes for the foothills/mountains and plains/rolling hills settings.

During the Late Prehistoric period, Margalef values decline from Woodland levels across habitats. One notable aspect of the Margalef values for the Late Prehistoric period is that there is no appreciable difference in species richness among habitats. The values for alluvial valley sites (D_{Mg} = 1.009 ± 0.102), foothills and mountains (D_{Mg} = 1.037 ± 0.196), and plains and rolling hills (D_{Mg} = 1.021 ± 0.1804) overlap extensively. In all

Table 6.2. Mean Margalef D_{mg} values (and SE) by time period and habitat setting, calculated using a GLM with gamma function.

Setting	Paleoindian	Archaic	Woodland	Late Prehistoric
Alluvial Valleys	1.24 (.28)	.82 (.12)	1.41 (.21)	1.01 (.10)
Foothills/Mountains	.70 (.08)	.83 (.13)	2.41 (1.20)	1.04 (.20)
Plains/Rolling Hills	.24 (.06)	1.11 (.56)	1.51 (.53)	1.02 (.18)

regions, the values are uniformly low, suggesting that the diets of the Great Plains people at this time were focused on only a few species.

Simpson's Index (1-D′)

The foothills and mountains (1-D′ = 0.243 ± 0.037) and plains and rolling hills (1-D′= 0.107 ± 0.034) settings during the Paleoindian period have the lowest Simpson's Index values for any period or habitat (Figure 6.5; Table 6.3). Simpson's Index values for alluvial valleys (1-D′= 0.580 ± 0.080) are significantly higher than for plains and rolling hills, and for foothills and mountains (p=0.0001 and p<0.0001), respectively, which differ significantly from each other (p=0.006).

Evenness values rise in both plains and rolling hills (1-D′ = 0.255 ± 0.141) and foothills and mountains (1-D′ = 0.416 ± 0.063) settings during the Archaic period, but drop in alluvial valley settings (1-D′ = 0.279 ± 0.043). The changes from Paleoindian values are significant for both alluvial valleys (p=.0009) and foothills and mountains (p=.017); however, these two do not differ significantly from each other during this period. If we ignore the

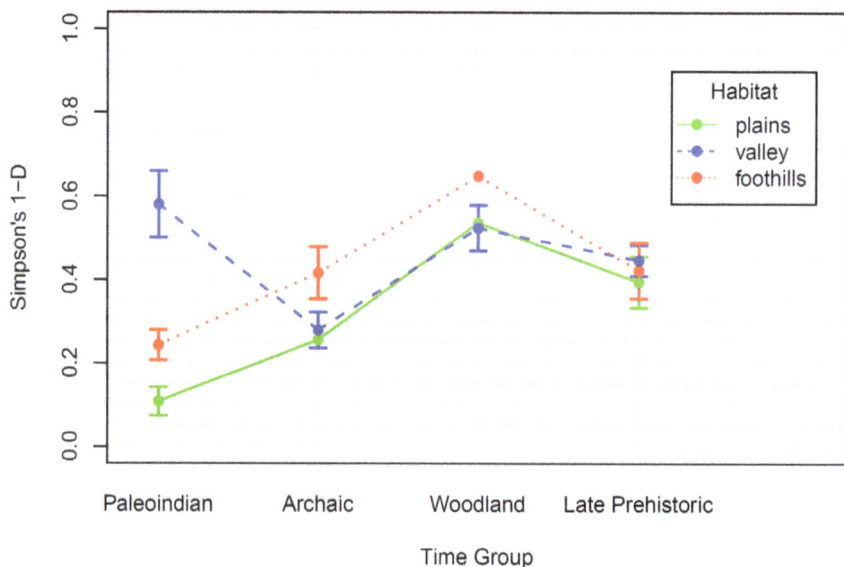

Figure 6.5. Estimates of mean Simpson's Index (1-D′) values with SE. This plot illustrates estimates across time and habitats (alluvial valleys, plains and rolling hills, and foothills and mountains) for the Paleoindian, Archaic, Woodland and Late Prehistoric periods. Means and SEs were calculated using a GLM using a beta distribution. Estimates without SEs had small sample size (see text). © The authors.

Table 6.3. Mean Simpson's Index 1-D' values (and standard errors) by time period and habitat setting, calculated using beta regression.

Setting	Paleoindian	Archaic	Woodland	Late Prehistoric
Alluvial Valleys	.58 (.08)	.28 (.04)	.52 (.05)	.42 (.07)
Foothills/Mountains	.24 (.04)	.42 (.06)	.65 (.17)	.45 (.04)
Plains/Rolling Hills	.11 (.03)	.26 (.14)	.54 (.13)	.40 (.06)

plains estimate because of sample size problems, evenness does statistically change between the Paleoindian and Archaic periods across all habitats. During the Woodland period, the Simpson's Index values rise across all habitats. The value for foothill and mountain sites (1-D' = 0.648 ± 0.168) reaches the highest value for any period or habitat, although this increase is reflective of just two sites. The values for the plains and rolling hills (1-D' = 0.537 ± 0.128) and alluvial valleys (1-D' = 0.524 ± 0.055) are almost the same, even though their sample sizes are quite different (4 vs. 22 sites, respectively). Only the increase in the value for alluvial valleys is significant compared to Archaic levels (p=0.0009). There is no statistically significant difference across habitats at the 0.05 level, suggesting a similar, moderate representation of various taxa in the diets. However, we should emphasize that there is a notable increasing trend of species evenness during the Woodland period.

During the Late Prehistoric, Simpson's Index values for all habitats decrease from Woodland levels. As observed with the Margalef values, Simpson's Index values for alluvial valley sites (1-D' = 0.446 ± 0.037), foothills and mountains (1-D' = 0.422 ± 0.067), and plains and rolling hills (1-D' = 0.395 ± 0.062) overlap extensively, and are not significantly different.

Large Mammal Abundance Index (AI_{lg})

During the Paleoindian period, AI_{lg} values are uniformly and moderately low (<.4) across all habitats, suggesting no significant differences in the use of large prey during this period (Figure 6.6, Table 6.4). During the Archaic period, however, AI_{lg} values fall for plains and rolling hill sites compared to Paleoindian levels, whereas values rise in both the foothills and mountains and alluvial valleys. However, only the increase in AI_{lg} value (AI_{lg} = 0.625 ± 0.059) for alluvial valleys (which reaches its highest level of any period) differs significantly from the Paleoindian period (p=0.004), and from the Archaic values for foothills and mountains (p=0.004) and plains and rolling hills (p=0.003). During the Woodland period, AI_{lg} values drop

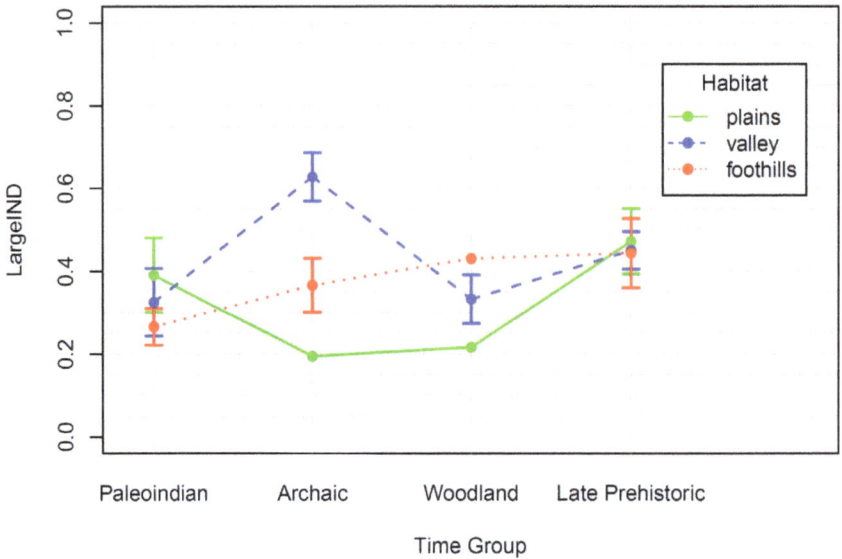

Figure 6.6. Estimates of mean Large Mammal Abundance Index (AI_lg) values with standard errors. This plot illustrates estimates across time and habitats (alluvial valleys, plains and rolling hills, and foothills and mountains) for the Paleoindian, Archaic, Woodland, and Late Prehistoric periods. Means and SEs were calculated using a GLM using a beta distribution. Estimates without SEs had small sample size (see text). © The authors.

Table 6.4. Mean large-bodied Abundance Index (AI) values (and standard errors) by time period and habitat setting, calculated using beta regression.

Setting	Paleoindian	Archaic	Woodland	Late Prehistoric
Alluvial Valleys	.33 (.08)	.63 (.06)	.34 (.06)	.47 (.05)
Foothills/Mountains	.26 (.04)	.37 (.07)	.43 (.22)	.44 (.08)
Plains/Rolling Hills	.39 (.09)	.20 (.13)	.22 (.10)	.47 (.08)

significantly in alluvial valleys compared to the Archaic period (p=0.0006), but across habitats there are no significant differences in AI_{lg} values.

As observed with the other analyses, during the Late Prehistoric period, AI_{lg} values are nearly identical across all habitats and at a generally higher level than in previous periods. Large prey seem to compose nearly 50 percent of the diets represented by faunal assemblages. This trend suggests that large-bodied fauna represented a large proportion of the animals hunted. These values reflect an increasing reliance on large prey compared to the Woodland period, although this increase is not significant.

Discussion

As discussed earlier in this chapter, the traditional view is that people on the Great Plains (and elsewhere) transitioned from hunting and gathering to farming through a mechanism of increasing resource intensification over time. In this study, we evaluated this hypothesis using a large dataset, finding no support for such a unidirectional intensification over time. Instead, the data show variability in the dietary diversification values, measured using the Margalef Diversity Index and Simpson's Index. Notably, these values do not increase uniformly over time. The results indicate that hunters on the Great Plains and in surrounding areas practiced flexible subsistence strategies. Their foraging and farming behaviors often varied in response to temporal and habitat differences in prey availability (e.g., Hill 2008; Knell and Hill 2012; Otárola-Castillo 2016). This study also sought to compare the Great Plains Paleoindian prey choice patterns we observed in our earlier work to evidence later in time. The data show that the patterns of faunal use found during the Paleoindian period are not consistent over time (Hill 2007a, 2007b, 2008; Hill and Knell 2013; Knell and Hill 2012; Otárola-Castillo 2016).

There is a high degree of variability across components. For any period, individual assemblages may show richness and AI_{lg} values that range from 0 to 1, and Margalef Diversity Index values that range between 0 and ~3.3 across habitats. In the broadest sense, both foragers and farmers preyed upon a modest number of species, often with one species numerically dominating the assemblage. The trend of low AI_{lg} values is an indication that large prey like bison were not necessarily the dominant prey in those diets. For the vast majority of time, however, large prey composed approximately 40 percent or less of the hunted diet, on average, across all habitats. Figures 6.7 and 6.8 directly compare Simpson's evenness and Margalef's richness values and the mean abundance of small, medium, and AI_{lg} values across time, differentiated by habitat. If one examines the temporal patterns, there are some intriguing changes, although they are not necessarily statistically significant.

Despite cooler, more variable climates and lower human population size than in later times, subsistence strategies during the Paleoindian period are not dramatically different from later periods (e.g., Figure 6.7). As we have shown previously, localities in the plains and rolling hills and in the foothills and mountains have very low average richness and evenness values (Hill 2007a, 2007b, 2008; Otárola-Castillo 2016). In terms of our expectations for diversification and specialization, the Paleoindian assemblages in the plains and rolling hills and in the foothills and mountains reflect a hyper-specialized (low richness/low evenness) subsistence strategy. The AI

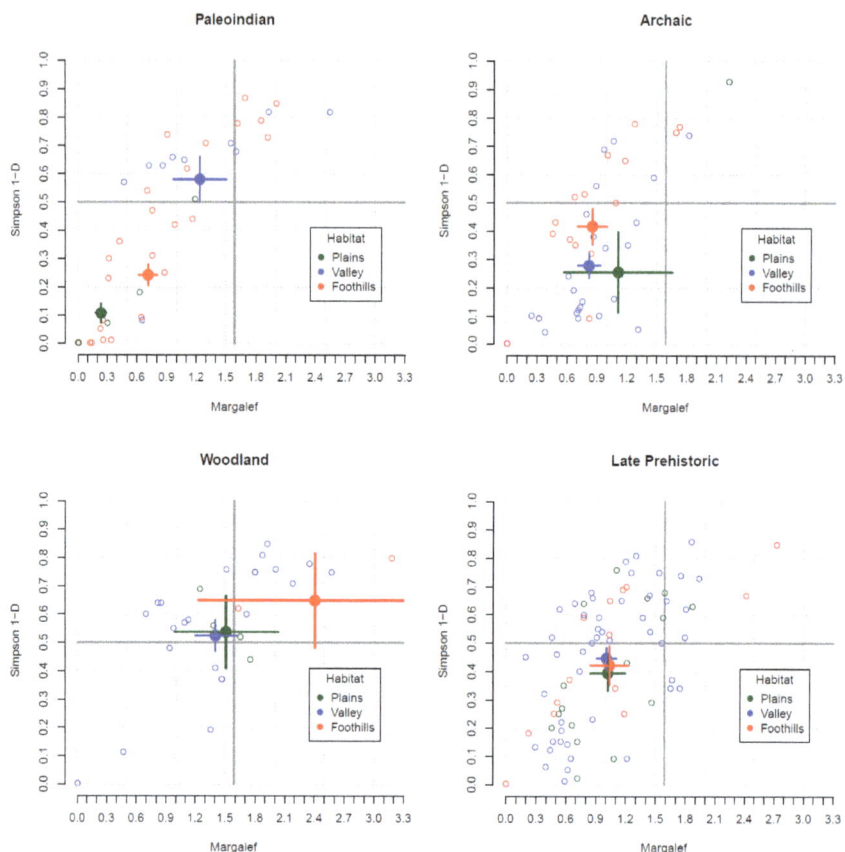

Figure 6.7. Bivariate plot exhibiting the variability in Margalef's Diversity Index (DMg) and Simpson's Index (1-D') values of site components in the three different habitats (alluvial valleys, plains and rolling hills, and foothills and mountains). Each panel separately illustrates the Paleoindian, Archaic, Woodland, and Late Prehistoric periods. Habitat means value with 95 percent confidence intervals are depicted for each habitat. © The authors.

values indicate (Figure 6.8) that, under this specialized adaptation, hunters likely focused on either large prey or small prey in the plains and rolling hills. In the foothills and mountains, however, the specialization would have been directed toward procuring medium-sized prey.

Paleoindian localities in alluvial valleys exhibit a generalist profile. These assemblages possess moderate to high richness values and moderate to high evenness values. In terms of the body size of prey chosen in alluvial settings, the primary focus would have been on small prey mixed with modest contributions from large and medium-sized prey.

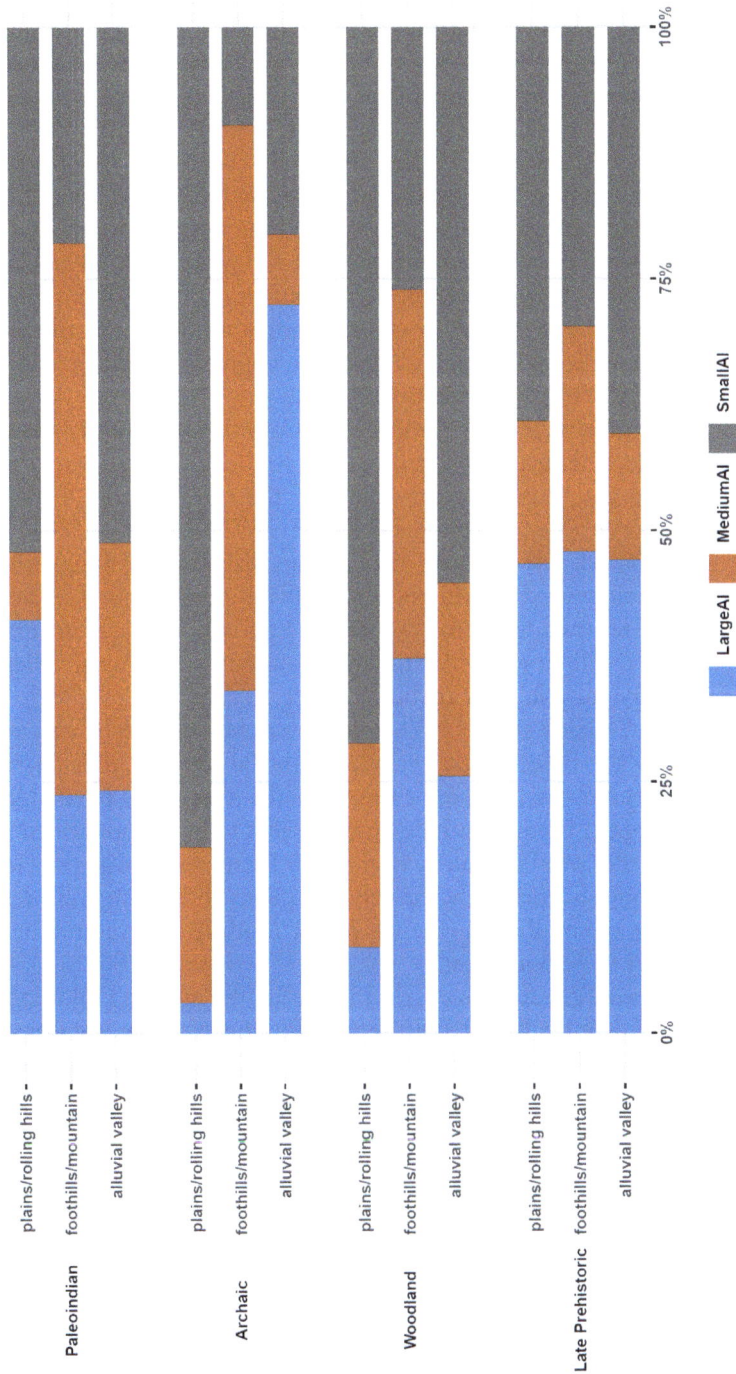

Figure 6.8. Stacked bar graph illustrating the variability in mean large–bodied Abundance Index (AIlg), medium–bodied Abundance Index (AIme), and small–bodied Abundance Index (AIsm) for three different habitats (alluvial valleys, plains and rolling hills, and foothills and mountains) during the Paleoindian, Archaic, Woodland and Late Prehistoric periods. © The authors.

The results of this study also challenge the traditional notion that Paleo-indian hunters were specialized hunters of big game such as proboscideans and bison (Frison 2001, 2004; Kornfeld et al. 2010). These foragers indeed had narrow diets, and, for sites in the plains and rolling hills, there is strong evidence of extensive use of large prey. However, in other settings, Paleo-indians seem to have specialized in deer, mountain sheep, and small prey, such as rodents and turtles, or enjoyed a more diverse mixture of prey. This duality in subsistence strategies likely represents the environmental con-straints under which Paleoindian hunters lived; the proverbial "When in Rome" aphorism seems to be an appropriate moniker for Paleoindian sub-sistence strategies. Indeed, the ability of Paleoindian foragers to maintain flexible strategies enabled them to shift between degrees of specialization and prey types, depending on the setting.

There is a noticeable paucity of Archaic sites from the plains and rolling hills in our sample. This gap likely reflects the well-documented erosion of upland surfaces and small alluvial valleys of the Great Plains during the middle Holocene (e.g., Bettis and Mandel 2002; Robertson 2011). Therefore, even though the Archaic sites in the plains and rolling hills show high species richness and evenness, it is difficult to ascertain whether these findings are representative for the Archaic period. We have greater confidence in our results for the foothill and mountain and alluvial valley settings, because the sample sizes are better. In general, our data show that the diets in Archaic plains and foothill sites were richer and slightly more even compared to the Paleoindian period; in alluvial settings, diets were less rich and even compared to earlier times. While a few sites have high Simpson and Margalef values, Archaic hunters seem to have maintained a hyper-specialized diet profile, such as in the very high use of large prey in alluvial valley settings. Surprisingly, the very few plains and rolling hill sites show a dominance of small prey, whereas in the foothills and mountains, medium-sized prey were dominant.

Because of the widespread climatic drying during the middle Holocene, we expected significant declines in the natural abundance of large-bodied fauna. Hill, Hill, and Widga (2008) demonstrated that bison experienced a significant reduction in body size during this period, which is consis-tent with the high levels of climatic stress and reduced quality of forage. Accordingly, people's low reliance on large-bodied fauna during this time was likely tied to the reduced abundance of large prey in dry grassland habitats. We should note, however, that hunters in the foothills and moun-tains and alluvial valleys maintained a specialized dietary focus on large and medium prey. We take this as an indication that large and medium prey populations were relatively abundant, at least during specific peri-ods. Alluvial valleys were likely always a common location for human residents and prey to go to get water. Given the increased temperatures and drought conditions during parts of the Archaic period, these habitats may have acted as refugia, tethering humans and prey to reliable water sources. Mountain springs and surface water sources may have been adequate to support medium-sized prey for humans to hunt. Human population sizes across the plains and in adjacent regions at this time were likely modest. As such, there is a low probability that humans could have depleted the large and medium-sized prey populations to the extent that foragers would have been forced to significantly broaden their diets.

By the Woodland period, the climate had ameliorated and become more grass-friendly, for example, with an apparent increase in precipitation levels. These changes could also have caused the size and number of bison herds to increase from middle Holocene levels. Archaeologists' identification of large bison jump sites across the Great Plains supports the notion that bison herds were at least occasionally quite large. However, the Woodland period was also a time of significant technological, social, and adaptive changes in the Great Plains, with the appearance of an incipient horticulture and increased sedentism in alluvial valleys. Developments in ceramic technology served to increase the efficiency and productivity of cooking plant resources. There is evidence of an increase in permanent human presence in the alluvial valleys. We imagine that human populations were growing at unprecedented rates during the Woodland period. However, even in the absence of population growth, decreased mobility during this period would have amplified hunting pressure on large prey populations. At the very least, sedentism likely limited hunters' ability to move easily to where bison were abundant. As a result, lower-ranked, but locally abundant, smaller prey likely became more attractive to many Woodland hunters.

As we expected, all these changes brought about modest reorganizations to the structure of faunal procurement. We must, however, acknowledge the potential effect of sampling problems. Our most rigorous sample for the Woodland period comes from alluvial valley sites. Overall, all sites move away from the hyper-specialized adaptation seen during the Archaic period toward a more generalized strategy (Figure 6.7). If the small sample of site components in the foothills and mountains is indeed representative, then some foragers might be classified as hyper-generalists. This strategy requires increases in the richness and evenness of prey selection over their values during the Archaic period. At this time, due to sample sizes, the best inferences come from alluvial settings. If we focus on prey size choice, Woodland hunters seem to have significantly reduced the number of large prey and increased the diversity of small prey compared to the Archaic period.

Our results show a dearth of habitat differences in terms of faunal use during the Late Prehistoric period (Figure 6.7). In effect, dietary diversity, evenness, and reliance on large prey are nearly identical across habitats. Most diets appear to have been hyper-specialized, with a uniform, moderately strong reliance on the use of bison. The data suggest that the inclusion of medium-sized prey in the diet was generally modest, while people were making moderate use of small prey; numerically, this use is only slightly lower than that of large prey (Figure 6.8).

The Late Prehistoric period saw significant increases in population size and sedentism. We expected the high population growth to exert increased hunting pressure and subsequently deplete local bison abundance. The reduction of local game animals is logical, especially in areas where Late Prehistoric people created large residential settlements. However, the relatively high use of bison found during the Late Prehistoric period suggests that people utilized some kind of mechanism to offset declines in availability. We believe that these people implemented changes in procurement strategies and technologies. In the northwestern plains, for example, large mass kills and jumps were used during this period. It is likely that in specific places, and at least seasonally, hunters increased their use of specialized procurement techniques to obtain substantial quantities of bison food products. Of course, jump kills do not characterize bison hunting everywhere on the plains. However, logistical, perhaps even modest-sized cooperative hunts were undertaken seasonally, scheduled around people's essential agricultural pursuits. If so, there could have been an increased supply of large prey-animals, even in the face of decreasing local availability.

Late Prehistoric people used small prey, such as rodents, fish, and birds, in proportions similar to bigger animals, probably because these types of prey were attracted to settlements and thus became locally abundant. Unlike bison hunts, which were likely planned and sometimes communal undertakings, various members of society (young and old individuals, as well as men, women, and children) could have participated in the collection of small prey, perhaps even while undertaking other activities, such as tending agricultural fields or collecting wood or water.

Conclusions

Popular accounts of indigenous life in the North American Great Plains portray a way of life and diet that was highly contingent on the vast herds of bison that roamed the region. Although romantic to some, this depiction is simplistic and does not acknowledge the multidimensional character of the plains' indigenous people. Our study examined evidence representing over thirteen thousand years of this region's cultural history, finding that people exhibited remarkable variation in behaviors and dietary strategies. We conclude that even though the plains people maintained a way of life associated with bison over time, bison were not the dominant species in their diet. Instead, people responded to marked climatic and habitat variability across space and time by adjusting their hunting strategies accordingly. To conduct this study, we developed a useful framework for understanding dietary strategies. We conceptualized a diversification and specialization "space" using indices of richness and evenness in order to characterize the hunting strategies of indigenous people on the Great Plains, and to quantify changes over time. We identified four discrete locations in the diversity space—diversification, hyper-diversification, specialization, and hyper-specialization—but did so out of pure convenience. In fact, these locations are not discrete, but comprise a continuous space that, in its current form, is relative to the assemblages in this sample. Nonetheless, we believe that this framework can be useful for comparing and measuring changes in the foraging strategies of small-scale societies over time.

The evolution of hunting strategies and dietary variation that we observed on the Great Plains zooarchaeological record does not support a model of progressive resource intensification from hunting and gathering to farming. Rather, the data support a model of constant diversification of continuous hunting strategies, starting with the Paleoindian and going through to the Late Prehistoric periods. In this model, hunters on the plains (and elsewhere) maintained a wide and diverse range of behavioral strategies. This highly flexible and diversified portfolio of dietary strategies enabled the people of the Great Plains to adapt their approaches to procuring food across different habitats and time periods.

Acknowledgments

We are grateful to various museums and their staff for providing access to the collections and materials used in this study, including the University of Kansas Natural History Museum, the Kansas State Historical Society, the University of Colorado, the Nebraska State Museum, the University of Texas, and the University of Wyoming. M.E.H. is grateful for the financial support received from the University of Iowa, the Arizona State Museum Thompson Fund (University of Arizona), the Emily W. Haury Education Fund for Archaeology (University of Arizona), and the George C. Frison Institute Paleoindian Grant (University of Wyoming), which facilitated museum visits. He also thanks Kevin Flaherty for his help in the early stages of data collection and for the statistical advice provided by

Rhonda R. DeCook, Feiran Jiao, and Barbara Monaco. E.O.C. is grateful to Sarah N. Coon for help with manuscript editing, and several undergraduate interns for help examining the literature in search of dietary data. Partial funding for this project was provided by Purdue University College of Liberal Arts' Exploratory Research in the Social Sciences award and the Margo Katherine Wilke research internship fund.

Reproducible Science Statement

All files, R code, and data necessary to replicate this manuscript are available as an R Markdown (.rmd) document from the Open Science Framework (DOI 10.17605/OSF.IO/NMQB2). For convenience, the R markdown file produces a .pdf pre-print of the manuscript. Reproducible files may be accessed here: https://osf.io/nmqb2/.

Erik Otárola-Castillo is an Assistant Professor at Purdue University, West Lafayette, Indiana, USA.

Melissa G. Torquato is a PhD candidate at Purdue University, West Lafayette, Indiana, USA.

Matthew E. Hill is an Associate Professor at the University of Iowa, Iowa City, USA.

Appendix 6.1. Summary Information for Archaeological Sites Used in This Study

SITE	Component	Habitat	Time Group	Total NISP	Species Count	Margalef Dmg	Simpson's 1-D'	Large AI	Medium AI	Small AI
13ML175	1995 excavations	AV	LP	6,482	10	1.22	0.09	0.00	0.01	0.99
14CO01	site	AV	LP	6,353	4	0.54	0.62	0.49	0.11	0.40
14CO03	site	AV	LP	11,575	6	0.77	0.47	0.64	0.08	0.28
14CO1509	site	AV	LP	984	5	0.59	0.01	0.99	0.00	0.00
14CO332	site	AV	LP	4,266	3	0.38	0.32	0.85	0.05	0.11
14CO382	site	AV	LP	12,922	5	0.74	0.40	0.77	0.08	0.15
14CO385	site	AV	LP	255	2	0.20	0.45	0.33	0.00	0.67
14CO501	site	AV	LP	37,008	7	0.87	0.23	0.87	0.04	0.09
14RY401	site	P/R	LP	224	11	1.88	0.63	0.05	0.62	0.33
25FT22	site	P/R	LP	7,287	6	0.56	0.27	0.01	0.10	0.90
25LP8	site	P/R	LP	274	5	0.72	0.15	0.89	0.08	0.03
34CD257	A	AV	W	12,595	15	1.52	0.76	0.00	0.06	0.94
34CD257	PV	AV	LP	1,636	10	1.26	0.75	0.01	0.04	0.95
34CD258	A	AV	LP	730	11	1.62	0.65	0.05	0.11	0.84
48SW13156	I	P/R	P	172	0			0.00	0.02	0.98
48SW8842	5	P/R	P	147	1	0.00	0.00	0.00	0.00	1.00
48UT375	Component 1	P/R	P	926	1			0.00	0.00	1.00
48UT375	Component 2	P/R	P	3,190	2	0.30	0.07	0.00	0.00	1.00
Agate Basin	Area 2-Folsom	P/R	P	1,910	10	1.19	0.51	0.54	0.45	0.01
Albert Bell	site	P/R	LP	1,022	5	0.58	0.35	0.80	0.08	0.12

(continued)

SITE	Component	Habitat	Time Group	Total NISP	Species Count	Margalef Dmg	Simpson's 1-D'	Large AI	Medium AI	Small AI
Allen	Occupation Level 1	AV	P	4,394	13	1.61	0.68	0.35	0.06	0.59
Allen	Intermediate Zone	AV	P	1,387	13	1.93	0.82	0.13	0.15	0.72
Allen	Occupation Level 2	AV	P	800	15	2.56	0.82	0.03	0.10	0.87
Annie Site (25DX30)	site	P/R	LP	2,058	7	1.11	0.76	0.24	0.17	0.59
Arthur (13DK27)	Middle Woodland	P/R	W	976	13	1.76	0.44	0.18	0.01	0.81
Ash Hollow	Lens A	P/R	LP	21	3	0.78	0.64	0.10	0.00	0.90
Ash Hollow	Lens B	P/R	LP	47	7	1.60	0.68	0.21	0.21	0.57
Ash Hollow	Lens C	P/R	LP	163	9	1.58	0.59	0.11	0.17	0.72
Ash Hollow	Lens D	P/R	W	174	8	1.39	0.56	0.16	0.09	0.75
Ash Hollow	Lens E	P/R	W	16	4	1.25	0.69	0.00	0.19	0.81
Ash Hollow	Lens F	P/R	A	10	5	2.23	0.93	0.00	0.30	0.70
Aubrey	Camp A and B; Pond C/E1; Red Sand S	AV	P	1,523	7	0.86	0.63	0.34	0.01	0.64
Avoca (14JN332)	1983 excavation	AV	LP	157	6	1.20	0.79	0.39	0.35	0.25
Bagnell (32MO16)	Heart River	AV	LP	5,460	5	0.47	0.15	0.83	0.05	0.12
Bagnell (32MO16)	Nailati Phase	AV	LP	9,532	5	0.44	0.12	0.83	0.04	0.13
Big Black	site	AV	P	836	0			0.41	0.02	0.57
Big Goose Creek	site	F/M	LP	209	14	2.73	0.85	0.00	0.24	0.76
Blood Run	site	AV	LP	1,926	13	1.75	0.34	0.43	0.01	0.56
Blue Point (32SW5734)	Component 1	P/R	P	120	1	0.00	0.00	0.10	0.25	0.65
Blue Point (32SW5734)	Component 2	P/R	P	80	1	0.00	0.00	0.00	0.01	0.99
Blue Point (32SW5734)	Component 3	P/R	A	299	1	0.00	0.00	0.06	0.01	0.93

SITE	Component	Habitat	Time Group	Total NISP	Species Count	Margalef Dmg	Simpson's 1-D'	Large AI	Medium AI	Small AI
Blue Stone (25HN45)	site	AV	LP	127	4	0.62	0.05	0.98	0.01	0.02
Bottleneck Cave	II	F/M	P	13	1	0.00	0.00	0.00	0.92	0.08
Bottleneck Cave	III	F/M	P	41	3	0.71	0.54	0.00	0.80	0.20
Bottleneck Cave	IV	F/M	A	58	4	0.77	0.53	0.00	0.79	0.21
Bottleneck Cave	VI	F/M	LP	241	10	2.42	0.67	0.01	0.01	0.98
Bradford House II	I	F/M	A	32	6	1.70	0.75	0.28	0.19	0.53
Bradford House II	II	F/M	W	59	13	3.19	0.80	0.15	0.37	0.47
Brewster (13CK15)	1970 excavations	AV	LP	7,768	8	0.86	0.68	0.23	0.05	0.73
Broken Kettle West (13PM25)	1968 excavations	AV	LP	1,350	15	1.94	0.73	0.00	0.35	0.65
Buffalo Pasture	site	AV	LP	2,918	14	1.67	0.37	0.64	0.07	0.28
Bunderbender	site	AV	LP	201	10	1.76	0.74	0.00	0.36	0.64
Cactus Flower (EbOp-16)	Occupation IV	AV	A	32	4	0.87	0.38	0.78	0.03	0.19
Cactus Flower (EbOp-16)	Occupation IX	AV	A	73	4	0.70	0.11	0.95	0.03	0.03
Cactus Flower (EbOp-16)	Occupation VI	AV	A	154	5	0.79	0.46	0.69	0.27	0.04
Cactus Flower (EbOp-16)	Occupation VII	AV	A	53	4	0.76	0.15	0.92	0.00	0.08
Cactus Flower (EbOp-16)	Occupation VIII	AV	A	660	7	0.92	0.10	0.95	0.02	0.03
Canterbury (5PE387)	site	F/M	LP	39	3	0.78	0.59	0.85	0.00	0.15
Cattleguard	site	F/M	P	3,517	2	0.12	0.00	1.00	0.00	0.00
Chan-ya-ta (13BV1)	House 6	P/R	LP	1,249	11	1.42	0.66	0.31	0.04	0.64
Colby	site	F/M	P	463	1	0.00	0.00	1.00	0.00	0.00
Cow Killer	Area 751	P/R	LP	2,615	12	1.47	0.29	0.04	0.77	0.19

(continued)

SITE	Component	Habitat	Time Group	Total NISP	Species Count	Margalef Dmg	Simpson's 1-D'	Large AI	Medium AI	Small AI
Cowan Site (13WD88)	site	AV	LP	11,233	14	1.81	0.62	0.02	0.04	0.94
Cramer (5PE484)	site	F/M	LP	48,859	11	1.19	0.25	0.97	0.00	0.02
Crandall (14RC420)	site	AV	LP	16,125	17	1.66	0.34	0.78	0.00	0.22
Cross Ranch	Nailati Phase	AV	LP	706	5	0.62	0.14	0.85	0.06	0.08
Dahnke-Reinke (32CS29)	1980s excavation-Early Woodland	AV	W	6,484	6	1.09	0.57	0.52	0.01	0.47
Dahnke-Reinke (32CS29)	1980s excavation-Late Woodland	AV	W	4,821	10	1.80	0.75	0.32	0.03	0.65
Dahnke-Reinke (32CS29)	1980s excavation-Middle Woodland	AV	W	11,845	6	0.98	0.55	0.58	0.00	0.42
DhPj-4	Level 1	AV	W	45	1	0.00	0.00	1.00	0.00	0.00
DhPj-4	Level 2	AV	A	18	1	0.00	0.00	1.00	0.00	0.00
Dixon (13WD8)	1994 excavation	AV	LP	3,949	11	1.45	0.54	0.15	0.10	0.75
Donovan	Level 1	P/R	LP	1,966	5	0.53	0.25	0.85	0.00	0.15
Donovan	Level 9	P/R	LP	1,935	6	0.66	0.21	0.88	0.00	0.11
Duncan (34WA2)	site	AV	LP	42,595	6	0.56	0.19	0.27	0.57	0.17
Edward I (34BK2)	site	AV	LP	2,336	8	0.91	0.52	0.46	0.04	0.50
Glen Elder (14ML1)	site	AV	LP	18	5	1.44	0.67	0.06	0.11	0.83
Gowen 1 (FaNq25)	site	AV	A	233	4	0.62	0.24	0.49	0.07	0.44
Gowen 2 (FaNq32)	site	AV	A	385	5	0.73	0.13	0.56	0.03	0.41
Heerwald	site	AV	LP	8,953	9	0.92	0.55	0.57	0.12	0.31
Helen Lookingbill	Layer 2/4	F/M	P	25	2	0.31	0.23	0.12	0.84	0.04

SITE	Component	Habitat	Time Group	Total NISP	Species Count	Margalef Dmg	Simpson's 1-D'	Large AI	Medium AI	Small AI
Helen Lookingbill	Layer 7/9	F/M	P	531	3	0.32	0.30	0.01	0.99	0.00
Hell Gap	Locality II–Alberta	F/M	P	1,316	2	0.14	0.00	0.99	0.01	0.00
Hell Gap	Locality I–Unknown	F/M	P	1,388	3	0.34	0.01	0.99	0.00	0.01
Hill	site	AV	A	164	5	0.89	0.56	0.75	0.04	0.21
Horner	I	F/M	P	2,154	3	0.26	0.01	0.99	0.00	0.00
Horsetheif (14HO308)	site	P/R	LP	3,330	4	0.46	0.20	0.94	0.02	0.04
Hulme	site	AV	LP	1,476	6	0.69	0.64	0.02	0.48	0.51
Indian Creek	site	AV	LP	356	7	1.04	0.51	0.58	0.26	0.16
Jackson	site	P/R	LP	4,464	7	0.72	0.02	0.96	0.00	0.04
Jake White Bull (39CO6)	site	AV	LP	330	4	0.55	0.15	0.65	0.02	0.33
Juan Baca (5LA1085)	site	F/M	LP	48	5	1.18	0.69	0.38	0.02	0.60
Jurgens	Area 2	AV	P	101	4	0.65	0.08	0.93	0.03	0.04
Kelso (25HO23)	site	AV	W	92	9	1.88	0.81	0.10	0.20	0.71
Lake Theo	Folsom	P/R	P	6,919	1	0.00	0.00	1.00	0.00	0.00
Landergin Mesa	site	AV	LP	1,854	8	0.97	0.54	0.41	0.22	0.37
Leavitt	site	AV	LP	106	9	1.80	0.52	0.55	0.10	0.35
Lewisville	(1949–1957 and 1978–1980)	AV	P	466	9	1.56	0.71	0.05	0.04	0.92
Lightning Spring (39HN204)	Stratum 1	F/M	LP	31	4	1.04	0.53	0.68	0.16	0.16
Lightning Spring (39HN204)	Stratum 10	F/M	A	39	2	0.32	0.09	0.08	0.77	0.15
Lightning Spring (39HN204)	Stratum 11	F/M	A	114	4	0.68	0.35	0.20	0.78	0.02
Lightning Spring (39HN204)	Stratum 12	F/M	A	24	2	0.46	0.39	0.13	0.88	0.00

(continued)

SITE	Component	Habitat	Time Group	Total NISP	Species Count	Margalef Dmg	Simpon's 1-D'	Large AI	Medium AI	Small AI
Lightning Spring (39HN204)	Stratum 14	F/M	A	11	2			0.27	0.73	0.00
Lightning Spring (39HN204)	Stratum 2	F/M	A	16	2	0.48	0.43	0.88	0.13	0.00
Lightning Spring (39HN204)	Stratum 3	F/M	A	27	1			0.96	0.00	0.04
Lightning Spring (39HN204)	Stratum 8	F/M	A	62	3	0.63	0.37	0.06	0.90	0.03
Lightning Spring (39HN204)	Stratum 9	F/M	A	12	2			0.83	0.17	0.00
Lime Creek	Zone I	AV	P	519	5	0.72	0.63	0.28	0.15	0.57
Lindenmeier	Folsom	P/R	P	593	5	0.63	0.18	0.88	0.01	0.11
Linger	SI 1977–1979	F/M	P	462	1	0.00	0.00	1.00	0.00	0.00
Logan Creek	Zone A	AV	A	200	3	0.38	0.04	0.97	0.01	0.03
Logan Creek	Zone B	AV	A	938	10	1.32	0.05	0.96	0.01	0.03
Logan Creek	Zone C	AV	A	236	9	1.47	0.59	0.58	0.02	0.40
Logan Creek	Zone D	AV	A	271	7	1.07	0.16	0.90	0.00	0.09
Logan Creek	Zone F	AV	A	61	2	0.24	0.10	0.93	0.07	0.00
Lundeen (14MD306)	site	AV	LP	5,988	11	1.16	0.65	0.11	0.08	0.81
MAD (13CF101)	Boyer	AV	W	2,726	14	2.19	0.71	0.23	0.49	0.28
MAD (13CF101)	Valley	AV	W	447	9	1.81	0.75	0.04	0.51	0.45
MAD (13CF102)	Valley	AV	W	119	6	2.01	0.76	0.06	0.15	0.79
MAD (13CF102)	Boyer	AV	W	449	8	1.41	0.41	0.41	0.39	0.20
MAD (13CF102)	Loseke	AV	W	4,410	12	1.72	0.60	0.51	0.28	0.21
Mangus	III	F/M	LP	117	2	0.23	0.18	0.07	0.64	0.29
Mangus	Red silt	F/M	LP	10	2	0.48	0.25	0.70	0.10	0.20
McIntoch	site	P/R	LP	3,787	11	1.22	0.43	0.16	0.01	0.83

SITE	Component	Habitat	Time Group	Total NISP	Species Count	Margalef Dmg	Simpson's 1-D'	Large AI	Medium AI	Small AI
Medicine Lodge Creek	23 ft-deep deer	F/M	P	65	5	1.16	0.44	0.03	0.35	0.62
Medicine Lodge Creek	Cody	F/M	P	28	4	0.99	0.42	0.07	0.14	0.79
Medicine Lodge Creek	Foothill-Mountain–North Paleoindian	F/M	P	14	6	2.01	0.85	0.29	0.36	0.36
Medicine Lodge Creek	Lovell Constricted–fir pit level	F/M	P	95	9	1.86	0.79	0.00	0.28	0.72
Medicine Lodge Creek	Pryor stemmed	F/M	P	52	8	1.92	0.73	0.02	0.48	0.50
Mondrian Tree (32MZ58)	1981 excavation – Zone 2	AV	A	67	5	0.99	0.34	0.79	0.15	0.06
Mondrian Tree (32MZ58)	1981 excavation – Zone 3	AV	A	77	4	0.72	0.12	0.94	0.01	0.05
Mondrian Tree (32MZ58)	1981 excavation – Zone 4	AV	A	131	6	1.07	0.72	0.38	0.54	0.08
Mondrian Tree (32MZ58)	1981 excavation – Zone 5	AV	A	23	3	0.67	0.19	0.87	0.04	0.09
Mondrian Tree (32MZ58)	1981 excavation – Zone 6	AV	A	36	2	0.32	0.09	0.81	0.03	0.17
Mondrian Tree (32MZ58)	1981 excavation – Zone 7	AV	A	30	4	0.97	0.69	0.50	0.30	0.20
Mummy Cave	Layer 1	F/M	P	35	4	1.30	0.71	0.00	0.14	0.86
Mummy Cave	Layer 4	F/M	P	33	6	1.70	0.87	0.00	0.52	0.48
Mummy Cave	Layer 6	F/M	P	46	4	0.91	0.74	0.00	0.38	0.63
Mummy Cave	Layer 8	F/M	P	85	4	0.76	0.31	0.00	0.98	0.02
Mummy Cave	Layer 9	F/M	P	108	1	0.00	0.00	0.00	0.99	0.01
Mummy Cave	Layer 10	F/M	P	145	4	0.65	0.09	0.00	0.94	0.06
Mummy Cave	Layer 11	F/M	P	95	2	0.23	0.05	0.00	1.00	0.00
Mummy Cave	Layer 12	F/M	P	179	5	0.88	0.25	0.00	0.91	0.09
Mummy Cave	Layer 14	F/M	P	17	3	0.76	0.47	0.00	0.76	0.24

(continued)

SITE	Component	Habitat	Time Group	Total NISP	Species Count	Margalef Dmg	Simpon's 1-D'	Large AI	Medium AI	Small AI
Munsell (5PE797)	site	F/M	LP	19	2	0.51	0.29	0.89	0.05	0.05
Myers-Hinderman	Unit 1	F/M	P	40	7	1.63	0.78	0.35	0.58	0.08
Myers-Hinderman	Unit 3	F/M	A	142	6	1.01	0.67	0.35	0.65	0.01
Myers-Hinderman	Unit 4	F/M	A	179	10	1.73	0.77	0.28	0.68	0.04
Myers-Hinderman	Unit 5	F/M	A	108	7	1.28	0.78	0.31	0.67	0.03
Myers-Hinderman	Unit 6	F/M	A	71	6	1.18	0.65	0.54	0.41	0.06
Myers-Hinderman	Unit 7	F/M	W	39	7	1.64	0.62	0.59	0.36	0.05
Myers-Hinderman	Unit 8	F/M	LP	46	5	1.04	0.65	0.48	0.52	0.00
Naze (32SN246)	Zone 1: Plains village	AV	LP	123	3	0.78	0.60	0.89	0.01	0.11
Naze (32SN246)	Zone 2: Middle Woodland	AV	W	381	3	0.47	0.11	0.58	0.24	0.18
Naze (32SN246)	Zone 3: Early Woodland	AV	W	71	4	0.82	0.64	0.58	0.27	0.15
Odessa Yates (34BV100)	1998–2000 excavations	AV	LP	22,388	8	0.86	0.50	0.88	0.04	0.08
Oliphant (14LT316)	1973 excavation	AV	LP	440	9	1.57	0.50	0.04	0.69	0.27
OV Clary	Middle	P/R	P	1,000	1	0.00	0.00	1.00	0.00	0.00
Oxbow Dam (DhMN-1)	Cultural Level 4-1995/96	AV	A	648	1	0.00	0.00	1.00	0.00	0.00
Oxbow Dam (DhMN-1)	Cultural Level 5 – 1995/96	AV	A	69	4	0.71	0.09	0.93	0.00	0.07
Oxbow Dam (DhMN-1)	Cultural Level 6 – 1995/96	AV	A	251	7	1.21	0.35	0.45	0.00	0.55
Phil (14JW48)	site	AV	LP	92	9	1.86	0.86	0.16	0.15	0.68
Phipps (13CK21)	1994 excavations	AV	LP	583	4	0.51	0.46	0.44	0.15	0.41
Phipps (13CK21)	pre-1970s excavations	AV	LP	4,829	8	0.87	0.66	0.34	0.14	0.52
Rainbow (13PM91)	Horizon A	AV	W	2,067	15	2.36	0.78	0.40	0.11	0.49

SITE	Component	Habitat	Time Group	Total NISP	Species Count	Margalef Dmg	Simpson's 1-D'	Large AI	Medium AI	Small AI
Rainbow (13PM91)	Horizon B	AV	W	850	12	2.58	0.75	0.03	0.02	0.96
Rainbow (13PM91)	Horizon C	AV	W	4,562	14	1.93	0.85	0.02	0.11	0.87
Rainbow (13PM91)	Horizon D	AV	W	1,151	10	1.36	0.19	0.12	0.05	0.83
SCHMIDT	Site	AV	LP	3,334	13	1.54	0.75	0.15	0.07	0.77
Sharp's (13ML42)	Site	AV	W	388	9	1.47	0.37	0.03	0.73	0.24
Sibbald Creek (EgPr-2)	Levels 0–10 cm	F/M	LP	95	6	1.10	0.34	0.81	0.13	0.06
Snake Blakeslee (5LA1247)	site	F/M	LP	983	8	1.21	0.70	0.64	0.04	0.32
Sorenson	IV	F/M	A	16	1	0.00	0.00	0.00	1.00	0.00
Sorenson	VI	F/M	LP	23	3	0.64	0.37	0.17	0.78	0.04
South Cannonball River (32SI19)	site	AV	LP	8,673	6	0.56	0.22	0.81	0.02	0.16
Stigenwalt	Archaic	AV	A	344	8	1.83	0.74	0.00	0.06	0.94
Sun River	Level IV	F/M	A	761	6	0.83	0.09	0.94	0.03	0.03
Sun River	Level V	F/M	A	626	5	0.68	0.52	0.65	0.33	0.02
Sun River	Level VI	F/M	A	1,391	6	0.84	0.32	0.03	0.82	0.14
Theodore Davis (25CC17)	site	AV	LP	118	6	1.37	0.59	0.59	0.26	0.14
Travis I (39CO213)	site	AV	LP	711	4	0.46	0.52	0.49	0.00	0.51
Trowbridge	site	P/R	W	5,078	12	1.66	0.52	0.00	0.52	0.48
Two Sisters	site	AV	LP	11,531	8	0.93	0.59	0.62	0.22	0.16
Upper Sanger (32OL12)	Heart River	AV	LP	497	5	0.65	0.09	0.89	0.04	0.07
Vera	site	P/R	LP	1,676	9	1.09	0.09	0.90	0.00	0.10

(continued)

SITE	Component	Habitat	Time Group	Total NISP	Species Count	Margalef Dmg	Simpson's 1-D'	Large AI	Medium AI	Small AI
Vermilion Lakes	Component 7	F/M	P	50	2	0.26	0.08	0.00	0.96	0.04
Vermilion Lakes	Component 8	F/M	P	109	3	0.43	0.36	0.02	0.77	0.21
Vermilion Lakes	Component 9a	F/M	P	17	4	1.11	0.62	0.00	0.82	0.18
Vermilion Lakes	Component 9b	F/M	P	11	1	0.00	0.00	0.00	1.00	0.00
Walker Gilmore (25CC28)	1968 excavation – Level 1	AV	A	50	6	1.30	0.43	0.00	0.02	0.98
Walker Gilmore (25CC28)	1968 excavation – Level 2	AV	W	78	4	0.70	0.60	0.00	0.10	0.90
Walker Gilmore (25CC28)	1968 excavation – Level 3	AV	W	91	6	1.13	0.58	0.04	0.20	0.76
Walker Gilmore (25CC28)	1968 excavation – Level 4	AV	W	110	5	0.85	0.64	0.01	0.07	0.92
Walker Gilmore (25CC28)	1968 excavation – Level 5	AV	W	74	5	0.94	0.48	0.03	0.22	0.76
Waugh	site	P/R	P	1,403	1	0.00	0.00	1.00	0.00	0.00
White Buffalo Robe (32ME7)	Heart River	AV	LP	2,147	4	0.40	0.06	0.84	0.02	0.14
White Buffalo Robe (32ME7)	Nailati Phase	AV	LP	1,469	3	0.29	0.13	0.60	0.04	0.36
Wilson Leonard	Early Paleoindian Bonebed: Units Isi, Isi/Icl, Igl/Isi, Isi/Isi-c, Isi/Icl/Isi-c	AV	P	311	3	0.47	0.57	0.12	0.74	0.14
Wilson Leonard	Unit II: (Golindria-Barber, St Mary's, Angostura)	AV	P	606	6	0.96	0.66	0.01	0.66	0.33
Wilson Leonard	Upper Unit I: (Wilson)	AV	P	430	6	1.08	0.65	0.00	0.75	0.24
Witt	Site	AV	LP	1,188	10	1.31	0.81	0.01	0.15	0.85
Yarmony (5EA799)	Ceramic locus	F/M	LP	68	1	0.00	0.00	0.03	0.43	0.53
Yarmony (5EA799)	Pithouse locus – House1&2	F/M	A	2,006	6	1.09	0.50	0.03	0.50	0.47
Yarmony (5EA799)	Pithouse locus – Midden F14	F/M	A	45	2			0.00	0.83	0.17

References

Adair, M. J. 2006. "Plains Plants." *Handbook of North American Indians* 3: 365–74.

———. 2012. "Refining Plains Woodland Chronology." *Plains Anthropologist* 57(223): 183–228.

Adair, M. J., and R. Drass. 2011. "Patterns of Plant Use in the Prehistoric Central and Southern Plains." In *The Subsistence Economies of Indigenous North American Societies*, ed. B. D. Smith, 307–52. Washington, DC: Smithsonian Institution.

Ahler, S. A., and D. L. Toom. 1995. *Archeology of the Medicine Crow Site Complex (39bf2), Buffalo County, South Dakota*. Springfield: State of Illinois.

Anderson, R. C. 2006. "Evolution and Origin of the Central Grassland of North America: Climate, Fire, and Mammalian Grazers." *The Journal of the Torrey Botanical Society* 133(4): 626–47.

Axelrod, D. I. 1985. "Rise of the Grassland Biome, Central North America." *The Botanical Review* 51(2): 163–201.

Balinsky, R. L. 1998. "Pleistocene to Holocene: Wilson-Leonard Microvertebrate Fauna and Its Paleoenvironmental Significance." In *Wilson-Leonard: An 11,000-Year Archaeological Record of Hunter-Gatherers in Central Texas*, ed. M. B. Collins, 1515–42. Austin: The University of Texas Press.

Bamforth, D. B. 2011. "Origin Stories, Archaeological Evidence, and Post-Clovis Paleoindian Bison Hunting on the Great Plains." *American Antiquity* 76(1): 24–40.

Barlow, K. R. 2002. "Predicting Maize Agriculture among the Fremont: An Economic Comparison of Farming and Foraging in the American Southwest." *American Antiquity* 67(1): 65–88.

Barnosky, C. W. 1989. "Postglacial Vegetation and Climate in the Northwestern Great Plains of Montana." *Quaternary Research* 31(1): 57–73.

Bayham, F. E. 1979. "Factors Influencing the Archaic Pattern of Animal Exploitation." *Kiva* 44(2–3): 219–35.

Beaver, J. E., and R. M. Dean. 2019. "Using Euclidean Distance in the Comparative Analysis of Taxonomic Abundance." *Journal of Archaeological Science: Reports* 25: 331–40.

Betancourt, J. L., K. A. Rylander, C. Peñalba, and J. L. McVickar. 2001. "Late Quaternary Vegetation History of Rough Canyon, South-Central New Mexico, USA." *Palaeogeography, Palaeoclimatology, Palaeoecology* 165(1–2): 71–95.

Bettinger, R. L., and M. N. Grote. 2016. "Marginal Value Theorem, Patch Choice, and Human Foraging Response in Varying Environments." *Journal of Anthropological Archaeology* 42: 79–87.

Bettinger, R. L., B. Winterhalder, and R. McElreath. 2006. "A Simple Model of Technological Intensification." *Journal of Archaeological Science* 33(4): 538–45.

Bettis III, E. A., and R. D. Mandel. 2002. "The Effects of Temporal and Spatial Patterns of Holocene Erosion and Alluviation on the Archaeological Record of the Central and Eastern Great Plains, USA." *Geoarchaeology: An International Journal* 17(2): 141–54.

Betts, M. W., and T. M. Friesen. 2004. "Quantifying Hunter-Gatherer Intensification: A Zooarchaeological Case Study from Arctic Canada." *Journal of Anthropological Archaeology* 23(4): 357–84.

Binford, L. R. 1980. "Willow Smoke and Dogs' Tails: Hunter-Gatherer Settlement Systems and Archaeological Site Formation." *American Antiquity* 45(1): 4–20.

———. 2001. *Constructing Frames of Reference: An Analytical Method for Archaeological Theory Using Hunter-Gatherer and Environmental Data Sets*. Berkeley: University of California Press.

Bird, D. W., and J. F. O'Connell. 2006. "Behavioral Ecology and Archaeology." *Journal of Archaeological Research* 14(2): 143–88.

Blackmar, J. M., and J. L. Hofman. 2006. "The Paleoarchaic of Kansas." *Kansas Archaeology*: 10–27.

Bleed, P. 1986. "The Optimal Design of Hunting Weapons: Maintainability or Reliability." *American Antiquity* 51(4): 737–47.

Boivin, N. L., M. A. Zeder, D. Q. Fuller, A. Crowther, G. Larson, J. M. Erlandson, T. Denham, and M. D. Petraglia. 2016. "Ecological Consequences of Human Niche Construction: Examining Long-Term Anthropogenic Shaping of Global Species Distributions." *Proceedings of the National Academy of Sciences* 113(23): 6388–96.

Boserup, E. 1965. *The Conditions of Agricultural Growth: The Economics of Agrarian Change under Population Pressure.* Chicago: Aldine.

Bousman, C. B. 1998. "Paleoenvironmental Change in Central Texas: The Palynological Evidence." *Plains Anthropologist* 43(164): 201–19.

Bozell, J. R., C. R. Falk, and E. Johnson. 2011. "Native American Use of Animals on the North American Great Plains." In *The Subsistence Economies of Indigenous North American Societies*, ed. B. D. Smith, 353–85. Washington, DC: Smithsonian Institution.

Brain, C. K. 1981. *The Hunters or the Hunted?* Chicago: University of Chicago Press.

Bright, J., A. Ugan, and L. Hunsaker. 2002. "The Effect of Handling Time on Subsistence Technology." *World Archaeology* 34(1): 164–81.

Brookfield, H. C. 1972. "Intensification and Disintensification in Pacific Agriculture: A Theoretical Approach." *Pacific Viewpoint* 13(1): 30–48.

Broughton, J. M. 1994a. "Declines in Mammalian Foraging Efficiency during the Late Holocene, San Francisco Bay, California." *Journal of Anthropological Archaeology* 13: 371–401.

———. 1994b. "Late Holocene Resource Intensification in the Sacramento Valley, California: The Vertebrate Evidence." *Journal of Archaeological Science* 21(4): 501–14.

———. 1997. "Widening Diet Breadth, Declining Foraging Efficiency, and Prehistoric Harvest Pressure: Ichthyofaunal Evidence from the Emeryville Shellmound, California." *Antiquity* 71(274): 845–62.

———. 1999. *Resource Depression and Intensification during the Late Holocene, San Francisco Bay: Evidence from the Emeryville Shellmound Vertebrate Fauna* 32. Berkeley: University of California Press.

———. 2002. "Prey Spatial Structure and Behavior Affect Archaeological Tests of Optimal Foraging Models: Examples from the Emeryville Shellmound Vertebrate Fauna." *World Archaeology* 34(1): 60–83.

Broughton, J. M., M. D. Cannon, and E. J. Bartelink. 2010. "Evolutionary Ecology, Resource Depression, and Niche Construction Theory: Applications to Central California Hunter-Gatherers and Mimbres-Mogollon Agriculturalists." *Journal of Archaeological Method and Theory* 17(4): 371–421.

Broughton, J. M., and E. M. Weitzel. 2018. "Population Reconstructions for Humans and Megafauna Suggest Mixed Causes for North American Pleistocene Extinctions." *Nature Communications* 9(1): 1–12.

Butler, V. L., and S. K. Campbell. 2004. "Resource Intensification and Resource Depression in the Pacific Northwest of North America: A Zooarchaeological Review." *Journal of World Prehistory* 18(4): 327–405.

Byerly, R. M., J. R. Cooper, D. J. Meltzer, M. E. Hill, and J. M. LaBelle. 2005. "On Bonfire Shelter (Texas) as a Paleoindian Bison Jump: An Assessment Using GIS and Zooarchaeology." *American Antiquity* 70(4): 595–629.

Byers, D. A., and J. M. Broughton. 2004. "Holocene Environmental Change, Artiodactyl

Abundances, and Human Hunting Strategies in the Great Basin." *American Antiquity* 69(2): 235–55.

Cannon, M. D. 2001. "Large Mammal Resource Depression and Agricultural Intensification: An Empirical Test in the Mimbres Valley, New Mexico." PhD dissertation, University of Washington, Seattle.

Cannon, M. D., and D. J. Meltzer. 2004. "Early Paleoindian Foraging: Examining the Faunal Evidence for Large Mammal Specialization and Regional Variability in Prey Choice." *Quaternary Science Reviews* 23(18–19): 1955–87.

———. 2008. "Explaining Variability in Early Paleoindian Foraging." *Quaternary International* 191(1): 5–17.

Clark, J. S., E. C. Grimm, J. J. Donovan, S. C. Fritz, D. R. Engstrom, and J. E. Almendinger. 2002. "Drought Cycles and Landscape Responses to Past Aridity on Prairies of the Northern Great Plains, USA." *Ecology* 83(3): 595–601.

Cleland, C. E. 1976. "The Focal-Diffuse Model: An Evolutionary Perspective on the Prehistoric Cultural Adaptations of the Eastern United States." *Midcontinental Journal of Archaeology* 1(1): 59–76.

Clifford, H. T., W. Stephenson, H. Clifford, and W. Stephenson. 1975. *An Introduction to Numerical Classification* 240. New York: Academic Press.

Coupland, G., K. Stewart, and K. Patton. 2010. "Do You Never Get Tired of Salmon? Evidence for Extreme Salmon Specialization at Prince Rupert Harbour, British Columbia." *Journal of Anthropological Archaeology* 29(2): 189–207.

Coupland, R. T. 1992. "Overview of the Grasslands of North America." *Ecosystems of the World* 8: 147–49.

Cribari-Neto, F., and A. Zeileis. 2010. "Beta Regression in R." *Journal of Statistical Software* 34(2): 1–24. URL http://www.jstatsoft.org/v34/i02/.

Dansgaard, W., S. J. Johnsen, J. Møller, and C. C. Langway. 1969. "One Thousand Centuries of Climatic Record from Camp Century on the Greenland Ice Sheet." *Science* 166(3903): 377–80.

Dean, R. M. 2007. "Hunting Intensification and the Hohokam 'Collapse.'" *Journal of Anthropological Archaeology* 26(1): 109–32.

———. 2017. "Fauna and the Emergence of Intensive Agricultural Economies in the United States Southwest." In *The Oxford Handbook of Zooarchaeology*, ed. U. Albarella, M. Rizzetto, H. Russ, K. Vickers, and S. Viner, 509–24. Oxford: Oxford University Press.

Dean, W. E., and A. Schwalb. 2000. "Holocene Environmental and Climatic Change in the Northern Great Plains as Recorded in the Geochemistry of Sediments in Pickerel Lake, South Dakota." *Quaternary International* 67(1): 5–20.

DeAngelis, J. A., and R. L. Lyman. 2018. "Evaluation of the Early Paleo-Indian Zooarchaeological Record as Evidence of Diet Breadth." *Archaeological and Anthropological Sciences* 10(3): 555–70.

Dunnell, R.C. 1967. "The Prehistory of Fishtrap, Kentucky: Archaeological Interpretation in Marginal Areas." PhD dissertation, Yale University, New Haven, CT.

Dyck, I., and R. E. Morlan. 2001. "Hunting and Gathering Tradition: Canadian Plains." *Handbook of North American Indians* 13(1): 115–30.

Earle, T. K. 1980. "A Model of Subsistence Change." In *Modeling Change in Prehistoric Subsistence Economies*, ed. T. K. Earle and A. L. Christenson, 1–29. New York: Academic Press.

Ellyson, L. J., L. Nagaoka, and S. Wolverton. 2019. "Animal Resource Use Related to Socioenvironmental Change among Mesa Verde Farmers." *Journal of Anthropological Research* 75(3): 361–92.

Fagan, B. M. 2018. *Ancient North America: The Archaeology of a Continent*. 5th edn. New York: Thames & Hudson.

Faith, J. T., and A. Du. 2018. "The Measurement of Taxonomic Evenness in Zooarchaeology." *Archaeological and Anthropological Sciences* 10(6): 1419–28.

Fladmark, K. R. 1975. *A Paleoecological Model for Northwest Coast Prehistory*. Ottawa: National Museum of Man, Mercury Series. Archaeological Survey of Canada Paper 43.

Flannery, K. V. 1968. "Archaeological Systems Theory and Early Mesoamerica." *Anthropological Archaeology in the Americas* 67: 87.

———. 1972. "The Cultural Evolution of Civilizations." *Annual Review of Ecology and Systematics* 3(1): 399–426.

Forbis, R. G. 1982. "One View of Plains Archaeology in Canada: The Past Decade." *Canadian Journal of Archaeology* 6: 157–66.

Forman, S. L., R. Oglesby, and R. S. Webb. 2001. "Temporal and Spatial Patterns of Holocene Dune Activity on the Great Plains of North America: Megadroughts and Climate Links." *Global and Planetary Change* 29(1–2): 1–29.

Frank, D. A., M. M. Kuns, and D. R. Guido. 2002. "Consumer Control of Grassland Plant Production." *Ecology* 83(3): 602–6.

Frank, D. A., and S. J. McNaughton. 1993. "Evidence for the Promotion of Aboveground Grassland Production by Native Large Herbivores in Yellowstone National Park." *Oecologia* 96(2): 157–61.

Frank, D. A., S. J. McNaughton, and B. F. Tracy. 1998. "The Ecology of the Earth's Grazing Ecosystems." *Bioscience* 48(7): 513–21.

Fredlund, G. G., C. B. Bousman, and D. K. Boyd. 1998. "The Holocene Phytolith Record from Morgan Playa in the Rolling Plains of Texas." *Plains Anthropologist* 43(164): 187–200.

Frison, G. C. 1970. "The Kobold Site, 24bh406: A Post-Althithermal Record of Buffalo-Jumping for the Northwestern Plains." *Plains Anthropologist* 15(47): 1–35.

———. 1998a. "The Northwestern and Northern Plains." In *Archaeology on the Great Plains*, ed. W. R. Wood, 140–72. Lawrence: University Press of Kansas.

———. 1998b. "Paleoindian Large Mammal Hunters on the Plains of North America." *Proceedings of the National Academy of Sciences* 95(24): 14576–83.

———. 2001. "Hunting and Gathering Tradition: Northwestern and Central Plains." In *Plains, Volume 13. Handbook of North American Indians*, ed. R. J. Mallie, 131–45. Washington, DC: Smithsonian Institution.

———. 2004. *Survival by Hunting: Prehistoric Human Predators and Animal Prey*. Berkeley: University of California Press.

Grayson, D. K., and D. J. Meltzer. 2002. "Clovis Hunting and Large Mammal Extinction: A Critical Review of the Evidence." *Journal of World Prehistory* 16(4): 313–59.

Gremillion, K. J. 2004. "Seed Processing and the Origins of Food Production in Eastern North America." *American Antiquity* 69(2): 215–33.

Gremillion, K. J., L. Barton, and D. R. Piperno. 2014. "Particularism and the Retreat from Theory in the Archaeology of Agricultural Origins." *Proceedings of the National Academy of Sciences* 111(17): 6171–77.

Gremillion, K. J., and D. R. Piperno. 2009. "Human Behavioral Ecology, Phenotypic (Developmental) Plasticity, and Agricultural Origins: Insights from the Emerging Evolutionary Synthesis." *Current Anthropology* 50(5): 615–19.

Halfen, A. F., and W. C. Johnson. 2013. "A Review of Great Plains Dune Field Chronologies." *Aeolian Research* 10: 135–60.

Haury, C. 2005. "Analysis of Fauna from the Rustad Site." *Plains Anthropologist* 50(196): 91–133.

Haynes, G., and M. J. Hutson. 2014. "Clovis-Era Subsistence: Regional Variability, Continental Patterning." In *Paleoamerican Odyssey*, ed. K. E. Graf, C. V. Ketron, and M. R. Waters, 293–309. College Station: Texas A&M University Press.

Hill, M. E. 2007a. "Causes of Regional and Temporal Variation in Paleoindian Diet in Western North America." PhD dissertation, University of Arizona, Tucson.

———. 2007b. "A Moveable Feast: Variation in Faunal Resource Use among Central and Western North American Paleoindian Sites." *American Antiquity* 72(3): 417–38.

———. 2008. "Variation in Paleoindian Fauna Use on the Great Plains and Rocky Mountains of North America." *Quaternary International* 191(1): 34–52.

———. 2013. "Sticking It to the Bison: Exploring Variation in Cody Bison Bonebeds." In *Paleoindian Lifeways of the Cody Complex*, ed. E. Knell and M. Muniz, 93–117. Salt Lake City: University of Utah Press.

Hill, M. E., M. G. Hill, and C. C. Widga. 2008. "Late Quaternary Bison Diminution on the Great Plains of North America: Evaluating the Role of Human Hunting versus Climate Change." *Quaternary Science Reviews* 27(17–18): 1752–71.

Hill, M. E., and E. J. Knell. 2013. "Cody in the Rockies: The Mountain Expression of a Plains Culture Complex." In *Paleoindian Lifeways of the Cody Complex*, ed. E. Knell and M. Muniz, 188–214. Salt Lake City: University of Utah Press.

Hofman, J. L. 1994. "Paleoindian Aggregations on the Great Plains." *Journal of Anthropological Archaeology* 13(4): 341–70.

Holliday, V. T. 1995. *Stratigraphy and Paleoenvironments of Late Quaternary Valley Fills on the Southern High Plains*. Boulder, CO: Geological Society of America.

Johnson, A. M., and A. W. Johnson. 1998. "The Plains Woodland." In *Archaeology of the Great Plains*, ed. W. R. Wood, 201–34. Lawrence: University of Kansas Press.

Johnson, E. 1986. "Late Pleistocene and Early Holocene Vertebrates and Paleoenvironments on the Southern High Plains, USA." *Geographie Physique et Quaternaire* 40(3): 249–61.

———, ed. 1987. *Lubbock Lake: Late Quaternary Studies on the Southern High Plains*. College Station: Texas A&M University Press.

Jones, E. L. 2004. "Dietary Evenness, Prey Choice, and Human–Environment Interactions." *Journal of Archaeological Science* 31(3): 307–17.

Kay, M. 1998. "The Central and Southern Plains Archaic." In *Archaeology on the Great Plains*, ed. W. R. Wood, 173–200. Lawrence: University of Kansas Press.

Kehoe, T. F. 1973. *The Gull Lake Site: A Prehistoric Bison Drive Site in Southwestern Saskatchewan*. Milwaukee: Milwaukee Public Museum.

Kelly, R. L., and L. C. Todd. 1988. "Coming into the Country: Early Paleoindian Hunting and Mobility." *American Antiquity* 53(2): 231–44.

Klein, R. G. 1976. "The Mammalian Fauna of the Klasies River Mouth Sites, Southern Cape Province, South Africa." *The South African Archaeological Bulletin* 31(123/124): 75–98.

Knell, E. J. 2007. "The Organization of Late Paleoindian Cody Complex Land-Use on the North American Great Plains." PhD dissertation, Washington State University, Pullman.

Knell, E. J., and M. E. Hill. 2012. "Linking Bones and Stones: Regional Variation in Late Paleoindian Cody Complex Land Use and Foraging Strategies." *American Antiquity* 77(1): 40–70.

Kornfeld, M. 1997. "Affluent Foragers of the Western Black Hills: A Settlement and Subsistence Model." In *Changing Perspectives of the Archaic on the Northwest Plains and Rocky Mountains*, ed. M. L. Larson and J. E. Francis, 56–84. Vermillion: University of South Dakota Press.

————. 2007. "Are Paleoindians of the Great Plains and Rockies Subsistence Specialists?" In *Foragers of the Terminal Pleistocene*, ed. R. B. Walker and B. N. Driskell, 32–58. Lincoln: University of Nebraska Press.

Kornfeld, M., G. C. Frison, and M. L. Larson. 2010. *Prehistoric Hunter-Gatherers of the High Plains and Rockies*. 3rd edn. Walnut Creek, CA: Left Coast Press.

Kornfeld, M., and M. L. Larson. 2008. "Bonebeds and Other Myths: Paleoindian to Archaic Transition on North American Great Plains and Rocky Mountains." *Quaternary International* 191(1): 18–33.

Kornfeld, M, M. L. Larson, C. Arnold, A. Wiewel, M. Toft, and D. Stanford. 2007. "The Nelson Site, a Cody Occupation in Northeastern Colorado." *Plains Anthropologist* 52(203): 257–78.

Küchler, A. W. 1965. "Potential Natural Vegetation of the Conterminous United States." *Soil Science* 99(5): 356.

Kuhn, S. L. 1994. "A Formal Approach to the Design and Assembly of Mobile Toolkits." *American Antiquity* 59(3): 426–42.

Lauenroth, W. K., I. C. Burke, and M. P. Gutmann. 1999. "The Structure and Function of Ecosystems in the Central North American Grassland Region." *Great Plains Research* 9(2): 223–59.

Leach, H. M. 1999. "Intensification in the Pacific: A Critique of the Archaeological Criteria and Their Application." *Current Anthropology* 40(3): 311–40.

Lehmer, D. J. 1971. *Introduction to Middle Missouri Archeology*. Washington, DC: Anthropological Papers No. 1, National Park Service.

Lenth, R. 2020. "Emmeans: Estimated Marginal Means, Aka Least-Squares Means. R Package Version 1.4.6." https://github.com/rvlenth/emmeans.

Levins, R. 1968. *Evolution in Changing Environments: Some Theoretical Explorations*. Princeton, NJ: Princeton University Press.

Liberty, M., and W. R. Wood. 1980. *Anthropology on the Great Plains*. Lincoln: University of Nebraska Press.

Lobdell, J. E. 1973. "The Scoggin Site: An Early Middle Period Bison Kill." *Wyoming Archaeologist* 16(3): 123–28.

Lyman, R. L. 1989. "Seal and Sea Lion Hunting: A Zooarchaeological Study from the Southern Northwest Coast of North America." *Journal of Anthropological Archaeology* 8(1): 68–99.

————. 1991. "Subsistence Change and Pinniped Hunting." In *Human Predators and Prey Mortality*, ed. M. C. Stiner, 187–99. Boulder, CO: Westview Press.

Mack, R. N., and J. N. Thompson. 1982. "Evolution in Steppe with Few Large, Hooved Mammals." *The American Naturalist* 119(6): 757–73.

Magurran, A. E. 2004. *Measuring Biological Diversity*. Malden, MA: Blackwell.

Malthus, T. 1798. *An Essay on the Principle of Population*. London: Reeves and Turner, St. Paul's Church-Yard.

Matson, R. G. 1983. "Intensification and the Development of Cultural Complexity: The Northwest versus the Northeast Coast." In *The Evolution of Maritime Cultures on the Northeast and Northwest Coasts of America*, ed. R. J. Nash, 125–48. Burnaby, Canada: Simon Fraser University.

Matson, R. G., and G. Coupland, eds. 1995. *The Prehistory of the Northwest Coast*. San Diego: Academic Press.

McNaughton, S. J. 1984. "Grazing Lawns: Animals in Herds, Plant Form, and Coevolution." *The American Naturalist* 124(6): 863–86.

Meltzer, D. J. 1999. "Human Responses to Middle Holocene (Altithermal) Climates on the North American Great Plains." *Quaternary Research* 52(3): 404–16.

———. 2015. "Pleistocene Overkill and North American Mammalian Extinctions." *Annual Review of Anthropology* 44: 33–53.

Metcalfe, D., and K. R. Barlow. 1992. "A Model for Exploring the Optimal Trade-Off between Field Processing and Transport." *American Anthropologist* 94(2): 340–56.

Miller, D. S. 2018. *From Colonization to Domestication: Population, Environment, and the Origins of Agriculture in Eastern North America*. Salt Lake City: University of Utah Press.

Morgan, C. 2015. "Is It Intensification Yet? Current Archaeological Perspectives on the Evolution of Hunter-Gatherer Economies." *Journal of Archaeological Research* 23(2): 163–213.

Morrison, K. D. 1994. "The Intensification of Production: Archaeological Approaches." *Journal of Archaeological Method and Theory* 1(2): 111–59.

Moss, M. L. 2012. "Understanding Variability in Northwest Coast Faunal Assemblages: Beyond Economic Intensification and Cultural Complexity." *The Journal of Island and Coastal Archaeology* 7(1): 1–22.

Mulloy, W. 1954. "The McKean Site in Northeastern Wyoming." *Southwestern Journal of Anthropology* 10(4): 432–60.

Munro, N. D. 2004. "Small Game Indicators of Human Foraging Efficiency and Early Herd Management at the Transition to Agriculture in South-West Asia." In *Proceedings of the Petits Animaux et Sociétés Humaines (du Complément Alimentaire aux Ressources Utilitaires)*, ed. J.-P. Brugal and J. Desse, 515–31. Valbonne: CNRS.

———. 2009. "Epipaleolithic Subsistence Intensification in the Southern Levant: The Faunal Evidence." In *The Evolution of Hominin Diets*, ed. J. Hublin and M. P. Richards, 141–55. New York: Springer.

Munro, N. D., G. Bar-Oz, J. S. Meier, L. Sapir-Hen, M. C. Stiner, and R. Yeshurun. 2018. "The Emergence of Animal Management in the Southern Levant." *Scientific Reports* 8(1): 1–11.

Nagaoka, L. 2002. "The Effects of Resource Depression on Foraging Efficient, Diet Breadth, and Patch Use in Southern New Zealand." *Journal of Anthropological Archaeology* 21: 419–42.

Neusius, S. W., and G. T. Gross. 2013. *Seeking Our Past: An Introduction to North American Archaeology*. New York: Oxford University Press.

Oswalt, W. H. 1976. *An Anthropological Analysis of Food-Getting Technology*. Hoboken, NJ: Wiley.

Otárola-Castillo, E. R. 2016. "A Spatio-Temporal Model of Hunter-Gatherer Foraging Ecology across the North American Great Plains throughout the Paleoindian Period: Development of Biological Theory and Statistical Methods to Link Human Evolutionary Biology, Ecology, and the Archaeological Record." PhD dissertation, Stony Brook University, NY.

R Core Team. 2020. *R: A Language and Environment for Statistical Computing*. Vienna: R Foundation for Statistical Computing.

Reid, K. C. 1983. "The Nebo Hill Phase: Late Archaic Prehistory in the Lower Missouri Valley." In *Archaic Hunter-Gatherers in the American Midwest*, ed. J. L. Phillips and J. A. Brown, 11–39. New York: Academic Press.

Reitz, E. J., and E. S. Wing. 1999. *Zooarchaeology*. Cambridge: Cambridge University Press.

Robertson, E. C. 2011. "Reassessing Hypsithermal Human–Environment Interaction on the Northern Plains." *Geological Society, London, Special Publications* 352(1): 181–94.

Schmits, L. J. 1978. "The Coffey Site: Environment and Cultural Adaptation at a Prairie Plains Archaic Site." *Midcontinental Journal of Archaeology* 3(1): 69–185.

Sellet, F. 1999. "A Dynamic View of Paleoindian Assemblages at the Hell Gap Site, Wyoming: Reconstructing Lithic Technological Systems." PhD dissertation, Southern Methodist University, Dallas, TX.

Semken Jr, H. A., and C. R. Falk. 1987. "Late Pleistocene/Holocene Mammalian Faunas and Environmental Changes on the Northern Plains of the United States." In *Late Quaternary Mammalian Biogeography and Environments of the Great Plains and Prairies*, ed. R. W. Graham, 176–313. Springfield: Illinois State Museum.

Shuman, B. N., and J. Marsicek. 2016. "The Structure of Holocene Climate Change in Mid-Latitude North America." *Quaternary Science Reviews* 141: 38–51.

Simpson, E. H. 1949. "Measurement of Diversity." *Nature* 163(4148): 688.

Smith, B. D. 2011. "A Cultural Niche Construction Theory of Initial Domestication." *Biological Theory* 6(3): 260–71.

———. 2015. "A Comparison of Niche Construction Theory and Diet Breadth Models as Explanatory Frameworks for the Initial Domestication of Plants and Animals." *Journal of Archaeological Research* 23(3): 215–62.

Smith, E. A. 2004. "Why Do Good Hunters Have Higher Reproductive Success?" *Human Nature* 15(4): 343–64.

Stiner, M. C. 2001. "Thirty Years on the 'Broad Spectrum Revolution' and Paleolithic Demography." *Proceedings of the National Academy of Sciences* 98(13): 6993–96.

Stiner, M. C., and N. D. Munro. 2002. "Approaches to Prehistoric Diet Breadth, Demography, and Prey Ranking Systems in Time and Space." *Journal of Archaeological Method and Theory* 9(2): 181–214.

Stiner, M. C., N. D. Munro, T. A. Surovell. 2000. "The Tortoise and the Hare: Small-Game Use, the Broad-Spectrum Revolution, and Paleolithic Demography." *Current Anthropology* 41(1): 39–79.

Stiner, M. C., N. D. Munro, T. A. Surovell, E. Tchernov, and O. Bar-Yosef. 1999. "Paleolithic Population Growth Pulses Evidenced by Small Animal Exploitation." *Science* 283(5399): 190–94.

Surovell, T. A., and N. M. Waguespack. 2008. "How Many Elephant Kills Are 14?: Clovis Mammoth and Mastodon Kills in Context." *Quaternary International* 191(1): 82–97.

———. 2009. "Human Prey Choice in the Late Pleistocene and Its Relation to Megafaunal Extinctions." In *American Megafaunal Extinctions at the End of the Pleistocene*, ed. G. Haynes, 77–105. New York: Springer.

Szuter, C. R., and F. E. Bayham. 1989. "Sedentism and Prehistoric Animal Procurement among Desert Horticulturalists of the North American Southwest." In *Farmers as Hunters: The Implications of Sedentism*, ed. S. Kent, 80–95. Cambridge: Cambridge University Press.

Theler, J. L. 2003. "Paleoenvironmental Interpretation from Burnham Site Gastropods: 1989 Results." In *The Burnham Site in Northwestern Oklahoma: Glimpses Beyond Clovis?*, ed. D. G. Wyckoff, J. L. Theler, and B. G. Carter, 169–89. Norman: Vol. 9. Sam Noble Oklahoma Museum of Natural History, University of Oklahoma Anthropological Society.

Thies, R. M., ed. 1990. *The Archeology of the Stigenwalt Site, 14lt351*. Topeka: Contract Archaeology Series No. 7, Kansas State Historical Society.

Thomas, D.H. 1969. "Great Basin Hunting Patterns: A Quantitative Method for Treating Faunal Remains." *American Antiquity* 34(4): 392–401.

Thurston, T. L., and C. T. Fisher. 2007. "Seeking a Richer Harvest: The Archaeology of Subsistence Intensification, Innovation, and Change." In *Seeking a Richer Harvest: The Archaeology of Subsistence Intensification, Innovation, and Change*, ed. T. L. Thurston and C. T. Fisher, 1–21. Boston, MA: Springer.

Tieszen, L. L., B. C. Reed, N. B. Bliss, B. K. Wylie, and D. D. DeJong. 1997. "Ndvi, C3 and C4 Production, and Distributions in Great Plains Grassland Land Cover Classes." *Ecological Applications* 7(1): 59–78.

Ugan, A., J. Bright, and A. Rogers. 2003. "When Is Technology Worth the Trouble?" *Journal of Archaeological Science* 30(10): 1315–29.

Walker, E. G. 1992. *The Gowen Site: An Early Archaic Site on the Northern Plains*. Ottawa: Archaeological Survey of Canada, Paper 145. National Museum of Man.

Waters, M. R. 2019. "Late Pleistocene Exploration and Settlement of the Americas by Modern Humans." *Science* 365(6449): 1–9.

Weaver, J. E. 1968. *Prairie Plants and Their Environment*. Lincoln: University of Nebraska Press.

Wedel, W. R. 1940. *Cultural Sequences in the Great Plains*, 12. Washington DC: Smithsonian Institute.

———. 1953. "Some Aspects of Human Ecology in the Central Plains." *American Anthropologist* 55: 499–514.

Weitzel, E. M. 2019. "Declining Foraging Efficiency in the Middle Tennessee River Valley Prior to Initial Domestication." *American Antiquity* 84(2): 191–214.

Wheat, J. B. 1978. "Olsen-Chubbuck and Jurgens Sites: Four Aspects of Paleo-Indian Bison Economy." *Plains Anthropologist* 23(82): 84–89.

Widga, C. C. 2004. "Early Archaic Subsistence in the Central Plains: The Spring Creek (25ft31) Fauna." *Plains Anthropologist* 49(189): 25–58.

———. 2006. "Bison, Bogs, and Big Bluestem: The Subsistence Ecology of Middle Holocene Hunter-Gatherers in the Eastern Great Plains." PhD dissertation, University of Kansas, Lawrence.

Widga, C. C., S. N. Lengyel, J. Saunders, G. Hodgins, J. D. Walker, and A. D. Wanamaker. 2017. "Late Pleistocene Proboscidean Population Dynamics in the North American Midcontinent." *Boreas* 46(4): 772–82.

Wiessner, P. 2002. "Hunting, Healing, and Hxaro Exchange: A Long-Term Perspective on !Kung (Ju/'Hoansi) Large-Game Hunting." *Evolution and Human Behavior* 23: 407–36.

Williams, M. W., P. D. Brooks, and T. Seastedt. 1998. "Nitrogen and Carbon Soil Dynamics in Response to Climate Change in a High-Elevation Ecosystem in the Rocky Mountains, USA." *Arctic and Alpine Research* 30(1): 26–30.

Winterhalder, B. 1986. "Diet Choice, Risk, and Food Sharing in a Stochastic Environment." *Journal of Anthropological Archaeology* 5: 369–92.

Wismer, M. A. 2018. "Hunt, Gather, Garden: Faunal Exploitation during the Adoption of Agriculture in the Tallgrass Prairie." PhD dissertation, University of Iowa, Iowa City.

Witty, T. A., and J. D. Reynolds. 1982. *The Slough Creek, Two Dog and William Young Sites, Council Grove Lake, Kansas*. Topeka: Kansas State Historical Society.

Yansa, C. H. 1998. "Holocene Paleovegetation and Paleohydrology of a Prairie Pothold in Southern Saskatchewan, Canada." *Journal of Paleolimnology* 19(4): 429–41.

———. 2006. "The Timing and Nature of Late Quaternary Vegetation Changes in the Northern Great Plains, USA and Canada: A Re-Assessment of the Spruce Phase." *Quaternary Science Reviews* 25(3–4): 263–81.

Zeder, M. A. 2012. "The Broad Spectrum Revolution at 40: Resource Diversity, Intensification, and an Alternative to Optimal Foraging Explanations." *Journal of Anthropological Archaeology* 31(3): 241–64.

———. 2015. "Core Questions in Domestication Research." *Proceedings of the National Academy of Sciences* 112(11): 3191–98.

———. 2016. "Domestication as a Model System for Niche Construction Theory." *Evolutionary Ecology* 30(2): 325–48.

Chapter 7

Challenges and Prospects of Richness and Diversity Measures in Paleoethnobotany

Alan Farahani and R. J. Sinensky

The measurement of taxonomic diversity and richness is central to the interpretive mission of the analysis of archaeological plant remains—a subdiscipline of archaeology commonly referred to as paleoethnobotany or archaeobotany (Hastorf and Popper 1988; Marston et al. 2014). Archaeologists using archaeological plant data often wish to assess whether some sites or time periods contained a richer assemblage of wild or domesticated plant foods (i.e., diet breadth), whether particularly diverse or narrow plant assemblages were formed by pre- and post-depositional natural processes (i.e., taphonomy), and how cultural practices may have modified the range of plant taxa deposited on any particular archaeological site (i.e., cultural formation processes). In all of these cases, the methods by which archaeologists and related researchers estimate the taxonomic richness or diversity of recovered plant remains has a direct bearing on the interpretation of these socio-natural phenomena of interest.

Measures developed by ecologists and other bioscientists are uniquely suited for paleoethnobotanical data because they have been established and refined to identify plant and animal biodiversity in a wide range of contemporary observational and experimental contexts at differing spatial resolutions. Nevertheless, despite important foundational work by paleoethnobotanists trying to address this issue (Lepofsky and Lertzman 2005; Lepofsky and Lyons 2003), diversity and richness measures are less commonly employed in paleoethnobotanical research in comparison to zooarchaeological and even lithic and other archaeological remains (cf. Baxter

2001; Buchanan et al. 2017; Eren 2012; Eren et al. 2012; Eren et al. 2016; Faith and Du 2018; Faith and Lyman 2019; Lyman and Ames 2007). Moreover, many of these infrequent applications present point estimates (e.g., sample mean) and/or single measures such as a single Shannon diversity index value to characterize an entire plant assemblage for a given site, or a temporal interval that may represent tens or sometimes hundreds of samples collected in the process of fieldwork or excavation.

This chapter illustrates the benefits on both theoretical and empirical grounds of specific implementations of diversity estimation techniques used widely in ecology and affiliated biosciences that match the nature of paleoethnobotanical sample-based abundance and incidence data. The theoretical challenges inherent to archaeological plant assemblages are discussed in consideration of the assumptions of most measures of diversity and richness. Following that, the utility of these measures is highlighted through the analysis of the richness and diversity of large archaeological plant assemblages from three discrete temporal intervals at the site of Las Capas, located in the Sonoran Desert of the US Southwest. A major conclusion is that the implementation of diversity and richness estimation tools, broadly favored in studies of biodiversity, allows for a more accurate comparison of human–plant relationships in the past at a number of temporal and spatial scales, albeit while paying close attention to the specific mathematical and theoretical assumptions inherent in these approaches.

Definitions of Richness and Diversity

The concepts that underlie the terms "richness" and "diversity" exhibit great variation in the paleoethnobotanical literature, and the two terms are often conflated. Archaeologists interested in the abundance of different artifact "types" have long noted that richness and diversity are representative of two different concepts (Kintigh 1984, 1989). Here, we utilize the most common accepted definitions of richness and diversity derived from ecology and affiliated biosciences (e.g., Maurer, McGill, and Magurran 2011). The latter approach to richness and diversity is particularly appropriate for paleoethnobotany, given the analogous research questions in plant-based ecology and the analytic methodologies needed to answer them—for example, the number of species represented in a particular area, the taxonomic diversity of a given area after environmental disturbance at a number of spatial or temporal scales (Huston 2014), or the relationship between taxonomic richness and elevation (Poulos and Camp 2010; Toledo-Garibaldi and Williams-Linera 2014).

In this framework, richness is defined as the total number of identifiable categories, or in the case of paleoethnobotanical research, formal Linnean taxonomic groups such as families, genera, or species (see Fritz and Nesbitt 2014). A formalization can be found in (Eq. 1):

$$(Eq.\ 1)\ S = \sum j_i$$

where j is the ith identifiable taxonomic category. What this formalization underlines is that any such measure of richness is a straightforward tabulation of the total number of identified discrete taxonomic groupings, regardless of item abundance (Magurran 2004: 76). Therefore, if an assemblage has ten genera, the corresponding richness (S) would equal ten, regardless of the abundances (i.e., counts) within each genus.

By contrast, diversity refers to the apportionment or the abundance of individuals *across these taxonomic groupings* (Maurer, McGill, and Magurran 2011: 56–57; Magurran 2004: 115). As a result, individuals (i.e., counts) may be apportioned such that more individuals are found across a more restricted number of taxa (i.e., dominance) or spread equally among all taxa (i.e., evenness). The calculation of diversity has been modeled using many different approaches depending on the statistical parameters of interest and the assumptions of diversity; for example, more emphasis on dominance (McNaughton, Berger-Parker) or on evenness (Camargo, Shannon, RAD beta). An extended description of these measures will not be provided here as they are treated in great detail in the ecological literature (Avolio et al. 2019; Magurran 2004, 2011; Maurer, McGill, and Magurran 2011). The focus of this chapter is on the specific contribution of rarefaction (discussed below), although the application of these diversity measures to paleoethnobotany still awaits further research.

The distinction between richness and diversity in paleoethnobotanical assemblages must be stressed, as an assemblage may be particularly rich in the total number of taxa (i.e., high S), but the apportionment of individuals may be heavily dominant across a few taxa. For instance, a researcher comparing an assemblage (a_1) to another assemblage (a_2) may note that $S_{a_1} > S_{a_2}$ by a difference of five taxa and conclude that a_1 was a richer assemblage (Table 7.1). While a_1 is a richer assemblage (higher S), the *anthropological*

Table 7.1. Two hypothetical assemblages (a_1, a_2) illustrating the counts of individuals across nine distinct taxa ($T_1 ... T_9$).

	T_1	T_2	...	...	...	...	...	...	T_9	S	$1/D$
a_1	210	210	5	3	2	7	3	1	10	9	2.39
a_2	145	142	144	150	0	0	0	0	0	4	3.99

interpretation of a_1 may change if it is noted that >90 percent of identified specimens are found in two taxa of a_1, whereas 90 percent of specimens are nearly equally distributed across taxa in a_2. Therefore, diversity and richness encode two distinctive sources of information about taxonomic variability in any given assemblage.

As mentioned previously, there are a number of diversity measures available, each with their own assumptions. One such diversity measure is the Inverse Simpson index, which is the sum of the squared proportional abundances of all taxa (Eq. 2, see also Table 7.2), known as *1/D*.

$$(Eq.\ 2)\quad \frac{1}{D} = \frac{1}{\Sigma p_i^2}$$

Using this formula would generate a value of 2.39 for a_1 (lower diversity) and 3.99 for a_2 (higher diversity), illustrating that while $S_{a1} > S_{a2}$, it is nonetheless the case that $1/Da_1 < 1/Da_2$ (Table 7.1). While the Inverse Simpson index has been called "the most robust measure available" among diversity indices such as the Shannon and Hurlburt (Jost 2010; Magurran 2004: 115), it is incumbent upon researchers using archaeological plant remains to identify the underlying reasons for the use of one metric over another (i.e., based on the performance of the metric for that data or on specific considerations of the data itself). In addition to the specifics of each of

Table 7.2. Common measures of richness and diversity.

Type	Formula	Description
Richness	$S = \sum j_i$	A base accounting of the number of taxa, where j_i is the ith distinct taxonomic category.
Margalef	$S_{margalef} = \dfrac{S-1}{\ln NISP}$	S adjusted by the natural log of the assemblage *NISP*, where *NISP* is the total number of identified remains (total abundance).
Menhinick	$S_{menhinick} = \dfrac{S}{\sqrt{NISP}}$	S adjusted by the square root of the assemblage *NISP*, where *NISP* is the total number of identified remains (total abundance).
Chao 1	$S_{chao} = S_{obs} + \dfrac{f_1^2}{2f_2}$	Observed S adjusted by an estimate of the number of species present, but not observed, where f_1 is the number of singleton taxa, and f_2 is the number of doubleton taxa.
Diversity measures		
Inverse Simpson	$1/D = \dfrac{1}{\Sigma p_i^2}$	The inverse of the probability that two random individuals belong to the same taxon, where p is the proportion that the ith taxon comprises of the assemblage.
Shannon	$D_{shannon} = -\sum p_i \ln p_i$	An information theoretic diversity index, where p is the proportion that the ith taxon comprises of the assemblage.

Note: See Magurran and McGill (2011) for further descriptions and additional measures.

these measures and metrics, researchers must also consider a range of challenges inherent to the interpretation of archaeological plant assemblages.

Theoretical Challenges Inherent in Archaeological Plant Assemblages

Although applications of richness and diversity in paleoethnobotany have close analogs in ecological research, there are a number of key theoretical and empirical differences that must be considered before and after such analyses are implemented. Chief among them is the fact that fifty years of research by a number of paleoethnobotanists—such as van der Veen (1999, 2007), Jones (1987), Hillman (1984), Miksicek (1987), Minnis (1981), and Dennell (1972, 1976)—have shown that archaeological plant assemblages are highly filtered subsets of the plants that were actually used in the past, which in turn are highly filtered subsets of the vegetation that existed within a greater vegetative community and ecosystem.

There are many human and non-human processes that mediate between the vegetative landscape and what is ultimately deposited onto archaeological sites, and because people are culturally *selective* in which plant parts they ultimately desire for culinary, medicinal, or other reasons, archaeological contexts are intentionally or incidentally *constructed* environments, rather than so-called natural ones, as in the case of much ecological research (Crumley, Lennartsson, and Westin 2018; Levis et al. 2018; Rowley-Conwy and Layton 2011). The role of human vegetation management and its subsequent impact on the composition of the archaeological plant assemblage is especially evident for past communities with increased dependency on domesticated plants, where the "ambient vegetation" is often a highly managed field with its own agro-ecosystem (Rivera Núñez, Fargher, and Nigh 2020). And even when plant parts pass through this cultural filtering process, post-depositional preservation factors subsequently affect what ultimately *survives* in the archaeological record (Miksicek 1987; Schiffer 1976, 1983).

There is also variation in the *origins* of archaeological deposits that are sampled and compared. Consider two groups of ten samples (A, B), in which group A and B derive from deposits dating to two distinct time periods at the same site. An analyst wishes to compare the richness of plant remains dating to each of these periods, and determines that the richness of deposits dating to period A is much greater than for deposits dating to period B. Further investigation reveals, however, that the deposits dating to period A are the byproduct of crop processing, and thus contain a larger number of plant remains of non-food origin and intent (i.e., are not desired for consumption by the community). In contrast, the samples dating to period B derive exclusively from a well-preserved storage structure, where only processed food plants were kept. Is it appropriate to compare the richness of these assemblages?

Even if the comparison of richness were restricted to likely food items, the problem of culturally mediated deposition remains. It is possible that the deposits dating to period A represent processing activities for only a subset of the total food plants used by the community, whereas the probability is much higher that the storage structure (unless specialized) will represent a much broader cross section of available food plants. And finally, there is still the issue as to whether the archaeological contexts assigned in the course of excavation (posthole, pit, etc.) have any direct bearing on the archaeological plant remains found in them (i.e., whether the plant remains found in a pit are in fact evidence of what had been stored there; see Fuller, Stevens, and McClatchie 2014; Miksicek 1987). Therefore, there may be good theoretical reasons for grouping together deposits with distinct depositional origins, but these concerns are not strictly answerable through the interpretation of even robust diversity and richness measures or estimates, as the algorithmic implementation will compute, regardless of the data we provide to it.

In addition, routine paleoethnobotanical analyses lead to measures of richness that are biased downward due to the influence of taxonomic "double-counting." For instance, paleoethnobotanists frequently assign specimens to broader taxonomic groupings such as family (Poaceae, grasses), but also to more precise taxonomic levels such as genus (*Hordeum* spp., multiple barley species) or species (*Zea mays*, maize). If five specimens are identified as Poaceae, two as *Hordeum* spp., and one as *Zea mays*, it is possible that the specimens grouped under Poaceae represent more than one grass genus or species (Table 7.3). This is because the majority of plant parts that preserve in archaeological deposits in the broadest range of environmental conditions are typically seeds or durable dry fruits such as caryopses, achenes or nuts (Gallagher 2014; Minnis 1981; Pearsall 2015; White and Shelton 2014), especially after carbonization (Gremillion 1997; Hastorf 1999; Hastorf and Popper 1988; Hastorf and Wright 1998; VanDerwarker et al. 2016).

Table 7.3. Hypothetical inventory of identified plant remains from one assemblage, with taxonomic categories and richness (S) at the top.

	Poaceae	*Hordeum* spp.	*Zea mays*	S
Counted	5	2	1	3 (observed)
Maximum species represented	5	2	1	8 (potential)
Minimum species represented	1	1	1	3 (potential)

Moreover, only certain taxa produce seeds or dry fruits distinctive enough to be identified beyond family or genus. As a consequence, it is usually easier to identify more distinctive remains of certain plants (such as *Hordeum* spp. or *Zea mays*), whereas there can be a broad swath of grass (Poaceae) caryopses (i.e., grains) that are difficult to distinguish (Adams 2001: 69–70; Adams and Murray 2004), and yet may represent tens if not hundreds of species of grasses once present on the landscape. Therefore, a richness (*S*) of 3 based on these three taxonomic groupings is likely biased downward, as the true number of distinct taxonomic categories could be as high as eight (5 Poaceae + 2 *Hordeum* spp.+ 1 *Zea mays*). In this sense paleoethnobotanists are not *overcounting* the number of on-site taxa but rather *underestimating* the range of plant types that were deposited and/or used on any given site.

There may be ways to mitigate such downward biases, such as modeling the upper (maximum potential richness) and lower (minimum potential richness) boundaries of observed taxa, but this decision would still be an a priori consideration based in part on our assumptions regarding the range of taxa that we expect to recover at an archaeological site. As with the preceding richness and diversity measures, our research questions, and our choices to partition data into various contexts (pits, middens, etc.), or other groupings (primary refuse, secondary refuse, etc.) are integral to our empirical analyses. Researchers must carefully identify these operating archaeological assumptions in order to generate meaningful interpretations of taxonomic abundances and densities of archaeological plant remains.

Sample Size and Sampling Effort Effects

Apart from considerations of archaeological context, depositional pathways, and issues of taxonomic undercounting, the number of samples collected and the number of specimens recovered affects the identification of richness and diversity. Numerous ecologists and archaeologists have shown that richness is highly dependent on , that is the total number of identified specimens (i.e., plant remains for paleoethnobotanists, Baxter 2001; Chao et al. 2009; Cowgill 1989; Gotelli and Colwell 2001). As the number of identified specimens increases, so too do the represented taxa, and the relationship between the two is roughly log-linear, where there is usually an exponential increase in the number of taxa identified in the first few specimens that plateaus asymptotically as additional specimens are identified (Figure 7.1). As a result, several richness indices have been developed that attempt to incorporate and offset the effects of increasing sample size, and these include Margalef's (1951), Menhinick's (1964), and Chao's (1984,

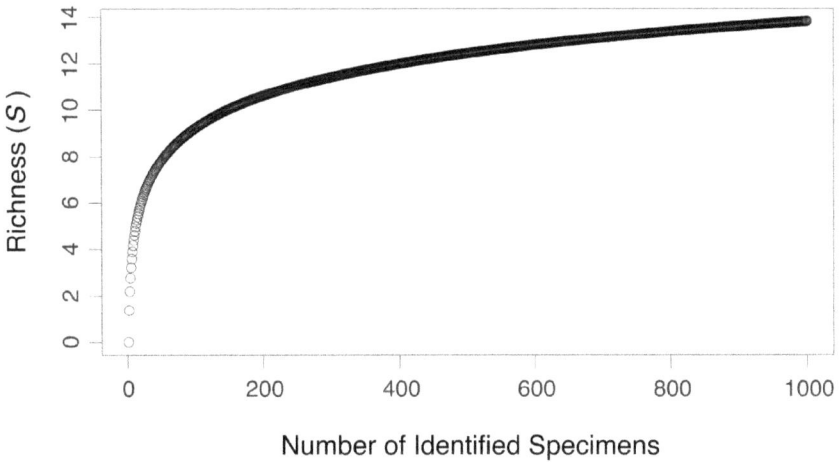

Figure 7.1. Hypothetical relationship between the number of identified specimens (usually counts of plant seeds, or similar disseminules) to the total number of taxa represented among them. © The authors.

1987), although each of these indices generates a point value only (Table 7.2). While N in the ecological formulation of these indices usually refers to one parameter (the counts of individual species), in paleoethnobotanical research, however, there are two distinct sources of N, namely, the total number of analyzed samples (N) and the total number of specimens identified across all samples ($NISP_N$).

As Lee (2012: 653) has argued, one of the most important parameters in estimating the density plant of taxa or remains at an archaeological site is the number of *samples* (in Lee's terminology, elements) collected during excavation, and not necessarily the number of individuals (i.e., NISP) per sample. This is because archaeological plant remains are obtained from discrete, physical samples collected from a bounded space (usually processed by some form of flotation if they are macrobotanical). As a consequence, there are a number of sampling effects that are due to the non-random spatial distribution of the archaeological remains of plant taxa. An increasing total number of samples (N) will affect total taxonomic richness, as each additional sample adds some variable amount of plant remains ($NISP_N$), which in turn increases the probability of adding a new taxonomic category up to some asymptotic point.

Since zooarchaeologists have also sought to identify the relationship between sample size, richness, and diversity in faunal assemblages, zooarchaeology is an instructive analog for paleoethnobotany. In zooarchaeological analyses, primary concern is how each individual identified faunal element contributes to the total number of identified taxa (or diversity; Faith and Lyman 2019: 197–218). How each element is collected in the field is essential; except in particular cases of "batch" sampling, most faunal remains are either hand-collected during excavation, or are retrieved from wet or dry sieving (Reitz and Wing 2008: 117–52). Therefore, the total number of identified specimens collected in this manner may be a reliable indicator of the taxonomic abundance (Faith and Lyman 2019: 57–59).

However, paleoethnobotanists do not collect *individual seeds* but rather *individual samples* of *varying volumes* from which seeds and other plant parts are extracted and then identified. These volumes are measurements, usually in liters (L), of the amount of archaeological sediment that is physically collected in the process of sampling. And because samples recovered from contexts closer to each other are more likely to contain a similar number and richness of recovered plant types (i.e., spatial autocorrelation; see Bacaro et al. 2016; Fortin et al. 2012; Ricotta et al. 2019), comparison of assemblages must also include comparison of the number of samples collected and the amount of archaeological sediment processed in aggregate. The reasons for this can be seen in Table 7.4. Although assemblage a_1 contains fewer of identified plant taxa (S), it has more total samples collected (N) and an accompanying larger amount of sediment processed (V_N). For its size, a_2 is a comparatively rich assemblage given the fewer number of samples collected as well as total sediment processed. As a corollary, the density of identified specimens in a_2 (2,000 seeds in 250 liters of processed sediment, or 8 seeds per liter) is much greater than a_1 (1,000 seeds in 500 L, or 2 seeds per liter). The notion of "comparatively rich" can be empirically assessed via a richness measure such as Margalef's or Menhinick's (see Table 7.2 for equations), both of which incorporate sample size (in this case $NISP_N$) in their calculations (Table 7.4). As a result, the estimation of richness must incorporate the total number of identified specimens ($NISP_N$) but also the total number of samples (N) in establishing differences in taxonomic richness or diversity between paleoethnobotanical assemblages. Paleoethnobotanical assemblages from archaeological sites can thus be defined by five separate components:

1. The total number of samples collected (N)
2. The total number of specimens identified across all samples ($NISP_N$)
3. The total amount of sediment collected across samples (V_N, measured in volume of sediment processed, usually liters (L), aka "sampling effort")
4. The amount of sediment collected per sample (V_i)
5. The number of items recovered per sample ($NISP_i$)

Table 7.4. Two hypothetical assemblages, with accompanying sampling information.

	N	$NISP_N$	V_N	S	$S_{Margalef}$	$S_{Menhinick}$	$\dfrac{NISP_N}{V_N}$
a_1	50	1,000	500	12	1.57	.374	2
a_2	25	2,000	250	13	1.58	.292	8

Note: For reference to each sampling parameter, please see the enumerated list provided in the text.

One of the major questions in the estimation of $NISP_N$ and S then for any given paleoethnobotanical assemblage is the effect and influence of sampling effort, or the volume of archaeological sediment collected per sample. Kadane (1988) provides a formalization of this relationship using the Poisson distribution in which the number of seeds in a sample ($NISP_i$) are modeled as a direct outcome of a Poisson process ($e^{-\lambda}\lambda^x/x$), where the number of seeds per deposit would be $NISP_i = V_i\lambda$, where λ is the dispersion parameter, or a constant value against which the volume (V_i) is multiplied to yield the predicted number of specimens per sample. The assumption latent to this, however, is that plant remains are uniformly distributed throughout an analyzed archaeological deposit (ibid.: 207). The number of seeds recovered in paleoethnobotanical samples, like many count data, however, are not uniformly distributed throughout excavated archaeological sediments but are *overdispersed*—that is, that the variance exceeds the mean (Ver Hoef and Boveng 2007). This violates a key assumption of the Poisson distribution, and a better distributional model for the data would be a negative binomial with a modification to allow a dispersion parameter θ, theta (Lindén and Mäntyniemi 2011).

Consequently, it is an empirical question as to whether the number of plant remains in any paleoethnobotanical assemblage is predicted by the volume of any given sample. This association is important because it determines whether sample volume must be considered *alongside* the total number of samples and identified specimens when considering past plant taxonomic abundance. Further research on the relationship of volume to the total number of plant remains recovered is necessary, but the following is an example that is illustrative of this process in which the number of samples, plant remains recovered, and volume are compared from two separate archaeological sites.

The first assemblage is from the archaeological site of Dhiban, located in the Hashemite Kingdom of Jordan, which has a multi-temporal inhabitation (ca. 1000 BCE–CE 1500). These deposits were sampled extensively from 2009 to 2019, and represent over 2,500 L of analyzed sediment across

211 samples (Farahani 2018). The second assemblage is from the site Las Capas, located in the Sonoran Desert of Arizona (USA). Las Capas also has a multi-temporal inhabitation (ca. 1200–700 BCE), and its deposits were sampled extensively by Desert Archaeology, Inc. (DAI) from 1998 to 2009, and represents over 6,000 L of sampled sediment across more than 1,300 analyzed samples (Diehl 2015, 2005; Sinensky and Farahani 2018a).

In order to compare the number of identified specimens recovered across samples and sample volumes at these two sites, a basic iterative resampling algorithm without replacement was written in R (R Core Team 2020). This procedure calculated the mean number of seeds and total volume of sediment from one to the total number of samples (1…max(N)), with fifty random draws at each step (Figure 7.2, Table 7.5). The results demonstrate that samples taken from Dhiban tended to be larger in sediment volume than those from Las Capas (Figure 7.2:A). The number of identified specimens, however, is in fact greater in the Las Capas assemblage for the same total sampled volume (i.e., density; Figure 7.2:B), whereas both sites exhibit roughly similar numbers of identified plant remains for an equivalent number of analyzed samples (Figure 7.2:C). How can this be the case?

These data illustrate the importance of *sampling effects*, especially volume, on the estimation of total abundance. The density of remains at Dhiban is

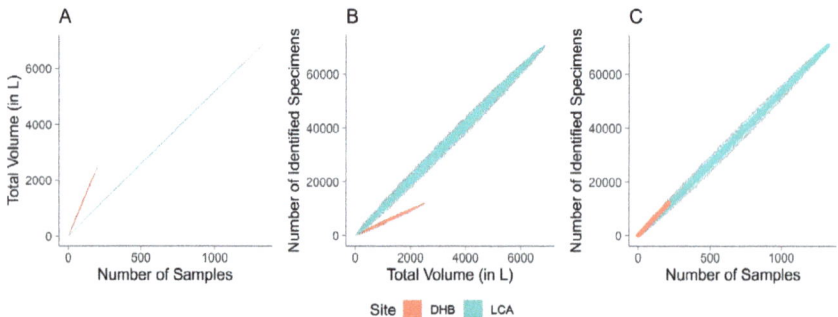

Figure 7.2. A comparison of the sampling outcomes of two archaeological sites from Jordan (Dhiban, DHB) and Arizona (Las Capas, LCA). (A) illustrates the total volume associated with increasing numbers of samples collected, (B) illustrates the average number of plant remains recovered from each site by total volume, while (C) does the same but by total number of samples. The ribbons in all cases are one standard deviation. © The authors.

Table 7.5. Summary statistics for the assemblages described in Figure 7.2.

Site	N	$V_N(L)$	$NISP_N$
DHB	211	2,548.5	12,136
LCA	1,324	6,873.6	70,824

likely lower than at Las Capas because samples at Dhiban tended to represent a larger volume of collected sediment—as a result, total specimen abundance at Dhiban is *less dense* than at Las Capas due to the consistent effect of the greater volume denominator (i.e., 5 items / 10 L is denser than 5 items / 100 L). There is much room for continued research on identifying the specific sampling effects of varying sample volume on NISP and abundance, but the use of the *number of samples* rather than the *total volume* may represent one way to reduce the effects of varying sample volumes.

In conclusion, the estimation of the richness and diversity of archaeological plant assemblages is contingent upon the *total number of samples collected*, as both the amount of archaeological sediment collected and the total NISP are correlated to the number of collected and analyzed samples. These results echo the recommendations drawn from decades of ecological field sampling, where Bonar, Fehmi and Mercado-Silva (2011: 21) note that "the more heterogeneity among samples, the more samples must be taken to estimate the parameter with a given degree of confidence. In addition, the more samples taken the better the chance of collecting rare species."

Empirical Modeling of Diversity in Paleoethnobotanical Assemblages

There is still much room for optimism regarding the analysis of richness and diversity in paleoethnobotanical assemblages, despite these theoretical challenges. Advances in open-source computation, especially in the R and Python languages, have made a panoply of robust diversity and richness measures more accessible for practicing paleoethnobotanists, and less onerous to input and visualize. In addition, a variety of implementations are available based on specific assumptions and arrangements of the data, such as whether the data are incidence-based (presence/absence) or abundance-based (NISP; i.e., raw count). In R there are the *vegan* (Oksanen et al. 2019), *iNEXT* (Hsieh, Ma, and Chao 2016, 2020), and *ade4* (Dray, Dufour, and Thioulouse 2020) packages; in Python there is *scikit-bio* and *ECOpy*, and the stand-alone free software *EstimateS* (Colwell and Elsensohn 2014). We expect that the accessibility and functionality of computational resources will improve and that new resources will be available by the time this chapter is published.

Rarefaction, Richness, and Diversity

As noted above, the total number of identified specimens *and* the total number of samples must be incorporated in any calculation of richness and diversity for paleoethnobotanical assemblages. Ecologists have developed a suite of methods bundled under "rarefaction" to offset the effect of sample size as measured in total samples (N) as well as the total number of identified specimens ($NISP_N$). The computation and visualization of rarefaction is an especially important component of the R packages *vegan* and *iNEXT*, as well as *EstimateS*.

Rarefaction is a statistical resampling technique that uses the available data to estimate the richness of a sample of a smaller total size (Cayuela, Gotelli, and Colwell 2015; Chao and Jost 2012; Chao et al. 2014; Colwell et al. 2012; Gotelli and Colwell 2001, 2011). The basic resampling sequence involves a resampling x times without replacement of n samples from a pool of N samples, at random, with the average richness plotted against the total number of samples (N) or individuals ($NISP_N$). Average richness can be calculated in many ways and these software packages and language platforms provide a means to compute and display a variety of these measures using either N or $NISP_N$ (e.g., Chao1, Chao2, ACE, etc.; see Colwell et al. 2012). Figure 7.3:A displays an annotated rarefaction curve in order to introduce the reader to the component parts of a typical plot.

If resampling takes place at the level of *samples*, then rarefaction is said to be *sample-based*, while if it takes place at the level of *individual counts*, then it is said to be *individual-based* (Gotelli and Colwell 2001). Given the preceding discussion, most paleoethnobotanical contexts require a *sample-based* approach due to the collection mechanism of archaeological plant remains in the field, namely carbonized plant remains derived from bulk or pinch flotation samples (d'Alpoim Guedes and Spengler 2014). A major advantage of sample-based rarefaction is therefore the reduction of inter-sample and inter-assemblage heterogeneity introduced by the varying numbers of individuals in samples of different volumes. In addition, there are *incidence-based* and *abundance-based* methods. Incidence-based methods use the presence and absence of taxa across samples alone when calculating average richness, while abundance-based methods incorporate the actual total counts within taxa.

Two "views" of a sample-based rarefaction conducted on the hypothetical paleoethnobotanical data provided in Table 7.4 are displayed in Figure 7.3:B. In both cases the y-axis represents *average expected richness* for a given number of samples or individuals. It is important to note that both graphs derive from a hypothetical calculation of *one* sample-based rarefaction—they display two visualizations of the same data and same calculation. As resampling in a rarefaction happens *either* at the level of the sample *or* of the individual, then a sample-based resampling procedure

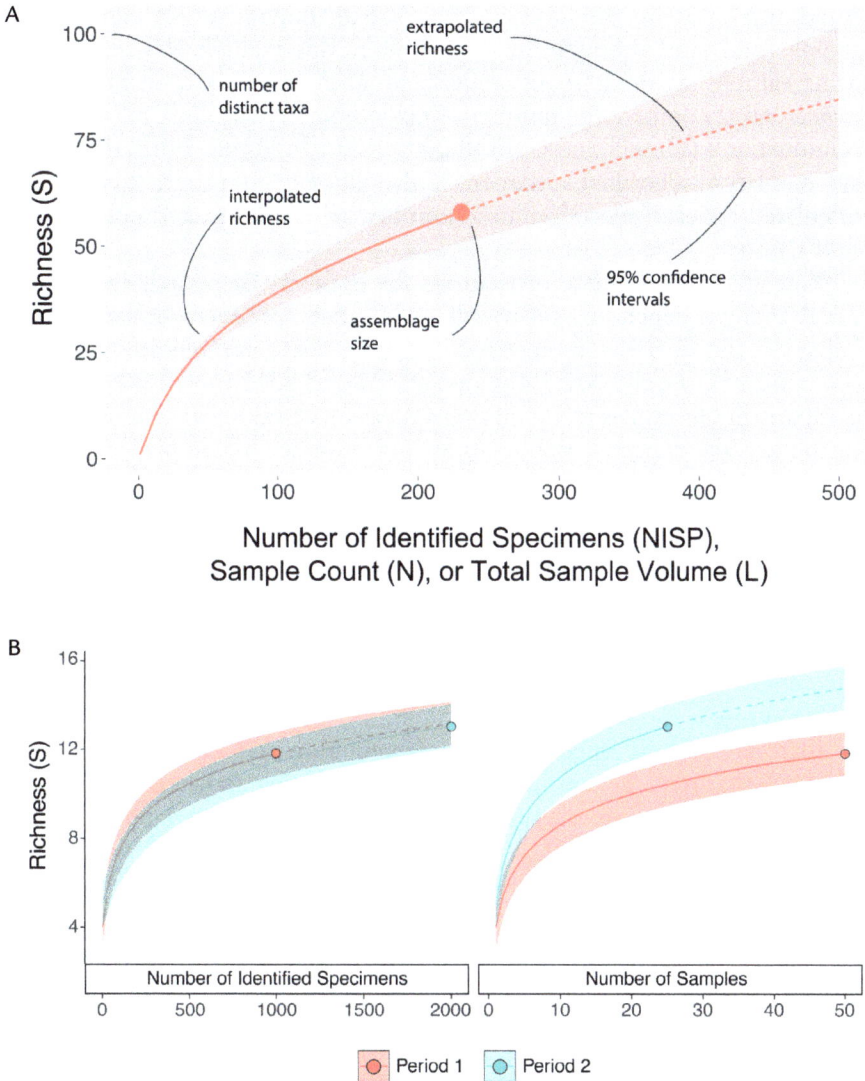

Figure 7.3. Sample-based rarefaction curves, comparing the number of identified specimens (NISP), or the total number of samples (N), or the total sample volume (in liters) to total richness (S): (A) An annotated sample-based rarefaction curve illustrating the component parts of a typical visualization for paleoethnobotanical data; (B) Sample-based rarefaction curves comparing richness to NISP and N for the data presented in Table 7.4. Here the hypothetical data are calculated on abundance data, hence the unit of resampling is the physical sample, not the number of individuals (NISP), although the average number of identified specimens (individuals) per sample is calculated as well in a sample-based rarefaction. © The authors.

could also calculate the (average) number of individuals per cumulative sample total. And although the rarefaction in this example was conducted using samples as the basis of analysis, all analyses focused on *taxonomic richness* must compare the number of taxonomic units against the number of individuals (Gotelli and Colwell 2001: 382). In Figure 7.3:B, the average number of identified specimens is also illustrated on the x-axis, as it is calculated for each successive total number of samples in a sample-based rarefaction.

Note that the estimate of richness for each of the periods in Figure 7.3:B changes depending on whether identified specimens or samples is being visualized. This difference has long been noted in ecological research (Gotelli and Colwell 2001; Longino and Colwell 2011), and it is because a comparison of samples to richness is a measure of *taxonomic density*—that is, the average expected richness per total number of samples (Colwell, Mao, and Chang 2004). As a result, it is common for two assemblages to show a difference in taxonomic density, but a negligible difference in taxonomic richness (i.e., average expected richness per total number of identified specimens) or even an opposite trend. This is because sample-based rarefaction captures the difference in patterns of *areal* abundance at the level of each discrete sample (here, N), while individual-based analysis theoretically models *individual* abundance that is assemblage-wide (here, $NISP_N$; Gotelli and Colwell 2001: 386–87).

There are several aspects of the interpretation and evaluation of rarefactions that must be considered by those analyzing archaeological plant remains. First, there are many cases in which the curves have not reached their asymptote—the point at which additional analysis does not result in greater richness. If so, then it is not possible to state what the "actual" richness of an assemblage is, but rather, two or more curves must be compared at their equivalent points of samples, specimens, or volumes. Gotelli and Colwell (2001: 385) also point out that genera reach their asymptotes faster than species-based analyses, and it is therefore likely that the broader taxonomic groupings assigned by paleoethnobotanists affect the rate at which an asymptote is reached.

Second, the terminal (right-most) points of the curves in these hypothetical rarefactions are left open, rather than closed. That is because this calculation must rely on the *unconditional variance* of the resampling estimate—closed curves (aka "banana plots") inaccurately represent *conditional variance* (Colwell, Mao, and Chang 2004; Colwell et al. 2012; Colwell and Elsensohn 2014). As the terminal point along the curve (right-most) also represents the point at which the greatest amount of accumulated variability exists within each assemblage, the confidence intervals will likely be open and widest. By contrast, confidence intervals are likely to be narrower in the earlier (left-most) portions of the curve because less variability exists at smaller sample sizes. Unconditional variance for sample-based rarefaction was introduced by Colwell, Mao, and Chang (2004), while unconditional variance for individual-based rarefaction was introduced by Colwell et al. (2012).

Not all existing software implementations model these curves with unconditional variance—currently, the packages with active implementation are *iNEXT* and *EstimateS*. However, most of the functions in the *vegan* package (*specaccum, rarefy,* etc.) are predicated on the conditional variance and therefore generate closed plots. There are also many algorithms for computing how best to resample an assemblage and then compute diversity indices: numerous proposals have been made to identify the models that link individual-based and sampled-based rarefaction, such as the Poisson and multinomial (see Colwell et al. 2012). It is therefore important to understand how different models, estimators, and underlying probability distributions affect the predicted outcomes of richness.

Finally, the rarefaction curves in Figure 7.3:B extend past the total number of samples collected, or the corresponding total number of identified specimens—that is, there is *extrapolation* beyond the observed totals. By contrast, there is *interpolation* of values between the observed numbers of samples or specimens. Extrapolation beyond observed totals is possible, and this is a primary goal of the *iNEXT* package in R (Hsieh, Ma, and Chao 2016). While the point of comparison along interpolated richness curves is typically limited to the terminus of the smallest assemblage, or the "reference sample size," extrapolation facilitates comparison between assemblages by doubling the size (or more) of the reference sample, thereby allowing the use of a greater amount of data (see discussion below). As with the methods above, however, it is critical to understand how extrapolation is mathematically calculated, and to assess whether such an estimate is appropriate for the assumptions underlying any given paleoethnobotanical assemblage.

In the following section we present an archaeological case study that utilizes a sample-based rarefaction to identify changes in diversity and richness in archaeobotanical assemblages recovered from functionally similar cultural features dating to three discrete temporal intervals.

Archaeological Case Study

Our archaeological case study comes from the site of Las Capas, which is found on the floodplain of the Santa Cruz River in the Sonoran Desert of Southeastern Arizona. The site was excavated by DAI in 1998–99 (Mabry

2008) and 2008–9 (Vint 2015; Vint and Nials 2015), and contains a well-preserved system of canal-fed agricultural fields, habitation structures and subterranean cooking and storage pits that date primarily to 1220–730 BCE (see Vint 2018 for an overview of the Archaic period in the Tucson Basin). Based on a broad suite of high-quality radiocarbon dates recovered from discrete strata, features have been divided into three distinct temporal intervals, 1220–1000 BCE, 930–800 BCE, and 800–730 BCE.

DAI employed a blanket sampling strategy, collecting approximately 6 liters of sediment from each 10 cm arbitrary or stratigraphic level excavated into thousands of cultural features. Macrobotanical plant remains were extracted from archaeological sediments via flotation. A subset of over thirteen hundred samples have been analyzed, yielding over seventy thousand taxonomically identifiable reproductive plant parts representing cultivated and foraged taxa, including maize, a variety of cacti and leguminous trees, and a broad array of ruderal annual plants encouraged by farming activities. The data in our analysis include those presented by Diehl (2005, 2015) and Sinensky (2013), and are available in Supplemental Table 2 ("Las Capas Flotation Data") in Sinensky and Farahani (2018b) (also see Appendix 7.1).

One of our major research questions was the extent to which the use of local plant resources was impacted by a series of moderate-intensity flood events in 930–800 BCE that caused disruptions to irrigation infrastructure. These floods are visible as discrete deposits of coarse alluvial sediments, which had inundated canals. Based on ecological studies of the effects of environmental disturbance events of varying intensity and frequency on plant richness, we hypothesized that this disturbance may have led to a greater richness and diversity of plants within the Las Capas agro-ecosystem that ultimately translated into greater foraged and farmed dietary diversity (following Connell 1978; Huston 1979, 2014; Kershaw and Mallik 2013; Yuan et al. 2016; but cf. Fox 2013; Sheil and Burslem 2013).

In order to identify the potential effects of these flood events, we calculated a variety of diversity and richness measures from the identified plant assemblages (see Sinensky and Farahani 2018a: 291–93). One approach to analysis could have been the generation of a single diversity index value (Shannon, Simpson, etc.) for each of the assemblages that date to these three time periods. Nevertheless, there are large differences between the total numbers of samples collected per time period, the total amount of flotation volume represented, and the number of identified specimens (Table 7.6).

We chose a class of rarefaction techniques to offset the effect of sample size as measured in total volume and the total number of identified specimens, and utilized a sample-based rarefaction that randomly resa-

Table 7.6. Summary data for the Las Capas paleoethnobotanical assemblage discussed in this chapter, including the date range associated with sampled deposits, the number of analyzed samples (N), the total volume of those samples (in liters), the number of identified plant remains $NISP_N$, the base richness (S), and an Inverse Simpson's index value (1/D).

Date Range	N	$V_N(L)$	$NISP_N$	S	1/D
800–730 BCE	633	3,345.2	39,099	38	1.64
930–800 BCE	217	1,137.5	16,233	35	3.19
1220–1000 BCE	474	2,390.9	15,492	37	2.32

mples *n* samples without replacement from the total pool of N samples weighted by sampling effort (i.e., sample volume) (Colwell et al. 2004, 2012; Gotelli and Colwell 2001; Oskanen et al. 2019). As mentioned previously, the estimation of average richness for a given number of samples represents *taxonomic density*. This was implemented in R using the *vegan* package (Oksanen et al. 2019) and the species accumulation curves (*specaccum*) function using the "random" method (Figure 7.4:A). This particular function incorporates "sampling effort" through declaration of an optional series of weights (here, the flotation volumes of each sample), which generates "the average effort per site, or sum of weights per number of samples" (Oskanen et al. 2019). The average species richness is then calculated from a linear interpolation of a single random permutation matrix of weights (here, the sample volumes) and of accumulated taxa.

In order to identify *taxonomic diversity*, we also utilized a sample-based rarefaction and measured mean expected richness based on the Inverse Simpson index, and we visualized NISP rather than total sample size in order to compare assemblages directly (Figure 7.4:B). This was implemented using the *EstimateS* software (Colwell and Elsensohn 2014). In both cases, we also calculated single point values of richness and diversity. As per our expectations, mean richness and diversity are greatest in the period with moderate intensity environmental disturbance (930–800 BCE), even when considering the same total analyzed volume or number of identified botanical specimens across periods. Note, however, that the outputs of the *specaccum* function model *interpolated* richness and the *conditional variance* of the rarefaction curves, and therefore do not permit a more accurate comparison of the smallest assemblage with the other time periods for an equivalent number of samples or volume. A more accurate comparison requires modeling the *extrapolated* richness and *unconditional variance* of all three assemblages to the terminus of the largest assemblage, which we implemented in R using the *iNEXT* package.

The computation of rarefaction in *iNEXT* involves the generation of Hill numbers, which calculate richness and diversity using a modification

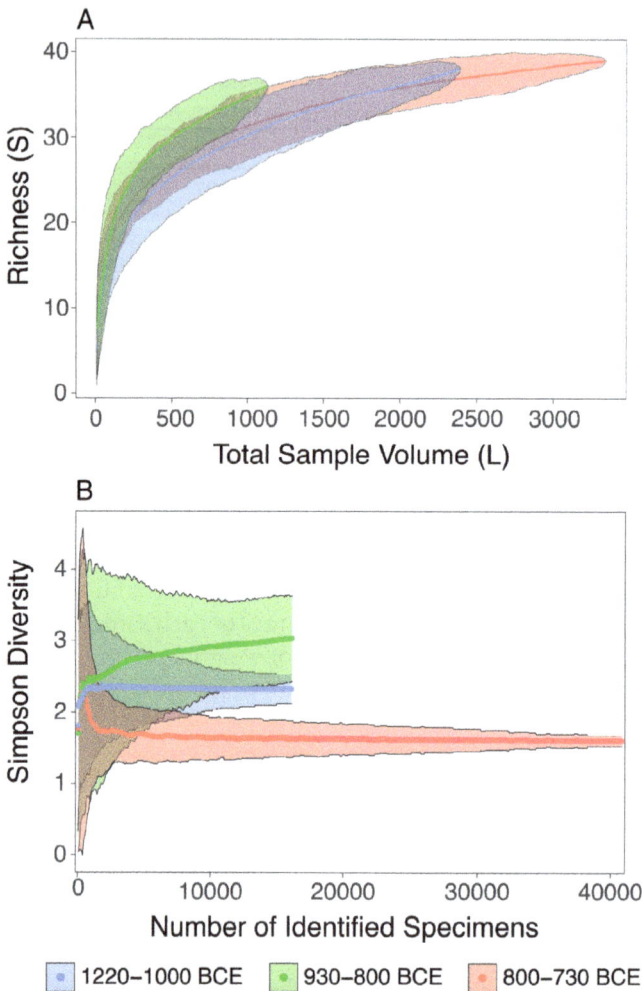

Figure 7.4. Taxonomic density (A) and diversity (B) computed from the three temporal phases at Las Capas, as reported in Sinensky and Farahani 2018. In both cases, analyses were conducted using a sample-based rarefaction. The color and fill of each curve represent a different temporal phase, as shown in the legend. © The authors.

of a single parameter "q", itself an equation that integrates species richness and relative abundances (Hill 1973; Jost 2006, 2007; MacArthur 1965). Ecologists have recently advocated the use of Hill numbers as a solution to the problem of "too many diversity indices" that exist for possible use in rarefaction or other applications, especially in biodiversity research (Chao, Chiu and Hsieh 2012; Chao et al. 2014; Ellison 2010). There are separate equations for deriving Hill numbers from abundance versus incidence data (see the extended discussion in Chao et al. 2014: 48–49). When q=0, basic richness is estimated; when q=1, the diversity index is "the exponential of Shannon entropy based on the relative incidences in the assemblage from which the sampling units are drawn," also known as Shannon diversity; while when q=2, the equation converges to Simpson diversity, specifically the "inverse Simpson concentration based on relative incidences" (Chao et al. 2014: 49, Appendices *passim*).

Using this implementation of Hill numbers on abundance data, the calculation of q=1, or Shannon diversity, reports the diversity of "typical" species, while when q=2, Simpson diversity reports the diversity of "dominant" species. The primary benefit from the use of Hill numbers is that each number models a *related yet distinctive component of diversity* in each assemblage—and therefore when rarefaction curves modeling the unconditional variance of all three indices are depicted side by side, they comprise a "diversity profile." We calculated a *sample-based* rarefaction in *iNEXT* using incidence data (presence or absence of taxa across samples), and an *individual-based* rarefaction using abundance data (total numbers of individuals identifiable to each taxon, $NISP_N$).

The *iNEXT* output of the sample-based rarefaction on incidence data reveals complementary but distinct results to our earlier analyses (Figure 7.5). First, we note that the *iNEXT* implementation models the extrapolated unconditional variance of all three assemblages to the terminus of the largest assemblage, and therefore provides a more robust comparison between assemblages (although richness extrapolation is only reliable beyond double the size of the reference sample in certain instances; see Chao et al. 2014: 53 for details). Second, for each Hill number "incidence data is interpreted as the effective number of *equally frequent* species in the assemblage from which the sampling units are drawn" (Chao et al. 2014: 49). For the sample-based calculation, all three Hill numbers reveal that the period of environmental disturbance, 930–800 BCE, contains the greatest richness per total number of samples (taxonomic density, Figure 7.5, q=0), and is also the most diverse (non-dominant, Figure 7.5, q=1, q=2). The extrapolated results (dotted lines) also illustrate the greater amount of variability present in the richness estimates of the samples dating to the period of environmental disturbance, which is visible as wider confidence intervals, a point to which we will return.

Nevertheless, the individual-based rarefaction on abundance (or count) data (Figure 7.5) provides results distinct from the sample-based rarefaction. As previously discussed, the individual-based rarefaction does not sample from a "list" of physical samples, but instead aggregates the total number of identified remains per identified taxonomic grouping (e.g., *Hordeum* spp.: 1,500, *Zea mays*: 10,000, etc.) and then samples from this

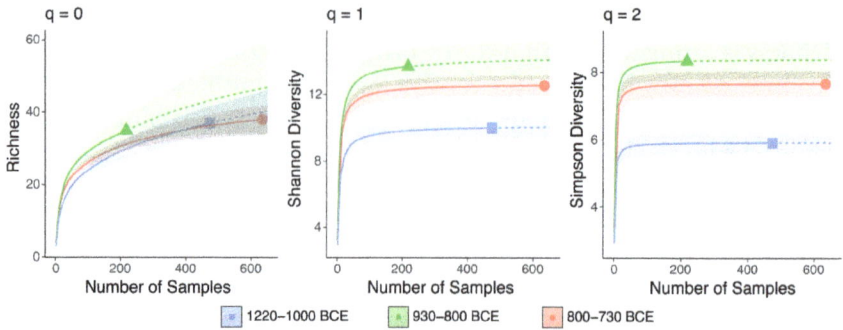

Figure 7.5. An inventory of Hill numbers calculated from *sample*-based rarefaction on *incidence* data using the *iNEXT* package. When q=0, the curves yield species richness; when q=1, the curves represent Shannon diversity; and when q=2, the curves represent Simpson diversity. © The authors.

"list" of specimens. The rarefaction results illustrate that taxonomic richness during the 930–800 BCE interval is slightly less than the earlier period (1220–1000 BCE) for an equivalent number of identified specimens, but both are greater than the last period (800–730 BCE). Nevertheless, the confidence intervals overlap for the richness estimates of all three of these periods, indicating a considerable amount of variation in the assemblages of each. Moreover, the extrapolation line for the mean expected richness of plant remains in the period of environmental disturbance, 930–800 BCE, suggests that this interval would likely be the richest with increased sampling.

The estimation of Shannon (Figure 7.6, q=1) and Simpson diversity (Figure 7.6, q=2) from the *iNEXT* individual-based abundance data also shows that for an equivalent number of identified specimens, the 930–800 BCE assemblage is far more diverse than the assemblages dating to the earlier and later periods. It is important to contrast these results with those generated using *EstimateS*. The *EstimateS* output (Figure 7.4:B; also see Supplemental Table 3 ['Las Capas EstimateS Output'] in Sinensky and Farahani 2018b) is calculated from a *sample*-based rarefaction on *abundance* data, and the visualization shows the mean Inverse Simpson index value for each successive total number of identified specimens. Because of the specific computation available in *EstimateS*, the average number of identified specimens (in this case, plant remains) is provided for each successive total number of samples alongside a suite of richness and diversity measures. As a consequence, because the *EstimateS* sample-based algorithm calculates the average number of individuals from abundance data, it is possible to ascertain the amount of *abundance* variability present in each time period, as counts are incorporated in the overall average calculation.

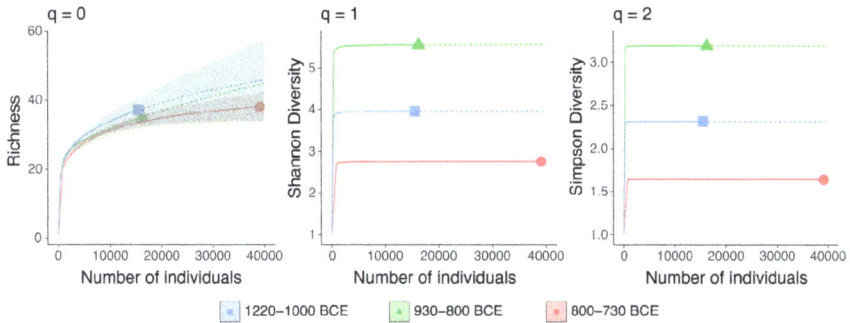

Figure 7.6. An inventory of Hill numbers calculated from *individual*-based rarefaction on *abundance* data using the *iNEXT* package. When q=0, the curves yield species richness; when q=1, the curves represent Shannon diversity; and when q=2, the curves represent Simpson diversity. © The authors.

While both the *EstimateS* and *iNEXT* analyses reveal the same temporal trends at Las Capas in terms of the decreasing diversity in plant types (930–800 BCE > 1220–1000 BCE > 800–730 BCE), the estimation of variability as is visible in dispersion around the mean is not present in the *iNEXT* output of the individual-based rarefaction (Figure 7.6). The reason for this is that *iNEXT* sample-based rarefaction does not currently generate the expected number of individuals. Moreover, the individual-based rarefaction is based on *individual abundance*, and not samples, and so sample-level diversity among individuals cannot be identified either. This is certainly not a limitation of *iNEXT*; rather, it reveals an important question for any archaeologist or other person analyzing past plant richness and diversity: to what extent is variation a meaningful signal of past human practices?

As has been shown, the calculation of rarefaction and accumulation curves can mitigate the effects of sample heterogeneity. It is possible to more confidently assert that the diversity and richness seen in response to the moderate intensity flood events of 930–800 BCE is not due to sample size or other related issues, but rather is capturing changes in agro-ecosystemic practice in the ancient Las Capas community. In addition, and in partial answer to the previous rhetorical question, the confidence intervals created in the sample-based rarefactions (figures 7.4:B and 7.5) also provide an important quantification of the amount of *variability* in the assemblages of each of these periods. The wide confidence intervals show that there is far more variability across the 930–800 BCE deposits, even when on average they are more diverse. The assemblage dating to this period is large in absolute numbers, representing at least sixteen thousand identified plant specimens. Therefore, the variability during this interval is not likely a function of small sample size, but of actual variation in human behavior across constructed contexts in response to flood events.

Not only are these changes to agro-ecosystemic practice visible in the fluctuating diversity and richness of botanical assemblages in response to the flood events, they are corroborated by a contemporary decline in the density and ubiquity of the primary agricultural crop, maize (Sinensky and Farahani 2018a: 291), and by geoarchaeological studies of agricultural soils from ancient fields and canals that demonstrate less intensive irrigation and canal upkeep compared to earlier and later periods (Nials 2015; Sinensky and Farahani 2018a: 287–89). We argue that this is due to changing farming and foraging practices, which we have discussed elsewhere at length (Sinensky and Farahani 2018a). By comparison, the following interval (800–730 BCE), during which floodplain conditions were optimal for irrigation agriculture, exhibits low diversity despite a high total-assemblage richness. This shows that inter-deposit variability is low, likely because these samples are consistently dominated by the primary food crop (maize) and a narrow range of associated ruderal taxa (as observed in sample-by-sample paleoethnobotanical analysis).

Discussion

Based on the previous overview of richness and diversity measures in paleoethnobotanical research, rarefaction, and the archaeological case study from Las Capas, the following discussion follows two themes: interpretive and technical. By interpretive, we ask in what way the results from rarefaction or accumulation curves can inform our interpretations of the human past. As for technical concerns, we summarize the relative advantages and disadvantages of the computational and statistical options available for measuring diversity and richness at the time of this writing. We then conclude with suggestions for the implementation of such metrics in future paleoethnobotanical research.

Interpretation of Taxonomic Richness and Diversity

It may appear that interpretation of the rarefaction curves generated for each of the time periods at Las Capas is straightforward—greater richness and diversity translate to a confirmation of the proposed environmental disturbance hypothesis. Nevertheless, this interpretation is not as straightforward as it appears, because it is the routine food cultivation, collection, preparation and consumption practices of hundreds of community members in the past that generate the diversity observed in each archaeobotanical assemblage. Which past cultural practices are leaving the traces of diversity that we are able to detect using rarefaction thousands of years later? This raises an interpretive problem—namely, what the calculated taxonomic density and richness might *mean* within the space of paleoethnobotanical interpretation. Like any discipline, the interpretation of the results of rarefaction is directly tied to the nature of the data we are investigating, and in this case, is largely a function of the practices of past communities who left these traces. The interpretation of rarefaction of contemporary plants collected in random quadrats on a mountain slope is different than a rarefaction of a three-thousand-year-old plant assemblage collected from what was once the residence of an extended household.

In that vein, it has been noted previously in this chapter that the identification of depositional routes is tantamount in the analysis of archaeological plant remains—why were some plants burnt by past communities (if indeed they were burnt by them), and how did they come to be part of the archaeological record? The question of depositional pathways of archaeological plant remains is likely closely associated with the interpretation of taxonomic density. For example, the greater amount of taxonomic density that can be seen in the period 930–800 BCE in the Las Capas data implies that a more even distribution of plant types (Shannon and Simpson diversity, q=1, q=2) was being *deposited* by Las Capas community members, and hence entered the archaeological record through these depositional acts in the places that were later sampled.

Nevertheless, there is considerable variability across sampled contexts (visible in the wider confidence intervals for this temporal interval), and this too likely points to intentional or unintentional spatial differences in the practices that resulted in the deposition of plant food remains. It is useful to contrast the variability in taxonomic density in the 930–800 BCE interval with the subsequent period, 800–730 BCE, when the Las Capas community deposited a similarly diverse yet less variable array of plants (note the partially overlapping confidence intervals in the sample-based rarefaction, Figure 7.5, q=1 and q=2). The fact that this most recent interval (800–730 BCE) shows a more similar diversity profile in taxonomic density to the period of disturbance before it, even as the productivity of irrigation agriculture rebounded to pre-disturbance levels, suggests that social memory of the spatially bound *practices* adopted in response to the disturbance events were maintained in some capacity (Sinensky and Farahani 2018a: 295–96).

Even still, the individual-based rarefaction reveals that there is a far more restricted, or dominant, range of plant types *assemblage-wide* in this most recent interval, in contrast to the high diversity of the preceding 930–800 BCE interval (Figure 7.5, q=1 and q=2). Therefore, the information being provided by both the sample-based (Figure 7.5) and the individual-based (Figure 7.6) computation of Hill numbers reveals complementary but slightly diverging trends about the same assemblage. The lower diversity of the most recent interval in the individual-based calculation as compared to its higher value in the sample-based calculation implies that while the practices that occurred at the spatial level of a *sample* generated a somewhat more diverse assemblage similar to the period before it (taxonomic density), the broader practices of growing, handling, depositing, and burning plant remains at the scale of the site-wide assemblage were heavily biased towards a restricted range of activities that resulted in the *overall* deposition of maize and a narrower set of disturbance plants encouraged by agricultural activities (taxonomic richness).

But the question of interpretation still remains. Do these differences in taxonomic richness and density represent (a) more in-field plant diversity in response to environmental disturbance, (b) a broader diet that we can detect due to culinary accidents, or (c) increased food processing on-site, and hence more probability of deposition due to an increased scale of processing—or some combination of all three? These richness and diversity measures do not, in fact, provide a "smoking gun" to decide between these alternatives, which must be investigated using a wider variety of paleoethnobotanical measures, such as weighted proportions of collected plant taxa, and additional lines of archaeological evidence—for example, comparison to artifactual (groundstone), paleoecological, or paleoenvironmental data. Nevertheless, these measures themselves provide the foundational starting point for any discussion regarding the taxonomic density and richness of archaeological plant remains.

Technical Concerns

It is also clear from the preceding example that the specific statistical assumptions underlying a chosen model will impact data interpretation. For instance, the *iNEXT* package in R is an implementation of statistical theory developed in several key papers regarding the use of Hill numbers in the rarefaction of abundance and incidence data (Chao et al. 2014; Chao and Jost 2012; Colwell et al. 2012; Hsieh et al. 2016). A key element of the calculation of these Hill numbers using rarefaction is the concept of *coverage-based rarefaction* (Chao and Jost 2012), which is also derived and visualizable in *iNEXT*, although not presented graphically here. In this approach, samples are compared based on a notion of "sample completeness." Samples standardized by size alone vary in completeness, and thus only those samples with similar levels of "coverage" should be compared. Although the preceding discussion did not touch upon this aspect of the calculation of rarefaction using the *iNEXT* package, it is nonetheless critical. Future research will be necessary to demonstrate how the concept of *sample coverage* (or just "coverage") can be extended and explained in terms of paleoethnobotanical data, and it is important to acknowledge this aspect of the underlying computation of *iNEXT* rarefaction. As a consequence, archaeological researchers using these tools must familiarize themselves as much as possible with the technical details of various implementations to be able to accurately model and compare assemblages across time and space. We hope that we have demonstrated several key issues that paleoethnobotanists and any researchers using archaeological plant data ought to consider when using richness and diversity measures to answer questions about the past.

Conclusion

Paleoethnobotanists have interpreted fluctuating plant food diversity as indicative of warfare (VanDerwarker, Marcoux, and Hollenbach 2013; VanDerwarker and Wilson 2016), socioeconomic differentiation (Lentz 1991; Turkon 2004), imperial interventions (Farahani 2018; Morehart and Eisenberg 2010; van der Veen 2008), divergent mobility strategies (Bonzani 1997; Lepofsky 2000; Rocek 1995; Wagner 2008), and human-induced environmental change (Marston 2011, 2017; Pearsall 1983; VanDerwarker 2006, 2010). At times, conclusions have been drawn from either simple numerical tabulations of identified taxa, or single point values of diversity indices (Shannon, Simpson, etc.) without considering the relative strengths or weaknesses of such measures. Indeed, there is now broader consensus amongst ecologists and statisticians that variants of the "diversity profile" presented previously are one solution to this issue. The use of rarefaction and accumulation techniques, even on already published data, might reveal additional dimensions of interpretation that previous methods did not.

In addition, estimates of richness and diversity in paleoethnobotany are dependent on more than the statistical parameters of interest and the assumptions of diversity. The methods employed by paleoethnobotanists during analysis—for example, only sorting larger plant remains and sub-sampling smaller fraction sizes (see Fritz and Nesbit 2014)—may make certain approaches less applicable for modeling richness and diversity for a given assemblage. Moreover, it may or may not be appropriate to include samples recovered from all archaeological contexts or deposits on theoretical grounds. Paleoethnobotanists should therefore be transparent regarding why particular measures, indices, or models are employed in their analyses. After choosing appropriate methods, any measure or estimate of richness and diversity must then control for the total number of samples collected. We hope that this fact alone encourages archaeologists to collect more samples at their field sites across a wide variety of contexts in order to form robust estimates of the richness and diversity of past plants (Guedes and Spengler 2014: 78–79; Lennstrom and Hastorf 1992). Additional research focused on the interpretative and technical aspects of rarefaction pertinent to paleoethnobotanical applications will improve their utility for investigating human–plant relationships. Broader engagement by paleoethnobotanists with current analytic methodologies favored by plant-based ecologists, and collaborative research that brings together bioscientists, statisticians, and paleoethnobotanists, will ultimately help facilitate such improvements.

In conclusion, the use of rarefaction and accumulation techniques is critical in establishing an empirically robust baseline discussion of taxonomic richness and diversity that exists in paleoethnobotanical assemblages, given variability across samples. A careful consideration of depositional and taphonomic processes is necessary, as it is not possible to "plug and pray" data into these model frameworks, and expect them to generate incontrovertible scientific data. In that respect, like in many other sciences, it is necessary to move away from point values and binary "reject–accept thinking," and towards capturing and displaying the variation in these data, and visualizing uncertainty. These approaches will then facilitate more precise detection of past human–plant relationships through the noise of sampling, taphonomy, and a myriad of other factors.

Acknowledgments

The authors would like to thank R. Lee Lyman, Sarah Oas, and two anonymous reviewers for suggestions that improved the quality of this manuscript. In addition, we thank Anne Chao and Robert Colwell for insightful conversation and recommendations that increased the accuracy and clarity of this manuscript. Any remaining errors are ultimately ours. Research and excavations at Las Capas were funded by Pima County, Arizona. Desert Archaeology, Inc. (DAI)'s 2008–9 project was administered by the Tres Rios Reclamation Facility and the Pima County Office of Sustainability and Conservation, Cultural Resources and Historical Preservation Division.

Alan Farahani is founder and analyst at SciScope Solutions.

R. J. Sinensky is a PhD candidate at the University of California, Los Angeles.

Appendix 7.1. Abundance of Reproductive Plant Parts Recovered from the Las Capas Site, Southeastern Arizona, 1220–730 BCE

	800–730 BCE	930–800 BCE	1220–1000 BCE
Total Volume (L)	3,345.2	1,137.5	2,390.9
Total Number of Samples (N)	633	217	474
Achnatherum hymenoides	8	2	0
Asteraceae	46	161	88
Astragalus spp.	142	42	5
Atriplex spp.	18	22	85
Boerhaavia spp.	124	30	6
Carnegiea gigantea	67	18	230
Cereus sp.	0	1	1
Chenopodium / Amaranthus type	30,240	8,428	9,655
Cleome / Polanisia type	236	280	133
Cucurbitaceae	15	1	1
Cyperaceae	39	93	19
Dasylirion spp.	1	0	1
Descurainia pinnata	223	179	39
Echinocereus / Mammillaria type	37	8	444
Ephedra sp.	0	1	0
Eschscholtzia sp.	1	0	0
Euphorbiaceae	8	3	3
Ferocactus spp.	1	0	5
Garryaceae	5	0	0
Hordeum spp.	3	6	1
Juglans spp.	0	1	1
Juniperus spp.	4	0	1
Kallstroemia spp.	4	0	2
Lamiaceae	224	214	55
Larrea sp.	1	0	1
Lepidium spp.	2,189	46	277
Mollugo sp.	6	23	14
Nicotiana spp.	1	0	0
Opuntia spp.	174	28	25
Oxalis sp.	0	1	0
Panicum spp.	10	10	9

(continued)

	800–730 BCE	930–800 BCE	1220–1000 BCE
Papaveraceae	0	1	0
Phaseolus sp.	0	1	1
Poaceae	421	241	149
Polygonaceae	277	37	43
Portulaca sp.	199	35	70
Prosopis / Acacia type	327	2,721	151
Rhus sp.	3	0	0
Solanaceae	3	1	5
Sphaeralcea spp.	2	98	7
Sporobolus spp.	351	1,597	36
Suaeda sp.	168	544	505
Trianthema portulacastrum	130	425	319
Vitis arizonica	0	0	2
Zea mays	3,391	934	3,103

Note: See Sinensky and Farahani (2018b) Supplemental Table 2 for sample-level data.

References

Adams, K. R. 2001. "Looking Back Through Time: Southwestern U.S. Archaeobotany at the New Millennium." In *Ethnobiology at the Millennium: Past Promise and Future Prospects*, ed. R. I. Ford, 49–99. Anthropological Papers 91. Ann Arbor: Museum of Anthropology, University of Michigan.

Adams, K. R., and S. S. Murray. 2004. "Identification Criteria for Plant Remains Recovered from Archaeological Sites in the Central Mesa Verde Region." https://www.crowcanyon.org/researchreports/Archaeobotanical/Plant_Identification/plant_identification.asp.

Avolio, M. L., E, J. Forrestel, C. C. Chang, K. J. La Pierre, K. T. Burghardt, and M. D. Smith. 2019. "Demystifying Dominant Species." *New Phytologist* 223(3): 1106–26.

Bacaro, G., A. Altobelli, M. Cameletti, D. Ciccarelli, S. Martellos, M. Palmer, C. Ricotta, D. Rocchini, S. Scheiner, E. Tordoni, and A. Chiarucci. 2016. "Incorporating Spatial Autocorrelation in Rarefaction Methods: Implications for Ecologists and Conservation Biologists." *Ecological Indicators* 69: 233–38.

Baxter, M. J. 2001. "Methodological Issues in the Study of Assemblage Diversity." *American Antiquity* 66(4): 715–25.

Bonar, S. A., J. S. Fehmi, and N. Mercado-Silva. 2011. "An Overview of Sampling Issues in Species Diversity and Abundance Surveys." In *Biological Diversity: Frontiers in Measurement and Assessment*, ed. A. E. Magurran and B. J. McGill, 11–24. Oxford: Oxford University Press.

Bonzani, R. M. 1997. "Plant Diversity in the Archaeological Record: A Means Toward Defining Hunter-Gatherer Mobility Strategies." *Journal of Archaeological Science* 24(12): 1129–39.

Buchanan, B., A. Chao, C.-H. Chiu, R. K. Colwell, M. J. O'Brien, A. Werner, and M. I. Eren. 2017. "Environment-Induced Changes in Selective Constraints on Social Learning during the Peopling of the Americas." *Scientific Reports* 7: 44431.

Cayuela, L., N. J. Gotelli, and R. K. Colwell. 2015. "Ecological and Biogeographic Null Hypotheses for Comparing Rarefaction Curves." *Ecological Monographs* 85(3): 437–55.

Chao, A. 1984. "Nonparametric Estimation of the Number of Classes in a Population." *Scandinavian Journal of Statistics* 11: 265–70.

———. 1987. "Estimating the Population Size for Capture–Recapture Data with Unequal Catchability." *Biometrics* 43(4): 783–91.

Chao, A., C.-H. Chiu, and T. C. Hsieh. 2012. "Proposing a Resolution to Debates on Diversity Partitioning." *Ecology* 93(9): 2037–51.

Chao, A., R. K. Colwell, C.-W. Lin, and N. J. Gotelli. 2009. "Sufficient Sampling for Asymptotic Minimum Species Richness Estimators." *Ecology* 90(4): 1125–33.

Chao, A., N. J. Gotelli, T. C. Hsieh, E. L. Sander, K. H. Ma, R. K. Colwell, and A. M. Ellison. 2014. "Rarefaction and Extrapolation with Hill Numbers: A Framework for Sampling and Estimation in Species Diversity Studies." *Ecological Monographs* 84(1): 45–67.

Chao, A., and L. Jost. 2012. "Coverage-Based Rarefaction and Extrapolation: Standardizing Samples by Completeness Rather than Size." *Ecology* 93(12): 2533–47.

Colwell, R. K, A. Chao, N. J. Gotelli, S.-Y. Lin, C. X. Mao, R. L. Chazdon, and J. T. Longino. 2012. "Models and Estimators Linking Individual-Based and Sample-Based Rarefaction, Extrapolation and Comparison of Assemblages." *Journal of Plant Ecology* 5(1): 3–21.

Colwell, R. K., and J. E. Elsensohn. 2014. "EstimateS Turns 20: Statistical Estimation of Species Richness and Shared Species from Samples, with Non-Parametric Extrapolation." *Ecography* 37(6): 609–13.

Colwell, R. K., C. X. Mao, and J. Chang. 2004. "Interpolating, Extrapolating, and Comparing Incidence-Based Species Accumulation Curves." *Ecology* 85(10): 2717–27.

Connell, J. H. 1978. "Diversity in Tropical Rain Forests and Coral Reefs." *Science* 199(4335): 1302–10.

Cowgill, G. L. 1989. "The Concept of Diversity in Archaeological Theory." In *Quantifying Diversity in Archaeology*, ed. R. D. Leonard and G. T. Jones, 131–41. Cambridge: Cambridge University Press.

Crumley, C. L., T. Lennartsson, and A. Westin. 2018. *Issues and Concepts in Historical Ecology: The Past and Future of Landscapes and Regions*. Cambridge: Cambridge University Press.

d'Alpoim Guedes, J., and R. Spengler. 2014. "Sampling Strategies in Paleoethnobotanical Analysis." In *Method and Theory in Paleoethnobotany*, ed. J. M. Marston, J. D. Guedes, and C. Warinner, 115–46. Boulder: University of Colorado Press.

Dennell, R. W. 1972. "The Interpretation of Plant Remains: Bulgaria." In *Papers in Economic Prehistory*, ed. E. S. Higgs, 149–59. Cambridge: Cambridge University Press.

———. 1976. "The Economic Importance of Plant Resources Represented on Archaeological Sites." *Journal of Archaeological Science* 3(3): 229–47.

Diehl, M. W. 2005. "Early Agricultural Period Foraging and Horticulture in Southern Arizona: Implications from Plant Remains." In *Subsistence and Resource Use Strategies of Early Agricultural Communities in Southern Arizona*, ed. M. W. Diehl, 73–90. Anthropological Papers 34. Tucson: Archaeology Southwest.

———. 2015. "Macrobotanical Data from Las Capas, AZ AA:12:111(ASM)." https://www.archaeologysouthwest.org/pdf/las%20capas_online_macrobot.pdf

Dray, S., A.-B. Dufour, and J. Thioulouse. 2020. "Package 'Ade4'—Version 1.7-15—Analysis of Ecological Data: Exploratory and Euclidean Methods in Environmental Sciences."

https://mran.revolutionanalytics.com/snapshot/2020-02-09/web/packages/ade4/ade4
.pdf.

Ellison, A. M. 2010. "Partitioning Diversity." *Ecology* 91(7): 1962–63.

Eren, M. I. 2012. "Were Unifacial Tools Regularly Hafted by Clovis Foragers in the North
American Lower Great Lakes Region? An Empirical Test of Edge Class Richness and
Attribute Frequency among Distal, Proximal, and Lateral Tool-Sections." *Journal of
Ohio Archaeology* 2: 1–15.

Eren, M. I., A. Chao, C.-H. Chiu, R. K. Colwell, B. Buchanan, M. T. Boulanger, J. Darwent,
and M. J. O'Brien. 2016. "Statistical Analysis of Paradigmatic Class Richness Supports
Greater Paleoindian Projectile-Point Diversity in the Southeast." *American Antiquity*
81(1): 174–92.

Eren, M. I., A. Chao, W.-H. Hwang, and R. K. Colwell. 2012. "Estimating the Richness
of a Population When the Maximum Number of Classes Is Fixed: A Nonparametric
Solution to an Archaeological Problem." *PLoS ONE* 7(5): e34179.

Faith, J. T., and A. Du. 2018. "The Measurement of Taxonomic Evenness in Zooarchaeology." *Archaeological and Anthropological Sciences* 10: 1419–28.

Faith, J. T., and R. L. Lyman. 2019. *Paleozoology and Paleoenvironments: Fundamentals,
Assumptions, Techniques.* Cambridge: Cambridge University Press.

Farahani, A. 2018. "A 2500-Year Historical Ecology of Agricultural Production under Em-
pire in Dhiban, Jordan." *Journal of Anthropological Archaeology* 52: 137–55.

Fortin, M.-J., P. A. M. James, A. MacKenzie, S. J. Melles, and B. Rayfield. 2012. "Spatial Statistics, Spatial Regression, and Graph Theory in Ecology." *Spatial Statistics* 1:
100–109.

Fox, J. W. 2013. "The Intermediate Disturbance Hypothesis Should Be Abandoned."
Trends in Ecology and Evolution 28(2): 86–92.

Fritz, G., and M. Nesbitt. 2014. "Laboratory Analysis and Identification of Plant Macrore-
mains." In *Method and Theory in Paleoethnobotany*, ed. J. M. Marston, J. D. Guedes, and
C. Warinner, 115–45. Boulder: University of Colorado Press.

Fuller, D. Q., C. Stevens, and M. McClatchie. 2014. "Routine Activities, Tertiary Refuse
and Labor Organization: Social Inferences from Everyday Archaeobotany." In *Ancient
Plants and People: Contemporary Trends in Archaeobotany*, ed. M. Madella, C. Lancelotti,
and M. Savard, 174–217. Tucson: University of Arizona Press.

Gallagher, D. E. 2014. "Formation Processes of the Macrobotanical Record." In *Method
and Theory in Paleoethnobotany*, ed. J. M. Marston, J. D. Guedes, and C. Warinner, 19–34.
Boulder: University of Colorado Press.

Gotelli, N. J., and R. K. Colwell. 2001. "Quantifying Biodiversity: Procedures and Pitfalls in
the Measurement and Comparison of Species Richness." *Ecology Letters* 4(4): 379–91.

———. 2011. "Estimating Species Richness." In *Biological Diversity: Frontiers in Measurement and Assessment*, ed. A. E. Magurran and B. J. McGill, 39–54. Oxford: Oxford
University Press.

Gremillion, Kristen J, ed. 1997. *People Plants and Landscapes: Studies in Paleoethnobotany.*
Tsucaloosa: University of Alabama Press.

Hastorf, C. A. 1999. "Recent Research in Paleoethnobotany." *Journal of Archaeological Research* 7(1): 55–103.

Hastorf, C. A., and V. S. Popper, eds. 1988. *Current Paleoethnobotany: Analytical Methods and
Cultural Interpretations of Archeological Plant Remains.* Chicago: University of Chicago
Press.

Hastorf, C. A., and M. F. Wright. 1998. "Interpreting Wild Seeds from Archaeological Sites:
A Dung Charring Experiment from the Andes." *Journal of Ethnobiology* 18: 211–27.

Hill, M. O. 1973. "Diversity and Evenness: A Unifying Notation and Its Consequences." *Ecology* 54(2): 427–32.

Hillman, G. C. 1984. "Traditional Husbandry and Processing of Archaic Cereals in Recent Times: The Operations, Products and Equipment Which Might Feature in Sumerian Texts." *Bulletin on Sumerian Agriculture* 2: 1–31.

Hsieh, T. C., K. H. Ma, and A. Chao. 2016. "iNEXT: An R Package for Rarefaction and Extrapolation of Species Diversity (Hill Numbers)." *Methods in Ecology and Evolution* 7(12): 1451–56.

———. 2020. "Package 'iNEXT', Version 2.0.20—Interpolation and Extrapolation for Species Diversity." Wiley Online Library. http://chao.stat.nthu.edu.tw/wordpress/software_download/.

Huston, M. A. 1979. "A General Hypothesis of Species Diversity." *The American Naturalist* 113(1): 81–101.

———. 2014. "Disturbance, Productivity, and Species Diversity: Empiricism vs. Logic in Ecological Theory." *Ecology* 95(9): 2382–96.

Jones, G. 1987. "A Statistical Approach to the Archaeological Identification of Crop Processing." *Journal of Archaeological Science* 14(3): 311–23.

Jost, L. 2006. "Entropy and Diversity." *Oikos* 113(2): 363–75.

———. 2007. "Partitioning Diversity into Independent Alpha and Beta Components." *Ecology* 88(10): 2427–39.

———. 2010. "The Relation between Evenness and Diversity." *Diversity* 2(2): 207–32.

Kadane, J. B. 1988. "Possible Statistical Contributions to Paleoethnobotany." In *Current Paleoethnobotany: Analytical Methods and Cultural Interpretations*, ed. C. A. Hastorf and V. S. Popper, 206–14. Chicago: University of Chicago Press.

Kershaw, H. M., and A. U. Mallik. 2013. "Predicting Plant Diversity Response to Disturbance: Applicability of the Intermediate Disturbance Hypothesis and Mass Ratio Hypothesis." *Critical Reviews in Plant Sciences* 32(6): 383–95.

Kintigh, K. W. 1984. "Measuring Archaeological Diversity by Comparison with Simulated Assemblages." *American Antiquity* 49(1): 44–54.

———. 1989. "Sample Size, Significance, and Measures of Diversity." In *Quantifying Diversity in Archaeology*, ed. R. D. Leonard and G. T. Jones, 25–36. Cambridge: Cambridge University Press.

Lee, G.-A. 2012. "Taphonomy and Sample Size Estimation in Paleoethnobotany." *Journal of Archaeological Science* 39(3): 648–55.

Lennstrom, H. A., and C. A. Hastorf. 1992. "Testing Old Wives' Tales in Palaeoethnobotany: A Comparison of Bulk and Scatter Sampling Schemes from Pancán, Peru." *Journal of Archaeological Science* 19(2): 205–29.

Lentz, D. L. 1991. "Maya Diets of the Rich and Poor: Paleoethnobotanical Evidence from Copan." *Latin American Antiquity* 2(3): 269–87.

Lepofsky, D. 2000. "Socioeconomy at Keatley Creek: The Botanical Evidence." In *The Ancient Past of Keatley Creek Site*, ed. B. Hayden, 75–86. Burnaby, BC: Archaeology Press.

Lepofsky, D., and K. Lertzman. 2005. "More on Sampling for Richness and Diversity in Archaeobiological Assemblages." *Journal of Ethnobiology* 25(2): 175–88.

Lepofsky, D., and N. Lyons. 2003. "Modeling Ancient Plant Use on the Northwest Coast: Towards an Understanding of Mobility and Sedentism." *Journal of Archaeological Science* 30(11): 1357–71.

Levis, C., B. M. Flores, P. A. Moreira, B. G. Luize, R. P. Alves, J. Franco-Moraes, J. Lins, E. Konings, M. Peña-Claros, and F. Bongers. 2018. "How People Domesticated Amazonian Forests." *Frontiers in Ecology and Evolution* 5: 1–21.

Lindén, A., and S. Mäntyniemi. 2011. "Using the Negative Binomial Distribution to Model Overdispersion in Ecological Count Data." *Ecology* 92(7): 1414–21.

Longino, J. T., and R. K. Colwell. 2011. "Density Compensation, Species Composition, and Richness of Ants on a Neotropical Elevational Gradient." *Ecosphere* 2(3): 1–20.

Lyman, R. L., and K. M. Ames. 2007. "On the Use of Species-Area Curves to Detect the Effects of Sample Size." *Journal of Archaeological Science* 34(12): 1985–90.

Mabry, J. B. 2008. *Las Capas: Early Irrigation and Sedentism in a Southwestern Floodplain.* Anthropological Papers 28. Tucson: Archaeology Southwest.

MacArthur, R. H. 1965. "Patterns of Species Diversity." *Biological Reviews* 40(4): 510–33.

Magurran, A. E. 2004. *Measuring Biological Diversity.* Oxford: Blackwell.

———. 2011. "Measuring Biological Diversity in Time (and Space)." In *Biological Diversity: Frontiers in Measurement and Assessment,* ed. A. E. Magurran and B. J. McGill, 85–94. Oxford: Oxford University Press.

Margalef, R. 1951. "Diversidad de Especies En Las Comunidades Naturales." *Publicaciones Del Instituto de Biología Aplicada* 9: 5–27.

Marston, J. M. 2011. "Archaeological Markers of Agricultural Risk Management." *Journal of Anthropological Archaeology* 30(2): 190–205.

Marston, J. M., J. D. Guedes, and C. Warinner, eds. 2014. *Method and Theory in Paleoethnobotany.* Boulder: University of Colorado Press.

———. 2017. *Agricultural Sustainability and Environmental Change at Ancient Gordion.* Gordion Special Studies 8. Philadelphia: University of Pennsylvania Press.

Maurer, B. A., B. J. McGill, and A. E. Magurran. 2011. "Measurement of Species Diversity." In *Biological Diversity: Frontiers in Measurement and Assessment,* ed. A. E. Magurran and B. J. McGill, 55–65. Oxford: Oxford University Press.

Menhinick, E. F. 1964. "A Comparison of Some Species-Individuals Diversity Indices Applied to Samples of Field Insects." *Ecology* 45(4): 859–61.

Miksicek, C. H. 1987. "Formation Processes of the Archaeobotanical Record." *Advances in Archaeological Method and Theory* 10: 211–47.

Minnis, P. E. 1981. "Seeds in Archaeological Sites: Sources and Some Interpretive Problems." *American Antiquity* 46(1): 143–52.

Morehart, C. T., and D. T. A. Eisenberg. 2010. "Prosperity, Power, and Change: Modeling Maize at Postclassic Xaltocan, Mexico." *Journal of Anthropological Archaeology* 29(1): 94–112.

Oksanen, J., F. G. Blanchet, R. Kindt, P. Legendre, P. R. Minchin, R. B. O'Hara, G. L. Simpson, P. Solymos, M. Henry, H. Stevens, and H. Wagner. 2019. "Package 'Vegan'— Community Ecology Package, Version 2.5-6." https://cran.r-project.org; and https://github.com/vegandevs/vegan.

Pearsall, D. M. 1983. "Evaluating the Stability of Subsistence Strategies by Use of Paleoethnobotanical Data." *Journal of Ethnobiology* 3(2): 121–37.

———. 2015. *Paleoethnobotany: A Handbook of Procedures.* 3rd edn. Walnut Creek, CA: Left Coast Press.

Poulos, H. M., and A. E. Camp. 2010. "Topographic Influences on Vegetation Mosaics and Tree Diversity in the Chihuahuan Desert Borderlands." *Ecology* 91(4): 1140–51.

R Core Team. 2020. "R: A Language and Environment for Statistical Computing." R Foundation for Statistical Computing, Vienna, Austria. https://www.R-project.org/.

Reitz, E. J., and E. S. Wing. 2008. *Zooarchaeology.* 2nd edn. Cambridge: Cambridge University Press.

Ricotta, C., A. T. R. Acosta, G. Bacaro, M. Carboni, A. Chiarucci, D. Rocchini, and S. Pavoine. 2019. "Rarefaction of Beta Diversity." *Ecological Indicators* 107: 105606.

Rivera-Núñez, T., L. Fargher, and R. Nigh. 2020. "Toward an Historical Agroecology: An Academic Approach in Which Time and Space Matter." *Agroecology and Sustainable Food Systems* 44: 975–1011.

Rocek, T. R. 1995. "Sedentarization and Agricultural Dependence: Perspectives from the Pithouse-to-Pueblo Transition in the American Southwest." *American Antiquity* 60(2): 218–39.

Rowley-Conwy, P., and R. Layton. 2011. "Foraging and Farming as Niche Construction: Stable and Unstable Adaptations." *Philosophical Transactions of the Royal Society B: Biological Sciences* 366(1566): 849–62.

Schiffer, M. B. 1976. *Behavioral Archaeology*. New York: Academic Press.

———. 1983. "Toward the Identification of Formation Processes." *American Antiquity* 48(4): 675–706.

Sheil, D., and D. Burslem. 2013. "Defining and Defending Connell's Intermediate Disturbance Hypothesis: A Response to Fox." *Trends in Ecology and Evolution* 28(10): 571–72.

Sinensky, R. J. 2013. "Risk Management and Dietary Change at the Early Agricultural Village of Las Capas." MA thesis, Northern Arizona University, Flagstaff, AZ.

Sinensky, R. J., and A. Farahani. 2018a. "Diversity-Disturbance Relationships in the Late Archaic Southwest: Implications for Farmer-Forager Foodways." *American Antiquity* 83(2): 281–301.

Sinensky, R. J., and A. Farahani. 2018b. "Diversity-Disturbance Relationships in the Late Archaic Southwest: Implications for Farmer-Forager Foodways. Supplemental Materials." *American Antiquity* 83(2): https://doi.org/10.1017/aaq.2017.74.

Toledo-Garibaldi, M., and G. Williams-Linera. 2014. "Tree Diversity Patterns in Successive Vegetation Types along an Elevation Gradient in the Mountains of Eastern Mexico." *Ecological Research* 29(6): 1097–1104.

Turkon, P. 2004. "Food and Status in the Prehispanic Malpaso Valley, Zacatecas, Mexico." *Journal of Anthropological Archaeology* 23(2): 225–51.

van der Veen, M. 1999. "The Economic Value of Chaff and Straw in Arid and Temperate Zones." *Vegetation History and Archaeobotany* 8(3): 211–24.

———. 2007. "Formation Processes of Desiccated and Carbonized Plant Remains: The Identification of Routine Practice." *Journal of Archaeological Science* 34(6): 968–90.

———. 2008. "Food as Embodied Material Culture: Diversity and Change in Plant Food Consumption in Roman Britain." *Journal of Roman Archaeology* 21: 83–109.

VanDerwarker, A. M. 2006. *Farming, Hunting, and Fishing in the Olmec World*. Austin: University of Texas Press.

———. 2010. "Simple Measures for Integrating Plant and Animal Remains." In *Integrating Zooarchaeology and Paleoethnobotany: A Consideration of Issues, Methods, and Cases*, ed. A. M. VanDerwarker and T. M. Peres, 65–74. New York: Springer.

VanDerwarker, A. M., D. N. Bardolph, K. M. Hoppa, H. B. Thakar, L. S. Martin, A. L. Jaqua, M. E. Biwer, and K. M. Gill. 2016. "New World Paleoethnobotany in the New Millennium (2000–2013)." *Journal of Archaeological Research* 24(2): 125–77.

VanDerwarker, A. M., J. B. Marcoux, and K. D. Hollenbach. 2013. "Farming and Foraging at the Crossroads: The Consequences of Cherokee and European Interaction through the Late Eighteenth Century." *American Antiquity* 78(1): 68–88.

VanDerwarker, A. M., and G. D. Wilson. 2016. "War, Food, and Structural Violence in the Mississippian Central Illinois Valley." In *The Archaeology of Food and Warfare: Food Insecurity in Prehistory*, ed. A. M. VanDerwarker and G. D. Wilson, 75–105. Cham, CH: Springer International Publishing.

Ver Hoef, J. M., and P. L. Boveng. 2007. "Quasi-Poisson vs. Negative Binomial Regression: How Should We Model Overdispersed Count Data?" *Ecology* 88(11): 2766–72.

Vint, J. M. 2018. "The Southwest Archaic in the Tucson Basin." In *The Archaic Southwest: Foragers in an Arid Land*, ed. B. J. Vierra, 66–97. Salt Lake City: University of Utah Press.

———, ed. 2015. *Implements of Change: Tools, Subsistence and the Built Environment of Las Capas, an Early Agricultural Irrigation Community in Southern Arizona.* Anthropological Papers 51. Tucson: Archaeology Southwest.

Vint, J. M., and F. L. Nials, eds. 2015. *The Anthropogenic Landscape of Las Capas, an Early Agricultural Irrigation Community in Southern Arizona.* Anthropological Papers 50. Tucson: Archaeology Southwest.

Wagner, G. E. 2008. "What Seasonal Diet at a Fort Ancient Community Reveals about Coping Mechanisms." In *Case Studies in Environmental Archaeology*, ed. E. J. Reitz, J. Sylvia, S. J. Scudder, and C. M. Scarry, 277–96. Interdisciplinary Contributions to Archaeology. New York: Springer.

White, C. E., and C. P. Shelton. 2014. "Recovering Macrobotanical Remains: Current Methods and Techniques." In *Method and Theory in Paleoethnobotany*, ed. J. M. Marston, J. D. Guedes, and C. Warinner, 95–114. Boulder: University of Colorado Press.

Yuan, Z. Y., F. Jiao, Y. H. Li, and R. L. Kallenbach. 2016. "Anthropogenic Disturbances Are Key to Maintaining the Biodiversity of Grasslands." *Scientific Reports* 6(1): 1–8.

Chapter 8

Quantifying Evenness of Paleoindian Projectile Point Forms within Geographic Regions of Eastern North America

Matthew T. Boulanger, Ryan P. Breslawski, and Ian A. Jorgeson

***

The earliest well-documented human occupation of North America is recognized archaeologically by the widespread presence of bifacially worked projectile points with prominent channels—flutes—driven upward from their bases on one or both sides. These fluted points are one of the preeminent "index fossils" (*sensu* Lyman and O'Brien 2006) in American archaeology, signaling that a site dates to between ca. 13,300 and 11,900 cal BP, usually referred to as the Paleoindian Period.

Every student of North American archaeology has learned that the age of fluted points was established during the late 1920s and early 1930s in the American West, first at Folsom, New Mexico (Cook 1927; Figgins 1927) and then at Blackwater Draw, New Mexico (Cotter 1937a, 1937b, 1938). The Late Pleistocene ages of these points were inferred through their direct association with now-extinct fauna such as mammoth and bison. Less well known is that archaeologists working east of the Mississippi River Valley had previously recognized fluted points as a distinctive artifact class (Shetrone 1936). Before the revelations of Folsom and Blackwater Draw, Brown (1926) defined the *Coldwater*[1] point as a distinctive fluted form in Mississippi. Similarly, Beauchamp (1897; see also Ritchie 1944) referred to New York's *Seneca River* points. The key difference between these eastern finds and those of the West was the absence of direct association with extinct megafauna that would allow archaeologists to establish an approximate age. Indeed, Beauchamp considered his *Seneca River* points to be products of the historically encountered Iroquoian tribes because, he suggested, the points evidenced great skill in manufacture, and thus must necessarily have been produced by a culture substantially more advanced than those of the Stone Age.

The widespread acceptance that fluted points were the earliest clear evidence of human occupation in the Americas led to a growing recognition that not all fluted points look like those from the type sites in the Southwest, and that fluted points from the East seemed to be different from those in the West. Archaeological research over the last half-century has made clear that across much of the Great Plains and American Southwest, *Clovis* points are followed in time by fluted *Folsom* point forms that show some degree of standardization in size, shape, and hafting (Ahler and Geib 2000; Amick 1995; Buchanan 2006; Buchanan and Collard 2010; Collard et al. 2010; Crabtree 1966; Judge 1970; Tunnell and Johnson 1991; Wormington 1957). *Folsom* points are exceedingly rare in the East. Their eastern limit of distribution seems to be in central Illinois and Wisconsin (Loebel, Lambert, and Hill 2016). Indeed, although the earliest fluted point forms certainly appear to be *Clovis*-like, later fluted-point forms in the East take on a bewildering variety of sizes and shapes (Anderson 1990b; Anderson et al. 2010; Anderson, O'Steen, and Sassaman 1996; Bradley 1997; Bradley et al. 2008; Brennan 1982; Bullen 1968; Goodyear 1982; Lewis 1954; MacDonald 1968; Mason 1962; O'Brien, Darwent, and Lyman 2001; Robinson et al. 2009; Thulman 2007, 2012). This has led to a proliferation of extensionally defined projectile-point "types," a general confusion in the names of different forms, and inconsistencies in how point specimens are classified. Illustrating this point, there remains some debate concerning whether the earliest fluted points in the East are morphologically identical to—or at least related to—so-called "western" *Clovis* points; or, whether there are multiple distinctive fluted-point forms that are superficially similar to *Clovis* and that represent regionalized traditions within the East (Bradley et al. 2008; Buchanan, O'Brien, and Collard 2014; Eren and Desjardine 2015; Miller, Holliday, and Bright 2014; Morrow 1995, 1996, 2019).

Regardless of whether the earliest *Clovis*-like forms in the East represent a single cultural tradition, or whether they represent distinctive regional forms, there is widespread agreement that greater diversity in later (e.g., non-*Clovis*-like) fluted-point forms exists in the East compared to the West. Mason's (1962) statement that the greatest diversity of fluted-point forms is known from the American Southeast has often been repeated—albeit with acknowledgments that this statement requires evaluation against the empirical record (Anderson and Faught 1998; Beck and Jones 2010; Brennan 1982; Broster et al. 2013; Bryan 1991; Miller and Gingerich 2013b; O'Brien, Darwent, and Lyman 2001; O'Brien et al.

2014). Although Mason's (1962) paper was written when there was only a limited amount of Paleoindian data across the continent, over fifty years of systematic research at regional (e.g., Brennan 1982) and continental scales (Anderson 1990a, 1990b) have largely borne out his conclusion of greater diversity in fluted-point forms in the East.

Trying to make sense of this diversity is not, however, a straightforward endeavor. Various state-level surveys are conducted by different researchers, who record different attributes and traits, exert varying levels of effort to identify materials, and record materials for which varying scales of contextual data (i.e., provenience) exist. Moreover, we know that the distribution of fluted points across the East is itself biased by numerous factors relating to historical and modern land use, and to artifact-collector behaviors (Anderson et al. 2019; Lepper 1983, 1985; Loebel 2012; Prascinas 2011; Seeman and Prufer 1982, 1984; Schaefer 2005). Thus, the total number of fluted points in a particular area likely reflects more than simply the local rate of Paleoindian tool production, use, and discard. Moreover, the absence of a unified taxonomic framework for classification of point specimens means that two specimens that are otherwise morphologically identical—but found in different states or by researchers with differing backgrounds—may be referred to by different names. As has been pointed out elsewhere (Boulanger 2015; O'Brien et al. 2014), when different researchers use different criteria to distinguish the same point type (*Clovis*), the type as a construct becomes increasingly meaningless.

Despite some criticisms, large-scale region- and state-based surveys have provided significant insight into the variation of Paleoindian point forms, their geographic distributions, and the significance of these factors to deciphering the peopling of the Americas (Anderson 1990b; Anderson et al. 2019; Anderson and Faught 2000; Anderson et al. 2010; Steele, Adams, and Sluckin 1998). As noted by Eren et al. (2016), nearly all researchers discussing fluted-point diversity in the East have implicitly or explicitly considered richness as the metric by which diversity is measured. Eren et al. summarize the situation concisely when they note three concerns about past statements about Eastern fluted-point diversity: (1) previous studies of point diversity have used extensionally defined projectile-point "types" as the unit of classification in assessing diversity; (2) over reliance on impressionistic qualitative statements of richness—the number of different forms within a population—rather than systematic quantitative assessments; and (3) the fact that richness can be strongly dependent on sample size. As we noted above, local sample sizes in this case appear to be biased by numerous factors related to modern-day land use and cover.

Here, we discuss a novel method of classifying fluted Paleoindian projectile-point forms and quantifying multiple scales of formal diversity within ecological regions of potential cultural significance. The methods discussed here address some of the criticisms offered by Eren et al. (2016) by: (1) using systematic, consistent, and replicable classes for defining formal variation; (2) quantifying diversity in a manner that provides estimations of diversity as well as the analytical uncertainty around those estimations; and (3) integrating sample size as a factor in our measurements of diversity within multiple scales of geographical and ecological inclusivity to account for visibility/recovery biases. A further benefit of the analyses presented here is that diversity of forms and the proportions of each form are measured within regions of geographic significance rather than within the confines of modern political boundaries, thereby attempting to measure diversity within geographic areas that are more likely to have been culturally significant to Paleoindian peoples thirteen thousand years ago.

Methods

We use a database of projectile-point specimens that subsumes and expands upon data used in earlier studies relating to Paleoindian projectile-point morphology in the East (Boulanger 2015; Eren et al. 2016; O'Brien et al. 2001, 2014, 2016). A total of 1,480 fluted points recovered from the East are included here. Of these, 93.5 percent (n = 1385) are reported to at least county-level provenience, 5.6 percent (n = 83) are reported to state-level provenience, and 0.8 percent (n = 12) have uncertain provenience to two or more counties (Table 8.1). Additional details concerning the measurements and the points used in this analysis can be found in Boulanger 2015 and O'Brien et al. 2014, and a complete listing of points used herein is available from the senior author.

We recorded a series of measurements and nominal attributes from each specimen in the dataset, with a focus on attributes that relate to blade and haft morphologies (Figure 8.1). From these data, we derived five variables for use in classifying each point in our sample (Figure 8.2). These derived variables are: (1) tang angle (the degree of flaring at the base); (2) basal indentation ratio (the relative depth of basal concavity); (3) constriction ratio (the degree of "waistedness" at the base); (4) location of maximum blade width; and (5) width:length ratio.

As with earlier studies, we use a paradigmatic classification to establish formal classes (analytical units) of projectile points. As discussed elsewhere (e.g., Dunnell 1971; Eren et al. 2016; O'Brien et al. 2001, 2016), using paradigmatic classes allows us to avoid the ambiguity and subjectivity of traditional culture-historical point "types," thus ensuring that our analytical units are entirely replicable (see Dunnell 1971, 1986; Lyman and O'Brien

Table 8.1. Number of fluted points from each state in the East by the scale of reported provenience.

| State | Scale of Provenience | | | |
	County	*Multiple Counties*	*State*	*Σ*
Alabama	108		1	109
Arkansas	20			20
Connecticut	6			6
Delaware	10			10
Florida	77		5	82
Georgia	10		2	12
Illinois	21			21
Indiana	65		5	70
Iowa	7			7
Kentucky	114		13	127
Louisiana	4		4	8
Maine	41		1	42
Maryland	21			21
Massachusetts	27			27
Michigan	2			2
Mississippi	32	1		33
Missouri	63		2	65
New Hampshire	8			8
New Jersey	28		2	30
New York	87		2	89
North Carolina	38		2	40
Ohio	69	9	5	83
Pennsylvania	168	1	23	192
South Carolina	46		8	54
Tennessee	192	1	6	199
Vermont	18			18
Virginia	68		2	70
West Virginia	26			26
Wisconsin	9			9
Σ	1,385	12	83	**1,480**

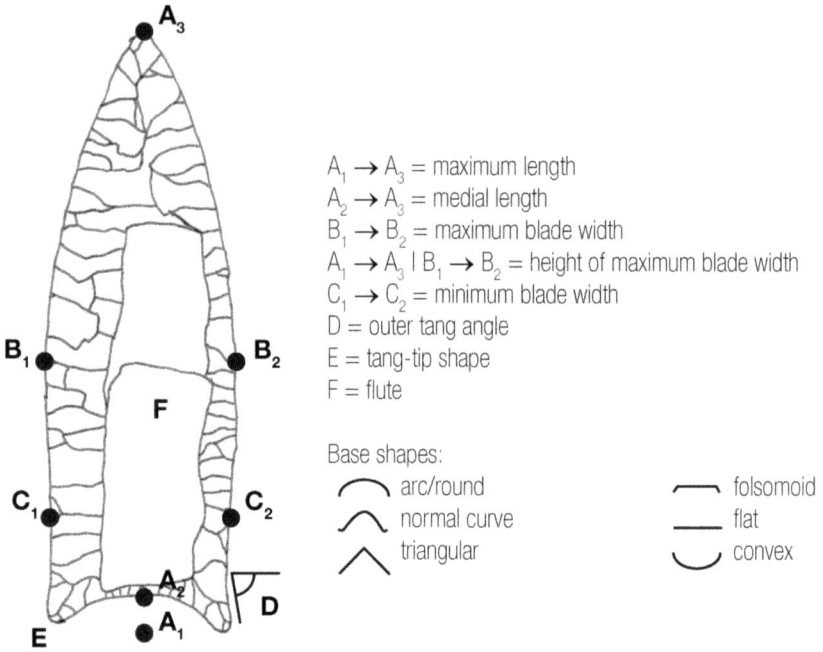

$A_1 \rightarrow A_3$ = maximum length
$A_2 \rightarrow A_3$ = medial length
$B_1 \rightarrow B_2$ = maximum blade width
$A_1 \rightarrow A_3 \mid B_1 \rightarrow B_2$ = height of maximum blade width
$C_1 \rightarrow C_2$ = minimum blade width
D = outer tang angle
E = tang-tip shape
F = flute

Base shapes:

arc/round   folsomoid
normal curve   flat
triangular   convex

Figure 8.1. Measurements and nominal attributes recorded from each fluted-point specimen. © The authors.

2002a, 2002b; O'Brien and Lyman 2000 for discussions of the fundamental differences between intensionally [deductively, theoretically] defined paradigmatic classes and extensionally [inductively, empirically] derived "types"). In past uses of these data (e.g., O'Brien et al. 2016), we used a classification in which each dimension possessed $n > 3$ states. Here, we have simplified the classification by reducing both the number of dimensions and the number of states within each dimension. Given the continuous distributions of each of these variables (Figure 8.2), and the somewhat exploratory nature of our study, we devised our classification to be as simple as possible by specifying only two states for each dimension. For tang angle, we arbitrarily selected 90° as the midpoint between states—essentially distinguishing "eared" points from lanceolate or "leaf-shaped" ones. States for the remaining dimensions were defined by whether the observed value was less than or greater than the median value of the overall sample. Using this classification, a maximum of thirty-two different point-form classes are possible. Every class is populated by at least one archaeological specimen, meaning that all possible morphospaces defined by our classification are populated (Table 8.2).

I. Outer Tang Angle
1. < 90 (eared)
2. > 90 (lanceolate)

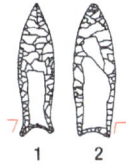

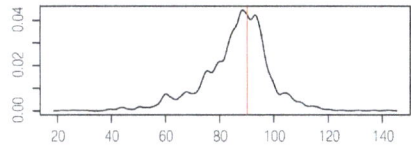

II. Basal-Indentation Ratio
1. < 0.06 (Shallower)
2. > 0.06 (Deeper)

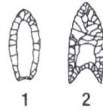

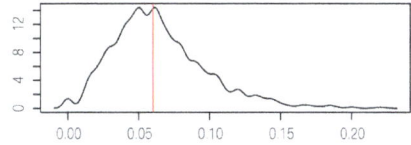

III. Constriction Ratio
1. < 0.875 (more parallel)
2. > 0.875 (more constricting)

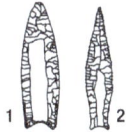

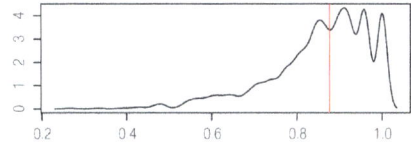

IV. Maximum Width Height
1. < 0.458 (towards proximal)
2. > 0.458 (towards distal)

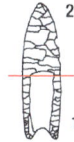

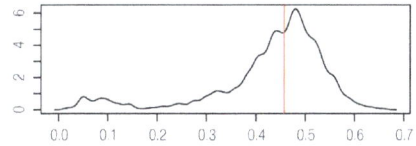

V. Width:Length Ratio
1. < .384 (more rectangular)
2. > .384 (more square)

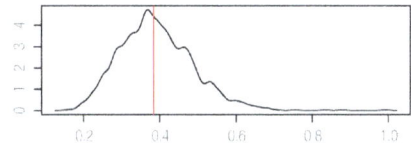

Figure 8.2. Graphical summary of the paradigmatic classification used in this study, as well as the distributions of observed measurements for each dimension in the sample (n = 1480). © The authors.

As noted above, our database includes a total of 1,480 individual specimens from across the eastern United States. Point specimens from neighboring Canadian provinces were removed from our larger database because of the absence of geographic and physiographic data for those areas. Our database is certainly not as large as the PIDBA database (Anderson et al.

Table 8.2. Paradigmatic classes defined by our classification, the total number of specimens assigned to each class, and the most-commonly represented point type names (as assigned by reporting authors) within each class. Serial order corresponds to that used in Figures 8.7, 8.8, and 8.10.

Serial Order	Class	Count	Most-Common Types Represented
1	11111	71	Cumberland (39), Clovis (13)
2	11112	15	Clovis (4), Gainey (2), Dalton (2)
3	11121	168	Cumberland (78), Clovis (45), Gainey (3)
4	11122	69	Clovis (21), Cumberland (8), Gainey (4)
5	11211	50	Clovis (15), Cumberland/Barnes (7), Gainey (5)
6	11212	37	Clovis (10), Gainey (7), Barnes (2)
7	11221	21	Clovis (8), Cumberland/Barnes (6)
8	11222	32	Clovis (11), Quad (2)
9	12111	13	Clovis (3), Dalton (3), Cumberland (2)
10	12112	24	Dalton (6), Clovis (5), Gainey (3)
11	12121	21	Clovis (7), Cumberland (7), Ross County Fluted (1)
12	12122	29	Clovis (7), Gainey (2), Quad (2)
13	12211	66	Clovis (12), Dalton (8), Gainey (5)
14	12212	128	Gainey (18), Clovis (16), Vail-Debert (10), Bull Brook (8)
15	12221	23	Clovis (11), Cumberland (3), Gainey (2)
16	12222	82	Gainey (13), Clovis (10), Vail-Debert (9)
17	21111	41	Clovis (24), Northumberland (3), Gainey (2)
18	21112	24	Clovis (7), Crowfield (2), Gainey (1)
19	21121	59	Clovis (33), Northumberland (7), Gainey (6)
20	21122	57	Clovis (25), Northumberland (9), Crowfield
21	21211	38	Clovis (21), Gainey (2), Bull Brook (1)
22	21212	24	Clovis (9), Gainey (5)
23	21221	19	Clovis (11), Gainey (2), Kings Road-Whipple (2)
24	21222	8	Clovis (5), Gainey (1), Folsom (1)
25	22111	25	Clovis (12), Gainey (1)
26	22112	25	Clovis (4), Dalton (2)
27	22121	37	Clovis (24), Gainey (4), Vail-Debert (1)
28	22122	42	Clovis (16), Crowfield (5), Gainey/St. Louis (5)
29	22211	71	Clovis (27), Redstone (8), Gainey (7)
30	22212	94	Clovis (20), Gainey (6), Redstone (5)
31	22221	26	Clovis (17), Gainey (2), Vail-Debert (2)
32	22222	41	Clovis (9), Vail-Debert (4), Barnes (3)

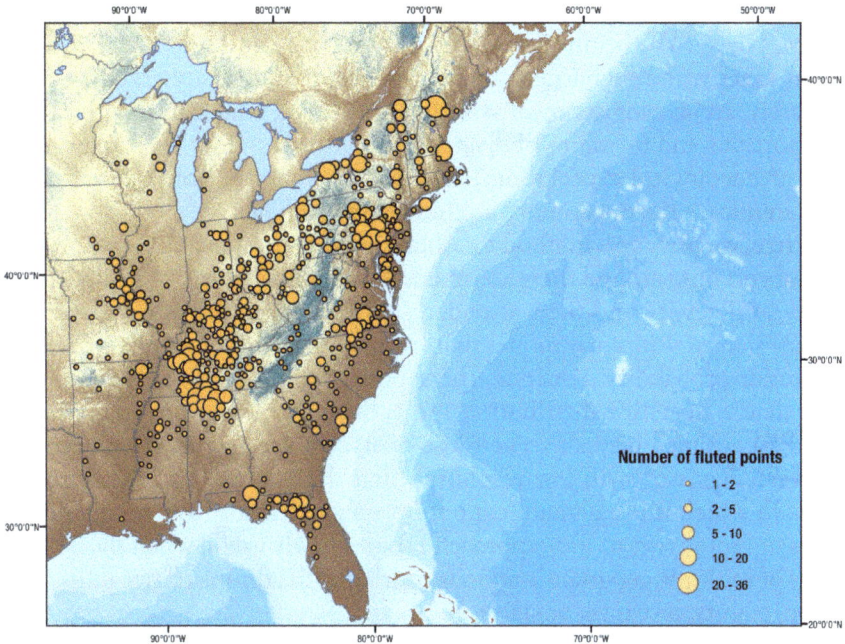

Figure 8.3. Locations and quantities of fluted-point specimens included in the present study. Note: Fluted points from localities in Canada were excluded because of limitations of the GIS files used in this study. © The authors.

2019), and there are some regions (e.g., the northern Midwest, the extreme Southeast) in which our database is relatively deficient (Figure 8.3). Yet our data have the advantage of having been collected by only two individuals recording identical metric variables (Boulanger 2015; O'Brien et al. 2001).

Statistical Modeling of Evenness

In addition to providing a replicable and consistent method of classifying point forms, paradigmatic classification allows us to establish a fixed number of possible classes. This is particularly useful when attempting to quantify formal diversity in projectile points, as it allows the number of artifact classes (K) to be researcher-defined, and thus imposes a natural upper bound on the number of possible classes. Fixing the maximum number of possible classes allows us to focus on evenness, in this case measured with the widely used Shannon evenness index (E_{H}). This differs from other classification schemes (e.g., extensionally described projectile-point types) in which there may be no upper bound on the number of possible classes. Paradigmatic classification thereby makes it possible to discuss artifact classes in terms of proportions, where each class k_i in K has proportions $p_1, p_2, ..., p_K$. With infinite sampling effort, we can know these proportions exactly, and therefore calculate a measure of diversity exactly. Unfortunately, archaeologists must work with samples, which means that class proportions and measures of diversity are estimates. If we want to evaluate our archaeological expectations, we need to obtain reliable estimates and communicate the uncertainty around those estimates.

Here, we provide a method for obtaining class proportion estimates and the uncertainty around those estimates, from which we then calculate measures of diversity and their attendant uncertainties. This is done through a Bayesian multinomial model that expresses artifact class proportions as posterior probability densities. These posterior densities are then used to calculate a posterior distribution for a diversity measure of interest. The method outlined here also allows use of artifact specimens whose recovery provenience is of such low resolution that the artifact (and therefore the class to which it is assigned) cannot be assigned to a single geographic or physiographic region. This approach is particularly useful when the boundaries of multiple geographic regions overlap with administrative units (e.g., town, county, province, or state).

Artifact Class Distributions

An observed sample of artifact counts across classes follows a *multinomial distribution*, where the observed count for each class k_i is a function of the total counts across classes K and the probability p_i of observing class k_i. The probability vector $\Theta_1, \Theta_2, ..., \Theta_K$ (henceforth Θ) corresponds to the true proportions of each artifact class, summing to 1. Our goal is to estimate Θ.

The Model

The model outcome consists of artifact counts C across K artifact classes in J unique regions. As such, observations take the form of a *[J, K]* matrix. We can express the multinomial likelihood for counts across K artifact classes in region j_j of J as

$$C_j \sim multinomial\ (\Theta_j).$$

To make model specification easier, Θ_j is estimated with parameters on the normal scale (as opposed to a scale constrained within 0–1) using the softmax function,

$$\Theta_j = softmax(X_j),$$

where X_j is a vector of real parameter values that, once exponentiated and standardized, sum to 1 (i.e., the target Θ_j vector). Fitting the model to observed artifact count data provides posterior distributions for X_j, and therefore Θ_j.

Prior Distributions for Parameter Values

Values in each X_j vector were assigned a prior probability of $N(0, \sigma_j)$, and each σ_j received its own prior probability distribution. This "hyper prior" takes the form

$$\sigma_j = \exp(\omega + \varphi_j), \qquad \omega \sim N(1,0.5) \qquad \varphi_j \sim N(0,0.5).$$

σ_j controls the degree of dispersion in the parameter values contained in the vector X_j. Therefore, it is responsible for the amount of heterogeneity in artifact class proportions in region j_j. More positive values in X_j correspond to artifact classes that dominate the region, whereas more negative values correspond to relatively rare artifact classes. ω is the average log dispersion in X_j across all regions J. φ_j is an offset from ω specific to region j_j.

The fixed parameter values for ω and φ_j were chosen based on trial simulations from prior parameter values, as well as model sensitivity tests for simulated datasets with known parameter values. The selected values allow for a wide degree of scenarios, ranging from regions dominated by a single artifact class (e.g., where class k_i has a proportion greater than 0.9) to regions where artifact proportions are uniform across classes. In cases where region j_j has few data, the degree of dispersion in artifact class proportions shrinks toward the average degree of dispersion estimated across all regions J (ω). In other words, when data are sparse for region j_j, the model assumes that the dispersion of artifact class proportions in region j_j is more likely to look like the average dispersion of artifact class proportions for the other observed J-1 regions.

Model Fitting

Models were fitted with Hamiltonian Monte Carlo simulation in Stan (Stan Development Team 2020) with four chains. Each chain ran with 5,000 warm-up iterations and 5,000 sampling iterations, producing 20,000 total sampling iterations. Model convergence was checked by visual inspection of trace plots, confirming the absence of divergent iterations, and ensuring that all R-hat values were below 1.01. Effective sample sizes for all parameters are above 1,500, ensuring reasonably precise posterior distributions.

Integrating Contextual Uncertainty

A long-standing concern regarding the recovery and reporting of Paleo-indian projectile points (and indeed, any archaeological material) in the East is uncertainty in artifact provenience. Regarding fluted points, the vast majority of known finds derive from private collectors who may or may not have recorded a precise find spot. We are therefore left with large numbers of point specimens for which the only known context is a general topographic feature (lake, valley, floodplain), a county (or multiple counties), or simply the state in which it was found. Rolingson (1964), for example, includes several points that are assigned only to the State of Kentucky. This broad-scale provenience is often difficult to reconcile with studies conducted at finer scales. Further, large, modern, publicly available databases often generalize provenience of finds to at least the county level to protect archaeological sites from illicit looting (Anderson et al. 2019). Archaeologists working with such data have often measured diversity within modern administrative units under the assumption that those units may serve as useful proxies for roughly spatially congruent regions of archaeological interest.

However, as discussed above, historic and modern land-use practices bias the recognition of Paleoindian sites and the recovery of Paleoindian material culture. Consequently, aggregating these archaeological phenomena by modern sociopolitical boundaries may mask significant trends and introduce false patterns.

Our model avoids these issues by probabilistically assigning point classes to regions of geographical, ecological, and geological similarity based on the extent to which a particular county or state falls within those regions. This is done by first fitting the model to those data from modern administrative units contained entirely within individual regions of interest. If we know with certainty that an artifact class was recovered from a particular county, and if that county is entirely within the boundaries of a specific region of interest, we know with certainty that the point class was recovered from that region. But what happens if more than one ecological region or geological province is present in a county? To which of these should the point specimen be assigned? The spatial relationship between the point class and the region is uncertain. Fitting the model to the total number of points recovered only from administrative units contained entirely within individual regions provides posterior probabilities for each artifact class within each region. Using these posterior probabilities, we simulate dataset permutations that probabilistically assign the remaining artifacts to the regions.

For N dataset permutations, N posterior Θ matrices are first sampled from the fitted model. Recall that each row j of Θ contains K artifact class probabilities that sum to one. With this information, we then calculate the probability of each region j_j membership for every regionally unassigned artifact z:

$$prob\left(j_j \mid z\right) = \frac{\theta_{z[j,k]} \times area_{z[j]}}{\sum_{w=1}^{J} \theta_{z[w,k]} \times area_{z[w]}}$$

$prob(j_j \mid z)$ The probability of region j_j, given artifact z.

$\theta_{z[j,k]}$ The probability of observing artifact z, which belongs to class k, given region j_j (θ). This value is sampled from the posterior of the model fitted to all artifacts located in administrative units contained entirely within individual regions.

$area_{z[j]}$ The area of region j_j in the administrative unit containing artifact z.

J The number of regions. The w index in the denominator is substituted for the j index in the numerator.

In simpler terms, the probability that artifact z is associated with region j_j is equal to the product of the probability of observing artifact z given j_j and the area of j_j in the administrative unit containing artifact z, standardized by the sum of all such products for every region j_w in the administrative unit.

Once regional probabilities are obtained for every unassigned artifact, regions are probabilistically assigned to those specimens. This is repeated over N permutations. The model is then fitted to every dataset permutation, and N posterior diversity densities are obtained for each region. Finally, the N posterior diversity densities are summed and standardized within each region to obtain a posterior diversity value distribution that averages across the dataset permutations. This process allows us to include projectile point specimens (and the classes to which they are assigned) of varying scales of provenience. That is, it does not matter if a specimen has only state-level provenience, or if it is uncertain exactly what county the artifact was found in. The model output factors in this uncertainty when associating a particular specimen with an environmental region of interest, and it builds regional membership uncertainty into each posterior diversity density.

The role of uncertain regional membership varies, depending on the dataset at hand. If most administrative units are divided up among multiple regions, then the dataset permutations will vary greatly, and the posterior diversity densities for each region will be wide. In cases where most administrative units are contained entirely within regions, dataset permutations will be similar, and the posterior diversity densities will not change much during this step. In the former scenario, many permutations may be necessary to capture the uncertainty in regional diversity values that is driven by uncertain artifact memberships in those regions. In the latter scenario, very few permutations may be necessary to capture this uncertainty (or, permutations will quickly become redundant, and the summed and standardized posterior diversity densities across permutations will remain stable).

Regions of Geographic/Physiographic Interest

We are particularly interested in identifying differences in projectile point forms between populations of Paleoindians in the East. Earlier work has shown that there are significant differences in projectile-point forms between populations, but for reasons discussed previously, these differences were aggregated by modern sociopolitical boundaries (i.e., states and counties). We seek to use environmental variables of differing scales of geographic inclusivity in our analysis, because we suspect that geographic and physiographic variables likely influenced spatial and temporal variation in human behavior, including the production of projectile-point forms.

Glaciated/Unglaciated. Some archaeologists hold that Clovis technology, including projectile points, is present throughout the unglaciated landscape of North America, but that it is absent from those portions of the continent that were once beneath glacial ice (e.g., Ellis and Lothrop 2019). Available radiocarbon dates suggest that early Paleoindian culture began later and lasted longer in glaciated regions than in unglaciated regions (Lothrop et al. 2016; Miller and Gingerich 2013a, 2013b). If this is indeed the case, we might anticipate both greater richness in point forms (more point classes) as well as greater evenness (greater parity in the *frequencies* of these classes) south of the extent of glaciation because people were there longer and therefore had more time to innovate with weaponry systems. The corollary prediction would be that in formerly glaciated regions, point forms may show lower richness—perhaps representing only a subset of forms from the south, and certain kinds of fluted forms will be more common—resulting in relatively lower evenness. We note that shifts in richness values often result in shifts in evenness index values, and thus one potentially fruitful avenue of research may lie in the comparison of relative differences in these metrics within and between aggregated samples.

Here, we use data compiled by Dalton et al. (2020) and Dyke, Moore, and Robertson (2003) to delineate the maximum extent of North American glaciation during the Pleistocene at roughly 20,000 cal BP (Figure 8.4). Note that we do not suggest a Paleoindian occupation of eastern North America at this particular time. Rather, we assume that the first people to enter the East likely did so south of glacial ice, and that recession of glacial ice likely had some effect on the earliest of Paleoindian populations, including uncertainty of floral and faunal communities adapting to newly available land, the drying out of proglacial lakes and wetlands, and the generally less hospitable climate and environment associated with proximity to the glacial front. By using the total extent of glaciation in our model, we are conservatively estimating the opening up of new terrain during the earliest occupation of the East.

Biotic Communities. Paleoindians entering into and living within the East encountered a variety of biotic communities, created by complex combinations of geology, climate, flora, and fauna. The exact biomes present in the East during the Pleistocene–Holocene transition were not necessarily analogous to those present today (Semken 1983), and the boundaries of these biomes shifted through time as plant and animal populations adapted to changes in global climate and local environments. Williams

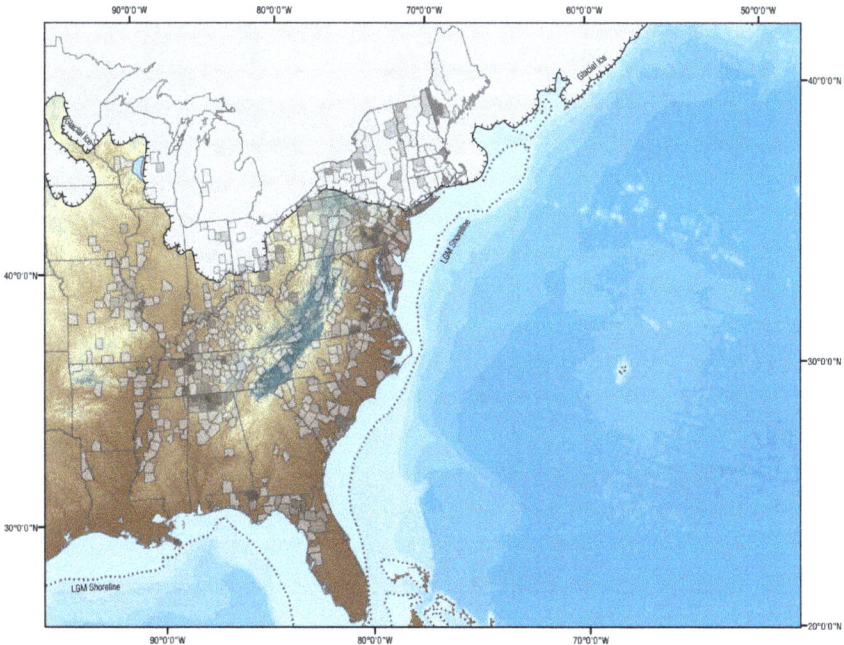

Figure 8.4. Extent of glaciation at ca. 20,000 cal BP (ca. 18,000 ^{14}C YBP) from Dalton et al. (2020) and Dyke et al. (2003), showing United States counties from which projectile point specimens are included. Note: Darker shading indicates greater numbers of specimens. © The authors.

and colleagues (2004) used fossil pollen data from across North America to model the distributions of biotic communities at roughly 1,000-year intervals, spanning the end of the Pleistocene and into the late Holocene. These biomes are broad-scale communities based on plant functional types rather than proportions of pollen counts by species. We use the biomes calculated for the millennium centered on 13,000 cal BP (Figure 8.5), as this appears to be the period during which fluted-point-making Paleoindians arrived in and began populating the East (Boulanger and Lyman 2014; Lothrop et al. 2016; Miller and Gingerich 2013b).

Because these biotic communities are based on estimated proportions of various plant taxa, they likely reflect in some way the forms of animal life inhabiting them—however, cross-referencing with the paleontological and archaeological records would certainly strengthen this assumption (Faith and Lyman 2019; Lyman 2017). If Paleoindian foragers were adapting their stone-tool technologies to the availability of different prey and prey-behavior within these biomes, we may anticipate increased fre-

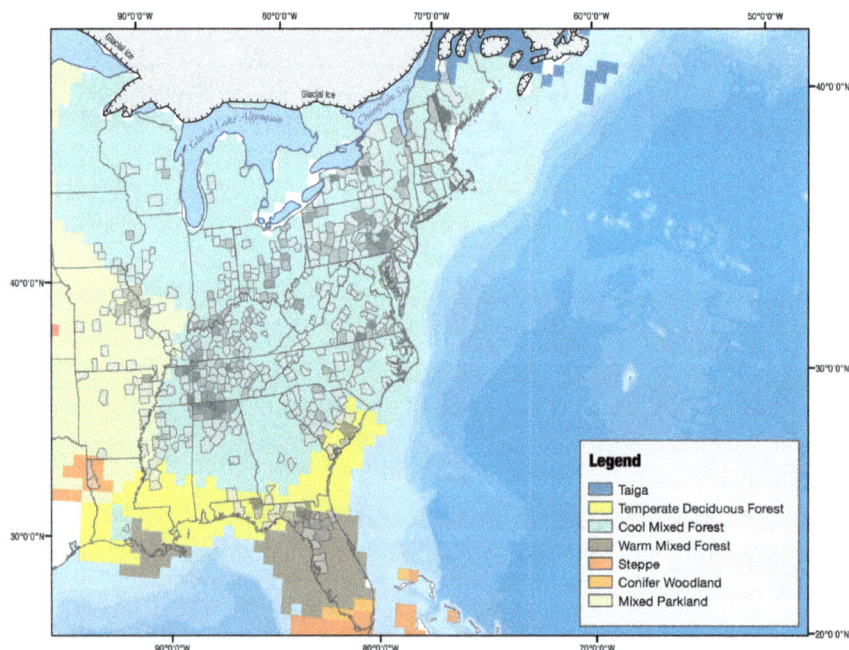

Figure 8.5. 13,000 cal BP biomes calculated for eastern North America by Williams et al. (2004). Glacial boundaries, proglacial lakes, and the Champlain Sea inlet at 11,000 ^{14}C YBP are shown from Dalton et al. (2020) and Dyke et al. (2003). As in Figure 8.4, counties with fluted-point specimens are shown and shaded by the number of specimens. © The authors.

quencies of certain attributes of those technologies in a manner similar to the emergence of *Folsom* points on the plains as bison come to dominate the landscape. Similarly, as groups of foragers adapt to the biomes in which they reside and decrease the extent of their seasonal movements, we might anticipate less frequent sharing of information across biomes, resulting in regionalization of projectile-point forms (O'Brien et al. 2016).

Physiographic Provinces. Physiography is the classification of landscapes based on similarities in topography, bedrock lithology and structure, geomorphic history, and geological processes of landscape formation. Thus, physiographic regions are generalized categories of similar landscapes. Here, we use the meso-scale physiographic provinces established by Fenneman (1946) to represent the finest-scale geographic regions in our analyses (Figure 8.6). We note that some attributes (e.g., topography, bedrock) used to define physiographic regions operate at a temporal scale that greatly exceeds the temporal scale of Paleoindian occupations. Others (e.g., geomorphology) may have been strongly influenced by landscape changes during the Holocene. Thus, our use of physiographic provinces does not assume that exactly the same regions existed at the end of the

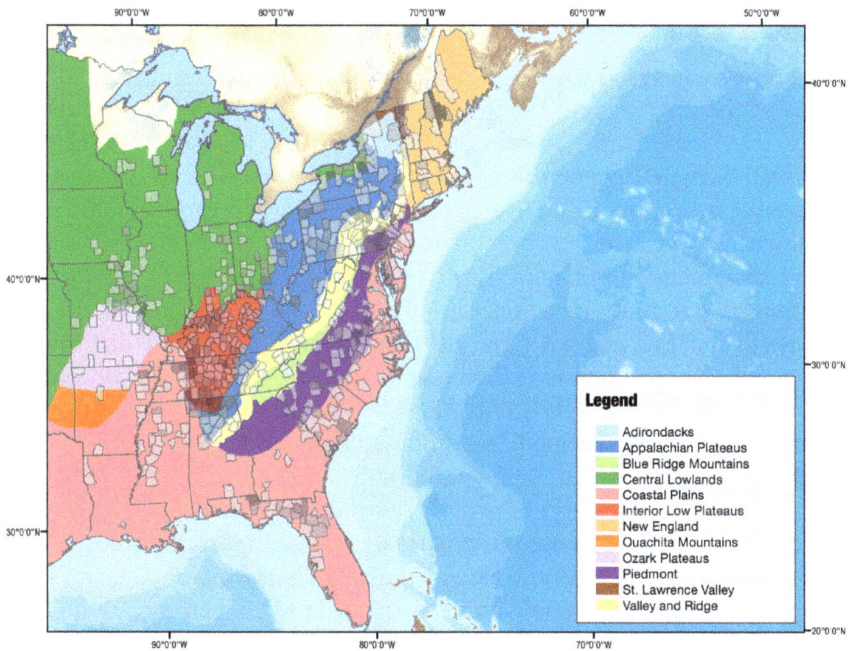

Figure 8.6. Physiographic provinces (Fenneman 1946) in the eastern United States. As in Figure 8.4, counties with fluted-point specimens are shown and shaded by the number of specimens. © The authors.

Pleistocene, but rather that underlying differences exist between these regions today, and that at least some of these differences existed during the late Pleistocene, regardless of the specific expression on the landscape in terms of floral and faunal compositions.

Results

Our modeling of evenness of point-class proportions allows us to make several observations about Paleoindian point diversity in the East as it relates to the landscapes in which Paleoindians lived. We present our results in subsections based on the geographic regions within which we have estimated point-class evenness. To interpret our modeled evenness values (E_H), recall that greater evenness means a more equitable distribution of all possible point forms, whereas lower evenness values signify greater inequity in the proportions of point forms—that is, lower values indicate that certain point forms are much more common, whereas higher values indicate greater parity in the frequencies of point forms.

Glaciated vs. Unglaciated Landscape

Our results suggest a greater evenness of point forms in unglaciated portions of the East than in the glaciated portion (Figure 8.7). These differences are notable across all permutations of our model, and are particularly noticeable when these permutations are pooled to provide robust estimates of evenness (Figure 8.7B). The greater uncertainty in estimates for evenness within glaciated portions of the East reflects the fact that far fewer point specimens in our database have been recovered from the northern portion of our study area. Yet, the differences in evenness estimates are robust (Table 8.3 and 8.4). The median E_H of the posterior distribution for the unglaciated region is 0.932, with the 95 percent highest probability density interval (HPDI) encompassing evenness values from 0.920 to 0.943. By contrast, the median evenness value for the glaciated region is 0.850 (95 percent HPDI: 0.814–0.883).

One intriguing way of viewing these results is to examine which of our point classes are represented in greater or lesser proportions among these regions (Figure 8.7C). In the case of the unglaciated region, the two most frequently represented point classes are 11121 (11.7 percent) and 11111 (8.1 percent). These classes describe essentially identical point forms, differing only in whether the maximum blade width is above or below the median value in the sample (0.458, or, just below half of the length). The

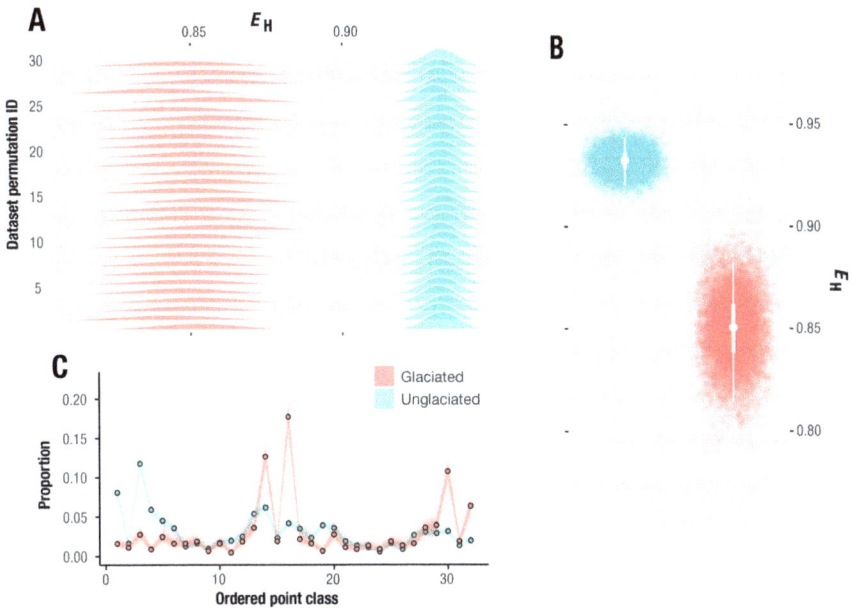

Figure 8.7. Results of modeling point-form evenness in glaciated and unglaciated landscapes showing the posterior probabilities for evenness values. (A) Distributions of modeled evenness values over 30 permutations of the model. (B) Samples drawn from the pooled posterior probability distribution of all models showing the estimated median evenness value, and the uncertainty in those estimations (X axis is jittered to enhance visibility). (C) Proportions of each point class within glaciated and unglaciated portions of the East across all permutations of the model. Note that the order of point classes in C is the same as in Table 8.2. © The authors.

states of the other dimensions indicate that points assigned to these two classes have eared bases, shallow basal indentations, straight sides, and are generally narrow relative to their length. These are point specimens that would typically be referred to as *Eastern Clovis* and *Cumberland*. While these two classes are the most frequently represented, they are only slightly more common than other forms (and hence, greater evenness). In contrast, the three most-commonly represented classes in the glaciated East—12222 (17.7 percent), 12212 (12.6 percent), 22212 (10.7 percent)—make up nearly 40 percent of the estimated sample population. Note the character states that are identical within these classes include deep basal indentations, constricted bases, and a greater width:length ratio. Similar to the two most frequent classes in the unglaciated region, the two most frequent classes (12222 and 12212) in the glaciated region differ only in the ver-

Table 8.3. Median evenness (E_H) values modeled for different biogeographic regions, as well as the 95 percent highest probability density interval (HPDI) of the modeled distributions. The final two columns provide the probability of each region having the minimum and the maximum evenness within each set of model comparisons.

	Median	95% HPDI	p Minimum	p Maximum
Glaciated Landscape				
Unglaciated	0.932	0.920–0.943	0.000	1.000
Glaciated	0.850	0.814–0.883	1.000	0.000
13,000 cal BP Biomes				
Cool Mixed Forest	0.932	0.921–0.942	0.000	0.657
Warm Mixed Forest	0.889	0.768–0.969	0.093	0.173
Temperate Deciduous Forest	0.788	0.697–0.868	0.905	0.000
Mixed Parkland	0.913	0.866–0.953	0.002	0.170
Physiographic Province				
Coastal Plain	0.921	0.895–0.944	0.000	0.039
Central Lowlands	0.915	0.876–0.948	0.000	0.036
New England	0.714	0.642–0.784	0.421	0.000
St. Lawrence Valley	0.871	0.540–0.982	0.088	0.120
Valley and Ridge	0.911	0.847–0.960	0.000	0.063
Appalachian Plateaus	0.921	0.883–0.952	0.000	0.068
Piedmont	0.926	0.882–0.961	0.000	0.116
Interior Low Plateaus	0.845	0.810–0.877	0.000	0.000
Ozark Plateaus	0.925	0.803–0.984	0.001	0.236
Ouachita Mountains	0.869	0.351–0.983	0.147	0.132
Blue Ridge Mountains	0.861	0.523–0.980	0.100	0.105
Adirondacks	0.818	0.339–0.979	0.243	0.084

tical position of the maximum blade width. This trait may be sensitive to resharpening of the projectile blade. Although we specifically eliminated point specimens from our database that showed clear evidence of extensive resharpening, perhaps our expectations regarding the influence of even minor resharpening need to be recalibrated.

Regardless, a comparison of the posterior distributions from our model shows that there are robust differences in evenness values, and that unglaciated portions of the East are much more even in terms of projectile-point classes. We also note that a direct comparison of the frequencies of various classes shows that those classes that are most frequent in each region are different.

Table 8.4. Comparison of modeled evenness (E_H) distributions for projectile-point classes in (A) unglaciated and (B) glaciated regions, and the probabilities of each distribution being greater than the other.

		p > A	p > B
A	Unglaciated	NA	1.000
B	Glaciated	0.000	NA

Biotic Communities

The biomes modeled by Williams and colleagues (2004) suggest that much of the eastern United States was covered in a broad expanse of what they classify as "Cool Mixed Forest," a biome characterized by the presence of boreal conifer species (*Pinus* and *Picea*) as well as more temperate deciduous species (*Quercus*, *Fraxinus*, and *Ostryal*). Based on their data, this biome would have been dominated by conifer species during the Last Glacial Maximum (LGM), thus we can conceptualize this broad biotic community as one in which conifers are decreasing in abundance over time. The southern reaches of our study area were covered in biomes characterized by relatively higher abundances of species favoring warmer temperatures—and which eventually expanded northward during the Holocene—including *Carya*, *Quercus*, *Tsuga*, and *Fagus*.

Results from our modeling of evenness within these biomes demonstrate that the large swath of Cool Mixed Forest is the area of greatest point-form evenness in the East (Figure 8.8, Table 8.5), and that this biome has the highest probability of possessing the greatest point-class diversity (Table 8.3). A casual glance at Figure 8.5 should reveal why this is the case: this biome encompasses nearly the entirety of the eastern United States, from central Mississippi, Alabama, and Georgia in the south to northern Maine and northern Wisconsin in the north. Not surprisingly, this biome therefore contains the vast majority of our projectile point specimens. And the same point classes that were the most prevalent in the glaciated/unglaciated model are also the most frequently represented within the Cool Mixed Forest biome (Figure 8.8).

The biomes that encompass the far southern portion of the East (Temperate Deciduous Forest and Warm Mixed Forest) have lower point-class evenness despite having greater uncertainty around the evenness estimate. Of these, the Temperate Deciduous Forest has the least class evenness of all the biomes (median = 0.788). Even considering the uncertainty around the median, this biome has 90.5 percent probability of being the biome with the least evenness. As shown in Figure 8.8C, two classes are by far the most common in this region: 11122 (24.4 percent) and 11121

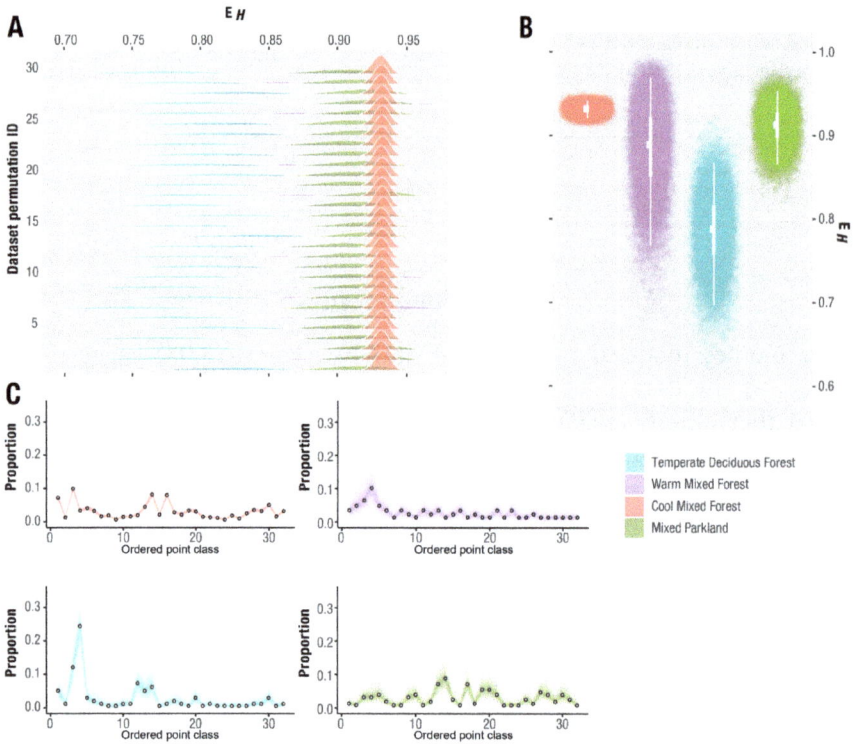

Figure 8.8. Results of modeling point-form evenness within reconstructed biomes of 13,000 cal BP (Williams et al. 2004). (A) Distributions of modeled evenness values over 30 permutations of the model. (B) Samples drawn from the pooled posterior probability distribution of all models showing the estimated median evenness value, and the uncertainty in those estimations (X axis is jittered to enhance visibility). (C) Proportions of each point class within each biome. Note that certain point classes are much more prevalent in some regions than in others. © The authors.

(12.1 percent). The only difference between these two classes is the fifth dimension in our classification, the width:length ratio, which as discussed above may reflect resharpening of point specimens. Most of the actual specimens assigned to these two classes were described as belonging either to the *Cumberland* or *Clovis* types. The *Cumberland* type is almost exclusively associated with the American Southeast (Lewis 1954). As noted above, class 11121 is also the most abundant class in the unglaciated region of the East, seemingly suggesting that our analysis is independently identifying at least some degree of regionalization in projectile-point form.

Classes 11122 and 11121 are also the most frequent point classes in the far-southern Warm Mixed Forest biome, comprising more than 16.6

Table 8.5. Comparison of modeled evenness (E_H) distributions for projectile-point classes in reconstructed biomes at 13,000 cal BP, and the probabilities of each distribution being greater than the other.

		p > A	p > B	p > C	p > D
A	*Cool Mixed Forest*	NA	0.813	1.000	0.801
B	*Warm Mixed Forest*	0.187	NA	0.906	0.330
C	*Temperate Deciduous Forest*	0.000	0.094	NA	0.003
D	*Mixed Parkland*	0.199	0.670	0.997	NA

percent of the total sample. No other point classes exceed 5 percent in their representation. As shown in Figure 8.8B, the median evenness value calculated for the Warm Mixed Forest is 0.887, but because significantly fewer point specimens have been recovered from the area covered by this biome, the uncertainty around this value is quite large.

Lastly, the Mixed Parkland biome, which encompasses the far western portion of our area of interest, has a relatively high median evenness value (0.903). As with the Warm Mixed Forest, fewer specimens have been recovered from this biome, leading to a greater degree of uncertainty around this value. Despite this uncertainty, our modeling approach allows us to calculate that the Mixed Parkland has a 67 percent probability of being more even than the Warm Mixed Forest, a 99.7 percent probability of being more even that the Temperate Deciduous Forest, but only a 20 percent probability of being more even than the Cool Mixed Forest. We find it interesting that the most common point classes in this biome are dissimilar to those observed for the other biomes. Class 12212 (8.9 percent) occurs in about the same frequency as it does in the Cool Mixed Forest; however, classes 12211 (7.2 percent) and 21111 (7.1 percent) are not as prevalent in the other biomes. Moreover, the most frequent classes in the other biomes (e.g., 11122, 11121) do not appear in any significantly greater frequency in the Mixed Parkland (Figure 8.8C).

Physiographic Provinces

Modern physiographic provinces (Fenneman 1946) are the finest-scale geographic province within which we modeled point-class evenness. Unlike the unglaciated/glaciated landscape or modeled biomes, definitions of physiographic provinces are based on a suite of topographic, geological, ecological, and geomorphological characteristics. Thus, attempting to explain significant differences in point class frequencies are quite difficult. However, our results point to some intriguing differences among these provinces.

As shown in Figure 8.9, several provinces simply have too few point specimens recovered from within their boundaries to reliably estimate point-class diversity. Four of these provinces are particularly rugged and rural landscapes, perhaps pointing to strong biases in the recovery and visibility of archaeological remains. The long-tailed distributions of evenness estimates for the Adirondacks, the Blue Ridge Mountains, the Ouachita Mountains, and the Ozark Plateaus (Figure 8.9B) all suggest that simply too few fluted points have been recovered (or, perhaps more correctly, are present in our database) to reliably estimate evenness. We suspect that the paucity of fluted-point specimens in the Ozark Plateaus and Ouachita Mountains provinces is likely a result of both recovery biases as well as our own focus, from the outset of this project (O'Brien, Darwent, and Lyman 2001), on recording fluted-point finds east of the Mississippi River Valley. However, in the cases of the Adirondacks and the Blue Ridge Mountains, the lack of fluted points seems more to do with recovery bias and perhaps an underlying lack of Paleoindian sites in these mountainous regions.

The posterior distribution of E_H for the St. Lawrence Valley is similarly long tailed, spanning values from 1 to less than 0.5. Again, this reflects few

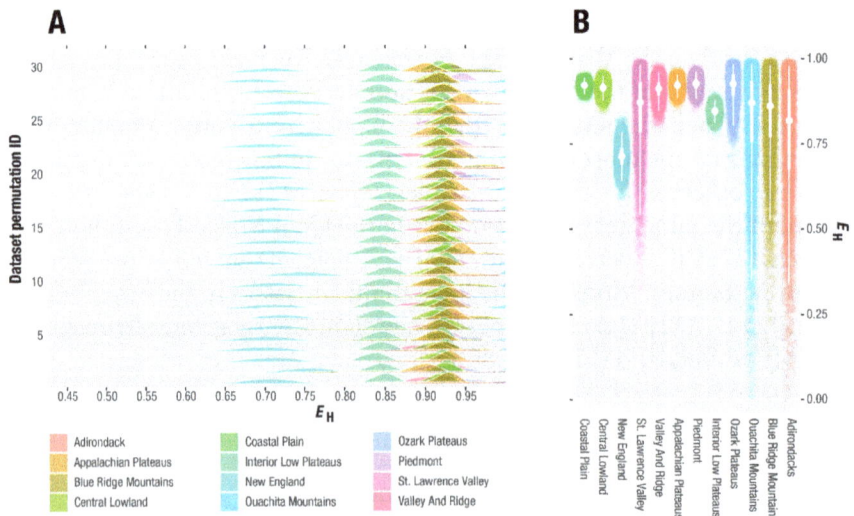

Figure 8.9. Results of modeling point-form evenness within physiographic provinces (Fenneman 1946). (A) Distributions of modeled evenness values over 30 permutations of the model. (B) Samples drawn from the pooled posterior probability distribution of all models showing the estimated median evenness value, and the uncertainty in those estimations (X axis is jittered to enhance visibility). Note the extreme uncertainty in evenness estimates within several of the provinces. © The authors.

specimens; however, in this case we cannot attribute this paucity to the ruggedness or ruralness of the landscape. Rather, we suspect that the lack of points from this province has more to do with two factors: first, this is the smallest physiographic province in our analysis, reflecting the well-known species–area relationship (e.g., Lyman and Ames 2007); and second, much of the St. Lawrence Valley was submerged beneath the Champlain Sea (an inlet of the North Atlantic) until ca. 12,000 cal BP, which is effectively the tail end of the period during which fluted points were produced. This would suggest that fluted points found within much of this physiographic province likely post-date ca. 12,000 cal BP, and that the amount of time during which fluted points could have been deposited in this province is significantly shorter than other provinces in our analysis.

Results of our modeling suggest a high degree of evenness among most physiographic provinces. The Coastal Plain, Central Lowland, Valley and Ridge, Appalachian Plateaus, and Piedmont all have median evenness estimates in excess of 0.91 (Table 8.3). And, although the dispersal of uncertainty around these medians varies, our model comparison suggests there is little support for any of these being greater than the other (Table 8.6). In short, our model suggests that these regions all have similar evenness in fluted-point forms.

The New England physiographic province shows the lowest E_H estimates in our model, indicating less diversity in point classes. The median evenness value for this province is 0.714. More significantly, the 95 percent HPDI for the New England province (0.642–0.784) does not overlap with the 95 percent HPDIs for any of the other well-resolved provinces (Table 8.3). Thus, even when adjusting for uncertainty in sample size and recovery bias, the New England province has the least diversity of point forms in the East. Indeed, when comparing the modeled evenness distribution of New England against those of all other provinces (excepting the poorly resolved provinces), the probability of it being greater is effectively zero (Table 8.6).

The two most-abundant classes within the New England province— 12222 (25.07 percent) and 12212 (18.56 percent)—are also among the most abundant in the Piedmont, Interior Low Plateaus, Appalachian Plateaus, and Central Lowlands provinces (Figure 8.10). However, the combined frequency of these classes in any other province does not exceed 17 percent. The relative abundances of these two classes combined in New England is 43.64 percent. The New England province has less diversity (evenness) in point forms not because it has unique projectile-point forms, but because certain forms are two to three times more common there than they are elsewhere in the East.

Table 8.6. Comparison of modeled evenness (E_H) distributions for projectile-point classes in modern physiographic provinces, and the probabilities of each distribution being greater than the other.

		p > A	p > B	p > C	p > D	p > E	p > F	p > G	p > H	p > I	p > J	p > K	p > L
A	Coastal Plain	NA	0.612	1.000	0.709	0.628	0.495	0.423	1.000	0.472	0.693	0.734	0.788
B	Central Lowlands	0.388	NA	1.000	0.681	0.547	0.401	0.345	0.997	0.428	0.668	0.709	0.769
C	New England	0.000	0.000	NA	0.141	0.000	0.000	0.000	0.001	0.002	0.202	0.162	0.308
D	St. Lawrence Valley	0.291	0.319	0.859	NA	0.337	0.289	0.271	0.587	0.293	0.516	0.528	0.610
E	Valley and Ridge	0.372	0.453	1.000	0.663	NA	0.382	0.337	0.966	0.407	0.653	0.691	0.755
F	Appalachian Plateaus	0.505	0.599	1.000	0.711	0.618	NA	0.435	0.998	0.476	0.693	0.735	0.787
G	Piedmont	0.577	0.655	1.000	0.729	0.663	0.565	NA	0.998	0.513	0.714	0.750	0.804
H	Interior Low Plateaus	0.000	0.003	1.000	0.413	0.034	0.002	0.002	NA	0.093	0.431	0.450	0.566
I	Ozark Plateaus	0.528	0.572	0.998	0.707	0.593	0.524	0.487	0.907	NA	0.701	0.730	0.787
J	Ouachita Mountains	0.307	0.332	0.798	0.484	0.347	0.307	0.286	0.569	0.299	NA	0.507	0.591
K	Blue Ridge Mountains	0.266	0.291	0.838	0.472	0.309	0.265	0.250	0.550	0.270	0.493	NA	0.592
L	Adirondacks	0.212	0.231	0.692	0.390	0.245	0.213	0.196	0.434	0.213	0.409	0.408	NA

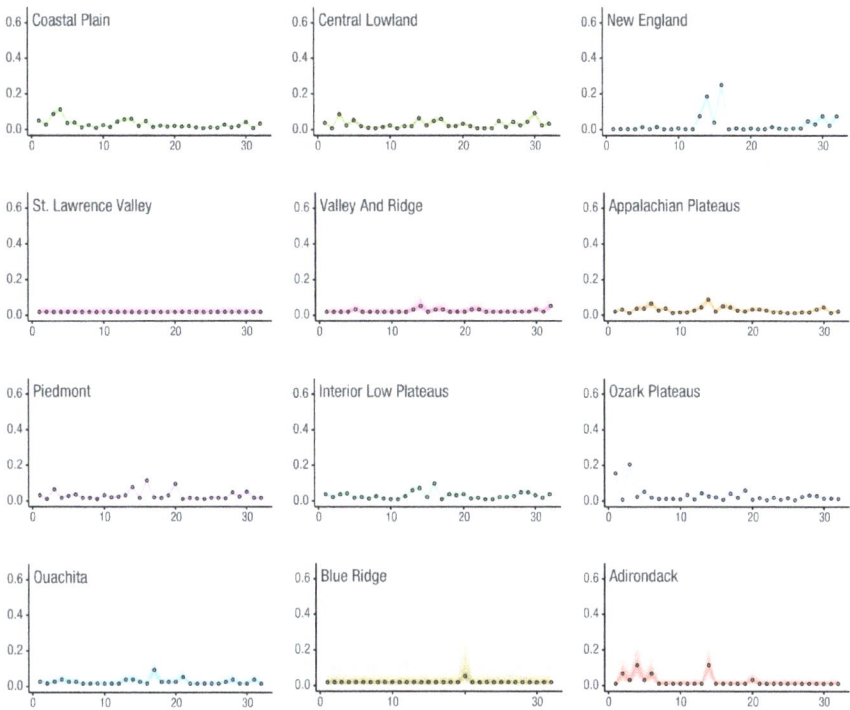

Figure 8.10. Proportions of each point class within physiographic provinces across all permutations of the model. Note that certain point classes are much more prevalent in some provinces than in others. © The authors.

Conclusions

Our use of paradigmatic classification and a Bayesian model to estimate evenness in Paleoindian fluted projectile point form reveals significant differences among and between regions of geographic significance. Using several scales of analysis, which emphasize differing aspects of geology, biotic classification, and physiography, we note that there is significant variation in projectile-point form and in the dispersion of forms throughout eastern North America. And, most importantly, we find significant differences in both absolute measures of evenness (diversity) as well as variability in estimates of evenness within geographic and physiographic regions across the East.

The model we lay out here allows for the integration of uncertainty in provenance of projectile-point specimens regardless of geographic scale. We believe this is a particularly useful innovation, given the lack of firm or precise contexts for many of the fluted points that have been recovered. We also note the Bayesian model allows for the pooling of uncertainty in provenance for these finds, thus resulting in more accurate estimations of point-form diversity.

The approach described here is unhindered by traditionally used extensionally defined projectile point types and qualitative comparisons. The results show a clear distinction in the evenness (diversity) of point forms, and those forms that are most common, between glaciated and unglaciated regions of the East. These results provide empirical support for more qualitative discussions of possible differences between these regions (e.g., Ellis and Lothrop 2019). Our data and earlier studies (e.g., Eren et al. 2016) show there is clearly something different about the Paleoindian occupation of the glaciated region of the East, as well as the New England province, that distinguishes them from the rest of the East. Our data are also consistent with findings of greater point-form diversity in certain parts of the Southeast (ibid.), and we can now confidently say that the Southeast appears to have both greater richness *and* evenness in point forms.

What exactly these differences in point-form diversity mean remains somewhat opaque. Within New England specifically and the glaciated Northeast in general, we find it intriguing that the most abundant point forms appear to represent a subset of those used elsewhere in the East. Acknowledging that point forms are not necessarily equivalent to people, what our data may be showing is a kind of founder's effect, whereby Paleoindians moving into a previously uninhabited area bring with them their particular recipe for producing fluted points, and this particular form becomes the most abundant in the region.

We also note that those regions with the greatest evenness in point forms also contain a greater abundance of bedded cryptocrystalline rocks (i.e., chert and flint) suitable for the production of flaked-stone tools. In contrast, the highly metamorphosed terrain of the Appalachian Highlands and New England tend to have far smaller and more nodular deposits of chert, as well as coarser-grained materials (also in smaller package sizes) such as quartzite, felsite, and rhyolite. This is particularly apparent when comparing the deep and expansive chert beds of Illinois, Indiana, Ohio, western Tennessee, and western Kentucky to the highly fragmented, indurated, and spatially restricted deposits of chert found in eastern New York, Vermont, Maine, and Massachusetts.

Perhaps differences in width:length ratios of point forms relate to the overall package size of chert obtainable from outcrops in these regions. Moreover, greater ease of access to high-quality raw materials might also encourage experimentation and innovation in projectile-point manufacture—if the cost of resupplying your resources is low, you can take greater risks (and conserve less) with those resources.

This is, of course, speculation, but it is speculation that has testable predictions. Chert and flint points in the glaciated region, in New England, and in the upper portions of the Cool Mixed Forest biome should show greater evidence of resharpening and recycling compared to those found in the South; however, we point out that the generally shorter, stubbier, and deeply indented points that seem to be most common in the Northeast are not simply scaled-down versions of their eastern and southern counterparts. Some other mechanisms are also at work. Although our study is largely an inductive one, the ability to quantitatively estimate diversity in a systematic manner lends itself to the formulation of testable hypotheses that ultimately move us away from describing diversity, and towards explaining it.

Acknowledgments

The model reported here was executed on the ManeFrame II high-performance computing cluster at Southern Methodist University. The R code for our model is available on request from the authors, as is a summary list of the various fluted-point specimens in our dataset. We thank Michael O'Brien, John Darwent, and R. Lee Lyman for their contributions to the dataset used here, and for the numerous conversations that led to ideas being explored here. We thank Jack Williams for generously sharing the paleo-biome data from his and colleagues 2004 paper, which allowed us to incorporate the spatial extent of the paleo-biomes in our model. Lastly, we thank Metin Eren and Briggs Buchanan for their invitation to present this research, for their voluminous patience, and for their dedication to bringing this volume to fruition.

Matthew T. Boulanger is a Lecturer at Southern Methodist University, Dallas, Texas, USA.

Ryan P. Breslawski is a PhD candidate at Southern Methodist University, Dallas, Texas, USA.

Ian A. Jorgeson is a PhD candidate at Southern Methodist University, Dallas, Texas, USA.

Note

1. Here, we italicize formal names for projectile point types that have been used, and sometimes defined, by archaeologists as a means of distinguishing them as ideational units, and to clarify to the reader when we are talking about artifact forms rather than cultural units or time periods.

References

Ahler, S. A., and P. R. Geib. 2000. "Why Flute? Folsom Point Design and Adaptation." *Journal of Archaeological Science* 27: 799–820.

Amick, D. S. 1995. "Patterns of Technological Variation among Folsom and Midland Projectile Points in the American Southwest." *Plains Anthropologist* 40: 23–28.

Anderson, D. G. 1990a. "A North American Paleoindian Projectile Point Database." *Current Research in the Pleistocene* 7: 67–69.

———. 1990b. "The Paleoindian Colonization of Eastern North America: A View from the Southeastern United States." In *Early Paleoindian Economies of Eastern North America*, ed. K. B. Tankersley and B. L. Isaac, 163–216. Greenwich, CT: JAI Press.

Anderson, D. G., D. Echeverry, D. S. Miller, A. A. White, S. J. Yerka, E. Kansa, S. Whitcher Kansa, C. R. Moore, K. N. Myers, J. J. Wells, T. G. Bissett, and A. M. Smallwood. 2019. "Paleoindian Settlement in the Southeastern United States: The Role of Large Databases." In *New Directions in the Search for the First Floridians*, ed. D. Thulman and I. Garrison, 241–75. Gainesville: University Press of Florida.

Anderson, D. G., and M. K. Faught. 1998. "The Distribution of Fluted Paleoindian Projectile Points: Update 1998." *Archaeology of Eastern North America* 26: 163–87.

———. 2000. "Paleoindian Artefact Distributions: Evidence and Implications." *Antiquity* 26: 163–87.

Anderson, D. G., D. S. Miller, S. J. Yerka, J. Gillam, D. Johanson, A. C. Goodyear, and A. M. Smallwood. 2010. "Paleoindian Database of the Americas 2010: Current Status and Findings." *Archaeology of Eastern North America* 38: 63–90.

Anderson, D. G., L. D. O'Steen, and K. E. Sassaman. 1996. "Chronological Considerations." In *The Paleoindian and Early Archaic Southeast*, ed. D. G. Anderson and K. E. Sassaman, 3–15. Tuscaloosa: University of Alabama Press.

Beauchamp, W. M. 1897. *Aboriginal Chipped Stone Implements of New York*, Volume 4(16) of Bulletin of the New York State Museum. Albany: University of the State of New York.

Beck, C., and G. T. Jones. 2010. "Clovis and Western Stemmed: Population Migration and the Meeting of Two Technologies in the Intermountain West." *American Antiquity* 75: 81–116.

Boulanger, M. T. 2015. "Phylogenetic and Morphometric Analyses of Eastern Fluted-Point Forms." PhD dissertation. Columbia, MO: University of Missouri, Columbia.

Boulanger, M. T., and R. L. Lyman. 2014. "Northeastern North American Pleistocene Megafauna Chronologically Overlapped Minimally with Paleoindians." *Quaternary Science Reviews* 85: 35–46.

Bradley, B. A. 1997. "Sloan Site Biface and Projectile Point Technology." In *Sloan: A Paleoindian Dalton Cemetery in Arkansas*, ed. D. F. Morse, 53–57. Washington, DC: Smithsonian Institution Press.

Bradley, J. W., A. Spiess, R. A. Boisvert, and J. Boudreau. 2008. "What's the Point? Modal Forms and Attributes of Paleoindian Bifaces in the New England Maritimes Region." *Archaeology of Eastern North America* 36: 119–72.

Brennan, L. A. 1982. "A Compilation of Fluted Points of Eastern North America by Count and Distribution: An AENA Project." *Archaeology of Eastern North America* 10: 27–46.

Broster, J. B., M. R. Norton, D. S. Miller, J. W. Tune, and J. Baker. 2013. "Tennessee's Paleoindian Record: The Cumberland and Lower Tennessee River Watersheds." In *In the Eastern Fluted Point Tradition*, ed. J. A. M. Gingerich, 299–314. Salt Lake City: University of Utah Press.

Brown, C. S. 1926. *Archeology of Mississippi*. Mississippi: Mississippi State Geological Survey.

Bryan, A. L. 1991. "The Fluted-Point Tradition in the Americas—One of Several Adaptations to Late Pleistocene American Environments." In *Clovis: Origins and Adaptations*, ed. R. Bonnichsen and K. L. Turnmire, 15–33. Corvallis: Center for the Study of the First Americans, Oregon State University.

Buchanan, B. 2006. "An Analysis of Folsom Projectile Point Resharpening Using Quantitative Comparisons of Form and Allometry." *Journal of Archaeological Science* 33: 185–99.

Buchanan, B., and M. Collard. 2010. "A Geometric Morphometrics-Based Assessment of Blade Shape Differences among Paleoindian Projectile Point Types from Western North America." *Journal of Archaeological Science* 37: 350–59.

Buchanan, B., M. J. O'Brien, and M. Collard. 2014. "Continent-Wide or Region-Specific? A Geometric Morphometrics-Based Assessment of Variation in Clovis Point Shape." *Archaeological and Anthropological Sciences* 6: 145–62.

Bullen, R. B. 1968. *A Guide to the Identification of Florida Projectile Points*. Gainesville: Florida State Museum.

Collard, M., B. Buchanan, M. J. Hamilton, and M. J. O'Brien. 2010. "Spatiotemporal Dynamics of the Clovis–Folsom Transition." *Journal of Archaeological Science* 37: 2513–19.

Cook, H. 1927. "New Geological and Paleontological Evidence Bearing on the Antiquity of Mankind in America." *Natural History* 27: 240–47.

Cotter, J. L. 1937a. "The Occurrence of Flints and Extinct Animals in Pluvial Deposits near Clovis, New Mexico: Part IV, Report on Excavation at the Gravel Pit, 1936." *Proceedings of the Academy of Natural Sciences of Philadelphia* 89: 1–16.

———. 1937b. "The Significance of Folsom and Yuma Artifact Occurrences in the Light of Typology and Distribution." In *Twenty-Fifth Anniversary Studies*, ed. D. S. Davidson, 27–36. Publications of the Philadelphia Anthropological Society. Philadelphia: University of Pennsylvania Press.

———. 1938. "The Occurrence of Flints and Extinct Animals in Pluvial Deposits near Clovis, New Mexico: Part VI, Report on Field Season of 1937." *Proceedings of the Academy of Natural Sciences of Philadelphia* 90: 113–17.

Crabtree, D. E. 1966. "A Stoneworker's Approach to Analyzing and Replicating the Lindenmeier Folsom." *Tebiwa* 9: 3–39.

Dalton, A. S., M. Margold, C. R. Stokes, L. Tarasov, A. S. Dyke, R. S. Adams, S. Allard, H. E. Arends, N. Atkinson, J. W. Attig, P. J. Barnett, R. L. Barnett, M. Batterson, P. Bernatchez, H. W. Borns Jr., A. Breckenridge, J. P. Briner, E. Brouard, J. E. Campbell, A. E. Carlson, J. J. Clague, B. B. Curry, R.-A. Daigneault, H. Dubé-Loubert, D. J. Easterbrook, D. A. Franzi, H. F. Friedrich, S. Funder, M. S. Gauthier, A. S. Gowan, K. L. Harris, B. Hétu, T. S. Hooyer, C. E. Jennings, M. D. Johnson, A. E. Kehew, S. E. Kelley, D. Kerr, E. L. King, K. K. Kjeldsen, A. R. Knaeble, P. Lajeunesse, T. R. Lakeman,

M. Lamothe, P. Larson, M. Lavoie, H. M. Loope, T. V. Lowell, B. A. Lusardi, L. Manz, I. McMartin, F. C. Nixon, S. Occhietti, M. A. Parkhill, D. J. W. Piper, A. G. Pronk, P. J. H. Richard, J. C. Ridge, M. Ross, M. Roy, A. Seaman, J. Shaw, R. R. Stea, J. T. Teller, W. B. Thompson, L. H. Thorleifson, D. J. Utting, J. J. Veillette, B. C. Ward, T. K. Weddle, and H. E. Wright Jr. 2020. "An Updated Radiocarbon-Based Ice Margin Chronology for the Last Deglaciation of the North American Ice Sheet Complex." *Quaternary Science Reviews* 234: 106223.

Dunnell, R. C. 1971. *Systematics in Prehistory*. New York: The Free Press.

———. 1986. "Methodological Issues in Americanist Artifact Classification." *Advances in Archaeological Method and Theory* 9: 149–207.

Dyke, A. S., A. Moore, and L. Robertson. 2003. "Deglaciation of North America: Thirty-Two Digital Maps at 1:7,000,000 Scale with Accompanying Digital Chronological Database and One Poster (Two Sheets) With Full Map Series." Ottawa: Geological Survey of Canada. Open File 1574.

Ellis, C. J., and J. C. Lothrop. 2019. "Early Fluted-Biface Variation in Glaciated Northeastern North America." *Paleoamerica* 5(2): 121–31.

Eren, M. I., A. Chao, C. H. Chiu, R. K. Colwell, B. Buchanan, M. T. Boulanger, J. Darwent, and M. J. O'Brien. 2016. "Statistical Analysis of Paradigmatic Class Richness Supports Greater Paleoindian Projectile-Point Diversity in the Southeast." *American Antiquity* 81: 174–92.

Eren, M. I., and A. Desjardines. 2015. "Flaked Stone Tools of Pleistocene Colonizers: Overshot Flaking at the Redwing Site, Ontario." In *Clovis: On the Edge of a New Understanding*, ed. A. M. Smallwood and T. A. Jennings, 109–20. College Station: Texas A&M University Press.

Faith, J. T., and R. L. Lyman. 2019. *Paleozoology and Paleoenvironments: Fundamentals, Assumptions, and Techniques*. Cambridge: Cambridge University Press.

Fenneman, N. M. 1946. *Physical Divisions of the United States*. Washington DC: United States Geological Survey.

Figgins, J. D. 1927. "The Antiquity of Man in America." *Natural History* 27: 229–39.

Goodyear, A. C. 1982. "The Chronological Position of the Dalton Horizon in the Southeastern United States." *American Antiquity* 47: 382–95.

Judge, W. J. 1970. "Systems Analysis and the Folsom–Midland Question." *Southwestern Journal of Anthropology* 26: 40–51.

Lepper, B. T. 1983. "Fluted Point Distributional Patterns in the Eastern United States: A Contemporary Phenomenon." *Midcontinental Journal of Archaeology* 8: 269–85.

———. 1985. "The Effects of Cultivation and Collecting on Ohio Fluted Point Finds: A Reply to Seeman and Prufer." *Midcontinental Journal of Archaeology* 10: 241–50.

Lewis, T. M. N. 1954. "The Cumberland Point." *Oklahoma Archaeological Society Bulletin* 2: 7–8.

Loebel, T. J. 2012. "Pattern or Bias? A Critical Evaluation of Midwestern Fluted Point Distributions Using Raster Based GIS." *Journal of Archaeological Science* 39: 1205–17.

Loebel, T. J., J. M. Lambert, and M. G. Hill. 2016. "Synthesis and Assessment of the Folsom Record in Illinois and Wisconsin." *Paleoamerica* 2: 135–49.

Lothrop, J. C., D. L. Lowery, A. E. Spiess, and C. J. Ellis. 2016. "Early Human Settlement of Northeastern North America." *Paleoamerica* 2(3): 192–251.

Lyman, R. L. 2017. "Paleoenvironmental Reconstruction from Faunal Remains: Ecological Basics and Analytical Assumptions." *Journal of Archaeological Research* 25: 315–71.

Lyman, R. L., and K. M. Ames. 2007. "On the Use of Species–Area Curves to Detect the Effects of Sample Size." *Journal of Archaeological Science* 34: 1985–90.

Lyman, R. L., and M. J. O'Brien. 2002a. "Classification." In *Darwin and Archaeology: A Handbook of Key Concepts*, ed. J. P. Hart and J.E. Terrell, 69–88. Westport, CT: Bergin & Garvey.

———. 2002b. "The Epistemological Nature of Archaeological Units." *Anthropological Theory* 2: 237–56.

———. 2006. *Measuring Time with Artifacts: A History of Methods in American Archaeology*. Lincoln: University of Nebraska Press.

MacDonald, G. F. 1968. *Debert: A Palaeo-Indian Site in Central Nova Scotia*. Anthropological Papers, No. 16. Ottawa: National Museum of Man.

Mason, R. J. 1962. "The Paleo-Indian Tradition in Eastern North America." *Current Anthropology* 3: 227–346.

Meltzer, D. J. 1988. "Late Pleistocene Human Adaptations in Eastern North America." *Journal of World Prehistory* 2: 1–52.

Miller, D. S., and J. A. M. Gingerich. 2013a. "Regional Variation in the Terminal Pleistocene and Early Holocene Radiocarbon Record of Eastern North America." *Quaternary Research* 79: 175–88.

———. 2013b. "Paleoindian Chronology and the Eastern Fluted Point Tradition." In *The Eastern Fluted Point Tradition*, ed. J. A. M. Gingerich, 9–37. Salt Lake City: University of Utah Press.

Miller, D. S., V. T. Holliday, and J. Bright. 2014. "Clovis Across the Continent." In *Paleoamerican Odyssey*, ed. K. E. Graf, C. V. Ketron, and M. R. Waters, 207–20. College Station: Texas A & M University Press.

Morrow, J. E. 1995. "Clovis Projectile Point Manufacture: A Perspective from the Ready/Lincoln Hills Site, 11JY46, Jersey County, Illinois." *Midcontinental Journal of Archaeology* 20(2): 167–91.

———. 1996. "The Organization of Early Paleoindian Lithic Technology in the Confluence Region of the Mississippi, Illinois, and Missouri Rivers." PhD dissertation. St. Louis, MO: Washington University in St. Louis.

———. 2019. "On Fluted Point Morphometrics, Cladistics, and the Origins of the Clovis Culture." *Paleoamerica* 5: 191–205.

O'Brien, M. J., M. T. Boulanger, B. Buchanan, R. A. Bentley, R. L. Lyman, C. P. Lipo, M. E. Madsen, and M. I. Eren. 2016. "Design Space and Cultural Transmission: Case Studies from Paleoindian Eastern North America." *Journal of Archaeological Method and Theory* 23: 692–740.

O'Brien, M. J., M. T. Boulanger, B. Buchanan, M. Collard, R. L. Lyman, and J. Darwent. 2014. "Innovation and Cultural Transmission in the American Paleolithic: Phylogenetic Analysis of Eastern Paleoindian Projectile-Point Classes." *Journal of Anthropological Archaeology* 34: 100–19.

O'Brien, M. J., J. Darwent, and R. L. Lyman. 2001. "Cladistics is Useful for Reconstructing Archaeological Phylogenies: Palaeoindian Points from the Southeastern United States." *Journal of Archaeological Science* 28(10): 1115–36.

O'Brien, M.J., and R. L. Lyman. 2000. *Applying Evolutionary Archaeology: A Systematic Approach*. New York: Springer.

Prasciunas, M. M. 2011. "Mapping Clovis: Projectile Points, Behavior, and Bias." *American Antiquity* 76: 107–26.

Ritchie, W. A. 1944. *The Pre-Iroquoian Occupations of New York State*. Rochester Museum Memoir 1. Rochester: Rochester Museum of Arts and Sciences.

Robinson, B. S., J. C. Ort, W. A. Eldridge, A. L. Burke, and B. G. Pelletier. 2009. "Paleoindian Aggregation and Social Context at Bull Brook." *American Antiquity* 74: 423–47.

Rolingson, M. A. 1964. *Paleo-Indian Culture in Kentucky: A Study Based on Projectile Points*. Studies in Anthropology 2. Lexington: University of Kentucky Press.

Schaefer, C. A. 2005. "A Question of Bias in the North American Fluted-Point Sample." MA thesis. Florida State University, Tallahassee.

Seeman, M. F., and O. H. Prufer. 1982. "An Updated Discussion of Ohio Fluted Points." *Midcontinental Journal of Archaeology* 7: 155–69.

———. 1984. "The Effects of Cultivation and Collecting on Ohio Fluted Point Finds: A Cautionary Note." *Midcontinental Journal of Archaeology* 9: 227–33.

Semken Jr., H. A. 1983. "Holocene Mammalian Biogeography and Climatic Change in the Eastern and Central United States." In *Late Quaternary Environment of the United States, Volume 2: The Holocene*, ed. H. E. Wright, 182–206. Minneapolis: University of Minnesota Press.

Shetrone, H. C. 1936. "The Folsom Phenomena as Seen from Ohio." *Ohio Archaeological and Historical Quarterly* 45: 240–56.

Stan Development Team. 2020. *RStan: the R interface to Stan*. R package v.2.21.2, http://mc-stan.org/.

Steele, J., J. Adams, and T. Sluckin. 1998. "Modeling Paleoindian Dispersals." *World Archaeology* 30: 286–305.

Thulman, D. K. 2007. "A Typology of Fluted Points from Florida." *Florida Anthropologist* 60(4): 63–75.

———. 2012. "Discriminating Paleoindian Point Types from Florida Using Landmark Geometric Morphometrics." *Journal of Archaeological Science* 39: 1599–1607.

Tunnell, C., and L. Johnson. 1991. "Comparing Dimensions for Folsom Points and Their Byproducts from the Adair-Steadman and Lindenmeier Sites and Other Localities." Archeological Reports Series, No. 1. Austin: Texas Historical Commission.

Williams, J. W., B. N. Shuman, T. Webb, P. J. Bartlein, and P. L. Leduc. 2004. "Late-Quaternary Vegetation Dynamics in North America: Scaling from Taxa to Biomes." *Ecological Monographs* 74(2): 309–34.

Wormington, H. M. 1957. *Ancient Man in North America*. Popular Series No. 4. Denver, CO: Denver Museum of Natural History.

Chapter 9

Thinking about Diversity in Material Culture at Multiple Scales

Steven L. Kuhn

———⚉———

Archaeological interest in diversity of classes of artifact or species as the subject of analysis can be traced back almost sixty years. Not much more needs to be said in this chapter about the story of diversity studies in archaeology (see Buchannan and Eren, this volume; O'Brien and Thomas, this volume). Of course, archaeologists are not the only community of researchers interested in variation in diversity. Geneticists, ecologists, and biogeographers, among others, have particularly strong interests in assessing diversity of genes and species. Some of the most widely cited papers on the relationships between sample size and species diversity in archaeofaunas (e.g., Grayson 1981) took explicit inspiration specifically from research in ecology.

Archaeologists pride themselves in borrowing methods and techniques from other fields. This sort of "lateral recycling" makes intellectual sense. However, in borrowing ideas about measurement and analysis of diversity, archaeologists adopted only part of the apparatus that had developed in fields such as ecology. For around fifty years, biologists have considered the phenomenon of diversity and multiple scales. Archaeologists often think at multiple temporal and spatial scales, but discussions of how to measure diversity by archaeologists have, by and large, been concerned with diversity at a single scale. It would benefit our field to look more seriously at multi-scalar approaches.

This chapter briefly reviews multi-scalar approaches to diversity in ecology, and their potential applications in archaeology. These examples discussed are explicitly programmatic and hypothetical. My purpose is not to advance a specific method or describe a particularly important case study, but to suggest avenues for expanding the ways archaeologists think about and use diversity analysis. In keeping with my own interests and knowledge, I focus mainly on applications to the study of material culture, rather than biological remains, and on the archaeology of hunter-gatherers. Some of the examples discussed will not be surprising: a number of common models for interpreting variation in and among assemblages are actually based on ideas about diversity at different scales, though they are seldom explicitly presented as such. Obviously, the causal models for variation in diversity at different scales cannot be adopted directly from ecology or biogeography. The factors that influence diversity of species in ecosystems are different from the ones that influence the distribution of artifact classes across archaeological landscapes. Taking a multi-scalar perspective would also involve adjusting both the basic units of analysis and the physical or temporal scale of those units. However, the benefit would be a broader and richer field for studying the factors that influence variation in the number and distributions of different kinds of thing within and among archaeological sites.

Concepts of α β and γ Diversity

Following pioneering work of R. H. Whittaker (1972) and R. J. Whittaker, Willis, and Field (2001), ecologists and biogeographers often partition taxonomic diversity into alpha, beta, and gamma components. Alpha diversity refers to the number of taxa represented within the minimum spatial component of the system under study. The minimum unit could be a patch, a sampling unit, or other similarly small area. Gamma diversity refers to the number of species represented in the entire system under consideration, such as a community, an ecosystem or a continent. Beta diversity is another sort of phenomenon: it is not about the numbers of taxa or classes, but about the differences *among* minimal sampling units in associations between classes.

Alpha and gamma diversity are typically assessed either by counting the number of different classes present (sample richness), or using measures generically referred to as Hill numbers, such as the Shannon-Wiener index or Simpson's index, which integrate class richness and evenness of representation (Chao, Chiu, and Jost 2014; Colwell and Chao, this volume). Beta diversity requires a very different kind of measurement. Typically, it is assessed in terms of either the number of distinct species assemblages within the ecosystem, or the average degree of overlap/non-overlap in taxonomic representation among various assemblages. More recently, the concept of *zeta diversity* has been proposed, conceived as species overlap among multiple large-scale units (communities, ecosystems, etc.) (Hui and McGeoch 2014). However, this concept is not yet widely used, so I will not discuss it further here.

Measures of diversity at different scales are not independent at either the causal level or at the level of measurement. Most obviously, levels of alpha and gamma diversity constrain beta diversity. If there are only a few species or classes of thing in a study area, there cannot be many different kinds of assemblage. To take the obvious example, imagine a situation in which there are only two kinds of artifact, type A and type B. There can be only three possible types of assemblage: ones that contain only type A, ones that are pure type B, and assemblages that contain both. Although it may seem extreme, this hypothetical example it is not so very different from the situation with Mode 1/Oldowan artifact assemblages from East Africa, as Isaac noted more forty years ago (Isaac 1976: 282). What this means is that, just as one cannot directly compare levels of class richness across assemblages of different size, one should not compare beta diversity across study areas with very different gamma diversity values. The mathematical relationships between α, β, and γ diversity, and the importance and definition of quantitative independence, have been a topic of considerable discussion among quantitative ecologists (e.g., Chao et al. 2012; Jost 2007). However, in the absence of widespread application of multi-scalar approaches to diversity in archaeology, these debates are peripheral to the current discussion.

It is easy to understand how concepts of α, β, and γ diversity could be mapped onto archaeological evidence. Alpha diversity would be measured at the level of individual assemblages. This is the scale of most archaeological analyses of diversity to date. Beta diversity refers to differences among these sample units. We might call it inter-assemblage variation. However, it is conceptualized and measured differently. Archaeologists typically measure variation in assemblage content in terms of proportional representation, using metrics such as the Brainerd-Robinson index of similarity (Brainerd 1951; Robinson 1951). In ecological applications, beta diversity measurement involves distance or similarity metrics based on matching or presence/absence (Anderson, Ellingsen, and McArdle 2006; Koleff, Gaston, and Lennon 2003) that are less widely used in archaeology. Gamma diversity is the total richness of classes within the sample universe. In an archaeological context it might refer to a site, a region, or the entire range of a particular archaeological "culture." Comparison of taxonomic richness across regions or continents may be a less familiar analytical strategy for most of us.

It is important to emphasize that the scales of alpha and gamma diversity used by ecologists vary: the minimal units of observation can be as small as individual patches or sample units, or they can be as large as entire communities; the maximum units can be communities, ecosystems, or continents. In archaeology, we typically begin with alpha diversity at the assemblage level. But there is no reason we could not scale up or down according to the dynamics of interest. For example, alpha diversity could be assessed at the level of entire sites or site clusters. As will be discussed below, flexibly expanding or shrinking spatial scales of observational units presents a potentially powerful analytic strategy.

Of course, the purpose and conceptual justification for a concern with diversity vary across the disciplines. Perhaps most fundamentally, ecologists have long considered diversity at various scales as functionally important and desirable properties of systems, promoting stability and resilience (Goodman 1975; Holling 1973; McCann 2000; Pianka 2011: Ch. 18). By contrast, the long-term viability of the archaeological record does not depend on the number of pottery types or animal species it contains. On the other hand, much like biogeographers, archaeologists are keenly interested in how specific historical, ecological and evolutionary processes produced patterns of standing diversity. Equally fundamentally, plants and animals have very different properties from artifacts: among other things, they move and reproduce all by themselves. Researchers studying community assembly are often concerned with the dispersal potential of different species. This phenomenon has no clear analog among artifacts, although it could be reconceptualized as "content bias" or "direct bias" (Richerson and Boyd 2005), the inherent learnability or attractiveness of an idea or practice. Nonetheless, both fields are concerned with the influence of environmental gradients and barriers on functional and neutral variation.

Studies of diversity have been applied to a very broad range of questions in ecology. The first applications of multi-scalar diversity analysis in ecology focused on functional properties of organisms interacting with environments. In his original paper on the topic, Whittaker (1972) understood species diversity as a consequence of the evolutionary interactions among species across a series of resource gradients defining a niche-space hypervolume. From this functional adaptive perspective, factors such as rainfall and temperature regimes, elevation, and environmental structure are key influences. As in so many other areas of biology, neutral theory came to prominence in ecology around the turn of the millennium. Neutral theories (Hubbell 2001; Rosindell, Hubbell, and Etienne 2011; Rosindell et al. 2012) sought to explain variation in diversity as a consequence of rates of speciation, dispersal and environmental permeability, and "ecological drift." In principle at least, these neutral models provided viable alternative working hypotheses to adaptive or functional models of diversity, enabling more effective testing of the latter. The complementary focus on adaptive and neutral approaches to understanding patterns in class representation have obvious parallels in the study of material culture. Archaeologists' interests in how aggregations of things (sites, assemblages) accumulated are similar in many fundamental ways to interests in the ways assemblages of species came to be. Long-standing questions about functional variation among artifact classes and assemblages are comparable to functional/ adaptive studies of variation in beta diversity of biological taxa. In archaeological applications we must consider both the natural and the social or cultural environments, but the basic causal structures are similar, in that factors external to the artifact or technology in question influence its abundance and geographic distribution. One of the earliest papers on the topic focused specifically on the adaptive origins of cultural diversity (Hardesty 1980). More recent developments in studies of cultural transmission implicate approaches to archaeological diversity more closely to aligned with applications of neutral theory in biogeography (Lyman and O'Brien 2000; Neiman 1995; Premo and Scholnick 2011; Shennan and Wilkinson 2001; Steele 2004). Consideration of how geological forces and other non-anthropogenic processes influenced assemblage formation also present another kind of neutral approach, albeit one based on the dynamics of sediment accumulation and loss rather than random changes in trait frequencies.

α Diversity in Material Culture

Alpha diversity is a good place to begin this discussion because it is relatively familiar. Zooarchaeologists have applied a variety of measures of alpha diversity at the assemblage level for assessing the effects of climate change, environmental gradients, or overharvesting on faunal spectra from archaeological deposits. Faunal assemblage richness and diversity have also been investigated in connection with questions about ecological specialization. A good deal less attention has been paid to alpha diversity in artifact assemblages. In part this may be attributable to the lack of easily transportable theory. There are robust empirical models for how species diversity ought to vary with temperature, moisture levels, elevation, levels of competition and other factors (Ews et al. 2004; Paine 1966; Pianka 1966; Ricklefs and Schluter 1994; Shmida and Wilson 1985). Theoretical diet breadth models provide testable predictions for how resources should be added to the diet as preferred foods become scarce or consumer populations expand (Broughton 1997; Stiner and Munro 2009; Winterhalder and Smith 2000). There are far fewer formal models predicting small-scale variation in simple diversity of artifact forms, as opposed to frequencies of specific functional types. Another obstacle is the lack of a common typological system for assigning things to classes. For better or worse, the Linnean taxonomic system still prevails across biology. Classifications of material culture are much more specific to regions, time periods and even schools of thought. This is an obvious obstacle to large-scale comparisons.

In fact, archaeologists already apply informal models of alpha diversity in artifact classes (though not typically identified as such) when identifying different kinds of sites in hunter-gatherer settlement systems. Mobile people often stage their activities across the landscape. Some places, often called home bases or residential camps, are host to a wide range of activities generating diverse kinds of debris. At other locales, such as hunting stations or stone workshops, the range of activities and the diversity of material left behind is much narrower. Building on this premise, archaeologists often use a number of distinct artifact classes represented in an assemblage to diagnose "site function" (Andrefsky 2005: Ch. 8): sites or assemblages with diverse classes of artifact are thought to represent base camps, whereas sites or assemblages with narrow inventories are called "special activity" or "task specific" locations.

While this is a reasonable starting place, it is not all about human decisions. A number of factors unrelated to strategies of land use may affect diversity in artifact assemblages. Sample size is the most obvious: following basic sampling theory, larger assemblages should contain more classes of artifacts. More interestingly, if people made a range of artifact forms, and if they tended to use and deposit them in different places, then the spatial scale of sampling units ought to be correlated with levels of diversity. If different kinds of artifacts were used in different areas, horizontally extensive excavations are likely to sample more kinds of activities than smaller ones. Based on first principles, we might expect that very small sample units will underestimate alpha diversity, even correcting for numbers of objects counted. The nature of the relationship between sample area and diversity could even provide clues as to underlying spatial structure, even if that structure is not accessible directly. Consider two occupation areas, one partitioned into a series of discrete activity zones and the other covered with a homogeneous carpet of mixed debris. In the first example, the simple spatial extent of a sample unit (an excavation or survey area) should be positively correlated with alpha diversity, independent of the number of finds. Conversely, if material is distributed more or less uniformly across the area sampled, the size of the sample unit will have no influence on alpha diversity, aside from the effect of larger numbers.

The temporal grain or resolution of an assemblage, the amount of time over which it accumulated, also ought to influence artifact diversity, again independent of sample size. Few archaeological assemblages represent single components or single events. Most contain debris from several, perhaps many occupations or visits spread over years, decades or centuries. The larger the number of occupational events sampled by a particular assemblage, the greater the range of processes and activities likely to be represented. An assemblage that accumulated over a few annual cycles in a seasonal environment will sample more kinds of activity than an assemblage created in a single season, even if the numbers of person-hours represented are similar. Assemblages that formed over centuries or millennia may even contain debris from intervals of rapid culture change and innovation, leading to the appearance of even greater alpha diversity. What this means is that the relationship between assemblage diversity and the temporal "grain" of the archaeological record may tell us interesting things about dynamism in technology over long durations. If artifacts were used for a narrow range of purposes, and if these changed slowly over time, then, correcting for total assemblage size, "single-component" assemblages should look very much like ones that accumulated over long periods. If the range of applications and artifact forms was larger, and/or if artifact forms evolved relatively quickly, then temporal grain of the record ought to have a pronounced effect on alpha diversity. Holding other factors constant, variation in α diversity among assemblages could even serve as a rough index of temporal duration.

β Diversity in Material Culture

The notion of beta diversity should be familiar to archaeologists studying material culture—although it is measured differently, it sounds very much like "inter-assemblage" variation. Archaeologists have devoted substantial time and energy to describing and interpreting inter-assemblage variation. One of the best-known discussions of the topic is the famous "Bordes–Binford debate" (Binford 1973; Binford and Binford 1966; Bordes 1961; Bordes and de Sonneville-Bordes 1970). While the debate continues to resonate among some scholars, thinking has moved on considerably.

One widely discussed factor contributing to beta diversity in hunter-gatherer lithic assemblages is the organization of land use systems. In a seminal series of papers, Lewis Binford argued that hunter-gatherer land use systems formed a spectrum in the distribution of activities across the landscape (Binford 1976, 1980). At one extreme were people (termed "foragers") who moved their base camps very frequently from place to place, situating them as close as possible to key subsistence resources. Foragers tended to exploit resources in short day trips out from residential bases, and so created a limited variety of "site types" and assemblages, mainly base camps and specialized resource procurement localities. At the other end of the spectrum were so-called "collectors," who shifted their bases of operation less frequently, choosing instead to exploit diverse resource patches through logistical forays over varying distances. Such a strategy resulted in a greater range of sites and assemblage types, including temporary camps, specialized activity sites, and staging areas for resource transport. This continuum continues to influence thinking about the ways past foragers used landscapes, and the resulting structure of the archaeological record. The important implication for the current discussion is that the ways people organized their activities in time and space ought to have had a significant impact on the beta diversity of the artifact assemblages they left behind. As foraging and land use are closely tied to environmental variables (Binford 2001; Grove 2009; Hamilton et al. 2016; Hamilton et al. 2007; Kelly 1992, 2013), these ideas can even provide a baseline of expectations about levels of beta diversity in assemblages in different times and places.

The geological environment may also have a strong influence on lithic assemblage diversity, through its effects on the temporal resolution of assemblages (Davies, Holdaway, and Fanning 2015; Fanning et al. 2009; Holdaway and Fanning 2008). For a very large part of the prehistoric record, assemblages are defined based on geological criteria: they are sets of material objects contained within an identifiable "package" of sediments. Rhythms of change in sedimentary regimes as well as simple rates of sediment accumulation determine the amount of time each assemblage represents, and the number of events it samples. Consequently, they ought to influence beta diversity. Assemblage "grain" has opposing effects on beta and alpha diversity (see also Premo 2014). Long periods of accumulation increase alpha diversity but reduce beta diversity. For reasons discussed in the previous section, assemblages that sampled relatively brief intervals of time and small numbers of events may differ substantially from one another. By contrast, a group of assemblages that each accumulated over many decades probably contains the detritus from something close to the maximum possible range of activities, which would tend to make them more similar to one another. Another general implication is that geological environments could have a strong influence on general perceptions of both intra- and inter-assemblage variability. Holding other variables constant, a region or period represented mainly by single-component, open-air occurrences ought to manifest more beta diversity than a region or period where the record consists mainly of deep cave sequences with comparatively poor temporal resolution.

A more exciting potential application of beta diversity concerns the effects of population structure on beta diversity. Recent findings from archaeology, genetics, and skeletal biology have pushed researchers to consider the effects of population structure on behavioral and biological evolution among late Pleistocene hominins in Africa (Scerri et al. 2014; Scerri et al. 2018). The implication is that interactions among semi-independent populations may have shaped or directed the evolution of "modern" behavior and anatomy. While the initial focus was on Africa, similar processes may have characterized late Pleistocene Eurasia, particularly in areas with multiple hominin populations (Greenbaum et al. 2018). To date, discussions of archaeological evidence of population structure in Pleistocene humans have relied on narrative rather than formal models. However, the potential exists for more rigorous approaches to testing for population structure. One of the central challenges is distinguishing the effects of simple isolation by distance from the effects of more abrupt barriers to cultural exchange. Statistics such as Fst and the Mantel test for autocorrelation provide one set of tools for investigating these questions (Guillot and Rousset 2013; Legendre, Borcard, and Peres-Neto 2005; Premo and Scholnick 2011; Shennan, Crema, and Kerig 2015).

In theory, population structure ought to leave very clear effects on beta diversity at a large scale. In unstructured populations, high levels of interconnection and information exchange between local groups should lead to homogenization of material culture, lowering beta diversity (see Lycett, this volume). In more structured populations, mutual isolation will lead to divergence, raising levels of beta diversity. However, population structure could affect strongly adaptive traits and neutral traits differently. Neutral traits, here defined as features of material culture that do not interact strongly with the natural environment, should diverge more in highly structured contexts, and could tend to homogenize when boundaries between populations are more open. Beta diversity in traits with high adaptive value, features of material culture that provide clear advantages in particular environmental circumstances, should reflect environmental structure as much as population structure. However, to the extent that barriers between populations prevent the spread of innovations with high adaptive value, they could inhibit homogenization of material culture. At least one study of variation in ethnographic material culture is consistent with this proposition. Jordan and Shennan (2009) find that patterns of geographic variation in traits such as basketry and cradles closely parallel other evidence for phylogeny, whereas construction of dwellings carries a stronger environmental signal. In order to investigate population structure through analyses of diversity it would probably be necessary to adjust the sizes of basic units of analysis, scaling up from single sites/assemblages to site clusters or regional groupings. However, the potential benefits of being able to address an important evolutionary hypothesis using archaeological evidence would certainly make the effort worthwhile.

γ Diversity in Material Culture

Archaeologists have focused on gamma diversity less than diversity at smaller scales, although the idea was incorporated into Kintigh's highly influential 1984 paper, using simulation to assess assemblage diversity (Kintigh 1984). Although we may recognize that some regions have much broader ranges of material culture than others, there are few ready-made models to help us understand this. This is in part because the scale of analysis exceeds that of the traditional "anthropological gaze," which focuses on individuals and communities. The kinds of dynamics that underly regional or macro-regional patterning are less familiar to many of us. On the other hand, it may well be an appropriate scale from which to approach the study of macro-evolutionary patterning in human cultures (Perreault 2019).

One predictive model that we do have about γ diversity concerns environmental differences in material culture complexity and diversity among hunter-gatherers. It has been well established that the complexity and number of distinct artifacts used for procuring food increase with latitude (Collard et al. 2011; Collard, Kemery, and Banks 2005; Oswalt 1976; Torrence 2001). The general explanation is that foragers in high latitudes must focus on resources (medium and large game animals in particular) that are both elusive and highly seasonal. Both factors increase the value of highly specialized, and presumably more effective, foraging tools. Hunter-gatherers living at lower latitudes are typically less dependent on large animals, and have a wider array of foraging options, reducing the advantages of investing in costly material aids. Diet breadth, especially the incorporation of avian and aquatic prey, further amplifies technological diversity: the challenge of extracting food from environments that humans cannot easily navigate increases the value of efficient technological assistance. There are obstacles to applying such models to archaeological evidence, the most salient one being the fact that archaeological sites very seldom yield up entire artifacts; usually, all we have to work with are the most durable stone and sometimes osseous elements of composite artifacts. Consequently, material archaeological remains probably underestimate both the complexity and diversity of implements. Nonetheless the models provide a useful baseline for evaluating how foraging groups in different times and places responded technologically to environmental variation. Departures from the expectations generated by the empirical model should provide valuable clues about the effects of other factors, such as demography and even hominin cognition, on diversity of material culture at large scales (Kuhn 2009; Kuhn and Stiner 2001).

In neutral biogeography, one of the important influences on gamma diversity is *permeability* (Boucher et al. 2014; Hubbell 2001). Two of the main sources of novelty in biology, especially over relatively short intervals, are migration and gene flow. All other things being equal, presence of permanent or periodic barriers can limit overall diversity in a system. Large areas that are isolated from neighboring regions by geographic barriers are deprived of one of the main sources of new species or genes. Partial isolation is one of the main pillars of the theory of island biogeography (MacArthur and Wilson 1967). The same ought to be true of systems of cultural evolution. Regions with permeable boundaries—conditions that encourage cultural exchange—ought to have greater diversity in both neutral and adaptive traits. Places that are very much isolated from neighboring areas ought to have lower cultural diversity, holding other important variables constant. Interestingly, there may be evidence of such effects in island populations of another "cultural" organism, namely birds, which acquire songs through learning (Aplin 2019; Lachlan et al. 2013). Archaeologists are well aware of inter-regional differences in diversity in material culture: the comparative simplicity and lack of variety in East Asian Paleolithic material cultures (Bar-Yosef and Wang 2012; Dennell 2016; Lycett and Norton 2010) is an obvious example. It would be worth approaching this question in terms of how permanent or periodic barriers to movement from neighboring areas may have constrained the accumulation of diversity.

Population structure, and more generally the flow of information among sub-populations, could also affect gamma diversity within a region. The effects of structure on gamma diversity are partially opposite to its effects on beta diversity, at least for neutral traits. The sheer number of neutral traits in existence ought to scale with effective population size, which is strongly influenced by levels of between and within group integration (Premo and Hublin 2009). Thus, regions with little internal structure could develop higher levels of gamma diversity in environmentally insensitive traits. On the other hand, we might expect diversity in more adaptively linked dimensions of material culture to behave differently. In part, levels of gamma diversity will depend on the structure of habitats within the area studied. If habitats are comparatively homogeneous throughout the study area, we should not expect as much diversity in material culture to evolve. If the area contains many different kinds of resources and environmental affordances, patchily distributed, it is reasonable to predict a similarly varied set of technological responses, resulting in relatively high gamma diversity. Environmental structure aside, the connectedness or isolation of human populations should also affect gamma diversity in features of material culture with high adaptive value. Where populations are well connected, and where information flows freely among them, it would be reasonable to expect particularly advantageous technological solutions to spread very quickly. If these innovations were added to existing material culture inventories, they would increase gamma diversity overall. On the other hand, "selective sweeps," where novel forms replace older ones, would restrict gamma diversity.

Conclusion

Archaeologists first "borrowed" diversity analysis from biogeography and community ecology some sixty years ago (O'Brien and Thomas, this volume). At this point, analyses of assemblage richness and diversity have become standard procedure in some areas of archaeological research, and in zooarchaeology in particular. Systematic analyses of taxonomic diversity in archaeofaunas have provided key insights into phenomena such as evolving foraging strategies and human impacts on prey populations. However, to date, formal studies of diversity in archaeology have focused mostly on diversity at the smallest (α) scale: the number and representation of classes contained within individual assemblages. Much less attention has been focused explicitly on diversity at larger (β and γ) scales. The field would benefit from expanding our approaches, thereby exploiting previous lessons from biogeography and genetics about the expression and study of diversity at larger spatial.

Of course this will not be easy, which probably explains why it has not been done already. Well-developed theory from ecology and biogeography explaining species diversity is a helpful place to start, but obviously the dynamics of cultural evolution and biological evolution are not identical. A second challenge stems from the fact that, as archaeologists, we often have limited control over the ways we sample the world: our basic units of analysis are often dictated by factors beyond our control. Archaeologists have to cope with the spatial and temporal structure imposed by geological factors, as well as by the history of research in a particular area. Fortunately, the temporal and spatial structure imposed by geology can be conceived and modeled as another sort of independent, non-behavioral influence of the partitioning of diversity. On the positive side of the equation, a number of widely used informal models of behavioral variation in time and space already implicate diversity at inter-assemblage and regional scales, even if these are not currently formalized as questions about diversity. Incorporating formal and explicit consideration of diversity at multiple scales would expand the range of questions we can address, and the kinds of answers we can obtain, through studies of material culture and other sorts of archaeological material.

Acknowledgments

My thanks to Briggs Buchanan and Metin I. Eren for inviting me to contribute to the volume. Comments from Lee Lyman and two anonymous reviewers were very helpful in clarifying this chapter.

Steven L. Kuhn is the Riecker Distinguished Professor at the University of Arizona, Tucson, Arizona, USA.

References

Anderson, M. J., K. E. Ellingsen, and B. H. McArdle. 2006. "Multivariate Dispersion as a Measure of Beta Diversity." *Ecology Letters* 9(6): 683–93.

Andrefsky, W. J. 2005. *Lithics: Macroscopic Approaches to Analysis*. 2nd edn. Cambridge: Cambridge University Press.

Aplin, L. M. 2019. "Culture and Cultural Evolution in Birds: A Review of the Evidence." *Animal Behaviour* 147: 179–87.

Bar-Yosef, O., and Y. Wang. 2012. "Paleolithic Archaeology in China." *Annual Review of Anthropology* 41(June): 319–35.

Binford, L. R. 1973. "The Mousterian and the 'Functional' Argument." In *The Explanation of Culture Change: Models in Prehistory*, ed. C. Renfrew, 227–54. London: Duckworth.

———. 1976. "Forty-Seven Trips: A Case Study of the Character of Some Formation Processes of the Archaeological Record." In *Contributions to Anthropology: Interior Peoples of Northern Alaska*, ed. E. S. Hall, 299–350. Ottawa: Archaeological Survey of Canada.

———. 1980. "Willow Smoke and Dogs' Tails: Hunter-Gatherer Settlement Systems and Archaeological Site Formation." *American Antiquity* 45(1): 4–20.

———. 2001. *Constructing Frames of Reference: An Analytical Method for Archaeological Theory Building Using Ethnographic and Environmental Data Sets*. Berkeley: University of California Press.

Binford, L. R., and S. R. Binford. 1966. "A Preliminary Analysis of Functional Variability in the Mousterian of Levallois Facies." *American Anthropologist* 68(2): 238–95.

Bordes, F. 1961. "Mousterian Cultures in France." *Science* 134(3482): 803–10.

Bordes, F., and D. de Sonneville-Bordes. 1970. "The Significance of Variability in Palaeolithic Assemblages." *World Archaeology* 2(1): 61–73.

Boucher, F. C., W. Thuiller, T. J. Davies, and S. Lavergne. 2014. "Neutral Biogeography and the Evolution of Climatic Niches." *American Naturalist* 183(5): 573–84.

Brainerd, G. W. 1951. "The Place of Chronological Ordering in Archaeological Analysis." *American Antiquity* 16(4): 301–13.

Broughton, J. M. 1997. "Widening Diet Breadth, Declining Foraging Efficiency, and Prehistoric Harvesting Pressure: Ichthyofaunal Evidence form the Emeryville Shellmound, California." *Antiquity* 71: 845–62.

Chao, A., C.-H. Chiu, T. C. Hsieh, and B. D. Inouye. 2012. "Proposing a Resolution to Debates on Diversity Partitioning." *Ecology* 93(9): 2037–51.

Chao, A., C.-H. Chiu, and L. Jost. 2014. "Unifying Species Diversity, Phylogenetic Diversity, Functional Diversity, and Related Similarity and Differentiation Measures Through Hill Numbers." *Annual Review of Ecology, Evolution, and Systematics* 45(1): 297–324.

Collard, M., B. Buchanan, J. Morin, and A. Costopoulos. 2011. "What Drives the Evolution of Hunter-Gatherer Subsistence Technology? A Reanalysis of the Risk Hypothesis with Data from the Pacific Northwest." *Philosophical Transactions of the Royal Society B* 366(1567): 1129–38.

Collard, M., M. Kemery, and S. Banks. 2005. "Causes of Toolkit Variation among Hunter-Gatherers: A Test of Four Competing Hypotheses." *Canadian Journal of Archaeology* 29: 1–19.

Davies, B., S. J. Holdaway, and P. C. Fanning. 2015. "Modelling the Palimpsest: An Exploratory Agent-Based Model of Surface Archaeological Deposit Formation in a Fluvial Arid Australian Landscape." *The Holocene* 26(3): 450–63.

Dennell, R. W. 2016. "Life Without the Movius Line: The Structure of the East and Southeast Asian Early Palaeolithic." *Quaternary International* 400: 14–22.

Ews, J., U. Brose, V. Grimm, K. Tielborger, M. C. Wichmann, M. Schwager, and F. Jeltsch. 2004. "Animal Species Diversity Driven by Habitat Heterogeneity/Diversity: The Importance of Keystone Structures." *Journal of Biogeography* 30: 79–92.

Fanning, P. C., S. J. Holdaway, E. J. Rhodes, and T. G. Bryant. 2009. "The Surface Archaeological Record in Arid Australia: Geomorphic Controls on Preservation, Exposure, and Visibility." *Geoarchaeology* 24(2): 121–46.

Goodman, D. 1975. "The Theory of Diversity–Stability Relationships in Ecology." *The Quarterly Review of Biology* 50(3): 237–66.

Grayson, D. K. 1981. "The Effects of Sample Size on Some Derived Measures in Vertebrate Faunal Analysis." *Journal of Archaeological Science* 8(1): 77–88.

Greenbaum, G., D. E. Friesem, E. Hovers, M. W. Feldman, and O. Kolodny. 2018. "Was Inter-Population Connectivity of Neanderthals and Modern Humans the Driver of the Upper Paleolithic Transition Rather than its Product?" *Quaternary Science Reviews* 216: 316–29.

Grove, M. 2009. "Hunter-Gatherer Movement Patterns: Causes and Constraints." *Journal of Anthropological Archaeology* 28(2): 222–33.

Guillot, G., and F. Rousset. 2013. "Dismantling the Mantel Tests." *Methods in Ecology and Evolution* 4(4): 336–44.

Hamilton, M. J., J. Lobo, E. Rupley, H. Youn, and G. B. West. 2016. "The Ecological and Evolutionary Energetics of Hunter-Gatherer Residential Mobility." *Evolutionary Anthropology* 25(3): 124–32.

Hamilton, M. J., B. T. Milne, R. S. Walker, and J. H. Brown. 2007. "Nonlinear Scaling of Space Use in Human Hunter-Gatherers." *Proceedings of the National Academy of Sciences USA* 104(11): 4765–769.

Hardesty, D. L. 1980. "The Use of General Ecological Principles in Archaeology." *Advances in Archaeological Method and Theory* 3: 157–87.

Holdaway, S. J., and P. C. Fanning. 2008. "Developing a Landscape History as Part of a Survey Strategy: A Critique of Current Settlement System Approaches Based on Case Studies from Western New South Wales." *Journal of Archaeological Method and Theory* 15(2): 167–89.

Holling, C. S. 1973. "Resilience and Stability of Ecological Systems." *Annual Review of Ecology and Systematics* 4(1): 1–23.

Hubbell, S. P. 2001. *The Unified Neutral Theory of Biodiversity and Biogeography*. Princeton, NJ: Princeton University Press.

Hui, C., and M. A. McGeoch. 2014. "Zeta Diversity as a Concept and Metric That Unifies Incidence-Based Biodiversity Patterns." *The American Naturalist* 184(5): 684–94.

Isaac, G. L. 1976. "Stages of Cultural Elaboration in the Pleistocene: Possible Archaeological Indicators of the Development of Language Capabilities." *Annals of the New York Academy of Sciences* 280(1): 275–88.

Jordan, P., and S. J. Shennan. 2009. "Diversity in Hunter-Gatherer Technological Traditions: Mapping Trajectories of Cultural 'Descent with Modification' in Northeast California." *Journal of Anthropological Archaeology* 28(3): 342–65.

Jost, L. 2007. "Partitioning Diversity into Independent Alpha and Beta Components." *Ecology* 88(10): 2427–39.

Kelly, R. L. 1992. "Mobility/Sedentism: Concepts, Archaeological Measures, and Effects." *Annual Review of Anthropology* 21: 43–66.

———. 2013. *Lifeways of Hunter-Gatherers: The Foraging Spectrum.* Cambridge: Cambridge University Press.

Kintigh, K. 1984. "Measuring Archaeological Diversity by Comparison with Simulated Assemblages." *American Antiquity* 49(1): 44–54. doi:10.2307/280511.

Koleff, P., K. J. Gaston, and J. J. Lennon. 2003. "Measuring Beta Diversity for Presence–Absence Data. *Journal of Animal Ecology* 72(3): 367–82.

Kuhn, S. L. 2009. "The Paradox of Diet and Technology in the Middle Paleolithic." In *Transitions in Prehistory: Essays in Honor of Ofer Bar-Yosef,* ed. J. J. Shea and D. Lieberman, 55–74. Oxford: Oxbow Books.

Kuhn, S. L., and M. C. Stiner. 2001. "The Antiquity of Hunter-Gatherers." In *Hunter-Gatherers: Interdisciplinary Perspectives,* ed. C. Panter-Brick, R. H. Layton, and P. A. Rowley-Conwy, 99–142. Cambridge: Cambridge University Press.

Lachlan, R. F., M. N. Verzijden, C. S. Bernard, P. P. Jonker, B. Koese, S. Jaarsma, W. Spoor, P. Spate, and C. Ten Cate. 2013. "The Progressive Loss of Syntactical Structure in Bird Song along an Island Colonization Chain." *Current Biology* 23(19): 1896–901.

Legendre, P., D. Borcard, and P. R. Peres-Neto. 2005. "Analyzing Beta Diversity: Partitioning the Spatial Variation of Community Compositional Data." *Ecological Monographs* 75(4): 435–50.

Lycett, S. J., and C. J. Norton. 2010. "A Demographic Model for Palaeolithic Technological Evolution: The Case of East Asia and the Movius Line." *Quaternary International* 211(1): 55–65.

Lyman, R. L., and M. J. O'Brien. 2000. "Measuring and Explaining Change in Artifact Variation with Clade-Diversity Diagrams." *Journal of Anthropological Archaeology* 19: 39–74.

MacArthur, R. H., and E. O. Wilson. 1967. *The Theory of Island Biogeography.* Princeton, NJ: Princeton University Press.

McCann, K. S. 2000. "The Diversity–Stability Debate." *Nature* 405(6783): 228–33.

Neiman, F. D. 1995. "Stylistic Variation in Evolutionary Perspective: Inferences from Decorative Diversity and Interassemblage Distance in Illinois Woodland Ceramic Assemblages." *American Antiquity* 60(1): 7–36.

Oswalt, W. 1976. *An Anthropological Analysis of Food-Getting Technology.* New York: Wiley.

Paine, R. T. 1966. "Food Web Complexity and Species Diversity." *The American Naturalist* 100(910): 65–75.

Perreault, C. 2019. *The Quality of the Archaeological Record.* Chicago: University of Chicago Press.

Pianka, E. R. 1966. "Latitudinal Gradients in Species Diversity: A Review of Concepts." *The American Naturalist* 100(910): 33–46.

———. 2011. *Evolutionary Ecology*. eBook. http://www.zo.utexas.edu/courses/bio373/ERP-EvolEcol.html.

Premo, L. S. 2014. "Cultural Transmission and Diversity in Time-Averaged Assemblages." *Current Anthropology* 55(1): 105–14.

Premo, L. S., and J.-J. Hublin. 2009. "Culture, Population Structure, and Low Genetic Diversity in Pleistocene Hominins." *Proceedings of the National Academy of Sciences* 106(1): 33–37.

Premo, L. S., and J. B. Scholnick. 2011. "The Spatial Scale of Social Learning Affects Cultural Diversity." *American Antiquity* 76(1): 163–76.

Richerson, P. J., and R. Boyd. 2005. *Not by Genes Alone*. Chicago: University of Chicago Press.

Ricklefs, R. E., and D. Schluter, eds. 1994. *Species Diversity in Ecological Communities*. Chicago: University of Chicago Press.

Robinson, W. S. 1951. "A Method for Chronologically Ordering Archaeological Deposits." *American Antiquity* 16(4): 293–301.

Rosindell, J., S. P. Hubbell, and R. S. Etienne. 2011. "The Unified Neutral Theory of Biodiversity and Biogeography at Age Ten." *Trends in Ecology and Evolution* 26(7): 340–48.

Rosindell, J., S. P. Hubbell, F. He, L. J. Harmon, and R. S. Etienne. 2012. "The Case for Ecological Neutral Theory." *Trends in Ecology and Evolution* 27(4): 203–8.

Scerri, E. M. L., N. A. Drake, R. Jennings, and H. S. Groucutt. 2014. "Earliest Evidence for the Structure of Homo Sapiens Populations in Africa." *Quaternary Science Reviews* 101: 207–16.

Scerri, E. M. L., M. G. Thomas, A. Manica, P. Gunz, J. T. Stock, C. Stringer, M. Grove, H. Groucutt, A. Timmermann, G. Rightmire, F. d'Errico, C. Tryon, N. Drake, A. Brooks, R. Dennell, R. Durbin, B. Henn, L. J. Lee-Thorp, P. deMenocal, M. Petraglia, J. Thompson, A. Scally, and L. Chikhi. 2018. "Did Our Species Evolve in Subdivided Populations across Africa, and Why Does It Matter?" *Trends in Ecology and Evolution* 33(8): 582–94.

Shennan, S. J., E. R. Crema, and T. Kerig. 2015. "Isolation-By-Distance, Homophily, and 'Core' vs. 'Package' Cultural Evolution Models in Neolithic Europe." *Evolution and Human Behavior* 36(2): 103–9.

Shennan, S. J., and J. R. Wilkinson. 2001. "Ceramic Style Change and Neutral Evolution: A Case Study from Neolithic Europe." *American Antiquity* 66(4): 577–93.

Shmida, A., and M. W. Wilson. 1985. "Biological Determinants of Species Diversity." *Journal of Biogeography* 12(1): 1–20.

Steele, J. 2004. "Population Structure and Diversity Indices." In *Simulations, Genetics and Human Prehistory*, eds. S. Matsumura, P. Forste, and C. Renfrew, 187–91. Cambridge: MacDonald Institute of Archaeology.

Stiner, M. C., and N. D. Munro. 2009. "Approaches to Prehistoric Diet Breadth, Demography, and Prey Ranking Systems in Time and Space." *Journal of Archaeological Method and Theory* 9(2): 181–214.

Torrence, R. 2001. "Hunter-Gatherer Technology: Macro- and Microscale Approaches." In *Hunter-Gatherers: An Interdisciplinary Perspective*, ed. C. Panter-Brick, R. Layton, and P. Rowley-Conwy, 13–73. Cambridge: Cambridge University Press.

Whittaker, R. H. 1972. "Evolution and Measurement of Species Diversity." *Taxon* 21(2/3): 213–51.

Whittaker, R. J., K. J. Willis, and R. Field. 2001. "Scale and Species Richness: Towards a General, Hierarchical Theory of Species Diversity." *Journal of Biogeography* 28(4): 453–70.

Winterhalder, B., and E. A. Smith. 2000. "Analyzing Adaptive Strategies: Human Behavioral Ecology at Twenty-Five." *Evolutionary Anthropology* 9(2): 51–72.

Chapter 10

Measuring and Comparing Class Diversity in Archaeological Assemblages

A Brief Guide to the History and State-of-the-Art in Diversity Statistics

Robert K. Colwell and Anne Chao

⬥

Thirty years ago, Leonard and Jones (1989) published an edited volume focused on applications of the concept of diversity in archaeology. The fifteen original papers in the volume explored the challenges posed in quantifying, comparing, and interpreting the diversity of archaeological materials in space and time. Most of the methods and concepts discussed had been adapted from those prominently applied in ecology at the time, or were developed *de novo* in parallel with contemporaneous approaches in ecology.

In the intervening years, technological advances unimaginable in 1989 have opened new doors to diversity-relevant data for archaeology and related fields—high-resolution GPS, accessible GIS tools, LIDAR, stable isotope methods, micro-CT scanning, high-performance computational clusters, and others. The ongoing effects of climate change have confronted ecologists and conservation biologists with the need to quantify, analyze, and model temporal changes in diversity and spatial distributions, converging on the temporal interests of the historical sciences, including archaeology.

Meanwhile, diversity statistics—our own expertise—has become a discipline in its own right, with both incremental and ground-breaking advances on several fronts. In this contribution, we outline the current state-of-the-art of class diversity quantification and estimation, and indicate best practices—as we see them—while attempting to relate these advances to the particular characteristics of archaeological data—as we understand them—and to the studies collected in this symposium volume.

The Common Currency of Diversity

The notion that diversity comprises two components, richness and even-ness—thought by many to be separable, but in fact inseparably intertwined—dominated ecology for decades (Magurran 1988; Peet 1974; Pielou 1969, 1975). By the time archaeology inherited the richness/evenness rubric from ecology, with all of its practical, terminological, and conceptual issues, a mul-titude of indices had been proposed, most aimed at quantifying diversity by somehow taking both components into account (Bobrowsky and Ball 1989). Debates over the virtues and drawbacks of each of these indices added to the sense, in some quarters (famously, Hurlbert 1971), that all were arbi-trary, and thus that the diversity concept itself lacked any rigorous meaning. The issue remained contentious for decades (Magurran and McGill 2011).

The discovery that we now recognize as having cut through this Gord-ian knot had already been introduced to ecology from physics in 1965 by MacArthur (1965), extended by Hill (1973), applauded in a major review by Peet (1974), but then subsequently ignored for decades by most ecol-ogists (Hill 1973 was cited twice, in passing, in the Leonard and Jones volume [Conkey 1989; Rothschild 1989]). Thirty years later, Jost (2006) took up the sword again, and showed rigorously—and explained compel-lingly—that the natural and universal currency of the diversity of classes (species, artifacts) in an assemblage is the simplest and most intuitive of all. That currency is just the "equivalent number" of classes that would yield the observed value of a diversity measure in a hypothetical assemblage in which all classes occurred with equal frequency. Following a multi-author *Ecology* forum (Ellison 2010), a clear consensus has now emerged, among ecologists, that Hill numbers should be the species diversity measure of choice (Bebber and Chao, this volume; Farahani and Sinensky, this vol-ume; Kuhn, this volume).

Hill Numbers, Diversity Profiles, and Evenness

With measures of diversity properly transformed to units of class equiv-alents, the three most commonly used measures—richness (class count), Shannon diversity (exponential of Shannon entropy), and Simpson diver-sity (inverse of Simpson concentration index) emerge as waypoints along a mathematically unified continuum of increasing orders of Hill numbers, as indexed by q,

$$^qD = \left(\sum_{i=1}^{S} p_i^q \right)^{\frac{1}{(1-q)}}, q \geq 0, q \neq 1,$$

where S is the number of classes and p_i denotes the relative abundance of class i, $i = 1, 2, ..., S$. For $q = 1$, we must take a limit to get Shannon diversity:

$$^1D = \lim_{q \to 1} {}^qD = exp\left(-\sum_{i=1}^{S} p_i \ln p_i\right).$$

The index q can best be viewed as a weighting factor for the influence of common classes on measures on diversity. For richness ($q = 0$), each *class* counts equally, regardless of rarity or commonness. For Shannon diversity ($q = 1$), each *individual* (each item or each incidence) counts equally, so that common classes count more than rare ones. For Simpson diversity ($q = 2$), the *commonest classes count disproportionately* (Table 10.1).

Because diversity ^qD is a continuous function of q, we can construct a diversity profile for any assemblage, with ^qD as a function of q (Figure 1 of Hill 1973; Chao and Jost 2015). When class frequencies are completely even, the profile is a horizontal line at the level of class richness. Otherwise, the profile is a decreasing function of order q. The steepness of its slope reflects the unevenness (variation) among class abundances. If class richness is fixed, the more uneven the distribution of class frequencies, the more steeply the profile declines. This property of the diversity profile turns out to offer a path towards constructing and understanding a corresponding evenness profile, as detailed below.

Evenness is a measure of the closeness of an observed vector of relative abundances p_i to a vector with the same number of classes in which all p_is are equal (Chao and Ricotta 2019), or "parity in the frequencies of classes" (Boulanger, Breslawski, and Jorgeson, this volume). The concept of evenness has a long history of application in archaeology, sometimes quantified by Simpson diversity (^2D) or related measures (e.g., Otárola-Castillo, Torquato, and Hill, this volume; Stemp and Macdonald, this volume), but this approach confounds richness and evenness (Jost 2010). Hill (1973,

Table 10.1. Terminology for diversity statistics, with archaeological examples.

Assemblage	A set of related artifacts, defined in space or in time, united by some common feature of material, use, or provenience
Class	A predefined category within a classification system for artifacts (e.g., ceramic types, stone tool types, knapping styles, taxa of plant or animal remains)
Sampling unit	An excavation site, a quadrant within a site, a temporal stratum within a site, or any other predefined unit that (at least in principle) could be replicated, even if not exactly, within a study

(continued)

Table 10.1. *Continued.*

Data types	Abundance data	Counts of "individuals" (e.g., individual projectile points, pottery sherds, MNI, NISP), in each of several classes in one or more sampling units
	Incidence data	Counts of the number of sampling units in which each of several classes has been detected ("presence" frequencies)
Reference sample	Abundance data	A list of the number of individuals for each of several classes from a single sampling unit
	Incidence data	A matrix of *1*s (detected) and *0*s (not detected) for several classes in several sampling units (by convention, classes are rows and sampling units are columns)
Rare class frequencies	Abundance data	*Singleton*: a class represented by only one individual in an abundance-based reference sample *Doubleton*: a class represented by exactly two individuals in an abundance-based reference sample
	Incidence data	*Unique*: a class represented in only one sampling unit in an incidence-based reference sample *Duplicate*: a class represented in exactly two sampling units in an incidence-based reference sample
Hill numbers S = number of classes p_i = proportional abundance or incidence of class i	$q = 0$	Richness (class count) $^0D = S$
	$q = 1$	Shannon diversity $^1D = exp(-\sum_{i=1}^{S} p_i \ln p_i)$
	$q = 2$	Simpson diversity $^2D = 1/\sum_{i=1}^{S} p_i^2$
Completeness	$q = 0$	*Class list completeness*: The proportion of the total number of *classes* in an assemblage (observed and unobserved) that belong to the observed *classes* in a reference sample
	$q = 1$	*Class inventory completeness*: Turing-Good *sample coverage*: the proportion of the total number of *individuals* (for abundance data) or *incidences* (for incidence data) in an assemblage (observed and unobserved) that belong to the observed *classes* in a reference sample
	$q = 2$	*Common class inventory completeness*: The proportion of the total number of *individuals* for abundance date) or incidences (for incidence data), *weighted by class abundance* or *incidence frequency* (observed and unobserved) in an assemblage that belong to the observed *classes* in a reference sample
Rarefaction/ extrapolation (R/E)	Individual-based	R/E of classes as a function of the number of accumulated individuals
	Sample-based	R/E of classes as a function of the number of accumulated sampling units
	Completeness-based	R/E of classes as a function of sample completeness

1997) proposed a definition of evenness as the ratio of diversity to class richness: i.e., $^qE^* = {}^qD/S$, for $q > 0$. Because ^qD takes values between 1 and S, the evenness index $^qE^*$ ranges from $1/S$ to 1. Thus, as the minimum $1/S$ depends upon S, the index $^qE^*$ is not independent of class richness. As shown by Chao and Ricotta (2019), a consequence of this dependence on class richness is that samples with different levels of variation among class abundances may yield the same value of $^qE^*$, leading to ambiguity in comparing evenness among assemblages. To remove the dependence of $^qE^*$ on richness, Jost (2010) transformed $^qE^*$ to a class of evenness measures in the range of [0, 1]. The resulting evenness measure of order q is expressed as

$$^qE = ({}^qD-1)/(S-1), q > 0.$$

(For $q = 0$, abundances are disregarded, so it is not meaningful to evaluate evenness.)

By constructing an evenness profile, with ^qE plotted as a function of q, this set of measures can be applied to meaningfully compare evenness, even if class richness varies among assemblages. Linking the evenness profile to the diversity profile, Chao and Ricotta (2019) showed that the corresponding "unevenness" measure $(1-E)$ is equal to the normalized slope of a line plotted in the corresponding Hill-number diversity profile, connecting the points on the profile with diversity orders 0 (richness) and any $q > 0$. Compared to diversity, quantifying evenness or unevenness among class abundances is even more complicated and extensively discussed (reviewed by Chao and Ricotta 2019). Underlying any measure of diversity or evenness is the vector of relative abundances, p_i, which is subject to sources of error that have themselves become the subject of methods of estimation (Chao et al. 2015; Boulanger, Breslawski, and Jorgeson, this volume).

Samples and Assemblages

Many of the authors in the Leonard and Jones volume (1989) struggled with the conceptual issues that bedeviled the idea of "diversity" (richness vs. evenness vs. "composite" measures), with discordant conclusions and terminology, now a bit dated, that we need not explore here. But the most prominent practical issue that emerged, in nearly every chapter in the 1989 volume (and earlier—e.g., Jones, Grayson, and Beck 1983) is the inevitable dependence of all measures of diversity, but especially richness, on sample size or sampling effort in archaeology, making diversity comparisons perilous, at best. As in ecology, the objective of diversity measurement in archaeology is not simply to put a number on the diversity of objects in a *sample* from an assemblage, but rather, to make inferences about the diversity of the *assemblage* itself, or the statistical universe of similar assemblages (Dunnell 1989).

Hill numbers and the diversity and evenness profiles make no assumptions about the statistical distribution of rarity or commonness of classes. In this sense, they are nonparametric measures of diversity. The diversity profile, itself, responds sensitively to the frequency distribution of classes in an empirical sample (Gotelli and Chao 2013). But how can we make statistically valid comparisons among samples or assemblages that differ in sample size or sampling effort—a difference not reflected in the diversity profile? This crucial objective is now being met by integrating several fundamental advances in biodiversity statistics, detailed in the sections below.

Statistical Sampling Models

Early applications of statistical sampling models to diversity data, beginning with the pioneering work by Fisher, Corbet, and Williams (1943), opened new avenues to estimation and analysis. These models are not to be confused with specific, parametric models fitted to observed data (e.g., Preston 1948), or with regression models that assume a particular, parametric relation between variables—for example, a linear relation between richness (or log richness) and log sample size (Thomas 1989). A formal, statistical sampling model links data—according to the way it is collected and organized—to a wealth of mathematical and statistical tools.

The idea of rarefying (subsampling) datasets to produce comparable sample sizes was initially attempted by a brute force approach in ecology (Sanders 1968), but the idea quickly inspired the use of sampling models and analytical, combinatorial formulations (Hurlbert 1971; Simberloff 1972), for both expected richness of subsamples and conditional variance of richness (Heck, van Belle, and Simberloff 1975). (More on conditional vs. unconditional variances and confidence intervals later.)

Rarefaction by these methods was soon applied not only in ecology but also in paleontology (Raup 1975), which of course shares many of the challenges faced by archaeology and other historical sciences. In archaeology, however, rarefaction was reinvented by Kintigh (1989), using repeated random draws from a frequency distribution based on pooled data, rather than applying the analytical formula of Hurlbert and Simberloff (which would give, precisely, the expectation of the Kintigh curve). By examining variation among randomizations, Kintigh estimated a conditional confidence interval, allowing the identification of unusually rich or poor individual samples, given the dataset. Kintigh's ingenious approach was used, rather effectively, in a qualitative way, by several contributors to the Leonard and Jones volume.

Meanwhile, the further development and exploitation of formal statistical sampling models for diversity data opened several distinct paths. But before we follow them, we take a detour to introduce a second kind of diversity data.

The Surprising Power and Realism of Replicated Incidence Data

Suppose an archaeologist wants to characterize the diversity of ceramic production (e.g., Rice 1989) at a study site. Separate collections are made from a variety of excavated plots within a site. In each collection (which we call a *sampling unit*), each pottery fragment is identified by class, using some recognized system. Suppose (as we suspect) it is often not possible to determine whether a group of sherds of the same class from the same sampling unit represent one or several pots, but that what we really want to know is the diversity of pots, not the diversity of fragments—the same issue arises with paleoethnobotanical sampling (Farahani and Sinensky, this volume). Instead of counting up the number of sherds of each class in each sampling unit, we simply record the detection (presence) or non-detection (presumed absence) of each ceramic class in each sampling unit. (We assume, based on spacing of the sampling scheme, that sherds from any individual pot are unlikely to appear in more than one sample.) When all the sampling units have been scored, we have what has come to be called *replicated incidence data* (Gotelli and Colwell 2001)—a matrix of classes x sampling units, filled with 0s and 1s. What have we lost by not counting (if we could) the number of pots of each class in each sampling unit, then pooling the data to get a single, *abundance*-based dataset for the site?

The answer, surprising to many people, is that we have lost virtually nothing (Chao et al. 2014; Chao and Colwell 2017; Colwell et al. 2012), provided that the number of sampling units is not too small, and all are collected and recorded in a similar manner. If we add up the 1s for each class of pot fragment, across sampling units, we get the *incidence frequency* for each class—the number of samples that included at least one sherd of that class. Suppose all the ceramic fragments are randomly distributed among all the sampling units. Clearly, rare classes will have low overall abundance frequencies and low incidence frequencies, and common classes will have high abundance frequencies and high incidence frequencies. Because the number of sampling units is inevitably limited, whereas counts of individuals have no fixed limit, the correspondence is not exact, but by applying the appropriate sampling model, little information is lost, because inferences are mainly based on infrequent (rare) classes (Figure 10.1).

Anyone who has ever sampled anything in the field, potsherds included, will immediately protest: "But of course the [*whatever it is that I study*] are *not* randomly distributed among sampling units!" Nevertheless, pooling abundance data from a set of sampling units and applying abundance-based rarefaction makes precisely this assumption. The consequence is that the diversity predicted for a smaller (rarefied) sample, by abundance-based rarefaction, is inevitably an overestimate of what one would actually find for the same number of artifacts organized into sampling units, because clustering of artifacts slows the rise of the empirical diversity as sampling units accumulate (Chazdon et al. 1998; Colwell and Coddington 1994; Colwell, Mao, and Chang 2004). Suppose we want to compare the diversity of two assemblages—one with substantially more artifacts than the other—using pooled abundance data from a set of sampling units for each assemblage. If we make the comparison based on rarefied abundance data, a diversity measure for a subset of the larger assemblage that

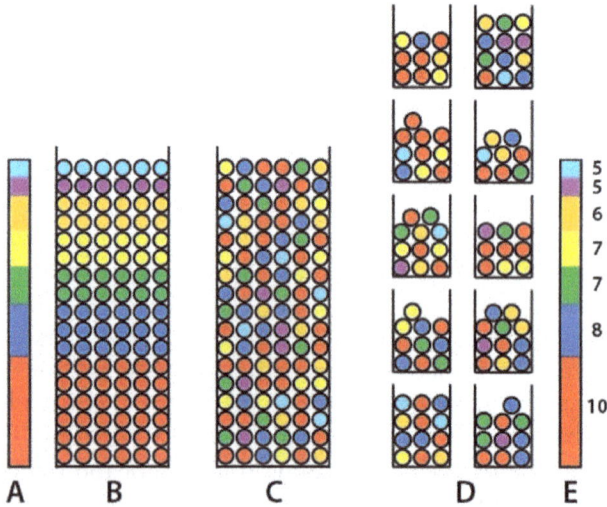

Figure 10.1. Why incidence frequencies closely reflect abundance, for random samples. (A) A frequency distribution of colors. (B) An urn of colored balls, sorted by color, matching the relative abundance of balls of different colors in frequency distribution A. Red balls are the commonest, light blue balls the rarest. (C) The urn is shaken to randomize the position of the balls in B. (D) Balls are drawn at random from the mixed urn in C, creating 10 random samples, each with 8 to 12 balls. (E) The incidence frequencies (the number of samples in which each color occurs at least once—the numbers next to the color bar) closely match the abundance frequencies in A. Red balls are the most frequent, light blue balls the least frequent. © The authors.

has been rarefied to match the smaller one could appear spuriously richer than the latter, when in fact both follow the same curve as samples are accumulated (Figure 10.2).

By contrast, in addition to simplifying the scoring of sampling units and avoiding pseudoreplication—by not having to assume that each sherd came from a different pot—the incidence approach takes account of spatial heterogeneity among sampling units (or temporal heterogeneity, if they are time-transgressive) (Chao and Colwell 2017; Colwell, Mao, and Chang 2004; Colwell et al. 2012; Smith, Stewart, and Cairns 1985). If the samples are, indeed, spatially or temporally structured, the incidence frequencies will reveal it. Thus, with replicated incidence data, we gain a more realistic and accurate depiction of the ceramic diversity at the site—allowing realistic diversity comparisons—than we could have produced by counting sherds of each class in each sample, and pooling the samples.

Replicated incidence data can be applied to virtually every statistical objective that can be achieved with abundance data, with almost no loss of power (Chao and Colwell 2017). Both kinds of data can be analyzed under

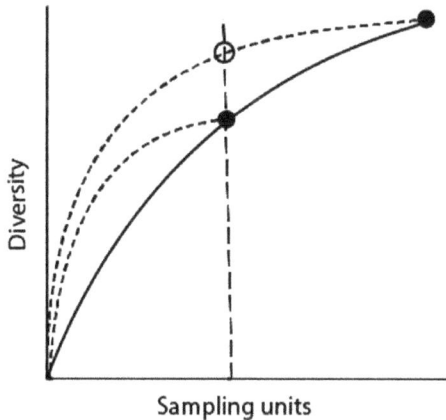

Figure 10.2. The perils of using abundance-based R/E when samples are spatially or temporally heterogeneous. The filled circles are a smaller and a larger reference sample, each from a different but (not known to the researcher) identical assemblage. The diversity (any Hill number) of the two assemblages is to be compared. The solid curved line is the sample-based rarefaction curve for the larger sample. Because the assemblages are actually identical, however, the sample-based rarefaction curve for the smaller sample coincides, up to its reference sample size, with the curve for the larger sample. The curved dashed lines are the abundance-based rarefaction curves for the two samples. The open circle marks the expected diversity of the larger sample, when rarefied by abundance-based rarefaction to the reference sample size of the smaller assemblage. The inference that the large sample is more diverse is erroneous, when spatial or temporal structuring is taken into account. © The authors.

a single statistical framework, under the following analogy: each incidence is analogous to an "individual," and the proportional incidence frequencies play the same role as class proportional abundances. As with abundance data, Hill numbers based on incidence data can be similarly formulated by replacing class proportional abundances with class proportional incidence frequencies. For q = 0, the incidence-based Hill number reduces to species richness, and the measures with q =1 and q = 2 can be interpreted as the effective number of frequent and highly frequent species in the assemblage, respectively. Incidence-based diversity profiles and evenness measures can also be analogously defined or derived.

Alan Turing and Estimators of Asymptotic Diversity

Alan Turing and his colleagues at Bletchley Park had the urgent job of cracking the Enigma code in order to understand as much as possible about the imminent moves, strengths, and weaknesses of the Nazi forces. But they also needed to estimate how much they did *not yet know* (McGrayne 2011)—specifically, how many coded letter combinations (classes) existed in the Enigma code-of-the-day alphabet cypher, but that had not yet been found in intercepted code segments.

Turing's surprising intuition was that the frequencies of the rarest recorded combinations—those with only one or two instances in intercepted code—held most of the information about the number of classes still unseen (Good 1953, 2000; Good and Toulmin 1956). In the terminology of biodiversity statistics (Table 10.1), these frequencies are *singletons* (only one instance) and *doubletons* (exactly two instances) for abundance data; or *uniques* (found in just one sampling unit) and *duplicates* (found in exactly two sampling units), for replicated incidence data (Colwell and Coddington 1994). Turing reasoned that, if many singletons appeared in a code segment, there were likely to be unseen classes, as well.

Chao (1984, 1987) applied Turing's concept to class diversity data (and to capture/recapture data, which shares the same structure), with many fruitful consequences (Chao and Colwell 2017). Later Chiu et al. (2014) extended Turing's approach to higher frequencies (Chao 2016; Chao et al. 2017a). For our purposes, the key application of this approach is the development of estimators of asymptotic (total) diversity of assemblages, for Hill numbers (Chao et al. 2014).

For richness, these are the well-known estimators Chao1 (for abundance data) and Chao2 (for replicated incidence data)—names bestowed on these measures by Colwell and Coddington (1994). Depending on the order q, asymptotic estimates obtained from sampling data may be subject to some downward bias, but the bias decreases with q. As demonstrated by Chao and Jost (2012) and Chao et al. (2014), Shannon diversity (q = 1) and Simpson diversity (q = 2) can be accurately inferred by asymptotic estimators, if the data are not too sparse.

For class richness (q = 0) in hyperdiverse assemblages, even if common species are highly heterogeneous in abundance, the Turing–Good frequency formulas imply that the Chao1 estimator is nearly unbiased as long as singletons have approximately the same mean abundances as undetected classes (Chao et al. 2017a)—a reasonable assumption for many datasets. Likewise, the Chao2 estimator is nearly unbiased if uniques have approximately the same detection (incidence) probabilities as undetected classes (Chao and Colwell 2017). However, even if undetected classes a have lower mean abundance than singletons (for abundance data), or a lower mean detection probability than uniques (for incidence data), these estimators represent a valid lower bound on class richness. Using estimators of asymptotic richness for class richness, Shannon diversity, and Simpson diversity, an asymptotic diversity profile can be plotted, in the same way that a diversity profile for observed data is plotted, displaying asymptotic diversity estimates as a function of Hill order q.

Rarefaction and Extrapolation (R/E) of Hill Numbers for Abundance Data and Replicated Incidence Data

As Sanders (1968) first proposed (for species richness of benthic invertebrates in deep-sea dredge samples), rarefaction of abundance-based samples can reduce the confounding effect of sample size by subsampling larger samples to match the size of the smallest samples. For decades, ecologists applied *individual-based rarefaction*, using the formulas of Hurlbert and Simberloff. Meanwhile, *sample-based rarefaction* (Gotelli and Colwell 2001) of replicated incidence data, for richness, was introduced to ecologists as "randomized species accumulation curves" (Colwell and Coddington 1994), gaining wide acceptance through the freeware application *EstimateS* (Colwell and Elsensohn 2014). [*EstimateS* relied on resampling algorithms for sample-based rarefaction, until replaced after a decade by an explicit combinatorial formula (Colwell, Mao, and Chang 2004) that turned out to be forty years old (Chiarucci et al. 2008; Shinozaki 1963).]

A unified approach to nonparametric extrapolation of individual-based and sample-based rarefaction curves was introduced for richness estimation by Colwell et al. (2012). This breakthrough exploited statistical sampling models to produce a seamless transition from rarefaction curves to extrapolation curves, joined at the observed richness of the *reference sam-*

ple (a single abundance sample or the pooled richness of a set of replicated incidence sampling units) (Figure 10.2). For the extrapolation part, an asymptotic richness "target" is required. The recommended asymptotic estimators are Chao1 for abundance data and Chao2 for incidence data, for their strong performance under a wide range of underlying relative frequency distributions and their statistically rigorous foundations.

Development of analytical formulas for rarefaction and extrapolation (R/E) of the full range of Hill numbers (with richness, as usual, a particular case), soon followed (Chao et al. 2014). For class richness (q = 0), the sample size for an assemblage should be extrapolated, at most, to double the size of the reference sample (the full, empirical sample). For Hill numbers of orders q = 1 (Shannon diversity) and q = 2 (Simpson diversity), if data are not too sparse, the extrapolation can be reliably extended to infinity. If a visual inspection shows that the R/E curve stabilizes and levels off (which happens for $q \geq 1$ in many applications, as sample size increases), the bias of the asymptotic estimator is limited or negligible and thus can be used to infer the true diversity. By contrast, a curve that is still increasing at the reference sample size (typically for class richness) signifies that the asymptotic estimator represents only a statistical lower bound—which may, nonetheless, be substantially greater than the observed diversity of the reference sample. In this volume, Bebber and Chao, Farahani and Sinensky, and Faith and Du apply rarefaction and extrapolation techniques to several kinds of archaeological data.

Confidence Intervals and Comparing Assemblages: What Is the Question?

Suppose a zooarchaeologist aims to compare the richness of vertebrate species in the diet of two ancient societies, based on bones recovered from middens that bear evidence of butchering or cooking. The archaeologist is able to gather data from 20 middens from Society A and 20 from Society B. Each midden is a *sampling unit*, scored for the detection or nondetection of each food species, yielding a single *reference sample* of replicated incidence data for A, and another for B (Table 10.1). Each reference sample is subjected not only to rarefaction, but also to extrapolation up to twice the size of the reference sample. Let us say that neither curve reaches a clear asymptote, but the curve for A consistently lies above the curve for B. Was the diet of A significantly richer than the diet of B, or is the difference not enough to conclude that they differed, based on these samples?

To construct a confidence envelope (say, 95 percent) around each curve, we need an estimate of variance for each level of accumulated sampling units. Until 2004, confidence intervals (envelopes) for sample-based rarefaction (including the closed-form equation of Ugland, Gray, and Ellingsen 2003) were derived from the conditional variance—the variance among randomizations, conditional on the sample itself. This approach assumes that the set of individual artifacts or sampling units in a reference sample constitute the statistical universe. Conditional confidence intervals are "banana-shaped"—narrow for small numbers of samples, because the number of possible combinations is small, and narrowing to zero for all sampling units, pooled, because only one such combination exists (see Farahani and Sinensky, this volume, for examples).

By contrast, the unconditional variance (and derived confidence envelopes) treats the reference sample as a sample from a larger universe—the assemblage, itself—that the archaeologist is trying to compare with a contrasting assemblage. It estimates the variation in diversity that would arise if an additional sample of size m (where m is the number of artifacts or sampling units accumulated at some point on the R/E curve) were taken from the entire assemblage in the same way, without expanding the spatial or temporal scope of sampling. Unconditional confidence intervals remain "open" when all sampling units in the reference sample are pooled.

Changxuan Mao derived the first unconditional variance estimator for replicated incidence data (Colwell, Mao, and Chang 2004), to the best of our knowledge. For abundance data, the conditional variance estimator of Heck, van Belle, and Simberloff (1975) was used from 1975 to 2012, when an unconditional estimator was finally introduced by Colwell et al. (2012). For unified R/E curves, the extrapolation portion requires a different approach for estimating unconditional variance. Using a bootstrap approach, Anne Chao derived such measures for both abundance data and replicated incidence data (ibid.). Remarkably, the confidence intervals for rarefaction and extrapolation, although based on completely different mathematical methods, join seamlessly at the reference sample. Unconditional confidence intervals have since been derived for the general case of Hill numbers (Chao et al. 2014).

What can we conclude about the significance (or not) of differences between a pair of R/E curves? If the 95 percent unconditional confidence intervals do not overlap over some interval of sample unit accumulation (for replicated incidence data) or individual accumulation (for abundance data), then the two reference samples differ significantly at $P < 0.05$, over that interval. However, if the confidence intervals do overlap to some extent, it is not possible to conclude whether the reference samples differ significantly in diversity or not (Colwell et al. 2012; Gotelli and Colwell 2011), and rigorous statistical tests (e.g., a two-sample normal test based on the diversity difference divided by its standard error) must be performed to determine whether a difference is statistically significant.

Rarefaction and Extrapolation by Sample Completeness

Returning to the example of the previous section, we supposed that the zooarchaeologist collected 20 samples from middens for each of the two societies, by design. It might seem perfectly fair to compare R/E curves, at any level of sample accumulation or extrapolation, because the confounding effect of sample size (number of accumulated sampling units) has been accounted for. However, suppose that the R/E curve for Society A levels off substantially more than the curve for Society B, while still remaining above the curve for B. The slope at the end of the rarefaction (or R/E) curve is a valid indicator of the completeness of the reference sample. The steeper the terminal slope, the less complete the reference sample.

Chao and Jost (2012) argued that the diversity of reference samples should be compared at similar degrees of *completeness*, in addition to comparing them at similar numbers of sampling units (for incidence data) or similar numbers of individuals (for abundance data)—especially if there are indications that reference samples to be compared differ substantially in degree of completeness. We return to this topic below, but first we expand on the history and current status of the idea of sample completeness.

The idea of quantifying sample completeness has two independent origins. For richness (Hill order $q = 0$), the ratio of observed richness to estimated asymptotic richness has long been used as a measure of sample completeness (e.g., Beck et al. 2012). In general terms, this measure estimates the proportion of the total number of classes in an assemblage (observed and unobserved) that is represented by the observed classes in a reference sample.

For abundance data, Turing and Good (Good 1953, 2000) originated the concept of *sample coverage* as a measure of completeness—the proportion of the total number of individuals in an assemblage (observed and unobserved) that belong to the observed classes in a reference sample. Turing and Good introduced a surprisingly simple and powerful estimator for sample coverage: $C = 1-f_1/n$, where f_1 is the number of singletons in a reference sample of size n. Chao and Jost (2012) introduced a more accurate version of the Turing–Good coverage estimator that incorporates f_2, the number of doubletons in the sample.

Subtracting the sample coverage from unity gives the proportion of the community belonging to unsampled classes—the *coverage deficit*. The coverage deficit of the sample can also be derived as the probability that a new, previously unsampled class would be found if the sample were enlarged by one individual—which turns out to be, precisely and satisfyingly, the terminal slope of the rarefaction curve (Chao and Jost 2012; Chao 2016).

Chao and colleagues (2020) recently extended and unified the concept of sample completeness in two ways. First, a single, continuous mathematical expression was developed to encompass estimates of *class list completeness* (q = 0, observed class count divided by estimated asymptotic class richness), *class inventory completeness* (q =1, measured by the improved Turing–Good sample coverage estimator), and *common class inventory completeness* (q =2, with each class proportionally weighted by its squared proportional abundance) (Table 10.1). In this way, for abundance data, a sample-completeness profile can be constructed, on the model of a diversity or evenness profile for the corresponding Hill numbers.

Second, Chao et al. (2020) extended the Turing–Good concept of sample coverage to incidence-based sample coverage for replicated incidence data, which is the form that would apply to our hypothetical ceramic diversity study, above. With that extension in hand, they further defined a sample-completeness profile for incidence data, exactly corresponding to the profile for abundance data.

When sample-completeness profiles reveal substantial differences in completeness among reference samples to be compared, a fair comparison can nonetheless be made by applying coverage-based rarefaction and extrapolation (Chao and Jost 2012; and Faith and Du, this volume). The coverage-based R/E curve plots diversity estimates (a Hill number, usually richness, Shannon, or Simpson diversity—or evenness) as a function of Turing–Good sample coverage (abundance-based or incidence-based). First, the diversity of each reference sample is extrapolated up to double the reference sample size. Then, a cutoff for comparison, C_{max}, is defined as is the level of coverage reached by the sample that attains the lowest coverage when extrapolated, among samples to be compared—"max" because it is the highest level of coverage we can use for comparison. For any coverage up to C_{max}, diversity and evenness estimates, with bootstrapped confidence intervals, can then be compared at equal coverage.

Alpha, Beta, and Gamma Diversity

Ecologists have long been concerned with measuring changes in assemblage composition (turnover) and changes in diversity along spatial gradients, from landscapes (Whittaker 1960) to continents (Rahbek and Graves 2001), and along temporal gradients, from decades (Dornelas et al. 2014) to millennia (Blois et al. 2013). Ever since Whittaker (1960, 1972) introduced the concepts of alpha, beta, and gamma diversity, a large and often contentious literature has developed around the challenge of measuring species turnover in space and time, and the closely related matter of quantifying similarities and dissimilarities among local or time-specific assemblages.

A wide range of beta diversity and related (dis)similarity concepts have been proposed, and the list of its measures seems endless (e.g., see Anderson et al. 2011). In ecology, there are two major approaches to beta diversity: the variance framework, derived from the total variance of a class-by-assemblage abundance matrix (Legendre and De Cáceres 2013); and the diversity decomposition framework, based on partitioning Hill numbers (Jost 2007; Whittaker 1972). Chao and Chiu (2016) bridged the two approaches by proving that they both converge to the same classes of species compositional (dis)similarity measures, including the multiple-assemblage generalizations of the classic Sørensen and Jaccard indexes, and the Horn (1966) and Morisita–Horn (Morisita 1959) measures.

An advantage of adopting the decomposition approach is that it leads to an intuitive and understandable interpretation: gamma diversity refers to the effective number of classes (Hill number of order q) in the pooled assemblage, whereas alpha diversity refers to the average effective number of classes among assemblages. Beta diversity is simply gamma diversity divided by alpha diversity, for any diversity order q (applying Whittaker's "multiplicative" definition of beta diversity, but using Hill numbers). Beta is then expressed in units of "assemblage equivalents" of compositional change between assemblages. Regardless of the values of alpha and gamma diversity, beta diversity always attains a *fixed minimum* value of unity if all N assemblages are identical in terms of class identity and abundance, and beta diversity attains a *fixed maximum* value of N (the number of assemblages) when no classes are shared among assemblages (i.e., complete turnover). Because beta diversity, therefore, lies in the range of $[1, N]$, it can be monotonically transformed to (dis)similarity measures in $[0, 1]$.

Another advantage of the decomposition approach is that it can be extended to phylogenetic and functional diversity, thus providing a unified partitioning theory that leads to phylogenetic and functional (dis)similarity measures (Chao, Chiu, and Jost 2014). Kuhn (this volume) explores the many parallels, and some important differences, between ecology and archaeology, in the study of multi-scale diversity.

Special Tools for Special Situations: Super-Duplicates, Genomics, and Bounded Classifications

In an archaeological context, for abundance data, the original Turing–Good frequency formula (Good 1953; Good and Toulmin 1956) would estimate the true mean proportional frequency of classes that appeared exactly r times. These are the expected—true—proportions of classes that are undetected ($r = 0$), singletons ($r = 1$), doubletons ($r = 2$), and more abundant classes, based on the observed class frequencies. When some classes are actually present but remain undetected, all observed class frequencies (especially rare, observed classes) are greater than their true values in the assemblage (Chao et al. 2017a). Chiu et al. (2014) developed a more accurate version of the Turing–Good frequency formula, and Chao and Colwell (2017) extended it to replicated incidence data. With these developments, it proved feasible to solve two, unrelated problems in class richness estimation.

A very simple data collection protocol records a list of all classes detected in a series of sampling units, and notes which of those classes occur in just one sampling unit (uniques). The number of classes found in exactly two sampling units (duplicates) and higher frequencies are not recorded. Thus, all we know is the number of uniques and the number of *super-duplicates* (classes that occur in two or more sampling units). Using an incidence-based Turing–Good frequency estimator, Chao et al. (2017b) developed an estimator for the true number of doubletons, and then applied Chao2 to estimate true richness. The method was successfully tested on a range of simulated assemblages and on empirical datasets for which the observed number of duplicates was recorded. The method was also applied to a survey of reef fish species, based on 116 scuba dives (sampling units), in which the observer (co-author Ditch Townsend, citizen scientist and the inspiration for this new richness estimator) kept a list and photographs of all species seen, and noted which of them he had seen on only one dive.

In the analysis of genomic data (in archaeology, it might be ancient DNA or environmental metagenomics), sequencing errors are common, and most appear as spurious singletons, inflating nonparametric estimates of genomic diversity. Using an abundance-based Turing–Good frequency estimator, Chiu and Chao (2016) developed an estimator for the true number of singletons, based on recorded frequencies of doubletons, tripletons, and quadrupletons, then used Chao1 to estimate true genomic richness. The estimator was successfully assessed with simulated distributions and empirical datasets.

A third tool—of special interest to archaeologists—is an asymptotic estimator of class richness for abundance data, for classifications with a fixed upper limit to the number of classes. The absolute lower bound for any richness estimate is always the observed number of classes, although a statistically estimated lower bound may be higher. As for an upper bound for estimates of class richness, when the total possible number of classes greatly exceeds any realistic sample (e.g., the insect species in a rainforest) or is unknown (the potential number of artifact classes, in our example, below, from Thomas and Colwell 2020; or the number of words in a language lexicon), no fixed upper bound need be taken into account, in setting confidence intervals around an estimate of asymptotic richness. But archaeological classifications frequently define a fixed set of classes, sometimes based on paradigmatic classifications—crossed classifications, with modes defined within dimensions (Bebber and Chao, this volume; Eren and Buchanan, this volume; Boulanger, Breslawski, and Jorgeson, this volume; Buchanan et al. 2017; Eren et al. 2016; Leonard and Jones 1987). In such cases, confidence intervals around asymptotic richness estimates must be bounded on the upper side as well as the lower side. To meet this challenge Eren et al. (2012) developed a doubly bounded richness estimator, which they applied successfully to archaeological data (Eren and Buchanan, this volume).

An Archaeological Example

We illustrate diversity estimation and analysis here by applying many of the tools described above to an archaeological dataset, from the Alta Toquima site (26Ny920), a high-elevation, summer-only, family residential village in Nevada. The site was occupied during episodes of extended drought between about 420–200 BC and AD 1400 (Thomas 2014). House foundations define the outlines of thirty-one pit-houses at Alta Toquima. The dataset that we analyzed contrasts the diversity of artifact classes between assemblages documented from inside eighteen of these houses (*intramural* samples) and assemblages recovered from *extramural* contexts at the site.

The dataset consists of 23 sampling units collected in the intramural context (each one collected from a separate point within a house foundation) and 22 sampling units collected in the extramural context (between house-sites, but within the village). For each sampling unit, the number of individual artifacts representing each of 39 artifact classes (Table 27.12 in Thomas and Colwell 2020) was recorded. In all, the intramural sampling units included 26 artifact classes, and the extramural sampling units included 23 classes.

Incidence-Based Analysis

For incidence-based analysis, the original abundance data matrices—intramural and extramural—were transformed to their incidence equivalents. With artifact classes as rows and sampling units as columns, each abundance value $a_{ij} > 0$ was replaced with a 1, indicating that artifact class i was detected in sampling unit j. *Incidence counts* are defined by the row sums of these matrices—the number of sampling units in which each artifact class was detected. The *incidence count frequencies* (Q_k) represent the number of artifact classes that were each detected in exactly k sampling units (Table 10.2a), for each dataset. The set of frequencies Q_k, and the number of sampling units T, are all that is needed for the subsequent analyses.

To compare the diversity of artifacts in the two assemblages, the incidence datasets are subjected to a sequence of steps, each based on comparing intramural vs. extramural diversity along a continuum of Hill numbers (indexed by q): $q = 0$ (artifact class richness), $q = 1$ (Shannon diversity of artifacts), and $q = 2$ (Simpson diversity of artifacts). To compare the artifact diversity of intramural vs. extramural assemblages, we develop and plot three sets of Hill-number profiles (sample-completeness profiles in Figure 10.3a, observed and asymptotic diversity profiles in Figure 10.3c,

Table 10.2. Data summary for incidence and abundance data.

(a) Incidence data. Incidence-based class frequency counts for the Alta Toquima Intramural and Extramural sites. Q_i denotes the number of classes that were detected in i sampling units.

(1) Intramural site: $S_{obs} = 26$, $T = 23$ (sampling units), $U = 112$ (total number of incidences); estimated sample completeness for $q = 0, 1,$ and 2 is, respectively, 77.0%, 92.4%, and 98.8%.

i	1	2	3	5	6	7	8	10	12	13
Q_i	9	5	1	2	2	1	2	2	1	1

(2) Extramural site: $S_{obs} = 23$, $T = 22$ (sampling units), $U = 105$ (total number of incidences); estimated sample completeness for $q = 0, 1,$ and 2 are, respectively, 88.5%, 95.6%, and 99.0%

i	1	2	3	4	5	7	8	9	15
Q_i	5	4	2	4	1	1	2	3	1

(b) Abundance data. Abundance-based class frequency counts for the Alta Toquima Intramural and Extramural datasets. f_r denotes the number of classes represented by r artifacts.

(1) Intramural dataset: $S_{obs} = 26$, $n = 613$ (number of artifacts); estimated sample completeness for $q = 0, 1,$ and 2 is, respectively, 70.3%, 98.7%, and 100%

r	1	2	3	5	6	9	12	14	32	36	66	189	197
f_r	8	3	2	1	1	4	1	1	1	1	1	1	1

(2) Extramural dataset: $S_{obs} = 23$, $n = 369$ (number of artifacts); estimated sample completeness for $q = 0, 1,$ and 2 is, respectively, 85.2%, 98.9%, and 100%

r	1	2	3	4	5	6	7	8	9	12	17	20	24	31	65	139
f_r	4	2	2	3	1	1	1	1	1	1	1	1	1	1	1	1

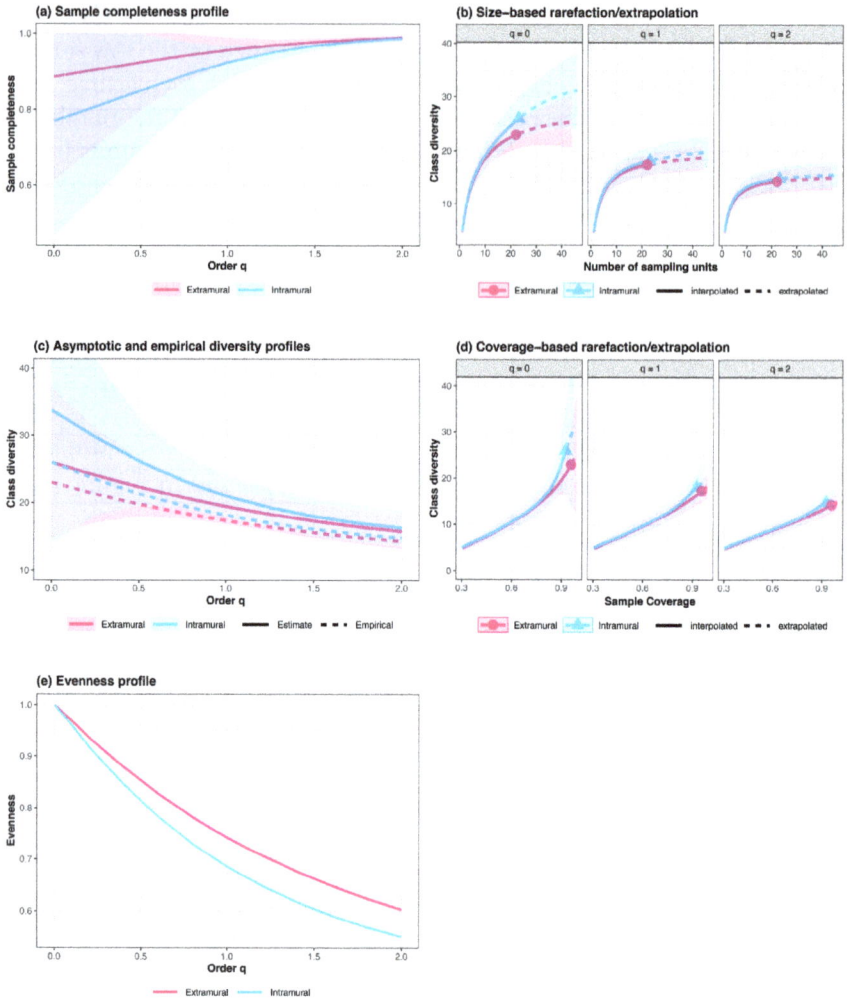

Figure 10.3. Results for incidence analysis for the Alta Toquima intramural and extramural datasets. (a) Estimated sample-completeness profile for diversity orders $0 \leq q \leq 2$. (b) Sample-based rarefaction (solid curve segments) and extrapolation (dashed curve segments); extrapolation is extended to double the size of the reference sample. (c) Observed (dotted lines) and asymptotic (solid lines, with confidence intervals) diversity profiles, for diversity orders $0 \leq q \leq 2$. (d) Coverage-based rarefaction (solid curve segments) and extrapolation (dashed curve segments); solid dots and triangles mark observed data points. (e) Evenness profiles for diversity orders $0 < q \leq 2$, computed for the coverage value of C_{max}, in this case 97.5%. Shaded areas in (a)–(d) show 95% confidence bands obtained with a bootstrap method with 100 replications. The numerical values for the three special cases of $q = 0$, 1, and 2 appear in Table 10.3 (left half). © The authors.

and evenness profiles in Figure 10.3e) and two rarefaction/extrapolation comparisons (sample-based in Figure 10.3b and coverage-based in Figure 10.3d). For all these analyses, we used the expanded online freeware application iNEXT (Hsieh, Ma, and Chao 2016).

STEP 1 (Figure 10.3a). *Assessment of sample completeness profile.* Figure 10.3a shows that estimated sample completeness for the intramural dataset is consistently lower than estimated completeness of the extramural dataset for $q \leq 2$, although the two confidence intervals overlap. For $q > 2$, the sample completeness estimates for the two datasets are close to the maximum level of unity. This result (detailed in the left half of Table 10.3) suggests that a higher proportion of infrequent classes in the intramural assemblage remained undetected, compared with the extramural assemblage.

STEP 2 (Figures 10.3b and 10.3c). *Sample-based rarefaction/extrapolation and asymptotic diversity.* Figure 10.3b shows the curves for sample-based rarefaction and extrapolation for diversity orders $q = 0$ (class richness), $q = 1$ (Shannon diversity), and $q = 2$ (Simpson diversity), for the intramural and extramural datasets. For the latter two diversities, the curves nearly stabilize, so that asymptotic diversity estimates for Shannon and Simpson diversities adequately approximate true diversities, allowing inferences about entire assemblages. However, neither of the curves for class richness ($q = 0$) levels off, even when extrapolated to double the reference (empirical) sample size. For richness, then, the intramural and extramural datasets do not contain sufficient information to accurately estimate true class richness within each assemblage. Thus, the asymptotic estimates for $q = 0$ (the Chao2 richness estimate) represent minimum class richness.

Within each dataset, the extent of undetected diversity can be assessed by comparing the estimated asymptotic diversity profile (solid lines in Figure 10.3c) with the corresponding observed/empirical diversity profile (dashed lines in Figure 10.3c). For class richness ($q = 0$), the asymptotic richness estimate for the intramural assemblage is 33.7 classes, higher than the estimate of 26 classes for the extramural assemblage (Table 10.3, left half). Because these estimates are lower bounds, as explained above, the degree of difference in true class richness for the assemblages cannot be precisely assessed. The minimum number of undetected classes within the intramural assemblage is 7.7 classes ($\geq$ 23 percent), as shown in Step 1 (Table 10.3, left half), whereas at least 3 classes ($\geq$ 11.5 percent) remain undetected in the extramural assemblage.

Table 10.3. The numerical values for the three special cases of q = 0, 1, and 2 for incidence-based data (left half) and abundance data (right half) for Alta Toquima intramural and extramural datasets. Blue font marks the higher value between the intramural and extramural datasets/assemblages.

Intramural/Extramural data (Incidence data converted from abundance data)				Intramural/Extramural data (Abundance data based on row totals)			
STEP 1. Sample completeness profiles							
	$q = 0$	$q = 1$	$q = 2$		$q = 0$	$q = 1$	$q = 2$
Intramural	77.0%	92.4%	98.8%	Intramural	70.3%	98.7%	100%
Extramural	88.5%	95.6%	99.0%	Extramural	85.2%	98.9%	100%
STEP 2. Asymptotic analysis							
	$q = 0$	$q = 1$	$q = 2$		$q = 0$	$q = 1$	$q = 2$
Intramural				Intramural			
Asymptotic	33.7	21	16.3	Asymptotic	36.6	7.4	4.6
Empirical	26	18.1	14.8	Empirical	26	7.2	4.6
Undetected	7.7	2.9	1.5	Undetected	10.6	0.2	0
Extramural				Extramural			
Asymptotic	26	19.4	15.8	Asymptotic	27	9.3	5.2
Empirical	23	17.3	14.3	Empirical	23	8.9	5.2
Undetected	3	2.1	1.5	Undetected	4	0.3	0.1
STEPS 3 and 4. Non-asymptotic coverage-based rarefaction and extrapolation analysis; evenness							
Maximum standardized coverage C_{max} = 97.5%				Maximum standardized coverage C_{max} = 99.4%			
Diversity	$q = 0$	$q = 1$	$q = 2$	Diversity	$q = 0$	$q = 1$	$q = 2$
Intramural	31.3	19.8	15.5	Intramural	31.7	7.3	4.6
Extramural	24.3	17.9	14.6	Extramural	24.8	9.1	5.2
Evenness	Pielou J'	$q = 1$	$q = 2$	Evenness	Pielou J'	$q = 1$	$q = 2$
Intramural	0.87	0.62	0.48	Intramural	0.58	0.21	0.12
Extramural	0.90	0.73	0.58	Extramural	0.69	0.34	0.18

The asymptotic Shannon diversity estimate for the intramural assemblage (21.0 class equivalents) is greater than the estimate for the extramural assemblage (19.4 class equivalents; Table 10.3, left half). Likewise, the asymptotic Simpson diversity estimate for the intramural assemblage (16.3 class equivalents) is greater than the estimate for the extramural assemblage (15.8 class equivalents; Table 10.3, left half). As explained above, these asymptotic values represent accurate estimates of the true Shannon and Simpson assemblage diversities. The difference between the two assemblages is 1.6 class equivalents (21–19.4) for Shannon diversity and 0.5 class equivalents (16.3–15.8) for Simpson diversity, but the two 95 percent confidence bands in Figure 10.3c overlap, so we cannot conclude that the difference at $P \leq 0.05$ is significant. Table 10.3 (left half) displays the undetected Shannon and Simpson diversities within the intramural and the extramural assemblages.

STEP 3 (Figure 10.3d). *Coverage-based rarefaction/extrapolation and non-asymptotic diversity.* When sampling data do not contain sufficient information to accurately estimate true diversity, fair comparisons of diversity across multiple assemblages should be made by standardizing sample completeness—that is, by comparing diversity for a standardized fraction of an assemblage's individuals (for abundance data) or, here, incidences. For class richness, although the Alta Toquima data are insufficient to infer the true richness of the full intramural and extramural assemblages, inference can be made up to a standardized completeness (sample coverage) value of C_{max} = 97.5 percent (Figure 10.3d, left panel). (Recall that C_{max}—the highest level of coverage we can use for comparison—is the level of coverage reached by the sample that attains the *lowest* coverage when extrapolated to twice the size of the reference sample, among samples to be compared.). Here, the richness represented by the remaining 2.5 percent of the incidences cannot be estimated from the data, due to insufficient information. In this example, coverage-based rarefaction/extrapolation curves enable us to make sensible inferences and fair comparisons of diversity profiles and their normalized slopes (as measures of evenness, Figure 10.3e) for any standardized assemblage fraction up to 97.5 percent.

   At a standardized coverage of 97.5 percent, the corresponding richness (q = 0) estimate is 31.3 classes for the intramural assemblage and 24.3 classes for the extramural assemblage. The difference in class richness between the two assemblages for a fraction of 97.5 percent is thus 7.0 classes (31.3–24.3), and the intramural assemblage is 1.3 times richer than the extramural assemblage, although the two 95 percent confidence intervals overlap. For Shannon diversity (q =1), for 97.5 percent assemblage fractions, the difference in diversity between the two sites is about 1.9 class equivalents (19.8–17.9); for Simpson diversity, the difference is about 0.9 class equivalents (15.5–14.6; Table 10.3, left half). These values differ very little from those of the entire assemblages discussed in Step 2.

STEP 4 (Figure 10.3e). *Evenness.* For a fixed value of sample coverage, we can evaluate the magnitude of the normalized slopes ${}^{q}E$ of the diversity profile (Figure 10.3c) for any value of $q > 0$, yielding an evenness profile for each dataset. These values are objective measures of evenness among class abundances or, here, among relative class incidence frequencies (Chao and Ricotta's (2019) Evenness $E3$). Figure 10.3e shows the evenness profile for diversity orders $0 < q \leq 2$, spanning diversity orders from (near)-richness (q arbitrarily close to 0) to Shannon ($q = 1$) and Simpson ($q = 2$) class diversities. For all values of q, evenness is computed for the coverage value of C_{max}, in this case 97.5 percent. All these evenness measures are standardized to the range $[0, 1]$ to adjust for the effect of differing class richness. The evenness profiles consistently show that evenness among class occurrences in the extramural site is higher than that in the intramural site. Table 10.3 (left half, last three rows) gives the values of ^qE for $q = 1$ and 2, as well as Pielou's (1969) widely used J' index of evenness, applied to artifact class incidence frequencies.

Abundance-Based Analysis

For abundance-based analysis, we analyzed the total number of individual artifacts of each artifact class, summed over all sampling units, from the original abundance data matrices—separately for intramural and extramural. With artifact classes as rows and sampling units as columns, these *total abundance data* are the marginal row sums. The row sums correspond directly (and are approximated by) the incidence counts for the same data (Figure 10.1). Likewise, the abundance frequencies (the number of species with total abundance of 1, 2, 3, ... individuals) correspond to incidence frequencies for incidence data. Table 10.2b gives the vector of abundance frequencies, which are sufficient to compute all diversity statistics discussed here.

Table 10.3 (right side) and Figure 10.4 record the results for diversity analysis of abundance data, corresponding directly with the analogous analyses of the incidence datasets that were derived from the same, original, replicated abundance data. The analyses based on abundance data show that the estimated diversity profiles for the intramural and extramural (Figure 10.4c) assemblages cross at around $q = 0.5$ (between richness, $q = 0$, and Shannon diversity, $q = 1$). Thus, for these abundance data, the ordering of diversity depends on the order q. For richness ($q = 0$), as in the incidence analysis, the intramural assemblage is consistently more diverse than the extramural assemblage (for class richness at a standardized assemblage fraction of 99.4 percent; Figure 10.4d and Table 10.3, right side). For Shannon diversity ($q = 1$) and Simpson diversity ($q = 2$), however, the direction of difference is reversed—and this conclusion is valid for any standardized assemblage fraction up to 100 percent (Figure 10.4d). This

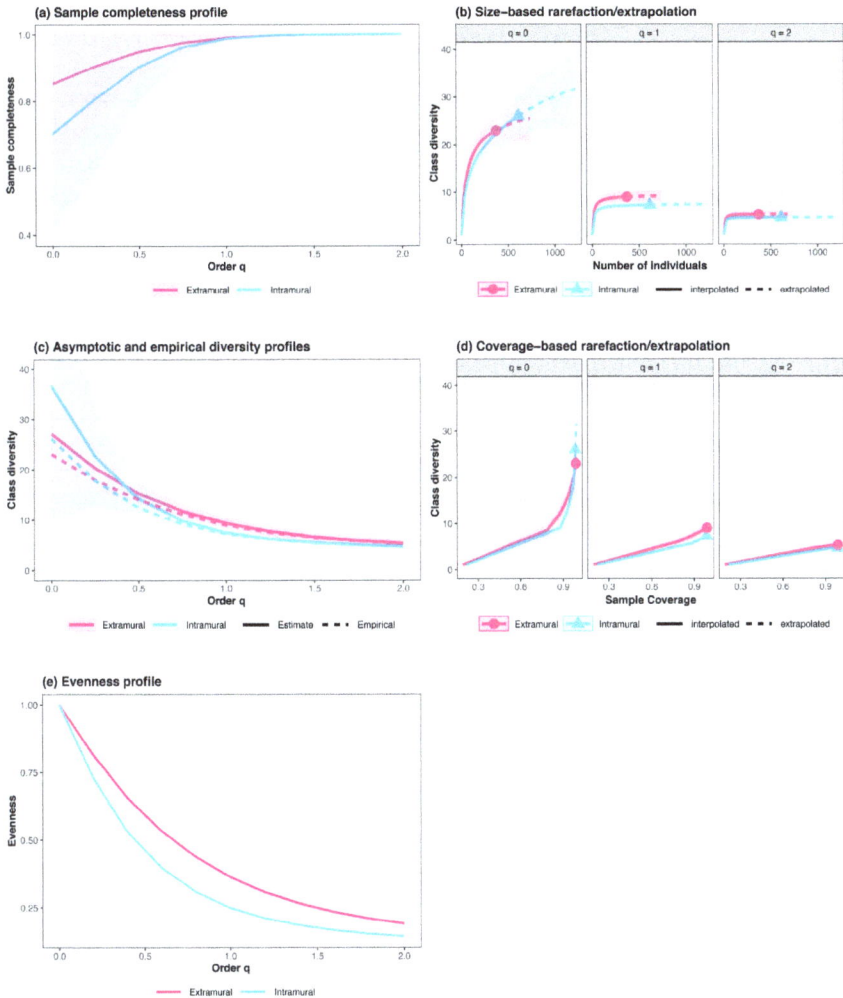

Figure 10.4. Results for abundance analysis for the Alta Toquima intramural and extramural datasets. See the Figure 10.3 caption for explanation. All numerical values for the three special cases of q = 0, 1, and 2 are shown in Table 10.3 (right half). © The authors.

reversal arises primarily from the presence more uneven abundance classes (Figure 10.4e and Table 10.3, right half, evenness data) and the dominance of two highly abundant classes (projectile points and pressure flaked bifaces) in the intramural site—a pattern damped by reducing the data to their incidence equivalents. Except for Shannon diversity, these differences in diversity for the abundance analyses are not statistically significant.

Comparison of Rarefaction Curves Based on the Two Different Types of Data

Figure 10.5 compares sample-based with abundance-based rarefaction curves for the intramural site (upper panels) and extramural site (lower panels) as a function of the rarefied fraction, rather than as a function of the number of accumulated sampling units (Figure 10.3b), the number of individual artifacts (Figure 10.4b), or coverage (figures 10.3d and 10.4d). The Y-axis (^qD) denotes the diversity or the effective number of classes for richness ($q = 0$; left panels), Shannon diversity ($q = 1$; middle panels), and Simpson diversity ($q = 2$; right panels), based on abundance data (red curves) and incidence data (blue curves).

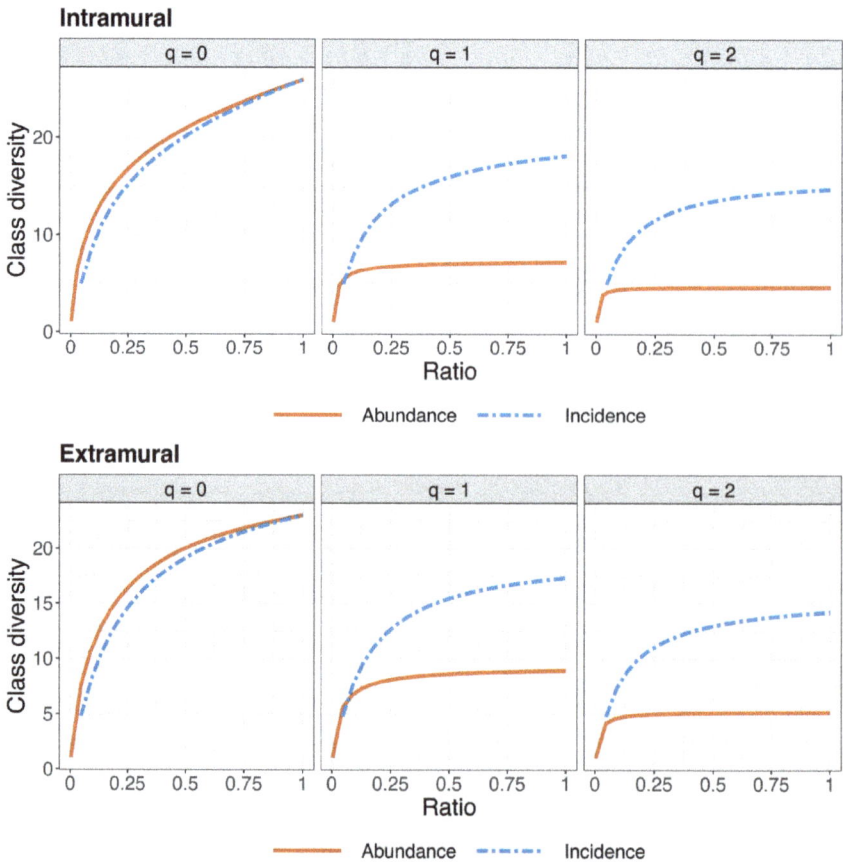

Figure 10.5. Comparison of incidence-based (blue) vs. abundance-based (red) rarefaction curves for the Alta Toquima intramural and extramural datasets. "Ratio" means rarefied fraction. See the text for interpretation. © The authors.

As discussed earlier, analysis based on replicated incidence data is more responsive than analysis based on abundance data to clustering or aggregation of artifacts. Thus, when artifact classes are spatially aggregated, treating dependent artifacts as "independent" data will generally result in overestimates for the species richness of any rarefied subsample (Figure 10.2 and left panel in Figure 10.5). As for Shannon diversity ($q = 1$, middle panels in Figure 10.5) and Simpson diversity ($q = 2$, right panels), the assumption of independence implied for abundance data may result in diversity underestimates, driven by exaggerated unevenness of abundances among classes. When a cluster of artifacts of the same class is found in a single sampling unit, each of the artifacts adds to the abundance count for that sampling unit, exaggerating the unevenness. In contrast, for incidence data, the entire cluster counts once.

Conclusions

Over the past three decades, after an extended and sometimes contentious period of exploration and experimentation, the concept of diversity has taken root in fertile statistical soil. Fundamental elements of diversity—class richness, evenness, and key classical measures of diversity—have been unified under the simple mathematics of Hill numbers, diversity profiles, and, most recently, evenness profiles. The demons of estimation and comparison of diversity based on sample data, long a source of frustration in many fields, including archaeology (Leonard and Jones 1989), will never be fully vanquished, but are now held at bay by statistically rigorous estimators of asymptotic diversity, and by integrated rarefaction and extrapolation of diversity (Hill numbers) from sample data, with unconditional confidence intervals. The concept of inventory completeness has been formalized, unified, and extended to completeness-based rarefaction and extrapolation. These advances have been primarily driven by the requirements of ecologists and evolutionary biologists, but we hope that most will find use in archaeology.

Acknowledgments

We are grateful to Metin Eren and Briggs Buchanan for organizing this symposium and for inviting us to participate, and to all the participants for educating us in the ways of archaeology and archaeologists. We thank David Hurst Thomas for his advice and for sharing the Alta Toquima data with us.

Robert K. Colwell is a Museum Curator Adjoint in Entomology at the Museum of Natural History, University of Colorado, Boulder, Colorado, USA; a Distinguished Research Professor and Distinguished Professor Emeritus at the University of Connecticut, Storrs, USA; and a Professor and Pesquisador Visitante Especial at the Universidade Federal de Goiás, Goiânia, Brazil.

Anne Chao is a Professor at the Institute of Statistics, National Tsing Hua University, Hsin-Chu, Taiwan.

References

Anderson, M. J., T. O. Crist, J. M. Chase, M. Vellend, B. D. Inouye, A. L. Freestone, N. J. Sanders, H. V. Cornell, L. S. Comita, and K. F. Davies. 2011. "Navigating the Multiple Meanings of β Diversity: A Roadmap for the Practicing Ecologist." *Ecology Letters* 14: 19–28.

Beck, J., J. D. Holloway, C. V. Khen, and I. J. Kitching. 2012. "Diversity Partitioning Confirms the Importance of Beta Components in Tropical Rainforest Lepidoptera." *The American Naturalist* 180: E64–E74.

Blois, J. L., J. W. Williams, M. C. Fitzpatrick, S. Ferrier, S. D. Veloz, F. He, Z. Liu, G. Manion, and B. Otto-Bliesner. 2013. "Modeling the Climatic Drivers of Spatial Patterns in Vegetation Composition since the Last Glacial Maximum." *Ecography* 36: 460–73.

Bobrowsky, P. T., and B. F. Ball. 1989. "The Theory and Mechanics of Ecological Diversity in Archaeology." In *Quantifying Diversity in Archaeology*, ed. R. D. Leonard and G. T. Jones, 4–12. Cambridge: Cambridge University Press.

Buchanan, B., A. Chao, C.-H. Chiu, R. K. Colwell, M. J. O'Brien, A. Werner, and M. I. Eren. 2017. "Environment-Induced Changes in Selective Constraints on Social Learning during the Peopling of the Americas." *Scientific Reports* 7: 44431.

Chao, A. 1984. "Non-Parametric Estimation of the Number of Classes in a Population." *Scandinavian Journal of Statistics* 11: 265–70.

———. 1987. "Estimating the Population Size for Capture–Recapture Data with Unequal Catchability." *Biometrics* 43: 783–91.

———. 2016. "My Entropy 'Pearl': Using Turing's Insight to Find an Optimal Estimator for Shannon Entropy." Methods Blog. British Ecological Society, Methods in Ecology and Evolution. https://methodsblog.com/2016/03/04/entropy-pearl/.

Chao, A., and C.-H. Chiu. 2016. "Bridging the Variance and Diversity Decomposition Approaches to Beta Diversity via Similarity and Differentiation Measures." *Methods in Ecology and Evolution* 7: 919–28.

Chao, A., C.-H. Chiu, R. K. Colwell, L. F. S. Magnago, R. L. Chazdon, and N. J. Gotelli. 2017a. "Deciphering the Enigma of Undetected Species, Phylogenetic, and Functional Diversity Based on Good–Turing Theory." *Ecology* 98: 2914–29.

Chao, A., C.-H. Chiu, and L. Jost. 2014. "Unifying Species Diversity, Phylogenetic Diversity, Functional Diversity, and Related Similarity and Differentiation Measures through Hill Numbers." *Annual Review of Ecology, Evolution, and Systematics* 45: 297–324.

Chao, A., and R. K. Colwell. 2017. "Thirty Years of Progeny from Chao's Inequality: Estimating and Comparing Richness with Incidence Data and Incomplete Sampling." *Statistics and Operations Research Transactions (SORT)* 41: 1–52.

Chao, A., R. K. Colwell, C.-H. Chiu, and D. Townsend. 2017b. "Seen Once or More Than Once: Applying Good–Turing Theory to Estimate Species Richness Using Only Unique Observations and a Species List." *Methods in Ecology and Evolution* 8: 1221–32.

Chao, A., N. J. Gotelli, T. C. Hsieh, E. L. Sander, K. H. Ma, R. K. Colwell, and A. M. Ellison. 2014. "Rarefaction and Extrapolation with Hill Numbers: A Framework for Sampling and Estimation in Species Diversity Studies." *Ecological Monographs* 84: 45–67.

Chao, A., T. C. Hsieh, R. L. Chazdon, R. K. Colwell, and N. J. Gotelli. 2015. "Unveiling the Species-Rank Abundance Distribution by Generalizing the Good–Turing Sample Coverage Theory." *Ecology* 96: 1189–1201.

Chao, A., and L. Jost. 2012. "Coverage-Based Rarefaction and Extrapolation: Standardizing Samples by Completeness Rather than Size." *Ecology* 93: 2533–47.

———. 2015. "Estimating Diversity and Entropy Profiles via Discovery Rates of New Species." *Methods in Ecology and Evolution* 6: 873–82.

Chao, A., Y. Kubota, D. Zelený, C.-H. Chiu, C. F. Li, B. Kusumoto, M. Yasuhara, S. Thorn, C. L. Wei, M. J. Costello, and R. K. Colwell. 2020. "Quantifying Sample Completeness and Comparing Diversities among Assemblages." *Ecological Research* 35: 292–314.

Chao, A., and C. Ricotta. 2019. "Quantifying Evenness and Linking It to Diversity, Beta Diversity, and Similarity." *Ecology* 100: e02852.

Chazdon, R. L., R. K. Colwell, J. S. Denslow, and M. R. Guariguata. 1998. "Statistical Methods for Estimating Species Richness of Woody Regeneration in Primary and Secondary Rain Forests of NE Costa Rica." In *Forest Biodiversity Research, Monitoring and Modeling: Conceptual Background and Old World Case Studies*, ed. F. Dallmeier and J. A. Comiskey, 285–309. Paris: Parthenon Publishing.

Chiarucci, A., G. Bacaro, D. Rocchini, and L. Fattorini. 2008. "Discovering and Rediscovering the Sample-Based Rarefaction Formula in the Ecological Literature." *Community Ecology* 9: 121–23.

Chiu, C.-H., and A. Chao. 2016. "Estimating and Comparing Microbial Diversity in the Presence of Sequencing Errors." *PeerJ* 4: e1634.

Chiu, C.-H., Y. T. Wang, B. A. Walther, and A. Chao. 2014. "An Improved Nonparametric Lower Bound of Species Richness via a Modified Good–Turing Frequency Formula." *Biometrics* 70: 671–82.

Colwell, R. K., A. Chao, N. J. Gotelli, S.-Y. Lin, C. X. Mao, R. L. Chazdon, and J. T. Longino. 2012. "Models and Estimators Linking Individual-Based and Sample-Based Rarefaction, Extrapolation, and Comparison of Assemblages." *Journal of Plant Ecology* 5: 3–21.

Colwell, R. K., and J. A. Coddington. 1994. "Estimating Terrestrial Biodiversity through Extrapolation." *Philosophical Transactions of the Royal Society (Series B)* 345: 101–18.

Colwell, R. K., and J. E. Elsensohn. 2014. "EstimateS Turns 20: Statistical Estimation of Species Richness and Shared Species from Samples, with Non-Parametric Extrapolation." *Ecography* 37: 609–13.

Colwell, R. K., C. X. Mao, and J. Chang. 2004. "Interpolating, Extrapolating, and Comparing Incidence-Based Species Accumulation Curves." *Ecology* 85: 2717–27.

Conkey, M. W. 1989. "The Use of Diversity in Stylistic Analyses." In *Quantifiying Diverstiy in Archaeology*, ed. R. D. Leonard and G. T. Jones, 118–30. Cambridge: Cambridge University Press.

Dornelas, M., N. J. Gotelli, B. McGill, H. Shimadzu, F. Moyes, C. Sievers, and A. E. Magurran. 2014. "Assemblage Time Series Reveal Biodiversity Change But Not Systematic Loss." *Science* 344: 296–99.

Dunnell, R. C. 1989. "Diversity in Archaeology: A Group of Measures in Search of an Application?" In *Quantifying Diversity in Archaeology*, ed. R. D. Leonard and G. T. Jones, 142–49. Cambridge: Cambridge University Press.

Ellison, A. M. 2010. "Partitioning Diversity." *Ecology* 91: 1962–63.

Eren, M. I., A. Chao, C.-H., Chiu, R. K. Colwell, B. Buchanan, M. T. Boulanger, J. Darwent, and M. J. O'Brien. 2016. "Statistical Analysis of Paradigmatic Class Richness Supports Greater Paleoindian Projectile-Point Diversity in the Southeast." *American Antiquity* 81: 174–92.

Eren, M. I., A. Chao, W. H. Hwang, and R. K. Colwell. 2012. "Estimating the Richness of a Population When the Maximum Number of Classes Is Fixed: A Nonparametric Solution to an Archaeological Problem." *PLoS ONE* 7: e34179.

Fisher, R., A. Corbett, and C. Williams. 1943. "The Relationship between the Number of Species and the Number of Individuals in a Random Sample of an Animal Population." *Journal Animal Ecology* 12: 42–58.

Good, I. J. 1953. "The Population Frequencies of Species and the Estimation of Population Parameters." *Biometrika* 40: 237–64.

———. 2000. "Turing's Anticipation of Empirical Bayes in Connection with the Cryptanalysis of the Naval Enigma." *Journal of Statistical Computation and Simulation* 66: 101–11.

Good, I. J., and G. H. Toulmin. 1956. "The Number of New Species, and the Increase in Population Coverage, When a Sample is Increased." *Biometrika* 43: 45–63.

Gotelli, N. J., and A. Chao. 2013. "Measuring and Estimating Species Richness, Species Diversity, and Biotic Similarity from Sampling Data." In *Encyclopedia of Biodiversity*, 2nd Edition, ed. S. Levin, 195–211. New York: Academic Press.

Gotelli, N. J., and R. K. Colwell. 2001. "Quantifying Biodiversity: Procedures and Pitfalls in the Measurement and Comparison of Species Richness." *Ecology Letters* 4: 379–91.

———. 2011. "Estimating Species Richness." In *Frontiers in Measuring Biodiversity*, ed. A. E. Magurran and B. J. McGill, 39–54. New York: Oxford University Press.

Heck Jr., K. L., G. van Belle, and D. Simberloff. 1975. "Explicit Calculation of the Farefaction Diversity Measurement and the Determination of Sufficient Sample Size." *Ecology* 56: 1459–61.

Hill, M. O. 1973. "Diversity and Evenness: A Unifying Notation and its Consequences." *Ecology* 54: 427–31.

———. 1997. "An Evenness Statistic Based on the Abundance-Weighted Variance of Species Proportions." *Oikos* 79: 413–16.

Horn, H. S. 1966. "Measurement of 'Overlap' in Comparative Ecological Studies." *The American Naturalist* 100: 419–24.

Hsieh, T., K. Ma, and A. Chao. 2016. "iNEXT: An R Package for Rarefaction and Extrapolation of Species Diversity (Hill Numbers)." *Methods in Ecology and Evolution* 7: 1451–56.

Hurlbert, S. H. 1971. "The Nonconcept of Species Diversity: A Critique and Alternative Parameters." *Ecology* 52: 577–86.

Jones, G. T., D. K. Grayson, and C. Beck. 1983. "Artifact Class Richness and Sample Size in Archaeological Surface Assemblages." In *Lulu Linear Punctated: Essays in Honor of George Irving Quimby*, ed. R. C. Dunnell, D. K. Grayson, and W. Koelz, 55–73. Ann Arbor, MI: Museum of Anthropology.

Jost, L. 2006. "Entropy and Diversity." *Oikos* 113: 363–75.

———. 2007. "Partitioning Diversity into Independent Alpha and Beta Components." *Ecology* 88: 2427–39.

———. 2010. "The Relation between Evenness and Diversity." *Diversity* 2: 207–32.

Kintigh, K. W. 1989. "Sample Size, Significance, and Measures of Diversity." In *Quantifying Diversity in Archaeology*, ed. R. D. Leonard and G. T. Jones, 25–36. Cambridge: Cambridge University Press.

Legendre, P., and M. De Cáceres. 2013. "Beta Diversity as the Variance of Community Data: Dissimilarity Coefficients and Partitioning." *Ecology Letters* 16: 951–63.

Leonard, R. D., and G. T. Jones. 1987. "Elements of an Inclusive Evolutionary Model for Archaeology." *Journal of Anthropological Archaeology* 6: 199–219.

———, eds. 1989. *Quantifying Diverstiy in Archaeology*. Cambridge: Cambridge University Press.

MacArthur, R. H. 1965. "Patterns of Species Diversity." *Biological Review* 40: 510–33.

Magurran, A. E. 1988. *Ecological Diversity and its Measurement*. Princeton, NJ: Princeton University Press.

Magurran, A. E., and B. J. McGill, eds. 2011. *Biological Diversity: Frontiers in Measurement and Assessment*. Oxford: Oxford University Press.

McGrayne, S. B. 2011. *The Theory That Would Not Die: How Bayes' Rule Cracked the Enigma Code, Hunted Down Russian Submarines, and Emerged Triumphant from Two Centuries of Controversy*. New Haven, CT: Yale University Press.

Morisita, M. 1959. "Measuring of Interspecific Association and Similarity between Communities." *Memoirs of the Faculty of Science, Kyushu University, Series E (Biology)* 3: 65–80.

Peet, R. K. 1974. "The Measurement of Species Diversity." *Annual Review of Ecology and Systematics* 5: 285–307.

Pielou, E. C. 1969. *An Introduction to Mathematical Ecology*. New York: Wiley.

———. 1975. *Ecological Diversity*. New York: Wiley Interscience.

Preston, F. W. 1948. "The Commonness, and Rarity, of Species." *Ecology* 29: 254–83.

Rahbek, C., and G. R. Graves. 2001. "Multiscale Assessment of Patterns of Avian Species Richness." *Proceedings of the National Academy of Sciences USA* 98: 4534–39.

Raup, D. 1975. "Taxonomic Diversity Estimation Using Rarefaction." *Paleobiology* 1: 333–42.

Rice, P. M. 1989. "Cermic Diversity, Production, and Use." In *Quantifying Diverstiy in Archaeology*, ed. R. D. Leonard and G. T. Jones, 109–17. Cambridge: Cambridge University Press.

Rothschild, N. A. 1989. "The Effect of Urbanization on Faunal Diversity: A Comparison between New York City and St. Augustine, Florida, in the Sixteenth to Eighteenth Centuries." In *Quantifying Diversity in Archaeology*, ed. R. D. Leonard and G. T. Jones, 92–99. Cambridge: Cambridge University Press.

Sanders, H. 1968. "Marine Benthic Diversity: A Comparative Study." *The American Naturalist* 102: 243–282.

Shinozaki, K. 1963. "Notes on the Species-Area Curve." 10th Annual Meeting of the Ecological Society of Japan (Abstract), 5.

Simberloff, D. 1972. "Properties of the Rarefaction Diversity Measurement." *The American Naturalist* 106: 414–18.

Smith, E., P. Stewart, and J. Cairns. 1985. "Similarities between Rarefaction Methods." *Hydrobiologia* 120: 167–70.

Thomas, D. H. 1989. "Diversity in Hunter-Gatherer Cultural Geography." In *Quantifying Diversity in Archaeology*, ed. R. D. Leonard and G. T. Jones, 85–91. Cambridge: Cambridge University Press.

———. 2014. "Exploring and Explaining Alta Toquima." *SAA Archaeological Record* 14: 32–37.

Thomas, D. H., and R. K. Colwell. 2020. "Class Richness: Sample-Based and Coverage-Based Approaches." In *Alpine Archaeology of Alta Toquima and the Mt. Jefferson Tablelands (Nevada)*, ed. D. H. Thomas, 776–812. Anthropological Papers of the American Museum of Natural History, Number 104. New York: American Museum of Natural History.

Ugland, K. I., J. S. Gray, and K. E. Ellingsen. 2003. "The Species–Accumulation Curve and Estimation of Species Richness." *Journal of Animal Ecology* 72: 888–97.

Whittaker, R. H. 1960. "Vegetation of the Siskiyou Mountains, Oregon and California." *Ecological Monographs* 30: 279–338.

———. 1972. "Evolution and Measurement of Species Diversity." *Taxon* 21: 213–51.

Diversity Metrics Are Convenient, but Their Archaeological Meanings Are Still Obscure

R. Lee Lyman

—⊗⊗⊗—

Often scientists cannot get numbers that compare well with theory until they know what numbers they should be making nature yield.
—T. S. Kuhn, *The Essential Tension*

As a celebration of the thirtieth anniversary of the publication of Robert (Bob) Leonard and George (Tom) Jones's 1989 *Quantifying Diversity in Archaeology*, this volume put together by Metin Eren and Briggs Buchanan is a good one. As O'Brien and Thomas point out in the Foreword, archaeology has made important advances both in measuring diversity (statistical freeware allowing numerous measures of diversity to be calculated in a fraction of a second) and toward understanding what particular measures might mean. One regular concern of the contributors to the Leonard and Jones volume was the influence of sample size (n of artifacts or ecofacts) on measures of diversity (often rendered as the number of kinds of phenomena). And while that is a concern found in many of the contributions making up this present compilation, it is not the focal point it once was. There is much to learn from all of these more recent contributions, and that is good.

I was a classmate of both Leonard and Jones, and we all took classes from Robert Dunnell in the late 1970s and early 1980s (not necessarily during the same academic term). The three of us also took classes from Donald Grayson. We all learned much from these mentors. Grayson taught us to worry about sample size effects on any quantitative measure of variability and diversity derived from archaeological phenomena. Several of the new contributions address sampling issues to great effect, for one thing distinguishing between individual-based rarefaction and sample-based rarefaction, demonstrating the greater accuracy and validity of the latter. Another thing regarding sampling is the difference between incidence (presence/absence) data and abundance data, and the demonstrable interrelatedness of the two when it comes to measures of diversity. In this respect, the chapter by Colwell and Chao is most welcome. These two individuals are not archaeologists, but it is wonderful to have these experts in diversity statistics summarize what is presently cutting edge in their field. Several archaeologist contributors have kept up to speed on these things (e.g., Bebber and Chao; Farahani and Sinensky; Faith and Du; Boulanger et al.), and they are to be commended.

Dunnell taught Leonard, Jones, me, and our fellow grad-students about the importance of classification and of the necessary articulation of formal theory (systematics) and explanatory theory. One of his favorite quotations—because it made the point so eloquently and in no uncertain terms—was penned by geneticist Richard Lewontin:

> It is not always appreciated that the problem of theory building is a constant interaction between constructing laws and finding an appropriate set of descriptive state variables such that laws can be constructed. We cannot go out and describe the world in any old way we please and then sit back and demand that an explanatory and predictive theory be built on that description. . . . There is a process of trial and synthesis going on . . . in which both state descriptions and laws are being fitted together. (Lewontin 1974: 8)

Sociologist Carlo Lastrucci made the same point a decade earlier, if not quite so plainly:

> The same facts [can obviously] be classified according to a variety of categories. . . . But there is no logically necessary reason why one type of classification is inherently superior to another; it depends upon the function the classification is to serve. Yet the function of a classificatory system can be rationalized only within the framework of a given theory . . . i.e., it is the theory [that] both justifies and gives meaning to the particular classification of facts. (Lastrucci 1963: 116)

The fascinating history of the (ongoing) development of chemistry's periodic table exemplifies the interaction between theory building and the construction of a classification that describes the phenomena of interest, provides explanations for the behaviors (e.g., associations, interactions) of those phenomena, and results in predictions (some accurate, some not, hence the "ongoing" development of this classification system) regarding unknown kinds of elements and the associations and interactions of particular elements (Scerri 1998, 2008). A recent call for the construction of a new classification of minerals, one that better captures the evolutionary history of planets and planetary systems than the current time-independent classification (Cleland, Hazen, and Morrison 2021), highlights the importance of not merely searching for elusive (and perhaps non-existent) "natural categories," but building, as Lewontin and Lastrucci emphasize, a classification system that serves a particular analytical purpose.

Because of Dunnell's emphasis on the fundamental importance of classification, it is likely that Leonard and Jones asked him to comment on the contributions to their book. Dunnell's (1989a) remarks are typical of his classroom lectures—deeply insightful, if tempered for publication and close public scrutiny. He noted good things about each chapter, but he also highlighted the weaknesses in many of them. The title of his chapter says it all: "Diversity in Archaeology: A Group of Measures in Search of Application?" In his view, there was too little concern among the contributors for the articulation of formal theory (classification) and explanatory theory, and minimal development of the latter with respect to artifacts and culture. The same old traditional artifact types, assemblages, components, units of whatever kind, were the things used to calculate diversity metrics (see also Cowgill's [1989] comments), and the explanations for those values were poorly linked to them theoretically. I perceive some improvement in this respect in Eren and Buchanan's collection (e.g., Kuhn's thoughtful suggestions), but I also perceive weaknesses (none of them insurmountable, if not easily surmounted), and it is to these I devote the remainder of my remarks.

A couple terms must be defined at the outset. I use the term *diversity* as a generic one that can mean any one or any combination of the three variables usually discussed under the topic of (archaeological) diversity: *richness* (the number of kinds or categories represented); *evenness* (the frequency distribution of specimens across the represented kinds); and *heterogeneity* (a combination of richness and evenness). The term *aggregate* means a combination of multiple individual things of the same scale; the scale can vary from combination to combination (e.g., from attributes of discrete objects, to discrete objects, to sets of discrete objects). Although the term *assemblage* is often found in the archaeological literature, and may be considered a synonym of how I have defined aggregate, the term *archaeological assemblage* is typically applied to sets of discrete objects (artifacts, ecofacts) thought to have implications above and beyond that of an aggregate (see below)—the distinction of the two will become important later. *Morphospace* refers to the total nature and range of formal variability—morphologies (shape), metrics (size), meristics (frequency), materials, etc.—that might be represented by an aggregate of specimens. *Measurement* is used as a synonym of description, and *metric* as a catchall or generic term for the various diversity statistics (e.g., Shannon index, Simpson index). *Systematics* refers to the hows, whys and results of classification, typology, and categorization.

The Importance of Units

Jones and Leonard argued that the term diversity is not a synonym for variation, but rather is a *measure* of variation. They cite statisticians who suggest that diversity, as generally defined in ecology, concerns "the nature or degree" (Jones and Leonard 1989: 2) of "apportionment of some quantity into a number of well-defined categories" (Patil and Taillie 1982: 548). Diversity metrics provide a quantitative measure of that "apportionment" or distribution of formal variation as it, in turn, has been measured by categories/classes/types of phenomena.

Reflecting (I believe) Dunnell's influence, Jones and Leonard emphasized that "the measurement of diversity rests on an unambiguous classification of the subject matter. This means that classes must be defined that are mutually exclusive, exhaustive, and composed at the same classificatory level" (Jones and Leonard 1989: 3). Mutually exclusive classes are those for which there is no chance any given specimen can be identified as more than one kind. An exhaustive set of classes is one in which all possible morphospace is included, such that all specimens in an aggregate can be categorized (which is not to say all defined classes will have empirical members; some may not). Same classificatory level refers to the fact that classes are equivalent in terms of the amount of morphospace each includes, and all classes are defined by the same combination of variables or attributes (also referred to as characters or dimensions). For instance, we would not want some categories to be exclusive and specific whereas others are inclusive and general (e.g., biological species *versus* biological genera; stone side-notched projectile points and stone corner-notched projectile points *versus* stone artifacts). I believe paradigmatic (Dunnell 1971) or dimensional classification is the best way, at least initially, to categorize or classify things (Lyman and O'Brien 2002; O'Brien and Lyman 2002). This is so because it meets the three requirements spelled out by Leonard and Jones, plus it forces analysts to be explicit about attributes (characters) and attribute states (character states) chosen (theoretically guided choices, preferably), and the units are clearly creations of the analyst and not dependent on the specimens under study (within the restriction of deciding you are classifying lithic projectile points, or ceramics, or bone fishhooks, and not a combination of formally disparate things such as baskets and bone tools).

Dunnell (1989a) identified two issues that plagued many of the contributions to the Leonard and Jones (1989) volume (see also Cowgill 1989). First was the minimal development and integration of explanatory theory with the classifications on which measures of diversity were founded; thus Dunnell commented, "most archaeological uses of diversity represent the application of a technique without a theoretical warrant" (Dunnell 1989a: 145). Simplistically, precisely what a particular value of a diversity metric signified in terms of human behavior (broadly construed) was not readily apparent for want of a theory linking archaeological observations with those behaviors. In this case, the observations are diversity metrics calculated on the basis of artifact types, and the human behavioral significance of some of the types is unclear. In their introduction to this volume, Buchanan and Eren (Chapter 1) highlight the absence of theory with their emphasis on testing multiple hypotheses; such rigorous testing will facilitate the building of archaeological diversity theory. Boulanger et al. (Chapter 9) are nearly uniquely explicit when they indicate that they are unsure what the diversity metrics they report mean, but they also go on to indicate that testable hypotheses can now be phrased in an effort to decipher those metrics. And though most other contributors list multiple possible explanations for the observations on diversity they report, I had the feeling they were fumbling a bit for want of a well-developed archaeological theory of diversity to help sort out the better and more appropriate hypotheses from those that simply accounted for the observed diversity metric(s).

The second issue Dunnell identified was that although the influence of the classifications and classificatory units used to measure diversity was recognized by most contributors to the Leonard and Jones volume, theoretical warrants for those units were not provided. In this new volume, Linnean biological taxa are the units used by some (Faith and Du; Farahani and Sinensky; Otárola-Castillo, Torquato, and Hill); these are very much industry standards in paleoethnobotany and zooarchaeology, but theoretical justification for use of these units to calculate diversity metrics here is difficult to find. One might think Linnean taxa, particularly species, are uncontroversial units in biology, but this is not at all true (Kenyon-Flatt 2021). Further, different categories such as skeletal parts (skulls *versus* vertebrae *versus* front leg bones *versus* hind leg bones) or plant parts (leaves, seeds, fruits, twigs) never enter the discussions here. In addition, given that animals are mobile, I wonder about the influence of the behaviors of the animals—regardless of species—on what is and what is not procured, regardless of taxonomic identity (e.g., Bird, Bird, and Codding 2009; Lyman 1989; Simmons and Ilany 1977; Stiner, Munro, and Surovell 2000). With respect to animals, Otárola-Castillo, Torquato, and Hill examine the diversity of body size classes of mammals as well as Linnean taxa, and that is good. However, they use body-size classes developed for Old World mammals rather than (for instance) Thomas's (1971) size classes developed for New World mammals. And, they do not apply any of the several statistical techniques for detecting gaps in empirical manifestations of continuous variables such as body mass (Lyman 2013, and references therein), so we are left to wonder about the basis for the boundaries between size classes (an aggregate boundary problem; see the next section). Both things—the classes themselves, and the boundaries between them—exemplify a lack of attention to theoretical linkages between classificatory units, research questions, and explanations. These observations are not meant to single out the efforts of Otárola-Castillo, Torquato, and Hill; their analyses are thoughtful and intriguing. I highlight their efforts here because their use of species as classificatory units is exceptionally well suited to illustrate the multifaceted slippery slope created by using categories or classes having little in the way of an explicit theoretical warrant.

Another indication of overlooking the importance of classificatory units is that only a couple of contributors provide sufficient information for the reader to know exactly of what the artifact types consist—the specific attributes and their combinations that define those types (Bebber and Chao; Andrews, Macdonald, and Morgan; Boulanger, Breslawski, and Jorgeson). One wonders how much the failure to delve deeply into the influence of systematics on measures of diversity can be held accountable for the seemingly groping search for an explanation of a calculated diversity metric, and the notices in several chapters that "more research is called for." And this raises a more general question: Why might a lack of concern for classification be present? In my view, this question pertains to archaeology in general, not just the study of archaeological diversity (reflecting Dunnell's influence on me).

The English language programmatic archaeological literature on systematics—its hows and whys, not its substantive studies (e.g., Hawley 1950; Perino 1971; Ritchie 1971; Suhm and Jelks 1962)—over the past one hundred years comprises a mere eight volumes (Adams and Adams 1991; Bonnichsen 1977; Dunnell 1971; Gardin 1970; Klejn 1982; Ramenofsky and Steffen 1998; Read 2007; Whallon and Brown 1982). Recent advanced texts focusing on modern archaeological method and theory typically include no discussion of the programmatics of systematics (Bentley, Maschner, and Chippindale 2008; Hodder 2012; Johnson 2020;

Prentiss 2019). And our introductory texts written for novices and wannabes (e.g., Fagan and Decorse 2005; Kelly and Thomas 2017; Renfrew and Bahn 2016) devote less than 3 percent of their pages to systematics (Lyman, unpublished data on 70 volumes). Perhaps I should not be surprised by the less than universal attention to systematics given by the contributors to this volume, or by archaeologists in general. If the literature summarized in this paragraph is an accurate barometer of the perceived (in)significance (or simple benign neglect) of archaeological systematics, I must conclude that archaeologists are simply not conditioned to think much about systematics—neither its analytical purposes nor its influences on analytical results.

Unfortunately, the problem is deeper than this. Even those who in the pages of this volume explicitly recognize and contend with the classification of artifacts largely ignore the systematics of larger units. Here I am thinking of assemblages, sites, and—in a few cases in this volume—large geographic regions containing multiple archaeological phenomena. It should be obvious that the boundaries of the aggregates of things for which measures of diversity are calculated will influence any diversity metric, because those boundaries dictate what is included in, and what is excluded from an aggregate. Given the near universal failure in this volume (Kuhn is a notable exception) to explicitly acknowledge the influence of the boundaries of the aggregates of things for which diversity metrics are calculated indicates this aspect of systematics warrants extended comment.

The Importance of Aggregates

Precisely how the spatial boundaries of a *site* are established is seldom explicit in textbook definitions of the concept (Table 11.1). Beginning about forty-five years ago, it was noted that the archaeological record is continuously distributed across landscapes, varying in its density of occurrence (Dancey 1974; Dunnell 1992; Dunnell and Dancey 1983; Foley 1981; Thomas 1975). This observation made explicit the fact that the spatial boundaries of an archaeological site are usually operationalized as some minimal density of artifacts per unit area: "a spatial *concentration* of material evidence of human activity" (Deetz 1967: 11, emphasis added). Of course, how dense is dense enough is an empirical matter. That is, the density of artifacts (broadly construed) will vary from spatio-temporal context to spatio-temporal context, and thus an analytical decision is required with respect to how dense is dense enough to argue a site is present at a particular location and has particular boundaries.

Table 11.1. Definitions of assemblage and site. Listed in chronological order of publication.

Assemblage (of artifacts)
- a set of artifacts "observed occurring together under conditions indicative of contemporary use" (Childe 1956b: 14–15)
- "all the artifacts (and the things used by man . . .) of a given culture in a given time and place" (Braidwood 1960: 173; see also Braidwood 1967: 84)
- "a spatial cluster of artifacts thought to represent something approaching a point in time" (Spaulding 1960: 450)
- "all the industries [chipped stone, ceramic, basketry, bone tool] taken together at one site" (Hole and Heizer 1966: 8)
- "an associated set of contemporary artefact-types; to be distinguished rigorously from the loose physical or geographical aggregate" (Clarke 1968: 665)
- "all the different artifacts found together in one layer, regardless of the materials from which they are made" (Hole and Heizer 1977: 381)
- "all artifacts of one culture or time period found within the context of an archaeological site" (Knudson 1978: 482)
- "all artifacts excavated at a site or from a specific recovery unit (for example, a burial assemblage)" (Rathje and Schiffer 1982: 390)
- "the whole set of artifacts representing the material culture inventory or repertoire used in a given cultural setting over a limited period of time" (Webster et al. 1993: 572) [sub-assemblage: "set of artifacts representing the tools used for a particular task" Webster et al. 1993: 583]
- "all of the artifacts, features, and other physical evidence (plant remains, animal remains, etc.) found in deposits associated with a single, continuous occupation of an archaeological site . . . sometimes treated as equivalent to 'collection,' extended to all the deposits from a site, or subdivided by type of material, as in 'faunal assemblage'" (Banning 2000: 294)
- "a gross grouping of all sub-assemblages assumed to represent the sum of human activities carried out within an ancient community" (Sharer and Ashmore 2003: G-2) [sub-assemblage: "a group of artifact classes, based on form and functional criteria, that is assumed to represent a single occupational group within an ancient community" Sharer and Ashmore 2003: G-15]
- "all the artifacts found at a site, including the sum of all sub-assemblages at the site" (Fagan and DeCorse 2005: 522) [sub-assemblage: "as association of artifacts denoting a particular form of activity practiced by a group of people" Fagan and DeCorse 2005: 533]
- "a related set of different things" (Price 2007: 111, G-1)
- "the entirety or individual subsets of the material culture recovered at an archaeological site or sites [can vary in terms of included material types, geographic space, or temporal duration]" Feder 2008: 404)
- "all of the materials—artifacts and ecofacts—collected from a site and representing all of the evidence of the activities at a site" (Sutton 2013: 363)
- "a group of artifacts recurring together at a particular time and place, and representing the sum of human activities" (Renfrew and Bahn 2016: 596)
- "a collection of artifacts of one or several classes of materials (stone tools, ceramics, bones) that comes from a defined context, such as a site, feature, or stratum" (Kelly and Thomas 2017: 358)

Site
- "the smallest unit of space dealt with by the archaeologists and the most difficult to define. Its physical limits, which may vary from a few square yards to as many square miles, are often impossible to fix. About the only requirement ordinarily demanded . . . is that [the site] be fairly continuously covered by remains of former occupation" (Willey and Phillips 1958: 18)
- "that place where an archaeologist digs. . . . a spatial concentration of material evidence of human activity" (Deetz 1967: 11)

(continued)

- "usually the scene of some past human activity" (Heizer and Graham 1967: 14)
- "location of archaeological remains" (Hole and Heizer 1977: 388)
- "any area where there is detectable evidence of past human activities" (Fladmark 1978: 1)
- "any area of the landscape that shows evidence of past human activities; a portion of the environment used by people" (Knudson 1978: 488)
- "a fairly continuous distribution of the remains of a former single unit of settlement" (Dancey 1981: 13)
- "a place that has material remains of human activities" (Rathje and Schiffer 1982: 396)
- "a spatially isolated area of concentrated archaeological remains, ranging from a scatter of stone fragments where someone sharpened a stone tool to cities inhabited for centuries" (Webster et al. 1993: 582)
- "a clustering of archaeological data, comprising artifacts, ecofacts, and features in any combination" (Sharer and Ashmore 2003: G-14)
- "any place where objects, features, or ecofacts manufactured or modified by human beings are found" (Fagan and DeCorse 2005: 532)
- "accumulation of artifacts and features, representing the places where people lived or carried out certain activities" (Price 2007: 112, G-10)
- "a place that people used in the past, and where physical evidence of their use of the place remains in the form of artifacts and/or ecofacts" (Feder 2008: 433)
- "a geographic locality where there is some evidence of past human activity, such as artifacts or features" (Sutton 2013: 368)
- "a distinct spatial clustering of artifacts, features, structures, and organic and environmental remains—the residue of human activity" (Renfrew and Bahn 2016: 603)
- "any place where material evidence exists about the human past; usually, 'site' refers to a concentration of such evidence" (Kelly and Thomas 2017: 358)

Assemblages of artifacts are often spatially bounded as well (Table 11.1). And rather than some minimum density of materials, typically a different variable is considered when specifying assemblage boundaries. To paraphrase Childe, an assemblage is a set of artifacts "observed occurring together under conditions indicative of contemporary use" (Childe 1956b: 14–15). More recently, Dibble et al. define an assemblage of lithic artifacts as "the totality of stone artifacts from a distinct context. Usually this context is defined geologically (e.g., a stratigraphic level), although anthropogenic features and certain techniques of excavation may also be used to define it" (Dibble et al. 2017: 830). Joyce and Pollard suggest the notion of an archaeological assemblage was founded on an early nineteenth-century geological concept of a "group of fossils distinctive of specific geological sediments" (Joyce and Pollard 2010: 295). In their view, the term took on its late twentieth-century archaeological connotations of a culturally and/or human behaviorally significant set of *associated* materials in the mid-twentieth century. (Exploring the history of the archaeological assemblage concept, including its apparent extra-disciplinary derivation, would likely prove to be not only a nifty project but a revealing one as well; it is beyond my scope here.)

Lucas observed the "concept of assemblage in archaeology is in many ways a very loose term, used in various ways, but two of its most common

meanings are a collection of objects associated on the basis of their depositional or spatial find-context, and a collection of one type of object found
within a site or area" (Lucas 2012: 193–97). He had in mind such things
as an assemblage from a stratum or a house floor as a depositional assemblage, and a lithic assemblage or ceramic assemblage as a typological (in
this case, material type) assemblage. Lucas went on to demonstrate that
both kinds of assemblage have spatial boundaries and the distinction between the two kinds of assemblage is a matter of analytical and interpretive emphasis. On the one hand, based on the unclear human behavioral
meaning of an assemblage of artifacts (plus its, to one degree or another,
time-averaged nature and its formational history including subtractive as
well as additive processes), some archaeologists suggest highly cautious
use of the term (Rezek et al. 2020). On the other hand, other archaeologists advocate broadening the concept to include aspects of an assemblage as a dynamically assembled, and potentially disassembled, aggregate
of phenomena (see papers introduced by Hamilakis and Jones 2017). All
of these suggestions deserve serious attention, particularly with respect to
measuring and interpreting the diversity of an aggregate/assemblage, but
my concern here is with the spatial boundaries of aggregates of whatever
kind or scale. How any given diversity metric is influenced by aggregate
boundaries is precisely why we need to think about those boundaries.

The industry standard of stratigraphic excavation (Lucas 2001; Praetzellis 1993) is recommended in introductory texts, and is emphasized in
advanced discussions of field methods (references in Ward, Winter, and
Dotte-Sarout 2016). In an otherwise important discussion of archaeological aggregates and their possible anthropological meaning, Kleindienst
(1967) overlooks the potential influence of stratigraphic boundaries on the
contents of aggregates of artifacts. This is typical of archaeology in general, although there is occasional recognition of the potential problems.
Ford (1962) was perhaps the first archaeologist working in the twentieth
century to explicitly question the validity of stratigraphic boundaries as *the*
means to define aggregates of artifacts within a site: "We must insist that
the vertical separation of potsherds and other cultural materials only by
the observable breaks in the deposit would be an archaeological variety of
cataclysmic geology.... It is as absurd to dig automatically in ten-centime-
ter levels as it is to separate collections only by visible stratification" (Ford
1962: 44). Clarke (1973: 14) comes close to making this point; Frankel
(1988) echoes Ford and cautions that stratigraphic excavation might make
culture change appear abrupt when in fact it was gradual; Lucas (2001:
167) states the problem, as do Dibble et al. (2017); and most recently Perreault (2019) explores some of the interpretive implications of differently
bounded aggregates (see Lyman 2003 for empirical examples). By using

stratigraphic boundaries to specify what is included and what is not included in an aggregate of artifacts conceived as an assemblage, we have bounded the aggregate extensionally, empirically, and in a way that has no necessary relationship to the variable, the diversity of which is of analytical interest. In short, theory behind the definition of aggregates—how and why to specify their boundaries in particular ways—does not exist.

Stratigraphic boundaries are analytically convenient, but they may be interpretively (theoretically) treacherous in the sense of creating aggregates the diversities of which have little to do with the properties of interest (Dunnell 2008). Although at a different level than the large aggregates under consideration here, visualize the model of temporally continuous variation in cultural phenomena, say a lineage of artifacts. How do we parse up that continuous variability into meaningful units? Paleontologists and archaeologists alike often utilize stratigraphic breaks and discontinuities as convenient boundaries between aggregates of phenomena that, when the average (or mode) of each aggregate is determined, have what seem to be discrete kinds representing discontinuous change (Figure 11.1). The kinds are, however, accidents of how a continuum has been sampled; they are accidents relative to culture change (the variable of interest) because they have been created by (potentially independent) geological processes (the variable bounding the aggregates).

Another way to highlight the importance of aggregate definition also reveals an aspect of diversity recognized by biologists that has, for the most part, gone unremarked in the chapters here; Kuhn is a notable exception. This aspect has much to do with specifying the boundaries of the aggregates whose diversity is the subject of interest. Ecologist Robert Whittaker (1960, 1972, 1975) distinguished and defined three kinds of diversity. Alpha (a) diversity concerns the variable as manifest within a biological community. Beta (b) diversity concerns difference (or similarity) in diversity across multiple communities, or between-community diversity; it can be measured across geographic space, or time, or both. Gamma (g) diversity is measured over a combination of communities; it can be thought of as regional, multi-community diversity (in contrast to that of a single community). That alpha diversity and gamma diversity (measures of inventory) vary in scale (inclusiveness) has long been recognized, as has the rather different nature of beta diversity (measures of similarity and/or difference) (Figure 11.2). These properties fostered debate about what exactly was being measured, how best to measure whatever it was that was being measured, and even if, whatever it was, was worthy of study (e.g., Gorelick 2011; Jurasinski and Koch 2011; Jurasinski, Retzer, and Beierkuhnlein 2009; Moreno and Rodríguez 2010, 2011; Tuomisto 2010a, 2010b, 2010c, 2011). This debate highlights the extreme complexity of the notion of di-

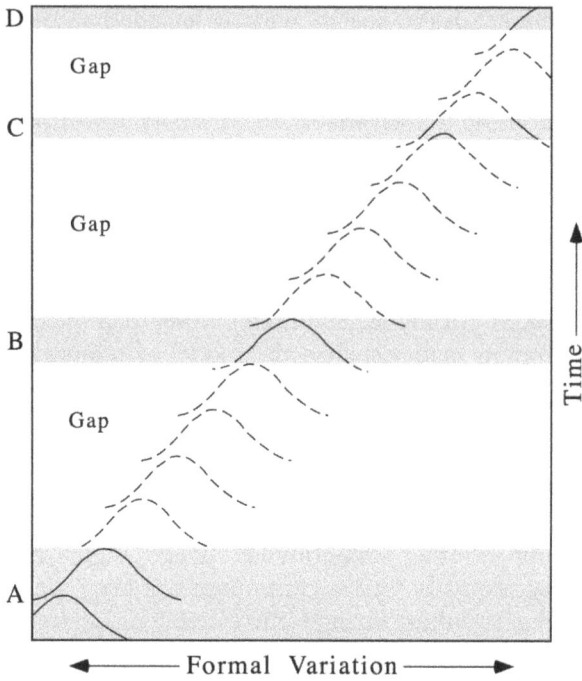

Figure 11.1. Paleontological model of how gaps in the stratigraphic record create gaps in the fossil record that can be conveniently used as boundaries between species. Each shaded bar labeled with a capital letter represents a stratum; each "gap" represents missing populations and strata. Each unimodal curve represents a population and its included formal variation; solid portions of each curve represent the parts of the population that are present; dashed portions of the curve represent the parts of the population that are absent from the fossil record. After Newell 1956. © The author.

versity within ecology and biology—where the concept has seen intensive examination (Maclaurin and Sterelny 2008), and where it is clearly understood that different metrics emphasize different variables making up a particular measure of diversity—and underscore that uncritical adoption of the concept(s) of diversity could lead to all sorts of problems in archaeology. To put a fine point on it, richness, as noted earlier, is generally defined as the number of kinds represented in an aggregate, so one would think richness should be a straightforward metric to calculate—a simple tally of types. But unbeknownst to many, richness can be calculated in several different ways (e.g., Alroy 2020; Gaston 1996; see Hiscock 2002 for discussion of factors that influence tallies of artifacts and thus, likely, the richness of types). Which one is appropriate in a given situation is not always clear. No wonder building explanatory theory is difficult in the home field of diversity (Whittaker, Willis, and Field 2001). And no won-

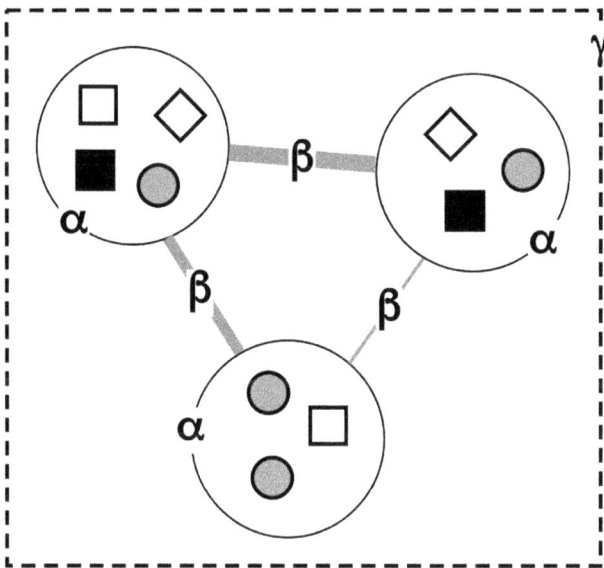

Figure 11.2. Illustration of alpha (α), beta (β), and gamma (γ) diversity. Each large circle represents an aggregate such as an artifact assemblage, and each symbol (open squares, diamonds, etc.) within a circle represents a different category (e.g., artifact type). The dashed box encloses all assemblages, and might represent a stratum or a site. For simplicity, diversity is calculated as richness. Alpha diversity is calculated for each assemblage (= 2, 3, or 4); gamma diversity is calculated for all assemblages combined (= 4); the magnitude of beta diversity, calculated as shared types, varies from one pair of assemblages to the next (= 1, 2, or 3) and is signified by the breadth of the gray line connecting two assemblages (greater breadth signifies more shared types). Modified after Jurasinski et al. 2009. © The author.

der archaeology does not seem to have progressed very far in constructing an explanatory theory of artifact diversity.

Concerning aggregate units, what might the differences between alpha and gamma diversity have to do with archaeology? Given the concepts were developed to label the diversity of one or more biological communities, what is a community? It should be clear a community is some kind of aggregate of organisms, but what kind? One widely accepted definition is that a community is "a group of organisms occurring in a particular environment, presumably interacting with each other and with the environment, and separable by means of ecological survey from other groups" (Mills 1969: 1427; see also Faith and Lyman 2019: 18–21). It is generally acknowledged today that the boundaries of adjacent communities can vary from rather distinct, abrupt, and obvious to relatively diffuse and imperceptible (Figure 11.3). Archaeological units, not unlike a biological com-

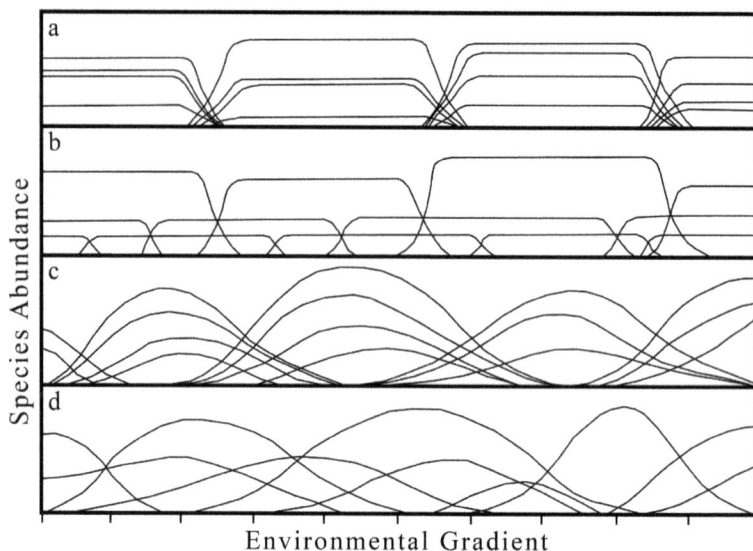

Figure 11.3. Models of variability in the abruptness of biological community boundaries along an environmental gradient. Each curve represents the frequency distribution of a species along the environmental gradient: (A) boundaries between communities are abrupt and self-evident; (B) boundaries between communities are diffuse and not apparent; (C) boundaries between communities are diffuse but evident; and (D) boundaries between communities are diffuse and not apparent. Note that each frequency curve could represent frequencies of a kind of artifact across geographic space (e.g., think site boundaries along the x-axis) or over time (e.g., think assemblage boundaries without stratigraphic breaks along the x-axis). After Whittaker 1975. © The author.

munity, are artifact assemblages and archaeological sites (Table 11.1). The archaeologist specifies the boundaries of each, whether aided by stratigraphic boundaries or not. The set of artifacts, features, ecofacts, whatever, in the aggregate is *inferred* to have some human behavioral significance, whether taphonomically skewed, time averaged, or representing a sample rather than a population (all things considered in depth by Farahani and Sinensky). With respect to the scale of aggregates, authors herein tend to keep their aggregates at the same scale when comparing diversity metrics, and that is as it should be. What is not considered sufficiently is what the implications might be if an archaeologist were to think they were measuring alpha diversity—however defined in terms of scale—rather than gamma diversity (or vice versa); and keep in mind that beta diversity concerns difference (or similarity) across space and/or change (or stasis) over time between either measures of alpha diversity or measures of gamma diversity.

Do not take the heading of this section, "The importance of aggregates," as suggesting that aggregates are not units in the same sense as the preceding section with the heading "The importance of units." In structuring the several previous pages in two distinct sections, I hope to underscore that artifacts as (often) discrete portable objects (e.g., Paleoindian projectile points, "Old Copper" projectile points, parfleces) and features, a term usually reserved for non-portable artifacts (e.g., floor plans, fire hearths, cache pits), are archaeological units of a smaller level than an archaeological unit at the level of an aggregate of such things. And while, as noted earlier, several authors in this volume display cognizance of the importance of classification of the lower levels (artifact, feature), several authors use higher level units (aggregates) ranging from ethnographic culture areas (Lycett), to physiographic units (Boulanger, Breslawski, and Jorgeson), to archaeologically delimited areas (Bebber and Chao), to continents (Andrews, Macdonald, and Morgan). Although warrants for using these kinds of units are offered, why these sorts of aggregates might be theoretically appropriate in terms of explanatory theory is given minimal consideration. This likely contributes to my impression of some fumbling and groping.

On to the Future

The contributions in this volume go some distance towards improving on what we thought we knew about archaeological diversity thirty years ago. It is clear the statistics have been improved considerably, and they are much more accessible (and diverse) via freeware. And we have come far in terms of figuring out exactly what some of the diversity metrics are tracking, and what they may mean in terms of biodiversity, ecology, biological evolution, and the like. But it should also be clear from close study of the chapters in this volume that archaeology still has some distance to go with respect to figuring out what particular values of selected diversity metrics actually mean in terms of human behaviors. Part of this difficulty resides in the too infrequent attention to archaeological systematics, both at the level of the phenomena being classified (e.g., stone tool use wear, stone projectile points, house floors) and at the level of the aggregates of things for which a diversity metric is desired. Why have we not progressed very far with respect to systematics or theory building?

The general disciplinary failure to deeply consider systematics—whether studying diversity or something else—seems to be at least partially a result of insufficient training regarding the fundamentals, the nuances, and the significance of systematics (Bingqi 1988 made a similar suggestion in a different context). My impression (and that is surely all it is at the moment) is that much of the literature on archaeological systematics that has appeared in the past couple decades indicates more interest in developing computer algorithms for sorting artifacts into types than consideration of the need for theory-guided classification, or the analytical goal of a particular classification. As noted above, paradigmatic classification forces one to think about attribute choice—do I want types that mark the passage of time, that distinguish spatial units of some scale, that monitor cultural transmission pathways, that track variability in resource extraction and/or processing? In short, what analytical work do I want my types to allow me to perform? Paradigmatic classes can be constructed such that each represents the same amount of hyperdimensional morphospace. This is critically important to the study of diversity. Think about the difference between change from two formally equivalent classes (1–2.9 cm long, and 3.0–4.9 cm long) to four formally equivalent classes that capture different amounts of morphospace than the first two classes (e.g., 1–1.9 cm long, 2.0–2.9 cm long, 3.0–3.9 cm long, and 4.0–4.9 cm long). There has indeed been a change in diversity (richness) from two kinds to four kinds, but that is a function of how formal variability has been parsed into units. Quantitative attributes (e.g., length, edge angle) capturing equal amounts of morphospace will be easy to specify; qualitative attributes (e.g., concave *versus* straight *versus* convex blade edge of a stone projectile point) will of course be more difficult to define in equal morphospace units, but thoughtful consideration should keep the magnitude of variability encompassed by distinct character states to a minimum. To reiterate, constructing a paradigmatic classification forces one to think about many very important things about systematics.

Diversity is a quantitative descriptive attribute of an aggregate of phenomena. The concept was developed for biota, specifically species. For an archaeologist to say the diversity of forms of artifacts (of whatever scale) reflects human behaviors presumes a one-to-one correspondence between the diversity of artifacts and the diversity of human behaviors. There is little in the way of robust theory to explain the diversity of human behaviors (but see Hamilton, Walker, and Kempes 2020), and there are very few middle-range theory linkages justifying the supposed correspondence between artifacts and behaviors. Theory building is going to be difficult. We need theory regarding the empirical manifestations of diversity—of whatever sort—in artifacts. Biologists and ecologists continue to study the empirical world, continue to argue about and develop ecological and biological units (e.g., communities, life zones, species), and continue to perfect quantitative metrics to build formal and explanatory theory. What should archaeologists do? We have had some success in figuring things out about the past by borrowing analytical techniques, models and theories from other disciplines. Some success has been attained in the study of cultural data by borrowing diversity theory from biology and ecology (e.g., ibid.). Similarly, as several chapters in this volume suggest, we need to be cognizant of cultural transmission theory as it provides some intriguing implications for the spatio-temporal distribution of kinds of material culture.

I suggest we focus some attention on discussions of diversity in paleontology. Significant insights to the history of life have come from studies of life's diversity by paleontologists (see Dunne 2018 for a brief introduction to the history of studying paleobiological diversity). I am not here trying to slyly advocate the adoption of Darwinian evolutionary theory as the explanatory theory of choice (e.g., O'Brien and Lyman 2000), though I do believe this theory in its current manifestations (Prentiss 2019) will facilitate building (and be some part of) a robust archaeological theory of diversity. Rather, I am suggesting archaeologists interested in studying (artifact) diversity should read the paleobiology literature, because this will likely save us much trial and error, and indicate ways to avoid repetition of mistakes already corrected. Paleontologists have, for instance, figured out which questions can be answered by the (temporal, spatial, formal) resolution of the available data, such as rates and causes of diversification and extinction at macroscales (as opposed to genetic, between-generation scales). Archaeologists have long acknowledged they study variability in artifact form (broadly construed) across time and space (e.g., Childe 1956a; Spaulding 1960; Willey 1953). Recent work in paleontology reveals intriguing patterns when simultaneous covariation of taxonomic richness (a measure of formal diversity and morphological diversity) with space and time is examined (e.g., Du and Behrensmeyer 2018; Louys, Price, and Travouillon 2021). Many of these patterns are readily accounted for by calling upon ecological and evolutionary theory. This is not to say we should mimic exactly what paleobiologists have done (even though we might analytically treat each artifact type as equivalent to a biological taxon or morphotype), but instead we can ask similar questions regarding the history of artifact typological diversity and morphological disparity (e.g., Lyman 2021b), invoke similar explanatory mechanisms (e.g., Close et al. 2019; Hautmann 2014), use similar sample assessment tools (e.g., Barnosky, Carrasco, and Davis 2005; Close et al. 2020), and even use similar graphs to analyze our data and to summarize what we have learned (e.g., Lyman 2019, 2021a). In the immediately preceding lines, I have cited a few articles that, together with the literature cited therein, provide an introduction to the paleobiological diversity literature.

To build just a bit on the issue of aggregates, these can be defined at virtually any scale or level. Biologists, for instance, recognize diversity within a community (alpha diversity), between communities (whether temporally or spatially segregated; beta diversity), within a landscape (gamma diversity), between landscapes (another scale of beta diversity), and within a biogeographic region (another scale of gamma diversity) (Whittaker 1977).

Archaeologists have long studied spatial variation and/or temporal change at all sorts of scales and resolutions, such as attributes of artifacts, artifacts as discrete objects, assemblages of artifacts, within and between site collections, variability across physiographic regions, differences between cultural areas, and other kinds of units and aggregates. Again, consultation of the paleobiological literature may provide guidance as to what might be reasonable questions to ask, and what the relevant scales of the studied analytical units (things, and aggregates of things) ought to be. Finally, we need to keep foremost in mind that "diversity is relative, and always constrained by method of measurement" (Shade 2017: 2). Insight results from comparison of diversity measures on different aggregates, noting similarities and differences in not only diversity metrics, but in contextual properties and sample sizes as well. We need to deeply consider which metric is appropriate given data quality (see Perreault 2019); Magurran (2004) provides an excellent introduction to many of the available diversity metrics.

As Eren and Buchanan note, there has been an apparent drop in interest in archaeological diversity over the past thirty years. This has likely contributed to less development of theory and less awareness of the significance of systematics than I had hoped for when I began to read this collection. In the middle to late 1980s, diversity (typically measured as richness, or as heterogeneity using the Shannon index, sometimes referred to as the Shannon–Weaver index) was something of a bandwagon onto which a large number of people wanted to climb. That bandwagon causes me to recall James Moore and Arthur Keene's "Archaeology and the law of the hammer": "Stated in its most elementary form, the law predicts that given a hammer, a young child will find that the world is poundable" (Moore and Keene 1983: 4). They go on to emphasize that a hammer is a tool, just as analytical methods are tools. And "methods, like tools, can be abused. The most obvious form of abuse involves using methods not because they fit the task at hand, but because they are methods we know and can easily apply" (ibid.). Part of the history of using diversity metrics in archaeology involved efforts to operationalize Binford's (1980) distinction of foragers and collectors in terms of artifact diversity. Measures of artifact richness were quite easy to determine and to compare. How many types of artifacts are represented in Assemblage X? Is that more, the same, or less than the number of types in Assemblage Y? And how about Assemblage Z? That those metrics might mean your assemblage represented a resource extraction camp used by foragers as opposed to a residential base used by collectors, well, that was *significant* in terms of the implicated human behaviors. The explanatory theory for diversity metrics was incompletely developed at the time, and seems to have not been developed much further today.

An as yet partially developed example of the interplay of units and theory building may enhance the points I have sought to make. A sketch of the example is all that is necessary. David L. Clarke (1968: 126) suggested "the apparent regulatory or insulator capacity of a culture system is proportional to its variety." That is, the greater the number of kinds of artifacts, the better a culture can mediate the effects of fluctuation in environment (broadly construed). Thus, "a rough relative measure of the regulatory or insulator control capacity of a culture system would be the number of differentiable artefact-types made by that system" (ibid.: 127). Clarke does not indicate the kind of units or types that would be appropriate. If I were working with stone tools, I would construct a paradigmatic classification of functional types (Steward 1954; Thomas 1974: 8–10) based on the use-wear damage evident on specimens (Dunnell 1978a, 1978b). Use wear is manifest as attributes resulting from artificial motion (Dunnell 1978a). Wear is empirical. If an object shows wear, it has been used, and if it has been used, it has (had) a function. Wear is thus equivalent to function. This is relational analogy (Hodder 1982) based on immanent properties and processes (Simpson 1970)—those that are not historically contingent, such as chemical and mechanical properties. Configurational (Simpson 1970) or formal (Hodder 1982) analogical reasoning is required if one wishes to attribute a particular function (e.g., cutting, scraping, piercing, engraving) to an item. Formal analogy is also (at least at present) required by those concerned with inferring the sort of material a stone tool edge has come in contact with, such as Stemp and Macdonald, hence their multiple calls for more experimental work.

The particular classification I would use is one developed by Dunnell (1978a) and his students (Beck and Jones 1989; Dunnell and Beck 1979; Dunnell and Campbell 1977; Jones, Grayson, and Beck 1983). Categories or classes are based on attributes (character states) of macroscopic edge and/or surface damage. The nature and position of damage is recorded (described) without any attempt to determine the specific function or behavior (e.g., cutting meat, scraping hides, engraving bone) that produced the damage. A particular discrete object may have been used in multiple ways (think a Swiss Army knife), so a single object may display multiple kinds of wear. Each damaged edge of a specimen is recorded as a "tool," thus the number of tools will be equal to or exceed the number of lithic specimens. The dimensions (characters) recorded are: kind of damage, location of damage, shape of damaged area, edge angle, and orientation of damage. The operating assumption is that the recorded damage represents wear related to use of the tool to undertake some activity. The empirical test implication to ensure the documented kinds of edge damage are not the result of some natural (non-human) process is that the classes represented by specimens should vary in diversity (which ones *are* represented) coincident with variability in the selective environment, whether across space or through time (Dunnell 1978a). The implication is based on the theory of the interaction of people with resources; different resources require different forms of human actions and tool morphologies in order for those resources to be extracted and processed or rendered humanly usable/consumable. Breadth of diversity of the represented functional classes (Clarke's concern) is expected to vary with the predictability and severity of environmental perturbations (Dunnell 1989b). Regardless of what people might *intend*, those populations with greater functional diversity of tools should be prevalent relative to those populations with less functional diversity in environments that fluctuate widely and unpredictably; the former have, as Clarke (1968) argued, a marked insurance buffer against such environments. Those without marked functional diversity in resource extraction and processing tools will have a less effective insurance policy, and selection will weed them out. Ethnographic evidence indicates that tool diversity and environment are related in complex ways (Collard et al. 2011), but Clarke's notion is a reasonable place to start.

Counting things and calculating indices of abundances (such as diversity metrics) is easy, and the increasing availability of computers—plus a dose of statistical knowledge—facilitates the calculations and manipulations of those abundances and indices. Further, there is seductive attractiveness to the idea that a shift from nominal to ordinal to interval/ratio scales of measurement is a hallmark of becoming scientific; seductive because such a shift (allegedly) makes observations more objective and less subjective, and also (allegedly) renders our observations more exact and precise (Porter 1995). As should now be clear from this chapter, while these things may be true in some cases, they are not necessarily true. Until we have robust theory, what those insights actually comprise (what diversity metrics mean in terms of human behaviors) will likely be controversial if not simply obscure. Important steps have been taken in this volume, as some initial baby steps were thirty years ago by Leonard and Jones and their colleagues. But many more steps are required. This will not be a sprint; it will be a marathon. However, I firmly believe that the finish line is attainable, and that the requisite effort to get there will be worth it.

Acknowledgments

I thank Metin Eren and Briggs Buchanan for the invitation and their faith in my abilities. Many of my ideas on archaeological systematics were initiated by the teachings of Robert C. Dunnell and honed by collaborations with both him and Michael J. O'Brien. My understanding of and interest in diversity and sampling was begun by lectures delivered by Donald K. Grayson. Subsequent discussions with students and colleagues too numerous to mention helped perfect my thinking.

R. Lee Lyman is Professor Emeritus at the University of Missouri, Columbia, USA.

References

Adams, W. Y., and E. W. Adams. 1991. *Archaeological Typology and Practical Reality.* Cambridge: Cambridge University Press.

Alroy, J. 2020. "On Four Measures of Taxonomic Richness." *Paleobiology* 46: 158–75.

Banning, E. B. 2000. *The Archaeologist's Laboratory: The Analysis of Archaeological Data.* New York: Springer.

Barnosky, A. D., M. A. Carrasco, and E. B. Davis. 2005. "The Impact of the Species–Area Relationship on Estimates of Paleodiversity." *Plos Biology* 3: e266.

Beck, C., and G. T. Jones. 1989. "Bias and Archaeological Classification." *American Antiquity* 54: 244–62.

Bentley, R. A., H. D. G. Maschner, and C. Chippindale, eds. 2008. *Handbook of Archaeological Theories.* Lanham, MD: AltaMira Press.

Binford, L. R. 1980. "Willow Smoke and Dogs' Tails: Hunter-Gatherer Settlement Systems and Archaeological Site Formation." *American Antiquity* 45: 4–20.

Bingqi, S. 1988. "New Issues in Archaeological Typology." *Chinese Sociology and Anthropology* 20: 68–72.

Bird, Douglas W., R. B. Bird, and B. F. Codding. 2009. "In Pursuit of Mobile Prey: Martu Hunting Strategies and Archaeofaunal Interpretation." *American Antiquity* 74: 3–29.

Bonnichsen, R. 1977. *Models for Deriving Cultural Information from Stone Tools.* Mercury Series, Archaeological Survey of Canada Paper no. 60. Ottawa: National Museum of Man.

Braidwood, R. J. 1960. *Archaeologists and What They Do.* New York: Franklin Watts.

———. 1967. *Prehistoric Men,* seventh edition. Glenview: Scott, Foresman, and Company.

Childe, V. G. 1956a. *Piecing Together the Past: The Interpretation of Archaeological Data.* London: Routledge & Kegan Paul.

———. 1956b. *A Short Introduction to Archaeology.* London: Frederick Muller.

Clarke, D. L. 1968. *Analytical Archaeology.* London: Methuen.

———. 1973. "Archaeology: The Loss of Innocence." *Antiquity* 47: 6–18.

Cleland, C. E., R. M. Hazen, and S. M. Morrison. 2021. "Historical Natural Kinds and Mineralogy: Systematizing Contingency in the Context of Necessity." *Proceedings of the National Academy of Science USA* 118: e2015370118.

Close, R. A., R. B. J. Benson, J. Alroy, A. K. Behrensmeyer, J. Benito, M. T. Carrano, T. J. Cleary, E. M. Dunne, P. D. Mannion, M. D. Uhen, and R. J. Butler. 2019. "Diversity Dynamics of Phanerozoic Terrestrial Tetrapods at the Local-Community Scale." *Nature Ecology and Evolution* 3: 590–97.

Close, R. A., R. B. J. Benson, J. Alroy, M. T. Carrano, T. J. Cleary, E. M. Dunne, P. D. Mannion, M. D. Uhen, and R. J. Butler. 2020. "The Apparent Exponential Radiation of

Phanerozoic Land Vertebrates is an Artefact of Spatial Sampling Biases." *Proceedings of the Royal Society B* 287: 20200372.

Collard, M., B. Buchanan, J. Morin, and A. Costopoulos. 2011. "What Drives the Evolution of Hunter-Gatherer Subsistence Technology? A Reanalysis of the Risk Hypothesis with Data from the Pacific Northwest." *Philosophical Transactions of the Royal Society B* 366: 1129–38.

Cowgill, G. L. 1989. "The Concept of Diversity in Archaeological Theory." In *Quantifying Diversity in Archaeology*, ed. R. D. Leonard and G. T. Jones, 131–41. Cambridge: Cambridge University Press.

Dancey, W. S. 1974. "The Archeological Survey: A Reorientation." *Man in the Northeast* 8: 98–112.

———. 1981. *Archaeological Field Methods: An Introduction*. Minneapolis, MN: Burgess.

Deetz, J. 1967. *Invitation to Archaeology*. Garden City, NY: Natural History Press.

Dibble, H. L., S. J. Holdaway, S. C. Lin, D. R. Braun, M. J. Douglass, R. Iovita, S. P. McPherron, D. I. Olszewski, and D. Sandgathe. 2017. "Major Fallacies Surrounding Stone Artifacts and Assemblages." *Journal of Archaeological Method and Theory* 24: 813–51.

Du, A., and A. K. Behrensmeyer. 2018. "Spatial, Temporal and Taxonomic Scaling in Richness in an Eastern African Large Scale Community." *Global Ecology and Biogeography* 27: 1031–42.

Dunne, E. 2018. "Patterns in Palaeontology: How Do We Measure Biodiversity in the Past?" *Paleontology Online* 8: 8.

Dunnell, R. C. 1971. *Systematics in Prehistory*. New York: Free Press.

———. 1978a. "Archaeological Potential of Anthropological and Scientific Models of Function." In *Archaeological Essays in Honor of Irving B. Rouse*, ed. R. C. Dunnell and E. S. Hall Jr., 41–73. The Hague: Mouton.

———. 1978b. "Style and Function: A Fundamental Dichotomy." *American Antiquity* 43: 192–202.

———. 1989a. "Diversity in Archaeology: A Group of Measures in Search of Application?" In *Quantifying Diversity in Archaeology*, ed. R. D. Leonard and G. T. Jones, 142–49. Cambridge: Cambridge University Press.

———. 1989b. "Aspects of the Application of Evolutionary Theory in Archaeology." In *Archaeological Thought in America*, ed. C. C. Lamberg-Karolvsky, 35–49. Cambridge: Cambridge University Press.

———. 1992. "The Notion Site." In *Space, Time, and Archaeological Landscapes*, ed. J. Rossignol and L. Wandsnider, 21–41. New York: Plenum Press.

———. 2008. "Archaeological Things: Languages of Observation." In *Time's River: Archaeological Syntheses from the Lower Mississippi River Valley*, ed. J. Rafferty and E. Peacock, 45–68. Tuscaloosa: University of Alabama Press.

Dunnell, R. C., and C. Beck. 1979. "The Caples Site, 45-SA-5, Skamania County, Washington." Reports in Archaeology no. 6. Seattle: University of Washington.

Dunnell, R. C., and S. K. Campbell. 1977. "Aboriginal Occupation of Hamilton Island, Washington." Reports in Archaeology no. 4. Seattle: University of Washington.

Dunnell, R. C., and W. S. Dancey. 1983. "The Siteless Survey: A Regional Data Collection Strategy." In *Advances in Archaeological Method and Theory*, Vol. 4, ed. M. B. Schiffer, 267–87. New York: Academic Press.

Fagan, B. M., and C. R. Decorse. 2005. *In the Beginning: An Introduction to Archaeology*, eleventh edition. Upper Saddle River, NJ: Pearson/Prentice Hall.

Faith, J. T., and R. L. Lyman. 2019. *Paleozoology and Paleoenvironments: Fundamentals, Assumptions, Techniques*. Cambridge: Cambridge University Press.

Feder, K. L. 2008. *Linking to the Past: A Brief Introduction to Archaeology*, second edition. New York: Oxford University Press.

Fladmark, K. R. 1978. *A Guide to Basic Archaeological Field Procedures*. Publication no. 4. Burnaby: Simon Fraser University.

Foley, R. 1981. "Off-Site Archaeology: An Alternative Approach for the Short-Sited." In *Pattern of the Past: Studies in Honour of David Clarke*, ed. I. Hodder, G. Isaac, and N. Hammond, 157–83. Cambridge: Cambridge University Press.

Ford, J. A. 1962. *A Quantitative Method for Deriving Cultural Chronology*. Technical Manual No. 1. Washington DC: Pan American Union.

Frankel, D. 1988. "Characterizing Change in Prehistoric Sequences: A View from Australia." *Archaeology in Oceania* 23: 41–48.

Gardin, J.-C., ed. 1970. *Archeologie et Calculateurs: Problèmes Sémiologiques et Mathématiques*. Paris: Centre Nationale de Recherche Scientifique.

Gaston, K. J. 1996. "Species Richness: Measure and Measurement." In *Biodiversity: A Biology of Numbers and Difference*, ed. K. J. Gaston, 77–113. Oxford: Blackwell Scientific.

Gorelick, R. 2011. "Commentary: Do We Have a Consistent Terminology for Species Diversity? The Fallacy of True Diversity." *Oecologia* 167: 885–88.

Hamilakis, Y., and A. M. Jones. 2017. "Archaeology and Assemblage." *Cambridge Archaeological Journal* 27: 77–84.

Hamilton, M. J., R. S. Walker, and C. P. Kempes. 2020. "Diversity Begets Diversity in Mammal Species and Human Cultures." *Scientific Reports* 10: 19654.

Hautmann, M. 2014. "Diversification and Diversity Partitioning." *Paleobiology* 40: 162–76.

Hawley, F. M. 1950. *Field Manual of Prehistoric Southwestern Pottery Types*, revised edition. Albuquerque: University of New Mexico Bulletin 291.

Heizer, R. F., and J. A. Graham. 1967. *A Guide to Field Methods in Archaeology: Approaches to the Anthropology of the Dead*. Palo Alto, CA: National Press.

Hiscock, P. 2002. "Quantifying the Size of Artefact Assemblages." *Journal of Archaeological Science* 29: 251–58.

Hodder, I. 1982. *The Present Past: An Introduction to Anthropology for Archaeologists*. London: B. T. Batsford.

———, ed. 2012. *Archaeological Theory Today*, second edition. Cambridge: Polity Press.

Hole, F. A., and R. F. Heizer. 1966. *An Introduction to Prehistoric Archeology*. New York: Holt, Rinehart and Winston.

———. 1977. *Prehistoric Archeology: A Brief Introduction*. New York: Holt, Rinehart and Winston.

Johnson, M. 2020. *Archaeological Theory: An Introduction*, third edition. Oxford: Blackwell.

Jones, G. T., D. K. Grayson, and C. Beck. 1983. "Artifact Class Richness and Sample Size in Archaeological Surface Assemblages." In *Lulu Linear Punctated: Essays in Honor of George Irving Quimby*, ed. R. C. Dunnell and D. K. Grayson, 55–73. Ann Arbor: University of Michigan Anthropological Papers no. 72.

Jones, G. T., and R. D. Leonard. 1989. "The Concept of Diversity: An Introduction." In *Quantifying Diversity in Archaeology*, ed. R. D. Leonard and G. T. Jones, 1–3. Cambridge: Cambridge University Press.

Joyce, R., and J. Pollard. 2010. "Archaeological Assemblages and Practices of Deposition." In *The Oxford Handbook of Material Culture Studies*, ed. D. Hicks and M. C. Beaudry, 291–309. Oxford: Oxford University Press.

Jurasinski, G., and M. Koch. 2011. "Commentary: Do We Have a Consistent Terminology for Species Diversity? We Are on the Way." *Oecologia* 167: 893–902.

Jurasinski, G., V. Retzer, and C. Beierkuhnlein. 2009. "Inventory, Differentiation, and Proportional Diversity: A Consistent Terminology for Quantifying Species Diversity." *Oecologia* 159: 15–26.

Kelly, R L., and D. H. Thomas. 2017. *Archaeology*, seventh edition. Boston, MA: Cengage Learning.

Kenyon-Flatt, B. 2021. "What Makes a Bird a Bird and a Beetle a Beetle: Biological Classification in the 21st Century." *Evolutionary Anthropology* 29(6): 346–47.

Kleindienst, M. R. 1967. "Questions of Terminology in Regard to the Study of Stone Age Industries in Eastern Africa: 'Cultural Stratigraphic Units.'" In *Background to Evolution in Africa*, ed. W. W. Bishop and J. D. Clark, 821–59. Chicago: University of Chicago Press.

Klejn, L. S. 1982. *Archaeological Typology*. Oxford: BAR International Series 153.

Knudson, S. J. 1978. *Culture in Retrospect: An Introduction to Archaeology*. Prospect Heights, IL: Waveland Press.

Kuhn, T. S. 1977. *The Essential Tension: Selected Studies in Scientific Tradition and Change*. Chicago: University of Chicago Press.

Lastrucci, C. L. 1963. *The Scientific Approach: Basic Principles of the Scientific Method*. Cambridge, MA: Schenkman Publishing Company, Inc.

Leonard, R. D., and G. T. Jones, eds. 1989. *Quantifying Diversity in Archaeology*. Cambridge: Cambridge University Press.

Lewontin, R. C. 1974. *The Genetic Basis of Evolutionary Change*. New York: Columbia University Press.

Louys, J., G. J. Price, and K. J. Travouillon. 2021. "Space–Time Equivalence in the Fossil Record, with a Case Study from Pleistocene Australia." *Quaternary Science Reviews* 253: 106764.

Lucas, G. 2001. *Critical Approaches to Fieldwork: Contemporary and Historical Archaeological Practice*. London: Routledge.

———. 2012. *Understanding the Archaeological Record*. Cambridge: Cambridge University Press.

Lyman, R. L. 1989. "Seal and Sea Lion Hunting: A Zooarchaeological Study from the Southern Northwest Coast of North America." *Journal of Anthropological Archaeology* 8: 68–99.

———. 2003. "The Influence of Time and Space Averaging on the Application of Foraging Theory in Zooarchaeology." *Journal of Archaeological Science* 30: 595–610.

———. 2013. "Taxonomic Composition and Body-Mass Distribution in the Terminal Pleistocene Mammalian Fauna from the Marmes Site, Southeastern Washington State, USA." *Paleobiology* 39: 345–59.

———. 2019. "Misunderstanding Graphs: The Confusion of Biological Clade Diversity and Archaeological Frequency Seriation Diagrams." *Studies in the History and Philosophy of Biological and Biomedical Sciences* 77: 101178 (pp. 1–13).

———. 2021a. *Graphing Culture Change in North American Archaeology: A History of Graph Types*. Oxford: Oxford University Press.

———. 2021b. "On the Importance of Systematics to Archaeological Research: The Covariation of Typological Diversity and Morphological Disparity." *Journal of Paleolithic Archaeology* 4: 3.

Lyman, R. L., and M. J. O'Brien. 2002. "Classification." In *Darwin and Archaeology: A Handbook of Key Concepts*, ed. J. P. Hart and J. E. Terrell, 69–88. Westport, CT: Bergin & Garvey.

Maclaurin, J., and K. Sterelny. 2008. *What Is Biodiversity?* Chicago: University of Chicago Press.

Magurran, A. E. 2004. *Measuring Biological Diversity*. Malden, MA: Blackwell.

Mills, E. L. 1969. "The Community Concept in Marine Zoology, with Comments on Continua and Instability in Some Marine Communities: A Review." *Journal of the Fisheries Research Board of Canada* 26: 1415–28.

Moore, J. A., and A. S. Keene. 1983. "Archaeology and the Law of the Hammer." In *Archaeological Hammers and Theories*, ed. J. A. Moore and A. S. Keene, 3–13. New York: Academic Press.

Moreno, C. E., and P. Rodríguez. 2010. "A Consistent Terminology for Quantifying Species Diversity?" *Oecologia* 163: 279–82.

———. 2011. "Commentary: Do We Have a Consistent Terminology for Species Diversity? Back to Basics and Toward a Unifying Framework." *Oecologia* 167: 889–92.

Newell, N. D. 1956. "Fossil Populations." In *The Species Concept in Paleontology*, ed. P. C. Sylvester-Bradley, 63–82. London: The Systematics Association Publication No. 2.

O'Brien, M. J., and R. L. Lyman. 2000. *Applying Evolutionary Archaeology: A Systematic Approach*. New York: Kluwer Academic/Plenum Press.

———. 2002. "The Epistemological Nature of Archaeological Units." *Anthropological Theory* 2: 37–56.

Patil, G. P., and C. Taillie. 1982. "Diversity as a Concept and its Measurement." *Journal of the American Statistical Association* 77: 548–61.

Perino, G. 1971. "Guide to the Identification of Certain American Indian Projectile Points." *Oklahoma Anthropological Society, Special Bulletin* no. 4.

Perreault, C. 2019. *The Quality of the Archaeological Record*. Chicago: University of Chicago Press.

Porter, T. M. 1995. *Trust in Numbers: The Pursuit of Objectivity in Science and Public Life*. Princeton, NJ: Princeton University Press.

Praetzellis, A. 1993. "The Limits of Arbitrary Excavation." In *Practices of Archaeological Stratigraphy*, ed. E. C. Harris, M. R. Brown III, and G. J. Brown, 68–86. London: Academic Press.

Prentiss, A. M., ed. 2019. *Handbook of Evolutionary Research in Archaeology*. Cham, Switzerland: Springer Nature.

Price, T. D. 2007. *Principles of Archaeology*. Boston, MA: McGraw Hill.

Ramenofsky, A. F., and A. Steffen, eds. 1998. *Unit Issues in Archaeology*. Salt Lake City: University of Utah Press.

Rathje, W. L., and M. B. Schiffer. 1982. *Archaeology*. New York: Harcourt Brace Jovanovich.

Read, D. W. 2007. *Artifact Classification: A Conceptual and Methodological Approach*. Walnut Creek, CA: Left Coast Press.

Renfrew, C., and P. Bahn. 2016. *Archaeology: Theories, Methods and Practice*, seventh edition. New York: Thames and Hudson.

Rezek, Z., S. J. Holdaway, D. I. Olszewski, S. C. Lin, M. Douglass, S. P. McPherron, R. Iovita, D. R. Braun, and D. Sandgathe. 2020. "Aggregates, Formational Emergence, and the Focus on Practice in Stone Artifact Archaeology." *Journal of Archaeological Method and Theory* 27: 887–928.

Ritchie, W. A. 1971. *A Typology and Nomenclature for New York Projectile Points*. New York State Museum and Science Service Bulletin no. 384. Albany: University of the State of New York.

Scerri, E. R. 1998. "The Evolution of the Periodic System." *Scientific American* 279(3): 78–83.

———. 2008. "The Past and Future of the Periodic Table." *American Scientist* 96: 52–58.

Shade, A. 2017. "Diversity Is the Question, Not the Answer." *The ISME Journal (International Society for Microbial Ecology)* 11: 1–6.

320 • R. Lee Lyman

Sharer, R. J., and W. Ashmore. 2003. *Archaeology: Discovering Our Past*. Boston, MA: McGraw Hill.

Simmons, A. H., and G. Ilany. 1977. "What Mean These Bones? Behavioral Implications of Gazelles' Remains from Archaeological Sites." *Paleorient* 3: 269–74.

Simpson, G. G. 1970. "Uniformitarianism: An Inquiry into Principle, Theory, and Method in Geohistory and Biohistory." In *Essays in Evolution and Genetics in Honor of Theodosius Dobzhansky*, ed. M. K. Hecht and W. C. Steere, 43–96. New York: Appleton.

Spaulding, A. C. 1960. "The Dimensions of Archaeology." In *Essays in the Science of Culture in Honor of Leslie A. White*, ed. G. E. Dole and R. L. Carneiro, 437–56. New York: Crowell.

Steward, J. H. 1954. "Types of Types." *American Anthropologist* 56: 54–57.

Stiner, M. C., N. D. Munro, and T. A. Surovell. 2000. "The Tortoise and the Hare: Small-Game Use, the Broad-Spectrum Revolution, and Paleolithic Demography." *Current Anthropology* 41: 39–73.

Suhm, D. A., and E. B. Jelks. 1962. *Handbook of Texas Archeology: Type Descriptions*. Texas Archeological Society Special Publication no. 1, Texas Memorial Museum Bulletin no. 4. Austin.

Sutton, M. Q. 2013. *Archaeology: The Science of the Human Past*, fourth edition. Boston, MA: Pearson.

Thomas, D. H. 1971. "Great Basin Hunting Patterns: A Quantitative Method for Treating Faunal Remains." *American Antiquity* 34: 392–401.

———. 1974. *Predicting the Past: An Introduction to Anthropological Archaeology*. New York: Holt, Rinehart and Winston.

———. 1975. "Nonsite Sampling in Archaeology: Up the Creek Without a Site?" In *Sampling in Archaeology*, ed. J. W. Mueller, 61–81. Tucson: University of Arizona Press.

Tuomisto, H. 2010a. "A Diversity of Beta Diversities: Straightening Up a Concept Gone Awry, Part 1: Defining Beta Diversity as a Function of Alpha and Gamma Diversity." *Ecography* 33: 2–22.

———. 2010b. "A Diversity of Beta Diversities: Straightening Up a Concept Gone Awry, Part 2: Quantifying Beta Diversity and Related Phenomena." *Ecography* 33: 23–45.

———. 2010c. "A Consistent Terminology for Quantifying Species Diversity? Yes, It Does Exist." *Oecologia* 164: 853–60.

———. 2011. "Commentary: Do We Have a Consistent Terminology for Species Diversity? Yes, If We Choose to Use It." *Oecologia* 167: 903–11.

Ward, I., S. Winter, and E. Dotte-Sarout. 2016. "The Lost Art of Stratigraphy? A Consideration of Excavation Strategies in Australian Indigenous Archaeology." *Australian Archaeology* 82: 263–74.

Webster, D. L., S. T. Evans, and W. T. Sanders. 1993. *Out of the Past: An Introduction to Archaeology*. Mountain View, CA: Mayfield Publishing Co.

Whallon, R., and J. A. Brown, eds. 1982. *Essays on Archaeological Typology*. Evanston, IL: Center for American Archaeology.

Whittaker, R. H. 1960. "Vegetation of the Siskiyou Mountains, Oregon and California." *Ecological Monographs* 30: 279–338.

———. 1972. "Evolution and the Measurement of Species Diversity." *Taxon* 21: 213–51.

———. 1975. *Communities and Ecosystems*, second edition. New York: Macmillan Publishing.

———. 1977. "Evolution of Species Diversity in Land Communities." In *Evolutionary Biology*, vol. 10, ed. M. K. Hecht, W. C. Steere, and B. Wallace, 1–67. New York: Plenum.

Whittaker, R. H., K. J. Willis, and R. Field. 2001. "Scale and Species Richness: Towards a General, Hierarchical Theory of Species Diversity." *Journal of Biogeography* 28: 453–70.

Willey, G. R. 1953. "Archaeological Theories and Interpretation: New World." In *Anthropology Today*, ed. A. L. Kroeber, 361–85. Chicago: University of Chicago Press.

Willey, G. R., and P. Phillips. 1958. *Method and Theory in American Archaeology*. Chicago: University of Chicago Press.

Index

abundance, xxiv, xxvi, 54, 83, 85, 89, 94,
    132, 138, 139, 140, 142, 144, 149, 150,
    151, 153, 154, 156, 179, 180, 181, 186,
    187, 188, 189, 190, 191, 192, 196, 197,
    198, 199, 202, 205, 233, 240, 251, 265,
    266, 269, 270, 271, 272, 273, 274, 275,
    276, 277, 278, 279, 280, 281, 284, 285,
    286, 287, 288, 289, 296
adaptation(s), 65, 125, 128, 133, 136, 152,
    155
alpha diversity, 116, 248, 249, 250, 251,
    252, 253, 254, 278, 305, 307, 308, 311
archaic, 8, 9, 10, 43, 44, 45, 46, 47, 48, 49,
    56, 57, 58, 59, 131, 135, 136, 137, 140,
    142, 145, 146, 147, 148, 149, 150, 152,
    153, 154, 155, 167, 194
assemblage, xxii, xxiv, 1, 12, 13, 52, 53, 54,
    56, 81, 82, 83, 84, 85, 87, 89, 90, 91,
    93, 94, 99, 100, 101, 103, 104, 140,
    142, 143, 144, 145, 151, 178, 179, 180,
    181, 182, 183, 186, 187, 188, 190, 192,
    193, 195, 197, 198, 199, 201, 202, 203,
    249, 250, 251, 252, 253, 254, 256, 258,
    264, 265, 266, 268, 270, 271, 272, 274,
    275, 276, 277, 278, 279, 283, 284, 285,
    286, 297, 302, 303, 304, 305, 307, 308,
    312

beta diversity, 248, 249, 251, 253, 254, 255,
    257, 278, 305, 307, 308, 311
bias, 49, 52, 105, 109, 146, 224, 236, 237,
    250, 273, 274
biases, 40, 184, 216, 236
biodiversity, xxiv, xxx, 178, 179, 196, 268,
    272, 309
biomes, 227, 228, 229, 232, 233, 234, 235,
    241

ceramic(s), 8, 9, 10, 11, 27, 93, 99, 136, 137,
    155, 168, 265, 269, 271, 277, 299, 302,
    304
chaos, 1, 52, 181, 190, 272, 273, 274, 279
character, 4, 5, 12, 13, 14, 49, 50, 52, 156,
    231, 298, 310, 313
classification, 3, 4, 5, 6, 7, 12, 13, 14, 48,
    49, 50, 58, 69, 70, 98, 101, 102, 104,
    105, 111, 130, 215, 216, 218, 219, 220,
    221, 229, 234, 239, 252, 265, 278, 279,
    280, 296, 297, 298, 299, 300, 301, 309,
    310, 313
classificatory, 66, 70, 102, 104, 296, 298,
    299, 300
classified, 7, 12, 13, 58, 70, 98, 155, 214,
    296, 309
Clovis, 2, 3, 6, 11, 13, 15, 27, 134, 214, 215,
    220, 226, 231, 234
completeness, 13, 53, 54, 55, 83, 202, 266,
    276, 277, 281, 282, 283, 284, 285,
    289
complexity, 81, 108, 111, 125, 129, 141,
    256, 305
coverage, xxiv, 13, 81, 82, 83, 84, 85, 87, 88,
    89, 90, 91, 92, 93, 94, 202, 203, 266,
    276, 277, 282, 283, 284, 285, 286,
    288
culture(s), xxi, xxix, 16, 28, 29, 30, 38, 40,
    45, 56, 66, 132, 133, 214, 216, 226,
    249, 253, 256, 297, 302, 304, 305,
    309, 313
culture history, xxviii, 16
    caterial culture(s), 34, 37, 65, 97, 99,
    126, 224, 247, 248, 251, 252, 253,
    255, 256, 257, 258, 302, 311
Copper Culture, 44, 45, 56, 57, 58
cultural transmission, 1, 27, 251, 310, 311

dimension(s), 4, 5, 9, 12, 26, 27, 29, 39, 40, 70, 203, 218, 219, 231, 234, 257, 280, 298, 313
  dimensional, 4, 49, 102, 138, 139, 298
  hyperdimensional, 310
  multidimensional, 156
diversity measures, xx, xxi, xxii, xxiii, xxv, xxix, xxx, 1, 2, 34, 97, 100, 104, 143, 144, 180, 181, 184, 198, 200, 202, 203, 312
Dunnell, Robert C., xx, xxiii, xxiv, xxx, 4, 5, 7, 296, 297, 298, 299, 300, 313
ecological, xxii, xxiii, 27, 30, 36, 40, 59, 70, 74, 93, 97, 102, 105, 125, 142, 180, 182, 185, 189, 192, 194, 216, 224, 235, 249, 250, 251, 307, 310, 311
evenness, xxi, xxii, xxiii, xxvi, 1, 6, 56, 98, 99, 116, 127, 138, 139, 140, 144, 145, 148, 149, 151, 152, 154, 155, 156, 157, 180, 213, 221, 226, 230, 231, 232, 233, 234, 235, 236, 237, 238, 239, 240, 248, 264, 265, 267, 268, 272, 277, 282, 283, 284, 285, 286, 287, 289, 297
evolution, 133, 157, 255, 257, 258, 309
  evolutionary, xxii, 1, 5, 16, 39, 40, 133, 250, 255, 256, 289, 297, 311

gamma diversity, 248, 249, 250, 256, 257, 258, 277, 278, 305, 307, 308, 311
Great Plains, 9, 26, 28, 29, 30, 31, 32, 34, 36, 37, 125, 126, 127, 129, 132, 133, 134, 135, 136, 137, 138, 140, 141, 142, 143, 144, 148, 151, 154, 155, 156, 157, 214

habitat(s), 127, 129, 131, 132, 137, 140, 142, 145, 146, 147, 148, 149, 150, 151, 152, 153, 154, 155, 156, 157, 159, 160, 161, 162, 163, 164, 165, 166, 167, 168, 187, 257
habitation, 44, 65, 194
heterogeneity, 56, 189, 190, 199, 223, 271, 297, 312
Hill number(s), 54, 195, 196, 197, 198, 202, 248, 264, 266, 267, 268, 271, 272, 273, 274, 275, 277, 278, 281, 289
Holocene, 9, 10, 11, 64, 65, 66, 74, 75, 85, 93, 127, 129, 133, 134, 135, 140, 154, 155, 227, 228, 229, 233

hypothesis, xxviii, 1, 5, 14, 15, 26, 36, 93, 126, 127, 128, 130, 151, 200, 255

Late Prehistoric, 10, 126, 127, 137, 141, 142, 145, 146, 147, 148, 149, 150, 152, 153, 156, 157
Lithic, xxi, 8, 9, 11, 97, 98, 100, 104, 105, 106, 107, 115, 178, 253, 254, 299, 303, 304, 313

material culture, xxi, xxx, 34, 37, 64, 97, 99, 126, 224, 248, 251, 252, 253, 255, 256, 257, 258, 302, 311

obsidian, 11, 97, 98, 99, 100, 103, 104, 111, 113

paleoethnobotany, 178, 179, 180, 182, 185, 186, 187, 203, 299
  paleoethnobotanical, 178, 179, 180, 183, 185, 187, 189, 190, 191, 193, 195, 200, 201, 202, 203, 204, 269
Paleoindian, 8, 9, 10, 11, 12, 14, 15, 27, 46, 65, 67, 68, 126, 127, 128, 129, 132, 133, 134, 135, 137, 140, 142, 145, 146, 147, 148, 149, 150, 151, 152, 153, 154, 157, 165, 168, 213, 215, 216, 224, 226, 227, 228, 229, 230, 236, 239, 240, 309
paradigmatic, 3, 4, 5, 6, 7, 12, 13, 14, 49, 50, 51, 102, 108, 109, 111, 113, 115, 216, 218, 219, 220, 221, 239, 280, 298, 310, 313
Pleistocene, 9, 10, 27, 64, 65, 66, 74, 75, 85, 89, 90, 91, 130, 133, 134, 213, 227, 228, 230, 255
probability, xxviii, 83, 155, 181, 183, 185, 193, 202, 222, 223, 225, 230, 231, 232, 233, 234, 235, 236, 237, 273, 276
projectile point(s), xxx, 7, 8, 9, 10, 11, 27, 47, 48, 93, 98, 115, 213, 214, 215, 216, 221, 224, 225, 226, 227, 229, 232, 233, 234, 235, 237, 238, 239, 240, 241, 266, 287, 298, 299, 309, 310

rarefaction, 3, 13, 14, 15, 53, 81, 82, 83, 84, 85, 87, 89, 90, 91, 92, 93, 94, 98, 99, 180, 189, 190, 191, 192, 193, 194,

195, 196, 197, 198, 199, 200, 201, 202, 203, 204, 266, 268, 270, 271, 273, 274, 275, 276, 277, 282, 283, 284, 285, 288, 289, 296
richness, xxi, xxii, xxiii, xxiv, xxvi, 1, 3, 12, 13, 14, 15, 28, 45, 46, 52, 53, 54, 55, 56, 58, 81, 82, 83, 84, 85, 88, 89, 90, 92, 93, 94, 98, 99, 100, 101, 102, 103, 104, 116, 127, 138, 139, 140, 143, 144, 145, 146, 147, 151, 152, 154, 155, 157, 178, 179, 180, 181, 182, 183, 184, 185, 186, 189, 190, 191, 192, 193, 194, 195–204, 215, 226, 240, 248, 249, 251, 258, 264, 265, 266, 267, 268, 272, 273, 274, 276, 277, 279, 280, 281, 283, 285, 286, 288, 289, 297, 306, 307, 310, 311, 312

sample size, xxi, xxii, xxiii, xxiv, xxvii, xxix, xxx, 2, 6, 13, 54, 81, 82, 83, 84, 85, 87, 88, 89, 90, 91, 92, 94, 98, 104, 105, 114, 143, 145, 146, 147, 148, 149, 150, 154, 155, 184, 185, 186, 190, 193, 194, 195, 199, 200, 215, 216, 223, 237, 247, 252, 253, 267, 268, 271, 273, 274, 276, 277, 283, 295, 296, 312
sampling, xxiv, xxvii, xxix, 34, 81, 83, 84, 92, 109, 146, 155, 184, 185, 186, 187, 188, 189, 194, 195, 197, 198, 204, 222, 223, 248, 252, 265, 266, 267, 268, 269, 270, 271, 272, 273, 274, 275, 276, 279, 280, 281, 285, 286, 288, 289, 296, 315
Shannon diversity, 13, 53, 54, 56, 179, 197, 198, 199, 264, 265, 266, 273, 274, 281, 283, 284, 285, 286, 287, 288, 289
Simpson diversity, 13, 53, 54, 55, 56, 98, 100, 104, 154, 181, 194, 195, 197, 198, 199, 201, 203, 264, 265, 266, 273, 274, 277, 281, 283, 284, 285, 286, 288, 289, 298, 301, 305, 307, 308, 309, 310, 312, 313

stone tool(s), xxiv, 2, 7, 8, 9, 10, 11, 49, 53, 64, 68, 74, 97, 98, 99, 101, 102, 104, 105, 106, 108, 109, 111, 114, 115, 116, 228, 240, 265, 302, 303, 309, 313

taxonomic, xxiv, 6, 48, 49, 81, 82, 86, 87, 130, 142, 178, 179, 180, 181, 183, 184, 185, 186, 187, 192, 194, 195, 196, 197, 198, 200, 201, 202, 204, 215, 248, 249, 252, 258, 300, 311
type(s), xxvi, xxvii, 1, 6, 7, 10, 14, 47, 48, 49, 51, 52, 56, 57, 58, 65, 66, 69, 70, 73, 82, 93, 97, 98, 99, 101, 102, 105, 109, 113, 114, 115, 126, 154, 156, 179, 184, 186, 199, 201, 214, 215, 216, 218, 220, 221, 228, 234, 240, 242, 249, 250, 252, 254, 265, 266, 288, 297, 298, 299, 300, 302, 306, 307, 310, 312, 313
typology, 5, 6, 48, 98, 298
typological, 101, 105, 252, 304, 311

unit(s), xxii, xxiv, 4, 6, 26, 27, 29, 32, 36, 48, 49, 85, 86, 87, 89, 94, 125, 191, 192, 197, 215, 216, 222, 224, 225, 226, 242, 248, 249, 250, 252, 255, 258, 264, 265, 266, 269, 270, 271, 272, 274, 275, 276, 278, 279, 280, 281, 286, 288, 289, 297, 298, 299, 300, 301, 302, 303, 305, 307, 308, 309, 310, 312, 313

variability, 27, 38, 39, 65, 66, 70, 71, 72, 73, 74, 75, 105, 126, 127, 128, 133, 140, 141, 151, 152, 153, 157, 181, 192, 193, 197, 198, 199, 200, 201, 204, 239, 254, 296, 298, 305, 308, 310, 311, 312, 314
variation, xxix, 4, 26, 27, 32, 39, 48, 51, 52, 56, 58, 81, 97, 98, 106, 126, 133, 138, 139, 142, 157, 179, 182, 198, 199, 200, 204, 215, 216, 226, 239, 247, 248, 249, 250, 251, 252, 253, 255, 256, 258, 265, 267, 275, 298, 305, 306, 312

woodland, 8, 126, 136, 137, 141, 142, 145, 146, 147, 148, 149, 150, 152, 153, 155, 160, 162, 166

www.ingramcontent.com/pod-product-compliance
Ingram Content Group UK Ltd.
Pitfield, Milton Keynes, MK11 3LW, UK
UKHW021035101225
3784IPUK00045B/3

9 781800 734296